Taught *to* Lead

The Education of the Presidents of the United States

Mason Crest Publishers
370 Reed Road
Broomall, PA 19008
www.masoncrest.com

1 3 5 7 9 8 6 4 2
First Printing

Library of Congress Cataloging-in-Publication Data

Taught to lead : the education of the presidents of the United States /
Fred L. Israel, general editor ; introduction by Arthur M. Schlesinger, Jr.
    p. cm.
  Includes bibliographical references and index.
  ISBN 1-59482-000-7
1. Presidents—United States—Biography. 2. Presidents—Education—United
States. 3. United States—Politics and government—Decision making.
4. Political leadership—United States. [1. Presidents—Education.]
  I. Israel, Fred L.
  E176.1.E34 2004b
  973'.09'9—dc22
                        2003025363

Taught to Lead

The Education of the Presidents of the United States

General Editor
Fred L. Israel
Department of History
City College of New York

Associate Editors
Michael Kelly
Department of History
The Gilman School

Hal Marcovitz
Staff Reporter
Morning Call (Allentown, PA)

Introduction by Arthur M. Schlesinger, jr.
Albert Schweitzer Chair in the Humanities
City University of New York

MASON CREST PUBLISHERS
PHILADELPHIA

Table of Contents

INTRODUCTION Arthur M. Schlesinger, jr. vi

FOREWORD Fred L. Israel, Editor viii

CHAPTER 1 George Washington 2

CHAPTER 2 John Adams 14

CHAPTER 3 Thomas Jefferson 26

CHAPTER 4 James Madison 40

CHAPTER 5 James Monroe 52

CHAPTER 6 John Quincy Adams 62

CHAPTER 7 Andrew Jackson 76

CHAPTER 8 Martin Van Buren 86

CHAPTER 9 William Henry Harrison 94

CHAPTER 10 John Tyler 106

CHAPTER 11 James K. Polk 116

CHAPTER 12 Zachary Taylor 126

CHAPTER 13 Millard Fillmore 136

CHAPTER 14 Franklin Pierce 146

CHAPTER 15 James Buchanan 158

CHAPTER 16 Abraham Lincoln 168

CHAPTER 17 Andrew Johnson 182

CHAPTER 18 Ulysses S. Grant 192

CHAPTER 19 Rutherford B. Hayes 202

CHAPTER 20 James A. Garfield 212

CHAPTER 21 Chester A. Arthur 224

CHAPTER 22   Grover Cleveland. 232

CHAPTER 23   Benjamin Harrison. 242

CHAPTER 24   William McKinley 252

CHAPTER 25   Theodore Roosevelt. 262

CHAPTER 26   William Howard Taft 274

CHAPTER 27   Woodrow Wilson 284

CHAPTER 28   Warren G. Harding 298

CHAPTER 29   Calvin Coolidge. 310

CHAPTER 30   Herbert Hoover 324

CHAPTER 31   Franklin D. Roosevelt 336

CHAPTER 32   Harry S. Truman 350

CHAPTER 33   Dwight D. Eisenhower 360

CHAPTER 34   John F. Kennedy. 376

CHAPTER 35   Lyndon B. Johnson. 388

CHAPTER 36   Richard M. Nixon 400

CHAPTER 37   Gerald Ford 412

CHAPTER 38   Jimmy Carter 424

CHAPTER 39   Ronald Reagan. 436

CHAPTER 40   George H. W. Bush 448

CHAPTER 41   Bill Clinton 460

CHAPTER 42   George W. Bush 470

A Selective Guide to Presidential Biographies 484

Internet Resources 490

Picture Credits 492

Contributors 496

Index 498

Introduction

It is singular that in the United States, a country fascinated both by education and by presidents, no one has written a book on the education of American presidents until this one. One reason may be that the link between American presidents and their education is complex and problematic.

Presidents, like everyone else, are shaped by the totality of their experiences of life. Anything may be a means to education for those who possess what T. S. Eliot called an "experiencing nature." "A whale-ship," observes Ishmael in *Moby Dick*, "was my Yale College and my Harvard." The greatest American autobiography deals very little with formal schooling but is entitled *The Education of Henry Adams*.

So experience shapes presidents. But there is a narrower definition of education as something taught in schools and colleges—as in answers to the question, "Where were you educated?" Formal instruction is tangible and measurable. History, however, reveals no necessary relationship between the quality of the schooling presidents had undergone as students and the quality of their performance in the White House.

Thus by common consent our three greatest presidents were George Washington, Abraham Lincoln, and Franklin D. Roosevelt. Washington and Lincoln had very little formal schooling. FDR had the best formal schooling the country could supply—Groton, Harvard, Columbia Law School. But, whatever their education, they were all great presidents.

Nor was it true that in Washington's and Lincoln's day college education was rare. After all, Washington's successors were John Adams, Harvard 1755; Thomas Jefferson, William and Mary 1762; James Madison, College of New Jersey (now Princeton) 1771; James Monroe, William and Mary 1776; and John Quincy Adams, Harvard 1787. Not until our seventh chief executive—Andrew Jackson—did the United States have another president who had not gone to college.

A total of nine presidents never attended college at all. Besides Washington, Jackson, and Lincoln, the educationally challenged in the nineteenth century were Martin Van Buren, Zachary Taylor, Millard Fillmore, Andrew Johnson, and Grover Cleveland. Even in the twentieth century, that century of higher education for the masses, we had one president who never made it to college. This was Harry S. Truman. Yet historians and political scientists customarily place Truman in the "near great" category.

On the other hand, the three most conspicuous "failed" presidents—James Buchanan, Dickinson 1809; Herbert Hoover, Stanford 1895; Richard M. Nixon, Whittier 1934—were all college men. An AB degree is thus no guarantee of success in the White House, nor is its absence a guarantee of failure.

But Washington, Lincoln, and Truman keenly lamented the inadequacy of their schooling. Washington and Lincoln hit upon the same adjective to describe their education—"defective." Washington believed that the radical American experiment in democracy required popular education to make it work. In his farewell address he called on his fellow citizens to promote "institutions for the general diffusion of knowledge. In proportion as the structure of a government gives force to public opinion, it is essential that public opinion should be enlightened."

President Washington had a specific institution in mind. "That a National University in *this* country is a thing to be desired, has always been my decided opinion," he wrote his vice president, John Adams, in 1795, "and the appropriation of ground and funds in the Federal City, have long been contemplated." The same year he told Jefferson of his dream of a university in the nation's capital where students would become "better acquainted with the principles of law, and government" and could learn from an international faculty "among whom some of the most celebrated characters in Scotland, in this line, I am told may be obtained." By recruiting students from all across the land, Washington added, a national university would "contribute to wear off those prejudices, and unreasonable jealousies, which prevent or weaken friendships and impair the harmony of the Union."

He took the case to Congress the next year in his eighth and last annual message. "The common education of a portion of our Youth from every quarter, well deserves attention…. A primary object of such a National Institution should be, the education of our Youth in the science of *Government*." Congress, Washington said, had no more pressing duty "than to patronize a plan for communicating it to those, who are to be the future guardians of the liberties of the Country."

The father of his country found very little support for his educational program. With renewed urgency he returned to the subject in the will drafted six months before his death in 1799. Here Washington expressed once again his "ardent wish" for a national university and left a substantial bequest toward its endowment. None of Washington's successors, however, has echoed his call for a national university.

Lincoln as an aspiring young politician called education "the most important subject which we as a people can be engaged in," and as president in 1862 he signed the Morrill Land Grant Act, providing public funds for state universities and colleges. Thus two great presidents, denied much formal education themselves, strove to improve educational facilities and amenities for the future guardians of American liberties.

The story of forty-two men (no women so far, alas) with diverse educational preparations for the presidency is compelling in its variety and its drama. And a word should be said about the vivid and imaginative illustrations that accompany and enhance the text.

The conclusion of this work? Surely it is that there are many roads to the White House.

—Arthur M. Schlesinger, jr.

Foreword

I n the Declaration of Independence of 1776, Thomas Jefferson listed more than thirty grievances against the king of England. Eleven years later, in writing the Constitution of the United States, the Founding Fathers quite naturally rejected a hereditary monarch or powerful head of state. Instead, they established an elected chief executive with a specific term of office. Article II, Section 1 of the Constitution explains, "The executive Power shall be vested in a President of the United States of America. He shall hold Office during the Term of four Years." There are formal constitutional requirements: one must be a "natural born citizen," at least thirty-five years old, and a resident of the United States for fourteen years. The constitution refers to the president as "he." It was probably beyond the thought process of the Founding Fathers that a woman, or a man who was not white, would ever be considered. The Twenty-second Amendment (1951), which deals with term limitations, uses "person" in referring to the president, recognizing that a woman could serve in that office.

The United States was the first nation to have an elected president—and a president with a stated term of office. Every four years since the adoption of the Constitution in 1789, the nation has held a presidential election. Elections have been held even during major economic disruptions and war.

The forty-two white men who have served as president seem to have very little else in common.[1] Five were never elected. John Tyler, Millard Fillmore, Andrew Johnson, Chester Arthur, and Gerald Ford entered office through death, assassination, or resignation of their predecessor. Each failed to remain in office, either through personal choice or political fate.

Some of these forty-two men were surprisingly strong-willed, while others were simply miscast. Although Abraham Lincoln prevented the permanent break-up of the Union and Woodrow Wilson and Franklin D. Roosevelt each confronted a world war, most presidents were average men doing the best they could in a complicated job. Likewise, there does not seem to be a pattern in the kind of person whom the voters have chosen to be their leader. They have been as young as John F. Kennedy (forty-three) and as old as Ronald Reagan (sixty-nine), intellectuals like Madison, Taft, and Wilson or plain thinkers like the great Jackson and the failed Harding. Personality types have run the gamut, from the ebullient spirits of the two Roosevelts and Truman to the taciturn Coolidge and dour Nixon. The Adamses, John and John Quincy, were father and son, as are George H. W. Bush and George

---

[1] George W. Bush is the forty-third president of the United States. However, forty-two men have served in that office as Grover Cleveland is considered the twenty-second and twenty-fourth president because of his non-consecutive terms.

W. Bush. Benjamin Harrison's grandfather was William Henry Harrison of "Old Tippecanoe" fame. Theodore Roosevelt was Franklin's admired cousin. They have come from states across the country, from Vermont to California. Mostly they have come to the White House from Congress and from governors' mansions. Six generals have been elected to the presidency. And, except for the tragic Civil War that followed the 1860 election of Lincoln, the electorate has always accepted the peaceful transfer of power.

Many of these men sought the responsibilities of the presidency. Others landed there by accident. Regardless, each man occupied a position of power and did his best to exercise leadership as he understood it. Each had the opportunity to make major decisions both in foreign and domestic matters that affected the direction of the nation.

The aim of these forty-two essays is to focus on the education of the presidents of the United States. More than three hundred illustrations with detailed captions are included. Each illustration elucidates an aspect of that president's education. Most are being published for the first time.

As with other presidential comparisons, no clear pattern emerges from their varied educations. However, most presidents from Washington through Wilson had a form of a classical education that included Bible study. Of the twenty-five pre-1900 presidents, sixteen experienced some formal higher education. Lincoln was self-educated, as were Jackson, Van Buren, Taylor, Fillmore, Andrew Johnson, and Grover Cleveland. William Henry Harrison attended medical school and James Garfield studied for the ministry.

All seventeen presidents since 1900, with the exception of Harry Truman, attended college. These colleges vary from Harding's bankrupt Ohio Central and its three instructors to the prestigious schools of Harvard, Yale, and Princeton. Hoover majored in geology at Stanford and Lyndon Johnson was trained as an elementary school teacher at a rural Texas college. Eisenhower graduated from West Point and Jimmy Carter from Annapolis. Woodrow Wilson is the only president to hold an earned doctorate degree. And, with the exception of Taft and Wilson, almost all seventeen presidents since 1900 were average students.

Collectively, these essays and illustrations are also a microcosm of American education since the 1750s. Teachers, tutors, parents, relatives, textbooks, novels, nonfiction, and the Bible—each had an important part in the education of the presidents, and therefore in shaping American history.

—Fred L. Israel

Taught *to* Lead

The Education of the Presidents
of the United States

George Washington

Chapter One

No American is more completely misunderstood than George Washington. To his contemporaries, Washington—commander of the tattered colonial army (1775–1783), chairman of the Constitutional Convention (1787), and first president of the United States (1789–1797)—was indisputably first in war, first in peace, and first in the hearts of his countrymen. Thomas Jefferson spoke for the nation in 1792 when he urged Washington to seek a second term. "The confidence of the whole Union is centered in you," he told his chief. After Washington's death in 1799, Jefferson wrote, "Never did nature and fortune combine more perfectly to make a man great, and to place him in…an everlasting remembrance." Washington was the first leader in some 2,000 years to relinquish great power once he had held it. And he did it twice—both as a general at the end of the Revolutionary War and as president, stepping down from office after two terms.

But Americans were not satisfied with the realities—glorious though they were—of Washington's life. They wanted a flawless hero. And, mainly because of Mason Weems's apocryphal biography published in 1800, Washington soon came to be regarded as a demigod. Weems (1759–1825), an Episcopal clergyman, wrote *The Life and Memorable Actions of George Washington*. With the exception of the Bible, this ultra-fictionalized biography was the bestseller of its day and held its own through over seventy accredited and varying editions, including five in German. In its fifth edition, the best known of Weems's tales appeared in book form—the story of the destructive six-year-old boy with a hatchet who chops down a cherry tree, then confesses the deed to his confronting father. "With the sweet face of youth brightened with the inexpressible charm of all-conquering truth, he bravely cried out, 'I can't tell a lie, Pa; you know I can't tell a lie. I did cut it with my hatchet,'" wrote Weems. In the book, the youngster's father, Augustine "Gus" Washington Sr., responds, "Run to my arms, you dearest boy….for you have paid me for it a thousand fold." Today, two centuries after this anecdote first appeared, it still remains one of the very few episodes about Washington that most Americans are able to recite—and it remains the most memorable two pages that Weems ever wrote.

"I can't tell a lie, Pa; you know I can't tell a lie. I did cut it with my hatchet."

The anecdote of young George Washington and the cherry tree became popular because it illustrated honesty, the most important virtue, which is rewarded with paternal love. Honesty, George supposedly was told by his father "is the loveliest quality of youth." However, the story was immortalized when it was included in *McGuffey's Fifth Eclectic Reader*, an elementary school text, beginning with the 1846 edition. William McGuffey bestowed unending fame on the above print when he placed it in his *Reader*. These *Readers*, first published in 1836, went through scores of editions, were revised and enlarged, and sold more than 122 million copies. Even the simplest lessons contained obvious morals. The *Readers* introduced thousands of boys and girls to the treasures of literature. Their moral and cultural influence upon children in the thirty-seven states in which they were used contributed much to the shaping of the American mind in the nineteenth century.

THE LIFE
OF
GEORGE WASHINGTON;
WITH
CURIOUS ANECDOTES,

EQUALLY HONOURABLE TO HIMSELF,
AND
EXEMPLARY TO HIS YOUNG COUNTRYMEN

A life how useful to his country led!
How loved while living! how revered now dead!
Lisp! lisp his name, ye children yet unborn!
And with like deeds your own great names adorn.

Embellished with Six Engravings.

BY M. L. WEEMS,
FORMERLY RECTOR OF MOUNT VERNON PARISH.

The author has treated this great subject with admirable "success in a new way." He turns all the actions of Washington to the encouragement of virtue by a careful application of numerous accomplishments drawn from the conduct of the founder of our Republic from his earliest life."—H. Lee, *Major General U.S Army*.

PHILADELPHIA:
J. B. LIPPINCOTT COMPANY.
1891.

The hatchet and cherry-tree story first appeared in book form in 1806.

16   LIFE OF WASHINGTON

fond, and was constantly going about chopping every thing that came in his way. One day, in the garden, where he often amused himself hacking his mother's pea-sticks, he unluckily tried the edge of his hatchet on the body of a beautiful young English cherry-tree, which he barked so terribly, that I don't believe the tree ever got the better of it. The next morning the old gentleman, finding out what had befallen his tree, which, by the by, was a great favourite, came into the house; and with much warmth asked for the mischievous author, declaring at the same time, that he would not have taken five guineas for his tree. Nobody could tell him any thing about it. Presently George and his hatchet made their appearance. "George," said his father, "do you know who killed that beautiful little cherry tree yonder in the garden?" This was a tough question; and George staggered under it for a moment; but quickly recovered himself: and looking at his father, with the sweet face of youth brightened with the inexpressible charm of all-conquering truth, he bravely cried out, "I can't tell a lie, Pa; you know I can't tell a lie. I did cut it with my hatchet."—Run to my arms, you dearest boy, cried his father in transports, run to my arms; glad am I, George, that you killed my tree; for you have paid me for it a thousand fold. Such an act of heroism in my son is more worth than a thousand trees, though blossomed with silver, and their fruits of purest gold."

It was in this way by interesting at once both his heart and head, that Mr. Washington conducted George with great ease and pleasure along the happy paths of virtue. But well knowing that his beloved charge, soon to be a man, would be left exposed to numberless temptations, both from himself and from others, his heart throbbed with the tenderest anxiety to make him acquainted with that great being, whom to know and love, is to possess the surest defence against vice, and the best of all motives to virtue and

Mason Weems invented the story that young Washington could not tell a lie. Weems had met Washington several times, the earliest being in 1787. In 1800, one year after Washington's death, Weems had the idea for a fictionalized biography of Washington. His friend Matthew Carey, who had apprenticed in Benjamin Franklin's printing shop, was a well-known Philadelphia publisher. Carey issued the first editions of Mason Weems's biography of Washington. Sales were so outstanding that Weems, the first ordained Episcopal minister in the United States, continued to offer ideas for embellishing the story in successive editions. In its fifth edition (1806), the hatchet and cherry-tree story first appeared in book form. By the 1920s, more than seventy editions of the book had been published.

For several generations, descendants of Mason Weems were asked to autograph copies of their ancestor's book. This 1891 edition of *The Life of George Washington* is autographed: "With the compliments of the great-great-great grandson of the author. Robert Weems Tansill, Jr."

George Washington was born February 22, 1732[1], in Westmoreland County, Virginia. Without a doubt, the Washington family ranked among the privileged in colonial Virginia—and from his very first biographer stories have been told of the family's happy households, although personal relations between the children and their mother, Mary Washington, were most formal. The family's wealth came from vast tobacco plantations. Young George had to have heard everywhere discussions of business ventures and of speculative enterprises. Likewise, he had to have observed the methods of cultivation of both tobacco, the staple crop of the colony, as well as of grain crops. The Washingtons owned many slaves, and the youth probably witnessed the management of the black workforce. As a young adult, Washington viewed slavery with a crass insensitivity that only his later experiences would temper into compassion. Of the nine presidents who held slaves, he was the only one to free all of them in his will.

The major part of Washington's classroom education totaled seven or eight years. It hardly went beyond what today would be considered the elementary grades. His father, and later his older half-brothers, seem to have been his teachers. According to a biographical sketch written by his friend David Humphreys, Washington also was instructed by a tutor. There is little evidence of who that man was or whether there had been more than one teacher. Mason Weems wrote that young George attended a school run by a man names Hobby; a John Hobby did in fact operate a school near Fredericksburg. Weems also noted that a "Mr. Williams, an excellent teacher," next instructed Washington in Westmoreland County. A Henry Williams did run a school there. The yearly expenses would have been a thousand pounds of tobacco for board and two hundred pounds for instruction. However, Weems's statements can neither be proved nor disproved.

David Ramsay, in his popular biography *Life of George Washington* (1807), wrote that Washington's mother Mary had a major influence on his education, but what influence she had cannot be accurately assessed. It seems, though, that she was against her eldest son attending school any distance from home. She also stopped a plan for young George to join the Royal Navy, although his friends, the wealthy and powerful Fairfax family, would certainly have used their influence to get George a position under an outstanding commander. According to Ramsay, who interviewed family members, "it is justifiable to credit her with a decided influence in the way of discipline and morals." We do know that, widowed at age thirty-five, she did not remarry. We also know she was a most possessive person and that her son was the passion of her life.[2] When Washington was commander-in-chief of the Continental Army, and later when he was president, she bitterly complained that he neglected her. She preserved Washington's childhood school

---

[1] A change in the calendar during Washington's lifetime pushed his birthdate ahead eleven days.

[2] James Thomas Flexner wrote, "Although she lived into George's second term as president, she never budged from home to take part in any triumphant moment of his career, and all her comments that have been recorded…show her deprecating her son's achievements." (*George Washington*, vol. 1, pp. 19–20.) This evaluation does not contradict "that her son was the passion of her life."

copybooks, his earliest surviving writings. These are an indispensable source for studying the future president's education.

In later life, Washington complained his "defective education" prevented him from writing an autobiography. He always was a poor speller but Jefferson and Madison were no better. He would almost never discuss his education. One biographer noted that Washington "spelled like a gentleman—and the gentlemen of those early days were not good spellers." Yet his school exercises record instruction that was almost entirely practical. The earliest school papers have a 1741 date—he was then nine—and clearly are the work of a boy who had already learned to read, write, and do basic arithmetic. The bulk of the surviving papers date from 1744 to 1748. In total, three hundred and thirteen pages exist; they are loosely bound in four volumes and are held by the Manuscript Division of the Library of Congress.[3]

Washington's school notebooks reveal a practical education. Nearly half of the pages are exercises in mathematics—many of calculations in geometry and trigonometry, essential to understand land surveying. About fifty pages deal with practical land surveying problems. There are also lessons in which Washington had to copy lease and indenture forms, contracts, and deeds. There are pages of account keeping and of "ciphering" or handwriting exercises. At least ten pages deal with configurations of the stars and geography, both essential for navigation. All of these subjects were advantageous for a member of the Virginia gentry and essential for a plantation owner. Lacking among the notebooks is any instruction in the humanities.

When Gus Washington died in 1743, plans for young George's education changed. The eleven-year-old would not be able to follow his father and his two older half-brothers to Appleby Grammar School in Cumbria, England. (The school, founded by royal charter in 1574, is still in existence.) Instead, the next half-dozen years of Washington's life were spent living with his mother, his many relatives in Westmoreland County, and at Mount Vernon, home of his elder half-brother Lawrence.

During this period, Washington wrote in his copybook one of the most interesting documents of his education—the one hundred and ten maxims he called "Rules of Civility and Decent Behavior in Company and Conversation." They cover ten handwritten pages. (His handwriting had evolved from a childhood scrawl to a sprawling legible script.) This exercise had the most formidable influence on Washington's character. The rules, sort of a middle ground between crudeness and pomposity, were guidelines for gentlemanly good behavior—every action done in company ought to be with some sign of respect to those that are present (number one); in the presence of others, sing not to yourself with a humming noise nor drum with your fingers or feet (number two); if you cough, sleep, sigh or yawn, do it not loud but privately (number five); sleep not when others speak (number six); spit not into the fire (number nine); when you sit down, keep your feet firm and even; without putting one on the other or crossing them (number ten); kill no vermin, or

---

[3] The Washington Papers consist of over four hundred volumes of manuscripts, more than 75,000 pages. They were purchased from the family by the U.S. government between 1834 and 1849 for $45,000.

This University of Pennsylvania mandamus conferred the honorary Doctor of Laws Degree on George Washington, July 4, 1783, for "the establishment of Peace and the security of those important interests which were involved in the fate of the War." *Mandamus* is a Latin word that literally means "we command." In this instance, the Board of Trustees authorized the degree to be conferred on Washington. The school, founded in 1740 as the College and Academy of Philadelphia, became in 1765 with the establishment of the first medical school in America, the oldest university in the nation. Honorary degrees date back to medieval universities, a recognition of distinction without regard to academic attainment.

At about age twelve, Washington wrote in his copybook one of the most interesting documents of his education—the one hundred and ten "Rules of Civility and Decent Behavior and Conversation." They cover ten pages. His handwriting had evolved from a childhood scrawl to a sprawling legible script. This exercise had a great influence on Washington's character.

At the top, in Washington's handwriting, are the first twelve rules. Summarized in modern English, the future president is writing: treat everyone with respect; be considerate; do not embarrass others; when you speak, be concise; and do not draw attention to yourself through rude behavior.

On the right is the final of the ten pages, on which rules one hundred and four to one hundred and ten are listed. The one hundred and seventh rule advises to show interest in others' conversation but never talk when your mouth is filled with food. The final rule, "Labor to keep alive in your breast that little spark of celestial fire called conscience," means don't allow yourself to become jaded or cynical.

Washington practiced these rules as others follow the tenets of a religion. "There was a decided strain of romance in the makeup of George Washington," wrote biographer John C. Fitzpatrick, "and it was precisely to this romantic strain that these rules strongly appealed."

fleas, lice, ticks in the sight of others (number thirteen), keep your nails clean and short (number fifteen); be no flatterer (number seventeen); to the one who is your equal, or not much inferior, you are to give the chief place in your lodging (number thirty-two); when you reprove another, be unblamable yourself (number forty-eight); play not the peacock (number fifty-four); think before you speak (number seventy-three); rinse not your mouth in the presence of others (number one hundred and one). About twenty of the rules governed good table manners—"Put not your meat to your mouth with your knife....Neither spit forth the stones of any fruit pie upon a dish nor cast anything under the table....Talk not with meat in your mouth." Washington, as he groomed himself into a gentleman, memorized these maxims and practiced them throughout his life. For him, they became the civil religion that he faithfully followed. (Note that not one of these "gentlemen's rules of civility" deal with the humane treatment of a slave!)

Until the 1890s, it was assumed that Washington had composed the "rules of civility." Researchers then found that similar rules had been prepared in the 1590s by an order of French Jesuits as guide for young noblemen. Translations of the Jesuit rules subsequently appeared in both Latin and English, and may have been copied by Washington. Others have pointed out that the rules closely resemble popular courtesy books published in London during the early eighteenth century. For example, Richard Allestree's *Gentleman's Calling* and *Ladies Calling* went through many editions. These two volumes provided those rising in English society—particularly the crass new mercantile elite—with needed pointers about social behavior. Probably, either Washington's father or one of his two half-brothers purchased a book that included the rules during their student days in England. (Augustine Jr. had returned from Appleby in June 1742, shortly before Washington began writing out the "rules of civility.") It is also possible that Washington's polished half-brother Lawrence, who took an interest in Washington's education, lent him the book containing this gentleman's code. In any event, these rules of English upper-class decorum seemed appropriate to the Virginia society in which Washington lived—a society of wealthy families living opulently on their great plantations. They also defined Washington's conduct for the rest of his life.

John C. Fitzpatrick, the compiler and editor of *The Writings of George Washington* (thirty-seven volumes), wrote that Washington copied the "rules of civility" around 1744, when George was about twelve. This was the year after the death of Augustine Washington Sr., who had a large extended family, and, apparently, the implications of his complex, detailed, and most equitable will were more at the forefront than was the depth and period of mourning. Washington had a distant and deferential relationship with his father. It lacked emotion and feeling.

Washington's childhood idol was his half-brother Lawrence, who was about fourteen years his elder. As a result of Lawrence's long and careful schooling in England, he returned to Virginia a young gentleman with grace and manners that captivated young George. Lawrence was carefully courteous and deferential to the rich and powerful he came to know. He preferred horses to books. His greatest gifts were social. He was extremely cultured but probably gave the impression of a wider learning than he had mastered. In today's vernacular, Lawrence would be called a "social snob." A little more than two months after their father's death, Lawrence married into the Fairfax family, one of the wealthiest families not only in Virginia but in the American colonies. This assured Lawrence's place in the front rank of socially conscious Virginia society.

The Fairfaxes of Virginia lived like medieval feudal lords. The family owned more than five million acres in perpetuity between the Potomac and Rappahannock Rivers—a 1649 grant made by the future King Charles II—that the proprietor could do with as he pleased. Lawrence's father-in-law, Colonel William Fairfax, was a cousin and agent of Thomas, sixth Lord Fairfax, the great proprietor. William was George's favorite Fairfax: he took a strong liking to the colonel, and the older Fairfax reciprocated. He encouraged Washington to ride and hunt, and taught him how to dress in the latest fashion. It was the colonel, as well as Lawrence Washington, who introduced young George to Roman history and literature and to English aristocratic manners. Washington later wrote that of all the Fairfaxes he was most indebted to the colonel, who became his second father and his role model—and to the colonel, George had become like a son. In this atmosphere, George had every reason to consult his handwritten "rules of civility."

Around 1747, when young Washington was about fifteen, Thomas, sixth Lord Fairfax settled in Virginia. Biographers describe this fifty-four-year-old as a somewhat eccentric, crusty character, even a recluse and misogynist. Fairfax was an Oxford graduate, an outstanding hound-breeder and foxhunter, and the first true English nobleman George Washington ever saw. He also was the first English lord ever to come live in America, and he set the priorities and social standards in the Fairfax world. To visit the Fairfaxes was similar to visiting an ultra-aristocratic English family. Their plantation had drawing rooms, a music room, an enormous dining room and a grand library filled with guests dressed in the latest London fashions. Because of the Fairfax influence, George now read more. He read the first one hundred and forty-three issues of Joseph Addison's and Richard Steele's *Spectator,* which was filled with the wit and politics of English society. Addison and Steele were fond of using classical quotations and apparently Washington memorized many that he freely used in his later correspondence. Washington also learned about the London theater from the latest issues of *Gentleman's Magazine.* Fairfax had a fetish for clothing and annually purchased the best and the latest London styles—but he did not wear them, preferring "that rougher costume which better corresponded to his out-of-door habits." His Lordship could not be questioned and he did what he pleased.

Fairfax's biographers agree that he enjoyed the company of young men. Until his marriage, George Washington shared his time between the Fairfax estates, his brother's home at Mount Vernon, and his mother's plantation. When Lord Fairfax

These are the things which once possess'd Will make a life that's truly bless'd...

This prophetic poem appears in George Washington's "school exercise book." He was about nine years of age when he copied the poem from an issue of the London publication *Gentleman's Magazine*. (The spelling and punctuation have been modernized.)

These are the things which once possess'd
Will make a life that's truly bless'd:
A good estate on healthy soil
Not got by vice, nor yet by toil:
Round a warm fire, a pleasant joke.
With chimney ever free from smoke:
A strength entire, a sparkling bowl,
A quiet wife, a quiet soul.
A mind as well as body whole:
Prudent simplicity, constant friends,
A diet which no art commends:
A merry night without much drinking,
A happy thought without much thinking:
Each night by quiet sleep made short,
A will to be but what thou art:
Possess'd of these, all else defy,
And either wish nor fear to die.

At the bottom of the page are instructions on how to keep ink from freezing and moulding which Washington copied from the 1727 London edition of George Fisher's *The Instructor: or, Young Man's Best Companion:* "Put a few drops of brandy or other spirits into it and it will not freeze and to hinder its moulding put a little salt therein."

True Happiness
These are the things which once Possess'd
Will make a life that's truly bless'd
A Good Estate on healthy Soil,
Not Got by Vice, nor yet by toil:
Round a warm Fire, a pleasant Joke,
With Chimney ever free from Smoke:
A Strength entire, a Sparkling Bowl,
A quiet Wife, a quiet Soul,
A Mind as well as body, whole
Prudent Simplicity, constant Friend,
A Diet which no art Commends;
A Merry Night without much Drinking
A Happy Thought without much Thinking;
Each Night by Quiet Sleep made Short
A Will to be but what thou art:
Possess'd of these, all else defy
And neither wish nor fear to Die
These are things which once Possess'd
Will make a life that's truly bless'd

To keep Ink from Freezing or Moulding
In hard Frosty Weather, Ink will be apt to Freeze; which if once it Doth, it will be Good for Nothing for it taketh away all its Blackness & Beauty. To prevent which (if you have not the Conveniency of keeping it Warm) Put a few Drops of Brandy or other Spirits into it and it will not freeze And to hinder its Moulding Put a little Salt therein.

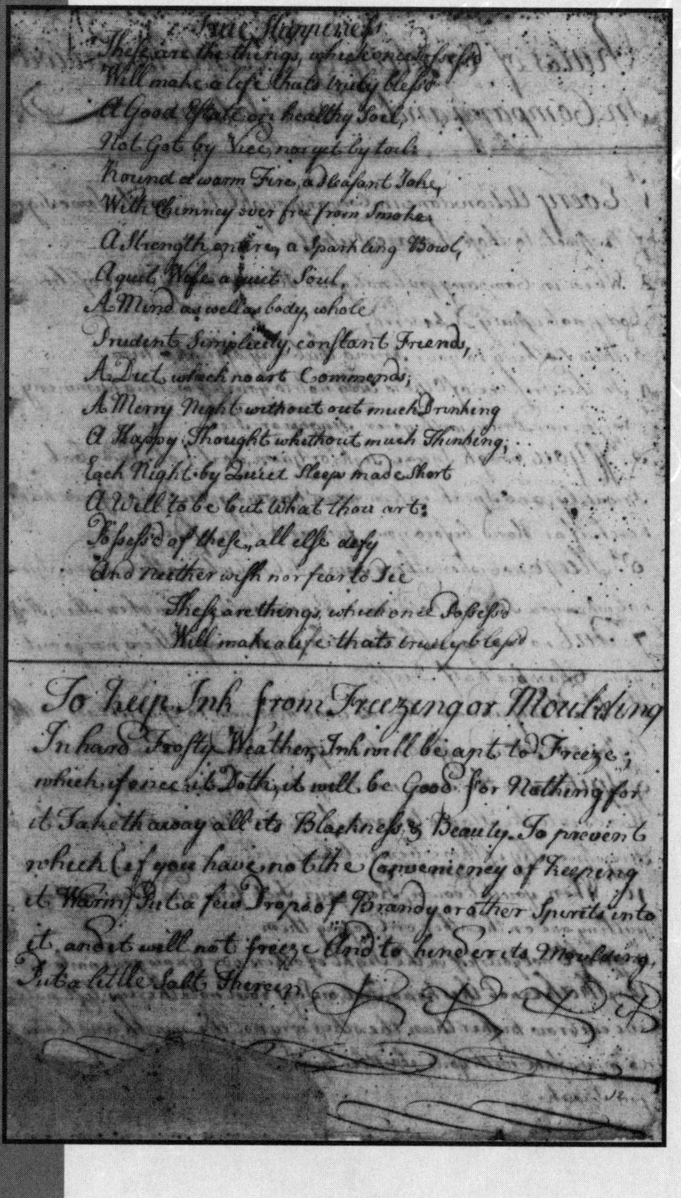

talked of battles and sieges and of an officer's gallant service, he probably made a soldier's life appear attractive to George. In his drawing rooms, Fairfax laid plans for opening up the vast new Virginia frontier. He had grown fond of tall, elegantly mannered George, now sixteen, and gave him the opportunity to have a fascinating experience—to be part of a surveying group that mapped the remotest parts of the Fairfax lands for new towns and settlements. This was George's farthest journey from home, a journey that included his first contact with the western wilderness. When Lord Fairfax died in 1781, Washington was genuinely moved. It is ironic that George Washington, the leader of the rebellion, learned his social graces from the Fairfaxes who educated him in an aristocratic lifestyle, the antithesis of the American Revolution.

Obviously, Washington absorbed ideas from the society in which he lived. Within the Virginia tidewater area, that low-lying coastal plain where the rivers rise and fall with the ocean tides, there were no less than eight strata of society. At the top were the landed proprietors (among them the Washingtons), while at the bottom were the black slaves; both groups were of immutable station. Other classes were small farmers, merchants, sailors, frontier people, indentured servants, and convict servants who worked on the plantations.

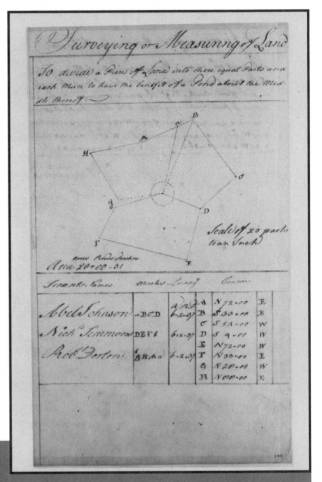

Washington completed the surveying problems shown on these pages when he was between fifteen and sixteen years old. The problems solved show that Washington had studied geography, geometric constructions, and the zodiacal configuration of the stars. "Surveying or Measuring of Land" account for thirty-nine of the one hundred and twenty pages in Washington's last extant notebook.

Washington's formal education ended when he was about sixteen. Only the surveying problems had carried him beyond what would today be considered the elementary school level.

In 1748, Thomas, sixth Lord Fairfax, gave sixteen-year-old Washington the opportunity to be part of a surveying group that mapped the remotest parts of the extensive Fairfax lands for new towns and settlements. During the thirty-one day expedition across the Blue Ridge Mountains, conducted in windy March and early April—ideal surveying weather, as tree leaves had to be down to sight through the theodolite—Washington studied the methods of experienced surveyors and wrote the field notes as they dictated them.

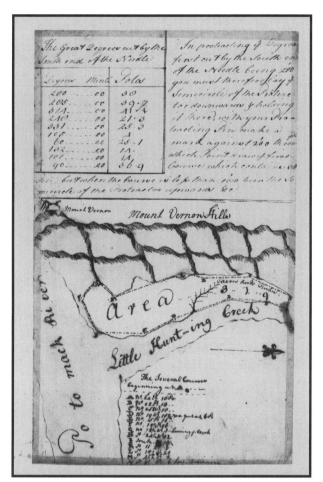

Everyone assumed that there would always be distinctions of social rank, an arrangement that seemed perfectly ordinary and proper at the time.

The planter class, an elite group, kept close ties with England and copied the manners of its aristocracy. Many lived in great Georgian mansions. They filled well-proportioned rooms with the finest imported furniture or hired artisans to carry out the designs of foreign cabinetmakers. Contemporary artists painted the gentry in all their imported finery. From the 1730s to the 1750s, the price of Virginia tobacco soared and rising profits made the planters' land more valuable. Washington doubtless understood the talk amongst his elders concerning surveying and patenting of western lands, of farming and horses, and of life along the Potomac, Rappahannock, and the James Rivers. Beyond these lands was the great, open, unclaimed Valley of the Ohio—with the promise of a fortune for young men of enterprise and courage.

From 1732 to the conclusion of the French and Indian War in 1763—that is, the first thirty years of Washington's life—nothing really happened politically that could have anticipated the American Revolution and the emergence of the "founding father" of a new nation, the first in modern history to successfully break away from its mother country. No person could have predicted how Washington or how any of his contemporaries would react to the political situation which subsequently developed. Washington's formal education was poor compared to the educations of such Patriot leaders as John Adams and Thomas Jefferson. He had not read the classics. He never learned a foreign language. He did not study law. He was uninterested in science. He was not intellectually inquisitive. However, by his early twenties, Washington's complicated character had emerged—he was moral, just, patient, ambitious, amicable, tenacious, and had the ability to make and maintain friendships. His responses were certain when his personal code of principles was involved. Even those who opposed him politically spoke generously of his fair mindedness and his sterling integrity. However, nothing in his education could have prepared him for the revolutionary events that followed.

—Fred L. Israel

John Adams

Chapter Two

Fifteen-year-old John Adams sat motionless on his horse, shocked at what he had been told. John had been ready to ride north from Braintree, Massachusetts, to Harvard College, outside Boston, where he was to take his entrance exams to continue his education. He had expected his teacher, Joseph Marsh, to travel with him and to be there through the testing on that June morning of 1751. John had just learned that Mr. Marsh felt sick and was afraid to travel. He would have to go alone.

The future second President of the United States was so unsure of his ability to pass the test that he almost turned his horse around to ride the short distance back home. Then John thought of how upset and disappointed his father would be if he failed to take the exams. He also realized that his father might be angry with Mr. Marsh for not going. John forced himself to turn his horse toward Boston and begin the journey by himself.

The day grew overcast with dark skies that threatened rain as John traveled the fifteen miles to Boston. From time to time he could see the slate gray Massachusetts Bay beyond the hills to his right. Finally, John crossed the Charles River and approached the four buildings that made up Harvard College in 1751. With some fear and uncertainty, John talked with Harvard President Edward Holyoke and several Harvard tutors. Then he was given an essay in English to be translated into Latin.

The ride back to Braintree was far different for John than his trip to Harvard. He had passed the exams and been accepted into Harvard as part of the class of 1755. John was lighthearted and enthusiastic on the way home, knowing that his father would be pleased with his success. Only about one half of one percent of young men went on to college in that time. Before long, John Adams passed by the Blue Hills, which were not far from his family's fifty-acre farm. It was on that farm that he had been born October 30, 1735, and where his education had begun.

Braintree (now Quincy) was a small village of approximately 1,500 people and a number of buildings, including a schoolhouse, a gristmill, a village store, several taverns, and a church. The Adams's farm was built right beside the shore road from Boston to Plymouth, at the base of Penn's Hill.

The Harvard University Archives

The Harvard University Archives are unique because they contain a continuous record of the oldest institution of higher learning in the United States. Many of the early college records were kept in bound volumes. These have been preserved intact.

In the 1930s, Samuel Eliot Morison compiled an "Inventory of the Harvard University Archives, to 1800." It remains the outstanding explanation and inventory of the archives for the seventeenth and eighteenth centuries. Morison's essay describes the record organization of the college—for example, "The College Books," "Corporation Records," "Overseers, Records," "Harvard College Papers," "President's Papers," "Professorship Papers," "Treasurer's Records," etc. In 1939, the Harvard Corporation established the Harvard University Archives as a unit within the University Library. The Archives mission was greatly enhanced by its move in 1976 from the top floor of Widener Library into much larger quarters in the Pusey Library. These archival records are an indispensable source for understanding the history of the college.

John Adams's student years at Harvard College, 1751–55, occurred in the middle of the thirty-two year administration of President Edward Holyoke (1737–69). This was a period of prosperity and progress for the college. Holyoke, who had been born in 1689, previously had been pastor of the Marblehead, Massachusetts, Congregational Church for twenty-one years. As president, Holyoke lessened the Calvinist dominance in the Harvard College curriculum. Textbooks he thought dated were replaced with newer works. Scottish philosopher David Fordyce's *Elements of Moral Philosophy* (1754) and John Locke's *An Essay Concerning Human Understanding* (1689) became required reading. Scientific instruction was modernized. Oratory was encouraged through regularly scheduled student debates. Academic awards were given to outstanding students for the first time in the college's history.

Holyoke was instrumental in the hiring of younger and less religiously dogmatic instructors, among them John Winthrop. Winthrop, a direct descendant of the colonial leader John Winthrop (1587/88–1649), was elected the second Hollis Professor of Mathematics and Natural Philosophy in 1738 at the age of twenty-four. Winthrop was the first important scientist and productive scholar on the teaching staff of Harvard College. In 1751, with Holyoke's approval, Winthrop introduced "elements of fluxions,"— now known as differential and integral calculus—into the Harvard mathematical curriculum. In addition to teaching,

Winthrop also gave public lectures and demonstrations in physical science. His research work, mainly in the field of astronomy, was carried out over a period of forty years, during which Winthrop came to be considered one of the outstanding scholars in the nation. Winthrop was young John Adams's favorite professor. Adams ecstatically recorded in his diary the clear night when he first gazed through Professor Winthrop's telescope at the satellites of Jupiter.

Nonetheless, during Adams's time at Harvard the college's curriculum was very similar to the Harvard of a century before. Latin and Greek were essential for all applicants. Entrance examinations were oral, except that the student usually had to write a Latin essay to test his skill in "making" Latin. All students were male. Student numbers had increased under President Holyoke but the largest graduating class before the American Revolution, that of 1771, numbered sixty-three. It was not until 1810 that another graduating class reached that figure. (Adams's graduating class of 1755 numbered twenty-seven.)

Most Harvard students were the sons of merchants, magistrates, and ministers from New England. Most students came from eastern Massachusetts and New Hampshire. Not a single New Yorker appears on the Harvard registration rolls between 1737 and 1790. About one student from the West Indies came to Harvard every two years or so from 1737 on. The median age of freshmen entering the college rose from a low of little over fifteen years in 1741 to seventeen years in 1769.

Inventories submitted by students burned out of their rooms after a 1764 fire list tables; chairs; feather beds; pictures and looking glasses; issues of leading London magazines such as Joseph Addison and Richard Steele's *The Spectator* and *The Tatler* and copies of England's popular *Gentleman's Magazine* (the periodical that gave the word "magazine" to the genre); books of popular plays; clothing; wigs and crisping irons; chafing dishes; tea sets; pipes and tobacco; rum and other liquors; corkscrews; and one Bible.

Harvard was noted for its outstanding classical education. It was this classical education that assisted Adams and his classmates later in politics and statesmanship. Eight of the fifty-six signers of the Declaration of Independence graduated from Harvard between 1740 and 1762. Each had been taught by Edward Holyoke. As these men became involved with the events that led to the American Revolution, they saw lessons for their own time in the writings of Plutarch and the orations of Cicero and Demosthenes, and they understood the logic of Plato's *Republic* and Aristotle's *Politics*.

The Harvard University Archives are unique because they contain a continuous record of the oldest institution of higher learning in the United States.

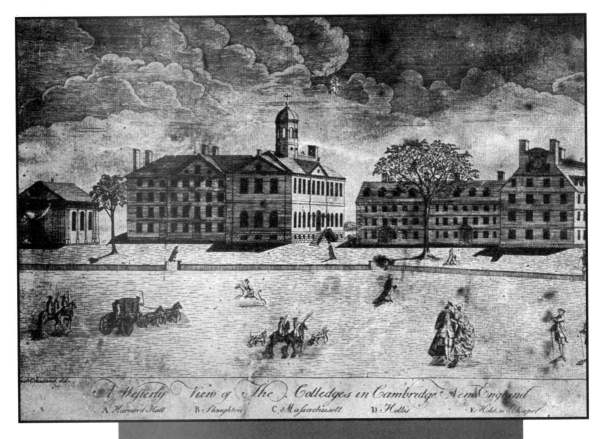

A Westerly View of The Colledges in Cambridge New England
A. Harvard Hall   B. Stoughton   C. Massachusett   D. Hollis   E. Holden Chapel

Old Harvard Hall, where John Adams studied, burned down on the night of January 24, 1764. It was replaced by the building with the steeple in the center of this 1767 drawing. The drawing was done by Joseph Chadwick and engraved by Paul Revere. It is the earliest engraving that shows Hollis Hall and the new Harvard Hall.

In 1764, Hollis Hall (the second building from left) was completed to house students because of growing enrollment. It was named after the English family that had sent continuous benefices to Harvard for almost fifty years.

To ensure that college property was kept in good condition—and to facilitate collection of fines for broken windows and other damages—Harvard was divided into districts. Students or tutors were assigned to inspect each district. The quarterly District Reports preserved in the Harvard Archives give a great deal of information about the condition of buildings and the occupants of college dormitory rooms. These reports ended in the mid-nineteenth century.

The Massachusetts Bay Colony, where John Adams was born, had been founded by Puritans in 1630. They were English settlers who firmly believed that the duty of humankind was to serve God. They wanted to see the Christian Church purified and restored to the condition they believed it had been in the time of Jesus. Because Puritans felt that the best way to do this was to know and obey the Bible, learning to read was essential for everyone. They wanted the whole population to be able to gain a basic understanding of the biblical Scriptures. Puritans had no concept of a separation between church and state; instead they believed religion and government should work together to create a righteous and just society.

The Puritan determination to educate all their citizens was seen early in the colony's history. Only five years after the founding of Massachusetts, the first Latin Grammar School was established in Boston. Just a year later, in 1636, Harvard College was begun for the purpose of training men for the Christian ministry. The Puritan leaders believed that the churches of New England needed an educated clergy. An act was passed in Massachusetts in 1647 that required every town of one hundred families or more to provide free grammar school education for their children. By 1750, about 75 percent of males and 65 percent of females in New England could read and write. That was the highest literacy rate in colonial America.

The Adams' family had settled in Massachusetts one hundred years before John was born. His father, Deacon John Adams (so-called because he was a deacon in the local church), had married Susanna Boylston of Brookline, a small village near Boston. Deacon John and Susanna had three sons: John was the eldest, followed by Peter and Elihu. Deacon John was a farmer and shoemaker. Though he had never been to college, he wanted his eldest son to have a college education. It was his desire that John become a minister like his uncle. Deacon John's other two sons would join him working on the farm.

John Adams's first taste of studying occurred in his own home. Most literate parents in those days educated their children in basic principles before they were five; John's parents began to teach him his ABC's and the fundamentals of reading. Their interest in education seems to have run in the family. Deacon John's mother, Hannah, was described as a person who had more books than was usual in those days, especially for a woman. She was a diligent reader, as was Deacon John. It would be years, though, before young John would discover this same interest for himself.

After home schooling by his parents, John continued on in his education by attending what was then called a "dame school." At about six years of age, children would attend a school in the home of a neighborhood woman, a "dame." In John Adams's case, that woman was Mrs. Belcher, the mother of another deacon in the family's local congregational church. For two years John left his home each morning and crossed the road to Mrs. Belcher's kitchen, where she taught the neighborhood children.

One primary educational tool from which John learned at the dame school was called a hornbook. This was a wooden frame, shaped like a paddle, with a sheet of paper containing letters of the alphabet or simple words mounted on it. The hornbook had a long handle, so John could hold it while studying. The frame was covered with a piece of transparent horn from a sheep or ox to keep the sheet from getting stained. A hole was cut into the handle and a rope inserted, so John could carry it on his belt or around his neck when it was not in use.

A second important educational tool was one used in New England schools throughout the eighteenth century—the *New England Primer*. The primer is believed to have been created by Benjamin Harris, a London printer who came to Boston around 1686. The *New England Primer* began with written prayers and then continued with the alphabet and words with increasing levels of difficulty. This was followed by rhymes to remember the alphabet such as

In ADAM'S Fall
We sinned all.
Heaven to find;
The BIBLE Mind.

There were rhymes for each letter of the alphabet from A to Z. Next in the *New England Primer* were poems, hymns, and a lengthy catechism, which was a summary of religious teaching in the form of questions and answers. The purpose of the primer was to give children instruction in both their letters and in religion.

When John was about eight, he completed the dame school and began attending the Braintree Latin School. This was a public school run at the time by Joseph Cleverly, a graduate of Harvard College and a reader at the Episcopal Church in Braintree. The heart of the curriculum in the school was Latin, the foundation for many other languages and a necessary tool for higher education in the eighteenth century. John also learned Greek, the language in which the New Testament had originally been written.

Two other important subjects studied at the Latin school were rhetoric and logic. The aim of rhetoric was to teach a student to write and speak with ease and confidence. Because Latin schools were designed to prepare young men for Harvard, it was almost certain that those who attended college would one day become pastors, teachers, or lawyers. These were all professions in which writing and public speaking were important. Logic was equally necessary, Puritans believed, because it helped students develop rational, sound thinking.

It was under Mr. Cleverly's teaching that young John Adams almost gave up on school. John believed that even though his schoolmaster knew a lot, he was a lazy teacher and did little to encourage his students to want to learn. John increasingly disliked the classroom and tried to avoid going to school. He had always been a person who loved the outdoors, so he often skipped class and went out to play. Because he lived near the ocean, he would swim in the quiet bays near his home, fly kites in the breezes off the bay, and play marbles. In the winter John would ice skate and walk through the fields. Above all, he loved hunting and liked to sit on the

In their meeting of April 29, 1755, the Harvard Overseers approved plans for the class of 1755's commencement. John Adams was in this class, along with twenty-six other students.

The Overseers also approved recommendations for curriculum and financial changes. Mention is made of rent money from a farm in Norfolk, England, donated to Harvard by a London merchant named Pennoyer in 1670. These rents were paid to Harvard College until 1903 when the Overseers ordered the property sold.

In the middle paragraph, the Overseers approved an inquiry into recent student disturbances. Judging from these records and those of the faculty, the most frequent student disturbances involved "indecent tumultuous noises" and "hollowing" or "huzzas" in the Yard late at night—sometimes followed by throwing a brick through a tutor's window.

On this list of Overseers are family names that had been associated with Harvard for several generations—Foxcroft, Willard, Hutchinson, Sewall, Chauncey, Whoolwright, and Pemberton.

At the March 24 meeting, a student was excused for one week to assist his father in rebuilding their house that was "consumed by fire."

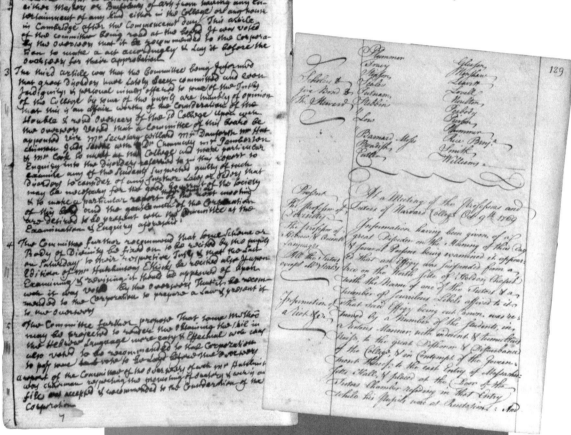

Pages from Harvard faculty records for 1769. The faculty voted to excuse students so they might return home to recuperate from an illness or for another specific purpose. For example, at the March 24 meeting, a student was excused for one week to assist his father in rebuilding their house that was "consumed by fire." At the October 9 meeting (right) an inquiry was held into an effigy of a tutor that was "suspended from a tree on the North side of the Holden Chapel." When college authorities cut the effigy down, a "number of students" acted in a "riotous manner with indecent and tumultuous noises to the great disruption of the college."

ground for hours watching for crows and squirrels to shoot. Sometimes he carried his gun to school in the morning and hid it in a neighbor's barn. Then, as early as he could, John slipped away from class, picked up the gun, and headed for the woods.

In spite of his feelings toward his teacher, John seemed to have an inborn desire to learn. John believed that Mr. Cleverly did not spend enough time in class to cover mathematics adequately, so he managed to get his own copy of the book used at the Latin school, Edward Cocker's *Decimal Arithmetic*, and studied it at home by himself. He went through the entire book and surpassed the other students in his class.

One day John begged his father to let him leave school and join his two brothers on the farm. Deacon John couldn't understand why his oldest son was more enthusiastic about work and sports than about studies. He decided to show John how hard life was as a farmer. The next morning the two went off to spend the entire day in the marshes gathering thatch. That night, though John was wet and tired, he still wanted to work on the family farm instead of continuing in school. His father didn't give in, however, and the very next day John was back at school.

Finally, when Adams was fourteen, he told his father that his real problem was with his schoolmaster. He asked Deacon John to approach Joseph Marsh, minister of the Congregational parish of Braintree, who ran a private Latin school near the Adams's farm. At the time, Marsh accepted only students from other towns, who boarded with him. John wanted his father to plead with Mr. Marsh to let him attend his private school. The next morning, the first words John heard from his father were, "I've persuaded Mr. Marsh to take you—and you must go this day!"

Marsh was able to inspire John and earn his respect. For the first time, young John began to enjoy the classroom. In less than two years, Marsh was convinced that young Adams was ready to take the entrance exams for Harvard. John was prepared for the next step in his education.

When Adams arrived at Harvard in the late summer of 1751, the college had undergone many changes. The college was named after a young minister, John Harvard, and had originally existed primarily to prepare ministers for Puritan congregations in New England. By 1708, however, when the college elected its first non-clergyman president, Harvard had already moved away from Puritanism. The curriculum continued to broaden through the eighteenth century, and more of the school's graduates became lawyers or doctors than ministers. There was more critical thinking even when it came to discussing theological ideas.

John Adams loved his years at Harvard. He once wrote that it was there that he experienced a "growing curiosity, a love of books and a fondness for study, which dissipated all my inclination for sports, and even for the society of ladies." He read constantly and concentrated on mathematics and philosophy. His knowledge of Latin, Greek, rhetoric, and logic grew deeper. When John entered Harvard, each class had a tutor who would work with them through their college years. Professor Joseph Mayhew was tutor for the class of 1755; he had been one of the men who had examined John for admittance to Harvard.

Adams and his twenty-three fellow classmates had a regular routine they followed the entire school year. They got up before sunrise, said prayers and ate breakfast, then attended classes from 8 A.M. to 5 P.M. with a break for lunch. There were lectures by professors and, often twice a week, debates on issues prepared by their class tutors. After dinner, the students would study until bedtime. The school year began in late August and continued until the end of December, when they were given a five-week winter break. School would then resume until the end of June, when they would have a six-week summer vacation before beginning their next year.

One powerful incentive that moved John Adams to learn was the presence of so many good students in his class. He was competitive and wanted to do better than his classmates. Throughout his four years, he never envied the gifts of fellow students but enjoyed the challenge he received from them. Their friendships caused John to pursue his studies with greater determination than ever. Many of his classmates went on to notable careers. One of these was Samuel Locke, who eventually became the president of Harvard. Another was John Wentworth, who went from college to become the last royal governor of New Hampshire. Tristram Dalton, also in the class of 1755, became one of the first U.S. Senators from Massachusetts.

Adams entered college with his father's expectation that he would become a minister. However, as the years at Harvard passed, events caused John to consider other options. During his junior year, John learned that his pastor in Braintree, Lemuel Bryant, was in a dispute with members of his congregation. Some congregants were critical of Reverend Bryant's preaching and his actions. John read published arguments on both sides and saw much narrowness of opinion. He seriously questioned whether he wanted to pursue a career that might put him in the same kind of conflict.

At this same time, Adams joined a group of students who spent evenings in readings and discussion. When he once read aloud some dramatic material, many of his fellow students told him he had a gift for public speaking and urged him to consider becoming a lawyer. Something responded inside of John, and he began to think seriously about law as a profession. He reasoned that his parents would accept a change in his career. He was certain that he could convince his father of the logic of such a decision, and he knew his mother had no great desire for him to become a pastor.

The real obstacle that stood in Adams's way was a lack of money. There were no law schools in America in the eighteenth century, so the only way to become a lawyer was to study as an apprentice under an established lawyer. In order to do that, John would have to pay a fee to a lawyer to tutor him and somehow find the money for his room, board, and necessities. It would take him at least two years before he would be ready to practice law himself. John Adams knew that he could not ask his father for any more financial assistance.

In his last year of Harvard, Adams decided to become a teacher while he grappled with the final choice for his lifetime career. Before graduation, he accepted a position as Latin master in a grammar school in Worcester, sixty miles west of

Harvard student room assignments, circa 1754. John Adams lived in Massachusetts Hall, Room 31 (his entry is on line nine). Adams described the shared room as being the "lowermost northwest chamber" of the building. Among Adams's classmates listed on this room directory were John Hancock, Thomas Sparhawk (with whom Adams roomed in their senior year), and Joseph Stockbridge, the wealthiest student in the class.

Boston, where he moved after he received his bachelor of arts degree in 1755. Once there, the town boarded him for three weeks, and then Adams found a room in the home of a prominent doctor, Dr. Nahum Willard. One incentive for Adams to live with the Willards was their large library. He realized he would have access to these many books as a border in the Willard home.

Adams's move to Worcester was a difficult one. After the stimulating environment of college, he found the townspeople to be less interesting. Worcester was about the size of Braintree, but much more isolated. He also found teaching frustrating because his students seemed dull. Adams would often select the smartest student to lead the class while he sat at his desk reading or writing.

However, he was able to spend many evenings discussing ideas with leading citizens of Worcester. Of particular interest at the time were new religious ideas flooding the colonies. Adams read a theological book, Thomas Morgan's *The Moral Philosopher*, and argued over its theology with his new friends. He also pored over many of Dr. Willard's medical books and for a time thought about medicine as a career.

Adams's uncertainties about his future continued. At times he disliked himself for his inability to make up his mind. Yet, when he began to visit the courts in Worcester and listen to gifted lawyers, Adams found his interest in law growing stronger. Finally, he decided to make law his career. As a result, he entered into the final stage of his formal education. At the end of the summer of 1756, Adams contacted a Worcester lawyer, James Putnam, about the possibility of becoming his apprentice. Mr. Putnam agreed to tutor him, and Adams moved in with the Putnam family to begin a two-year program studying law.

Adams's law education became more practical after he began attending court with Putnam to watch him in action. After a time, he began to prepare briefs— statements or summaries of Putnam's cases going to trial. Adams continued this practice of reading, discussing, visiting court, and working on briefs for two years. In October of 1758, he finished his law studies with Putnam. Through an oversight, Putnam neglected to give Adams the recommendation needed for him to practice law. So Adams introduced himself to Attorney General Jeremy Gridley, who liked him and gave him the necessary certificate and recommended him to the court. This letter of recommendation was almost equivalent to a law degree.

Adams decided to return to his parent's home because Braintree was in the Boston judicial district where he would have more opportunities than in distant Worcester. Once Adams was settled, he visited some prominent lawyers in the bustling city of Boston to seek their support and advice. He also sized up his opposition among other young lawyers in the area. He realized that some of them had influential friends who could help them advance in their careers. With that advantage over him, Adams decided to develop a plan of reading over the next few years so that he would have a greater knowledge of the law.

Adams was encouraged to continue his reading by his friend Jeremy Gridley, who allowed Adams to use his extensive library. Pointing to his books, Gridley once told Adams, "There is the secret of my eminence." John spent much time in Gridley's library, filling his mind with as much of the law as he could. He had learned to continue his own education through a consistent habit of reading.

On October 25, 1764, John Adams, who was then twenty-eight, married nineteen-year-old Abigail Smith, from the nearby town of Weymouth. Daughter of a pastor, Abigail was a remarkably well-read and intellectual woman. Like John, she loved to read and was an excellent writer. The two of them carried on a lengthy correspondence for years when John became active in politics and was gone for lengthy periods of time. John and Abigail Adams would have five children, including John Quincy Adams, the sixth president of the United States.

John and Abigail moved to Boston in 1768, where John continued his practice and became well respected among its citizens. Adams became widely known throughout the city in 1770 when he agreed to defend some British soldiers stationed in Boston who had killed some townspeople. That episode became known as the Boston Massacre. Most of the soldiers were acquitted, and though Adams was disliked at the time, his willingness to protect the innocent—no matter who they were—eventually won him great respect.

As resistance to Great Britain grew in America, John Adams became one of the most outspoken advocates for a war of independence. In 1774, Adams was a delegate from Massachusetts to the Continental Congress and headed the committee to draft the Declaration of Independence. After the colonies gained their freedom, Adams served the United States as its first American minister to Great Britain. In 1789, he was elected vice president under George Washington, and in 1797 was elected president.

After serving one term, and losing his bid for a second term to Thomas Jefferson, Adams retired to Braintree. There he had the time once again for his books and study. "Learning, he said, "is not to be obtained by chance, but must be sought after with vigor." He died on July 4, 1826, the fiftieth anniversary of the signing of the Declaration of Independence, just a few hours after the death of Thomas Jefferson. Adams was buried next to his beloved Abigail, who had died in 1818.

Perhaps John Adams's life can best be summarized by biographer David McCullough: "As his family and friends knew, Adams was both a devout Christian and an independent thinker, and he saw no conflict in that. He was hardheaded and a man of 'sensibility,' a close observer of human folly as displayed in everyday life and fired by an inexhaustible love of books and scholarly reflection."

—Bill Thompson

Thomas Jefferson
Chapter Three

"I cannot live without books," wrote Thomas Jefferson to his friend, John Adams, as both were nearing the end of their lives. As he wrote these words, Jefferson could look back on a life filled with reading and intense study. Jefferson remembered how he had developed this love of learning during his childhood in Virginia. He had acquired it first from his father, Peter, who was determined to develop his own mind in spite of his lack of formal education.

Both Thomas Jefferson and his father, Peter, were born in the southern colony of Virginia, where public education was not a high priority. Unlike some of the northern colonies, where the government insisted on providing schools for its children, Virginia authorities left education to the Anglican clergy. The Episcopalian pastors, called rectors, were expected to educate the young through sermons, classes, and personal visits. Any education beyond that was the responsibility of individual families—if they could afford to hire tutors for their children.

When Peter Jefferson was a boy, his father taught him to read and write but did not provide any other education. However, Peter was determined to educate himself, and he began to acquire books early in his life. Books were rare in Virginia then, especially on the frontier. Peter began to develop a small library that included the Bible and works by Shakespeare and other English writers. Peter learned the techniques of mapping while traveling throughout Virginia as a surveyor. Along with Joshua Fry, Peter Jefferson made the first detailed map of Virginia. It was published in 1751 and used extensively for many years.

Peter married Jane Randolph in 1739 and took her to his farm in Goochland County, near the Southwest Mountains of Virginia. He named it Shadwell in honor of his wife's birthplace in England. Peter's interest in education grew as a result of his marriage. The men of the Randolph family, who owned vast estates in Virginia, had all graduated from the College of William and Mary in Williamsburg, Virginia. When Thomas Jefferson was born on April 13, 1743, Peter was determined to educate his son and one day send him to the College of William and Mary.

The College of William and Mary

The College of William and Mary at Williamsburg, Virginia, is the second-oldest institution of higher education in the United States (after Harvard College). King William III and Queen Mary II of England chartered the college in 1693 to train Anglican clergymen and colonial civil servants. The scholastic honor society Phi Beta Kappa was organized there in 1776. Seven signers of the Declaration of Independence—including Thomas Jefferson, its author; John Marshall, the fourth chief justice of the U.S. Supreme Court; and James Monroe, later the fifth U.S. president—were college alumni, as was President John Tyler. George Washington was the college's first American chancellor (1788–99).

In March 1760, Thomas Jefferson entered the College of William and Mary. He completed his studies there two years later. His chief intellectual stimulus while a student came from his association with Dr. William Small, who held the first chair of mathematics and then that of natural philosophy (science). Small aroused in Jefferson an interest in science that was destined to persist throughout his life. The professor also introduced Jefferson to Virginia's governor, Francis Fauquier, and to George Wythe, the most noted teacher of law of his generation.

Small's appointment to William and Mary was an attempt by Governor Fauquier to break the clerical domination of the college. Small considered himself an apostle of the Enlightenment, a teacher who must pass on to his students the need to question all dogma. He remained at the college for only six years (1758–64) because of difficulties with his colleagues. His aloofness, his perceived feigned migraines, and, above all, his inborn sense of intellectual superiority caused the cancellation of his teaching contract, undoubtedly by mutual consent. Small returned to England.

Small recognized that Jefferson was uniquely talented. That a polymath of such rare quality should be at William and Mary at the right moment to teach the polymath of them all is one of the happiest coincidences in educational history.

In 1775, just before the outbreak of the American Revolution, Jefferson wrote to Small that he was sending "half of a little present he had laid by"—three dozen bottles of Madeira that had aged for eight years in the Monticello cellars. Small had no opportunity to enjoy the wine, for he had been dead for two months when Jefferson sent off the gift. Jefferson wrote nothing as an obituary, though for the rest of his life Small's name would enter again and again into his conversation and correspondence, always followed with an expression of affection, respect, and indebtedness.

"I cannot live without books," wrote Thomas Jefferson…. As he wrote these words, Jefferson could look back on a life filled with reading and intense study.

When Thomas Jefferson was born on April 13, 1743, Peter was determined to educate his son and send him to the College of William and Mary one day.

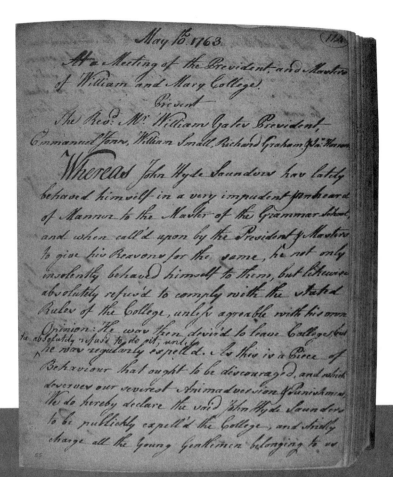

On May 10, 1763 William Small was one of four "Masters," in addition to the college president, present at a discipline hearing for John Hyde Saunders of Williamsburg. The young man had been "very impudent....to the Master of the Grammar School." He was "insolent" and "absolutely refus'd to comply with the stated Rules of the College." Saunders was expelled. Young Saunders's father had built the stables for the college. In 1772, he was awarded the contract to build "the new west wing," the first major construction undertaken at the school in forty years.

Most punishments recorded in the Faculty Minutes were imposed for drunkenness or for brawling with the local boys of Williamsburg. Extant records indicate that Small became involved in faculty discussions mainly when the purchase of scientific equipment was discussed. The Reverend William Yates, listed in this document, served as the fifth president of William and Mary (1761–68). Dumas Malone, who wrote a multi-volume biography of Jefferson, quoted John Page, Jefferson's classmate and friend, who described how they "suffered" from Yates's "arid teaching."

The earliest memory Thomas Jefferson had was from when he was two years old. Someone handed him up to a slave sitting high on one of his fathers' horses. He sat on a pillow so he could manage the long trip ahead of them. At that time the Jefferson family moved east to Tuckahoe Plantation, to run the estate owned by Peter Jefferson's wife's cousin who had died. It would be Tom's home for the next six years and where he received his first formal education.

Thomas Jefferson began the first phase of his formal education at Tuckahoe in an "English school." The Randolph and Jefferson children attended a one-room schoolhouse built on the grounds of the estate. Thomas studied along with his two older sisters, the Randolph children, and several of their cousins. Their teacher was an Anglican churchman who taught them the basics of reading, writing, and arithmetic.

As was typical in colonial days, the rector included the recitation of prayers and Bible reading in his instruction. Jefferson never took to religion, however, and was not sure about prayer. According to one story, Jefferson left the classroom one day and decided to test the power of prayer by asking for dinnertime to come quickly because he was hungry. As his life progressed, Thomas Jefferson became convinced that religion and education should be kept separate.

Peter spent much time and energy in personally developing his son's education. In the evenings, he taught Tom penmanship, insisting that he be precise and neat. Tom learned mathematics, how to keep accounts accurately, and how to work systematically. His father instilled in Tom his commitment to books, and it seems probable that Tom began reading books in his father's library even before he went to the English school at age five. Tom was taken on walks through the woods around Tuckahoe, and developed an interest in animal and plant life. Peter also began to teach his young son the basics of surveying, which had provided such a good living for him on the frontier.

Peter Jefferson was a physically strong man whose courage was well known. He told Tom that it is the strong in body who are both strong and free in mind. Therefore, along with his studies, Tom was taught to love the outdoors. The young boy was instructed to set aside four hours a day for physical exercise. He walked through the countryside, rode a horse, and hunted and fished in the Southwest Mountains, enjoying his childhood.

When the Jefferson family returned to Shadwell, Tom, then about nine years old, began a second phase in his education. He was enrolled at a school between Shadwell and Tuckahoe taught by the Reverend William Douglas. It was a Latin school, where Jefferson learned the classical languages of Latin and Greek. Douglas also introduced Tom to French. Because the school was far from home, Tom boarded there and visited his home every three or four months. Jefferson loved to learn and later said that there was nothing more "sublime" than reading literature in their original languages.

Tom was not completely happy at Douglas's school. He felt that the clergyman was only a "superficial Latinist" and was even worse in teaching Greek.

However, he did develop a talent on his own. During the six years he attended Douglas's school, Jefferson started to teach himself how to play the fiddle. He practiced three hours a day and gradually became an accomplished violinist.

Tragedy deeply affected Thomas Jefferson's life in 1757, when he was fourteen years old. His father died suddenly, leaving Tom with the responsibility for seven younger siblings. It was a difficult time for him, as he recalled years later:

> When I recollect that at fourteen years of age, the whole care and direction of my self was thrown on my self entirely, without a relation or friend qualified to advise and guide me, and recollect the various sorts of bad company with which I associated from time to time, I am astonished that I did not turn off with some of them, and become as worthless to society as they were...

Yet, it was his continued interest in education that protected him.

Jefferson eventually inherited 5,000 acres from his father's estate. The income from this land supported him while he continued to develop his knowledge. Thomas always felt there were two things his father left him that were most valuable. One was his father's library of forty books, a real treasure in those days. The other was Peter's deathbed wish that Thomas would pursue a classical education. Thomas Jefferson always remembered his father with great love and respect, admiring him for his kindness, his physical strength and his love of learning.

After his father's death, Tom's guardians sent him to a new Latin school established in the parish of Fredericksville at Hanover. It was run by the Reverend James Maury, who became like a second father to Jefferson. Reverend Maury was a demanding teacher but one who had a great intellect and a gift for teaching. Jefferson boarded there for two years and found it to be one of the most enjoyable times of his life. Reverend Maury continued to teach him Latin, Greek, and French, but now Jefferson felt he was in a "real" Latin school. He spent much of his time in Maury's four-hundred-volume library, pouring over its books.

In addition to the classical languages, Jefferson began to read some English literature, geography, history, and math. He studied English composition and learned how to speak in clear and persuasive grammar, although this shy young man always shunned public speaking. Maury took his students on field trips through the Virginia countryside and taught them zoology, geology, physics, and chemistry.

Jefferson's classmates realized that he was a serious student. He would sit under an oak tree and study Latin and Greek while the other students played. Jefferson studied the next day's lesson before he joined his friends. Maury taught him some of the same lessons as his father had—especially the value of self-discipline and patience.

During the two years at Maury's school, Jefferson began a practice that would continue for the next fifteen years, throughout his entire school experience. He started to keep a literary commonplace book. In it, Jefferson wrote down selected

The College of William and Mary was founded in 1693. To support the school and to pay for the construction of its first building, the Virginia House of Burgesses enacted a special "importation tax" upon "skins and furrs" as well as a new tobacco tax. Faculty salaries were paid from this tax. Good tobacco crops meant higher salaries, while failed years resulted in almost no wages. (Today, this would be similar to having one's salary pegged to the rise and fall of the stock market.) This tobacco tax, its enforcement and collection, remained a point of contention between Virginia tobacco planters and the college until the American Revolution. In the above document, the president of William and Mary ordered that the "books" of a James River tobacco planter be audited for the period October 15, 1763, to September 28, 1764, because it "appears to us that no payment has been made to the College."

Bursar's Books, College of William and Mary, 1763–64

When Jefferson attended William and Mary from 1760 to 1762, the enrollment was slightly more than one hundred students. (Slaves who were servants to the wealthier boys were not counted.) Less than a dozen Native Americans, or Indians, were enrolled in a special school with the aim of converting them to Christianity and to amalgamate them into "white society." The "college is at present in a very peaceable & thriving Way, & has now more Scholars in it, than it has ever had from its Foundation," President William Stith wrote to the Bishop of London in 1753.

Two years later, the Virginia tobacco crop failed. To cope with the desperate situation, the colonial legislature passed a law that for the next ten months—until the harvesting of the 1756 crop—all debts legally payable in tobacco could be paid in paper money at a rate fixed by law. Fortunately, 1756 and 1757 yielded outstanding tobacco crops. Nevertheless, the paper money law was reenacted. The William and Mary faculty considered the legislature's act as an attack upon them and the college, both dependent upon the price of tobacco and both opposed to being paid in paper money. In 1755 and 1756, faculty members, along with a quarter of Virginia's total Anglican clergy (whose salaries also were dependent upon the price of tobacco), protested to the Bishop of London about being paid in paper money rather than from the fees raised through the tobacco tax. But their protests were to no avail.

The above document details faculty salaries for 1763–64. The column on the right is the sums due in pound sterling. The column on the left is the sum actually paid in the depreciated local currency.

passages from the books he was reading. He summarized what he read and picked out what he felt were the key ideas and most inspiring thoughts. The earliest portions are from the writings of Horace, Virgil, and Ovid, who Jefferson studied while at Maury's school. Later, when he attended college, Jefferson continued to write in his commonplace book, adding selections from such Greek writers as Homer, Euripides, and Herodotus.

Jefferson eventually published the *Literary Commonplace Book* in the 1780s. It was a small book, four by six inches, with one hundred and twenty-three pages. The book was divided into sections of prose, classical poetry, English poetry, English dramatic verse, and miscellaneous poetry.

After two years at Maury's Latin school, Jefferson was ready to begin a new phase of his formal education. In March 1760, just before his seventeenth birthday, Jefferson left Shadwell for the one hundred and twenty-eight mile trip to Williamsburg, Virginia. He wanted to fulfill his father's dream—and secure his own future—by enrolling in the College of William and Mary. Thomas Jefferson also understood that in Williamsburg he would make contact with influential people who could further his ambitions.

Williamsburg was the largest town Thomas Jefferson had ever seen. It was the capital of the Virginia colony, the seat of political life, and the social and cultural heart of all the southern colonies. The mile-long Duke of Gloucester Street was the heart of the town with the college at one end and the capitol building at the other. When Jefferson enrolled in college, the town had about two hundred one-story houses with many large mansions. The population was normally between one thousand and fifteen hundred, but when the General Court and House of Burgesses were in session in the spring and fall, the population doubled. It was an exciting place to study for a young man arriving from the Virginia frontier. Here, at the seat of the provincial government, Jefferson witnessed history in the making and politics in practice.

The oldest higher education institution in the South, the College of William and Mary had been chartered in 1693 by King William III and Queen Mary II. From its beginning, the school was intended to be both a seminary for Anglican clergy and a college for the sons of the wealthy Virginia planters. In 1760, the college had six professors, including one who taught in the Indian School, which was devoted to the conversion and teaching of Native Americans. There was a struggle going on at the time of Jefferson's attendance between those who wanted the college to be secular and those who felt its first priority should be religious.

Jefferson enrolled in the Philosophy School, much like a liberal arts school today, and was eager to study the classics and mathematics. There he met William Small, one of the three men in Williamsburg who would have a powerful influence on his life. Young Jefferson was taught solely by Small, who had arrived in Williamsburg shortly before Jefferson. He was the only non-clergyman on the faculty. Small had been educated at Aberdeen, Scotland, and had a brilliant mind. He was well trained in science, then called natural philosophy, and taught a variety of other subjects.

Soon, Jefferson was learning logic, physics, ethics, philosophy, history, and rhetoric. Professor Small appreciated Jefferson's eagerness to learn, and the two became close friends. It was Small who introduced Thomas Jefferson to the ideas of the Enlightenment, a movement that had spread across Europe and into the colonies. This philosophy rejected many traditional ideas about religion and politics and encouraged people to use reason alone for guidance. Later in his life, Jefferson credited William Small as determining the direction of his life.

Jefferson continued to consume books. He read Montesquieu, Voltaire, and Rousseau in French, Cicero in Latin, and English authors like Shakespeare, Chaucer, and Milton. The scope of his reading was broad and included the science of Isaac Newton, which challenged many popular scientific theories. He began to teach himself Spanish and even Anglo-Saxon so that he could understand the roots of English common law.

Professor Small introduced Jefferson to the second man who would alter his life, George Wythe, the most noted lawyer of his generation in Virginia. Wythe and his wife had no children, and so they treated Tom as if he were their son. Jefferson thoroughly enjoyed his friendship with Wythe and considered him his "faithful and beloved mentor." They were to remain friends for many years. Wythe would one day sign the Declaration of Independence, which was written by Thomas Jefferson.

Jefferson was next introduced to Governor Francis Fauquier, an important figure in Virginia society and the third man to make a lasting impression on him. The three older men and student Thomas Jefferson became fast friends and met together regularly. The four often had dinner at the Governor's Palace near the college. Jefferson loved these informal dinners and felt that he heard more interesting and meaningful conversation there than at any time in his life. Fauquier was also a good musician and often asked Jefferson to play the violin in quartets that he arranged.

At the same time that Jefferson was enjoying the company of these established leaders of Virginia, he was also a typical college student. He was a recognized member of a close-knit social group made up of the children of the great families of Virginia. Jefferson and some of his teenage friends from Maury's Latin school, who were also attending William and Mary, formed a secret club. They called it the Flat Hat Club, and spoke what they dubbed "pig Latin." They met in the Apollo Room of the Raleigh Tavern, just up Duke of Gloucester Street from the House of Burgesses. These friends would have a major influence on Jefferson's career.

Jefferson graduated from the College of William and Mary in two years and entered the final phase of his formal education. In 1762, he decided to study law under George Wythe. He became a part of a group of young men also studying with this famous lawyer which included John Marshall, later the fourth chief justice of the U.S. Supreme Court; James Monroe, one day to become the fifth president of the United States; and Henry Clay, secretary of state under John Quincy Adams.

"Desperate Debts," Bursar's Books, College of William and Mary, 1764–68

In the 1760s the College of William and Mary was close to bankruptcy. Most of the sums due the college just did not come in. Tobacco-duty frauds continued unabated. For almost twenty years, the college had not received one penny of the revenue due it on imported skins and furs. This "desperate debts" page listed money overdue the college. Interest charges were regularly added. Benjamin Harrison, the Revolutionary statesman and governor of Virginia, is among those listed on this page as owing the school money in 1764–65. Harrison, who served in the House of Burgesses (1749–75), also owned one of the largest estates in Virginia. The sums due were from the unpaid tobacco tax. Likewise, John Carter, another large Virginia landholder, is listed as delinquent in paying the tobacco tax to William and Mary for 1764–67.

Norborne Berkeley, Baron de Botetourt (c. 1718–1770)

Thomas Jefferson considered his academic studies at William and Mary to be decidedly useful. Without a doubt, this was because of William Small. The other three or four faculty members were dullards.

In 1785, twenty-three years after leaving William and Mary, Jefferson wrote a rousing testimonial to the teaching that he had received:

> But why send an American youth to Europe for education? What are the objects of an [sic] useful American education? Classical knowledge, modern languages, chiefly French, Spanish, and Italian; Mathematics, Natural philosophy, Natural history, Civil history, and Ethics. In Natural Philosophy, I mean to include Chemistry and Agriculture, and in Natural history, to include Botany, as well as the other branches of those departments. It is true that the habit of speaking the modern languages cannot be so well acquired in America; but every other article can be as well acquired at William and Mary college as at any place in Europe.

Actually, Jefferson was describing the major academic changes that had occurred at William and Mary after he left the school. One person who stands out for having had a profound effect upon raising standards was Norborne Berkeley, Baron de Botetourt.

Lord Botetourt was appointed governor of Virginia in 1768. He was related to the prominent Berkeley family of Virginia and London. Instead of appointing a deputy to perform his duties, Botetourt went out to the colony in person, becoming the first royal governor in almost seventy-five years to take up permanent residence in Virginia. He brought over with him a resplendent coach and a team of cream-white Hanoverian horses. Botetourt promptly summoned the Virginia General Assembly. Dressed in a red coat, decorated with gold braiding, he was driven to the Capitol in his glittering coach drawn by his horses in their silver mounted harnesses—the whole an imitation of King George III opening the British Parliament. He delivered his address as if reading it from the royal throne. Some present said he even imitated the mannerisms of the monarch. But the burgesses were not awed by this pomp and circumstance. When they reasserted their rights not to be transported overseas to be tried by English juries, Botetourt rebuked them for their boldness and dissolved them as a body. Most of the burgesses reassembled at a local tavern. They unanimously adopted a resolution offered by George Washington that they would neither import nor buy any article that was subject to a parliamentary tax. This resolution began a path to the American Revolution.

Botetourt died in 1770, two years after his arrival in Virginia. During this brief period, he took an active role in the college as rector of the William and Mary Board of Visitors. Exacerbated by student vandalism and the continued insolvency of the school, Botetourt set about to improve both its physical and academic fabric.

His intervention in the academic life of William and Mary was immediate. To encourage scholarship, the governor offered two gold medals annually, one for classical learning and the other for achievement in natural philosophy [science]. These medals were to be awarded after a vigorous and thorough competition. These honors were given to students enrolled in the college for at least one year and who also demonstrated "moral conduct as members of society" as well as academic merit. The Botetourt Medals were the first medals presented by an academic institution in America. The College of William and Mary still awards the Lord Botetourt Medal on Commencement Day to the graduating senior who ranks first academically.

Botetourt's interest in the education at William and Mary was a real one. He took part in student's oral examinations. Until Botetourt, and in the almost eighty years since the college had received its royal charter, the college had not conferred one bachelor's degree. Botetourt had the scientific apparatus, which had been in storage since William Small departed, dusted off and used again. Encouraged by him, the F.H.C., a scholastic society which when Jefferson had been a student had by his own account "no useful object," suddenly took on the preparation of a highly sophisticated reading list and began plans for the purchase of a considerable library.

After Botetourt's death in 1770, a marble statue was erected in his honor. It stands in the quadrangle of the College of William and Mary.

Under Wythe's direction, Jefferson studied the writings of English jurists Sir William Blackstone and Edward Coke. Jefferson also studied English law as well as Virginia colonial law.

Thomas Jefferson continued to show the self-discipline that had helped him become such a good student. He awoke each morning at five, read ethics, religion, and natural law until eight, and then studied law until lunch. In the afternoon he returned to his study of law and then would visit friends. In late afternoon he would read history and at night, for relaxation, read literature. Jefferson studied approximately fifteen hours a day. In addition to that heavy schedule, Jefferson continued to set aside two hours every day for walking.

For the next five years, from 1762 to 1767, Jefferson studied under George Wythe. Whenever the General Court was in session and Wythe was in Williamsburg, Jefferson went to his home to read in his excellent library. Jefferson was given cases to research and prepare for Wythe and then went with him to the General Court in Williamsburg. When Wythe traveled to county courts around Virginia, Jefferson often went with him. During the latter part of his association with Wythe, Jefferson began to argue cases by himself in the courts. He was practically Wythe's law partner. In April of 1767, when Jefferson was twenty-four, he was admitted to the Virginia bar. He would practice law until 1774, when the courts were closed by unrest in the colonies.

Jefferson's formal education came to an end when he was twenty-four, but he continued to expand his knowledge and skills throughout his life. After he became a successful lawyer, he returned to Shadwell and began to build a new house on his estate. He leveled the top of a mountain and began to build on the summit. He named his new home Monticello ("small mountain"). Building on a height was unknown in the colonies, but it was an idea Jefferson had learned from books he had

Front and back views of copper striking of the Botetourt Medal, done as a proof, c. 1772

read on architecture. He was especially influenced by the sixteenth-century Italian, Andrea Palladio, whose text *Four Books of Architecture* taught Jefferson that there were laws of architecture, just as there were laws of mathematics and physical laws.

When he was twenty-eight, Jefferson met and married Martha Wayles Skelton, the twenty-three year old widow of a former classmate from William and Mary; she had a young son from her previous marriage. They were married on January 1, 1772, at The Forest, an estate owned by Martha's wealthy lawyer father. They settled at an incomplete Monticello. The Jeffersons had a happy marriage, which produced six children before Martha died after childbirth on September 6, 1782. Jefferson mourned his wife deeply and never remarried.

Thomas Jefferson's political career began when he was only twenty-six. He was first elected to the House of Burgesses in 1769, representing Albemarle County. He would serve in the House of Burgesses until he became a member of the Continental Congress in 1775. Thomas Jefferson was the principal author of the Declaration of Independence in 1776. This famous document, written without reference to a single book, showed the brilliance of his mind and the depth of his knowledge.

Jefferson was governor of Virginia from 1779 until 1781, during the American Revolution. He was elected to Congress in 1783 and served until 1785. He sailed for Europe in 1785 as the minister to France for the new United States of America and remained there until 1789. After his return to America, he became the first secretary of state under George Washington, a position he held from 1790 to 1793. Jefferson was elected vice president under John Adams and served in that position from 1797 until 1801.

In 1801, Jefferson became the third president of the United States, in an election decided by the House of Representatives when the electoral vote ended in a tie between Jefferson and Aaron Burr. He was elected to a second term in 1804. While president, Thomas Jefferson oversaw the Louisiana Purchase, which greatly increased the size of the United States, and authorized the Lewis and Clark expedition.

Thomas Jefferson retired from politics in 1809, at the end of his second term as president, and returned to his beloved Monticello. Home in Virginia, Jefferson founded the University of Virginia at Charlottesville in 1825, designing its buildings and managing its construction.

Late in his life, Jefferson sold his collection of 6,487 books for $23,950 to the U.S. government to replace a library that had been destroyed by British troops when they burned Washington, D.C., during the war of 1812. The money helped Jefferson pay an enormous debt he had because of a bad loan to a friend and debts inherited from his father-in-law. Jefferson's extensive collection had to be carried to Washington in eleven wagons, and became the basis for the developing Library of Congress. However, it was not long before his love for books led Jefferson to purchase new volumes and begin another library at Monticello.

In 1826, as Jefferson passed his eighty-third birthday, he became increasingly ill. His good friend and correspondent, former president John Adams, was also in very poor health. The two had both signed the Declaration of Independence in 1776 and were hoping to live until its fiftieth anniversary on July 4. As the fourth approached, Jefferson passed in and out of consciousness. He kept asking, "Is it the fourth yet?" Finally, in the early hours of July 4, 1826, Jefferson died, just a few hours before John Adams.

Thomas Jefferson was a lifelong student. He never stopped learning and never stopped being optimistic about what education could do. He believed that each new generation would build upon the knowledge of the past and work toward the well-being of human beings. For him, education was essential to a good life and to a beneficial existence. "Education," he once wrote, "engrafts a new man on the native stock, and improves what in his nature was vicious and perverse into qualities of virtue and social worth."

The value of education instilled in him by his father served him well. On the simple stone over his grave in the family burial ground at Monticello, he is described as he wished to be remembered, not as the holder of great offices, but as the author of the Declaration of Independence, and the Virginia statute for religious freedom, and the father of the University of Virginia.

—Bill Thompson

James Madison

Chapter Four

During March 1751, James and Nellie Madison traveled for three days over the rough dirt roads of colonial Virginia. They were on the way to Nellie's parents' home on the Rappahannock River, just across from the tidewater town of Port Royal. The couple was fifty miles away from their own home, but Nellie wanted to be with her mother when she gave birth to her first child.

At midnight on March 16, 1751, the baby arrived. It was a boy, whom the couple named James after his father. As Nellie held her son for the first time, she had no idea what the future held in store. Virginia was still a colony of Great Britain, and the United States did not yet exist. Yet this infant would one day be a key figure among the men who formed the government of the United States, as well as the country's fourth president.

James Madison Jr. was born into a prosperous family. Ambrose Madison, the grandfather of baby James, had settled in Orange Country on five thousand acres in 1729. With his wife, Frances, and three children, he developed an estate, which he called Mount Pleasant. (It would later be renamed Montpelier.)

Ambrose died in 1731, leaving his thirty-one-year-old widow to manage the tobacco estate herself. With her twenty-nine slaves, Frances became a successful Virginia planter, selling her tobacco crop in England. She was interested in developing the education of her children and made sure that her contacts in London sent her books and the *Spectator*, the leading magazine of the day. Her son James, educated as a child by Frances, began to help on the estate when he was only nine years old.

James Madison Sr. eventually inherited Montpelier and continued developing it. Soon, Montpelier was the largest plantation in the county, with more than one hundred slaves. When James was twenty-six years old, he married seventeen-year-old Nellie Conway. It was just a little more than eighteen months later that the couple welcomed their first child, James Jr. A few weeks later, they returned to Montpelier and continued their life there, along with James' mother, Frances. James and Nellie would have eleven more children, but only seven of the Madison children lived to maturity.

Grandmother Frances was James Jr.'s first teacher. There were no public

Princeton University (The College of New Jersey)

Princeton University, founded as the College of New Jersey in 1746, is the fourth-oldest institution of higher education in the United States. At the time, no college existed between Yale in New Haven, Connecticut, and the College of William and Mary in Williamsburg, Virginia. Princeton's John Witherspoon was the only college president to sign the Declaration of Independence (1776). It was in Princeton's Nassau Hall in 1783 that General George Washington received the formal thanks of the Continental Congress for his conduct of the American Revolution. Nine of the fifty-five members of the Constitutional Convention (1787) were Princeton graduates—more than from any other college.

Like its predecessors—Harvard, William and Mary, and Yale—Princeton was established by a religious denomination. It came into being because of the Great Awakening, that famous religious revival during the second quarter of the eighteenth century. Emphasizing the need of a personal religious experience, revivalists like Gilbert Tennent, his father and brother, and George Whitefield attracted multitudes of adherents by their fiery exhortations to sinners to repent. In the Presbyterian Church, these believers were known as New Lights (as opposed to the Old Sides, who preferred a more conservative religious doctrine). It was the New Light group that was instrumental in the founding of Princeton to educate ministers for their rapidly increasing churches. In 1748, Jonathan Belcher, the colonial governor of New Jersey, gave the new school his personal library of four hundred and seventy-four volumes, instantly making the college library one of the largest in the colonies.

Serious education came into young James Madison's life when his father sent him to the small local school of Edinburgh-trained Donald Robertson. Years later, when he was president of the United States, Madison wrote that Robertson was "a man of great learning, and an eminent teacher." Robertson instilled in Madison a love for learning. Madison's next tutor was Thomas Martin, a Presbyterian minister who had graduated from the College of New Jersey at Princeton in 1762. Martin served as a "family teacher" as he taught James, his three brothers and sister, and some neighbors children as well. Martin directed Madison to Princeton. Young Madison appreciated the opportunity to travel nearly three hundred miles from his native Virginia. And so, in 1769, eighteen-year-old James Madison set off to Princeton accompanied by Thomas Martin, Martin's brother, and Sawney, a Madison family slave and servant.

Student life at Princeton in the early 1770s was dominated by routine. There were about eighty students. Nassau Hall, which opened in 1756, contained the classrooms, a kitchen and dining area, and the student living quarters. Madison's classmate Philip Vickers Fithian, recorded the following schedule:

5-5:30 A.M. Dressing period. "The Bell rings at five, after which there is an Intermission of half an hour, that everyone may have time to dress, at the end of which it rings again, and Prayers begin; And lest any should plead that he did not hear the Bell, the Servant who rings goes to every Door and beats till he wakens the Boys."

5:30 Morning Prayers. "After Morning Prayers, we can, now in the winter, study by candle Light every Morning."

8:00 Breakfast. "From eight to nine is time of our own, to play, or exercise."

9:00-1:00 Recitation.

1:00 Dinner. "We all dine in the same Room, at three tables. After dinner till three we have Liberty to go out at Pleasure."

3:00-5:00 Study.

5:00 Evening Prayers

7:00 Supper.

9:00 "At nine the Bell rings for Study; And a Tutor goes through College, to see that every Student is in his own Room; if he finds that any are absent, or more in any Room than belongs there, he notes them down, and the day following calls them to an Account. After nine any may go to bed, but to go before is reproachful."

John Witherspoon, president of the College of New Jersey, 1768–94

James Madison's arrival at Princeton coincided with the arrival of John Witherspoon as the new college president. Witherspoon's years at Princeton are considered one of the must illustrious administrations in the college's history. Witherspoon, a descendant of John Knox and the choice of the New Lights, held views that were welcome to those of the Old Side. The traditional classical and religious education was maintained but Witherspoon introduced into the curriculum the study of eighteenth-century philosophy, French, modern history, and oratory. He insisted upon a mastery of the English language. Witherspoon altered the college's original mission. It was his conviction that an education should fit a man for public usefulness, not only for the pulpit. Book learning for its own sake did not appeal to him. From 1768 to 1776, the College of New Jersey increased its student body, the faculty, and the college endowment. From the favorable comments of Madison and others who studied at Princeton before the American Revolution, it seems that life at the college was progressive and stimulating.

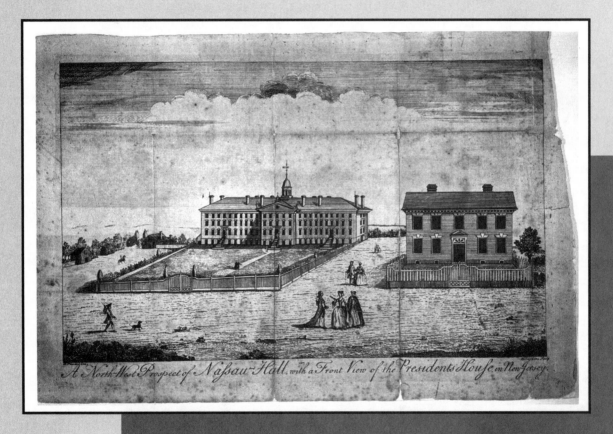

A North-West Prospect of Nassau-Hall, with a Front View of the Presidents House, in New Jersey.

Copper Engraving of Princeton's Nassau Hall and the President's House, 1764, by Henry Dawkins.
Henry Dawkins, a Philadelphia artist, copied this 1764 engraving of Nassau Hall and the president's house at Princeton from a drawing by William Tennant, class of 1758. James Madison lived in Nassau Hall for three years, 1769–72.
Witherspoon is credited with first applying the word *campus* (Latin for "field") to the college setting rather than calling it a yard, as was usual then. His description stuck, and gradually the word campus was adopted by universities throughout the nation.

schools in Virginia at this time, so most children received their educations at home. Frances taught her grandson reading, writing, and arithmetic, and encouraged him to read the *Spectator* before he was in his teens. He remembered the benefits he received from the magazine all his life. "It was good," James wrote to a young nephew years later, "for stirring in your mind a desire for improvement, a taste for learning and a lively sense of the duties, the virtues and the proprieties of life."

Jemmy, as young James was called, was a typical Virginia boy and loved taking long walks, horseback riding, and hunting and fishing with his many cousins who lived nearby. Yet Jemmy's first love was books and study. He enjoyed reading in his father's library more than playing outdoors.

When Jemmy was still young, the Madison family moved into a new brick mansion just a half mile away. This estate would be his home for the rest of his life.

For Jemmy, one of the most important rooms in the new home was the library. He read any book he could understand. Many of the books were religious and included *The Gospel Mystery of Sanctification*, *Warning to a Careless World*, and *The Nature of Sin*. These books expanded Jemmy's mind and gave him an interest in the the study of divinity. However, the library also contained books such as *The Motion of Fluids* and *The Dictionary of Arts and Sciences*, which described the latest scientific studies and discoveries. Jemmy read from those as well, and during his childhood developed an interest in science.

When Jemmy was ten, his Grandmother Frances died. To continue his education, Jemmy was sent to a boarding school run by Donald Robertson. Robertson had been educated at Aberdeen and Edinburgh in Scotland and had started his school along the Mattapony River just four years before eleven-year-old Jemmy arrived to join some of his cousins already attending the school.

It was while Madison studied with Robertson that he came alive intellectually. When, as an old man, Madison looked back over his life, he recalled the education he received at Robertson's school: "All that I have been in life I owe largely to that man." He studied English and mathematics during his first year, beginning his studies with a book called *Rudiments*. After this Jamie—as Robertson called the young man—went on to study Latin and Greek. He read Latin writings by the Roman poets Virgil, Horace, and Ovid as well as the Roman historians Cornelius Nepos and Sallust. In his final year, Madison concentrated on Greek and read many Greek classics, including the biographer Plutarch, the philosopher Plato, and the historian Herodotus.

Madison also studied Spanish and French. Unfortunately, in learning these languages he accidentally picked up Robertson's strong Scottish accent. This would make his conversation in the languages almost impossible to understand, as he would find out later in college. Madison also studied geography, history, and a variety of literature. Robertson's large library contained writings by the French essayist Montaigne and the political philosopher Montesquieu as well as the English philosopher John Locke. Madison read these and began developing his interest in the workings of government.

Before Madison arrived at Robertson's boarding school, he had begun a commonplace book like many other young men of his day. It is dated 1759, when Madison was only eight years old, but it probably contains things he copied at Robertson's school and possibly during his college years. It is a twenty-four-page notebook in which he copied some of the poems he was reading as well as articles from the *Spectator* and his own thoughts about authors he was reading. It shows clearly his ability to understand ideas and summarize them well. He was interested in the nature of human beings and the theories of government.

Another notebook that Madison filled out, dated 1766, was called "Notes on a Brief System of Logic." It has one hundred and twenty-two pages, and in them Madison included summaries of lectures given by his teacher and notes taken during class. There are references to writers such as Socrates and Euclid. At the end of the notebook are drawings and astronomical charts, including "The Solar System from Copernicus," a sixteenth-century Polish astronomer. Because some of the thinking is so mature, some scholars surmise that many of the notes might have been done when he was in college several years later.

Madison graduated from Donald Robertson's school on September 9, 1767, and returned to Montpelier for the next phase of his education. Reverend Thomas Martin had become rector at the Brick Church, not far from Montpelier. He lived at the Madison home; in return, he acted as tutor for the family. With Martin's guidance, Madison's understanding of Greek and Latin continued to deepen over the next two years.

The greatest influence Thomas Martin had on young Madison's life, however, was to direct him toward the College of New Jersey, later to be called Princeton University. Martin had graduated from that school just five years before coming to Montpelier and often spoke about its advantages. Thomas's brother, Alexander, also a recent graduate of the College of New Jersey, often visited Thomas Martin at Montpelier, and he too raved about the college.

Both brothers, though active churchmen, were opposed to the power of the Episcopal Church in Virginia. They disapproved of the establishment of a state-supported church that was financed through government taxes, which was the case in the Virginia Colony. Because William and Mary College in Williamsburg had been founded by the Episcopal Church and was closely connected to the political leaders of Virginia, they did not speak favorably of it. The College of New Jersey had been created by "New Side" Presbyterians, who stressed evangelism and religious freedom. Madison, who had witnessed the oppression of Baptists by the Episcopal Church in Virginia, appreciated a Presbyterian college that did not support the power of the clergy. When Madison was eighteen years old, he decided to go to the College of New Jersey.

Madison arrived in Princeton during the spring of 1769. The College of New Jersey had been founded in 1746 and so was only twenty-three years old when Madison arrived. Yet, it was probably the most diverse of the five colleges in America, with students coming from each of the colonies. When Madison attended

These Board of Trustees minutes were written while James Madison was a student at Princeton, 1769–71.

The page on the left focuses on financial problems. President John Witherspoon set the college on a sound financial basis, often raising funds by traveling through the colonies to recruit students. Although Princeton punished students who engaged in games of chance, officials saw no contradiction in holding a lottery for the benefit of the college. For example, in 1772 Delaware held a lottery for the "College of New Jersey, the Presbyterian Congregation of Princetown [Princeton], and the United Presbyterian Congregations of New Castle in Christiana Bridge." The proceeds to these three groups constituted fifteen percent of the prize money.

On the right page, dated September 26, 1770, the Board of Trustees conferred honorary doctorates of divinity on five ministers. The following day, September 27, the Board dealt with raising money in other colonies for support of the college. Noteworthy here is the mention of Richard Stockton, class of 1748. In 1766 Stockton, as a trustee of the college, was asked by the board to offer the college presidency to John Witherspoon, then living near Glasgow, Scotland. Stockton, a future signer of the Declaration of Independence, was received in London by King George III. He was given the freedom of the city of Edinburgh at a public dinner. However, Stockton could not convince Mrs. Witherspoon to move from Glasgow to Princeton. Undaunted, Stockton wrote to his wife: "I have engaged all the eminent clergymen in Edinburgh and Glasgow to attack her in her intrenchments and they are determined to take her by storm, if nothing else will do." Finally, after prolonged negotiations, Mrs. Witherspoon yielded and the Stockton mission was successful.

When James Madison was a student at Princeton, the library contained about two thousand books. This total included the five hundred or so volumes that John Witherspoon brought with him from Scotland when he assumed the college presidency in 1768. Witherspoon consistently ordered more books, with special emphasis on works in English. The above page from the Board of Trustees minutes (left) deals with the appointment of a new librarian. Among his other tasks, the librarian was given the responsibility of cataloging the books and maintaining better management of the library.

the College of New Jersey, only nineteen of the eighty-four students attending were from New Jersey. In his graduating class, only one of the twelve graduates was from New Jersey. That was a contrast to other colonial colleges, where the student bodies were made up mostly of men from the colonies in which the schools were located.

The president of the college in 1769 was a Presbyterian clergyman, Dr. John Witherspoon, who had come from Scotland the year before. He was considered a man of great learning who had much personal charm. In Scotland, Witherspoon had been exposed to the Enlightenment, a movement that rejected traditional social, religious, and political ideas. Witherspoon brought their books and ideas to Princeton. Witherspoon was conservative in his theology but liberal in his politics. He had a strong influence on Madison and other students of the college at a time when the colonies were being stirred by ideas of freedom from Great Britain. The College of New Jersey graduated more signers of the Declaration of Independence than any of the other colonial colleges.

Madison was tested when he entered the College of New Jersey and, because of his excellent early education, was able to enroll as a sophomore. Along with another student, he received permission to accelerate his studies so he could finish the remaining three years in two and graduate in 1771. In order to complete the accelerated schedule, Madison went for weeks with only five hours of sleep a night. He became thoroughly engrossed in his studies.

School began in November and continued for twenty-one weeks until April. After a five-week break, school resumed in May and went for another twenty-one weeks until September. Madison studied a variety of subjects. He continued to develop his knowledge of the classics, and in his first year studied astronomy, geography, algebra, rhetoric, French, and debating. Later he took mathematics and natural philosophy (physics and astronomy). Witherspoon himself taught courses in history and moral philosophy to Madison when he was a senior.

Life was full for Madison; he not only excelled in his studies but made many friends. The students had classes in Nassau Hall and also lived there together, three men to a room. One of Madison's friends was a college tutor, Samuel Stanhope Smith, who eventually succeeded Witherspoon as president of the College of New Jersey. Another friend was William Bradford, who studied divinity while in Princeton and later became a lawyer.

Right after entering college, Madison joined the newly formed American Whig Society. This was a literary organization in which friendships were developed as literature and essays about the issues of the time were read, discussed, and debated. The private debates, on such issues as freedom from British rule, whetted Madison's appetite for government.

In 1770, another literary society was formed, the Cliosophic Society, which began a "paper war" with the Whigs; one of its leaders was Aaron Burr. The public debates between the two societies often became more exciting than class work. Leaders of both societies would write satires that ridiculed the other.

Madison was one author for the Whigs, along with Philip Freneau and Henry Brackenridge, who were both excellent poets.

While not the equal of Freneau and Brackenridge in poetry, Madison wrote one satire that mocked Moses Allen, the founder of the Cliosophics. He called him "Great Allen" and assigned him a place in "Pluto's realm" (hell). Some of Madison's satires were too vulgar to be printed and were later repressed by his friends and biographers. Because Madison's humorous side was often unrecorded, later generations often thought of him as formal and stuffy. Yet the satires show a casual side of Madison. It was all in good fun, though. Moses Allen would become a pastor and visit Madison at Montpelier.

It was in Princeton that Madison realized how poorly he had learned French. President Witherspoon entertained a French diplomat as a guest of the college. Hearing that the young student had learned French fluently in Virginia, Witherspoon asked Madison to interpret for him. However, Madison spoke with such a Scottish burr that the Frenchman could not understand one word he said. This episode became one of Madison's favorite dinner stories for the remainder of his life.

The political situation in the American colonies greatly affected the College of New Jersey during Madison's years there. During the 1760s, the colonies were arguing with the British Parliament over the right of England to tax the colonies without their consent. The Townshend Acts of 1767 placed duties on many American imports. Boston merchants decided not to import goods from England, and many American cities, including New York and Philadelphia, joined the boycott.

In the summer of 1770, when Madison was in his second year at the College of New Jersey, the students learned of a letter written by the merchants of New York to the merchants of Philadelphia. The letter asked the Philadelphia merchants to join them in importing goods once again from England. The students felt this letter was a blow to the growing American desire for independence from Great Britain. Madison joined the other students at Princeton in a protest. They all dressed in black and marched outside Nassau Hall. A hangman they had hired then burned a copy of the letter to the tolling of a bell.

As graduation drew near, Madison's health grew worse, perhaps due to his overstudy and lack of sleep. Madison had some serious illnesses and many bouts of a nervous disorder that left him exhausted. He also suffered from hypochondria and believed that he would not live long or have a healthy life. Perhaps for these reasons, he was the only graduating senior who did not take part in the commencement ceremonies.

After Madison graduated in September of 1771, he received his father's permission to do graduate study under President Witherspoon. Madison stayed on for six months, taught solely by President Witherspoon. He learned some Hebrew, which had not been part of the college curriculum. He continued to read John Locke, David Hume, and others who shaped the Enlightenment worldview. Madison also studied some books on law and theology. In the spring of 1772, Madison left Princeton and returned to the family estate. His former tutor, Thomas Martin, had died, and his father needed another tutor for the younger Madison children. James Madison decided to fill that role.

Leaving Princeton did not end the education of James Madison. In fact, during the next three years he added greatly to his knowledge. His first responsibility was the teaching of his youngest siblings. However, he had a great deal of time to read, study, and meditate. He wanted to keep learning and to use his time for developing his understanding of the world. As he corresponded with his former college friend, William Bradford, they exchanged lists of books they wanted to have for their libraries.

Madison did a great deal of study in the New Testament, taking notes on William Burkett's book *Expository Notes*, which had been recently purchased by his father. He did not consider the Christian ministry as a career, but he did say that divinity was the most sublime of all sciences. He encouraged William Bradford to "season his other studies with a little divinity now and then, which like the philosopher's stone…will turn them…into the nature of itself and make them more precious than gold."

In this page from the minutes for 1771, the Board of Trustees raised student fees in order to make repairs to their living quarters. The Trustees also appointed William Churchill Houston as professor of mathematics and natural philosophy (science). Houston graduated from Princeton in 1768 and remained there first as master of the college grammar school and then as a tutor. Houston was Madison's tutor in 1770. Subsequently, Houston became a revolutionary leader as captain of the Somerset County, New Jersey, militia (1776), deputy secretary of the Continental Congress (1775–76), and a delegate to the Constitutional Convention (1787).

The study of government was a subject that increasingly interested Madison. He felt that the principles and forms of modern governments were too important to be ignored by anyone who had a thirst for knowledge. As he studied privately at Montpelier, he was well aware of the abuses of the government in Virginia. The established Episcopal Church persecuted anyone who disagreed with its doctrines. Five Baptist ministers were in jail for publishing their religious ideas, even though they were accepted Christian teachings. Frustrated over the oppressive atmosphere in Virginia, he wrote to Bradford in Pennsylvania, "I want again to breathe your free air."

Madison's political life began in 1774 when he was elected to the Committee of Safety in Orange County, chaired by his father. In 1776, he was elected a member of the Virginia House of Delegates, where he met Thomas Jefferson for the first time. The two began a friendship that lasted the rest of their lives. Madison worked hard to enact Jefferson's bill for religious freedom. Madison also worked closely with Jefferson and Patrick Henry for the independence of the Virginia colony. After the revolution he was a member of the Virginia House of Delegates and opposed the reestablishment of the Episcopal Church in Virginia. He was able to defeat all attempts to use tax money to support any Christian denomination in the newly formed State of Virginia.

The Princeton University archives have a complete record of the Board of Trustees minutes, a few dating back to the founding of the college in 1746. However, the military campaigns fought during the American Revolution in and around Princeton, and subsequent fires, destroyed most of the early college records.

This entry of June 26, 1860, is interesting because it explains how commencement exercises were held. The board ordered the procedure to be the same as the previous year: "The candidates for the first degree in the Arts, with the exception of Valedictory orator, delivered their speeches in the morning of Wednesday, the day of Commencement. There was then an intermission in the exercises for an hour. After which the Master's Oration was pronounced, the degrees were conferred and the Valedictory addresses were made. The whole exercises were concluded with prayer and with a benediction. The permission for music is the same as it was last year, and the expense will be the same, vig. one hundred and twenty-five dollars."

The president of the Board of Trustees also noted "with pleasure" that the buildings of the college and the surrounding grounds were maintained in excellent condition. He also announced that Nassau Hall had been rebuilt after the 1855 fires and he offered a prayer for its completion "without the loss of a single life, and without any serious or lasting injury. Let us be thankful."

The Board of Trustees accepted the gift of the late Professor Matthew B. Hope's 1,600-volume library. Hope was remembered by graduates of that period as one of Princeton's most inspiring teachers.

Before Jefferson went to Paris in 1785, he agreed to buy a number of books for Madison, particularly those that concerned ancient and modern republics. Jefferson also sent Madison thirty-seven volumes of the *Encyclopedie Methodique,* which Madison described as a complete scientific library. He pored over these books to learn the history of European nations and to discover the strengths and weaknesses of their governments.

In 1787, Madison was elected a delegate to the Constitutional Convention. It was here that his skills in political science and logic would become evident. Because of his great involvement in the debates surrounding the Constitution, and his work to have the document approved, Madison is often called the Father of the Constitution. His extensive notes and journals are the principal sources of information about the convention and the process of drafting the Constitution.

Madison was determined to help create a strong central government that would last. Once the Constitution was written, he wanted to make sure it would be approved by the people. He wrote a number of essays about the Constitution, explaining the document and encouraging the states to ratify it. Madison's essays, along with similar essays by John Jay and Alexander Hamilton, became known as the Federalist Papers. These influential essays convinced Americans to approve the Constitution. It became the basis for the U.S. government in 1789.

Madison was elected to the House of Representatives from Virginia in 1789. He continued his work in establishing the new government and sponsored the first ten amendments to the Constitution—the Bill of Rights.

Marriage came late for James Madison. He met a widow, Dorothea "Dolley" Payne Todd, when he was forty-three and married her on September 15, 1794. Dolley Madison became a charming first lady when Madison became president in 1809.

Madison was secretary of state for eight years under President Thomas Jefferson, then served two terms as president. He retired on March 4, 1817, and returned to Montpelier. He continued to receive new books, as well as newspapers and reports from political, educational, and scientific organizations. Madison wrote articles and letters, and spent a great deal of time organizing his own papers. He also served as rector of the University of Virginia from 1826 to 1836.

Madison was described in his retirement by one visitor as a man who "sparkled in conversation," who had a remarkable command of the English language, and was profound and far-reaching in his views. Even when he was unable to read in his old age, Dolley would sit at his side and read for him. His mind never stopped searching for knowledge. He died peacefully on June 28, 1836, at the age of eighty-five.

Throughout James Madison's life, he always acknowledged the importance of education, particularly as it related to government. In a letter to his friend W. T. Barry, dated August 4, 1822, he wrote: "A popular government without popular information, or the means of acquiring it, is but a prologue to a farce or a tragedy, or perhaps both. Knowledge will forever govern ignorance, and a people who mean to be their own governors must arm themselves with the power which knowledge gives."

—Bill Thompson

James Monroe
Chapter Five

I t was a hot, difficult march for James Monroe, a young college student from Virginia. It was late summer of 1776, and he had enlisted in the military and was joining several hundred other men heading for New York. When they arrived on the island of Manhattan with the other troops from Virginia, he and the others were exhausted. However, their spirits were high because they were anxious to face the British army. The Virginians joined General George Washington's men already camped at Harlem and settled in. Just a few days later, word came that the British had invaded Manhattan just six miles south of the Americans. Monroe waited with the Continental army for the British advance north.

Monroe was furious when he heard that poorly trained troops from Connecticut had run from the British without offering any resistance. He wanted the English to arrive so he and his fellow soldiers could show them the courage of Virginia men. When the British did reach Harlem, the fresh Virginia infantry held back the strong and continuous British attacks. The next day, General Washington honored the young men from Virginia for their bravery. He was especially impressed by the courage of the broad-shouldered, six-foot-tall Monroe.

This experience of warfare was a world away from the life that James Monroe had known in Virginia, four hundred miles south of the Harlem battlefield. Monroe was born in Westmoreland County on April 28, 1758. His home in Westmoreland County, between the Potomac and Rappahannock Rivers, was not far from where George Washington had spent his youth. James was the oldest son of Spence and Elizabeth Monroe, whose ancestors had settled there more than a century before his birth.

Early colonists had first farmed the fertile soil of Virginia on the peninsula where Westmoreland County was located. Raising tobacco was hard on the soil, so every three or four years a planter would have to move to new fields and let the older land lay fallow. By the time Monroe was born, the soil of Westmoreland County had become poor through over cultivation, and the land was profitable only to those great Virginia families that owned thousands of acres.

The time that James Monroe spent at William and Mary (1774–76) coincided with the most disruptive period in the college's history. William and Mary was identified with the Church of England, the state religion. By 1775, at the outset of the Revolution, many American-based Anglican ministers, including two of the six college professors (a third was in London for his ordination), took up the Tory cause.

In this September 14, 1775, entry from the Journal of the Meetings of the President and Masters, the Reverend John Camm, the Loyalist president of William and Mary, dismissed James Innes from his position as head usher of the grammar school. (An usher would be equivalent to a college tutor today—somewhere between a student and a faculty member.) Innes was accused of "neglecting his Duty for the three last months by repeatedly absenting himself from the College for days & weeks together, without asking permission to be absent, behaving herein as if he had no superior in the Society to whom he thought himself accountable for his conduct." At the bottom of this entry is the cryptic admonition: "No Arms or Ammunition shall be brought into the College and kept there by the students."

James Innes had entered William and Mary in 1771. By 1775, he had become the captain of the Williamsburg volunteers and therefore an anathema to the Tory college president. In his five years as an undergraduate and usher—the five years that led up to the Revolution—Innes was not only eager for the fighting against the British to begin but he also was determined to enlist his fellow students in the revolutionary cause. Innes was extremely popular, except with the college leaders. As an usher living in the ambiguous world between faculty and undergraduates, Innes aroused agitation among the students and anguish among his professors.

Innes influenced young James Monroe. He encouraged Monroe's decision to leave William and Mary and join the Williamsburg volunteers. This decision affected the rest of Monroe's life.

War disrupts the College of William and Mary

In 1774, at age sixteen, James Monroe entered the College of William and Mary. But the advent of the American Revolution soon interrupted his academic studies. In 1776, at age eighteen, he enlisted in a Virginia regiment of the Continental Army.

Students at the College of William and Mary were absorbed by the crisis with Great Britain, as was the rest of America. Yet, routine continued. Solemn young men attended meetings of earnest societies to debate philosophical issues. Reverend William Henley, a professor of moral philosophy who was the most popular of the faculty members, gave lectures on the "Elementary Ideas of Poetry" to those gentlemen of Williamsburg who chose to pay a fee to attend. Whenever he spoke, the Great Hall at the college was usually filled to capacity.

However, Henley opposed the Revolution. An American bishop in an independent United States, he reasoned, would weaken the connection to the Church of England. The relationship, he wrote, would be no better than "a Mongrel Episcopate." In late 1775, after the outbreak of war, Henley left Virginia for England, where he lived for the next forty years.

By coincidence, Henley later taught George Gordon, Lord Byron, at Harrow, an English boarding school for boys that had been founded in 1571. During the last years of Henley's life, his former student Monroe was secretary of state and secretary of war of the United States, which at the time was fighting Great Britain in the War of 1812. At the same time, Lord Byron had become Britain's most famous man of letters.

Although he could trace his ancestry to British royalty, Spence Monroe had inherited only five hundred acres of land and was not a wealthy man. Yet, he was still considered part of the gentry, or ruling class, although he was at the lower end of the social ladder. None of the Monroe ancestors had been able to afford college. Few had held important political positions, because Virginia's government was run by members of wealthy families with large landholdings: the Carters, the Randolphs, the Byrds, and the Lees. However, James's mother, Elizabeth Jones Monroe, came from a wealthier family. Her brother, Joseph Jones, was an important judge in Fredericksburg. He would prove to be a powerful asset to James Monroe as the young man matured.

James grew up in a world of agriculture and for the rest of his life he loved being close to the soil where he felt a sense of peace. He lived near the major north-south road that connected Williamsburg, the Virginia capital, with a ferry that crossed the Potomac. As a result, even when he was a boy James was well informed about the political events of his day.

Like all of the children of the gentry, James began his education at home. His first teachers were his parents, who taught him to read and write. His mother was an educated woman, unusual for the time. From his early years, however, James's education developed as much through experience as through formal schooling. When he was seven, he watched as his father organized a boycott with a hundred other Westmoreland County men against the Stamp Act of 1765. The British had put a tax on all paper used by the colonists for official documents, a decision deeply resented throughout the colonies. James saw how effective the protest was when the British repealed the Stamp Act a year later.

When James was eleven years old, he started to attend his first formal school, Campbelltown Academy, where he studied from 1769 to 1774. It was considered the best grammar school in Virginia. Monroe later wrote, "Twenty-five students only were admitted into his academy, but so high was its character that youths were sent to it from more distant parts of the then colony." The founder of the school, and its teacher, was the Reverend Archibald Campbell, who was then rector of Washington Parish, where the Monroe family lived and worshiped.

Reverend Campbell had come to Virginia from Scotland in 1741 and had established his academy about nine years later. He was called "a clergyman of great respectability" and was known for his learning, especially his knowledge of Greek studies. Reverend Campbell was also called "a disciplinarian of the sternest type" and did not allow the students much time for play. He was an excellent teacher and emphasized mathematics and Latin.

Monroe's father had gone to the academy, as had most of the children of the gentry in Westmoreland. When James Monroe first began his studies, he developed a close friendship with young John Marshall, and the two would remain lifelong friends The boys undoubtedly found ways to have fun together in spite of their strict teacher. Eventually they both became lawyers in Richmond (Marshall would eventually become chief justice of the U.S. Supreme Court) and, as adults, loved to play cards and billiards together and went to the theatre as often as possible.

While at Campbelltown, Monroe learned Latin and Greek and received a well-grounded classical education. He read Pope's "Essay on Man" and some of his "Moral Essays." As Monroe continued his studies, the political situation in the colonies was becoming increasingly unstable. Boycotts and demonstrations were common. In 1773, Boston citizens dumped tea in the harbor and defied British authority. The students heard the citizens of Westmoreland County openly speaking against England.

Both of Monroe's parents died within months of each other in 1774, leaving James as heir of the Monroe estate. His father's death left him with the responsibility for the welfare of his two brothers, Andrew and Joseph, as well as his sister Elizabeth. Fortunately for James Monroe, his uncle, Judge Jones, was executor of the estate. The Judge was a wealthy man and a member of the House of Burgesses, the Virginia legislature, which made him part of the group that ruled Virginia. The Joneses had no children and treated teenage James as their own son.

Judge Jones believed Monroe was ready for advanced education. Both James and his uncle had hoped that James could go to Europe for his studies. Most children of the gentry went to England for advanced schooling, because this was considered superior to the educational opportunities available in colonial America. However, the political situation made that difficult. With his uncle's connections,

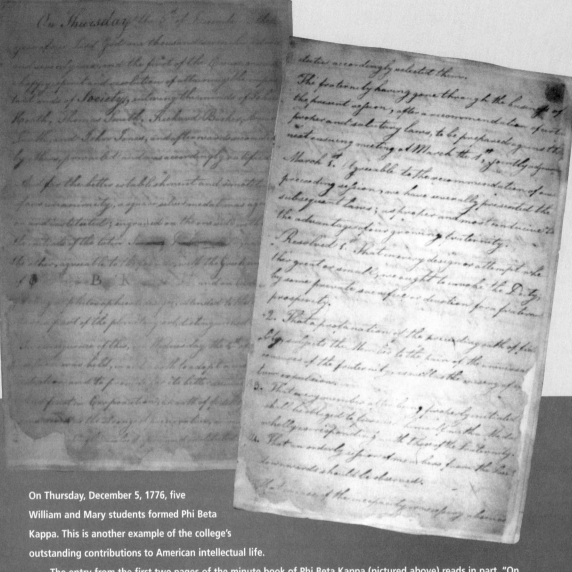

On Thursday, December 5, 1776, five William and Mary students formed Phi Beta Kappa. This is another example of the college's outstanding contributions to American intellectual life.

The entry from the first two pages of the minute book of Phi Beta Kappa (pictured above) reads in part, "On Thursdy, the 5th of December, in the year of our Lord God one thousand seven hundred and seventy-six, and the first of the Commonwealth, a happy spirit and resolution of attaining the important ends of Society entering the minds of John Heath, Thomas Smith, Richard Booker, Armstd Smith, and John Jones, and afterwards seconded by others, prevailed, and was accordingly ratified.

"And for the better establishment and sanctitude of our unanimity, a square silver medal was agreed on and instituted, engraved on the one side with S.P., the initials of the Latin S[ocietas] P[hilosophas], and on the other, agreeable to the former, with the Greek initials FBK, and an index imparting a philosophical design, extended to the three stars, a part of the planetary orb, distinguished."

Phi Beta Kappa was the first undergraduate secret society at an American college. It began as a social fraternity, but has evolved to become the leading advocate of the liberal arts and sciences at the undergraduate level. Today, Phi Beta Kappa elects more than 15,000 new members annually from its nearly 270 chapters across the United States. Membership is open to both men and women undergraduates who excel in academics.

and probably with his financial support as well, sixteen-year-old Monroe went to Williamsburg in June of 1774 to attend the College of William and Mary.

James Monroe did very well in his entrance exams, which included the classical materials he had studied under Campbell. Monroe soon discovered, however, that he was in an entirely new environment. All of his life he had lived among planters, who generally opposed the authority of the British crown. Now Monroe found himself in a school where some of the professors were Tories who supported the authority of the British crown.

Monroe was introduced to his roommate, John Mercer, who was fifteen and came from a wealthy family. The two became good friends and started their classes together. Both were immediately affected, however, by the political developments in Williamsburg. Not long after Monroe and his roommate began their studies, the governor of Virginia, John Murray, the Earl of Dunmore, tried to show his authority by dissolving the Virginia House of Burgesses.

The burgesses continued to assemble, meeting instead in the Apollo Room of Raleigh Tavern, just down the street from the college. They met twice that summer in opposition to the governor. Monroe was especially aware of the conflict because his uncle, Joseph Jones, was one of the burgesses. Both students and faculty at William and Mary discussed the clash between the governor and the burgesses. For a while, teaching and studying took a backseat to politics.

When the struggle quieted, Monroe returned to his studies. Only sixteen, he discovered that he was not fully prepared for the work he was asked to do. Some years later, Monroe wrote to a nephew about his first six months at the college: "I had been examined…and [was] found well qualified to enter the philosophical school." But when he began his advanced mathematics course, Monroe discovered, "I was altogether unqualified" and "made a ridiculous figure." When his winter vacation came, Monroe decided to stay on in Williamsburg and use that time for intense study. When he returned to the classroom after two months, "I had made such good use of my time that I obtained the approbation and praise of the professors."

Through the first part of 1775, the College of William and Mary went about the business of education. Then in April, the governor again created a crisis. He sent soldiers to seize some gunpowder that belonged to the city of Williamsburg. Some patriots discovered the plan, and bands of men gathered to protect the powder. Governor Dunmore agreed to pay for it, calming some of the citizens. However, the whole matter aroused the college students, and they began to join townspeople at frequent meetings being held throughout the city. Monroe went to these meetings and joined other students as they spent time drilling on the college campus.

During that same time, a twenty-year-old worker at the college, James Innes, spoke openly on campus about the need to arm. He created a military group of interested students; Monroe was impressed by him and joined the militia. Like many other students, Monroe purchased a rifle and kept it in his room against school rules. Innes was considered a nuisance in the eyes of the college professors.

He was accused of taking students to a tavern, getting them drunk, and causing a disturbance late at night. Finally, in June 1775 Innes left the college and went to fight in the new Continental Army, much to the relief of the faculty.

Also in June 1775, a British general met with the burgesses and tried to work out a compromise with them. They remained defiant, however, and Governor Dunmore, concerned by some of their radical comments, sought refuge in a British warship on the James River. The burgesses quickly set up a committee to take over the government of the capital. Fighting broke out between the British soldiers and the citizens of Williamsburg.

After the British army fired on militiamen at Concord, Massachusetts, Monroe joined a group of twenty-four men, made up of college students and older males, and attacked the Governor's palace on June 24. At seventeen, Monroe was the youngest member of the group. There was no resistance at the palace, and the rebel band easily walked off with two hundred muskets and three hundred swords. The weapons were donated to the Virginia militia.

In spite of his involvement in these military adventures, Monroe continued in his studies. The colonists began to take over the entire Virginia colony over the next year, and throughout the American colonies people were preparing for war. Monroe knew he had to make a choice. In the spring of 1776, Monroe and his roommate, John Mercer decided to suspend their college careers and join the patriot cause. They enlisted, along with other students from William and Mary, in the Third Virginia Regiment. They were made lieutenants and joined in the long march toward Washington's army camped on the island of Manhattan. However, if Monroe thought he was leaving his studies behind, he would discover that opportunities to learn were everywhere.

After the battle at Manhattan, Monroe was among Washington's troops as they retreated through New Jersey. The American army reached the Delaware River by December. When Washington decided to attack Trenton on Christmas Day, Monroe was with a group of fifty men who were sent ahead toward the city. Monroe was seriously wounded at Trenton and spent three months recovering in Bucks County, Pennsylvania. He eventually rejoined Washington and when the Continental Army was camped at Valley Forge during the next winter, Monroe shared a cabin with his old friend, John Marshall, who had also enlisted.

Monroe felt that the many new relationships he was making in the military were valuable, because they gave him a greater knowledge of other parts of the world. He realized that when his experience was limited only to Virginia, his perspective on events had been limited also.

One of the men who most influenced Monroe during this time was Pierre S. DuPonceau, an eighteen-year-old from France. The young Frenchman was highly intelligent and spoke excellent English. He began to share with Monroe the writings of French philosophers, subjects Monroe had never studied. The two young men had the same interest in reading and shared books with one another. They had long talks about what they were reading and became extremely close.

Front and back views of the oldest extant Phi Beta Kappa key, which was given to William Short in 1780.

Short attended William and Mary from 1777 to 1781, and was the president of the society from 1778 to 1781. After leaving the college, he had a distinguished career in government. Short was Thomas Jefferson's private secretary during his mission to France, 1785–87. From Paris, Jefferson, John Adams, and Benjamin Franklin sent Short to The Hague to meet with a Prussian envoy and arrange a commercial treaty between Prussia and the United States. Short also served as minister to the Netherlands, 1792–93.

DuPonceau gave Monroe popular plays by Nicholas Rowe, who incorporated politics throughout his dramas. The Frenchman also loaned Monroe sermons by preacher James Watson, who had liberal ideas on Christianity. DuPonceau encouraged Monroe to read books by French philosopher Mark Akenside, who placed ancient Greek ideas above those of the Christian faith. This period of study gave Monroe a broader concept of the war against Great Britain. He came to believe that he was involved in a battle to free *all* humankind from oppression.

When it became apparent that he would not receive a field command, Monroe resigned from the army on December 20, 1778, and returned to Virginia. For a year he tried to find a position in the Virginia state militia but could not. He met and became friends with Thomas Jefferson, who had become governor of Virginia in 1779. Jefferson appreciated the warmth and sincerity of the young former soldier and became his mentor. Through Jefferson's friendship, a new period of education began for the twenty-one-year-old Monroe. Jefferson encouraged Monroe to study law as a way of entering politics and helping to develop the new nation.

In 1780, Monroe "submitted the direction of his studies" to Jefferson and reentered William and Mary as his apprentice. Jefferson was interested in helping his apprentices learn the basic principles of law. Monroe and two other young men began to study the writings of a liberal lawmaker, Edward Coke, and a famous English jurist, Sir William Blackstone. The young apprentices were allowed to study the law cases of Jefferson and were given the large collection of the statutes of Virginia to read.

The final stage of their apprenticeship was to read the great books of western civilization, both ancient and modern. Among them were the writings of the philosopher and historian David Hume, the English philosopher John Locke, and the French philosopher Jean Rousseau. Ancient authors included the Greek moralist Plutarch, the Roman historian Tacitus, and the Greek stoic Epictetus.

Monroe's gratitude to Jefferson was expressed in a letter he wrote to his teacher in September 1780:

> Your kindness and attention to me in this and variety of other instances has really put me under such obligations to you that I fear I shall hardly ever have it in my power to repay them....You became acquainted with me and undertook the direction of my studies and believe me I feel that whatever I am at present in the opinion of others or whatever I may be in future has greatly arise from your friendship. My plan of life is now fixed, [and] has a certain object for its view...

Monroe expected to study next with the famous Virginia lawyer, George Wythe, Jefferson's early teacher in Williamsburg. Wythe had recently become a law professor at William and Mary, and Monroe looked forward to learning from him. However, Jefferson told Monroe he was moving to Richmond, Virginia, where the capital had been relocated, and invited Monroe to go with him. Monroe sought advice from his uncle, who encouraged him to continue his association with Jefferson. Monroe went with Jefferson and shortly after settled down on an estate not far from Richmond. There he continued the study of law, still under Jefferson's tutelage.

By October of 1781, Monroe had finished the books Jefferson had given him and made plans to go to Europe to complete his education. He wrote to Jefferson, "Since my return from Richmond I have...read all the books you mention of the subject of law." He was interested, he wrote Jefferson, not only to study for the sake of being able to practice law, but also to better himself. What could be acquired from books, Monroe wrote, "will qualify a man not only for public office, but enable him to bear prosperity or adversity...by giving him resources within himself, of pleasure and content which otherwise he would look for in vain from others."

Monroe was not able to go, however. The next spring, with the fighting of the American Revolution ended, he was elected to the House of Delegates from

King George County. His political career had begun. Monroe became a member of the Continental Congress in 1783 and a U.S. Senator in 1790. He finally traveled to Europe when he became minister to France in 1794.

In 1785, while a member of the Continental Congress, Monroe met Elizabeth Kortright, only sixteen years old but "a statuesque beauty with raven hair and blue eyes." They were married a year later, on February 16, 1786, and had two daughters.

Monroe's career continued without a break. He was governor of Virginia twice, minister to Great Britain, secretary of state and secretary of war. He was elected president in 1816 (the first president to have been a senator) and again in 1820. Monroe retired on March 4, 1825, and moved into a new home, Oak Hill, in Virginia. When his wife died in 1830, he went to live with a daughter and son-in-law in New York City.

President James Monroe died in New York on July 4, 1831. He was the third president to die on the anniversary of the Declaration of Independence.

James Monroe's public career was greatly influenced by three major factors: the American Revolution; the principles of the Republican Party, which he helped found (this party eventually evolved into the Democratic Party); and his diplomatic experiences. The Monroe Doctrine was one of the most important principles in U.S. foreign policy, as it closed the Americas to further colonization by European powers like France, Spain, and Great Britain.

Perhaps one of the best remarks to be made about James Monroe was spoken about him while he was still in his twenties. Thomas Jefferson said "Turn his soul wrong side outwards and there is not a speck on it."

—Bill Thompson

John Quincy Adams
Chapter Six

Imagine a twelve-year-old giving language lessons to a French ambassador. This happened to young John Quincy Adams aboard a ship, *La Sensible*, soon after it sailed out of the French port of Nantes. Just one year in France had helped John Quincy, who was then called Johnny, learn French. He was traveling with his father, John Adams, to their home in Quincy, Massachusetts. Another passenger on *La Sensible* was Chevalier Anne Cesar de La Luzerne, the new French ambassador to the United States.

John Adams entered the lounge of the ship one day and found Johnny sitting with the French ambassador. Next to them was the ambassador's private secretary. John Adams could see that the two men were fascinated by his son. They were reading aloud a lecture by an English jurist, Sir William Blackstone. Their English was rather poor, and Johnny was correcting each word and syllable they spoke. He was giving them no praise for their efforts and showed little sympathy for their mistakes.

Rather than resent this, the two Frenchmen told John Adams that they could not do without his son, "little John." He was an enormous help to them in learning the English language, and they were grateful that he used no flattery and was firm with them. John Adams was pleased that his son had been able to help them. Young Johnny Adams, one day to become the sixth president of the United States, was a unique young person who experienced an unusual childhood.

John Quincy Adams was born in Quincy (then Braintree), Massachusetts, on July 11, 1767. Johnny lived with his parents, Abigail and John, in a frame house just across the street from where his father had lived as a boy. He had an older sister, Abigail (Nabby), and two younger brothers, Charles and Tom. John Adams practiced law and had his offices in the front room of their home. Johnny enjoyed the same kind of early boyhood as his father and grandfather had. He loved to walk through the marshes, to hunt in the wooded hills, and to fish in the streams flowing into the nearby bay.

Education was a priority in the Adam's household. Both Abigail and John Adams were dedicated to passing on to their children their own love of learning and of books. They taught Johnny to read and write by the time he was five, and by

March 20. 1778.

The Subscribers, being a Committee appointed by the Corporation having examined the Steward's accounts of disbursements for commons from Nov: 14. 1777 to March 12. 1778 inclusively, beg leave to represent to the Reverend Corporation that they find,

That the Steward had Stores remaining on hand Nov: 14. 1777 — — £ 99. 15. 0

That in the time above specified he purchased Provisions to the amount of — 609 ~ 8. 11

That he has received from the College woodlot fourteen loads of wood a 60/ — 42 : 0 . 0
Also one load of faggots — V. 10. 0
That there must be charged for wear of table-linen — 4. 10. 0

That no charge be allowed for the Laundress this quarter because a full allowance was made the last quarter, and the students were dismissed as many days before the last quarter-day, as they have been convened before the present —

That from the above sum there must be deducted as follows for Provisions charged as sittings 26.16.1½
Stores unexpended — — 309. — — 757. 3. 11

335: 16. 1¾

That the neat expense for Provisions is — 421. 7. 9¼

Examination of the Harvard steward's accounts, March 20, 1778.

This committee reviewed the Harvard steward's account book. Among other things, it was noted that there was no laundry charge between November 1777 and March 1778 as "the students were dismissed as many days before the last quarter-day, as they have been convened." The Continental Army had sent General Burgoyne's surrendered troops to be housed in the college buildings. This caused most classes to be cancelled during the winter 1777–78 term.

the time he was six he was expected to write letters. However, though Johnny participated in the normal activities for a boy his age, he was also exposed to the conflicts that were occurring between the British and the American colonists. That struggle, which led to the Revolutionary War, greatly affected John Quincy Adams's upbringing and early education.

Colonial resistance to British authority was beginning to break into physical violence while Johnny was very young. His father had taken the family to live in Boston as his law practice began to prosper. During the winter of 1770, British troops fired on a mob not far from their home, killing five colonists. This skirmish became known as the Boston Massacre. John Adams was the only lawyer who would defend the British soldiers, for which some people scorned him. As a result of the unrest in Boston, in early 1771 John moved his wife and children back to the farm in Quincy, eleven miles south of Boston. The family returned to Boston in 1772, but after further troubles with the British they returned to Quincy to stay.

Much of Johnny's early education was left to Abigail because John was busy establishing his legal practice. He later became involved in the colonies' fight for independence from Britain. Because of that, he spent much time in Philadelphia as a member of the Continental Congress. Though absent from home, his letters to Abigail expressed his concerns for the education of his family. "Above all cares of this life let our ardent anxiety be to improve the minds and manners of our children," he wrote. "Let us teach them not only to do virtuously, but to excel."

The political situation in Massachusetts grew worse in 1775, and Abigail became anxious about the education of her children. Public schools were not operating, and she had to find other ways to teach Johnny. Her husband had two law clerks, John Thaxter and Nathan Rice, who became Johnny's tutors for a time. Johnny especially liked Thaxter, his father's cousin, who helped Johnny with some of the basics, such as Latin, which he had started learning from by his parents. John Adams helped by writing regularly from Philadelphia and including Latin sentences for Johnny to translate.

Abigail watched over Johnny's progress and asked him to read to her from Rollin's *Ancient History*, a text that had been translated from French. In his letters, John Adams encouraged Abigail to make sure Johnny was taught geography and the skill of copying, which was then considered essential to learning. Johnny developed a daily schedule of reading that included the *Complete History of England* by Tobias Smollett. John Adams also wrote directly to his oldest son, challenging him to prepare to learn Greek. He wanted him to have the pleasure one day of reading the *History of the Peloponnesian War* by historian Thucydides in the original Greek.

Bible reading was a regular practice for everyone in the family, and John Quincy developed a habit of reading the Bible for an hour each day. He also loved fairy tales and pored over the *Arabian Nights*. For Johnny, the characters in the stories seemed to be real people. He read many Shakespeare plays, such as *The Tempest*, *As You Like It*, and *Much Ado About Nothing*. Reading them made him feel as though he was in an enchanted world. He tried to understand *Paradise Lost* by John Milton, because his parents both loved it. Johnny did not finish reading this difficult epic poem, though, until he had become an adult.

One day in the spring of 1775, Abigail and the children climbed Penn's Hill behind their home, where they could look north toward Boston. They saw the city of Charlestown in flames—it had been set on fire by British troops. Another day, from the same spot, they heard the roar of cannon from a battle on Breeds Hill just outside Boston. (This battle became popularly, though erroneously, known as the Battle of Bunker Hill.) Because of John Adams's position in the Continental Congress, Abigail and her children feared that one day British soldiers might snatch them from their home and take them hostage into Boston. In spite of their anxieties, both Abigail and John instilled strong patriotic feelings in their four children. Abigail had Johnny memorize "How Sleep the Brave," a heroic poem honoring warriors who had died in battle. He quoted it every day after he said the Lord's Prayer.

Realizing that Johnny's education had been severely interrupted by the confusion of war, Abigail was determined to send him to the Governor Dummer

Academy, north of Boston. This would prepare him to enter Harvard College, the school from which his father had graduated. However, in November 1777 Congress asked her husband to be a member of a commission being sent to France to win its support for the American cause. John Thaxter suggested that Johnny travel with his father because he would learn much from the experience. With the approval of Abigail and John, ten-year-old Johnny was at his father's side as the ship *Boston* sailed out of Massachusetts Bay on February 13, 1778.

For three days and nights the *Boston* was tossed around by a severe hurricane, making John Adams regret that he had brought his young son. Though strong winds continued throughout the voyage, Johnny handled it well and even used the time for study. A French surgeon on the ship, Dr. Nicholas Noel, took a liking to Johnny and began teaching him French. At other times, Johnny wandered the ship and spent time with the captain, who taught him about the compass, about navigation, and how to work the sails of the *Boston*.

At the end of March, the ship had reached the coast of France. The passengers left the storm-battered ship at Bordeaux on April 1. After several days, John Adams and his son continued on to Paris and reached the bustling city on April 8. Both Adamses were impressed by the sights and sounds of Paris, which was so much larger than Boston. Johnny was placed in a boarding school in Passy, a suburb of Paris, along with several other American boys, including Benjamin Franklin's grandson. This was Johnny's first formal school education. The academy was run by M. LeCoeur, who emphasized French and Latin. Johnny also learned fencing, dancing, drawing, and music, subjects not considered important back home in Massachusetts.

The students began school each morning at 6 A.M. At 8 A.M. they had a break for breakfast and then went to class again from 9 A.M. to noon. There was another break for dinner and play, followed by afternoon classes from 2 P.M. until 4:30 P.M. The students had thirty minutes for play and then took their final classes from 5 P.M. until 7:30 P.M. They ate supper and played games before going to bed at 9 P.M. The only day off was Sunday, when they attended church. In spite of the busy schedule, Johnny loved the school and learned to speak and write the French language with much greater fluency than his father.

Johnny turned eleven that summer and began to develop a love for the theater, particularly comedies. Johnny had begun to keep a diary so that he would remember the things he was experiencing. His diary and letters home were filled with the names of famous actors and with the titles of Shakespeare plays he had attended. Although Abigail was concerned about his morals—she wrote to Johnny that he should be careful—John Adams replied to his wife that she did not have to worry, because Johnny was a good student and well-behaved.

The Commission was having little success in France, and at the end of 1778 Congress decided to recall the commissioners. The two Adamses left Paris at the beginning of March 1779 and prepared to head home. They had difficulty finding a ship to take them back to America and spent three months together reading

Harvard During and After the American Revolution

The American Revolution (1775–81) brought profound change to Harvard College. The overwhelming number of students, faculty, and alumni opposed Great Britain and sided with the revolutionaries. Under the leadership of John Hancock, whose titles also included treasurer of Harvard, the Second Massachusetts Provincial Congress met at Cambridge in February 1775. They framed measures to prepare the colony for war. Of the 1,224 Harvard graduates living on January 1, 1776, only 196 (16 percent) were loyalists.

Numerous battles between the British and the Massachusetts militia—and later the Continental Army—occurred in Massachusetts between April 1775 and March 1776, when the British evacuated Boston. More than a thousand militiamen were quartered in the college. Half a ton of lead from the roofs was molded into bullets. Brass knobs and box locks disappeared. Some buildings never recovered and were eventually torn down. Within days of British General Sir William Howe's decision to evacuate Boston, taking with him about a thousand loyalists, the Harvard Corporation conferred on General George Washington an honorary doctor of laws degree.

The college labored under great difficulty during the war. Student enrollment fell off: from 1778 through 1783 the average size of the graduating classes was thirty students, compared to an average class of forty-six during the period 1771 to 1777. Trade and transportation were so disrupted that it was often difficult to obtain supplies for the college community. One student wrote home in 1777 that the steward never knew one day if he would have food for the commons the next day. The textbook shortage became so acute that in 1778 the college president petitioned the State of Massachusetts for the authority to plunder sequestered Tory libraries for books. During the winter of 1777–78, the students had to be sent home because the college buildings were needed as prisons to house the British soldiers captured in the surrender of General John Burgoyne's army after the Battle of Saratoga. Very few members of the Harvard war classes attained distinction.

Equally startling was the tolerance of college authorities toward irregularities during this time. Students slipped away for a year or more and returned to their old standing without examination or a "make up," provided they paid the college fees for the period of their absence. One "student" appeared at Cambridge for the first time on July 18, 1780, passed examinations in seven subjects, paid two years' tuition, and obtained his bachelor's degree the following day. In the summer of 1780, a group of students told President Samuel Langdon, "As a man of genius and knowledge we respect you; as a man of piety and virtue we venerate you; as a President we despise you." Langdon resigned.

Eighteen-year-old John Quincy Adams entered Harvard with advanced standing in October 1785. He already had been the private secretary to the American minister to Russia in St. Petersburg (1781), and to his father, statesman John Adams, in Great Britain (1782–83). He had traveled widely in Europe, often on his own. He had attended a Paris boarding school with Benjamin Franklin's grandson and studied at a Latin school in Amsterdam. With his mother Abigail, he shared the delights of the French theater. He knew Latin and Greek, and he spoke French, Dutch, and German. He also had met many of the leading cultural and political European figures of the day. His father, himself a Harvard graduate (Class of 1755), wrote from London congratulating John Quincy on his admission "into the seat of the Muses, our dear Alma Mater, where I hope you will find a Pleasure and Improvements equal to your Expectations."

Adams was a serious student. He wrote to his sister that in his first year at Harvard, he had to relearn his Greek grammar, study the New Testament, read four of the eight books in Xenophon's *Cyropedia* (which describes the education of the ideal ruler) and five or six books in Homer's *Iliad*. "In Latin," Adams wrote, "I have but little else to go through but Horace, part of which I have already done. In English, I have to study Watts' Logic, Locke on the Human Understanding, and something in Astronomy."

Joseph Willard, the college president, enforced authority and standards. He wore a white wig and a black gown. Students were expected to take off their hats when the president entered Harvard Yard. Students wore a blue-gray coat, with a vest, and black or olive trousers. Certain distinctions in dress marked different classes—no buttons on cuffs for freshmen; buttons on cuffs for sophomores; ornamental coat fastening for juniors, except on cuffs; and ornamental fastenings on the cuffs for seniors. (Apparently, students loathed these class distinction markings and they were eventually abandoned.) On July 16, 1787, John Quincy Adams graduated from Harvard as a member of the newly founded chapter of Phi Beta Kappa.

and studying. John helped his son translate some works of the Roman author Cicero. Johnny also read *Don Quixote*. John wrote Abigail that their son was growing in body and mind and was known for "his general knowledge, which for his age is uncommon." His knowledge was practical as well. While waiting in port, Johnny was befriended by some sailors who taught him to swim, a sport he practiced for the rest of his life.

Finally on June 17, 1779, John Quincy boarded *La Sensible* with his father, and they began a six-week journey back across the Atlantic. This return trip was more pleasant than their rough sail the year before, and it wasn't long before Johnny was helping the French ambassador with his English. *La Sensible* reached Massachusetts on July 31, and Johnny and his father were warmly greeted by Abigail and the children. John Quincy was looking forward to entering an American school and starting his preparation for Harvard.

After only three months at home, John Adams was asked by Congress to return to Paris. John decided to take nine-year-old Charles and let Johnny attend a

This May 29, 1783, fourth-quarter tuition bill for Samuel Abbot included a charge for "sizings," or extra expenses. For example, meat was served at dinner but jelly, ale, beer, and other items cost extra. These costs were called sizings.

Abbot also received financial credit for being a Hollis scholar. Thomas Hollis (1659--1731), a London merchant, was an outstanding benefactor of Harvard College. He endowed the Hollis Professor of Divinity as well as scholarship funds for poorer students.

Sums here are in the British form of pounds, shillings, and pence. This currency system continued to be used in the newly formed United States until the Coinage Act of 1792 instituted dollars and cents.

regular school. However, Abigail thought a European education would be better for her oldest son, and so both Johnny and Charles boarded the ship on November 13, 1779, with their father.

After they arrived in France, they spent some time in French cities, enjoying their culture. Finally, John, Johnny, and Charles reached Paris on February 9, 1780. Almost immediately, the two boys were placed in an academy in Passy run by the Pechigny family. John Quincy returned to the study of Latin and also had classes in Greek, geography, mathematics, drawing, and writing. He was overwhelmed by all his subjects and asked his father's advice on what he should concentrate. Adams advised him to give his attention to Latin and Greek and to develop his penmanship.

Just as John Quincy had settled into the academy and was enjoying translating some French fables into English, his father decided to make another move. Adams felt the French were hindering his attempts to make peace with the British. He made plans to leave for Holland and seek their support for American independence. John Adams and his sons left for France on July 27, 1780, just after Johnny turned thirteen. During August, as the family traveled through Holland, John Quincy studied Dutch, attempting to prepare himself for school in yet another country.

On September 30, the two boys were placed in a famous Latin school in Amsterdam, which had been established in 1342. Johnny hated it. The head of the school disliked the fact that Johnny couldn't speak Dutch and put him in an elementary grade. That humiliated Johnny and he became rebellious. John Adams quickly took the boys out of the Latin school and made arrangements for two private tutors to teach his sons.

John Thaxter had come to Europe as John's secretary, so he became one of the tutors. The other tutor was Benjamin Waterhouse, from Massachusetts, who was studying medicine at the University of Leyden. Johnny and Charles lived at Waterhouse's home while their father worked and lived at The Hague, the center of the Dutch government. At the age of thirteen, Johnny became an independent student at the university, which at the time was probably the best school in Europe. He took lessons from his tutors and attended lectures at the university.

Adams wrote from The Hague and told his oldest son to attend lectures in medicine, chemistry, and philosophy and to write him with full reports of what he was learning. John Quincy wrote back, "We went to hear a medicinal lecture by Professor Horn. We saw several experiments there. In the afternoon we went to hear a law lecture by Professor Pestel. Each lecture lasts an hour." Then he added, "I continue writing in Homer, the Greek grammar, and Greek testament every day."

By January 1781, Johnny was formally admitted to the University of Leyden. By that spring his father was concerned that his son was strong in Greek and Latin but ignoring his own language. He asked Johnny to begin reading English poets, telling him, "You will never be alone with a poet in your pocket." John Quincy not only read English poets, but he began writing poetry himself, a practice he kept up all his life.

In July, just after he turned fourteen, another radical change took place in Johnny's life. In later years he was convinced that this change damaged his education and continued the upheavals he had experienced since he was a small boy. Francis Dana, who had come to Europe as secretary to the peace commission that included John Adams, was sent to Russia by the American Congress. He needed a secretary who could speak French, the language of the Russian court in those days. John recommended his son because he was so fluent in French.

Dana and young Adams began their two-month, two thousand-mile trip across Europe. Though Johnny left his formal education behind, he learned much as he saw the differences between his own country and the small states he visited in modern-day Germany and Poland, as well as Russia. He felt that the rulers of these countries valued their animals more than their farmers. The two reached St. Petersburg at the end of August 1781 and were impressed by its beauty and size.

There was an immediate problem for Johnny however. There were no schools for him in St. Petersburg, and the few private tutors available were far too expensive. Johnny realized he would have to educate himself while there, and he began searching bookstores in the city and spending time in an English library. Johnny read all eight volumes of David Hume's *History of England*, and a five-volume work by Macauley, also called *The History of England*. He read Adam Smith's *The Wealth of Nations*, and Robertson's three-volume study *The History of Charles V*. He took up the study of German and became even better at French.

John Adams was pleased with his son's letters and realized that John Quincy was quite mature for his age. Adams was deeply concerned, however, that Johnny was not learning some of the basics of grammar and that he was not developing any friendships among Americans. The next year, when John Quincy told his father he wanted to return to Holland, John Adams gave him permission. Johnny left St. Petersburg on October 30, 1782, and set out for Stockholm, Sweden, the easiest winter route to Western Europe. On his own now, Johnny spent months traveling through Sweden, Denmark, and Germany and did not reach The Hague until April 21, 1783.

In Holland, John Quincy decided to continue studying independently with his father as his tutor. He read the New Testament in Greek, and, with his father's encouragement, read sermons as a way of relaxing. Johnny went with his father to Paris in August 1783 and attended the theatre again. He translated Caesar and Horace and copied English poets.

The American Revolution had officially ended with the signing of the Treaty of Paris in September 1783. After helping to negotiate this treaty, Adams traveled to England with his son in October 1783. In London, Johnny met two famous American painters, Benjamin West and John Singleton Copley. They introduced him to the finest artworks in the country.

Abigail and Nabby sailed for Europe in July of 1784 to meet Johnny in London. While he waited for them to arrive, John Quincy went to the House of

A page from the records of the Harvard Overseers meeting, October 13, 1785. At this meeting, the Harvard Overseers confirmed the appointment of Eliphalet Pearson, the first principal of Phillips Academy at Andover, as Hancock Professor of Hebrew and Oriental Languages. Pearson— called "the elephant" by students as a pun on his name and as a tribute to his bulk—was a dominant personality in the college for many years. John Quincy Adams was a student in Pearson's class during 1786–87.

Eliphalet Pearson kept an informal "Journal of Disorders." These are a few of his entries for 1788–89:

Dec 9, 1788. Disorders coming out of chapel. Also in the hall at breakfast the same morning. Bisket, tea cups, saucers, and a KNIFE thrown at the tutors. At evening prayers, the Lights were all extinguished by powder and lead, except 2 or 3. Upon this a general laugh among the juniors—

December 15. More disorders at my public lecture, than I ever knew before. The bible, cloth, candles, and branches, I found laid in confusion upon the seat of the desk. During lecture several pebbles were snapped, certain gutteral sounds were made on each side the chapel, beside some whistling.

December 16. Still greater disorders at Doctor Wigglesworth's public lecture. As he was passing up the alley, two vollies of stones, one from each side, were thrown at him.

February 24. Mackey was drunk in bed, and Dennie and Trapier were also highly intoxicated.

April 2. On Tuesday morning of this week, the Front door of Harvard was barred, the inner kitchen door tied to the buttery door, the chapel and hall doors braced too by a bench, the bell rope cut off, and the scuttle door fastened down by a board laid over it across the balcony.

The library at Harvard was the largest college library in the nation during the eighteenth century. It was located in the upper west rooms of Harvard Hall. The librarian had ten alcoves in which to arrange the books. Each Harvard librarian had his own book arrangement system.

The above is the charging list for James Bowdoin, 1786–88. Bowdoin's political career began in 1753 when he was elected to the Massachusetts General Court, and his active role in state politics continued until the state ratified the Constitution thirty-five years later. In 1785, when he was elected governor of Massachusetts, he resigned as a Harvard Overseer as the governor was ex officio president of Harvard's senior governing board.

On November 14, 1787, the governor borrowed, signed for, and returned volume one of the Encyclopedia Britannica (second entry). Volume two was subsequently delivered to him. The Britannica is the oldest English language general encyclopedia. The first edition appeared in 1768. The second edition, which was published in Edinburgh between 1777 and 1784, was enlarged from three to ten volumes. This edition contained a new section of biographical articles and the expansion of the geographic chapters. It also updated the history sections. Bowdoin probably borrowed the second edition. No one knows exactly why the governor borrowed these volumes, but volume two does mention "James Bowdoin" several times. Eventually, the governor's son would donate the land and money to start Bowdoin College in honor of his father.

Commons to listen to debates among the leading politicians in England. When Abigail first saw Johnny after five years, she did not recognize him. At seventeen, he was fully grown. After their reunion, the entire family went to Paris and lived there for the next nine months. Johnny continued his Latin and math studies with his father's help and did some trigonometry and geometry. He also spent time with Thomas Jefferson, who was then U.S. minister to France, and with the Marquis de Lafayette, who had served in the American army during the Revolution.

When John Adams was appointed the U.S. minister to England in 1785, John Quincy had a difficult choice. He could stay on in Europe as his father's secretary, or he could return to the United States and go to Harvard. After seven years in Europe, enjoying the company of important intellectuals and artists, it was hard to think of submitting himself to a small college in New England with its rules and regulations. When John Quincy finally decided to return to America and begin the life of a college student, John Adams wrote the president of Harvard College to ask that John Quincy enter as an upperclassman.

Johnny sailed from France in May 1785, and arrived in Boston on July 17, right after his eighteenth birthday. Riding overland to Boston, he stopped in Hartford, Connecticut. He met poet John Trumbull who gave him a copy of his poem "M'Fingal." At the same time, Johnny bought a book, *The Conquest of Canaan*, by the Reverend Timothy Dwight, which he read with delight.

In August, Johnny met with Joseph Willard, the president of Harvard. Willard suggested that Johnny needed additional study in order to be admitted as an upperclassman. Johnny went to Haverhill, Massachusetts, in October to stay with his uncle, the Reverend John Shaw, who agreed to act as his tutor. Johnny studied ten hours a day, sleeping late and then going to his books late at night.

John Quincy describes some of his studies: "Immediately upon going to Mr. Shaw's I began upon the Greek Grammar…I then undertook the Greek Testament, in which I went before I came here as far as the Epistle to Titus.…I also finished Horace and the Andria of Terence. In Logic I was equal with the class and in Locke about 70 pages behind them, Guthrie's Geography I had also finished." His aunt wrote to Abigail that Johnny went after knowledge like it was food. On March 14, he hurried back to Cambridge, and, after an examination by Willard, three professors, and four tutors, he was admitted to Harvard as a junior.

Johnny followed the traditional classic education with an emphasis on public speaking. He was elected to Phi Beta Kappa, a society for persons who gain high scholastic honors. While a member he joined in on many debates. Johnny also joined the A.B. literary society and gave speeches on many subjects. He enjoyed math and science and particularly liked astronomy.

For the first time, Johnny made friends among his own countrymen and developed some close relationships. Both of his brothers were also at Harvard, and they spent time together in Cambridge, traveling back to Quincy together on holidays. However, Johnny didn't have much good to say about the faculty. He criticized almost every faculty member, including the president, and only seemed to enjoy his Latin professor, Mr. James, who according to Johnny "knew his subject."

The class of 1787 had its commencement exercise on July 21. The topic of Johnny's speech was "Upon the Importance and Necessity of Public Faith to the Well Being of Community" and he received his degree along with his fifty classmates. Johnny was ranked number two in his class. His speech that day was published in the *Boston Centinel* on July 21. Less than a month later, Johnny took a stagecoach to Newburyport, a coastal town in Massachusetts, to begin his study of law under the guidance of lawyer Theophilus Parsons.

Parsons expected the men under him to work eight hours a day in his office and then four hours at home. John Quincy took a room with a woman named Mrs. Leather; her house was just a block from Parsons's law office. He began his reading assignments with Sir Edward Coke's *Reports* and *Institutes* and continued on with Sir William Blackstone's *Commentaries on the Laws of England*. He reread and enjoyed much more the *History of England* by David Hume and Edward Gibbons's *The Decline and Fall of the Roman Empire*. One book he read on his own was *Confessions* by Jean-Jacques Rousseau, which he considered the most amazing book he had ever read.

This period was the lowest time of John Quincy Adams's life. He became severely depressed during his first year in Newburyport and returned home to Quincy for a holiday in the summer of 1788. His parents had returned from Europe and he spent time with them. When he returned to his legal studies in the fall, his condition was worsened. Unable to study, he returned to Quincy and stayed there until March of 1789.

When John Quincy resumed his studies in April, his spirits began to improve. He became involved in a more active social life, began writing poetry, and had his first romance. By the summer, Adams had shown great improvement, and he visited his parents in New York City where his father had become the first vice president of the United States. Later that year, when President Washington visited Newburyport, it was John Quincy who wrote the address honoring him.

In July of 1790, John Quincy Adams received his master's of arts degree from Harvard. At the age of twenty-three he opened a law office in Boston. Soon, though, he began a career in public service that continued to the very end of his life. He was appointed to be U.S. minister to the Netherlands by President Washington in 1794 and later served as minister to Prussia (a state in modern-day Germany). He was a Massachusetts state senator, a U.S. senator, minister to Russia, minister to Great Britain, and secretary of state before he ran for president in 1824. He served one term as president and finished his public career as a member of the House of Representatives, in which he served for seventeen years. His speeches in Congress earned him the nickname "Old Man Eloquent."

John Quincy Adams married Louisa Catherine Johnson on July 26, 1797. He had met her in France when she was four years old and he was twelve, and they met again as adults in London, where they married. The couple had three sons who lived to maturity.

John Quincy Adams died on February 23, 1848, at the age of eighty, two days after suffering a stroke on the floor of the House of Representatives. It was written about John Quincy Adams: "He was…esteemed for his fearless conscientiousness, his ardent patriotism, his vast and various acquirements, and his unfaltering devotion to human freedom." He never stopped learning, reading and writing almost until the day he died.

—Bill Thompson

Andrew Jackson
C h a p t e r   S e v e n

News traveled slowly through the backwoods country of the Carolinas. Printing presses were unheard of in such villages as Hillsboro, Salisbury, and Waxhaw, so when the news arrived, it usually came in the form of a newspaper toted by a traveler from Columbia, Charleston, or Savannah, or even one of the great northern cities, such as Philadelphia or New York.

Chances are the newspaper was several days or even weeks old, but that mattered little to the people of those tiny, cloistered colonial towns, hungry for information about the outside world. This was particularly true in the summer of 1776, as fervor rose for revolution, not only in Philadelphia, where delegates to the Continental Congress were debating independence, but also in places like Waxhaw, South Carolina, where patriotic feelings were vivid and loyalists knew they would not be welcome.

Sometime in the midsummer of 1776 a newspaper did arrive in Waxhaw, and soon talk traveled throughout town and into the neighboring farm fields that it contained news of a most important event. As was their custom, the people of Waxhaw gathered in the town center for a public reading of the newspaper. Most of them did not have the ability to read, so the responsibility to stand before the crowd and deliver the news, word by word, fell on one of the few qualified readers.

On many occasions, that job fell to Andy Jackson—then just nine years old but, nevertheless, the best reader in Waxhaw. Years later, Jackson would recall that special job in the town of his childhood, claiming he could "read a paper clear through without getting hoarse…or stopping to spell out the words." And so, on that late July day in 1776, Jackson stood before some thirty or forty residents of Waxhaw, and read, "When in the course of human events…."

It was, of course, the text of the Declaration of Independence that young Andrew Jackson had been called on to deliver to the people of Waxhaw. It is doubtful whether the tall, skinny, and squeaky-voiced youngster delivered Thomas Jefferson's words with the same passion or enthusiasm that they were delivered with when Colonel John Nixon first read them publicly in Philadelphia on July 8, 1776. Nonetheless, Andrew's oratory skills were probably good enough for the people of

LIFE

OF

ANDREW JACKSON,

CONDENSED FROM THE AUTHOR'S "LIFE OF ANDREW JACKSON,"
IN THREE VOLUMES.

BY JAMES PARTON,

AUTHOR OF THE "LIFE OF AARON BURR," "HUMOROUS POETRY OF THE ENGLISH
LANGUAGE," ETC.

NEW YORK:
PUBLISHED BY MASON BROTHERS.
BOSTON: MASON & HAMLIN. PHILADELPHIA: J. B. LIPPINCOTT & CO.
LONDON: D. APPLETON & CO., 16 LITTLE BRITAIN.
1863.

ANDREW JACKSON.
Engraved by H. B. Hall from a painting by Earl.
MASON BROTHERS N.Y.

James Parton (1822–91) ranks among the most successful writers of his generation. He also was Andrew Jackson's first major biographer. His three-volume *Life of Andrew Jackson* was first published in 1860, fifteen years after the President's death. Parton, who is referred to as the "father of modern biography," used primary written sources as well as interviews with people who had known the president. While Parton's conclusions are interpretive, he is praised for his historical methods. Subsequent Jackson biographers have built upon Parton's pioneering research work.

Parton wrote about Jackson's education: "He learned to read, to write, and cast accounts—little more. If he began, as he may have done, to learn by heart, in the old-fashioned way, the Latin grammar, he never acquired enough of it to leave any traces of classical knowledge in his mind or his writings....He was never a well-informed man. He never was addicted to books. He never learned to write the English language correctly, though he often wrote it eloquently and convincingly. He never learned to spell correctly, though he was a better speller than Frederic II, Marlborough, Napoleon, or Washington. Few men of his day, and no women, were correct spellers. And, indeed, we may say that all the most illustrious men have been bad spellers, except those who could not spell at all. The scrupulous exactness in that respect, which is now so common, was scarcely known three generations ago."

Waxhaw who, in just a few years, would make tremendous sacrifices for independence. And nobody in Waxhaw would sacrifice more than the Jacksons.

Andrew Jackson Jr. was born on March 15, 1767. His father Andrew and mother Elizabeth Hutchinson Jackson emigrated from Carrickfergus in Northern Ireland two years before Andy's birth. They made their way to Waxhaw, a tiny Presbyterian settlement a few miles below the North Carolina border near the Catawba River. Soon, the city of Charlotte would rise just to the north of Waxhaw.

Although they joined many family members in Waxhaw, no grant of prime agricultural land awaited the Jacksons when they arrived in South Carolina. Andrew and Elizabeth Jackson would become sharecroppers, forced to coax what few crops they could out of unforgiving red clay soil. In March 1767, a few days before the birth of his third son, Andrew Jackson Sr. injured himself while straining under the weight of a log. He died just a few hours later.

The man who would be elected seventh president of the United States was born to a widowed mother who was taken in by her sister, Jane Crawford, and her husband, James, earning her keep as a housekeeper and nurse for Jane, who was ill. In addition to Andy Jr., Elizabeth would raise her two older sons in the Crawford home—Hugh, three years old at the time of Andy's birth, and Robert, two years Andy's senior.

Robert V. Remini, the distinguished biographer of Andrew Jackson, writes, "It was also said—again unfairly—that the only secular book Jackson ever read from cover to cover was *The Vicar of Wakefield*. True, he prized the *Vicar* above all other books after the Bible, but the extent of the library he left upon his death raises doubts about his reading limitations."

Oliver Goldsmith's 1766 novel is the story of the Vicar's strength of character during times of great difficulty. Also, the book is a rejection of the ostentatious style of many novels of the time. Perhaps, Jackson identified both with the Vicar and with Goldsmith, who maintained his provincial manners in the midst of the sophisticated Londoners among whom he moved.

At left are the title and the opening pages from the second American edition of *The Vicar of Wakefield* (1820).

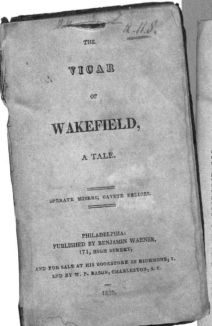

Elizabeth Jackson was not totally lacking in resources—family members in Northern Ireland, aware of the woman's plight, regularly sent her support, which is probably how Elizabeth was able to send her youngest and brightest child to school.

Andy started school at the age of five, attending what was known as an "old-field" school. In the rural South, old fields were fields that had been sapped of their rich soil by season after season of cotton, tobacco, and crop farming. As the fields were left fallow, pine trees would grow in place of the crops, eventually creating a dense, forested patch of land. In such old fields, it was not unusual for villagers to find a place for a school, clear away some pine trees, and erect a small building. Usually, the schools were built after an itinerant clergyman arrived in town and announced that he was qualified to teach school and would do so for a modest salary, as long as the villagers provided him with a school and, of course, pupils.

Students sat in rows on benches made from split logs. Long but thin wooden planks served as writing desks. Mud was slapped in the walls between the pine logs to keep the winter chill out and the warmth of the fireplace in, but the schools were damp and poorly lit.

Andy's first teacher in the old-field school of Waxhaw was Dr. William Humphries, who instructed his charges in reading, writing, and mathematics or, as it was more commonly known at the time, "casting accounts." Humphries was advised by the town fathers to teach the type of arithmetic a farm boy would need to know—how to count the coins paid by the miller for a bushel of corn, for example.

Books were scarce in Waxhaw and in his later years Andrew Jackson would never impress his contemporaries with his knowledge of literature. Nevertheless, as President Jackson would occasionally quote Shakespeare, it is obvious that he had read the Bard of Avon during his childhood. He also told people that as a boy, he read Oliver Goldsmith's *The Vicar of Wakefield*, a novel that may have served to inspire him to stand steadfast in his beliefs during times of great tragedy and turmoil in his personal life and political trials. He also read that most common of books found in the rural South, the Bible, although he did not become a deeply religious man until late in life.

As an adult, Jackson would often express an admiration for Sir William Wallace, the thirteenth-century Scottish hero who was executed after leading an uprising against the English. Wallace, Jackson said, was "the best model for a young man....We find in him the truly undaunted courage, always ready to brave any dangers, for the relief of his country or his friend." It is likely that Jackson learned about Wallace in Dr. Humphries' one-room schoolhouse.

While Jackson excelled as a reader, his lack of talent as a writer remains somewhat enigmatic. Well into his presidency, Jackson seemed the most challenged of writers, giving little thought in his official communications to grammar, spelling, or syntax. It was not unusual for Jackson to spell the same word four or five different ways on the same page. This may have been caused by his learning to write late in comparison to when he learned to read. Another theory, however, is that injuries he sustained as a young man, including a shattered shoulder and a bullet that remained in his chest for forty-five years, caused him so much pain when he moved his arm to write that he cared little how he spelled or wrote. As president, he turned over the drafts of speeches, essays, letters, and other communications to a team of secretaries, who would recopy his correspondence, making the appropriate edits. Yet, when he delivered his remarks through oration, Jackson was a most eloquent and electric speaker.

Outside of class, Jackson was a wild, unpredictable boy full of zest and mischief. He enjoyed playing practical jokes on his classmates, but didn't enjoy it as much when he was the butt of their humor. One time, some boys handed young Andy a gun loaded to the muzzle with gunpowder and dared him to fire it, knowing full well the blast would be too much for the skinny Jackson to shoulder standing up. Sure enough, the charge knocked Andy on his rump, but before any of his chums had the chance to make light of the situation, he was back on his feet and delivering this warning: "By God, if one of you laughs, I'll kill him." It is said that no one dared laugh.

Jackson could be a bully, but he also had a good heart and never picked on smaller boys. Instead, he was quick to protect young boys whenever he saw others pushing them around.

He also loved sports. Andrew never needed much encouragement to participate in a footrace, jumping contest, or wrestling match. He loved racing horses, too, and as an adult would become a fine horseman.

Years later, Dr. Cyrus L. Hunter, a physician from North Carolina, wrote that his father, the Reverend Humphrey Hunter, had attended school in Waxhaw with Andy Jackson. Here is how Cyrus Hunter described his father's school days with the future president:

> My father and Jackson, of the same Scotch-Irish stock, imbued with the same religious sentiments and reared under the same moral training, prosecuted their studies together with that cordiality of feeling which pertains to kindred souls. I have no recollection of my father narrating any remarkable passages of Jackson's boyhood. He spoke of his making commendable progress in his studies, or his ardent and rather quick temperament. The impression left upon my mind would lead me to say that he was an impulsive youth, ambitious, courageous and persevering in his undertakings.

At some point Andy withdrew from the old-field school and enrolled in a private academy taught by a Presbyterian minister, the Reverend James White Stephenson. Elizabeth Jackson had apparently decided that her youngest son should pursue a career in the ministry, and that desire was likely the reason for Andy's transfer. Events unfolding in Philadelphia in the summer of 1776 would cut short Andy's education and any future he might have pursued in the ministry. The country was at war, and in a few short years the horrors of war would reach Waxhaw and, in particular, the Jackson family.

Hugh Jackson was first to lose his life. Andy's oldest brother died in 1779 at the

Battle of Stono Ferry, helping to repel a British invasion. Hugh Jackson succumbed not to a gunshot or bayonet wound but to heat and exhaustion. He was sixteen years old.

Charleston and Savannah fell to the British in May 1780. British troops and loyalists swept through South Carolina, committing atrocities against the rebellious colonists. A force of three hundred British soldiers under the leadership of Lieutenant Colonel Banastre Tarleton arrived in Waxhaw, slaughtering one hundred and thirteen villagers and wounding another one hundred and fifty.

A regiment of South Carolina volunteers led by Colonel William Richardson Davie vowed to track down Tarleton. Many survivors of Waxhaw, anxious to avenge the massacre in their town, joined up. Two of them were Andrew and Robert Jackson, who were too young to fight. Still, they served the regiment as messengers and found themselves dodging gunfire at the Battle of Hanging Rock.

Following the battle, Andy and Robert returned to Waxhaw. While staying in the home of a cousin, they were discovered by a British officer, who had them arrested because they refused to shine his boots. The Jackson brothers both sustained stab wounds in the tangle with the officer. They were imprisoned in a crowded, filthy jail in the town of Camden, some forty miles from Waxhaw, where their wounds were left to fester. Elizabeth Jackson learned of their imprisonment, rode to Camden, and convinced the British authorities to release her two sons. Both boys caught smallpox in the jail; by the time she got them home through a driving rainstorm, they were both in a grave condition.

Robert died two days after returning to Waxhaw; Andy survived, but it would take Elizabeth a year to nurse her boy back to health. He would carry the scars of smallpox on his face throughout his life.

With the War of Independence drawing to a close, Elizabeth volunteered to nurse American prisoners held on ships in Charleston harbor. During this duty, she contracted cholera and died. Her final words to her son, as she left Waxhaw for Charleston, were, "Make friends by being honest and keep them by being steadfast." Andy was fifteen years old and now virtually on his own.

For a time he lived with an uncle, Joseph White, and found work as an apprentice in a saddler's shop. It was during this period that he met many young gentlemen who fled inland following the fall of Charleston. These young men were Andrew's age, and they introduced him to the world of drinking, gambling, and mischief making. When the British left Charleston in 1782 and his friends returned home, he went with them. He didn't last long in Charleston. A grandfather in Carrickfergus had left him a small inheritance, which he quickly lost gambling on cockfights and dice games.

He returned to Waxhaw penniless. With no other paths open to him, Jackson presented himself to the town fathers as qualified to teach school. He held the job for a year.

By 1784, he was on the move again. Coming to the conclusion that with a new country and new set of laws, there would be plenty of business available for a

THE
HISTORY
OF THE
LIFE AND ADVENTURES,
AND
HEROIC ACTIONS,
OF THE RENOWNED
SIR WILLIAM WALLACE,
GENERAL AND GOVERNOR OF SCOTLAND.

Wherein the old obsolete words are rendered more intelligible, and adapted to the understanding of such as have no leisure to study the meaning and import of such phrases, without the help of a glossary.

BY WILLIAM HAMILTON.

TO WHICH IS ANNEXED,
THE LIFE AND MARTIAL ACHIEVEMENTS
OF THAT VALIANT HERO,
ROBERT BRUCE,
KING OF SCOTLAND.

BY JOHN HARVEY.

EDINBURGH:
PRINTED FOR OGLE, ALLARDICE & THOMSON;
M. OGLE, GLASGOW ; OGLES, DUNCAN, & COCHRAN, LONDON ;
AND JOHNSTON & DEAS, DUBLIN.

1819.

THE
HISTORY
OF
SIR WILLIAM WALLACE.

BOOK I.

CHAP. I.

Of our ancestors, brave, true, ancient Scots,
Whose glorious scutcheons knew no bars, nor blots;
But blood untainted circled ev'ry vein,
And ev'ry thing ignoble did disdain ;
Of such illustrious patriots and bold,
Who stoutly did maintain our rights of old,
Who their malicious, and invet'rate foes,
With sword in hand did gallantly oppose :
And in their own, and nation's just defence,
Did briskly check the frequent insolence
Of haughty neighbours, enemies profest,
Picts, Danes, and Saxons, Scotland's very pest ;
Of such, I say, I'll brag and vaunt, so long
As I have pow'r to use my pen or tongue ;
And sound their praises in such modern strain,
As suiteth best a Scot's poetic vein.
    First, here I honour, in particular,
Sir William Wallace, much renown'd in war ;
Whose bold progenitors have long time stood,
Of honourable and true Scottish blood ;
And in first rank of ancient barons go,
Old knights of Craigy, baronets also ;
Which gallant race, to make my story brief,
Sir Thomas Wallace represents as chief.
So much for the brave Wallace father's side,
Nor will I here his mother's kindred hide :
She was a lady most complete and bright,
The daughter of that honourable knight
Sir Ronald Crawford, high sheriff of Air,
Who fondly doated on this charming fair

"Despite his limitations, Jackson was neither ignorant nor illiterate," concludes Robert Remini, Jackson's biographer. "He was a man of genuine intellectual power, formidable in speech and writing, and later in life, an excellent conversationalist." Remini quotes Jackson's 1822 recommendation to his young ward to read the history of the Scottish chiefs. "Considering his background, this recommendation was hardly unexpected. He always regarded Sir William Wallace as 'the best model for a young man....we find in him the truly undaunted courage; always ready to brave any dangers, for the relief of his country or his friend.'" Perhaps, as Remini says, Jackson could have been writing about himself.

William Wallace (c. 1270–1305) is one of Scotland's greatest national heroes, leader of the Scottish resistance forces during the first years of the long, and ultimately successful, struggle to free Scotland from English rule. (Wallace was the subject of Mel Gibson's 1995 film *Braveheart*.) Most stories surrounding Wallace have been traced to a late fifteenth century poet, Henry the Minstrel. In 1721, William Hamilton of Gilbertfield rephrased the old obsolete words into more intelligible English. It is Hamilton's edition that Jackson quoted both in letters and conversation.

Illustrated above are the title and introduction pages from an 1819 edition of William Hamilton, *The History of the Life and Adventures, and Heroic Actions, of the Renowned Sir William Wallace.*

young man familiar with America's unique legal system, Andrew resolved to become a lawyer. But his limited finances made law school out of the question; however, Spruce McCay, an attorney in nearby Salisbury, North Carolina, had agreed to take him in as a clerk. Under McCay, Jackson would read law, copy McCay's pleadings, run errands, and sweep the office.

He spent two years under McCay and six months under another lawyer, John Stokes—a survivor of the Waxhaw massacre—and would learn enough law to be admitted to practice before the courts of North Carolina on September 26, 1787. Later, he would become one of the more than twenty lawyers, from John Adams to Bill Clinton, to occupy the White House. His legal credentials would always be rather thin, though, due in large measure to his fondness for dancing, wooing women, drinking, and gambling that would occupy his idle hours while under the tutelage of McCay and Stokes. Indeed, his nights in Salisbury were rarely devoted to studying Spruce McCay's law books.

There was a dancing school in Salisbury where Jackson became one of the most devoted of pupils. He was so fine a dancer, in fact, that the proprietors of the school asked him to organize the academy's annual Christmas cotillion, which was one of Salisbury's most important social functions. Jackson took on the responsibility with delight and saw to all the arrangements, including the delivery of invitations to Salisbury's eligible women. As a gag, Jackson also delivered invitations to Molly Wood and her daughter, Rachel, the town prostitutes. Jackson believed the two women would never show up, but when Molly and Rachel strode into the dance hall dressed in their Christmas finest, happily displaying their invitations, all dancing jolted to a halt as the fine members of Salisbury society gaped at the two prostitutes in astonishment. Molly and Rachel were soon shown the door, and Jackson was given a vicious tongue-lashing for his ill-advised attempt at humor.

Whether that event ruined his chances for a law career in Salisbury, or whether he always believed his future in law was best pursued plying his trade in the wilderness, Jackson elected to leave town soon after he had been admitted to the bar. Along with his friend and fellow McCay law clerk John McNairy, Jackson headed into the western Carolina wilderness to establish a practice. There wasn't much work for lawyers on the frontier, but in 1788 McNairy won an appointment as judge in a newly opened territory that included the stockaded village of Nashville. Jackson decided to accompany McNairy into the hill country, concluding that wherever a judge could be found, a lawyer was sure to find business. Jackson was able to establish a profitable law practice in Nashville, mostly as a debt collector, and was helped along by McNairy who appointed him prosecuting attorney for the town.

His appointment to the job by McNairy marked the first of many political connections Jackson would use for his own profit and to further his own career. He would make friends with a politically active attorney named William Blount, who was soon to be appointed governor of North Carolina. In 1791, his friendship with Blount resulted in an appointment to the post of judge-advocate for a county

For the rest of his life, Jackson quoted versions of his mother's last words

Andrew Jackson's mother died when he was fourteen. His father had died before Jackson's birth. His older brothers also had died. Jackson's biographers agree about his deep sadness. For the rest of his life, Jackson quoted versions of his mother's last words—words he said were the best educational advice that he ever received.

John Eaton, Jackson's earliest biographer and longtime friend, quoted him as repeating her famous last words this way: "One of the last injunctions given me by her was never to institute a suit for assault and battery, or for defamation; never to wound the feelings of others, nor suffer my own to be outraged; these were her words of admonition to me; I remember them well, and have never failed to respect them; my settled course throughout life has been to bear them in mind and never to insult or wantonly to assail the feelings of any one and yet many conceive me to be a most ferocious animal, insensitive to moral duty, and regardless of the laws both of God and man." (John Eaton, *The Life of Andrew Jackson, Major General in the Service of the United States,* 1817 edition.)

In a December 4, 1838 letter to Martin Van Buren, Jackson gave this version of his mother's advice—"to indict no man for assault and battery or sue him for slander."

Versions of the last words of Jackson's mother were well known in Tennessee. In 1907, a Nashville publication summarized her advice. Above is that summary from *Taylor-Trotwood Magazine* (May 1907, pp. 142–43). The author, John Trotwood Moore, had devoted himself to researching Jackson's life.

militia. Other than his brief service under fire at the Battle of Hanging Rock, it would be Jackson's first taste of military service.

When Tennessee was admitted as a state in 1796, Jackson served as a delegate to the convention that drafted the state's constitution. He later won his first election, going to Washington as Tennessee's lone member of the U.S. House of Representatives. Later, he would serve as a circuit court judge and establish a plantation outside Nashville. In 1802, another friend, Tennessee Governor Archibald Roane, appointed Jackson major-general of the Tennessee militia. In that role, he would in 1815 repulse the British invasion at the Battle of New Orleans, which established Andrew Jackson as a national hero and likely presidential candidate. Jackson chose not to challenge his friend James Monroe in 1816 or 1820. Instead, he waited until 1824 to run for president. He won the majority of the popular vote and more electoral votes that year than John Quincy Adams or Henry Clay but not enough to win the presidency under the terms of the U.S. Constitution. The election was thrown into the U.S. House, where Clay supported Adams, thus denying Jackson the presidency.

Jackson would, however, overwhelm Adams four years later. Most Americans felt a kinship with "Old Hickory," a nickname he earned because the soldiers who served under him believed him to be as tough as a hickory tree. After being elected in 1828, Jackson made the presidency into a truly powerful position, using the spoils system to hire and fire thousands of federal workers, guaranteeing that only those beholden to him would hold government jobs. He forged the modern Democratic Party from the remnants of the old Jeffersonian Democratic-Republican Party that had been divided following the 1824 electoral college fight with Adams and Clay. Jackson also expanded the nation's borders, often at the expense of Native Americans who were pushed off their lands, and by forcing Nicholas Biddle's Second Bank of the United States to make loans at low interest, which sparked a land boom in the West.

Jackson was, indeed, tough as hickory, a trait in his character that people who knew him as a young man found hard to accept. In 1860, Jackson's biographer James Parton searched through Salisbury for acquaintances who remembered Jackson as a law student. He found one elderly woman, who related to Parton her reaction upon hearing the news, some thirty-six years before, that Andrew Jackson was a serious and viable candidate for president of the United States:

> What! Jackson up for president? Jackson? Andrew Jackson? The Jackson that used to live in Salisbury? Why, when he was here, he was such a rake that my husband would not bring him into the house! It is true, he might have taken him out to the stable to weigh horses for a race, and might drink a glass of whiskey with him there. Well, if Andrew Jackson can be president, anybody can!

—Hal Marcovitz

Martin Van Buren
Chapter Eight

In the late 1700s and early 1800s, the village tavern was more than just a place where a traveler could enjoy a tankard of ale while the coachman watered the horses. The tavern was a place where men of the village talked over the news, argued politics, convened town meetings, and even served as jurors and witnesses in cases involving petty infractions of the common law.

In Kinderhook, New York, a robust dialogue on the events of the day could usually be found at Abraham Van Buren's tavern. On the road between New York City and the state capital of Albany, Van Buren's tavern often served as a meeting place for some of the most important political figures of the day. It was not unusual for a farmer wandering into Van Buren's tavern for the purpose of quenching his thirst after a late harvest afternoon to find men such as John Jay, Alexander Hamilton, and Aaron Burr holding court and airing their opinions.

It is likely that Abraham's young son Martin helped keep tankards full while the men of the village talked over the disagreements between President John Adams and Vice President Thomas Jefferson, the XYZ Affair, the Reign of Terror in France, the growing abolitionist movement in America, or the ways in which the British continued to pose a threat to the United States nearly two decades after the War of Independence. Martin Van Buren was a bright boy, easily the best student at the local school, Kinderhook Academy, but young boys knew to keep their mouths shut when the men had important business to talk over. Still, the future president of the United States was like a sponge as a boy—he absorbed all he heard and formed his own opinions, particularly when it came to discussions of Thomas Jefferson's ideas about a minimalist government and the protection of human rights.

In Abraham Van Buren's tavern, the conversations were often conducted in Dutch. Dutch homesteaders had settled Kinderhook in the 1600s shortly after Henry Hudson sailed up the river that bears his name. Kinderhook, a Dutch word that means "Children's Corner," is located some five miles east of the river and about ten miles south of Albany.

Abraham Van Buren was a second-generation Dutch American who inherited the tavern in Kinderhook as well as an adjacent farm from his father.

Martin Van Buren was born December 5, 1782, in the family living quarters of the one-and-a-half-story clapboard tavern in Kinderhook. Born six years after the signing of the Declaration of Independence, Van Buren would become the first president not to have been a citizen of a country other than the United States.

Abraham Van Buren was a second-generation Dutch American who inherited the tavern in Kinderhook as well as an adjacent one hundred acre farm from his father. Abraham also inherited six slaves who worked on the farm and helped Martin's mother, Marie, in the tavern kitchen. Marie was a widow with three children when she married Abraham. They had five children of their own. Martin arrived third behind two older sisters and ahead of two younger brothers.

The Van Burens were not wealthy. Abraham Van Buren was a generous man and patrons of his tavern found him willing to extend credit or offer a loan. The fact that those loans were rarely paid back had much to do with the Van Buren family's modest circumstances. Still, they found the means to send their children to the local school. Kinderhook Academy was a run-down one-room schoolhouse in a hilly part of town. Little sunlight fell through the school's windows, which made reading difficult. The children were divided in rows not by class, but by age and size. Attendance was sporadic because the children were often needed in the fields. During the long winter months there were no crops to tend, but snowfall was often heavy and the young children found it difficult to trudge through the deep drifts. The teacher, David B. Warden, was dedicated and well educated himself, and the children of Kinderhook were well served by the school whenever they managed to attend.

Marie Van Buren insisted that her children keep up with their studies. Because little "Mat" was so bright, she was particularly keen on the boy pursuing his education. After all, Warden had raved to Mrs. Van Buren that her boy could read and write English better than any other student at the school—an impressive accomplishment, to be sure, because in most Kinderhook homes Dutch was spoken across the dinner table.

Martin had an aura that set him aside from the other Kinderhook students. He was a small and delicate boy with reddish-blond hair that hung to his shoulders. He had bright blue eyes that were fixed steadily on his lessons. What's more, he was a happy young man whose disposition made him a leader among his peers. His quick mind and poise gained him a measure of renown among the adults of Kinderhook, although it is likely that some of them were suspicious of this most

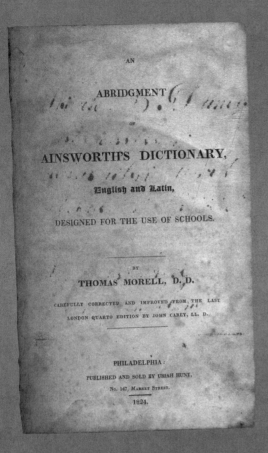

In his lengthy *Autobiography*, Martin Van Buren devotes less than one sentence to his schooling. Van Buren, the eighth president of the United States, learned Dutch as his first language. Descended from settlers who came to New Netherlands in 1631, his parents were frugal farmers and keepers of an inherited tavern who became respectable slave-owning citizens in the village of Kinderhook, near Albany, New York. Little is known about Van Buren's formal education. It is known that at the inadequate village school, he gained a fair knowledge of English and a smattering of Latin. We also know that his holography was almost illegible. After graduation at age fourteen, he became a clerk in the law office of a prominent local politician. It is here that Van Buren became fascinated with politics. He read little from law books but devoured almost every political pamphlet.

Latin, both as a spoken and literary language of the classical world, was a requirement in both public and private schools until the twentieth century. Above are pages from an 1824 edition of *Ainsworth's Dictionary, English and Latin, Designed for the Use of Schools.* First published in England in 1736, Ainsworth's *Dictionary* was a basic volume in almost every American school library through the mid-nineteenth century.

unusual young man. Years later, Van Buren wrote that Warden warned him about his "ardent, hasty, and impetuous" nature.

He studied Latin, grammar, rhetoric, and logic at the school. There were few books on the school shelves—the works of William Shakespeare were known to have been among them—but Martin had little interest in sonnets and plays, preferring instead to devour the Jeffersonian pamphlets he found on the tables in his father's tavern. In the tavern, the men talked about the rift between the Federalists and the anti-Federalists, who would soon become known as Democratic-Republicans (and eventually evolve into the modern Democratic Party). Over the years, Abraham Van Buren had found it bad business to take sides in political arguments. The tavern keeper maintained a staunch neutrality because he didn't want to lose customers of either persuasion. Nevertheless, Abraham soon found himself aligning with the Democratic-Republicans. His son, Martin, was turning into a Jefferson supporter as well.

In 1796, when Martin Van Buren was fourteen years old, he left Kinderhook Academy. It is likely that by that age, he had learned all that the village teacher was capable of teaching him, and few children would have continued in a village school past that age, anyway. The sons of farmers were needed in the fields. The sons of millers and tradesmen would have been expected to contribute their labor to the family welfare as well. Martin Van Buren, the son of a tavern keeper, would ordinarily have been expected to now devote himself full time to his father's business under the notion that, as the oldest son, he would one day inherit the tavern, just as Abraham Van Buren had inherited it from his father. The Van Burens, however, knew that their son was destined to be more than just a tavern keeper. James and John Van Alen, Marie Van Buren's two sons by her first husband, had become lawyers by working as apprentices to established attorneys. The Van Bureaus would have liked to send Martin to Columbia College in New York City, but their modest means made that impossible. Instead, Martin would receive his education in the law as his two half-brothers had found theirs. Francis Silvester, a busy Kinderhook lawyer and member of one of the town's most prominent families, agreed to take in the tavern keeper's boy as an apprentice.

Well into his adult years, even as he found himself a resident of the White House, Van Buren regretted his failure to obtain a formal education above what had been available to him at Kinderhook Academy. He felt that he had been forced to work harder to achieve his goals than men of lesser ability who were better educated. Van Buren wrote, "How often have I felt the necessity of a regular course of reading to enable me to maintain the reputation I had acquired and to sustain me in my conflicts with able and better educated men."

Nevertheless, for a man destined for a career as a master political intriguer, an apprenticeship under Francis Silvester was not a bad way to begin. By working for Silvester, Van Buren received more than just an education in the common law as it was practiced in Kinderhook. Silvester was also a close friend of the Van Ness family, wealthy Kinderhookers whose son William was pursuing a legal education himself at Columbia College. Martin benefited from this relationship, and Billy Van Ness and Martin Van Buren would later become very close friends.

Silvester was also an ardent Federalist, and he dressed the part. The dandified member of the bar was well tailored, spending no small amount of his income on stylish clothes and constantly admonishing his employees to always look their best. Van Buren, on the other hand, dressed like the son of a small-town tavern keeper. Although he took pains to keep a neat appearance, his coarse woolen clothes indicated his upbringing. This circumstance was rectified almost overnight. Several months after Martin joined Silvester's law firm, Francis's brother Cornelius, a Kinderhook storekeeper, spirited the boy away to Albany, where he outfitted young Martin in silken hose, silver buckles, and a suit of clothes that sparkled. From that day on, Van Buren had a tendency to overdress. (Some four decades later, that habit would cause problems during his presidential reelection campaign. In the campaign of 1840, the Whigs and their candidate, William Henry Harrison, mounted a vicious campaign against incumbent President Van Buren, accusing the president of being out of touch with the common people and pointing toward his ostentatious dress as proof of his snobbery. The smear campaign worked, resulting in Van Buren's ouster from the presidency. The fact that Harrison himself was a descendant of a prominent and wealthy family of Virginia planters must surely have been galling to the humble lad from Kinderhook.)

Van Buren was a busy employee of the Silvester law firm. In this era before photocopy machines, carbon paper, typewriters, or any other mechanized form of rendering words onto paper, Martin Van Buren's main job required him to copy, by hand, the long and elaborate pleadings that Francis Silvester would file in court on behalf of his clients. He also served writs and other papers and accompanied Silvester to court, toting the books and reams of papers his mentor would need for each case. Back in the office, he was also required to sweep up, dust the furniture, and keep the fireplace blazing.

Occasionally, Silvester permitted his apprentice the opportunity to take the lead in court. The courts of the era hardly resembled the solemn halls of justice found in county courthouses today. Taverns frequently served double-duty as courtrooms, and that's where Francis Silvester's caseload frequently led him, along with his eager apprentice.

In a tavern in the town of Valatic, not far from Kinderhook, Silvester had loaned out Van Buren to serve as an aide to Aaron Gardinier, a local attorney. The case was minor and the evidence was presented quickly. When it came time to voice closing arguments, Gardinier turned to his fifteen-year-old aide and said, "Here, Mat, sum up. You may as well begin early."

To face the jury, the diminutive Van Buren stood on a chair. History does not record whether Van Buren's courtroom oratory won the day for Gardinier's client;

nevertheless, the future president did report that Gardinier must have been satisfied with his performance because he paid him an extra fifty cents for the effort.

Van Buren's duties as a clerk in the Silvester law firm also required him to help out from time to time as a sort of night watchman in Cornelius Silvester's store, sleeping in the back room of the emporium on the clerk's night off. Like most people who had the pleasure of meeting Martin Van Buren, Cornelius had been impressed with the boy's intelligence and bearing, and foresaw a great future for his brother's apprentice. Cornelius was also aware that Van Buren regarded himself a Democratic-Republican. Cornelius was as much a Federalist as his brother, and he aimed to change the mind of the young apprentice. One night, while performing his overnight sentry duty on the cot in the rear of Cornelius's store, Van Buren found himself shaken awake by his employer's brother. It was well past midnight; nevertheless, Cornelius had selected that hour to win Van Buren over to the Federalist side. Later, Van Buren wrote:

> He placed himself by the [bed's] side, and for more than an hour occupied himself in presenting the reasons which ought to induce me to adopt the politics of the Federal party, and solicited me to do so with a degree of earnestness and obvious concern for my welfare which I could not but respect. After hearing him out, I replied calmly that I appreciated thoroughly the kindness of his feelings, and was well satisfied of the purity of his motives, but that my course had been settled after much reflection, and could not be changed. He paused a moment, and then took my hand and said he would never trouble me again on the subject, and would always remain my friend.

Van Buren remained with the Silvester law firm for six years. During that time, the rift between the Federalists and Democratic-Republicans continued to grow and become ever more vicious. In 1800, Jefferson defeated the Federalist John Adams for the presidency. Van Buren, long fascinated by politics, worked hard for the Jefferson campaign in Kinderhook. His labors so impressed Democratic-Republican leaders that they awarded him with a minor party post—delegate to a caucus meeting in Troy, New York, where his fellow Jeffersonian from Kinderhook, John P. Van Ness, was nominated for a seat in Congress.

Van Buren's activism on behalf of the Democratic-Republicans did not sit well with the Silvesters, although there is no evidence that either Francis or Cornelius sought retribution against the clerk. Still, Van Buren had worked for Francis Silvester for six years, and it is likely that by then he had learned all about the law that he was likely to learn as it was practiced in Kinderhook. In 1801, just before turning nineteen, he left Kinderhook to join his friend Billy Van Ness, the newly elected congressman's younger brother, as a clerk in a law practice in New York City. The departure from the Silvesters was without hard feelings on both sides.

When Van Buren arrived in New York, the city had not yet grown into the bustling East Coast metropolis it was destined to become. The wave of immigration that would cause New York's population to explode was still decades in the future. Still, in 1801 the population of New York was some 60,000 people, which made it one of the largest American cities of the day. If Van Buren believed that his clerkship under Billy Van Ness would lead to notoriety and wealth as an important big city barrister, he was mistaken. Van Ness had virtually no clients. Of course, as the son of a wealthy upstate family with considerable political connections—family friend Aaron Burr was now vice president—Van Ness always seemed to find a way to eke out an existence. For his part, Van Buren was forced to exist under far more humble circumstances. The two years he spent in New York were a time of poverty, missed meals, chilly nights in his rented room on Catherine Street, and lazy afternoons spent on New York's fashionable avenues watching the gentry stroll by. For a young man aiming to make his mark in the law, it was the worst of circumstances. For a young man whose first love was politics, however, Van Buren could not have asked for a better opportunity to learn about the intrigues of the city's powerful leaders.

At the time, the two most powerful families in New York were the Clintons and the Livingstons. De Witt Clinton was a member of the U.S. Senate and would soon become mayor of New York City. His uncle George was governor of New York State and destined to become vice president. Robert R. Livingston would serve as minister to France under Jefferson and negotiate the Louisiana Purchase. His brother Edward would serve a term as mayor of New York. What Van Buren found when he arrived in New York was internecine warfare breaking out between the leading Jeffersonian politicians in the city, with the Clintons and Livingstons on one side and Vice President Aaron Burr on the other.

One of the battlegrounds in this war was the political patronage system. With the Federalists ousted from power in the election of 1800, the Clintons and Livingstons swept Federalist workers from their city jobs and replaced them with committed Jeffersonians. Burr's allies received none of the jobs—all of the posts went to political workers who swore allegiance to the Clintons and Livingstons.

Burr struck back. He enlisted Billy Van Ness to write and publish a slanderous pamphlet under the pseudonym "Aristides" that attacked the Clintons and Livingstons as schemers who aimed to place their own man in the White House.

Both sides tangled for months, and both sides would suffer losses. Edward Livingston, serving as both mayor and United States attorney, would find himself engulfed in a scandal involving over $100,000 in missing federal funds. Livingston was forced to resign in shame and flee to Louisiana, where he performed penance by reforming the state's ancient Spanish and French laws. Burr was headed for trouble as well. His long-time feud with Alexander Hamilton ended on July 11, 1804, in Weehawken, New Jersey, when he killed Hamilton in a duel. Billy Van Ness, still devoted to the vice president, served as a second to

Burr on that misty morning in New Jersey. Later, a curious gambit staged by Burr to seize territory in the west resulted in his arrest on the charge of treason. He was acquitted, but his political career was over. Burr fled to Europe, returning to New York City in 1812 virtually penniless.

Van Buren's part in all these intrigues was no more than one would expect a poor law clerk to play—that of a fascinated observer who was fortunate enough to watch it all unfold from a ringside seat. In 1803, now overwhelmed by poverty, Martin Van Buren returned to Kinderhook to join his half-brother James Van Alen in a law practice. However, the two years he spent in New York City absorbing political lessons taught by such masters of the game as Billy Van Ness, De Witt Clinton, and Aaron Burr would serve him well years later when he joined forces with a scrappy ex-soldier named Andy Jackson to forge the modern Democratic Party.

—Hal Marcovitz

William Henry Harrison
Chapter Nine

W hen William Henry Harrison campaigned for president in 1840, his supporters in the Whig Party published a glowing biography of their candidate in which they extolled his humble "log cabin" lifestyle, as well as his military career as a fierce Indian fighter. A Baltimore newspaper soon picked up the story, reporting that the candidate's "table, instead of being covered with exciting wines, is well supplied with the best cider."

There is no question that Harrison made his mark as a military hero by putting down a Shawnee uprising at the Battle of Tippecanoe in 1811, but that business about hard cider and log cabins was stretching a point. True, Harrison had preserved an early settler's log cabin on his farm in Ohio, but he was by no means the type of man who could be found splitting rails down by the woodshed. He had been born into a wealthy and influential family in Virginia, the son of an aristocratic plantation owner and slaveholder who had signed the Declaration of Independence. America's ninth president studied for three years at Hampden-Sydney College in Virginia, where he absorbed the words of classical writers, finally ending his education in Philadelphia by spending a brief time as a medical student before turning to a career in the military.

Still, "Old Tippecanoe" did not discourage the voters from believing in his backwoods ways. His opponent in the 1840 election was the incumbent president, Martin Van Buren, who spent the campaign fending off the Whig allegation that he was a snob who dined on silver plates—an unfair charge inasmuch as Van Buren was the son of a New York tavern owner, born into far more humble circumstances than William Henry Harrison. The Whig Party would not exist much longer—it ran its last presidential candidate in 1852—but it made a considerable contribution to the American electoral system that is still very much felt today: the Whigs were the first political "spin doctors."

William Henry Harrison was born February 9, 1773, in Charles City County, Virginia. He was the seventh and youngest child of Benjamin Harrison V, whose family had arrived in Virginia in 1633, just twenty-five years after the founding of

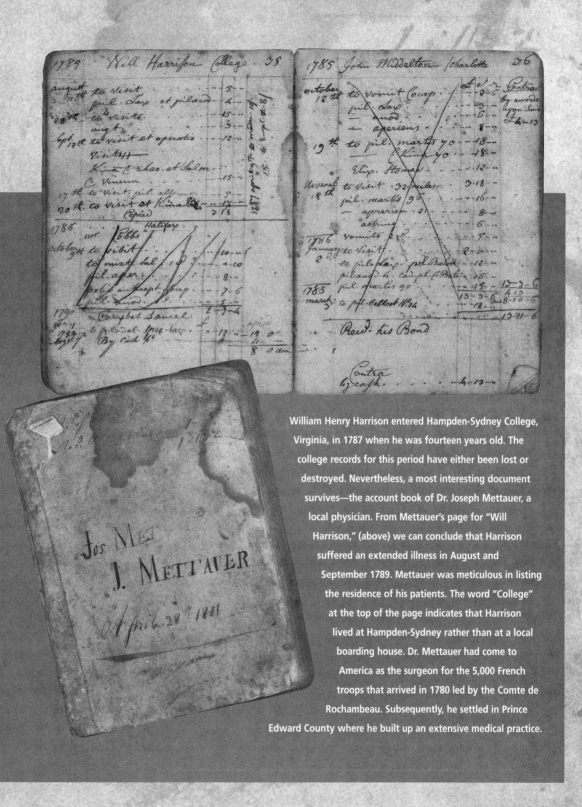

William Henry Harrison entered Hampden-Sydney College, Virginia, in 1787 when he was fourteen years old. The college records for this period have either been lost or destroyed. Nevertheless, a most interesting document survives—the account book of Dr. Joseph Mettauer, a local physician. From Mettauer's page for "Will Harrison," (above) we can conclude that Harrison suffered an extended illness in August and September 1789. Mettauer was meticulous in listing the residence of his patients. The word "College" at the top of the page indicates that Harrison lived at Hampden-Sydney rather than at a local boarding house. Dr. Mettauer had come to America as the surgeon for the 5,000 French troops that arrived in 1780 led by the Comte de Rochambeau. Subsequently, he settled in Prince Edward County where he built up an extensive medical practice.

William Henry Harrison attended the University of Pennsylvania Medical School in 1790–91. He is the only president of the United States to have been a medical student.

Established in 1765, the Pennsylvania Medical School was the first such school in America. John Morgan, a native of Philadelphia and the school's founder, had studied medicine in London and Edinburgh. In 1775, the Continental Congress appointed Morgan "director-general of hospitals and physician-in-chief" of the American army.

This page from the *Minutes of the Medical Faculty* lists medical degrees conferred in 1790. In addition to completing the necessary course of study, each degree candidate had to write a thesis and defend it before the medical faculty. For example, Joseph Pennington of Philadelphia gave a satisfactory explanation of his paper on "the Phenomena, causes and Effects of Fumintation" (rage, fury, or agitation). Several medical students chose to write their theses and defend them in Latin.

The online version of the *Guide to the Archives' General Collection of the University of Pennsylvania, 1740–1820*, is an outstanding source for studying higher education during the era of the American Revolution through primary documents.

the Jamestown colony. William's mother, Elizabeth Bassett Harrison, was old-time Virginia as well; she was distantly related to the family of George Washington. By the time William Henry was born, the Harrisons owned plantations, mills, and a shipyard, and resided at Berkeley, a grand estate extending for miles along both shores of the James River. George Washington and Patrick Henry were frequent guests at Berkeley. Benjamin's distant cousin and close family friend was Richard Henry Lee, the delegate to the Continental Congress in Philadelphia who made the formal motion for American independence on June 7, 1776. A nearby neighbor, but hardly a friend, was a man named John Tyler. For years, Tyler would prove to be a constant political irritation to Benjamin Harrison; in an ironic twist, his son would later serve as William Henry Harrison's vice president and successor.

Benjamin Harrison served as a delegate to the Continental Congress and as governor of Virginia. He was a slaveholder who vigorously disagreed with abolitionist views. As William Henry grew older, he would come to oppose slavery and, much to the embarrassment of his family, join an abolitionist society.

Tutors who lived on the Berkeley estate provided William Henry's early education. In 1781 Berkeley was burned during the waning days of the American Revolution and the Harrisons decided it was best to send their young children away for the duration of the war. William Henry was packed off to Lower Brandon, an estate in Prince George County owned by Benjamin's cousin Nathaniel Harrison. At Lower Brandon, William Henry attended classes at Brandon School, a private academy established on the estate grounds by Nathaniel. By the time he was fourteen, William Henry was well-versed in mathematics and reading. It is also likely that he received considerable instruction in Latin and Greek, which would have been typical for a child of his background during the eighteenth century.

He may also have impressed his tutors with his interest in the natural sciences, because when it came time to pick a college for William Henry, the decision was made to send him to Hampden-Sydney rather than to the College of William and Mary, where George Washington, Thomas Jefferson, and James Monroe had studied. In Harrison's time William and Mary was the preeminent college in Virginia and the South. The Reverend James Blair, a relative of the Harrison family, had been one of the founders of the school, and at the time William Henry was to begin formal schooling his older brother, Carter Bassett Harrison, was studying law at William and Mary.

Although Hampden-Sydney had only been in existence for four years when William Henry Harrison began school, it had already earned a reputation as an important training academy for future doctors. This designation was owed mostly to the residency at the school of Dr. Joseph Mettauer, a prominent Virginia physician. One of Mettauer's students was James A. Jones, who would go on to become surgeon-general of the U.S. Army.

The school would grow in reputation as a fine center of learning. Although no other future presidents attended Hampden-Sydney, among the school's earliest graduates were George Bibb, who would become a U.S. senator and treasury secretary; Moses Waddell, who would go on to found the University of Georgia; William Branch Giles, a future governor of Virginia; and Patrick Henry Shields, who helped establish the state of Indiana.

In 1787 William Henry Harrison left Berkeley for Prince Edward County to commence his formal education as a doctor. Initially, he took classes in Greek, Latin, and history. He was a good student, but hardly a scholar. His selection of reading material indicates that he may not have been as interested in medicine as his family might have believed. Instead, he fancied himself a student of history. He pored over Homer's *Iliad* and *Odyssey* and read Julius Caesar's *De Bello Gallico* and *De Bello Civili*. All those works describe the art of war in some fashion and, in Homer's case, the romantic adventure of war as well. The tale of Greek warriors participating in heroic battles far from friendly shores may have made quite an impression on young William Henry Harrison, who just a few years before had been packed off to safety by protective parents because he was too young to fight the Redcoats.

He was also a devoted reader of Cicero's *Orations*. Here, again, was plenty of fuel to feed a young mind that had thus far seen little of America beyond the tobacco fields of Berkeley. "Courage," Cicero wrote, "is considered the undertaking of dangers and the enduring of labors. Its parts are magnificence, confidence, patience, and perseverance. Magnificence is the thinking about and executing of great and lofty things with a certain large and splendid determination of spirit; confidence is that by which, in great and honorable things, the spirit places great confidence in itself with fixed hope; perseverance is a stable and permanent persistence in a well-considered calculation."

Harrison maintained a fondness for ancient Roman and Greek history. In his correspondence and speeches, he often referred to ways in which the leaders of those ancient realms responded to crises. "Alexander toiled and conquered to attain the applause of the Athenians," Harrison reminded Simón Bolívar in a letter to the Colombian leader in 1829 while serving as U.S. envoy to the South American country. In the letter, Harrison admonished Bolívar to maintain democratic principles in the face of a rebellion. His letter concluded, "Will you regard as nothing the opinions of [the United States] which has evinced its superiority…by having carried into actual practice a system of government, of which the wisest Athenians had but a glimpse of theory?"

Twelve years later, Harrison peppered his inaugural address with references to the Romans and Greeks. In a reference to Caesar's duplicitous friend Brutus, Harrison said, "It was the remark of a Roman consul in an early period of that celebrated Republic that a most striking contrast was observable in the conduct of candidates for offices of power and trust before and after obtaining them. They seldom carry out in the latter case the pledges and promises made in the former." Later, Harrison's friend and future secretary of state, Daniel Webster, claimed to have read the speech beforehand and edited out numerous other references to assorted Romans.

Harrison's inaugural address was, by the way, the longest on record—an ironic distinction inasmuch as Harrison's presidency was the shortest on record. The address included nearly 8,500 words and required some two hours to deliver. (By contrast, President George W. Bush spoke just over 1,600 words on the occasion of his inauguration one hundred and sixty years later.)

At Hampden-Sydney, philosophers Charles Rollin and Hugh Blair were also among Harrison's favorite authors. Both men wrote on the *belles lettres*—the use and study of language and rhetoric. Later, Harrison would boast that he had read through the pondering prose of Rollin—which filled some 3,000 pages—no fewer than three times by his seventeenth birthday.

At Hampden-Sydney, Harrison joined the Union Society, which had been founded by tutor David Wiley and thirteen students "for the promotion of literature and friendship." The society would soon accumulate an enormous library for the college. Otherwise, his residence at Hampden-Sydney is marked by two illnesses the subject of the Thesis of the graduate, and his place of nativity, or last residence.

4th That there be two terms for graduating in the university — the one in april, the other in September every year.

Resolved. 1st That each candidate for a degree in medicine be privately examined before the Medical professors upon the different branches of medicine, and if approved of, that he be directed to compose a Thesis upon a subject chosen for him, or consented to, by the professors, which thesis he shall defend publickly after, which, he shall be admitted to the degree of M.D.

2d That this Thesis be published, or not, at the option of the graduate.

3d That a new form of a Diploma be composed, and delivered to the graduates in medicine, in the English Language, which shall contain with the usual matters,

In these 1806 resolutions, the trustees of the University of Pennsylvania formally established a written thesis requirement for the M.D. degree. A "new form of Diploma" written in English rather than Latin was authorized. Also, two terms of attendance were required for graduation from medical school—"the one in April, the other in September."

The medical Faculty beg leave to inform the Trustees of the University, that the candidates for medical Degrees are ready for an examination & request them to appoint a meeting of the Trustees and Faculty for that purpose to morrow afternoon at 4 oClock.

W Shippen jr
Dean of M. F.

April 18. 1792

William Shippen, pioneer teacher of anatomy and obstetrics, was dean of the medical faculty of the University of Pennsylvania from 1765 to 1776 and from 1791 to 1802. In 1762, Shippen established the first American maternity hospital in Philadelphia. During the Revolutionary years, Shippen was chief physician and director-general of the Continental Army Medical Corps and later the organizer of the United States Army Medical Corps.

In this memorandum of April 18, 1792, Shippen informed the university trustees that "the candidates for medical degrees are ready for an examination and request them to appoint a meeting of the Trustees and Faculty for that purpose tomorrow afternoon at 4 o'clock."

suffered while matriculating at the college. The nature of those maladies remains unclear more than two centuries later, but there was no question be was under the care of Dr. Mettauer, who billed him for services rendered.

Of his years at Hampden-Sydney, Harrison wrote, "Inferior to many of my Class as a Latin and Greek scholar, I was considered but inferior to one in the Belles Lettres information and particularly in History. I was acquainted with the accounts of all the battles described by ancient Authors from Homer to Julius Caesar…This partiality for History is discoverable in my letters and speeches which have occasionally been published."

In 1790, at the age of seventeen, Harrison suddenly left Hampden-Sydney, spending a year in the state capital of Richmond as an apprentice to Dr. Andrew Leipner. He did not obtain a degree from Hampden-Sydney. Harrison's quick departure from the school may have been attributed to a change in the college administration—the president resigned the year before over a disagreement with school trustee Patrick Henry. It may also have been for religious reasons—Harrison's Episcopalian family may have been alarmed at the growing population of Methodists on the Hampden-Sydney campus. Whatever the reason for the hasty departure, Harrison's instructors must have believed he was now ready to prepare for a career in medicine, for without their endorsements it is unlikely that Dr. Leipner would have taken him on as an apprentice.

As Dr. Leipner's helper, it is likely that the future president would have performed minor medical procedures—dressing wounds or preparing sulfur compounds used as disinfectants. It was during his year in Richmond that Harrison made a foray into a social issue when he joined the Humane Society, an abolitionist organization of Methodists and Quakers headed by Robert Pleasants, a Virginia legislator long critical of Harrison's father for using slave labor. Once the governor found out about his son's zeal for social activism, the boy was recalled from Richmond and sent north to enroll in the medical department of the College of Philadelphia. Founded in 1765, it is the oldest medical school in America and today is the University of Pennsylvania's school of medicine.

In Philadelphia, Harrison was to be taken under the wings of two of his father's friends—Dr. Benjamin Rush and Robert Morris, both of whom had signed the Declaration of Independence. Rush was a professor at the medical school and staff physician at the nearby Pennsylvania Hospital, which was affiliated with the college. Morris, the financier of the American Revolution, was a prosperous Philadelphia banker. Harrison also found another familiar face on the medical school faculty: Dr. William Shippen, Richard Henry Lee's brother-in-law. Shippen, the first professor of obstetrics in America, was head of the school's department of anatomy, surgery, and midwifery.

Harrison arrived in Philadelphia in May 1791, taking most of his classes in Anatomical Hall on the campus of the College of Philadelphia. As a student under Rush, it is likely that Harrison would have learned the basics of anatomy and the techniques of healing as they were known then—doctors still bled their patients to rid them of disease in those days—but by the 1790s, Rush was also establishing himself as an authority on mental illness. (His 1812 book *Observations and Inquiries Upon the Diseases of the Mind* was the first psychiatric textbook published in the United States; it offered the groundbreaking opinion that insanity was a disease and not the result of demonic possession.) Still, in the 1790s not much was known about treating the mentally ill. Following his mentor around the corridors of Pennsylvania Hospital, Harrison may have seen the great surgeon's patients strapped into his "tranquilizer chair," a device invented by Rush to reduce the flow of the patient's blood to the brain. Rush's biographers have concluded that the uncomfortable device probably did no harm to anybody, but wasn't much help either.

Meanwhile, events were unfolding quickly that would prompt the future president to abandon his career as a physician after four months of formal training under Dr. Rush. Just after starting classes, he learned that his father had died. The aged revolutionary statesman had been ailing for some time.

William Henry Harrison inherited 3,000 acres from his father's estate, but found himself land rich and cash poor. The elder Harrison had made no plans to finance the boy's medical training—news that was delivered to William Henry in a letter written by an older brother. William Henry suddenly found himself without funds. By coincidence, Richard Henry Lee, then the governor of Virginia, was visiting Philadelphia. Harrison sought out his father's old friend for advice.

Lee suggested the military as a career. That summer, the Philadelphia newspapers reported many stories of threats by hostile Indians on America's western frontier. The idea obviously had great appeal to Harrison, who immediately left medical school and enlisted in the army. "In 24 hours from the first conception of changing my profession," Harrison later wrote, "I was an Ensign in the 1st U.S. Regiment of Infantry."

Morris found out about Harrison's decision and summoned the boy. Morris tried to talk him out of volunteering for the army, which at the time was undermanned and underfunded. In addition, Morris pointed out, life on the frontier facing hostile Indians was hardly the type of experience young Harrison had known in Virginia plantation society. However, Harrison was determined and Morris gave in, speculating that the western frontier was as good a place as any for a young man to embark on life's journey.

William Henry Harrison had a long and successful career as a soldier. He served as an aide-de-camp to General "Mad" Anthony Wayne at the Battle of Fallen Timbers in August 1794; this victory by the U.S. army opened Ohio to settlement. He rose steadily in the ranks, and was promoted to captain in 1797. The next year, Harrison resigned from the army to serve as secretary of the Northwest Territory, which encompassed the future states of Ohio and Indiana. After the Indiana Territory was separated from the Northwest Territory, Harrison served as governor for twelve years (1800–1812).

In 1811, Harrison became a national hero at the Battle of Tippecanoe when he put down an Indian uprising led by the chief Tecumseh, who organized a federation of tribes to repulse further settlement of Indian lands.

With the outbreak of the War of 1812, Harrison rejoined the army with the rank of brigadier general. He clashed again with Tecumseh at the Battle of the Thames in 1813. Harrison's troops defeated a combined force of British soldiers and Indian warriors. Tecumseh was killed in the battle, and his Indian followers scattered, never again to pose a threat to settlers in the Indiana Territory.

Following the war, Harrison and his wife, Anna Symmes Harrison, made their home on a farm in North Bend, Ohio, near Cincinnati. He was elected to the U.S. House of Representatives, but failed in a bid for the Senate. Later, he was sent as U.S. minister to Colombia, but was recalled by President Andrew Jackson after a series of diplomatic blunders. After returning to North Bend, the Harrisons suffered some economic misfortunes, and by the time the Whigs started their search for a

These pages list faculty salaries paid. (One John Matthias Kramer was discharged at mid-semester and paid half of his salary plus "a gratuity.") Also listed here are accounts with Peter Collinson and other London merchants for the purchase of medical books and medical instruments. Perhaps Collinson is best known for popularizing the writings of Carl Linnaeus, the noted Swedish botanist, whom Collinson met when the scientist lectured at Oxford in 1736.

The University of Pennsylvania agreed to pay for these ordered items with money raised from their next lottery. Throughout the eighteenth century, lotteries were used to obtain money for schools, churches, roads, bridges, canals, and other public projects. In 1748, funds obtained through a lottery were used to build Philadelphia's fortifications. And in 1826 a lottery was held to pay Thomas Jefferson's debts.

BOOK XIX.

CONTINUED.

SEQUEL

OF THE

HISTORY

OF

ALEXANDER'S SUCCESSORS.

SECTION VIII.

Fulvius the consul subdues the Ætolians. The Spartans are cruelly treated by their exiles. Manlius, the other consul, conquers the Asiatic Gauls. Antiochus, in order to pay the tribute due to the Romans, plunders a temple in Elymias. That monarch is killed. Explication of Daniel's prophecy concerning Antiochus.

DURING the expedition of the Romans in Asia,* some commotions had happened in Greece. Amynander, by the aid of the Ætolians, had re-established himself in his kingdom of Athamania, after having driven out of his cities the Macedonian garrisons that held them for king Philip. He deputed some ambassadors to the senate of Rome; and others into Asia to the two Scipios, who were then at Ephesus, after their signal victory over Antiochus, to excuse his having employed the arms of the Ætolians against Philip, and also to make his complaints against that prince.

The Ætolians had likewise undertaken some enterprises against Philip, in which they had met with tolerable success: but when they heard of Antiochus's defeat, and found that the ambassadors they had sent to Rome were returning from thence, without being able to obtain any of their demands, and that Fulvius the consul was actually marching against them, they were seized with real alarms. Finding it would be impossible for them to resist the Romans by force of arms, they again had recourse to entreaties; and

A. M. 3815.
Ant. J. C. 189.

* Liv. l. xxxvii. n. 1—11. Polyb. in Excerpt. Leg. c. 26—28.

VOL. VII.   B

After his nomination for president by the Whigs in 1839, Harrison was asked to comment on his education. In his script, he wrote, "Inferior to many of my Class at College as a Latin & Greek scholar, I was considered but inferior to one in Belles Lettres information & particularly in History....I had actually read through the ponderous Work of Rollin which treats of Grecian & Roman history three times before I was 17 years old." Reference here is to French historian Charles Rollin's *Histoire Romaine dupuis la Foundation de Rome jusqu'a la Bataile d'Actium (Roman History from the Founding of Rome until the Battle of Actium)*, which was published in sixteen volumes between 1742 and 1751. An English translation was available when Harrison was a student. For decades, Rollin's histories of the ancient world remained popular in the United States. Voltaire described Rollins as "one of the first French historians who wrote a good style in prose."

Rollin's eight-volume *Ancient History* (1829) was used in American secondary schools and colleges until the early 20th century. Many editions and condensations exist. The chronology at the end of each volume is still considered the most extensive and detailed of the ancient world. Later writers on ancient history, such as James Henry Breasted, relied heavily on Rollin's pioneering volumes.

presidential candidate Harrison was working as a clerk in a minor government office in Hamilton County, Ohio.

By the start of the 1840 presidential campaign, Harrison was sixty-eight years old and ailing. The Whigs took great pains to cover up his infirmities. Whig newspapers described the general as someone of "elastic vigor" who spoke in "trumpet-like" tones. As the campaign wore on, he assured Daniel Webster, "My health is indeed better than it has been for many years."

The real truth came out a year later. He took the oath of office on March 4, 1841, and made his long inaugural speech on a blustery, damp day. For all his verbiage, Harrison disclosed little more than his intention to follow Congress's lead. Old Tippecanoe did show an eerie prescience by assuring the American people that he would not serve a second term. Shortly after his inauguration, President Harrison caught a cold that developed into pneumonia, and he died on April 4, 1841, after just a month in office.

—Hal Marcovitz

This is a record of student tuition fees and charges for firewood and quill pens collected by the University of Pennsylvania, 1768.

John Tyler
Chapter Ten

Nine-year-old John Tyler was a delicate boy who was regarded as rather docile. Most boys John Tyler's age enjoyed hunting and fishing with their fathers on their comfortable Virginia estates and plantations. Not young John. He preferred to spend his spare time playing his violin and writing poetry. Any suspicions that he was a pampered sissy, however, were instantly dispelled one day in 1800, when John was attending a school led by a Mr. McMurdo, a dictatorial Scottish schoolmaster who brooked no shenanigans from the sons of the wealthy plantation owners that had hired him to teach their children. McMurdo kept a birch switch on his desk and did not hesitate to use it at the slightest provocation. There is no evidence that John ever felt the sting of McMurdo's switch. Still, years later he noted, "It was a wonder that he did not whip all the sense out of his scholars."

The incident that touched off the uprising in McMurdo's schoolhouse remains unclear. Nevertheless, the students were moved to revolt against McMurdo's cruelty, and much to the astonishment of all who knew him the leader of the rebellion was the ordinarily docile violin player, John Tyler. Evidently, the students surrounded McMurdo, overpowered him, tied his hands and feet, and locked him in the schoolhouse. A passerby who heard the man's pleas for help rescued the hapless schoolmaster after several hours of imprisonment.

Once freed from his bonds, McMurdo went immediately to Greenway, the estate where John lived with his father, Judge John Tyler Sr. The indignant McMurdo related the events of the day to the judge, naming his son as the ringleader. The elder Tyler was unmoved by McMurdo's complaint. Clearly, the stories of McMurdo's despotism had made it to the judge's ears, and he had no sympathy for the Scotsman. He dismissed McMurdo with the words *sic semper tyrannis*—the Latin phrase that serves as the motto for the state of Virginia, which means "ever thus to tyrants!"

John Tyler, tenth president of the United States, was born on March 29, 1790. He was one of eight children of John and Mary Armistead Tyler. Greenway, the Tyler estate, covered some 1,200 acres along the James River near Charles City,

Nine-year-old John Tyler was a delicate boy who was regarded as rather docile....He preferred to spend his spare time playing his violin and writing poetry.

The Sir Christopher Wren Building at the College of William and Mary is the oldest academic building in continuous use in the United States. It was constructed between 1695 and 1699, before Williamsburg was founded, when the capital of the Virginia colony was still located at Jamestown. The building was designed by Wren, the famed English architect, who also designed St. Paul's Cathedral in London. The Wren Building has been destroyed by fire three times, in 1705, 1859, and 1862. Each time the structure was rebuilt, and for more than three centuries it has been "the soul of the College." This daguerreotype was done in 1855 and is the oldest extant one of the college.

In 1802, at age twelve, John Tyler entered the secondary division of the College of William and Mary in Williamsburg, about thirty miles from Charles City. He boarded with his sister and brother-in-law. Tyler began his college-level studies in 1805 and graduated from the school with the class of 1807.

In this June 1807 letter to his classmate John Blow, Tyler described working on his senior oration.

Virginia. Charles City could be found about midway between Virginia's two great cities of the era, Williamsburg and Richmond.

The first Tyler to arrive in America was Henry Tyler, an Englishman who set foot in Virginia just forty-four years after the Jamestown colony was established in 1607. The Tylers would become wealthy and influential members of the Virginia planter aristocracy—a social class that produced George Washington, Thomas Jefferson, James Monroe, and James Madison, among others. The elder John Tyler fought in the American War for Independence alongside Patrick Henry. Following the war, he took up the practice of law and was soon appointed judge. He served in the Virginia legislature and later as governor. He also owned forty slaves and believed vehemently in the rights of states to determine their own destinies—an uncompromising philosophy his son would adopt as his own.

John's mother believed her son was destined for great accomplishments. It is said that on a moonlit night just a year after his birth, she saw her boy reaching skyward with his two chubby hands in a vain effort to grasp the moon. Astonished by what she saw, Mary Tyler is said to have remarked, "This child is destined to be a president of the United States, his wishes fly so high." Sadly, young John would barely get to know his mother. Mary Tyler died of a stroke when he was seven years old. John was often ill himself. He was a gaunt boy who endured stomach ailments, bouts of diarrhea, and frequent colds.

When John was twelve years old he enrolled in the preparatory school on the campus of the College of William and Mary in nearby Williamsburg. By the time he stepped onto the campus in 1802, the Tylers had long been associated with the school. His father and grandfather had both been students at William and Mary, and Judge Tyler would eventually serve on the Board of Visitors, the panel that oversaw the operation of the institution. In addition, two of John's aunts were married to William and Mary professors.

John lived off campus, boarding in the home of an older sister and her husband, a Judge James Semple, during the two years he spent in the preparatory school. After this he was accepted as a college student at William and Mary, the second-oldest college in the United States and the preeminent school for the sons of influential and wealthy Virginians. John Tyler's classmates included William Crittenden, who would serve under Tyler as attorney general; Winfield Scott, who would become an important military leader and a hero of the Mexican-American War; and Philip P. Barbour, who would be appointed to the U.S. Supreme Court by President Andrew Jackson.

By the time John started classes at William and Mary, more than a century after its founding in 1693, the school was still very selective in its choice of students. Enrollment was usually limited to no more than sixty students a year. Years after he left the White House, John returned to the Williamsburg campus to make a speech, noting at the time how selective the school had remained since he studied there. He said, "Of the number of sands upon the shore of time, she boasts not, but of those rare and precious gems, which have been garnered from their midst, and which shine and will shine forever on her illumined brow."

Despite its prestige, the college had been through a period of turmoil by the time John Tyler commenced his studies there. Thomas Jefferson, who had graduated from William and Mary in 1760, continued to exert considerable influence over the school long after he left the Williamsburg campus. In 1779, Jefferson served in the Virginia legislature and drafted a law titled "Bill for the More General Diffusion of Knowledge," which was intended to vastly change the William and Mary curriculum. Jefferson's legislation abolished William and Mary's divinity school and charged the college with adding courses in the arts and sciences to its curriculum. Jefferson's law also established new teaching positions at William and Mary, creating professorships in philosophy, medicine, languages, and legal studies. When John Tyler arrived at William and Mary just two decades later, the college was still wrestling with the mission Jefferson had laid. In 1804 the college's endowment was a paltry $130,000, and the Board of Visitors was finding it extraordinarily difficult to find the type of men whom Jefferson had envisioned teaching William and Mary students. The college's curriculum was still rather narrow during Tyler's matriculation; his courses were limited to mathematics, economics, and classic literature.

Still, he made the most of his opportunity. In economics class, Tyler was assigned to read *The Wealth of Nations*, the landmark treatise on economics by philosopher Adam Smith, who postulated that the government should provide only a minimum of influence over the economy, permitting businesses to grow on their own. Smith's theory became known as *laissez-faire*, or free trade. There is no question that Tyler was influenced by Smith's work. Later, while serving in Congress, he opposed tariffs—taxes assessed by the government on exports and imports. During his White House years, Tyler fought hard against establishment of a national bank, vetoing measures that would have established a government-controlled financial institution.

Among the other books John read in his William and Mary courses were David Hume's *History of England*, which provided important lessons to a future world leader on the pitfalls a powerful nation would do well to avoid, and the political satires of Tobias George Smollett, who lampooned England's society, culture, and military. John also had a taste for literature, perhaps stemming from his days as a young poet at Greenway. He enjoyed reading the works of such British men of letters as John Milton, Alexander Pope, Samuel Johnson, Oliver Goldsmith, Thomas Gray, and Joseph Addison. He was particularly fond of Addison, the essayist and poet whose writings appeared in the *Tatler* and the *Spectator*, liberal English political journals published by Sir Richard Steele. Addision was a staunch believer in the rights of men, constitutional government, and free trade. However, Addison was more than just a political commentator. He was a master storyteller who was regarded as an elegant craftsman of words. John wrote that Addision "is considered the best writer in the English language. He paints virtue in her most lovely colors, and makes each sensitive mind her lover and admirer."

John Tyler became fascinated with political economics as a student at the College of William and Mary. (Politics and economics had not yet been separated into separate subjects.) Adam Smith's recently published *An Inquiry into the Nature and Causes of the Wealth of Nations* was the text. Tyler committed Smith's arguments to memory. Tyler's subsequent speeches on the tariff and free trade delivered as a legislator and as president were drawn almost verbatim from this influential work. Indeed, Smith's persuasive arguments for government non-interference in the economy complemented Tyler's defense of states' rights.

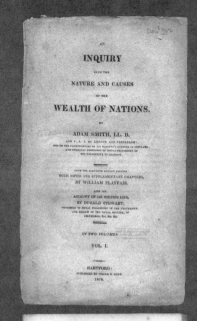

In 1776, Adam Smith published his seminal *Wealth of Nations*. He criticized the older economic system of mercantilism, with its regulatory and monopolistic practices. Smith urged that certain "natural laws" of production and exchange be allowed to work. Thomas Malthus, David Ricardo, and the so-called Manchester School followed Smith. Their doctrine was dubbed (by its opponents) *laissez-faire*, and, in its elaborated form, is still called classical economics.

Basically, classical economics held that there is a world of economic relationships autonomous and separable from government and politics. The economic world, in this view, is regulated within itself by certain "natural laws," such as the law of supply and demand and the law of diminishing returns. All persons should follow their own enlightened self-interest; as each knows his own interest better than anyone else—and the sum total of individual interests will add-up to the general welfare and liberty of all (except slaves). Government should do as little as possible, confining itself to preserving life and property. Government must provide reasonable laws and reliable courts to assure the discharge of private contracts, debts, and other obligations. Likewise business, education, charity, and personal matters should be left to private initiative.

There must be no tariffs—free trade should reign everywhere because the economic system is worldwide, unaffected by political barriers or national differences. As for the worker, according to classical economists before about 1850, he should not expect to earn more than a bare minimum living. Adam Smith called this principle the "iron law of wages." If the worker received more than a subsistence wage, he only would "breed" more children who would eat up excess profits. If discontented, the worker should see the folly of changing the system. For this *is* the system, the natural system.

The classical economic liberalism espoused by Adam Smith and his followers emphasized the free, unencumbered marketplace as the most efficient, equitable, and salutary mechanism for the distribution of goods and services in society. John Tyler repeatedly used these arguments in the South's struggle against all other interpretations of the Constitution.

Above are pages from an 1818 American edition of Adam Smith, *An Inquiry into the Nature and Causes of the Wealth of Nations*. The first American edition was published about 1790.

Tyler's favorite novelist, though, was the Englishman Edward Bulwer-Lytton, an unusual choice for a student so dedicated to fine writing. Although Bulwer-Lytton's novels are given credit for arousing the social consciousness of the British people, he is regarded by modern critics as a truly horrible wordsmith. It was Bulwer-Lytton who wrote the much-lampooned opening line "It was a dark and stormy night," which appears on the first page of his novel *Paul Clifford*. He was also the author of these familiar and well-worn words uttered by lawyers everywhere: "The pen is mightier than the sword."

Tyler particularly enjoyed Bulwer-Lytton's novel *Eugene Aram*. The novel told the fictionalized story of a real-life murderer hanged in 1759, yet portrayed as a hero by Bulwer-Lytton because of the man's intellectualism. John sat up one evening reading the novel until midnight, later writing that he found it "deeply and painfully interesting."

John received high grades at William and Mary in most subjects, but he had considerable trouble with penmanship. During his final year at William and Mary, Judge Tyler sent his son this rather strong rebuke: "I can't help telling you how much I am mortified to find no improvement in your handwriting, neither do you connect your lines straight, which makes your letters look so abominable. It is an easy thing to correct this fault, and unless you do so how can you be fit for law business of every description? Look at the handwriting of Mr. Jefferson, Wythe, Pendleton, Mercer, Nicolas, and all the old lawyers, and you will find how much care they took to write handsomely. Writing and cyphering well are absolutely necessary and cannot be dispensed with." There is evidence that John heeded his father's admonishments; historians who have examined John's presidential papers report that his handwriting was entirely legible.

John was a hard-working member of the student body at William and Mary and was well respected by his professors. Apparently, the hostility he had displayed toward McMurdo was an isolated incident in his young life, because he showed no such attitude toward his professors in Williamsburg. In fact, he was a favorite student of Bishop James Madison, the Episcopal clergyman who served as president of William and Mary, although there is one incident on campus that shows Bishop Madison was not always completely enamored with young Tyler. That incident occurred during commencement exercises in 1807. John was selected to deliver the commencement address in Bruton Parish Church in Williamsburg. Later, John wrote that his address was extremely well received by faculty members, who told him it was "the best commencement oration, both in style and matter, ever delivered at the institution within their recollection."

However, not everyone agreed. The topic for John's oration was whether more educational opportunities should be made available to women—a controversial topic at

"I can't help telling you how much I am mortified to find no improvement in your handwriting," wrote Tyler's father.

that time. Evidently, Bishop Madison didn't agree with young John's proposals to permit women to participate in higher education. During the speech, Bishop Madison stood in the back of the church, gesticulating wildly with his hands and walking cane whenever John voiced an idea with which the bishop disagreed, apparently hoping that John would pick up the signals, drop the idea, and move on to another topic. Instead, John ignored the bishop and kept on talking. (It would be another twenty-six years before the first American woman would be admitted to a college in the United States.)

In the society into which John was born, it was common for sons to follow their fathers into the family's trade or craft. The sons of farmers became farmers, the sons of blacksmiths learned the ironworking craft, and the sons of brick masons became masons themselves. In John's case, his father had been a lawyer and legislator. That was the course John selected for himself. Following his graduation from William and Mary he intended to study law, writing that he believed the profession of law was the "high road to fame."

At the time, there were few law schools in America. Most young attorneys learned the craft of law by serving as apprentices or clerks to established lawyers. They would spend several years reading law books and performing menial tasks, such as copying lengthy pleadings, running errands, and even sweeping the office. In most cases, they would earn little or no money for these services, receiving their pay in the form of lessons in the law their employers provided for them as well as commitments to eventually sponsor them for admission before the bar of their state courts.

John's clerkship lasted two years. He started off by studying under his father, Judge John Tyler, as well as a cousin, Samuel Tyler. Within a few months, though, the judge was elected governor of Virginia, and he left Charles City for the state capital in Richmond. John went with his father, intending to continue his legal studies in the capital.

John served as an aide to his father. In 1809, former President Jefferson paid his respects to Governor Tyler in Richmond. Jefferson stayed for dinner, and young John made sure the great statesman had two desserts. When Jefferson saw the two servings of plum pudding placed in front of him, he asked the young man whether he was getting "extraordinary" treatment. "Yes," Tyler admitted, "but this is an extraordinary occasion."

When not helping his father, Tyler made friends in Richmond and joined a literary society, whose members met occasionally to debate social and political issues and practice their speaking techniques. Such groups were common on college campuses and in cities where men aspired to careers in the law and public office. After joining the society, Tyler became friendly with a young man named Abel P. Upshur, who would later serve under President Tyler as secretary of state.

Meanwhile, Tyler continued to study law. Because his father was serving as governor, he no longer had the time to devote to his son's legal training. Tyler began a clerkship under Richmond attorney Edmund Randolph, who had served as attorney general and secretary of state under President George Washington. Other attorneys in practice in Richmond during Tyler 's clerkship included John Marshall, a chief justice of the Supreme Court, and William Wirt, soon to be President James Monroe's attorney general.

Tyler passed the bar examination at age nineteen. Under Virginia law, he was two years too young to practice law, but the examiner evidently never bothered to ask Tyler his age and he was admitted to the bar. It wasn't long before John Tyler had developed a thriving law practice. He gained a reputation as a brilliant criminal attorney with a dramatic speaking style. He was recognized as an articulate lawyer able to sway the emotions of many jurors into believing his clients were truly law-abiding citizens who had been falsely accused.

During this time in Richmond Tyler met Letitia Christian, daughter of a wealthy planter from New Kent County, Virginia. They married in 1813. By then, his political career was also off and running. In 1811, Tyler had been elected to a seat in the Virginia legislature representing Charles City. He briefly served with a company of volunteers, which had been raised to defend Richmond against British invasion during the War of 1812, but because the city was never threatened he saw no action during the conflict. After the war, he won election to the U.S. House of Representatives, served as governor of Virginia, and in 1833 was elected to the U.S. Senate. He had been a Democrat for much of that time, but split with his party and joined the Whigs, believing them to be defenders of states' rights, although he would eventually find himself incorrect in that assessment.

Meanwhile, an Army general named William Henry Harrison had become a national hero in 1811 when he put down an Indian uprising at the Battle of Tippecanoe. Harrison had been raised on a Virginia plantation not far from Greenway. In fact, Harrison's father, Benjamin Harrison, had been a long-time political foe of Judge John Tyler. The Harrison and Tyler families were never close, so it was truly ironic when the Whigs turned to Tyler in 1840 to serve as the vice presidential candidate on the ticket headed by General Harrison, who by then was living in Ohio.

The Whigs won the election for the aging general by portraying his opponent, the incumbent Martin Van Buren, as an elitist who was out of touch with the problems of common Americans. The so-called "hard cider and log cabin" campaign was highly effective—particularly for its motto, which remains one of the most familiar political slogans in American history, mainly for its alliteration and the jolly way it rolled off the tongue: "Tippecanoe and Tyler, too."

President Harrison would serve just one month in office. He caught pneumonia on the day of his inauguration and died shortly after. Tyler is said to have been shocked when he learned of the president's death—he had not even known Harrison was sick. One story that has circulated over the years reports that when officials arrived at Tyler's home to announce the death of the nation's chief executive, they found the vice president on his hands and knees playing marbles with his children. In any event, when Harrison became the first president to die in office, Tyler became the first vice president to ascend to the White House under the constitutional provision that provides for presidential succession.

Tyler would serve a single term in office, soon losing the support of the Whig Party. A true southerner, Tyler defended states' rights for his entire tenure in the White House. He would soon clash with the powerful Whig Senator Henry Clay, who believed in a strong national government. Clay supported the creation of a national bank, which Tyler opposed not only because of his devotion to *laissez-faire* economics but because he believed a national bank would impede the states in setting their own economic policies. Twice Clay pushed through legislation creating a national bank, and twice Tyler vetoed the legislation. In 1844, the Whigs refused to nominate Tyler for a second term, turning instead to Clay as their candidate. That fall, Clay was defeated for the presidency by James K. Polk.

After leaving the White House, Tyler retired to his Virginia estate. A believer in states' rights to the end, he supported the secession of the southern states in 1860–61. Soon after the outbreak of the Civil War, he was elected to a seat in the Confederate Congress. His service to the Confederacy would be brief. He died January 18, 1862.

—Hal Marcovitz

James K. Polk
Chapter Eleven

With his rural upbringing, young James K. Polk must have thought he had found a little piece of heaven when he arrived in Chapel Hill in January 1816. True, the North Carolina town was little more than a village consisting of just thirteen houses, two stores, and a tavern. A single muddy street ran through Chapel Hill, which the town fathers had somewhat optimistically named Grand Avenue. When Jim Polk followed Grand Avenue less than a quarter mile north out of Chapel Hill, he arrived at the campus of the University of North Carolina.

The school was just two decades old when Polk enrolled to commence his college education. Nevertheless, the college had grown quickly since it had been established as the first state university in the United States. By the time Polk arrived, the university was housed in three buildings. These buildings held classrooms and dormitories as well as a library, chapel, and meeting rooms where the school's two highly competitive student literary societies, the Dialectic and Philanthropic, held their meetings.

The university was located in some of the most beautiful terrain in North Carolina. The school's founders laid out the campus atop a ridge that offered the students a panoramic view of the forested North Carolina Piedmont. A student who gazed southeast through the cobalt blue Carolina sky could see smoke rising from the chimneys of Raleigh, the state capital, located some thirty miles away.

Polk had no trouble adjusting to university life. He soon became the top scholar on campus and a leader among his fellow students. Polk joined the Dialectic Society and took part in the group's lively and heated debates. In the 1800s, a college literary society was more than just a place where students could share their thoughts about books they read or recite essays or speeches they composed for the next day's class in rhetoric. The societies were also forums for political thought and social commentary.

In the early nineteenth century many college professors in America were also Protestant ministers or theologians, and had been raised and educated under strict moral codes that included a strong adherence to the lessons taught in the Bible. Few professors were willing to entertain radical thinking among students—even at North Carolina,

James K. Polk entered the University of North Carolina in 1815. The school consisted of a president, one professor, three tutors, and about eighty students. Nearby was the tiny community of Chapel Hill. Presbyterian instruction was the mainstay. Indeed, the president and the sole professor were Presbyterian ministers. Students attended chapel twice daily. On Sundays, black gowns were worn. Any student who questioned the existence of God was immediately expelled. After evening prayers, students were expected to return to their rooms to study. Tuition was ten dollars a term (later raised to fifteen dollars) and room was a dollar extra.

Polk was placed in the sophomore class, second half, because he did so well in the rigorous entrance examination that covered English grammar, Latin, and Greek. A classmate wrote that Polk "never missed a recitation nor omitted the punctilious performance of any duty." The future president, a timid person, formed a lifelong friendship at the university with John Y. Mason, who would later serve in Polk's cabinet, first as attorney general and then as secretary of the navy. Polk graduated in 1818, with first honors in mathematics and the classics. In June 1847 President Polk, accompanied by Mason, returned to Chapel Hill to attend graduation ceremonies.

These pages from the University of North Carolina Student Records and Faculty Reports, January 7, 1818, detail the academic examination of the university students conducted over several days in late 1817. Polk is listed in the twelve-member senior class that was examined on the Bible, moral and natural philosophy, rhetoric, and English grammar. The report concludes: "Distinctions might be made in scholarship, but it would be difficult at what point to stop. They are all approved."

These primary documents dealing with Polk's education are unique. They have been preserved in the archives of the University of North Carolina at Chapel Hill. Most southern college archives, as well as the schools themselves, were destroyed during the Civil War. In 1864, as General William T. Sherman's Union troops approached Chapel Hill, the university president rode out to meet him. He pleaded that the university buildings be spared. Sherman agreed but requested the use of the campus for his cavalry. Subsequently, the commander of the Union cavalry married the university president's daughter. This was truly scandalous at the time!

Each year, the entire University of North Carolina faculty tested the students. In late November 1816, Polk's fifteen-member junior class was examined in algebra, geometry, and English grammar. The final report noted, "In the class, James K. Polk, and William Moseley are the best scholars." Polk and Moseley, who later became governor of Florida, were roommates. In later years, the two friends reminisced about the "many tedious and laborious hours" they had spent in their room on the third floor of New College "attempting to discover the beauties of Cicero and Homer and the less interesting amusements of quadratic equations and conic sections."

"In the class, James K. Polk, and William Moseley are the best scholars."

where the senior year was totally devoted to philosophy, ostensibly to encourage the students to form their own ideas about how they planned to live the rest of their lives.

At North Carolina the college president, Reverend Robert Chapman, had modeled the school on the College of New Jersey (now Princeton University), a Presbyterian school. At North Carolina, Chapman insisted that prayer and Bible study be a part of the curriculum. The day commenced with solemn prayer in the school chapel. Prayers were said again just before supper. On Saturdays, students and faculty members were required to wear black robes and attend a public worship session.

While there were occasional tensions between Chapman and the students over the president's strict religious beliefs, there were political differences between the president and the student body. The Reverend Chapman was a devout member of the Federalist Party, which had dominated politics in the early years of the United States. However, by 1816 the Federalists were in decline and many Americans embraced the ideals of Thomas Jefferson's Republican Party. Nobody was more enthusiastic about the republican ideology than the young intellectuals on college campuses, who believed it was their destiny to lead the nation. The Reverend Chapman didn't see it that way, and he discouraged the espousal of Jeffersonian ideas on campus. By September 1816, relations between Chapman and the students were heading toward a confrontation. Clearly, some sort of student rebellion was in the air.

Jim Polk found himself caught up in the middle of it all. Even though he had been a student at North Carolina for just nine months, the other students were already impressed by his intelligence and poise and looked toward him for leadership. It must have surely angered Chapman when Polk, until then a faculty favorite, advised his fellow members of the Dialectic Society to stand up to the professors and speak their minds. "Stoop not from the true principles of honor to gain the favor of the faculty and thus succeed in your views of promotion," the future president of the United States told his fellow students.

Just a few years before making this statement, Jim Polk had not been the kind of erudite young man whose opinions were valued among members of the campus literary societies. He had grown up in rural Tennessee, and received a typical education for a boy whose family trade was farming—almost no formal schooling at all. After Polk made a name for himself in politics, his former neighbors recalled watching the president in his boyhood years skip barefoot down a dusty road, his pants rolled up to his knees and school books slung over a shoulder. That story may have been concocted by nineteenth-century Democratic Party managers eager to publicize Polk's humble beginnings; nevertheless, it cannot be denied that by the age of eighteen, the eleventh president of the United States could barely read and write. That was typical for a boy of Polk's backwoods upbringing, and if it were not for a childhood plagued by ill health it is likely he never would have set foot in Chapel Hill.

James Knox Polk was born November 2, 1795, in Mecklenburg County, North Carolina. His father was Sam Polk, whose Scotch-Irish ancestors had immigrated to America in the late 1600s. They settled in Maryland, but by the 1750s the Polks had decided to head south because they believed Maryland was getting too crowded for their liking. A year before Jim's birth, Sam Polk had married Jane Knox. She was the daughter of Captain James Knox, a wealthy Revolutionary War hero who died just weeks before his daughter's wedding. His estate left the couple well prepared for the hardships of life that awaited them.

Truth be told, though, the Polks would have fared quite nicely without Jane's inheritance. Sam's father was Ezekiel Polk, a wealthy North Carolina farmer whose talent as a surveyor led him to make some savvy investments in land. One of those investments was in middle Tennessee, some five hundred miles west of the Polk family's Mecklenburg homestead. In 1805, the land suddenly opened up to settlement—the Cherokees and Chickasaws having signed treaties giving up their rights to the territory. Years before, Ezekiel Polk had surveyed that territory and knew exactly where to stake his claim. Within months, Ezekiel Polk acquired thousands of acres near the Duck River in what would become known as Maury County. By the end of 1805 Ezekiel Polk had moved to Tennessee. A year later, enticed by Ezekiel's offer of several hundred acres of fertile bottomland, Sam and his brother William elected to leave Mecklenburg and start new lives in Tennessee as well. At the time Jim Polk, the oldest of Sam and Jane's five children, was eleven.

Sam and Jane Polk moved into a log cabin and began raising tobacco. The land was for the most part untamed and unsettled, and Ezekiel Polk found himself much in demand as a surveyor. Surveying expeditions into the Duck River wilderness often took days or weeks. Ezekiel would typically round up his two sons as well as his sons-in-law, cousins, nephews, and grandchildren and venture into the wilderness at the head of a large surveying party. Jim Polk was delighted to accompany the men on such missions, but he was a sickly, gaunt boy who tired easily. The boy was unable to keep up with the men—or even the other Polk boys his age. As a result, Jim would usually be left back in camp to tend to the horses while the others labored in the forests.

In addition to his lack of energy, as a child Jim often suffered from acute abdominal pains and raging fevers. Finally, his illness was diagnosed as a gallstone. Because doctors were not common in rural areas in 1812, the problem could not be cured until Sam Polk heard about a physician in Kentucky whose surgical skills were said to be remarkable. After a two hundred and thirty mile trip on horseback, Jim Polk went under the knife on Dr. Ephraim McDonald's operating table. Anesthesia was unknown in those days; the seventeen-year-old patient endured the incision with only brandy to dull the pain. He survived the operation, and after a period of convalescence returned to Maury County where he proudly showed off the small stone Dr. McDonald had cut out of his gut.

The surgery cured his abdominal pains, but Jim was still weak and unaccustomed to hard farm labor. Sam Polk proposed his boy learn the trade of a shopkeeper, and found Jim a job in a store in the nearby town of Columbia. The boy found the work not to his liking. Jim Polk had ambitions; clerking in a small town trading post was not

Literary societies provided important training at early American colleges. Students met periodically to debate public issues. Most students at Chapel Hill were members of either the Dialectic Society or its keen rival, the Philanthropic Society. Polk joined the former during his first term. Each society met once a week to debate a prearranged topic. Members were required to participate in these debates every other week and to present written compositions at the alternate meetings. The best essays were filed in the society archives. Eight of Polk's essays were so honored, and two of them still exist.

In Polk's first essay, "The Admission of Foreigners into Office in the United States," Polk worried about the deleterious influence immigrants might have on American society, including their possible formation of political factions and parties. Polk became a staunch Democrat but, in 1817, when the essay was written, many still considered political parties unnecessary. In the second essay, "The Powers of Invention," Polk expressed his strong faith in human progress through reason.

The Dialectic Society had libraries superior to that of the university itself. Polk donated many volumes, including John Eaton's 1817 biography of Andrew Jackson and a multi-volume set of Edward Gibbon's *Decline and Fall of the Roman Empire*. The Society strictly enforced its rules. Polk was occasionally fined for missing meetings and other infractions that included a ten cent fine for exchanging "threatening language" with another member.

Polk was an active member. He served as treasurer, secretary, and chairman of the executive committee. He also served two terms as society president—an unprecedented honor. The three pages above are from Polk's May 20, 1818, address to the Society thanking the members for electing him to a second term.

one of them. Now eighteen years old, Jim told his father he wanted to go to school.

Just south of Columbia, a congregation of Presbyterians had established a school in the Zion Church led by their minister, Robert Henderson. When Jim Polk enrolled in the school, he could barely make out the words on a printed page. Within a short time, Henderson had him reading the works of the classical Roman and Greek authors. Henderson was astounded by the pace at which this farm boy gulped down knowledge. After a year, Henderson told Sam Polk he had taught Jim all he was capable of teaching him. Young Jim Polk, Henderson said, "was diligent in his studies and his moral conduct was unexceptionable and exemplary."

Polk spent the next year at Bradley Academy, located some fifty miles northeast of Columbia in Murfreesboro, Tennessee. He studied under Samuel Black, a Presbyterian minister who led classes in Greek, Latin, mathematics, geography, philosophy, astronomy, the *belles-lettres*, logic, and literature. Classical Latin authors that Polk read at school included Lucian, whose dialogues were studied for their satirical content, and the historian Sallust, whose tales of the corruption of Rome and the deviousness of the traitor Catiline may have been used by Black to calibrate the moral compasses inside his students. Polk also tackled Julius Caesar's *De Bello Gallico* and *De Bello Civili*, which taught him something of the art of war, and studied the writings of the Roman poet Vergil, whose *Aeneid* tells the story of the wanderings of the warrior whose descendants would eventually found the city of Rome—important reading for a future commander in chief of an army that would later humble Mexico and seize its territory.

What's more, under Black Polk had cleansed himself of his farm boy ways and gained a certain academic polish, which may have helped him come to the attention of Sarah Childress, a wealthy Murfreesboro girl he met while attending Bradley Academy. The couple would marry in 1824.

After a year at Bradley Academy, Black declared Polk ready for college. Sam Polk, amazed at his son's progress, was anxious to see the boy continue his education. The choice of the college was simple—Sam's cousin, William Polk, served as a trustee for the University of North Carolina at Chapel Hill. The tuition was $10 a year, although during Jim's matriculation the fee was raised to $15.

Though Black and Henderson regarded him as the brightest of their students, few of their students had the intelligence or ambition for college, so Polk was nervous when he arrived in January 1816. He had to undergo a rigorous entrance examination—a committee of faculty members grilled him in his abilities to read English, Latin, and Greek—but Polk easily sailed through their questions. He did so well, in fact, that after a short consultation the faculty examiners concluded that his abilities already ranked him beyond the freshman level, and he was to be admitted as a member of the sophomore class.

He was one of about eighty students who would take classes at North Carolina that year. In addition to the dictatorial Reverend Chapman, the only

The above image is an 1813 paper cutout done of the University of North Carolina at Chapel Hill. The university was located on a great ridge from which one could look out across forested hills to see as far as Raleigh, the state capital, about thirty miles away. New College (later called South Building), the three-story structure on the right of the illustration, contained recreation rooms, the library, literary society meeting rooms, and the dormitory. Old East, the original two-story structure, is on the left of the illustration. The small village of Chapel Hill stood along a dusty road about three hundred yards from the university buildings.

other professor on campus at the time was Reverend Joseph Caldwell, who taught mathematics and philosophy. Tutors led most of the other classes.

Polk would not take his first class under Caldwell until his junior year. From that point on, he developed a close bond with Caldwell. Polk was an excellent math student, easily mastering the concepts of advanced geometry—no small feat for a boy whose prior exposure to mathematics had been limited to measuring out salt and sugar in the Columbia trading post. Caldwell also taught philosophy, which he had learned at the College of New Jersey under John Witherspoon, the sixth and most celebrated president of the university. Witherspoon had liberalized the curriculum at the College of New Jersey, adding lectures in eighteenth-century literature and rhetoric and placing more emphasis on the sciences. Witherspoon also subscribed to the theories of the English philosopher John Locke, whose defense of human rights and liberties may have had a lot to do with Witherspoon's participation in the Continental Congress and his decision to add his signature to the Declaration of Independence.

Witherspoon passed on those values to Caldwell, who in turn passed them on to Polk. Prior to enrolling at North Carolina, Polk had watched the rise of Jeffersonian political thought and the subsequent self-destruction of the Federalist Party. Back home, all the Polks, Jim included, were avid boosters of their fellow Tennessee citizen Andrew Jackson, who knew Sam Polk well. As a college student, Polk found himself focused on the growing national presence of the hero of the Battle of New Orleans.

The papers Polk wrote for class reflected the work of a budding eighteenth-century Democrat. One of his papers, titled "The Admission of Foreigners into Office in the United States," argued against permitting immigrants to hold elective office because Polk believed they would introduce an Old World monarchial government into what was then the world's only true democratic society. In the paper, he labeled the late Federalist Alexander Hamilton "a friend to aristocracy" and warned against "those who have been accustomed to cringe to the despots of Europe."

Most of his college papers were unabashedly patriotic. Polk believed wholeheartedly in the intellectual capabilities of Americans, and often pointed toward inventors and artists such as Benjamin Franklin, Benjamin West, and Robert Fulton to prove his point. He argued that only in a free democratic society could such "genius in rags" be permitted to blossom. By the time he left Chapel Hill, he had become an ardent Jeffersonian.

Caldwell was able to hone Polk's intelligence. Where Henderson and Black had merely opened the boy's eyes to knowledge, Caldwell taught Polk how to use his education. During his three years at North Carolina, Polk was twice elected president of the Dialectic Society—at the time an unprecedented achievement. He formed close friendships with students—his roommate, William D. Moseley, matched Polk in scholarship on campus and would later come close to nearly matching his friend's achievements in politics. Moseley would eventually serve as first governor of Florida.

Caldwell would take over as president of the college near the end of Polk's first year on campus and begin to do for North Carolina what Witherspoon had done for the College of New Jersey. For much of Polk's first year, however, the autocratic Reverend Chapman still reigned.

Events finally came to a boil one evening in September 1816 when Philanthropic member William B. Shepard defied Chapman's order to delete passages from his chapel oration. Angry words were exchanged and the chapel meeting broke up as students and faculty members shouted threats to one another. That night, the Chapel Hill dormitories were in tumult. The next morning, the Philanthropic members regrouped to plan their next move. They were thwarted by the faculty, though, which announced that anyone who would not sign a letter of recantation would be suspended.

That left everyone on campus quite unnerved. Even the members of the Dialectic Society, who had nothing to do with Shepard's rebellion, were upset by the situation. The Philanthropics accused the Dialectics of failing to come to their assistance, a charge that Polk refuted in strong language. Several of the Philanthropics refused to sign the letters of recantation; Chapman responded by suspending them. The ranks of the Philanthropics were soon down to just thirteen students.

When a bomb exploded on the doorstep of a tutor, the trustees of the college felt obliged to take action. Things did not go well for Chapman. Some of the trustees were fathers of young men enrolled at North Carolina; undoubtedly, they had been hearing complaints about the ill-humored autocrat for years. Chapman was ousted as president and Caldwell installed in his place. As for the students, they suffered losses as well. Shepard and another Philanthropic leader, George Dromgoole, were expelled. However, it would not be the last that Polk would see of either young man. Years later, Polk would serve alongside Shepard and Dromgoole in the U.S. House of Representatives—a legislative body that recognized Polk's leadership ability when it elected him speaker in 1835.

In May 1818, twelve college trustees arrived in Chapel Hill and spent a week interviewing members of the senior class. Polk astounded his inquisitors with the breadth of his knowledge. He was named top scholar and assigned the duty of delivering the salutatory address. Polk and the other graduating seniors reveled in the weeklong celebration on campus, which culminated in commencement exercises. Following graduation, Polk intended to pursue the practice of law, although he already knew his true ambition was to serve in public office.

In 1847, President James K. Polk visited the campus of the University of North Carolina to help dedicate a monument to Joseph Caldwell. As the students and faculty members of the now-thriving state university gathered before the president, Polk said, "It was here…that I spent near three years of my life. It was here that I received lessons of instructions to which I mainly attribute whatever success or advancement has attended me in subsequent life."

—Hal Marcovitz

Zachary Taylor
Chapter Twelve

When Zachary Taylor was twenty-three years old, he won a commission in the United States Army at the rank of lieutenant. Taylor considered his appointment to the military the fulfillment of a dream, and immediately sat down to compose a letter of thanks to Henry Dearborn, the secretary of war. Here is the text of young Taylor's letter:

> Sir
> I received your letter of the 4th of May in which you informed me that
> I was appointed a firs Lieutenant in the seventh regiment of Infantry in
> the service of the United States which appointment I doo accept.
> I am Sir with great respect
> your Obt. Servt.
> Zachary Taylor

Any high school or college English teacher would blanch at the composition, spelling, and grammar employed by Lieutenant Taylor in his correspondence with Secretary Dearborn. The truth is, however, that Zachary Taylor had no college English professor because he did not attend college. In fact, Taylor had barely any formal schooling to speak of. As a boy, he received just a brief education in tiny backwoods schoolhouses. By 1808, the year Zachary received his commission, he had long since devoted himself to tending the fields on the vast Taylor family property, where the nation's twelfth president learned the science of farming and, to a lesser degree, the art of war.

Nearly four decades later, Zachary Taylor found himself leading American soldiers in warfare against Mexico. By then, he had attained the rank of brigadier general and was, therefore, responsible for composing many letters and other communications to his superior officers as well as subordinates in the field. Some of those letters ran dozens of pages and contained explanations of complicated military maneuvers.

In one such letter, Taylor urged his superiors to authorize an invasion of Texas during the winter months, arguing that the climate of the rugged territory would be

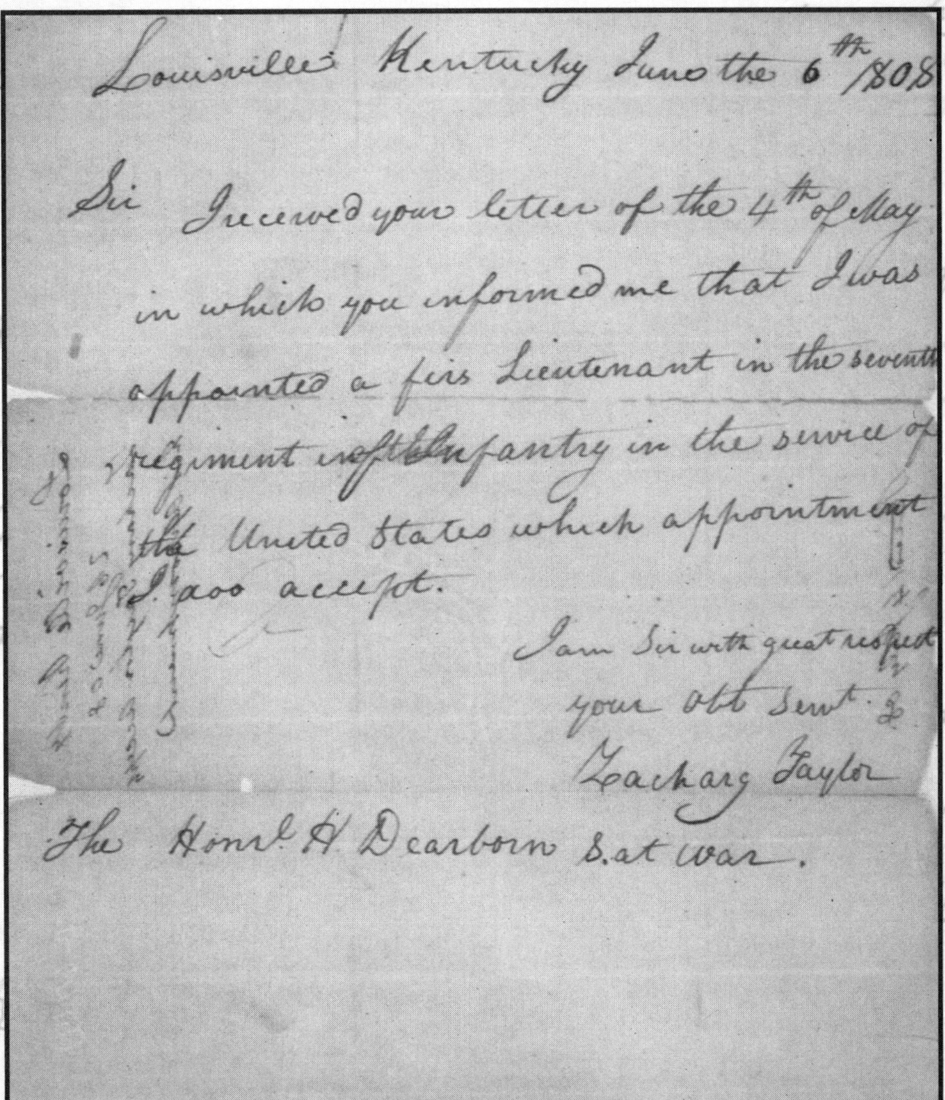

Louisville Kentucky June the 6th 1808

Sir   I received your letter of the 4th of May in which you informed me that I was appointed a firs Lieutenant in the seventh regiment of the Infantry in the service of the United States which appointment I doo accept.

I am Sir with great respect
your obt Servt &
Zachary Taylor

The Honl. H. Dearborn S. at War.

In May 1808, Zachary Taylor was commissioned a first lieutenant in the United States Army. Congress had provided for a new regiment, the Seventh Infantry, and Kentucky's congressional delegation had recommended Taylor to the officer staff. Also, Secretary of State James Madison, a longtime family friend, interceded on behalf of the young man.

   Above is the earliest known Taylor letter. It is addressed to the Secretary of War and was written on June 6, 1808. In it, Taylor accepted his army commission.

more favorable for the army's purposes than an advance in the summertime. Here is an excerpt from that letter, written on the eve of war with Mexico in 1845:

> On the hypothesis of an early adjustment of the boundary, and the consequent establishment of permanent frontier posts, I cannot urge too strongly upon the department the necessity of occupying those posts before the warm weather shall set in. A large amount of sickness is, I fear, to be apprehended, with every precaution that can be taken; but the information which I obtain leads me to believe that a summer movement would be attended with great expense of health and life. As in Florida, the winter is best for operations in Texas.

> I am, sir, very respectfully, your obedient servant,
> Z. Taylor.

No spelling errors. Complete sentences. Perfect grammar. Proper use of punctuation. Since winning his commission, had Zachary Taylor stayed up nights in his tent, reading spelling and grammar primers? No, the officer had no time for such pursuits. When not soldiering in the service of his country, he was home looking over his sprawling Louisiana plantation.

The difference between the two letters may be found in the fact that while Taylor certainly wrote his note of thanks to Secretary Dearborn, he may have simply dictated the correspondence regarding the inhospitable summertime climate of Texas, leaving it to a secretary to fix things up. Taylor's long-time aide-de-camp was Colonel William W. S. Bliss—a West Point graduate at the age of seventeen, speaker of six languages, and avid student of Kant and Goethe. He was also Taylor's son-in-law and, in all likelihood, the author of most letters and other communications that were issued under General Taylor's signature. Taylor said Bliss could be relied on for "trustworthy information, honest and competent advice, a friendly hand to supplement or subtract, and skillful pen to report, explain and, if necessary, discreetly color the facts." Zachary Taylor was so dependent on the colonel that he called him "Perfect Bliss."

Zachary Taylor was born on November 24, 1784, in Montebello, Virginia. Taylor would grow up to be president, but he would not join the ranks of the many presidents—among them Washington, Jefferson, Madison and Monroe—who would call Virginia home. Fact is, the Taylors were leaving Virginia for a new life in Kentucky when they stopped to visit a relative in Montebello just twelve miles from home. That is where Sarah Strother Taylor went into labor.

It can truthfully be said that Zachary Taylor was born in a log cabin. With no room in the main house to accommodate all visitors that day, the host family put the Taylors up in one of the outlying cabins ordinarily used by the field hands.

Taylor may have been born in a log cabin, but his family was far from poor. The first Taylors had migrated from England in the 1630s and settled in

Virginia just three decades after the founding of the Jamestown colony. By the time Zachary's father was born, the Taylors were wealthy and influential Virginia plantation owners. In fact, Zachary would share a great-grandfather with James Madison.

Zachary's father Richard graduated from William and Mary College in Virginia. He served in the War of Independence, seeing action under the command of General Washington at the Battle of Brandywine. He later served in the Virginia Assembly.

Richard Taylor was also a true pioneer. Before the war, he and his brother Hancock Taylor made their way south, examining territory that the American colonies obtained through Indian treaties. During the trip Richard procured some land five miles east of the tiny village of Louisville. On an autumn day in 1784, with his wife about to give birth to the third of their nine children, the Taylors set off to claim their property in Kentucky.

Following Zachary's birth, Sarah and the baby remained in Virginia for several months while Richard pushed on, anxious to begin the business of farming. In Kentucky, Richard established Hare Forest plantation, which eventually covered 10,000 acres in four Kentucky counties, making use of the labor of twenty-six slaves. In the beginning, though, the family lived in a log cabin Richard erected on the property along Beargrass Creek. In time, that cabin would be transformed into a magnificent mansion.

Richard Taylor was an educated and wealthy man who could have afforded to send his son to the finest schools in America. Sarah Taylor was well educated as well: as a member of the Virginia planter aristocracy, Sarah's lessons were taught by European tutors employed on the estate of the uncle who raised her. Zachary and his brothers and sisters, however, would receive just a small degree of the education their parents enjoyed.

Even for a family as well off as the Taylors, those early years in the Kentucky wilderness were rough and dangerous. Hostile Indians were said to be lurking behind every tree. Bears, wolves, and wildcats were also a concern. Recalled Thomas Cleland, Zachary Taylor's boyhood friend: "[Our] residence was on the edge of a dense cane-brake. Here we were saluted every night with the howling of wolves. In the meantime father had gone to look for his land. He was absent more than six weeks without our knowing the cause. The family was in painful suspense. The Taylor family, old and young, was very hospitable and kind to us. William, Hancock, and 'Little Zack,' as General Taylor was then called, were my playmates. Mrs. Taylor conceived a great fondness for my mother, and treated her as a sister."

An itinerant teacher named Elisha Ayers soon arrived in Beargrass country and was recruited by Richard Taylor to give lessons in the fundamentals of reading, writing, and mathematics to his children. Ayers was a Connecticut Yankee, but he was not a typical studious academic. He was a lanky, uncouth wanderer who traipsed from town to town in the backwoods South in search of work on the back

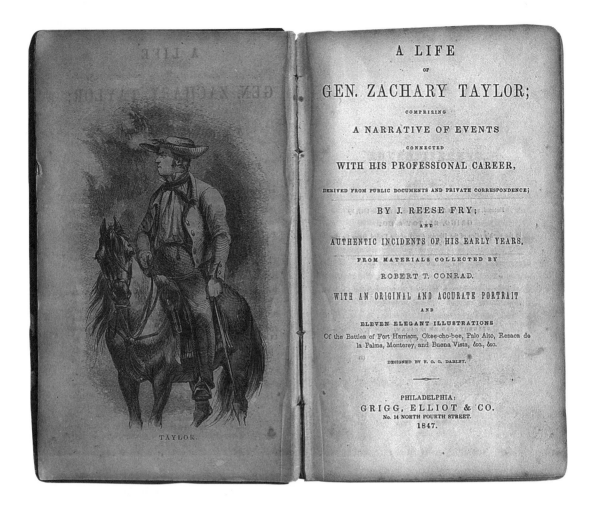

TAYLOR.

A LIFE
OF
GEN. ZACHARY TAYLOR;
COMPRISING
A NARRATIVE OF EVENTS
CONNECTED
WITH HIS PROFESSIONAL CAREER,
DERIVED FROM PUBLIC DOCUMENTS AND PRIVATE CORRESPONDENCE;
BY J. REESE FRY;
AND
AUTHENTIC INCIDENTS OF HIS EARLY YEARS,
FROM MATERIALS COLLECTED BY
ROBERT T. CONRAD.
WITH AN ORIGINAL AND ACCURATE PORTRAIT
AND
ELEVEN ELEGANT ILLUSTRATIONS
Of the Battles of Fort Harrison, Okee-cho-bee, Palo Alto, Resaca de
la Palma, Monterey, and Buena Vista, &c., &c.
DESIGNED BY F. O. C. DARLEY.

PHILADELPHIA:
GRIGG, ELLIOT & CO.
No. 14 NORTH FOURTH STREET.
1847.

of a mule. The Beargrass families built a schoolhouse for Ayers and enrolled their children. Ayers' specialty was mathematics.

Another teacher who provided much more practical guidance to the Beargrass children was Lewis Wetsel, a Kentucky mountain man who survived many tangles with hostile Indians. Wetsel is believed to have shown Zachary and his friends how to shoot straight—a skill to be valued in the Beargrass wilderness.

"The Kentuckians were then a warlike and chivalrous people and they were often engaged in offensive or defensive skirmishes with the Indians," Ayers recalled years later. "A number [of Indians] were known to be in the woods not far distant from the schoolhouse, and, on occasion, one of them was shot, wearing a British uniform. In their hostility to the Americans, they were encouraged and sustained by the British authorities on the northern frontier." There was a Mr. Wetsel in the neighborhood of the school, who, having been once chased by three or four Indians, loaded his rifle while running, and successively shot them all. This exploit made Wetsel famous, and he became the instructor of the young men and boys in his mode of maintaining a running fire. Among his pupils, it is believed, was young Zachary.

tinction increased. He received from President Washington a commission as collector of that port, New Orleans being then in possession of the Spaniards. He had been a personal friend of Washington, prior to his emigration from Virginia, and his worth was, therefore, familiar to that great man, from early knowledge as well as later report.

One of the chief cares of Colonel Taylor was the education of his children. During the first ten or fifteen years of his residence in Kentucky, the country being sparsely settled, and exposed to Indian enemies, this purpose could be accomplished only in a very partial degree. A school, for the rudiments of English merely, was established in his neighbourhood by Elisha Ayres, a native of Connecticut, who afterwards returned to that state, and now resides, a venerable gentleman of four-score years, at Preston, in the vicinity of Norwich. A letter from him, written during the past summer to the author of this volume, in answer to one of inquiry concerning the school-boy days of General Taylor, explains satisfactorily the circumstances in which they were passed, and exhibits the character of our hero, at that time, in a light worthy of his mature reputation.

In the language of Mr. Ayres, "the Kentuckians were then a warlike and chivalrous people, and they were often engaged in offensive or defensive skirmishes with the Indians. A number were known to be in the woods not far distant from the school-house, and, on one occasion, one of them was shot, wearing a British uniform. In their hostility to the Americans, they were encouraged and sustained by the British authorities on the Northern frontier. There was a Mr. Whetsel, in the neighbourhood of the school, who, having been once chased by three or four Indians, loaded his rifle while running, and successively shot them all. This exploit made Whetsel famous, and he became the instructor of the young men and boys in the neighbourhood, in his mode of maintaining a running fire. Among his pupils, it is believed, was young Zachary." It may be remarked, upon this recital of "young Zachary's" first training in the art of war, that he has apparently forgotten

TAYLOR'S FIRST LESSON IN THE ART OF WAR.

The United States had found a new military hero after General Zachary Taylor defeated the Mexican forces of General Pedro de Ampudia at the Battle of Monterey (1846) and then the army of General Antonio López de Santa Anna at the Battle of Buena Vista (1847). City after city gave the general a hero's welcome. Immediately, several biographies were published. The one written by Robert T. Conrad is perhaps the best for studying Taylor's education. Conrad, a well-known Philadelphia lawyer and a history buff, went to Kentucky and interviewed people who had known Taylor as a young man. Conrad gave his notes to J. Reese Fry, an outstanding journalist, who completed the Taylor biography in 1847. Subsequent Taylor biographies have relied on the Conrad/Fry account of Taylor's education. The etching above, "Taylor's First Lessons in the Art of War," is based on those interviews and is the oldest known engraving of "young" Taylor. The pages reprinted here are from an 1847 copy of A *Life of Gen. Zachary Taylor* by Fry and Conrad.

Elisha Ayers recalled teaching Taylor. He said the future president was "quick in learning, and still patient in study." As for Ayers, wanderlust is said to have afflicted him, and in time the rumpled New Englander mounted his mule for adventures elsewhere in the Kentucky hills. His place in the education of Zachary Taylor was taken by Kean O'Hara, a much more dedicated and accomplished teacher. The hardy pioneers who chose to make their homes in the Kentucky of the early 1800s could hardly have expected to see someone in their midst whose academic credentials matched those of Kean O'Hara. A scholar of classic literature, O'Hara found himself on the losing side of the Irish Revolution of 1798 and was exiled from his country. Kentucky Governor Isaac Shelby invited him to teach in his state, which had entered the Union just six years before and was sorely in need of qualified teachers. O'Hara established a school in Danville near Lexington, and then moved to Louisville, where one of his pupils was Zachary Taylor.

Later, O'Hara's son, Theodore O'Hara, would become an important American poet. In fact, he would serve under General Zachary Taylor in Mexico and write an ode to the Kentucky boys who fell in the Battle of Buena Vista titled "The Bivouac of the Dead." The poem eloquently spoke about the sacrifices of war. Ironically, the Battle of Buena Vista was Taylor's greatest victory, and was primarily responsible for making the general into a national hero and likely presidential candidate. In June of 1848, just a year after the Battle of Buena Vista, the Whig senator from Kentucky, John J. Crittenden, gave a speech in his home state promoting the candidacy of Zachary Taylor for president. During that speech, Crittenden insisted that Taylor was well educated. He said:

> Not mere scholastic learning—he has never graduated at a college—but his mind is richly stored with that practical knowledge which is acquired from both men and books. He is a deeply read man, in all ancient and modern history, and in all matters relating to the practical duties of life, civil and military. He is intimate with Plutarch...a Plutarch hero himself, as bright as ever adorned the page of history.

Certainly, much of that robust rhetoric can be attributed to partisan boosterism by the Whig spin-doctors of the era. Yet, if what Crittenden said is true and Taylor did study Plutarch at least at some point in his life, it is not out of the question that the general was inspired in that pursuit by Kean O'Hara. And what would he have learned from Plutarch? A Kentucky farm boy dreaming of a career in the military would have been enthralled by Plutarch's recitations of the lives of the fifteen great Greek heroes, particularly the military leaders and conquerors Plutarch selected for his list. For example, Plutarch told the story of Philpoemen, the brave Greek general "who in actual fighting was as good as the youngest, and in judgment as good as the oldest, so that there came onto the field of battle no better soldier or commander." Plutarch also wrote of Pelopidas, who led the Thebans to victory over the superior Spartans. And Plutarch wrote of Alexander the Great, conqueror of cities at the age of sixteen:

> The neighboring states and the cities of Greece rebelled against Macedonian rule now that they saw a boy on the throne. Alexander's council advised him to give up trying to subjugate the Greeks and to concentrate on his own resources on keeping the barbarian nations of the north under control. Treat the Greeks kindly, they said, and that will dissipate the first impulses of rebellion. But Alexander rejected this advice. If any sign of weakness were perceived at the beginning of his government, everyone would be encouraged to attack, so only bravery was their safety.

Plutarch's writing about the glory of war could easily inspire any farm boy to long for the day when he could join the military.

Kean O'Hara's influence on Zachary Taylor was brief. The young man was needed in his father's fields. For the rest of his boyhood, Zachary would devote his energies to tending the Taylors' widening Kentucky plantation.

Away from the Taylor family's calm and bucolic fields, tensions continued to escalate between the United States and its old enemy, Great Britain. In 1806, Taylor briefly joined a regiment of Kentucky volunteers, hastily formed in response to Aaron Burr's apparently treasonous plot to grab for land in the West. Two years later, the opportunity finally arrived for Taylor to obtain a commission in the U.S. Army.

Sadly, he found the opportunity to apply for the rank through the death of his brother, William Taylor, who had already won a commission as a lieutenant in the Army's Seventh Infantry. In early 1808 William died while skirmishing with hostile Indians in Louisiana. Richard Taylor called on his influential friends in Kentucky politics to back his son Zachary for the vacancy. Letters were written on Zachary's behalf, and on May 3, 1808, Secretary of War Dearborn issued the commission for the young man to join the Seventh Infantry of the United States Army. For most of the next forty years, Zachary Taylor would be a soldier.

He spent the first few months of his enlistment helping to recruit infantrymen, then accompanied the Seventh Infantry to camp in New Orleans just in time to endure the hottest summer in years in Louisiana. The army selected the swampy region known as Terre Aux Boeufs to bivouac the Seventh Infantry, so many of the men, including Taylor, contracted yellow fever. Taylor was sent home to Kentucky to regain his health. It would be two years before he resumed his profession as a soldier.

When he did rejoin the Seventh, it was at the rank of captain. He had also taken a wife during his two years away from the military. Her name was

Margaret Mackall Smith, and she was the daughter of a prominent Jefferson County, Kentucky, family.

Taylor returned to active duty in time to serve in the War of 1812. Following the war, his career would take him to Wisconsin, Minnesota, Missouri, and Louisiana, usually to put down uprisings by Native American tribes. In 1837, his defeat of the Seminoles at Lake Okeechobee in Florida won him promotion to brigadier general. It was during the Seminole War that Taylor's troops dubbed their commander "Old Rough and Ready," in recognition of his iron constitution in leading them relentlessly through the murky Everglades as well as his fondness for plain uniforms.

His greatest victories, however, were yet to come. In 1846, he led 2,300 men in the Battle of Palo Alto against a Mexican army that outnumbered his men three to one. A year later, at Buena Vista, he again led his troops to victory against a much larger Mexican force. The conquest of the Mexican army at Buena Vista effectively ended the war, enabling the United States to annex Texas. Zachary Taylor was now a national hero.

Throughout his military career, Taylor continued to rely on Colonel Bliss. During the Mexican-American War, dictator Antonio López de Santa Anna sent a message to Taylor, warning the general that he would be "cut to pieces with your troops" unless he surrendered. Taylor is said to have reacted angrily and most threateningly, but Bliss stepped in and penned a diplomatic reply, declining Santa Anna's request with a curt yet smug message that the United States Army does not respond to hollow threats. "In reply to your note of this date summoning me to surrender my forces at discretion, I beg leave to say I decline acceding to your request," said the simple note, signed by General Taylor.

In 1848, the Whigs offered Taylor the nomination for the presidency. There were many well-spoken Whigs who often provided the appropriate words for Taylor whenever he needed them, such as Senator Crittenden, Representative Alexander Stephens of Georgia, and a young congressman from Illinois, Abraham Lincoln. In that era, it was highly unusual for candidates to take an active part in their campaigns. Bliss was on hand, as well; when his father-in-law was elected president, Bliss would accompany him into the White House as a trusted aide.

His inaugural speech was short—President Taylor uttered just over a thousand words, and left many of his Whig supporters wondering where he stood on the few issues he did manage to address. Sitting just to the side of Taylor during the speech was President James K. Polk, the man he replaced in the White House. Later, Polk told people that Taylor spoke "in a very low voice and very badly as to his pronunciation and manner."

Zachary Taylor's presidency would be short. Although a southerner and slaveholder himself, Taylor was against permitting slavery in any new state joining the union. It was during his brief administration that Senator Henry

Clay drafted the Great Compromise, permitting California to enter as a free state in exchange for adoption of the Fugitive Slave Act, which gave southerners the right to pursue runaway slaves in the North. Taylor opposed the compromise and threatened to veto the Fugitive Slave Act, but the bill never reached his desk. On July 4, 1850, after serving just sixteen months in office, he visited the Washington Monument, which was then under construction. It was a hot and muggy day in the nation's capital and Taylor suffered from the heat. That night, he was stricken by cholera. He died five days later.

—Hal Marcovitz

Millard Fillmore
Chapter Thirteen

When Millard Fillmore was fifteen years old, his parents sent him to the nearby village of Sparta, New York, to learn the trade of wool-carding. Millard had been a good student in school—whenever he managed to attend—but the Fillmores were nearly destitute; their tiny farm hardly produced crops, and they desperately needed the few dollars their boy's salary as an apprentice would provide to supplement the family's meager income. Young as he was, he was sent to learn a trade because his sister Olive, though older, could not go into an apprenticeship and his brother was even younger than Millard.

Benjamin Hungerford was the man to whom Millard was apprenticed; Hungerford was a family friend who owned a wool-carding factory. Carding is the removing of dirt, twigs, and other impurities from raw wool, then preparing it to be spun. For years, carding was performed by hand, usually by girls and their mothers who would spend long hours combing the raw wool with stiff metal brushes until the fibers were smooth and could be spun into yarn. In 1797, a Massachusetts entrepreneur named Amos Whittemore invented a machine that could card wool, using large wooden implements with metal teeth fixed to cylinders. Each machine could card as much wool as dozens of workers.

Yet it was with some reluctance that Millard Fillmore agreed to work for Hungerford. It was 1815, and war with Great Britain (the War of 1812) had just ended. Millard had been too young to join the army, but as he grew older he harbored dreams of becoming a soldier. However, Millard's father Nathaniel convinced him to take up the trade, and so young Millard made his way to Sparta to become an apprentice to Hungerford.

William Scott, foreman of Hungerford's factory, would soon become Millard's close friend. Scott would later recall his first glimpse of the boy as he entered the factory: "He was dressed in a suit of homespun sheep's gray coat and trousers, wool hat, and stout cowhide boots. His light hair was long, his face was round and chubby, and his demeanor was that of a bright, intelligent, good natured lad, quite sedate, rather slow in his motions, with an air of thoughtfulness that gained my respect."

Millard Fillmore, who was born in 1800, wrote in his autobiography how his parents, a young New York State pioneer family, suffered the privations and hardships common to the frontier. Fillmore worked on his father's farm, became a clothier's apprentice in a carding mill, and attended school infrequently. However, he became fascinated with geography after seeing his first map in a copy of Jedidiah Morse's *The American Universal Geography.* Until the Civil War, most Americans' awareness of geography—and maps—came from Morse's volumes. They had no significant competitors.

Jedidiah Morse (1761–1826) is known as the "father of American geography." Dissatisfied with the treatment of America in the existing English texts, he prepared a series of "geographical lectures" which were issued in 1784 as *Geography Made Easy*, the first geography book published in the United States. By 1820, this famous text had passed through twenty-five editions. So successful was this first effort that Morse began a larger work which he published in 1789 as *The American Geographer* and in its later editions as *The American Universal Geography*. This work passed through at least seven U.S. editions, and almost as many European editions, and firmly established Morse's reputation. Morse also wrote the article "America" for the first American edition of the *Encyclopedia Britannica* (1790). In 1795, Morse published *Elements of Geography* for children. This slim book went through scores of editions. His son Samuel Morse is known as the "father of the telegraph" and the inventor of Morse code.

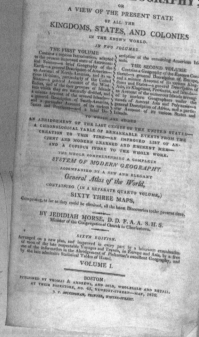

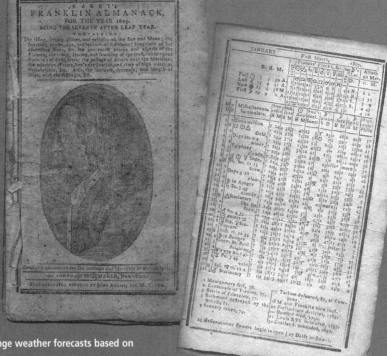

Fillmore wrote in his autobiography that he had learned to read because he "had taken all the schooling the surrounding country could offer." He could read, to be sure, but almost nothing except the Bible and a few spelling books that were available. Years later, he described the family library as "a Bible, a hymn book, and an almanac."

In Colonial days, the almanac was a publication of prime importance for its long-range weather forecasts based on esoteric interpretations of natural phenomena. Beginning as a source for astronomical information, the almanac rapidly grew into an indispensable publication for farmers that contained all sorts of information from recipes to prophecies. The most famous was Benjamin Franklin's *Poor Richard's Almanac*, which first appeared in 1732. It immediately became the most popular book published, second to the Bible. It was unequalled in reputation for proverbs, wit, and wisdom. All almanacs were important publications for they contained information necessary to every American farmer. Seven already were being published in Philadelphia in 1732, so it seemed unlikely that another would be successful. However, Franklin had new ideas that he felt would insure the success of his venture. Along with the usual information on the weather, tides, eclipses, and medicinal remedies, Franklin printed the maxims and pithy sayings that were even then making him famous. Each edition of Franklin's almanac saw an increase in sales until more than 10,000 were printed annually, approximately one for every hundred people in the colonies.

Franklin stopped writing for the almanac after 1748, when he began to devote most of his time to public affairs. However, his almanac continued to be issued by Matthew Carey, a well-known Philadelphia publisher and writer.

Millard's apprenticeship would last only a few months. Instead of learning the carding trade, his main duties required him to trudge into the woods every day to chop wood to burn in the factory fireplaces. Annoyed with the drudgery of this task, Millard finally confronted Hungerford, telling the factory boss that he hadn't left home to learn how to chop wood. Hungerford ordered Millard to obey him and return to the woodpile. "I will chastise you for your disobedience," Hungerford threatened. In those days, chastisement—or punishment—could include a beating.

Millard refused to step back. Instead, he raised his ax, and said, "You will not chastise me. If you approach me I will split you down."

Hungerford stood before Millard, his body frozen for a moment, then stepped back and walked away. Hungerford soon released Millard from his apprenticeship, permitting him to return home. Years later, Millard, who became the thirteenth president of the United States, had this to say about the incident: "I am inclined to think it was unjustifiable rebellion, or at least my threat of knocking him down was going too far, for I fear I should have executed it; and my only justification or apology is that I have an inborn hatred of injustice and tyranny which I cannot repress."

Born in the most humble of circumstances, Millard entered life on January 7, 1800—the first president of the United States born in the nineteenth century. His parents, Nathaniel and Phoebe Fillmore, had left Vermont in 1798 to settle in central New York State in what was then Onondaga County (now Cayuga County). They raised their children in a crude log cabin in virtual wilderness four miles from their nearest neighbor. Later, Millard would describe his childhood home as "completely shut out from all enterprises of civilization and advancement."

While raising his young family, Nathaniel Fillmore found it very hard to coax crops out of the rocky soil of his farm. In 1802, he lost the farm because of a defect in his deed. The Fillmores were forced to leave the homestead, moving some ten miles to land Millard's father leased near the village of Sempronius, now known as Niles. "My father took a perpetual lease of a small farm of about 130 acres," Fillmore wrote in his autobiography. "[The land] was wholly uncultivated and covered with heavy timber. He built a small log house and commenced clearing the land; and it was at this place and in these pursuits that I first knew anything of life." The Fillmores persevered and soon the land produced crops.

Millard first attended school in a one-room schoolhouse in the nearby village of New Hope. He was either nine or ten when he first took lessons; before this time he probably did not know how to read or write. Moreover, he was hampered by his father's unwillingness to let him attend school for more than a few months in the late fall and winter. In the spring and summer, Nathaniel needed him for labor on the farm.

His first teacher was a Connecticut Yankee named Amos Castle, who found Millard to be a quick learner. Although he was already behind many of his classmates, he advanced quickly and soon impressed Castle with his intelligence and hunger for knowledge. He learned to read with the help of *The American Spelling Book*, written by Noah Webster in 1783. The familiar book with the blue binding was the first attempt to show young students how to read and spell by breaking words into syllables. Some sixty million copies of Webster's spelling book were printed in the more than one hundred years that the book remained in publication.

Clearly, Millard Fillmore was proof that Noah Webster knew how to teach students to spell. After just a few weeks in Castle's school, the teacher awarded Millard a certificate congratulating the young farm boy for "spelling 224 words without missing."

The first novel that Millard read was William Rufus Chetwood's *Voyages and Adventures of Captain Robert Boyle*, the story of a swashbuckling hero who battled pirates, slave traders, and assorted other villains. This book, which was first published in England in 1730, was reprinted almost endlessly for the next century.

But spring soon arrived and Millard's father called the youth back to the fields. At nights, though, Millard was able to teach himself some simple arithmetic and somehow came into the ownership of Jedidiah Morse's *The American Universal Geography*, a school textbook for geography studies that had been in print for about fifteen years by the time Millard obtained his copy. Reading on his own in the Fillmore family cabin, Millard was able to acquaint himself somewhat with the nations of the world and their places on the face of the Earth.

The following winter, Millard enrolled in a Sempronius school led by a Mr. Western, from whom he learned grammar and mathematics. Again, he spent just a few months in school, then was recalled to his father's fields. It would be a pattern repeated each year until Millard was fifteen years old, when he spent those few unpleasant months chopping wood for Benjamin Hungerford.

After returning home from his apprenticeship in Sparta, he again tried to learn the wool-carding trade—this time in a New Hope factory owned by Zaccheus Cheney and Alvan Kellogg, who agreed to take him on for an apprenticeship of five years. This time, Millard found his apprenticeship much more agreeable; Cheney and Kellogg truly did teach him carding and gave him a measure of responsibility. Within a short time, he was maintaining the financial ledgers for the factory.

He was paid $55 a year by Cheney and Kellogg. His agreement with their company gave him time off to help his father on the farm and also attend school in the winter, usually a slow period in the carding business. His hunger for reading remained unquenchable, and finally he had the means to obtain books. In 1817 or 1818, Millard paid $2 to join the Sempronius library, which entitled him access to a small selection of books kept in the librarian's home.

He also bought his own dictionary and propped it up amid the noisy carding machines in the factory, stealing glances at the words and their definitions as he dashed back and forth across the factory floor, feeding the machines and removing the rolls of carded fibers.

In the winter of 1818, when business had slowed in the carding factory, Fillmore found a job as a schoolteacher in the town of Scott, near Cortland, New York. The job paid $10 a month. According to Fillmore, Scott was a "rough and uncultured" place, and the boys at the school were known to make trouble for the teacher. Indeed,

Fillmore obtained the job because the schoolboys had been abusive to the previous teacher and drove him out of town. It didn't take long for the boys of Scott to challenge Millard Fillmore. He very soon found himself in a confrontation with a boy who tested his authority. Fillmore responded by threatening the boy with the fireplace poker. That settled the argument. Fillmore, however, soon learned that parents were distressed that the new teacher had threatened the boy with a poker. At the meeting that followed, Fillmore explained that his action in raising the poker had been self-defense. His explanation was accepted, and he returned to his duties. That spring, after the school year ended, he found work in a sawmill, then returned to the carding factory.

During the following winter, work again fell off in the carding factory. This time, Millard decided to return to school. Although now nineteen and long past the age when most boys left school for work on the family farms or as trade craftsmen, Millard was determined to improve himself intellectually. He enrolled in a school in Sempronius and found room and board with a farm family, for whom he worked as a wood chopper.

It was at the school in Sempronius that he came under the guidance of Abigail Powers, a teacher just two years older than Millard. For Abigail, Millard Fillmore was a student very much out of the ordinary. Certainly, she had taught her share of farm boys in the two years she had been employed as a teacher, but Millard seemed much more intelligent and willing to learn than the other boys in her classes. And, of course, he was much older. She quickly realized that while Millard seemed bright and eager to learn, he lacked refinement. He was polite, but he was at a loss as to how to act in social situations. Abigail became his private tutor, determined to refine his social graces. Soon, she became his fiancée as well.

In 1819, Nathaniel and Phoebe Fillmore moved to a new farm in Montville, about eight miles from Sempronius, where they became tenant farmers on property owned by Judge Walter Wood, who presided over the courts of Cayuga County. Due to the rural nature of the region, Judge Wood had few official duties. Mostly, he was called upon to settle disputes over ownership of properties. In those days, accurate deeds and other property records were a rarity—a fact the Fillmores knew well. After all, a defective deed had caused the Fillmores to lose their first farm.

Nathaniel Fillmore had always been impressed with his son's interest in books and learning. Without telling Millard, Nathaniel asked Judge Wood if he would accept his son as an apprentice lawyer. Wood agreed, and on the young man's first day of work in his office, the judge handed him a copy of William Blackstone's *Commentaries on the Laws of England*.

The British legal scholar Sir William Blackstone had written this series of commentaries on law in 1765, and although the author concentrated on the laws of England, students of law in the United States found much to learn from the text. Blackstone's advocacy for the rule of common law over the power of the king had inspired the framers of the U.S. Constitution. Blackstone wrote of the rights of citizens to "petition the king and parliament to redress grievances." Twenty-five years later, the First Amendment to the Constitution ensured that citizens of the United

COMMENTARIES

ON THE

LAWS

OF

ENGLAND.

BOOK THE FIRST.

BY

WILLIAM BLACKSTONE, Esq.

VINERIAN PROFESSOR OF LAW,

AND

SOLICITOR GENERAL TO HER MA[JESTY]

OXFORD,

[PR]INTED AT THE CLAREND[ON]

M. DCC. LXV.

CONTENTS.

INTRODUCTION.

SECT. I.
On the STUDY of the LAW.   Page 3.

SECT. II.
Of the NATURE of LAWS in general.   38.

SECT. III.
Of the LAWS of ENGLAND.   63.

SECT. IV.
Of the COUNTRIES subject to the LAWS of ENGLAND. 93.

BOOK I.
Of the RIGHTS of PERSONS.

CHAP. I.
Of the absolute RIGHTS of INDIVIDUALS. 117.

CHAP.

INTRODUCTION.

SECTION THE FIRST.

ON THE STUDY OF THE LAW. *

MR VICE-CHANCELLOR, AND GENTLEMEN OF THE UNIVERSITY,

THE general expectation of so numerous and respectable an audience, the novelty, and (I may add) the importance of the duty required from this chair, must unavoidably be productive of great diffidence and apprehensions in him who has the honour to be placed in it. He must be sensible how much has the ho- to be placed in it. He must be sensible how much the honour depend upon his conduct in the infancy of a study, which is now first adopted by public academical authority; which has generally been reputed (however unjustly) of a dry and unfruitful nature; and of which the theoretical, elementary parts have hitherto received a very moderate share of cultivation. He cannot but reflect that, if either his plan of instruction be crude and injudicious, or the execution of it lame and superficial, it will cast a damp upon the farther progress of this most useful and most rational branch of learning; and may defeat for a time the public-

* Read in Oxford at the opening of the Vinerian lectures; 25 Oct. 1758.

A 2   [f]pirited

Fillmore wrote how his tenant farming parents uprooted their family almost annually in searching for better land in central New York State. When he was nineteen, Fillmore's father prevailed upon their then landlord, an aged county judge, to "try out Millard for two months as a clerk in his law office." As Fillmore recalled, early the next morning he called at Judge Wood's office. The wrinkled, old man greeted him, "shoved" the first volume of Blackstone's *Commentaries* into his hand, and directed, "Thee will please turn thy attention to this."

Sir William Blackstone's four-volume *Commentaries on the Laws of England* (1765–69) was the first great effort to reduce English common law to a unified and rational system. The preservation of liberty, Blackstone wrote, required a widespread understanding of what the English legal system was all about. Blackstone's *Commentaries* was the dominant law book and the basis of university legal education in both England and America until the 1860s. It is the most important legal treatise ever written in the English language.

Above are the title and preface pages from a facsimile of the first edition of book one, "Of the Rights of Persons." After two months of reading Blackstone, Fillmore admitted that he did not understand the book.

States have the right "to petition the government for a redress of grievances."

To work as an apprentice to Judge Wood, Millard had to gain the permission of Cheney and Kellogg, to whom he still owed another year under his apprenticeship in the carding factory. By now, Millard was a valuable employee of the two partners, and they were opposed to releasing him. They finally agreed to terminate his apprenticeship for the sum of $30, which Millard promised to pay out of his future earnings.

Cheney thought him foolish. "Do you see that young man yonder?" Cheney asked a friend after catching sight of Millard on a New Hope street. "He is, for a sensible young man, pursuing a very foolish course. He has been engaged with me in business for some time. He was far the best apprentice I ever had, and the best workman I ever had. He understands the business perfectly, yet he has abandoned his trade and gone to reading law!"

Millard boarded in Judge Wood's comfortable home, which was to be his compensation for assisting the judge in his practice. Otherwise, he earned a salary as a schoolteacher in Montville, which he used to repay Cheney and Kellogg, and made many trips back to Sempronius to see Abigail. During his apprenticeship with the judge, he read law books before school started in the morning and in the afternoon when classes were finished. His chief duty as Wood's apprentice may have been as a land surveyor—an important duty for a judge whose jurisdiction consisted primarily of settling property disputes.

Millard learned much about the law in his two busy years as an apprentice under Judge Wood, yet he soon found himself bored by the mundane duties Wood assigned him. During his apprenticeship he was employed by Elias Rogers of the town of Moravia to represent him in a lawsuit filed with a justice of the peace, a court official who presides over minor cases. Millard handled the settlement of the case for Rogers, who paid him a fee of $3. When Judge Wood learned of Millard's representation of Rogers, he angrily reprimanded his apprentice because he had not consulted with him before taking the case. Millard protested that he had only performed the work to earn a few dollars, but promised not to accept clients again without Wood's approval. Later, he said, "I don't think Judge Wood knew, or could realize, how important three dollars were to me in those days."

The friction over the Rogers' case prompted Millard to leave Wood's employment. Once again, he would have to pay off his employer because he was leaving before his apprenticeship was completed. He negotiated a settlement with the judge for $65, which he promised to pay out of his future earnings as an attorney. Although his parting with Judge Wood was hardly amicable, Millard would long remember an important piece of advice the judge had given him: "If thee has an ambition for distinction, and can sacrifice everything else to success, the law is the road that leads to honors."

For Millard, the road led to Buffalo, a city on Lake Erie west of Montville, where he found employment as a law clerk in the office of Asa Rice and Joseph Clary. He had little trouble gaining employment, for Buffalo was a growing city. Its several law firms all had heavy case loads and were in dire need of intelligent clerks

Fillmore left the White House in 1853. In those days, there were no national presidential libraries that collected the public and private papers of the nation's chief executives. In subsequent years, Fillmore was the first chancellor of the University of Buffalo, a founder of the Buffalo Historical Society and its first president, a founder of the Buffalo General Hospital, and a volunteer in various other civic, educational, and philanthropic endeavors.

Approximately twenty years after his death in 1874, Frank H. Severance, the secretary of the Buffalo Historical Society, collected Fillmore's scattered private papers as well as reminiscences of those who knew the former president. (The Society had asked Fillmore to write his autobiography in 1871. He stopped after about fifteen pages that deal with his youth and education. These pages are the primary source for this period of the former president's life.) In 1907, under Severance's direction, the Buffalo Historical Society published the *Millard Fillmore Papers*, including the brief autobiography, in two volumes.

who could help the attorneys prepare precise summaries. He earned no salary under Rice and Clary, and again had to take a job as a teacher. Nevertheless, Rice and Clary helped prepare Millard for his bar examination, and in February 1823 all his years of hard work and self-denial finally paid off when he passed the examination and was permitted to practice law in the state of New York.

The years of poverty would soon be behind Millard Fillmore. He became a busy lawyer, opening his own practice in the town of Aurora, where his parents had bought a farm. In 1826 he married Abigail; his seven years' labor had gained him his bride. Moving back to Buffalo in 1830, he launched his political career. Two years later, he was elected to the state assembly. Though he was elected largely on the basis of the political party to which he belonged, he was responsible for laws that banned the practice of jailing debtors. He also became a protégé of New York Whig newspaper publisher and political powerbroker Thurlow Weed, who guided Fillmore's career into the New York

State Legislature and then the United States Congress. In 1840, the Whigs captured control of the U.S. House of Representatives, and Fillmore become chairman of the powerful Ways and Means Committee. In that capacity, he took the lead in framing the protectionist Tariff Act of 1842.

Weed pushed him to run for governor of New York. Against Fillmore's better judgment, he ran in 1844 and was defeated by Silas Wright, the good friend of former president Martin Van Buren. (Fillmore attributed his defeat to "the Abolitionists and foreign Catholics.") Three years later Fillmore was elected comptroller of New York, which is the state's highest fiscal office. He had held office for just a year when he was selected to join Zachary Taylor on the Whigs' presidential ticket. The presidential nomination of Taylor, a hero of the Mexican War, had angered Northern Whigs because Taylor was a Southerner and slaveholder. Fillmore was selected as the candidate for vice president in part because he was a Northerner who gave geographical balance to the ticket. He owed his nomination for vice president to the influence of Henry Clay, who, angered at the choice of Taylor, refused to accept Abbot Lawrence, the Massachusetts cotton manufacturer, as the nominee for vice president. Clay declared he would not "have cotton at both ends of the ticket." Fillmore and Taylor never met until after the election, and when they did meet, they concluded that they didn't like each other.

Taylor's presidency was brief. He died in 1850, before the most important piece of legislation produced by Congress during his tenure reached the White House: the Fugitive Slave Act. The act, which would give Southern slaveholders more power to seek the return of slaves who had escaped to the Northern states, was drafted by Senator Henry Clay as part of what became known as the "Compromise of 1850." In exchange, Southern legislators had agreed to admit California into the Union as a free state, where slavery was prohibited. Although Taylor was a slaveholder, he wanted to preserve the United States, and made it clear before his death that he would not sign the bill. However, by the time the legislation reached the president's desk, Fillmore was the occupant of the White House. Although Fillmore and his Cabinet also wanted to preserve the Union, he signed the bill, believing it would help avoid Civil War.

The Abolitionist wing of the Whig Party seethed when Fillmore signed the Fugitive Slave Act. They refused to support him in the 1852 election, denying him the Whig nomination. It would be the last election for the Whig Party, which disintegrated after its defeat that year. Many former Whigs now joined a new party for the 1856 election—the Republican Party. Fillmore, though, joined the American Party, a coalition of former Whigs and anti-immigration zealots. They were nicknamed the "Know-Nothing Party" because party members, when asked questions by outsiders, were told to respond only "I know nothing." The party lasted only briefly. In the presidential election of 1856, Fillmore finished a distant third. He soon retired from politics.

Fillmore remained active in his retirement, eventually becoming the first chancellor of the University of Buffalo—a rewarding achievement for a man whose own education had suffered because of the terrible poverty of his youth.

—Hal Marcovitz

Franklin Pierce
Chapter Fourteen

He was a curly, blue-eyed child with "a sweet expression of face," according to his friend Nathaniel Hawthorne. In the opinion of many historians, young Franklin Pierce grew to become America's handsomest president. Photographs depict a dour but striking face with thin lips and a fine, straight nose beneath shocks of dark, wavy hair and protruding brows. He appears to be an intelligent, sensitive man of social graces, but with a countenance singed by personal grief. Pierce was a president buffeted by unhappiness and ill-prepared for the gathering storm of division that soon would overcome his nation. Standing a frail five feet, ten inches, harried by lung disease, Franklin Pierce was not destined for long life. Perhaps it was a mercy. From 1853, the year he took office as then America's youngest president, until his death sixteen years later, he would suffer a downward spiral of unpopularity, failure, bitterness, and sorrow.

One weekend in 1816, twelve-year-old Franklin faced a crisis that seemed far more unbearable to him than all the problems that ever could beset a head of state: he was homesick. His parents, determined that he would have a better education than they, had enrolled him at an academy in Hancock, New Hampshire, about fifteen miles from his hometown of Hillsborough. It was his first experience of leaving home, and he soon decided Hancock was not for him. Early that Sunday morning, he walked home. His family arrived from church to find him waiting with a carefully prepared argument of why he needed no further schooling.

To Franklin's puzzlement, his father listened quietly. Benjamin Pierce did not punish his son, or even scold him. After dinner, the parent hitched the horse and carriage and took Franklin for a drive. Instantly, the boy's dismay returned—they were on the road to Hancock. Halfway there, the father deposited Franklin at roadside, turned the horse, and silently drove away. Forlorn, Franklin had little choice but return to prep school and adjust.

Lessons of life were often harsh and usually effective in early America. They had to be. In New Hampshire's aptly named "Land of Hills," this kind of upbringing forged the likes of Daniel Webster and John Stark. Webster, twenty-four years old at Franklin's

Bridgton

CATALOGUE

OF THE

OFFICERS AND STUDENTS

OF

BOWDOIN COLLEGE,

MAINE,

OCTOBER, 1822.

—

BRUNSWICK:
JOSEPH GRIFFIN.
1822.

BOWDOIN COLLEGE.

MARCH, 1822.

—ooo—

TERMS OF ADMISSION.

Candidates for admisssion into the Freshman Class are required to write Latin grammatically, and to be well versed in Geography, in Walsh's Arithmetic, Cicero's Select Orations, the Bucolics, Georgics, and Aeneid of Virgil, Sallust, the Greek Testament, and Collectanea Græca Minora. They must produce certificates of their good moral character. The usual time for examination is the day after Commencement.—Candidates for admission into the other classes will be examined also in the books, which have been studied by the class, into which admission is requested.—Scholars from other Colleges, before they can be examined, must produce a certificate of their regular dismission.

COURSE OF STUDY.

FRESHMAN CLASS.

First Term. Xenophon in Græca Majora; Livy; Arithmetic in Webber.
Second Term. Græca Majora, (Vol. i.); Livy; Arithmetic continued.
Third Term. Græca Majora continued; Livy finished (5 books); Murray's English Grammar; Blair's Rhetoric; Review of the studies of the year.
During the whole year. Weekly translations into Latin and Greek; private Declamations; Recitations from the Bible every Sunday evening.

Franklin Pierce enrolled in Bowdoin College in October 1820. He was sixteen years old. In order to matriculate, Pierce had to write grammatically correct Latin and to sight translate Cicero's *Orations* and Virgil's *Aeneid*. The freshman year was divided into three parts. Reading assignments were in the Greek and Latin classics, plus each student had to master advanced arithmetic and English grammar. Mandatory Bible reading occurred every Sunday evening.

Located along the Maine coast in Brunswick, Bowdoin was chartered in 1794. The college admitted its first students in 1802 and awarded its first degrees in 1806.

The page on the left is the handwritten record of the Bowdoin College Library that list "Pierce" and the books that he withdrew, October 1821 through April 20, 1823. Among the books Pierce borrowed from the library was Lewis and Clark's *Expedition* (two vols.) [*History of the Expedition Under the Command of Captains Lewis and Clark to the Sources of the Missouri, Thence Across the Rocky Mountains and Down the River Columbia to the Pacific Ocean Performed During the Years* 1804–06]. This was the first edition (1814) of the most famous of all western travel narratives.

Pierce also withdrew from the library Oliver Goldsmith's popularly written book *Roman History, From the Foundations of the City of Rome to the Destruction of the Western Empire* (1769) and Simon Ockley's *History of the Saracens* (1718). The latter is an adventure book that describes the Saracens, a medieval Islamic people, their battles, sieges, religion, and customs. He borrowed books in Latin such as the illustrated *Antiquitatum Romanarum Corpus Absolutissimum cum Notis Doctissimis ac Locupletissimus Thomae Dempstieri, J.C. [A Complete Book of Roman Artifacts with an authoritative introduction by Thomas Dempstieri]* (1743).

Theodore L. Moody was Pierce's roommate at Bowdoin for two years. His library record from July 29, 1823 through June 30, 1824 (right) informs us that he borrowed and renewed, and borrowed several additional times, the Scottish philosopher David Hume's two-volume *Essays and Treatises on Several Subjects* (1767). Moody also renewed various volumes by British political theorist Edmund Burke at least ten times. These handwritten library records have survived more than one hundred eighty years. It is interesting to wonder if today's college library records will endure as long.

There were thirteen students in Pierce's class of 1824. In addition to a $24 yearly tuition, there was an added library fee of about $1.50. Room and board cost approximately $2 per week. A mandatory student debate on an assigned topic was held each Wednesday afternoon. All students, in alphabetical rotation, had to argue a given topic.

birth, was preparing for a law career that would lead him to fame as one of the country's greatest orators of all time. Crusty Brigadier General Stark, one of the most celebrated militia commanders of the Revolutionary War, by that time was retired to his farm.

Benjamin Pierce, Franklin's father, is far lesser known today but was highly respected throughout New England. He was a self-made man who rose to prominence from an upbringing as a poor colonial farmer. He had little education but steadfast conviction and courage. Raised by an uncle, seventeen-year-old Benjamin is said to have been plowing a field when he received the electrifying news of skirmishes between colonists and British soldiers at Lexington and Concord, Massachusetts—the outbreak of the American Revolution. It was April 1775. He literally walked from the field, took up arms, and spent the next seven years fighting for freedom. After the end of the Revolution, his meager soldier's pay allowed him to buy fifty acres near Hillsborough. Benjamin set about clearing his land, building a log home beside a creek, and finding himself a wife. His first, Elizabeth Andrews, died less than a year after their marriage. Two years later, he married Anna Kendrick. As their family grew, so did the local prestige of honest, plainspoken Ben Pierce. He was made an officer in the Hillsborough militia and was elected to the New Hampshire legislature. Later, he served as county sheriff and postmaster.

Soon after Franklin's birth, on November 23, 1804, the family built a larger home in Lower Hillsborough Village. The new republic offered hope for prosperity, and the Pierces understood what would be required for their nine children to achieve it: education. Meanwhile, the parents instilled characteristics that were hallmarks of early nineteenth-century New Englanders. His mother saw to it that Franklin grew firmly in the Episcopalian faith. His father passed along—as much by example as by words—love of country and the importance of upholding the law of the land. According to biographer Nathaniel Hawthorne, the youthful Franklin was remembered in old Hillsborough as kind, upright, and "very delightful." At the same time, he was a typical, fun-loving boy who roamed the forests and skated on the ponds in winter. He became an eager fisher—a passion he kept throughout his life.

When Franklin was seven, mounting tension between the United States and Great Britain led the two countries into another war. One of Franklin's older brothers and a brother-in-law served in the army during the War of 1812. At home in New Hampshire, the war was Franklin's introduction to politics. He observed his father's public and private discussions on the course of the conflict and other affairs of the nation. Benjamin Pierce, staunchly anti-Federalist, supported President Thomas Jefferson and the fledgling Democratic-Republican Party. Franklin did not understand what the conflict was all about, but he began to see that confusing complications could arise in a democracy when differing regional and economic interests clashed.

Franklin attended the regular Hillsborough school until he was twelve. Then he was sent to college prep schools, first in Hancock and then in Francestown, New Hampshire. He got along well with other students and went out of his way to earn their friendship. In one case, he reportedly spent his daily recess periods for weeks on end helping a lagging schoolmate catch up with class work. Hawthorne later wrote of Franklin's "sweetness of disposition and cordial sympathy," but he also had the reputation of a prankster who loved to romp and tussle with his cronies, sometimes at the expense of the furniture.

At Francestown Academy, Franklin labored under the stern instruction of Simeon Ingersoll Bard, "a walking dictionary and a strong disciplinarian," in the words of biographer Roy Franklin Nichols. Bard quizzed his young charges relentlessly until they knew their Latin, Greek, chemistry, geography, and arithmetic.

Their father had sent Franklin's older brother Ben to Dartmouth College, but then decided the politics of the Dartmouth administration and faculty weren't to his liking. Specifically, Dartmouth at the time was largely under the sway of Federalists (including Daniel Webster). Franklin, the father decided, would attend Bowdoin College in Brunswick, a small lumber town near the Maine coast. Bowdoin was a new college, in operation less than twenty years when Franklin arrived, but it would attain prestige in coming generations. At the time Franklin attended, Bowdoin consisted of two campus buildings and a plain chapel that doubled as the college library.

In autumn 1820, Franklin's parents personally accompanied him to Brunswick in the family's two-wheeled, horse-drawn carriage and settled him into a boarding house. He was the only freshman among the six student residents there, but he was not intimidated. He looked ahead eagerly to his years at Bowdoin. "My spirits were exuberant," he recalled later. "I was far from my home without restraint except such as the government of a college imposed."

Nineteen students were in his freshman class; five would drop out by their senior year. The likable sixteen-year-old quickly made many friends. By far the most important in his life was Nathaniel Hawthorne, who enrolled a year after Franklin. Hawthorne would become one of America's most famous authors, writing such books as *The Scarlet Letter*, *The House of the Seven Gables*, *Tanglewood Tales*, and *Twice-Told Tales*. Today, the writings of Nathaniel Hawthorne are much better known to Americans than is the presidential record of Franklin Pierce. Other classmates at Bowdoin during the early 1820s included Henry Wadsworth Longfellow, who would become one of America's best-loved poets, and John P. Hale, who eventually would pose fierce political opposition for the future president.

Much later, Hawthorne wrote a biography to help Pierce's presidential election campaign. The author recalled of his old friend, "He was then a youth, with the boy and man in him, vivacious, mirthful, slender, of a fair complexion, with light hair that had a curl in it: his bright and cheerful aspect made a kind of sunshine, both as regarded its radiance and its warmth; insomuch that no shyness of disposition, in his associates, could well resist its influence."

The Bowdoin student body was divided into two societies or, as Hawthorne defined them, "institutions": the "respectable conservative" and the "progressive." Both he and Pierce were progressives. Pierce became a skilled debater and took a keen interest in politics. He was also impressed by the writings of British

Pierce had to write grammatically correct Latin and to sight translate Cicero's *Orations* and Virgil's *Aeneid*.

In May 1823, Bowdoin College held its annual spring "exhibition," or Classical oratorical program. Pierce was chosen to participate. He wrote and read this essay in Latin—*De triumphis Romanorum* (The Roman Triumphs). According to his letters, he was "greatly relieved when it was over."

The fact that both Henry Wadsworth Longfellow and Nathaniel Hawthorne were students at Bowdoin during most of Pierce's collegiate years has made descriptions of the college plentiful. All biographers of these men give accounts of Bowdoin student life during the 1820s. Pierce exchanged letters with most of his classmates throughout his life, fulfilling a mutual pledge "of constant and continuous correspondence."

In 1852, the Democratic Party nominated Franklin Pierce as its candidate for president. During the campaign, Pierce wrote letters of appreciation to supporters but otherwise followed the advice of Democratic elders to do as little as possible and to say almost nothing about his views on any topic. With Pierce's approval, his college friend Nathaniel Hawthorne wrote the "authorized" campaign biography, *The Life of Franklin Pierce* (144 pages). About 13,000 copies were printed by late September. The New York City Democratic Party (Tammany Hall) purchased 5,000 copies for "immediate distribution." During the presidential campaign, Pierce and Hawthorne attended the fiftieth anniversary of the admission of the first students to Bowdoin. Among the new president's first appointments was that of Hawthorne to be American consul at Liverpool.

LIFE

OF

FRANKLIN PIERCE.

BY

NATHANIEL HAWTHORNE.

BOSTON:
TICKNOR, REED, AND FIELDS.
M DCCC LII.

14   LIFE OF

in aiding him in his lessons. These attributes, proper to a generous and affectionate nature, have remained with him through life. Lending their color to his deportment, and softening his manners, they are, perhaps, even now, the characteristics by which most of those who casually meet him would be inclined to identify the man. But there are other qualities, not then developed, but which have subsequently attained a firm and manly growth, and are recognized as his leading traits among those who really know him. Franklin Pierce's development, indeed, has always been the reverse of premature; the boy did not show the germ of all that was in the man, nor, perhaps, did the young man adequately foreshow the mature one.

In 1820, at the age of sixteen, he became a student of Bowdoin College, at Brunswick, Maine. It was in the autumn of the next year, that the author of this memoir entered the class below him; but our college reminiscences, however interesting to the parties concerned, are not exactly the material for a biography. He was then a youth, with the boy and man in him, vivacious, mirthful, slender, of a fair complexion, with light hair that had a curl in it: his bright and cheerful aspect made a kind of sunshine, both as regarded its radiance and its warmth; insomuch that no shyness of disposition, in his associates, could well resist its influence. We soon became acquainted, and were more philosopher John Locke. He joined the Athenaean Society, one of Bowdoin's two literary clubs, and was elected captain of the military drill company, the Bowdoin Cadets. Hawthorne described the boy commander's "air and step of a veteran…as well became the son of a revolutionary hero." In fact, until well into his college years, Pierce seems to have contemplated an army career.

One of Pierce's closest friends was an older student named Zenas Caldwell, "a pure-minded, studious, devoutly religious character…with the authority of a grave and sagacious turn of mind." Caldwell's strong religious beliefs had a marked impact on Pierce; during their senior year, when they roomed together, they prayed each night on their knees before going to bed.

Caldwell apparently typified many Bowdoin students, who tended to be significantly older than the lad from Hillsborough and, unlike Pierce, were working to pay for their own education. Naturally, they were more inclined than he to take their studies very seriously and learn all they could for the money they were paying. For the first two years, Pierce proved far more adroit in social activities than learning. "Carefree and irresponsible," Nichols chronicled, "he trailed along, getting his work from others if he couldn't do it himself." On at least one occasion, he openly admitted to a professor in class that he'd solved a difficult algebra problem by copying a fellow student's work.

As a result, Pierce's grades dropped him to the bottom of his class. "It could have been no easy task," Hawthorne reflected sympathetically, "to hold successful rivalry with students so much in earnest as these were." By other accounts, though, Pierce's descent into the academic cellar was his own doing. When he first read the student list at the beginning of his third year and saw his name at the bottom, he recoiled angrily and vowed to abort his education. But then he buckled down to his books, encouraged by Caldwell and other chums. He steadily improved his record until by graduation he ranked near the top among his peers.

Meanwhile, his ingrained patriotic and Episcopalian values from childhood took root. Hawthorne affirmed that during his final years at Bowdoin, Pierce's "habits of attention, and obedience to college discipline, were of the strictest character."

Franklin Pierce soon began to consider seriously what he might best be suited to do in life. Just as importantly, he began actually contributing to society. At Caldwell's request, Pierce spent the six-week winter break of his junior year teaching at the wilderness schoolhouse in Hebron, Maine. He stayed with the Caldwell family, who treated him as an honored guest. In return, he spent fireside evenings tutoring Caldwell's younger brother, who hoped to attend college. Perhaps the strongest evidence of his newfound dedication was his decision not to go home for the spring break that year. Instead, he remained on campus to prepare for the summer term.

College life two centuries ago was much different from today. Students had to follow rules that would appall their modern-day successors. At Bowdoin, they could not leave the vicinity of Brunswick or nearby Topsham unless their parents requested permission for them, could not shoot pool or play cards, could not "attend any theatrical entertainment or any idle show in Brunswick or Topsham," could not shout or sing loudly (which would dishonor "the character of a literary institution"), and could go hunting and fishing only with permission. Weekends were by no means a time for pleasure. To the contrary, the rules of Bowdoin stipulated: "Students must be in their rooms Saturday and Sunday evenings and abstain from diversions of every kind. They who profane the Sabbath by unnecessary business, visiting or receiving visits, or by walking abroad, or by any amusement, or in other ways, may be admonished or suspended." Students were fined for missing classes and daily prayers. The penalty for not sitting erect and attentive at chapel was fifty cents—a hefty fee in 1820, when a week's room and board cost about two dollars.

Six days of each week brought the same regimen: chapel at eight-thirty, an hour-long class at nine, an hour-long study period at ten, another class at eleven, two hours for lunch and exercise. Except on Saturday, students spent most of the afternoon in private study, with a final late-afternoon class followed by evening prayers conducted by the college president. Courses included arithmetic, English grammar, Latin and Greek translations, history, and "forensics" (speech/debates). In time, algebra, geometry, chemistry, religion, philosophy, and mineralogy were added to Pierce's subjects.

Boarding facilities were plain and chilly in winter. Students read by candlelight. Classrooms were likewise barren. On cold days, students had a practical incentive for arriving at class early rather than late: they coveted the seats closest to the fireplace. The library opened at noon each day for exactly one hour. Books in those years were held in great value, and check-out policies were strictly limited—freshmen, for example, could take out just one book at a time.

The school year was divided into three terms. It began in October and ended in early September, with a six-week vacation in winter, three-week break in spring, and four weeks in autumn between the old year and the new. Tuition, board, and other expenses totaled about two hundred dollars a year.

Despite the Bowdoin regimen, Pierce found time to enjoy the Maine coastal setting. He loved to walk the forest paths with his friends and explore along the Androscoggin River. They went swimming in fair weather, picked berries, and fished the river and hunted squirrels and birds. For amusement, they visited the riverside shanty of an old fortuneteller and brazenly frequented the village tavern in defiance of campus rules.

A pressing concern among college students today is whether they may keep a car on campus. Similarly, Franklin Pierce apparently lobbied his father for permission to keep a horse at Bowdoin—a privilege the elder Pierce granted during Franklin's senior year.

Franklin had risen high enough in his grades that he was chosen to give one of his class's commencement speeches. He was deeply disappointed that his father

Bowdoin College campus, 1823, oil on canvas, by John G. Brown

Bowdoin College is named for the Revolutionary War–era American statesman James Bowdoin (1726–90) who
also was the first president of the American Academy of Arts and Sciences (founded in 1780). In 1794, his son
James donated land and money to establish the college named in honor of his father. During their first week
on campus, Bowdoin students follow a tradition by signing the same Matriculation Book as did Hawthorne,
Longfellow, and Pierce.

did not attend his graduation, opting instead to attend a reception in Portsmouth, New Hampshire, for the Marquis de Lafayette, hero of the Revolution.

After graduating from Bowdoin in 1824, Pierce went to work as a clerk for several lawyers and judges in succession. In those times, many aspiring lawyers learned their profession not by attending law school, but by literally "reading law" under the tutelage of an established barrister. They had to familiarize themselves with *Commentaries on the Laws of England*, Sir William Blackstone's classic legal reference, and to master the details of their state and national constitutions.

Pierce also attended law school in Northampton, Massachusetts. Then, after two more clerkships, he was admitted to the bar in 1827. He began his law practice in Hillsborough—and lost his first case. It was a healthy jolt of realism that, in Hawthorne's words, "did but serve to make him aware of the latent resources of his mind."

Only twenty-three years old, Franklin Pierce was embarked on a remarkable career that would lift him from the losing counsel's humble table in a Hillsborough courtroom to the White House in Washington. The same year he became a lawyer, his father was elected governor of New Hampshire. Benjamin Pierce's wide-ranging influence in regional affairs of state would benefit his son's vocation. For his own part, Franklin Pierce had acquired at Bowdoin the public speaking and debating skills he would need for what was to come. He already possessed the outgoing personality that could build popularity among voters. He was a fine dresser, a young man who was fun to be around, who liked to please everyone, and who easily won the trust of new acquaintances.

At twenty-four, Pierce was elected to the New Hampshire state legislature. Four years later, he was elected to the first of two terms in Congress. In 1836, he became the youngest U.S. senator of his time.

Just before completing his Senate term, he resigned and returned to law practice. This he did at the urging of his wife Jane, a fragile, shy woman he had met at Bowdoin and married in 1834. Jane Pierce hated politics, and throughout his career, she discouraged her husband from the statesman's life.

During the 1840s, Pierce developed into one of the most persuasive lawyers in New England. Citizens from near and far packed the courtroom to hear him argue cases. It was a talent that would prove invaluable a decade later in his bid for president. Another priceless credential for national politics was a military record. Although Pierce's experiences in the Mexican War (1846–48) were less than heroic, he took his place among the popular returning veterans.

He was not the favored presidential candidate at the Democratic national convention in Baltimore in June 1852. After the four leading contenders repeatedly failed to win a majority of delegates' votes, he won the nomination as a compromise choice. He went on to defeat the Whig candidate, General Winfield Scott, in the general election.

Only forty-eight years old, Franklin had become the foremost American. But his was a tragic life. He and his wife lost all three of their sons in childhood. The third, Bennie, was killed in a train wreck in January 1853, just two months before Pierce took office as president.

Most historians consider Franklin Pierce one of America's weakest presidents. The great irony is that during his term in office (1853–57) the United States was unusually prosperous. The country was expanding steadily westward, connected by spreading railway systems, and factories were mass-producing a variety of products.

But a fatal divisiveness was brewing between North and South over the slavery issue. In a way, the president seemed in a unique position to bridge the differences between regions. A New Englander, Pierce nevertheless had strong political friendships with southern statesmen. He insisted compromise was the answer—but in the turbulent political arena of the 1850s, compromise only fueled the fire of dissension. Above all, Franklin was a patriot sworn to uphold the Constitution and preserve the federal union. Toward that end, he took great care—too much care, historians judge—to appease the South in the escalating crisis. He made significant proslavery political appointments and decisions. This steadily lost support for both him and the Democratic Party in the northern states. His hopes of a second term were doomed. Four years after he left office, the nation went to war. Franklin Pierce became what some historians call "the forgotten president."

Jane Pierce died in 1863, still in her fifties. A few months later, Pierce accompanied his old school friend Nathaniel Hawthorne to New England's idyllic White Mountains. Hawthorne was in failing health, and they hoped the secluded environment would help him. It did not; Hawthorne died one night in a bedroom next to Franklin Pierce's room. While others had forsaken the former president, the Bowdoin underclassman had remained faithful. Now he was gone.

Franklin Pierce's own death came in 1869 in Concord, New Hampshire.

—Daniel E. Harmon

James Buchanan
Chapter Fifteen

Weary from long nights of carousing, a bored young man named James Buchanan endured his geography teacher's lectures with no small measure of contempt. Buchanan was not alone. Virtually every student who took classes under Dr. Robert Davidson would report their hatred for the man who not only lectured them in the classroom, but served as head of the Dickinson College faculty as well.

Another of Davidson's students, Roger B. Taney, remembered the teacher years later. "He was not harsh or ill-natured in his intercourse with us, but he was formal and solemn and precise and, in short, was always the pedagogue in school and out of school," wrote Taney, who had studied at Dickinson College fourteen years before Buchanan. Taney, like Buchanan, would go on to a career that would culminate in high public office; he became chief justice of the Supreme Court of the United States.

Buchanan, Taney, and other students who passed through Davidson's classes were required to memorize and recite a poem written by Davidson, which purported to explain the mysteries of the globe in a few terse lines. The students thought the exercise was ridiculous; nonetheless, they memorized the verse. The poem included these lines:

Round the globe now to rove, and its surface survey,
Oh, youth of America, hasten away;
Bid adieu for awhile to the toys you desire,
Earth's beauties to view, and its wonders admire.

"Nothing, I think, impaired the respect of the class for Dr. Davidson more than his acrostic," recalled Taney. "It was so often…repeated among us in derision."

Buchanan was even less enamored with Davidson's teaching methods than Taney had been. By far the brightest of the students at Dickinson, the sixteen-year-old Buchanan found that it didn't require much in the way of study to pass his courses. Instead, he spent his nights not poring over the day's lessons, but in the taverns of Carlisle, Pennsylvania, drinking ale and smoking cigars in blatant violation of college rules. "Without much natural tendency to become dissipated," he later

In 1807, James Buchanan entered the junior class of Dickinson College in what was then a frontier town— Carlisle, Pennsylvania. Dickinson had been founded in 1784 through the efforts of Benjamin Rush, the revolutionary statesman, who believed that a college "with an open Bible" was needed in Pennsylvania west of the Appalachians. Buchanan found the school in "wretched condition" with no "efficient discipline." His behavior at Dickinson was far from exemplary. "I engaged in every sort of extravagance and mischief," he wrote. He was expelled in 1808 but was readmitted after pledging good behavior to his minister, a college trustee. Buchanan completed his senior year, graduating in September 1809. "I left college," he wrote, "feeling little attachment to the Alma Mater."

Forty-two students were enrolled at Dickinson in 1807—eight in the senior class, nineteen in Buchanan's junior, and the remainder were freshmen or assigned to the Latin preparatory school. (The college did not yet include a sophomore year.) The entire teaching staff included three instructors. Robert Davidson, an ordained Presbyterian minister, was the president. He taught history, geography, and philosophy. Davidson was particularly fond of astronomy, having written a short pamphlet on geography and astronomy in rhyme that each Dickinson student had to purchase and memorize. John Hayes was in charge of languages, and James McCormick handled mathematics. McCormick also lodged and boarded half a dozen students at his home, including Buchanan. "Mr. McCormick and his wife were as kind to us as if they had been our parents," recalled a Buchanan classmate. "[He] sometimes seemed quite distressed when, upon examining a pupil, he found him not quite as learned as he was himself."

Two of Buchanan's handwritten college notebooks have survived, both from 1808—"Lecture Notes on Trigonometry, Surveying, and Navigation," and "Questions and Answers on Mathematics, Astronomy and Natural Philosophy."

Illustrated above is a page in Buchanan's handwriting for an 1808 paper on navigation required in Professor McCormick's class. Next to it is a page from the noted astronomer Nathaniel Bowditch's book *The New American Practical Navigator* (c.1802 edition). This is an example of rote education so common in early eighteenth-century American colleges. Usually, there was a shortage of textbooks. Students were required to copy—and at the same time to memorize—from the few books available to the instructor.

explained, "and chiefly from the example of others, and in order to be considered a clever and spirited youth, I engaged in every sort of extravagance and mischief."

When his first year at Dickinson was completed, Buchanan passed his final examinations with ease and returned to his family's farm in nearby Mercersburg to relax for a few weeks while awaiting the start of the winter term and another year of rowdy behavior.

On one pleasantly warm, late summer day in September, Buchanan suffered a sudden and rude shock. There was a knock on the door. His father James answered and was handed a note by a messenger. The elder Buchanan opened the envelope and read the contents of the note silently to himself. It was clear from the man's expression that the correspondence contained the gravest of news. Without uttering a word, James glared at his son, tossed him the note, and stormed out of the room.

Young James read the letter, in which Dr. Davidson informed James's father that his vain, sarcastic, and carousing son would not be invited back for another year at Dickinson College. In fact, wrote Davidson, the boy would have been given the boot earlier if it had not been for the respect the faculty held for his father. "They had borne with me as best they could until that period," Buchanan recalled, "but they would not receive me again, and…the letter was written to [my father] to save him the mortification of sending me back and having me rejected. Mortified to the soul, I at once determined upon my course."

The story of Abraham Lincoln's humble beginnings are known to every school child—how the nation's sixteenth president was born in a log cabin and learned to read by the light of a cooking fire is part of the story of America. Less well-known, though, is the fact that Lincoln's immediate predecessor in the White House was also born in a log cabin on the edge of what was then America's frontier.

James Buchanan was born April 23, 1791, in Cove Gap, Pennsylvania, about one hundred and forty miles west of Philadelphia. At the time, Cove Gap was one of the last crossroads towns on the trail into America's wilderness. As such, the busiest place in town was the trading post and warehouse run by John Tom. Pioneers, trappers, homesteaders, soldiers, and others heading west all stopped at "Stony Batter," which is what Tom called his store, to take on supplies.

Tom's assistant at Stony Batter was James Buchanan Sr., a hard-working Presbyterian from County Donegal in the northern part of Ireland. Buchanan had emigrated to America in 1783 at the invitation of an uncle, Joshua Russell, who owned a tavern in Gettysburg. Buchanan arrived in the port of Philadelphia in the summer of 1783; he was met by his uncle who promised to look after the young man. They returned to Gettysburg, where Buchanan lived off the charity of Uncle Joshua only briefly. The ambitious, intelligent and industrious young immigrant was anxious to make his own way, and soon learned of an employment opportunity at John Tom's trading post some forty miles west of Gettysburg.

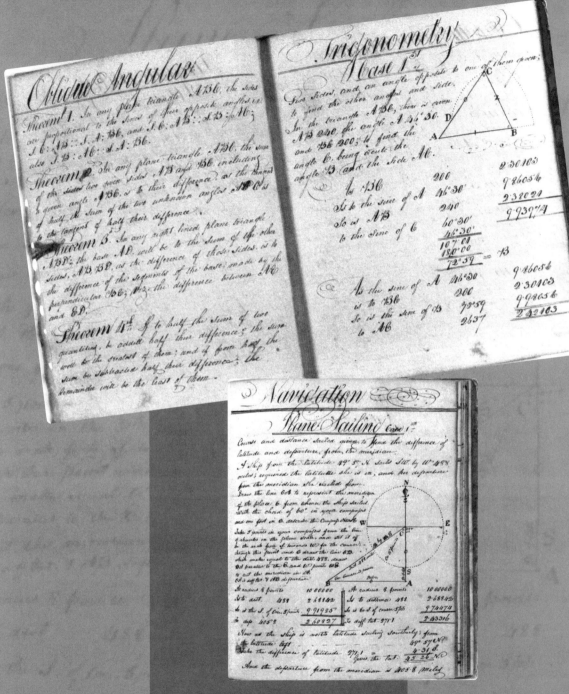

These pages are from James Buchanan's 1808 notebooks on navigation and mathematics. Buchanan found his courses at Dickinson College dull, and his memoirs are most uncomplimentary toward the school and its teaching staff.

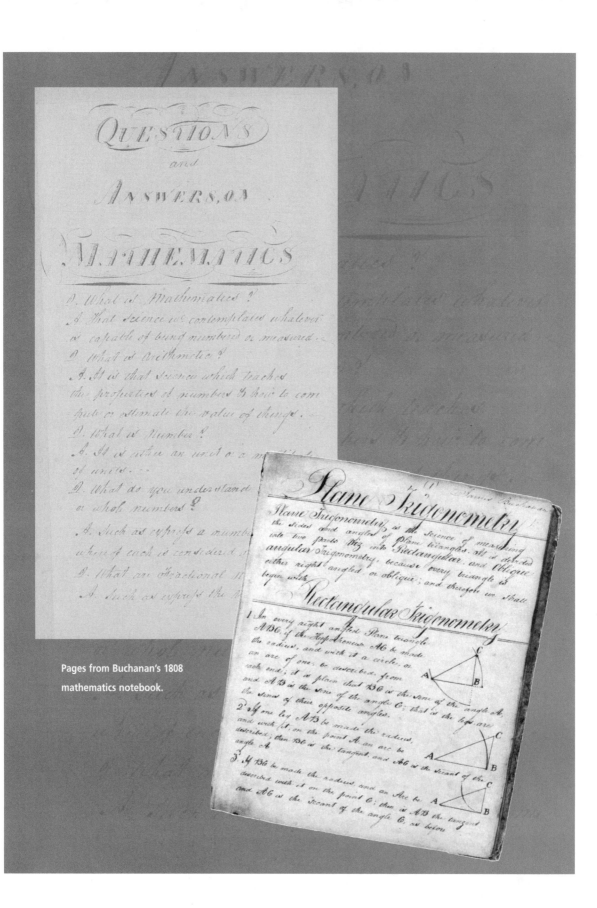

Pages from Buchanan's 1808
mathematics notebook.

Buchanan worked under Tom for four years, and during that time Tom turned a bustling business into a failed enterprise. In June 1787, James Buchanan, a frugal man who was careful to save his money, bought Stony Batter and a hundred surrounding acres for £142 at a tax auction.

Buchanan celebrated his venture into business by marrying his sweetheart, Elizabeth Speer, the daughter of a neighbor of his Uncle Joshua. The Buchanans moved into the log cabin in Cove Gap. Their first child, Mary, died shortly after her birth in 1789. Two years later, son James was born. He was the first of ten more children who would be born into the Buchanan family, although another girl and boy would also die in childhood. Nevertheless, the Buchanans were a robust family and they made father James proud. And there was no question that James was proudest of his oldest son and namesake.

Young James and the other Buchanan children received their early schooling from their mother. Elizabeth Buchanan was well-read; her favorite writers were the poets John Milton, Alexander Pope, and William Cowper, whose works she recited to her children. James was a good listener who absorbed his mother's lessons.

From the words of Milton, Buchanan undoubtedly absorbed some ideas regarding the eternal battle of good against evil, as well as the belief that good will come out of evil. From Cowper, James learned to love the rural life; after retiring from the presidency, Buchanan spent his last years on his rural Pennsylvania estate known as Wheatland and rarely set foot in a big city again. And from Pope, James's natural wit perhaps developed into sarcasm under the influence of Pope's acid invectives, which Buchanan would find useful in debating at Dickinson. It was a talent that would get him in trouble with the faculty but would serve him well as a lawyer and, later, as a lawmaker.

Elizabeth Buchanan also read the Bible to her children and told them stories about George Washington, whom the Buchanans idolized. James and Elizabeth named their youngest son after Washington and may even have met him when the president stayed briefly at Uncle Joshua's tavern in late 1794.

Another early and important teacher was his father. Helping around the Stony Batter trading post, James observed his father's attention to bookkeeping and his fondness for working with numbers. It was the elder Buchanan's belief that John Tom's failure could be attributed to the man's abysmal abilities when it came to calculating numbers. In his later years, son James would be an ardent bookkeeper himself. Even as an occupant of the White House, Buchanan kept scrupulous records of how much he spent and how much he was owed, down to the penny.

With his family growing and business at the trading post turning out to be very prosperous, James Buchanan decided to move out of Cove Gap and into a red-brick home he built on the main street of Mercersburg, a town not far from the Maryland border. Son James was sent to the Old Stone Academy, a one-room schoolhouse in Mercersburg. He was six years old when he enrolled in the school, which was led by a Presbyterian minister, the Reverend James R. Sharon. At the time, there was no law that compelled families to send their children to school.

Even though James was six, his father could have used his help at the trading post or in the fields of the family's adjacent farm. Nevertheless, in County Donegal the elder Buchanan had been sent to school (by his Uncle Samuel, who raised him), so he believed in education and was determined to see his son attend school. For the next ten years, James Buchanan attended school at the Old Stone Academy.

Under the Reverend Sharon and other teachers, James learned Greek, Latin, and mathematics. He was easily the brightest boy in school, although it should be pointed out that the student body at the Old Stone Academy never numbered more than a handful of pupils. Nevertheless, this very sharp young man soon came to the attention of the Reverend John King, the Presbyterian minister in Mercersburg whose authority included overseeing the school.

King was a trustee of Dickinson College. When James turned sixteen, King urged the elder Buchanan to send his boy to Dickinson, about forty miles northeast of Mercersburg. Elizabeth Dickinson had always wanted her eldest son to enter the ministry, but her husband had other ideas. By now, James Buchanan Sr. was the most prosperous businessman and farmer in Mercersburg. He realized that his growing assets would require a keen mind schooled in the complexities of the law to protect his holdings. His son would attend college with the goal of becoming a lawyer so that he might serve his father and look after the Buchanan family interests. In September 1807, James and his father saddled their horses and set out for Carlisle so the boy could enroll in Dickinson College.

The school had been founded in 1783 by Dr. Benjamin Rush, a noted Philadelphia physician and a signer of the Declaration of Independence who believed the young nation needed a college on its western frontier. (The fact that the college was established just a hundred miles west of Philadelphia illustrates where the frontier was in those days.) Rush convinced a number of esteemed citizens to donate to the college and serve on the board of trustees. Among them were James Wilson, soon to be a Supreme Court justice; William Bingham, one of the wealthiest men in Philadelphia; and Ephraim and Robert Blaine, ancestors of future presidential candidate James G. Blaine.

Rush also invited John Dickinson to join the board. A Philadelphian who maintained a farm in Delaware, Dickinson had served in the Continental Congress and later fought in the Continental Army, seeing action at the Battle of Brandywine. His "Letters from a Farmer in Pennsylvania," which were published in a Pennsylvania newspaper in 1767 and 1768, eloquently attacked British taxation policy and urged resistance to unjust laws. The letters earned Dickinson the reputation as "Penman of the Revolution." When Dickinson agreed to donate five hundred acres in Cumberland County as well as a selection of books for the school library, Rush had little trouble convincing the other trustees to name the school after him.

By the time James Buchanan arrived, the college had hardly grown into the prosperous institution its founders had expected. Funds were always short, and Dr. Rush frequently found himself scrambling for money to keep the college going. Since its founding, the college had used an ancient grammar school building on Liberty

Avenue in Carlisle as its main classroom facility. The old building was finally replaced in 1806 by a newly constructed classroom; nevertheless, the money troubles continued. "Suppose we add $10 a year to our tuition money?" Rush proposed in a letter to college officials in 1807. "Education in the present state of our country on an intensive plan should be considered a luxury; and placed only within the reach of persons in easy circumstances. Unless this be the case the proportion of learning will soon over-balance the proportion of labor in our country. Let a plain education…reading, writing and arithmetic be made as cheap as possible, and even free of expense to those who are unable to pay for it. In a Republic no man should have a vote who is unable to read."

Dr. Davidson was one of three professors at the college when Buchanan arrived to join the junior class. The others were Professor John Hayes, who taught languages, and Professor James McCormick, instructor in mathematics. Of the three, Buchanan admired McCormick the most. McCormick and his wife often provided lodgings to students in their home. Unlike the self-important Davidson, McCormick was patient and eager to enjoy a good laugh with his students. When one of his students tested poorly, McCormick would often become quite upset, believing that he had failed in his duty to educate the youth.

At first, Buchanan studied hard. Required reading at Dickinson included the ancient Roman and Greek literary masters—Homer and Cicero among them.

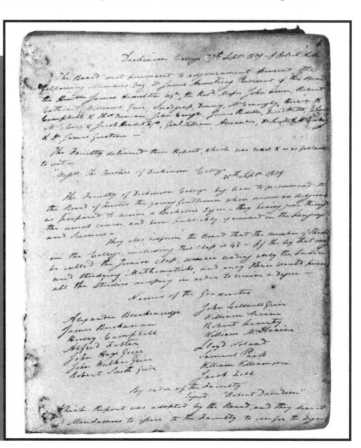

A page from the minutes of the Dickinson College board of trustees meeting, September 27, 1809. During that meeting formal approval was voted for the A.B. degree to be awarded to the fifteen graduates of the class of 1809—whom the board of trustees certified "as prepared to receive their Bachelor's degree, they having gone through the usual courses, and been publicly examined in the Languages and Sciences." Buchanan's name is second down, left column.

DICKENSON COLLEGE

This engraving, titled "Dickenson College, 1810" (the college name is misspelled), was based on a sketch done by Buchanan's classmate Alexander Brackenridge.

Cicero's "Catiline Debates" were of particular interest to Buchanan. The orations tell the story of how Cicero used the Roman Senate to unmask and denounce the traitorous Lucius Cataline. "When, O Catiline, do you mean to cease abusing our patience?" Cicero said. "How long is that madness of yours still to mock us? When is there to be an end of that unbridled audacity of yours, swaggering about as it does now?" For someone whose political career would take him first to the legislature of Pennsylvania and then to Congress, Cicero's eloquent arguments to a body of lawmakers surely must have provided Buchanan with inspiration.

Buchanan also pored through the writings of the school's chief benefactor, John Dickinson. There is no question that Dickinson was one of the nation's most devoted patriots. His letters stirred emotions in his fellow colonists and clearly set out a list of grievances that he felt King George was obliged to correct—but he also counseled the colonists against war. In his third letter, Dickinson explained the purpose of his open correspondence. He wrote: "The meaning of the [letters] is to convince the people of these colonies that they are at this moment exposed to the most imminent dangers; and to persuade them immediately, vigorously, and unanimously, to exert themselves, in the most firm, but most peaceful manner, for obtaining relief. The cause of liberty is a cause of too much dignity to be sullied by turbulence and tumult. It ought to be maintained in a manner suitable to her nature. Those who engage in it, should breathe a sedate, yet fervent spirit, animating them to actions of prudence, justice, modesty, bravery, humanity and magnanimity." Nine years later, when Dickinson was serving in the Continental Congress, he participated in the historic debate on independence during the summer of 1776. When the delegates voted for independence, Dickinson refused to sign the declaration. He believed it would lead to war with England, which he opposed.

John Dickinson was a man who stood on his principles, refusing to go along with the majority when he believed it would surely lead to war. More than eight decades later, President James Buchanan would find himself faced with a similar problem. It was Buchanan's steadfast belief that the U.S. Constitution provided no powers to the president to halt the secession of the southern states, which occurred during the last weeks of his administration. Sadly, he stood by that belief as the chasm separating North and South grew ever wider, making bloodshed inevitable.

Buchanan did return to Dickinson for his senior year. After receiving the letter of expulsion from Dr. Davidson, Buchanan approached the Reverend King and asked him to intercede. By then, Buchanan's hometown minister had become president of the Dickinson trustees. "He gave me a gentle lecture," Buchanan recalled. "He then proposed to me that if I would pledge my honor to him to behave better at college than I had done, he felt such confidence in me that he would pledge himself to Dr. Davidson on my behalf, and he did not doubt that I would be permitted to return."

Once back at Dickinson, Buchanan kept his word. He stayed out of Carlisle taverns, spent his nights on his school work, and reined in his sarcastic mouth when called on in class. He joined one of the school's two literary groups, the Union Philosophical Society, and led the organization's lively debates—often practicing his speeches while strolling through town. When the school year ended, the Union Philosophical endorsed Buchanan for senior class valedictorian. The faculty, still smarting over Buchanan's conduct the previous year, selected the choice of the school's other literary group, the Belles Lettres Society.

Buchanan was outraged. So were most of his fellow students, who believed him to be the far superior student. There was talk of a student rebellion—nobody would accept valedictory honors. Finally, the faculty reached a compromise: Buchanan would be permitted to deliver an address at the graduation, but not as valedictorian. Grudgingly, Buchanan agreed. On September 19, 1809, the nation's future president accepted his diploma from Dickinson College.

The graduation incident would forever weigh heavily on Buchanan. Years later, he wrote: "The other members of the society belonging to the senior class would have united with me in refusing to speak at the approaching commencement, but I was unwilling to place them in this situation on my account, and more especially as several of them were designed for the ministry. I held out myself for some time, but at last yielded on receiving a kind communication from the professors. I left college, however, feeling but little attachment towards the Alma Mater."

—Hal Marcovitz

Abraham Lincoln
Chapter Sixteen

Abraham Lincoln, who as the sixteenth president would lead the United States through the turbulent Civil War era (1861–1865), was born on February 12, 1809, in a log cabin situated in what is now Larue County, Kentucky. As a child, Abraham persevered through poverty, minimal school education, and the death of his mother. Still, as a mostly self-educated person, Abraham pursued a life that led him from his father's small log cabin to the nation's White House.

Abraham's father, Thomas Lincoln, was a farmer and landowner but was hardly prosperous. In 1816, Tom Lincoln, besieged by claims made against the ownership of his land, sold his farm and moved his family to Indiana, establishing a homestead along the Little Pigeon Creek in Spencer County.

For the Lincoln family, the early years in Indiana would be a time of hardship. The family spent most of the first year in a half-camp, a three-walled structure that barely provided any shelter at all. A campfire continually burned on the structure's open side—while it provided little heat, the flames kept wolves, bears, and other animals away from the door. Eventually, Tom used his skill as a carpenter to build a small log cabin for his family.

Food was scarce, so the Lincoln family ate whatever small game Tom could shoot. While Tom and Abraham spent most of their time clearing the barren land, it was a year before they could plant a crop of corn and pumpkins.

Years later, Abraham composed a humorous poem entitled, *The Bear Hunt*, which included a verse about his boyhood home:

> When first my father settled here,
> 'Twas then the frontier line:
> The panther's scream filled night with fear
> And bears preyed on the swine.

Although this poem illustrates Abraham's literary nature, neither his father nor mother, Nancy, could read or write. As children, Abraham and his older sister,

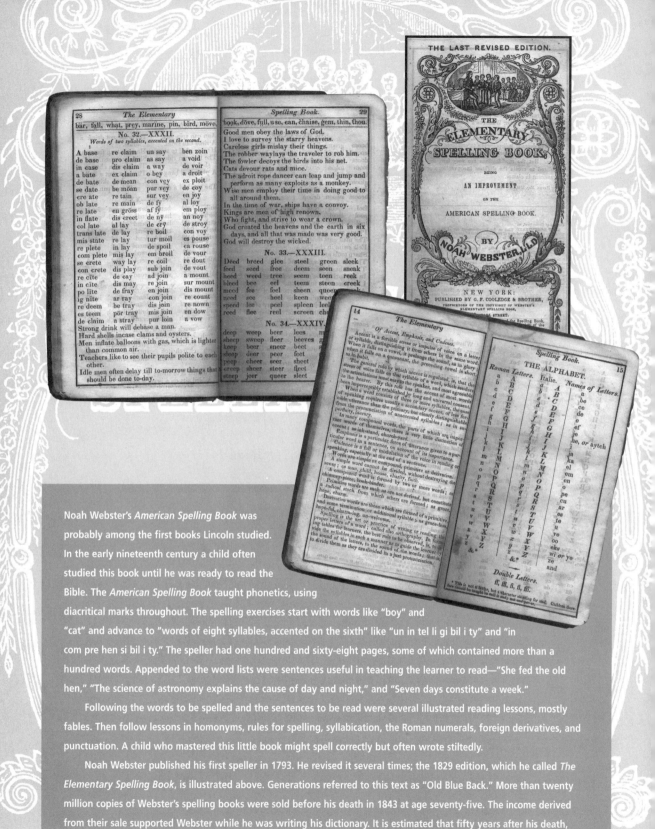

Noah Webster's *American Spelling Book* was probably among the first books Lincoln studied. In the early nineteenth century a child often studied this book until he was ready to read the Bible. The *American Spelling Book* taught phonetics, using diacritical marks throughout. The spelling exercises start with words like "boy" and "cat" and advance to "words of eight syllables, accented on the sixth" like "un in tel li gi bil i ty" and "in com pre hen si bil i ty." The speller had one hundred and sixty-eight pages, some of which contained more than a hundred words. Appended to the word lists were sentences useful in teaching the learner to read—"She fed the old hen," "The science of astronomy explains the cause of day and night," and "Seven days constitute a week."

Following the words to be spelled and the sentences to be read were several illustrated reading lessons, mostly fables. Then follow lessons in homonyms, rules for spelling, syllabication, the Roman numerals, foreign derivatives, and punctuation. A child who mastered this little book might spell correctly but often wrote stiltedly.

Noah Webster published his first speller in 1793. He revised it several times; the 1829 edition, which he called *The Elementary Spelling Book*, is illustrated above. Generations referred to this text as "Old Blue Back." More than twenty million copies of Webster's spelling books were sold before his death in 1843 at age seventy-five. The income derived from their sale supported Webster while he was writing his dictionary. It is estimated that fifty years after his death, Webster's spellers and dictionary still sold at the rate of a million copies a year.

Sarah, managed to attend only a few months at a log-cabin school in Kentucky, where teachers Zachariah Riney and Caleb Hazel taught them the alphabet and simple arithmetic. Abraham and Sarah were barely literate when their family established a new homestead in the Indiana wilderness.

It would be three years before Abraham and Sarah saw the inside of another schoolhouse. By then, Abraham's mother had died, and Thomas Lincoln had remarried. His new wife, Sarah Bush Johnston Lincoln, was a widow with three children. She brought books into the Lincoln cabin and insisted that all the children attend school. Abraham grew very fond of his stepmother; in later years he called her his "angel mother."

From the time Abraham was ten until he was fifteen, he spent parts of three years in school. As an adult, he estimated that his total time in school amounted to less than twelve months. Usually, Tom Lincoln allowed Abraham to leave the farm for only two or three months at a time.

In Indiana, three teachers—Andrew Crawford, James Swaney, and Azel Dorsey—instructed Abraham. They were typical teachers of the era—itinerants with a modest education who arrived in town and offered their services as schoolmasters. The local townspeople raised whatever money they could to pay their salaries and to also provide a cabin to serve as the schoolhouse. Most teachers moved on to another town after a year or two.

Of those years, Abraham said, "No qualification was ever required of a teacher beyond readin', writin', and cipherin' to the Rule of Three [proportion and ratio]. If a straggler supposed to understand Latin happened to sojourn in the neighborhood, he was looked upon as a wizard."

In the neighborhoods of Indiana, the one-room schools Abraham attended were called blab schools, because students were required to stand and speak their lessons aloud. Whenever students made a mistake, the teacher interrupted them with a correction. Teachers used this style of teaching because only a few outdated textbooks were available, which would make reading the lessons a difficult task. Among the few books Abraham used in those early years were *The New and Complete System of Arithmetic* by Nicholas Pike and the *New Guide to the English Tongue* by Thomas Dilworth.

Dilworth's book, originally published in 1740, provided the spellings for words up to four letters. After 1783 many schools had replaced this book with Noah Webster's *American Spelling Book*, which was the first book to show young students how to read and spell by breaking words into syllables. Approximately sixty million copies of Webster's spelling book were printed in the one hundred-plus years the book remained in publication. Because of the poverty of the folks who lived near Little Pigeon Creek, only a few copies of Webster's speller existed in the area. Perhaps this explains Lincoln's lifelong struggles with spelling. Until the end of his life, Abraham had a habit of spelling "beginning" with one "n" and writing "unanamous" when he meant "unanimous." He referred to his own inauguration as president as his "inaugeration."

Lincoln began reading the Bible as a child. He said that reading the Bible was the greatest comfort he and his sister had during the months that followed their mother's death in 1818 when he was nine years old. John L. Scripps's 1860 campaign biography *Life of Abraham Lincoln*, which Lincoln read and revised before publication, reported that it had been Nancy Lincoln's custom on the Sabbath to read a portion of the Scriptures aloud to her family and that after young Lincoln and his sister learned to read, they shared by turns in this Sunday reading.

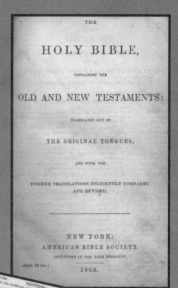

Robert H. Browne, while a soldier during the Civil War, spent considerable time in the Kentucky community where the Lincolns had lived. He gathered recollections of those who had known the family; these were published in 1907 as *Abraham Lincoln and Men of His Time*. Browne repeatedly was told that Lincoln's mother "had taught him to read the Bible when only five years old," and that "it did set everybody a-wonderin' to see how much he knowed, and him not mor'n seven."

Lincoln had the ability to quote in full almost any passage of Scripture, often giving chapter and verse. There is no evidence that he was ever an orthodox Christian; as an adult he seems to have been a philosophical theist who appreciated the wisdom and literary charm to be found in the Bible. Above all, he valued its moral precepts. After having interviewed local ministers and their families who knew young Lincoln, J. H. Spencer wrote about Lincoln in *A History of Kentucky Baptists* (1886):

> He...had to do much of his traveling on foot, and often barefooted...many a time...shoeless and coatless....He possessed only medium talents, but he hade an easy flow of common English words, his heart was thoroughly educated and deeply imbued with the grace of God, and he was an indefatigable laborer in the gospel of Christ.

Most of those whom Spencer interviewed seem to have been residents of what was then Hardin County, Kentucky.

The first book printed within the limits of the present United States of which any copy survives is a portion of the Bible (the so-called Bay Psalm Book, which was printed in Cambridge, Massachusetts, around 1640). During Lincoln's childhood the Bible was the number one book both read and owned in America. There were at least several dozen Bible societies in America when Lincoln was a child. In 1816, a union of these societies formed the American Bible Society. Its founding document set as its goal the placing of a Bible in every home, including those on the frontier.

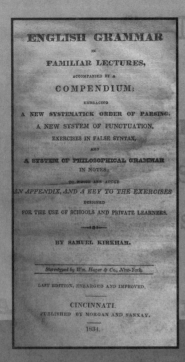

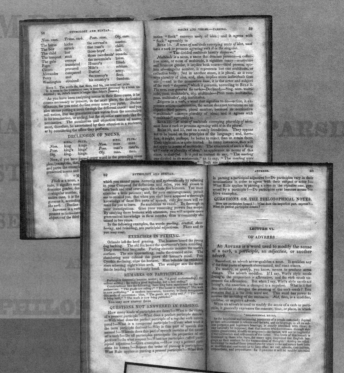

It is thought that the first book Lincoln studied was Dilworth's "Speller"—*A New Guide to the English Tongue*, by Thomas Dilworth. First printed in England in 1740, it was copied by many American printers. It soon ranked as the leading elementary textbook of the colonies and it remained in print for some time after the American Revolution. It was a combination speller, reader, and grammar text.

Historians also know that Lincoln familiarized himself with Samuel Kirkham's more sophisticated *English Grammar*. The first edition appeared in the early 1820s. The book went through many editions and it became the standard for at least a generation. (The pages shown above are from the 1834 edition of Kirkham's *Grammar*.)

The definitions in Kirkham's book are clear and concise—"A Verb is a word which signifies to BE, to DO, or to SUFFER; as I am; I rule; I am ruled." Good explanatory notes followed word definitions. Questions enabled the student to test his memory and his understanding. The student who mastered Kirkham's *Grammar* obtained an excellent knowledge of grammar as well as the ability to speak and write clearly.

Abraham probably had a better experience with *Pike's Arithmetic*, which was first published in 1788. The book included more than five hundred pages of lessons that showed students how to do addition, subtraction, fractions, volumes, square roots, and geometry. In later years, Abraham proved to be a gifted mathematician: he taught himself trigonometry while learning the craft of land surveying.

While Abraham Lincoln often showed a strong desire for knowledge, he told people he wasn't much of a reader. "I never read an entire novel in my life," he said. "I commenced *Ivanhoe* but never finished it."

Such a boast can be regarded as the false claim of a politician anxious to win approval from common voters of the era, not many of whom could be regarded as dedicated readers. In reality, Lincoln was an avid reader—interested in almost any book he could obtain. He most enjoyed reading history, and was particularly stirred by stories of the Founding Fathers during the American Revolution. Although books were hard to come by in rural Indiana during the 1820s and 1830s, Lincoln still managed to collect copies of literary classics, including *Aesop's Fables*, John Bunyan's *Pilgrim's Progress*, and Daniel Defoe's *The Life and Adventures of Robinson Crusoe*. As a boy, he read Mason Weems's *Life of George Washington*. He received his first lessons in oration from William Scott's *Lessons in Elocution*, which also gave him his first taste of Shakespeare.

This type of self-reliance served as a catalyst throughout Lincoln's life. When he was seventeen years old Lincoln pursued his interest in law by walking many miles from his family's log cabin near Gentryville in Spencer County to the town of Rockport, Indiana, where Judge John Pitcher permitted him to read his law books. Lincoln also walked to the town of Boonville, where attorney John A. Brackenridge maintained a law practice. Brackenridge was the local county prosecutor and members of the Indiana legal profession held his courtroom oratorical skills in high regard. Lincoln sat in the Boonville courtroom and listened to Brackenridge handle his cases; this helped Lincoln learn how to argue a case.

During this time of Lincoln's life, he had also used his ambition to start his own business. Abraham had found a job on the farm of James Taylor. Taylor's farm was located along Anderson's Creek, approximately sixteen miles from Lincoln's home in rural southern Indiana. Lincoln not only helped Taylor with the plowing and planting, but also with the operation of a ferryboat that Taylor sailed along the creek to the Ohio River.

While working for Taylor, Lincoln built a scow—a small boat propelled by a pole—to earn extra money by meeting riverboats in the middle of the Ohio and ferrying passengers to shore. Although Lincoln never obtained a license for his new endeavor, he began earning good money. On one occasion, a passenger paid him a dollar for the ride—an incredible amount of money for young Lincoln, who had never once in his short lifetime earned that much money in one day.

But Lincoln's sudden prosperity didn't continue on such a smooth course. Brothers John and Lin Dill also operated a ferry on the Ohio River, and they didn't appreciate an unlicensed ferryman moving in on their trade. The Dills could not

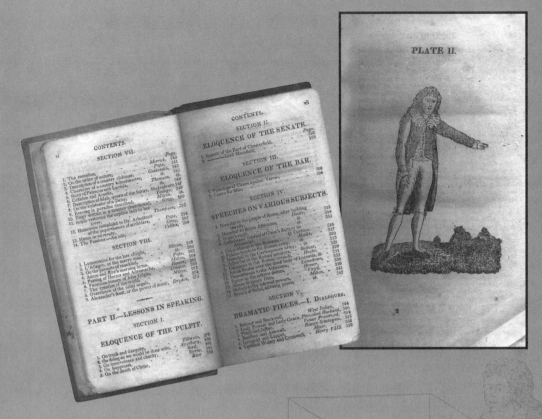

As a teenager, Lincoln read William Scott's *Lessons in Elocution, or a Selection of Pieces in Prose and Verse for the Improvement of Youth in Reading and Speaking to which are prefixed Elements of Gesture.* Lincoln probably read the 1805 edition; the pages shown here are from the 1817 edition.

Scott's *Lessons in Elocution* is crowded with selected passages, essays, and entire poems from several dozen writers, including John Milton, Alexander Pope, Thomas Gray, and Edward Gibbon. However, the largest section is devoted to Shakespearian gems from *Hamlet*, *Julius Caesar*, *Othello*, *As You Like It*, and *Henry IV*.

Scott's four hundred and thirty-six pages also contain lesser-known writers. For example, Lincoln frequently quoted from William Knox's "Address to a Young Student," which appears in the compilation. Knox, a fairly obscure Scottish writer who died in 1825, also wrote a poem that some Lincoln scholars consider his favorite. Also included in Scott's *Lessons in Elocution* are sections on "Elements of Gesture" as well as suggestions for voice modulation and projection.

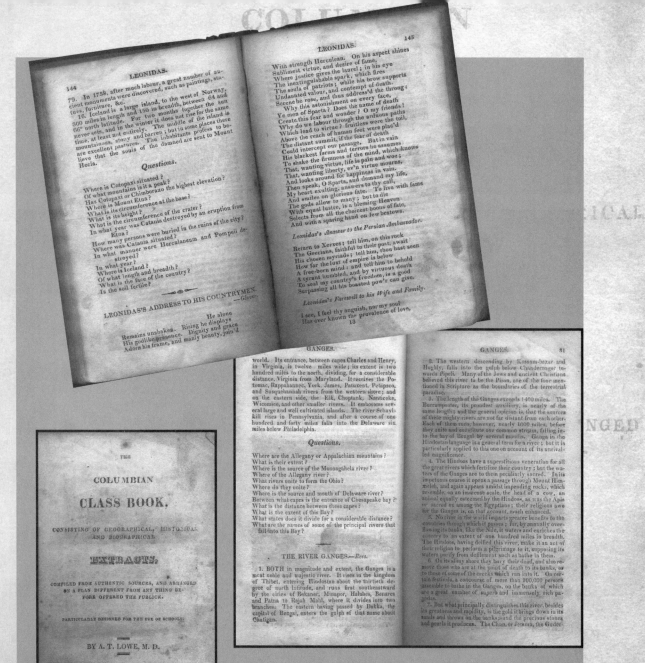

Before the American Revolution, most schoolbooks used in the colonies were imported from England. After the Revolution, publishers rushed forth with new books and compilations under such titles as *The Columbian Class Book*, *Columbian Orator*, and *The American Preceptor*. These books contained selections from both American and English literature.

We know that Lincoln read A. T. Lowe's *The Columbian Class Book* because his marked edition has been preserved. The first edition of this book appeared in 1824. It is a compilation of extracts from classical history books and selections from American and English prose. The first piece is a twenty-nine page essay on George Washington, followed by questions like "Where are the Allegany or Appalachian mountains" and "What rivers unite to form the Ohio." The section on Russia asks the reader to discuss "the state of literature and civilization in that nation."

bother Lincoln while he stayed on the Indiana side of the river, because the middle of the Ohio River was the border between Indiana and Kentucky. Under Kentucky law, however, it was forbidden for an unlicensed ferry to "set any person over a river," so when Lincoln ferried a passenger to the Kentucky side the Dills hurried to the local justice of the peace and swore out a complaint against their competitor.

Justice of the Peace Samuel Pate of Lewisport, Kentucky, issued a warrant for Lincoln's arrest. He was charged with a violation of "An Act Respecting the Establishment of Ferries." Although Lincoln probably could have settled the court matter with the Dills by paying a small fine, the self-driven seventeen-year-old chose to fight the charge. Lincoln could not afford a lawyer, so he decided to act as his own attorney. Using a gift for oration that would later spellbind the nation, Lincoln defended himself in the courtroom even though he had no formal education in law. He ultimately persuaded Justice Pate to drop the charges because he argued that meeting a riverboat halfway across the river did not constitute a journey "over" the river.

The Dills stormed out of the courtroom. Pate, impressed by Lincoln's argument, invited the young man to stay so they could talk about law: the conversation lasted hours. Justice Pate also invited Lincoln to visit his courtroom in the future. For months, whenever business on the river was slow, Lincoln spent his afternoons in Pate's courtroom, listening to the arguments made by practicing attorneys—absorbing real-life lessons not available at the finest American law schools of the time.

While Lincoln's knowledge grew as he watched court proceedings, his living quarters remained confined. The cabin, which measured eighteen feet wide by twenty feet long, housed not only Tom Lincoln's family, but often his cousins and in-laws as well. It was not unusual for as many as thirteen adults and children to be living in the log cabin. As Abraham Lincoln said of the cabin later, "There wasn't room to cuss the cat without gittin' its hairs in your teeth."

At age nineteen, Lincoln would leave the cramped cabin each day to work as a farmhand. He often raised the ire of his employers when they caught him sitting in the shade of a tree, concentrating on a book instead of pulling stumps. Later, Lincoln wryly commented, "My father taught me to work but he never taught me to like it."

In 1830 Tom Lincoln finally gave up his Indiana farm and moved the family to Macon County, Illinois. Now twenty-one, Lincoln spent a few months at the new farm before leaving the family for life on his own. He settled in New Salem, a town in Sangamon County about twenty miles northwest of Springfield, Illinois.

For the next six years, Lincoln labored in a number of jobs, gaining life-education as a postmaster, storekeeper, surveyor, and mill worker. He helped navigate a flatboat to New Orleans, and he also served in an Illinois militia during an Indian uprising known as the Black Hawk War. In 1834, Lincoln was elected to the first of four successive terms in the Illinois legislature. Throughout this period, he continued to look for ways to improve his skills as a writer and orator. In New Salem, he joined the New Salem Debating Society, a group of intellectuals led by Dr. John Allen, a graduate of Dartmouth College. Soon, the members of the society found themselves impressed with Lincoln's public speaking talents. Lincoln also became friendly with Mentor Graham, the town schoolmaster, who helped him improve his language skills.

While serving in the legislature, Lincoln met John Todd Stuart, a Springfield attorney and fellow lawmaker who encouraged Lincoln to study for a career as a lawyer. At the time, there were few law schools in the United States. Most young men trained for legal careers by finding jobs as clerks in established law offices. Usually working without pay, the apprentices were allowed to read their employer's law books while also accompanying the lawyer to court in exchange for completing office tasks such as copying pleadings, running errands, tending the fire, and sweeping floors at night. After a few years of such training, the employer normally sponsored the apprentice for admission to practice before the bar of the court.

Lincoln had no inclination to leave the legislature to engage in such an apprenticeship. Instead, during recesses in the legislature's sessions, Lincoln returned to New Salem, where he spent his idle hours studying law books he borrowed from Stuart.

"He was the most uncouth looking man I ever saw," recalled Henry E. Drummer, Stuart's law partner. "He seemed to have but little to say; seemed to feel timid, with a tinge of sadness visible in the countenance, but when he did talk all this disappeared for the time and he demonstrated that he was both strong and acute. He surprised us more and more at every visit."

In March 1834, the Sangamon County Circuit Court certified Abraham Lincoln as a person of good moral character—the first requirement needed to become a lawyer. Six months later, Lincoln took the bar examination in Sangamon County. The test proved to be much easier than he had expected, consisting mainly of a few general questions about the law. Lincoln celebrated his passing grade by treating his examiners to dinner. On September 9, 1836, he was issued a license to practice law. Two days later, Lincoln stepped into a Sangamon County courtroom representing a client who claimed to have been cheated out of four oxen. Lincoln lost the case. He was not discouraged, and soon formed a law practice in Springfield with William H. Herndon.

With his professional career moving forward, Lincoln also attended to his personal life. In 1842, Lincoln married Mary Todd, the daughter of a wealthy Kentucky family. The Lincolns would have four sons, although only one, Robert Todd Lincoln, reached adulthood.

Lincoln's political career eventually took him to Washington, where he served one term in the U.S. House of Representatives. He became an influential member of the Whig Party. Following the presidential election of 1852, the Whig Party collapsed, and Lincoln joined the newly formed Republican Party. In 1858, he campaigned for the U.S. Senate in Illinois, facing Democrat Stephen A. Douglas. It was during the Senate campaign that Lincoln voiced his feeling that civil war was inevitable unless all states either accepted or abolished slavery: "A house divided against itself cannot stand."

Jeremiah Day was president of Yale University and a professor of mathematics and natural philosophy. Day exerted an enormous influence on the development of Yale during the first half of the nineteenth century. His official association with the school lasted for sixty-nine years, from 1798 until his death in 1867. However, Day is best known for his textbooks. In 1814, he published *An Introduction to Algebra*. By 1850, sixty-eight editions of this slim volume had been published. No other American mathematical work has ever surpassed this record. Lincoln's marked-up copy has been preserved.

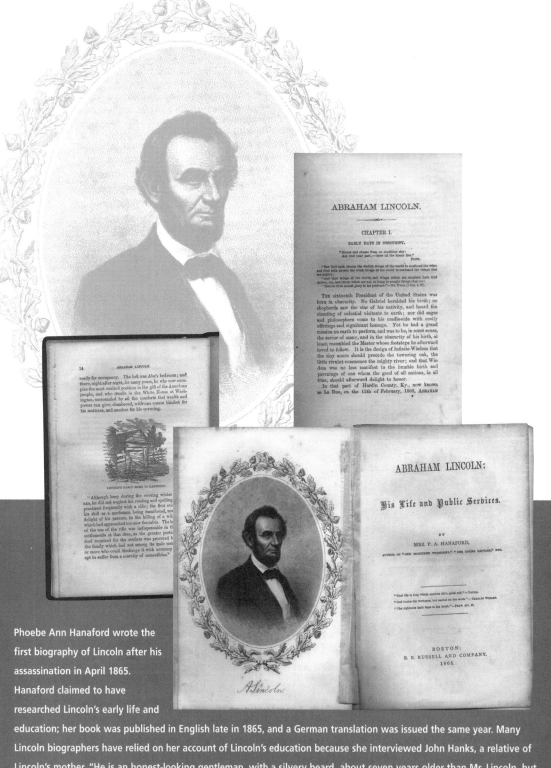

Phoebe Ann Hanaford wrote the first biography of Lincoln after his assassination in April 1865. Hanaford claimed to have researched Lincoln's early life and education; her book was published in English late in 1865, and a German translation was issued the same year. Many Lincoln biographers have relied on her account of Lincoln's education because she interviewed John Hanks, a relative of Lincoln's mother. "He is an honest-looking gentleman, with a silvery beard, about seven years older than Mr. Lincoln, but much more venerable in appearance," Hanaford wrote. "He can neither read nor write. He says that his cousin Dennis F. Hanks taught 'little Abe' his letters."

The campaign featured seven spirited debates with Douglas. Lincoln's easy backwoods manner soon found favor with the audiences who gathered around small-town stages to hear the two great orators. "I am not master of language," he told Douglas during one of the debates. "I have not a fine education; I am not capable of entering into a disquisition of dialectics, as I believe you call it."

Lincoln ultimately lost the election, but he had achieved national recognition in the Republican Party. In 1860, the party nominated him as its candidate for president. That fall, Lincoln defeated Douglas and two other candidates to win the presidency. When Lincoln took the oath of office in March 1861, Civil War seemed inevitable—the legislatures of seven southern states had already voted to secede from the Union. On April 12, 1861, Confederate troops fired on Fort Sumter in South Carolina. The Civil War had commenced.

The brutal and bloody struggle would last four years, finally ending in a victory by the Union forces. During the war, Lincoln used his gifts as an orator to calm the troubled nation. He hoped to convince the American people that the preservation of the Union and freedom for the slaves were worth the blood spilled on the battlefields. The Gettysburg Address (1863) and Lincoln's second inaugural address (1865) both contain some of the most important words ever spoken by an U.S. president. Lincoln concluded his second inaugural address, delivered just weeks before the Confederate surrender, with these words:

> With malice toward none, with charity for all, with firmness in the right, as God gives us to see the right, let us strive on to finish the work we are in, to bind up the nation's wounds, to care for him who shall have borne the battle, and for his widow and his orphan, to do all which may achieve and cherish a just and lasting peace among ourselves and with all nations.

On April 9, 1865, Robert E. Lee surrendered the Army of Northern Virginia to Union commander Ulysses S. Grant at Appomattox Court House, Virginia. Five days later, while attending a performance at Ford's Theater in Washington, D.C., Lincoln was shot by southern sympathizer John Wilkes Booth. Lincoln died the next morning, April 15, 1865, at the age of fifty-six. He was the first American president to be assassinated, and was mourned by the nation.

Years later, Lincoln's law partner William Herndon said that President Lincoln's lack of a formal education enhanced his ability to communicate with the American people.

"Had he gone to college...he would have lost...his strong individuality in his speech, his style, manner and method of utterance," Herndon said. "He would have been a rounded man in an artistic way...the flunky, smooth, sickly, weak artistic literature of the day, ocean wide and as shallow too, would, like the rising tide and reflux...have ground the rough corners off the man."

—Hal Marcovitz

Andrew Johnson
Chapter Seventeen

I f you know only one thing about Andrew Johnson, it's probably that he was
the first American president to face impeachment, in 1868. If you've made
a passing study of his career, you know he was the president who had the
unhappy distinction of succeeding the slain Abraham Lincoln in office. You
may have learned that he rather incompetently directed a spent and seething
nation through its first four years of Reconstruction—the hamstrung,
problematic chief of state who squabbled futilely but stubbornly against the
postwar congressional majority. By all accounts, many northerners and
southerners alike regarded him with mistrust.

There's much more to his story, of course. Few American presidents have
challenged historians like the seventeenth. Andrew Johnson was a walking study in
contradiction. For example:

- As a U.S. senator from Tennessee when the southern states
  seceded in 1860–61, he vigorously opposed secession and urged
  preservation of the Union. Yet he did not oppose the explosive
  issue of slavery (arguing that the Constitution condoned it), and
  was himself a slave owner.

- Aside from the secession question, he agreed with many southern
  political views at the time. Yet he openly loathed the wealthy
  plantation owners who largely directed those politics.

- He championed underdogs, especially working-class farmers and
  tradesmen. As a businessman, he often loaned money to poor people.
  Yet he voiced prejudices against impoverished blacks.

As for presidential firsts, Andrew Johnson is notable for more than one.
Did you know, for example, that he was the first and only president in history to
be elected to the U.S. Senate *after* leaving the White House? And did you know
he was the only president who never went to school? The exact nature of young

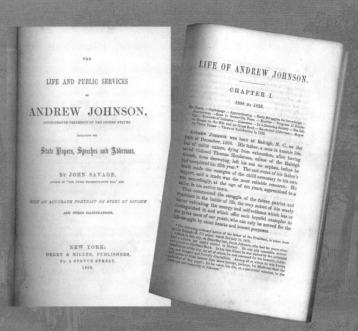

BIRTH-PLACE OF ANDREW JOHNSON, RALEIGH, N. C.

Andrew Johnson's father, "who for many years occupied a humble but useful station" as a bank porter and sexton in Raleigh, North Carolina, died in 1812 when Andrew was less than four years old. The Johnson family, which also included Andrew's mother and older brother, was reduced to abject poverty. At age seven, his mother apprenticed Andrew to a tailor. At one time, he was advertised as a "runaway." In 1826, Johnson, now eighteen, moved to Tennessee together with his mother and stepfather. He settled in Greeneville. In rating family economic backgrounds of the presidents, Andrew Johnson must rank as the poorest.

In 1860, John Savage, a Washington reporter and journalist, wrote biographical essays on those men prominently mentioned as potential presidential candidates. Four years later, he expanded the one on Andrew Johnson, then a vice-presidential nominee. And in 1865, after Lincoln's assassination, Savage published a five hundred-fifty-page biography of the new president. The few pages dealing with Johnson's childhood and education have been used by subsequent biographers as the principle source for this period of his life. Savage lists interviews for his information.

On November 8, 1818, Johnson's mother apprenticed her ten-year-old son Andrew to one James J. Selby to learn the tailor's trade. The contract called for him to remain with Selby until he was twenty-one. The responsibilities of the master and apprentice were defined in a form of contract called an "indenture." The actual Johnson indenture was not recorded until 1822 in the Wake County, North Carolina, Court Minutes. This document is reproduced above; Johnson's indenture is marked with a black arrow.

Apprenticeship was a system by which a youth was bound to a master workman for a period of years in exchange for maintenance and training in a craft. In the American colonies, both voluntary and court-mandated apprenticeship existed. With the latter, poor children were bound out to masters for support and trade training. In 1642, the laws of the Massachusetts Bay Colony required all masters to teach apprentices to read, as well as the principles of religion. This was the first compulsory education law in America.

Terms of an indenture were enforceable in the courts, and runaways could be compelled to return to their master to serve out their terms with additional periods added for the time they had been absent. In the mid-nineteenth century, indentures gradually ended because of machinery, technical schools, and labor unions that agitated against this system.

Andrew's education, in fact, is a bit of an enigma. It has forced historians to hedge their writing, cautious not to state details as certainties. One account says an aging neighbor taught Andrew the alphabet. An educated servant girl may have taught him to write. The accuracy of those and other reports is unproven.

Let's turn back in history almost two centuries and examine what is known about Andrew Johnson's upbringing, his mastery of a trade, and his "book learning."

He was born in a log cabin four days after Christmas in 1808. The Johnsons were "poor whites" in Raleigh, North Carolina. Jacob Johnson, his father, was a carpenter, janitor, bank porter, and common laborer with few possessions and no schooling—but a man of integrity and courage. Besides his assorted jobs, Jacob at different times served as Raleigh's constable, captain of its militia company, and sexton (the petty official who rang the town bell at appointed times).

When Andrew was just three years old and his brother William was eight, their father one winter day plunged into an icy millpond to pull out three drowning men whose boat had capsized. Everyone arrived safely on the bank, but Jacob was exhausted and fatally chilled. His health waned over a period of weeks and months, and he soon died. His wife and children were left in near poverty.

Raleigh, with about a thousand residents, had been designated North Carolina's capital. Although it did not impress veteran travelers, it was something of a commercial hub. It drew a regular influx of lawyers and state legislators, as well as merchants and farmers marketing their goods. Andrew, with his friends and cousins, wistfully watched these comings and goings from the distance of class separation. As "poor white trash," they could hardly aspire to become judges and statesmen, or even prominent merchants. So they were content to chase one another through Raleigh's dirt streets, play sandlot sports, and swim in the town millpond. Aging residents later would remember President Johnson as a "harum-scarum" youngster who more than once got into trouble by tearing his clothes in scrambling over fences.

Andrew's mother, the former Mary McDonough, was known in Raleigh as "Polly the Weaver." She earned meager wages by spinning and weaving cloth. She also was a laundress who washed the household linen of North Carolina's supreme court judges. That may seem an ignoble livelihood for the mother of a future president, but it helped put food on the family table, which was all that mattered. Even after she remarried a few years later, the family was dismally poor. Her new husband, by one account, was "a worthless ne'er-do-well."

No public schools existed in Raleigh in those times, and the family could spare no money for a paid, traveling tutor. For youngsters of Andrew's lowly class, learning a skill was far more necessary than learning words and numbers. It mattered much less that he could read a book or compose a letter than that he could earn a living as a tradesman.

Nevertheless, Andrew started to acquire the rudiments of an education— and a passion for learning more. At a Raleigh tailor shop, owner James Selby brought in educated citizens to read to his workers. In this era before public schooling, tradesmen like Selby were required to provide their apprentices with the rudiments of an education. The nature of the occupation—stitching and cutting cloth—allowed tailor apprentices to listen while they worked. The readers would bring in every sort of available publication, from month-old newspapers to poetry to reports from Congress. Andrew often dropped by Selby's shop to listen to the readings and the political discussions among the men who gathered there. Meanwhile, he picked up a working understanding of the tailor's craft.

Facing few choices for survival, Mary apprenticed both William and Andrew to Selby. They became indentured servants—"bound boys," which meant they could not take a job elsewhere without Selby's permission (and permission inevitably would carry a formidable price tag). Apprentices were, in a sense, child slaves. In most cases, they were bound to serve throughout their teen years, working twelve hours a day. Once they became proficient at their trade—which might take only a few months—their master enjoyed the benefit of practically free skilled labor.

To Raleigh's political upper class, the Johnson boys and their kind were only slightly more acceptable socially than African-American slaves. They were held in public contempt and sometimes mistreated. For the rest of his life, Andrew would harbor resentment toward the rich. At the same time, he was raised to believe whites, even those who were dirt poor like his own family, were superior to blacks.

When he went to work for Selby, Andrew was not quite ten years old. By contract, he was to serve as apprentice until age twenty-one. His "bondage" would last only a few years, though. In June 1824, he, William, and one or two friends fled Raleigh. According to one speculation, this resulted from a nighttime escapade in which the boys tossed wood chips against the window of a Raleigh home, trying to get the attention of the teenage girls inside. Unhappily for them, they attracted the girls' mother, who threatened to call down the law. The boys hardly paused until they'd reached the town of Carthage, fifty miles away.

With a ten dollar price on his head as a runaway apprentice, Andrew wandered to distant towns in the two Carolinas and Tennessee, earning a little money by tailoring. By this time, he apparently was literate. A man who got to know him in Laurens, South Carolina, where the teen-ager worked in a tailor shop for almost two years, later would report that Andrew frequently spent his free time reading.

The boy also found time for romance. He was heartbroken when, after an extended courtship, a Laurens girl refused to marry him. The young woman's mother reportedly would not accept a poor tailor lad for a son-in-law. It was a torturous blow that undoubtedly intensified young Andrew's loathing for the upper classes.

At one point during these years of wandering, he returned to Raleigh and tried unsuccessfully to reconcile with Selby, his old master. As long as he remained in North Carolina, Andrew would live in legal bondage unless he and Selby could come to terms. However, the elder tradesman's demand for payment was beyond Andrew's means.

In 1826, Andrew and his parents, with everything they owned stowed in a small horse cart, left Raleigh for the western frontier. Their passage through the Blue Ridge Mountains was an adventure marked by close encounters with wild animals. They arrived in the eastern Tennessee town of Greeneville, which Andrew found to his liking. After a brief exploration of other frontier communities, he returned to Greeneville and opened his own tailor shop. Still in his teens, with little education and an upbringing of poverty, he soon was to taste relative success as a businessman. Happily for him, Greeneville's only other tailor retired soon after he arrived.

Although he'd never attended school, Andrew had learned the rudiments of reading and writing while serving his apprenticeship in Raleigh, helped along by shop foreman James Litchford. He had shown a zeal for education and taken advantage of the instruction of a local man, Dr. William Hill, who read historic speeches to laborers from *The Columbian Orator* (also called the *American Speaker*). Not only had Andrew learned to read; this style of learning had instilled in him a passion for politics and public speaking.

Englishmen William Pitt and Charles James Fox were among his earliest statesmen heroes. The two had spoken boldly before Parliament on behalf of the American colonists before and during the Revolution. Fox, only in his twenties when the war began, warned his colleagues that the Americans possessed "a spirit which is unconquerable." In a speech reprinted in the *Orator*, Fox had pointed out the difficulties of winning a war against such passionate foes on the other side of the Atlantic. "[A]s long as there is a man in America, a being formed such as we are, you will have him present himself against you in the field."

Pitt, much older and in failing health, died two years after the Revolution began. In the decade leading up to the war, he argued forcefully for Great Britain to heed the colonists' complaints. "The Americans have been wronged," he stated in 1766, in a speech condemning the Stamp Act. "They have been driven to madness by injustice." In 1775, with fighting imminent, he told the British lords pointblank: "We shall be forced, ultimately, to retract; let us retract while we *can*, not when we *must*." And in 1777, the year before he died, Pitt lamented to Parliament, "If you conquer [the Americans], what then? You cannot make them respect you; you cannot make them wear your cloth. You will plant an invincible hatred in their breasts against you." All of these speeches were included in the *Columbian Orator*.

Young Andrew must have been enthralled by the maverick noblemen's historic words. To imagine them standing before the most powerful legislative body in the world, stating so eloquently their heartfelt opinions under the glares and scowls of angry opponents in such a hallowed chamber…what could be more noble? What could be more glorious?

At age eighteen, Andrew Johnson married sixteen-year-old Eliza McCardle of Greeneville. Better educated than he, she managed to improve his reading and writing skills somewhat—although his spelling hardly improved. (Like many people of his day, Johnson was an atrocious speller. Once, when his secretary pointed out that he'd misspelled his own name, he retorted, "It is a man of small imagination who cannot spell his name more than one way.") In the words of biographer Hans L. Trefousse, "Reading every book he could find, generally works on politics and oratory, he acquired a knowledge of some of the famous legends of antiquity, stories he tended to use over and over again."

Johnson and a Greeneville friend, Blackston McDannel, shared an interest in political affairs of the frontier. Since they often disagreed, they amicably staged public debates. They eventually organized a local debating society—a form of public entertainment quite common in towns of the day. Johnson also became an avid member of Greeneville's two college debating societies and developed an impressive public speaking talent. He joined the Polemic Society, the debating club at Greeneville College, and later began to walk four miles each way to attend Friday night gatherings of the Philomathean Literary Society at Tusculum Academy. On Saturday nights, the Tusculum students would flock to Johnson's tailor shop to continue the previous night's debates. According to historian George Fort Milton, "He borrowed continually from the private libraries of Greenville, few in number and restricted in quality, and made it a habit to seek out the heart of every person's knowledge by eager questioning and debate."

He didn't pursue only his own education, but the education of those he employed at his shop. Johnson reportedly paid a schoolboy fifty cents a day—an exceptional fee in those times—to come to his humble workplace and read aloud to himself and his laborers. These frontier tailors, wrote Milton, listened to "Eliot's debates, Jefferson's messages, and over and over again the Constitution of the United States."

Johnson's interest in politics was inspired largely by the success of Andrew Jackson, another lowly Carolina settler boy who had become a national military hero and in 1828 would be elected president. Greeneville citizens, most of them Jacksonians, congregated regularly at Johnson's tailor shop to discuss politics and current events. They were impressed when Johnson spoke. When he was only twenty, they elected him to a post as town alderman (councilman). In coming years, he became Greeneville's mayor, then a state legislator and, at thirty-four, a United States congressman. Johnson polished his speaking skills as his political career progressed. While his grammar was not the best, he spoke clearly, and the points he made were easy for his constituents to understand.

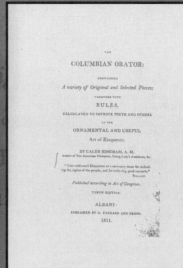

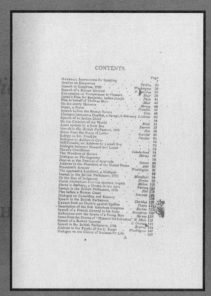

In his 1865 biography of Andrew Johnson, John Savage recounts that public-spirited citizens, who opposed the indenture system, came to Selby's tailor shop to read to the apprenticed young men. Johnson, we are told, listened attentively because he was determined to obtain an education. Selections from *The Columbian Orator* (1797) were read and reread. The book contained speeches of famous statesmen, both English and American, and Johnson memorized them. One of the readers was so impressed that he gave the book to Johnson. Apparently, Johnson kept this volume to the end of his life.

Caleb Bingham was a pioneer writer of textbooks. He wrote the second English grammar book published in the United States, a year after Noah Webster's grammar book was published. In 1797, Bingham published *The Columbian Orator*. Over fourteen years, the *Orator* went through eleven editions. The selections are secular and religious. Many selections are strongly patriotic, expressing enthusiasm for the young American republic. Until the appearance of such compilations, the Bible and the psalm book had been the principle school reading books.

Above are selections from *The Columbian Orator*, 1811 facsimile edition.

In 1853, Johnson ran successfully for governor of Tennessee. Four years later, he won a seat in the United States Senate. In the turbulent election year of 1860, his Tennessee delegation nominated him for president at the Democratic National Convention. The Democratic Party, hopelessly divided in the pending national crisis, chose Stephen A. Douglas, while southern Democrats put forth U.S. Vice President John C. Breckinridge as a sectional candidate. Johnson reluctantly supported Breckinridge, but urged the party to reunite.

Lincoln easily won the momentous election. As the southern states began to secede, Johnson was appalled. To his dismay, Tennessee joined the Confederacy. When it did, Johnson became the only U.S. senator from the South to declare loyalty to the Union. Lincoln responded by appointing him military governor of Tennessee in 1862. Two years later, Lincoln won reelection with Johnson as his running mate on the Republican-Union Party ticket.

Lincoln hoped not only to win the war, but also to reunite the divided country. Johnson's role in the administration, however, angered staunch antislavery leaders. Before the Civil War, when Johnson had become a successful businessman, he had acquired several slaves (possibly as many as ten) as household servants. He apparently had treated them kindly and provided for all their physical needs. During the war, as Tennessee's military governor, he had come to consider slavery wrong and had proclaimed freedom for all slaves in the state. Nonetheless, he never accepted blacks as the equals of whites. (Later, as president, he would oppose giving blacks the right to vote and oppose federal aid to freed slaves.) Northern politicians generally regarded him with suspicion, if not open contempt.

When Lincoln was assassinated in April 1865, Johnson became president and took immediate steps to restore the southern states to the Union. He offered amnesty to most southerners and pressed for the rebel states to be given renewed representation in Congress. Those issues, combined with the president's disinterest in assuring the rights and welfare of former slaves, alienated northern political leaders. His opponents, led by the so-called Radical Republicans, gained momentum in the 1866 congressional elections. The new Congress passed a series of measures to restrict the president's power during Reconstruction. Ultimately, Congress impeached him, but the Senate failed by one vote to actually remove him from office. He had no chance in the 1868 presidential race; his own party rejected him at its convention.

Andrew Johnson remained a man who defied stereotypes. He also demonstrated to the very end his ability to rise repeatedly from defeat and tragedy. He became so sick in the spring of 1869, the year after leaving the presidency, that newspapers mistakenly proclaimed him dead. One of his sons died shortly afterward. He ran for U.S. Senate later that year and lost. In 1872, he ran for Congress and lost. The Panic of 1873, which cost him much of his personal wealth, was followed by a bout with cholera that almost killed him.

From all of these troubles, he came back. In January 1875, he was elected by the Tennessee legislature to a U.S. Senate seat. He braced himself, expecting to be greeted with animosity in Washington. Remarkably, he found his desk in the Senate chamber covered with flowers and was applauded heartily as he took his seat. Some of the senators who had voted to remove him from office in 1868 now came forward to shake his hand.

Finally absolved, he died of a series of strokes only a few months later. By his instructions to survivors, he was wrapped in an American flag and a copy of the U.S. Constitution was placed beneath his head in the coffin. He was buried near Greeneville, Tennessee.

All his life, Andrew Johnson never was ashamed of his humble background. He believed the way he had acquired what education he had—basically on his own, without being nurtured by teachers—was the only way an individual truly could learn. He likewise was proud of his tailor's trade.

Interestingly, the "uneducated president" actively promoted education for common people. He made sure his own children obtained training beyond the basic school level. As Tennessee's governor in 1853, he proposed a special tax to fund school improvements. Six weeks after he became president, he stressed to a group of children visiting the White House that they ultimately were responsible for their own education. They could not receive an education simply by attending school, he said. Parents and teachers could help them only to a limited degree. Unless they sought knowledge for themselves, he told the young people, they would never truly become educated.

—Daniel E. Harmon

Ulysses S. Grant

Chapter Eighteen

In the 1830s, the Ohio Valley was on the frontier and transportation was uncomfortable and often perilous. Farmers, lawyers, doctors, and rural families dreaded the prospect of long-distance travel. Dirt roads were uneven. Ominous, shaded curves ahead might conceal robbers. Stream crossings could be risky after storms, when currents were quick and water depths unpredictable. Broken-down and wrecked wagons, crimes, injuries, and violent deaths were not uncommon.

Folks bound to or from the village of Georgetown, a small county seat in southwestern Ohio, often found themselves bundled aboard a horse-drawn wagon or carriage driven by a young boy—not even a teenager—named Hiram. Even though travelers did not know Hiram, they were advised to trust him, for he would get them to their destinations. And he invariably did. Passengers at journey's end would hop down, stiff and sore, but thankful for the skill of their driver.

Hiram is better remembered by the name Ulysses—the name by which he was known during his adult career as a Civil War general, and later as the eighteenth president of the United States.

As a youngster, Ulysses had little interest in becoming a military leader. He had ample inspiration for this career in his lineage, though. One of his grandfathers was said to have fought in the American Revolution at Bunker Hill (although no official records have been found to confirm the claim). Earlier forebears, one of them a militia commander, were killed in action during the French and Indian War (1754–63).

The oldest of six children, Ulysses was born in a tiny wooden house beside the Ohio River in Point Pleasant, Ohio, on April 27, 1822. His father, Jesse Grant, was a tanner, or leather-maker. Jesse Grant could read and write, but was not well educated. Hiram's mother, Hannah Simpson Grant, also was literate. She had grown up on a farm. They named their first child Hiram Ulysses Grant. As the boy grew older, he came to dislike his initials—H.U.G. Eventually, when a congressman endorsed Hiram for admission to West Point, the name incorrectly was entered in the records as "Ulysses Simpson Grant." Unable to persuade the West Point adjutant to correct the mistake, Ulysses accepted this as his name.

In the winter of 1838–39, Jesse Grant applied for, and received, an appointment for his son to the United States Military Academy at West Point, New York. This aroused no enthusiasm in the sixteen-year old. At West Point, young Grant was told that his congressman, who had appointed him, had reported his name as Ulysses Simpson Grant. Failing to obtain a correction from the authorities and also fearing that his actual initials "H.U.G." (Hiram Ulysses Grant) would make him an object of ridicule, he accepted the name bestowed upon him.

No high points mark Grant's four years at West Point. He finished twenty-first among the thirty-nine men who made up the graduating class of 1843. Academically only his work in mathematics was above average. In horsemanship, Grant had no peer among his fellow cadets, but in other respects he was a quiet and unassuming student. "Sam" Grant sought neither honors nor popularity.

He had no intention of remaining in the army. "If I could have escaped West Point without bringing myself into disgrace at home," the future war hero wrote in his *Memoirs*, "I would have done so."

Grant began his studies at West Point six years after Colonel Sylvanus Thayer resigned as superintendent of the academy after sixteen years of service. Thayer was truly the "father of the Military Academy." The academy, hardly more than a secondary school when Thayer took charge, claimed before he left a number of distinguished professors as instructors. Thayer organized the cadets into companies officered by members of their own body. He appointed an army officer as Commandant of Cadets, responsible for their military instruction and soldiery discipline. Thayer issued a strict set of regulations governing every phase of cadet life. The reforms that Thayer instituted and the many customs that he initiated still influence his successors.

The United States Military Academy at West Point, New York, was established by Act of Congress in 1802. The primary purpose of the academy is to instruct future officers of the U.S. Army. Graduates have served in every American war since the War of 1812.

In 1827, George Catlin (1796–1872) visited West Point. Catlin is noted for his many illustrations of Native Americans. His numerous paintings and drawings constitute an invaluable record of their culture. However, in 1827, prior to his travels among the Native American tribes, Catlin was commissioned to paint portraits of New York's governor, DeWitt Clinton, and members of the New York state legislature. At Clinton's invitation, Catlin journeyed with the governor from Albany for a day's visit to West Point. Here, Catlin completed drawings for two engravings of West Point scenes. These engravings are a wonderful visual history of the military academy at that time.

Pictured are "Artillery Drill on the Plain" (left), which shows the North and South barracks and the academic building (the institution's original structures) in the rear of the engraving, and "Parade Grounds—West Point."

Seth Eastman (1808–1875), a graduate of West Point, pursued a successful career with the United States Army, though he is best known today as a painter. His eastern landscape paintings are considered the predecessor of the Hudson River Valley landscape artists. This is a reproduction of Eastman's "View of the Hudson River Valley With a View of the Military Academy," painted in 1834.

Point Pleasant was only a village, planted some twenty-five miles upriver from Cincinnati. A year later, the family moved to Georgetown, Ohio, about twenty miles away. They built a brick house, and it was here that Ulysses began his formal education in a one-room schoolhouse typical of the times.

Early in his life, Ulysses decided that he preferred farm work to tanning. He planted crops, chopped firewood, and performed other chores. When called upon, he helped his father tan hides into leather, but he hated the sight of bloody animal skins. Jesse Grant was prosperous by frontier standards—he even served a term as Georgetown's mayor—but the tannery was a crude, smelly place, and Ulysses never got used to it. The sight of blood sickened him; throughout his life, he couldn't bear the sight of rare-cooked steak. He made it clear to his father that he had no intention of inheriting the tannery business.

But horses interested him enormously. He grew up around them. Ulysses had his first horseback ride before he was two, was driving wagon teams at eight, bought and trained his own colt at nine, and was plowing fields at eleven. By that time, he was providing his transport service, taking people and products via horse-drawn wagon between Georgetown and destinations many miles away. His wagon excursions served to instill in Ulysses a sense of boldness. They also began to reveal to the curious youngster a bit of the world outside his village, and made him long to see more. Meanwhile, he was earning a reputation as a trainer of wild horses. Ulysses was not very big—he would grow to only five feet seven inches tall—but he was powerful, even as a youngster. Physical strength was only a secondary asset in his mastery of animals. Most importantly, he seemed to understand them and to gain their confidence and respect.

Jesse Grant was keenly interested in politics and often expressed his views in the county newspaper. He bragged of the talents and potential of his son, to the boy's embarrassment. Otherwise, the Grants apparently were not inclined to show their feelings, either in public or private. Historians have read much into the president's comment that he never saw his mother cry. As a young cadet at West Point, Ulysses was away from home for two years before he earned his first leave. A stilted "How are you?" reportedly was as intimate a greeting as he got—or expected—when he finally visited his family.

When he was five, Ulysses was enrolled in Georgetown's small "subscription school," an enterprise paid for directly by those village parents who wanted their children to be educated. School was in session thirteen weeks in winter (older children were expected to work at home during warmer seasons). The fee per child for the school season was $1.50 to $2, or a supply of wheat, corn, and/or tobacco worth that amount. Alongside others much older (some of his classmates were teenagers), Ulysses was taught the literal basics: reading, writing, and arithmetic. He learned his numbers easily, and by age six he reportedly could read adult-level books. His father, who amassed a significant library of thirty or forty volumes, encouraged his son's reading. It is apparent that from an early age, the oldest child in the family was expected to acquire an advanced education that would elevate him above the tanner's lowly social status.

He was a quiet, modest, unexcitable boy, friendly but not sociable. A schoolmate recalled many years later that "when he said anything, he always said it short." He showed no leadership instincts but simply joined in the activities of other Georgetown boys. As a boy Ulysses was mild-mannered and sensitive. He reportedly didn't swear or tell off-color jokes. By his own recollection, he never did anything to provoke significant punishment by his parents, or even a severe tongue-lashing.

He was amazed by the harsh discipline he witnessed at school. Schoolmasters always were vigilant to correct any breach of discipline, real or perceived. "Switches were brought in bundles from a beech wood near the schoolhouse, by the boys for whose benefit they were intended," he later recalled. "Often a whole bundle would be used up in a single day."

In 1836–37, Ulysses' father sent him to a "seminary" across the river in Maysville, Kentucky, to further his education. The fourteen-year-old was bored, for he already had learned most of the lessons taught there. One new opportunity captured his interest, though: the debating society. Joining it, the quiet Ulysses began to develop some of the public speaking skills that would become obligatory when he became a national political figure. Later, he attended Presbyterian Academy in Ripley, Ohio.

Again, he found that he already knew most of what the instructors had to teach.

His father wanted Ulysses to attend West Point—perhaps in part because the government paid the expenses. In 1839, when the boy was seventeen, the official appointment came through their congressman, much to Jesse Grant's delight and his son's disgust. While West Point was a military school, most of its students at that time expected to pursue civilian professions. The academy was noted especially for training civil engineers. During the early nineteenth century, most graduates ultimately established careers outside the military after completing their obligations as Army officers (at the time Grant attended West Point, this obligation was eight years of military service). The young man did not even know his father had requested the appointment. Among other misgivings, Ulysses doubted he could live up to the requirements of a West Point cadet. He later recalled that he "had not the faintest idea of staying in the army even if I should be graduated, which I did not expect." His career ambition was to farm, or perhaps become a river trader. He was not opposed to attending college, but he had no desire to attend a military academy.

Glumly, he looked to the bright side. At least he would get to see some of the large eastern cities. Philadelphia and New York especially interested him. As for cadet life, he expected to find it unpleasant. Once enrolled, this anticipation was confirmed. His letters from the academy to relatives were dourly comic. "My pants sit as tight to my skin as bark to a tree," he wrote to R. McKinstry Griffith, a cousin, "and if I don't walk military, that is if I bend over quickly or run, they are apt to crack with a report as loud as a pistol" Yet, he didn't completely detest the academy. West Point was "decidedly the most beautiful place that I have ever seen," he wrote Griffith, praising the nearby Hudson River with "its bosom studded with hundreds of snow white sails." During his first year, he came to the conclusion that there was "much to dislike but more to like. I mean to study hard and stay if possible."

Most of the other cadets of his year were significantly older. Some already had attended college before receiving their academy appointments. Actually, the Ohio country boy barely met the physical requirements for entry to West Point. Cadets had to be at least five feet tall; Ulysses was five feet one inch tall at the time. He weighed one hundred and seventeen pounds. By graduation four years later, he would grow six inches but remain at practically the same weight.

Amused by his initials "U.S.," classmates at West Point jovially called him Uncle Sam Grant. Fellow cadets commonly referred to him as Sam (which probably irked him, because one of his younger brothers was named Samuel Simpson Grant). Ulysses didn't care much for nicknames. He preferred his original name, Hiram.

Cadets were housed in tiny, unheated rooms. In the dead of winter, they had to fetch water from outdoor wells. Barracks steps were slick with ice after water sloshed from hurriedly carried buckets and froze. Drummed out of bed at five A.M., the students lived each day according to a strict regimen. Unhappily for Ulysses, he never understood music—and as a result was reportedly one of the most pathetic marchers ever to fall in line at the academy.

West Pointers were taught an interesting curriculum grouped into eight departments: math, engineering, philosophy, history/ethics, science, drawing, tactics, and French. The sciences included chemistry, geology, and mineralogy. "Ethics" was a confusingly named course that included writing, grammar, speaking, and geography. French was especially important in U.S. colleges during the nineteenth century, when "foreign relations" primarily meant relations with England and France.

Ulysses did well in math—which, as it happened, was the most important subject at West Point. He also excelled at drawing. Cadets were required to learn drawing skills in the event they ever would need to sketch accurate battle maps in the field. Robert Walter Weir, the West Point drawing instructor, was a painter of renown. Surviving works suggest Ulysses had significant talent as an artist, but apparently he didn't pursue it seriously as an adult.

By contrast, he made poor showings in English, French, sciences, and battle tactics. In his memoirs, he recalled that he "rarely read over a lesson the second time." However, he was interested in literature and was elected president of The Dialectic, the

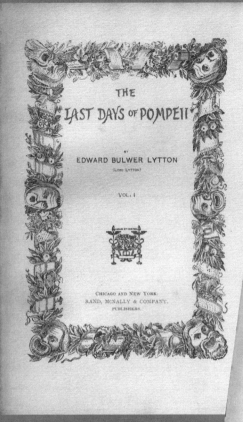

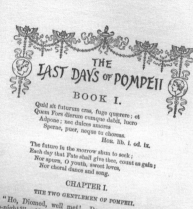

Grant found life at West Point to be a bore. In his memoirs, Grant wrote that he devoted more time to reading popular novels while at the academy than he did to studying his textbooks: "I read all of the works of Bulwer's then published, Cooper's, Marryat's, Scott's, Washington Irving's works, Lever's and many others that I do not now remember." These six were the most popular fiction writers in the English language during the 1830s and 1840s.

Frederick Marryat (1792–1848), an English naval officer and novelist, used his varied experiences at sea in a series of adventure novels published between 1830 and 1840. Walter Scott (1771–1832) ranks among the great historical novelists. Scott's *Ivanhoe*, set in twelfth-century England, is his most popular book. Grant read *Ivanhoe*, as well as Scott's *Quentin Durwood*, set in fifteenth-century France, and *The Talesman*, which deals with Palestine during the Crusades. James Fenimore Cooper (1789–1851) is considered America's first major novelist, and his books were bestsellers in their day. Grant read Cooper's frontier adventure stories *The Last of the Mohicans*, *The Pathfinder*, and *The Deerslayer*. Washington Irving (1783–1859) is known for such short stories as "The Legend of Sleepy Hollow" and "Rip Van Winkle." Irish novelist Charles James Lever (1806–1872) set his books in post-Napoleonic Europe. Grant read Lever's 1841 novel *Charles O'Malley*.

Perhaps the runaway fiction best seller of the nineteenth century was Edward Bulwer-Lytton's *The Last Days of Pompeii*. Published in 1834, the book went through many printings. Grant read the three-volume edition. The convoluted plot revolves around the constant intrigues of the characters that include romance, magic love-potions, betrayals, and heroism. In the background is the story of the Vesuvius volcano, which exploded in A.D. 79, leaving Pompeii buried under ash and rock. Illustrated here is the ornate title and opening page from the 1899 edition, the first to make use of glossy photographs.

West Point literary club. While he spent only as much time as necessary with his textbooks, he became an avid reader of what scholars call "light fiction." He later reminisced: "There is a fine library connected with the Academy from which cadets can get books to read in their quarters. I devoted more time to these than to books relating to the course of studies. Much of the time, I am sorry to say, was devoted to novels. . . . I read all of the works of Bulwer's then published, Cooper's, Marryat's, Scott's, Washington Irving's works, Lever's, and many others that I do not now remember"

Historians have observed one striking deficiency at the academy. Before the Civil War, West Point cadets learned little of military strategy, which might be called "the science of war." That is, they were educated in the tactics of fighting, but not in the techniques of maneuvering large armies into strong positions before and during battle. What strategy they learned was based on the writings of a Frenchman, Baron Henri Jomini, who had analyzed the European campaigns of Napoleon Bonaparte. Jomini's teachings were brilliant in their day, but by the mid-nineteenth century the methods of warfare had changed dramatically. By the time of the American Civil War, infantrymen would carry rifles that could be loaded more rapidly and fired accurately over far greater distances than Napoleonic muzzleloaders. That would make bayonet fighting at close quarters—the savage way in which many previous battles had been won—almost obsolete. Furthermore, Jomini had formulated army strategy during an era before railroads made it possible to transfer large forces easily and telegraph lines made communications among commanders quicker and more reliable.

Ulysses never fully embraced Jomini's military strategy (he later remarked that he never even read Jomini's writings). As events would prove, this apparent neglect as a student would work in his favor. Generals on both sides of the Civil War mapped strategy following Jomini's teachings. Midway through the great conflict, Grant and a few other Union generals began to understand that the accepted theories weren't working. Willing to disregard the old master's teachings, they proceeded to devise new strategies—and win the war.

Grant disliked the discipline of cadet life. As biographer Geoffrey Perret wrote, "A cadet could be a mathematical wizard, but if he forgot to button his coat properly or did not manage to tie his shoelaces to the satisfaction of some martinet, the demerits he received would count for as much as his genius." Ulysses sometimes was late for class, skipped chapel, and was a careless dresser. Although it was forbidden, he at least once visited a town pub.

Grant showed little interest in being a leader. After being promoted to sergeant in his third cadet year, he lost the stripes because of demerits and returned to the ranks. West Point drillmasters, commented biographer Lloyd Lewis, concluded that Grant was "a born private." Likewise, he was disinterested in dash and social graces. He did not dance and made few attempts to impress young ladies. One of his fellow cadets later would comment on Grant's "total absence of elegance."

In short, Grant tolerated West Point, yearning for the climax of this period of his life. One of his professors would recall that the young man "always showed himself a clear thinker and a steady worker." But many years later, in a moment of seething malcontent while serving as president of the United States, Grant confided that he looked forward to leaving public office as "the happiest day of my life, except possibly the day I left West Point." He graduated in 1843, ranked in the middle of his class academically. He was conspicuously low in conduct. In horsemanship, however, Grant was unrivaled. His crowning moment occurred during graduation week. The academy's riding master set the jumping bar at a formidable height above six feet and called out Cadet Grant from the line of mounted graduates on parade. Saddled atop a magnificent, sprightly chestnut named York—a mount no other cadet had fully mastered—Grant proceeded to the far end of the riding hall, turned, and spurred the animal forward. At the climax of a thundering, quickening gallop, York cleared the bar gracefully. It would be a quarter century before Grant's jump record was bested at West Point.

Other cadets during Grant's tenure included some who would become famous on both sides of the Civil War twenty years later. They included William T. Sherman, Thomas "Stonewall" Jackson, George B. McClellan, William S. Rosecrans, George E. Pickett, and A.P. Hill. One of his friends was a large, strapping cadet from Georgia, James Longstreet. In time, the two would become opposing army commanders.

With the formality of West Point behind him, Grant decided he rather liked the notion of soldiering. He hoped to serve his tour of duty as a cavalry officer. To his disappointment, he instead was assigned as a second lieutenant of infantry. After spending the summer of 1843 at home on furlough, recovering from a lung ailment, the young officer was sent to an Army post near St. Louis, Missouri. While stationed there, he met a young woman named Julia Dent. In time, they would be married. First, though, he got a taste of warfare. He served with distinction in the Mexican War—a conflict he personally opposed—from 1846 to 1848, and was made a captain in the Army in 1853. At that level, his career abruptly halted. In 1854, while assigned to a remote Army post in the Pacific Northwest, he was discovered drunk in public and was forced to resign his commission. Excessive drinking was to become a lifelong vice.

After failing as a farmer, the ex-captain found himself relegated to a clerk's job in his father's Galena, Illinois, leather shop when the Civil War began in April 1861. Ulysses was given a new Army command and quickly rose to the rank of brigadier general. After successes in important midwestern campaigns, President Abraham Lincoln appointed him overall commander of the Union armies.

With the surrender of Confederate General Robert E. Lee in April 1865, Ulysses S. Grant became America's foremost war hero. At the 1868 Republican national convention, he was the overwhelming choice as the presidential candidate. He defeated Democrat Horatio Seymour and went on to serve two terms in the White House. "The office," he remarked in his first inaugural address, "has come to me unsought." When Ulysses entered the White House, the process of restoring the Union after the catastrophic Civil War was already well underway.

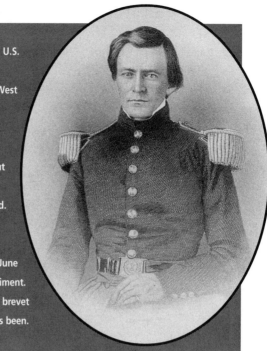

An engraving of Brevet Second Lieutenant U.S. Grant, Fourth U.S. Infantry, made circa 1845.

Upon graduation in June 1843 Grant—the best rider at West Point—requested a commission in the cavalry. There was no vacancy, so Grant was assigned to the Fourth Infantry. After serving two years in Missouri and Louisiana, in September 1845 Grant was assigned to General Zachary Taylor's small but efficient army at Corpus Christi, Texas. Later it moved to the Rio Grande River, where a conflict with the Mexicans occurred.

Grant was never in sympathy with the Mexican War. Nevertheless, he took part actively in all of General Taylor's battles except the last, Buena Vista (1847). At Monterey (May/June 1846), Grant was the only mounted officer in charge of his regiment. Grant emerged from the Mexican War as a first lieutenant and brevet captain, but no less averse to a military life than he had always been.

The pressing issue confronting his administration was the national economy.

He is remembered as largely a hands-off president. As a military commander, he had relied on his trusted subordinates to perform their duties with as little oversight as possible. As president, he assumed he could use the same approach. He expected Congress to establish public policies and his cabinet heads to see that they were carried out. He intended to function more as the nation's referee than as its leader. As one political observer surmised, the president had "no policy of his own," expecting his Republican Party to establish policy. The party, however, was wrenched by infighting between old-line leaders and reformers. Seeking to appease both sides, Ulysses pleased few political leaders of the day. When he did attempt to lend more clear direction during his second term in office, he often was ineffective. His administration was marred by numerous scandals. Grant is credited with exhibiting a steady resolve, however, and with making correct decisions on important issues in the face of withering political opposition. For the most part, however, historians have decided Grant was far more effective as a military commander than as president.

Some think of Ulysses S. Grant as a president with a mediocre mentality and an indifferent attitude toward education. To an extent, that perception stemmed from his own modest memoirs, in which he humorously characterized himself as a disinterested, restless student. "I was not studious in habit," he wrote of his West Point days, "and probably did not make progress enough to compensate for the outlay for board and nutrition." In reality, he arguably was one of the brightest Americans to rise from a frontier village upbringing and make his mark. Stricken with throat cancer, Grant died in 1885 at Mount McGregor, New York.

—Daniel E. Harmon

Rutherford B. Hayes
Chapter Nineteen

As a youngster, Rutherford B. "Rud" Hayes acquired his coltish sense of humor from his sister, Fanny, a tomboy who led him on childhood adventures into the woods near their Ohio home. Fanny taught her little brother some of his first lessons and knew how to draw the best out of Rud by playfully toying with his temperament. For example, during his first year at Kenyon College in Ohio, when Rud was uncharacteristically stricken by homesickness and melancholy, Fanny lifted his spirits by lampooning a recent letter Rud had received from their mother. Sophia Hayes complained in the letter that Fanny's approaching marriage would, of course, mean that she would soon leave "her Mother's house." In a letter to Rud intended to lift his spirits, Fanny joked about the "base ingratitude of a daughter leaving her Mother's house, a proper good brick one too."

Rud cheered up and stuck out his freshman year. His first year at Kenyon would be part of an educational experience that would lead young Rutherford B. Hayes to Harvard Law School; then to careers in law, the military, and politics; finally culminating in his election to the presidency of the United States. In 1875, a year before he defeated Samuel Tilden for president, Hayes addressed the prospect of his national candidacy in his diary. "How wild!" wrote Hayes, still prone to giddy outbursts well into his fifties. "What a queer lot we are becoming!"

It could be considered a miracle that Rutherford Birchard Hayes learned to laugh at all. Hayes's mother and father left New England in 1817 in search of a happy future. The couple owned a store in Dummerston, Vermont, but following the War of 1812 business slacked off and the Hayeses decided to look for opportunity elsewhere. They found it in the village of Delaware, Ohio, just north of Columbus, where they bought a one hundred and twenty-five acre farm.

Little but heartache awaited the family in Ohio. The first child of Sophia and the senior Rutherford Hayes was stillborn; their daughter Sarah would die of a childhood illness, and a son, Lorenzo, drowned when he fell through the ice while skating on a frozen lake. Finally, young Rud Hayes would never know his father.

In 1837, when Rutherford B. Hayes was fifteen, he entered Isaac Webb's preparatory school in Middletown, Connecticut. Webb, a former Yale tutor, accepted twenty "diligent boys of good character" into his school, where "thorough study, faithful instruction, and steady discipline" prevailed. School was in session from nine to noon, one to four, and six to nine. Hayes wrote to his family, "I study only nine hours and I learn the fastest I ever did in my life." The expense of tuition, room, and board at Webb's school was $250 a month—indeed a costly sum considering that the average wage earner received about one dollar per day.

Journal

In commencing this diary I have several objects in view, among which the principal are.

First to improve in composition. From having always neglected composition, and from the difficulty with which the mere mechanical execution of a piece of writing is affected, it is almost impossible for me to put my thoughts upon paper with sufficient clearness to be understood. When I sit down to write, even so unimportant an article as a letter, the ideas which had previously crowded into my mind suddenly vanish, leaving me to twirl my pen and thump my pate for ideas which are no longer its inmates.

Second, to obtain fluency in expressing my ideas.

In conversation I am often at great loss for words, which, to say the least, is very annoying; but it is in extempore speaking that I am most troubled by this deficiency. I think I have several of the qualifications requisite for a successful extempore speaker, such as, I fancy, a tolerable quick perception, and order in the arrangement of my ideas, but for want of fluency I am frequently prevented from succeeding in my extempore efforts.

Third, to promote decision of character.

This is a quality in which I am by no means deficient; but by recording my resolutions, I shall be more careful how I make them, and when they are formed, I shall be more careful to keep them.

Fourth, and last I expect to receive benefit and amusement in after days from the perusal of my youthful anticipations, broken resolves, ambitious hopes, strange desires, and half formed opinions.

In 1838, at age sixteen, Hayes began a journal. He made extensive entries regularly throughout his life. This voluminous diary is an incomparable record for understanding Hayes, his extended family, the politics of the period, and his presidency. Three presidents maintained such a detailed journal from youth to death—John Adams, John Quincy Adams, and Hayes.

"In commencing my diary," Hayes wrote, "I have several objects in view, among which the principal are: First to improve in composition….Second, to obtain fluency in expressing my ideas….Third, to promote decision of character. This is a quality in which I am by no means deficient, but by recording my resolutions, I shall be more careful how I make them, and when they are formed I shall be more careful to keep them. Fourth and last, I expect to receive benefit and amendment in after days from the perusal of my youthful anticipations, broken resolves, ambition, hopes, strange desires and half formed opinions."

The elder Rutherford Hayes died of typhus less than three months before Rud was born on October 4, 1822.

Sophia was forced to raise Rud and Fanny on her own. She was not entirely without resources. Sophia made a good profit leasing the Hayes croplands to tenant farmers. Also, her brother Sardis Birchard had accompanied the Hayes family to Ohio, where he became a wealthy merchant. Sardis, who never married, helped his sister with her living expenses and would pay for the education of his niece and nephew.

At first, that education occurred at home. Having lost a husband and three children to disease or accidents, Sophia was hesitant to let Rud and Fanny out of her sight. As young children, the brother and sister played together and learned their lessons together. Two years older than Rud, Fanny read William Shakespeare and Sir Walter Scott to her baby brother. Later, she taught him French.

When Rud was eight years old, a public school opened in Delaware. Sophia enrolled her children, who spent several miserable weeks in the institution taking instruction from a dictatorial schoolmaster named Daniel Granger, who was known to thrash misbehaving students and once brandished a knife at a pupil he caught whispering in class. Hearing these stories, Sophia gave in to her children's demands and withdrew them from Granger's school.

They had a much more pleasant experience in a private academy in Delaware conducted by Joan Hills Murray. It was at Murray's school that Rud first studied the history of the United States. He read the speeches of Patrick Henry, Daniel Webster, and Henry Clay and was soon able to recite them from memory. His favorite speech was Webster's "Reply to Robert Y. Hayne," with its stirring conclusion, "Liberty and Union, now and forever, one and inseparable." He was also the best speller in school.

Rud spent five years under the tutelage of Joan Hills Murray. By the time he was thirteen, his sister had already moved on to a girls' school in nearby Putnam, Ohio. Fanny was every bit as intelligent as her brother and was by far the best student at her school, but in the nineteenth century few careers were open to women. There was little need for Fanny to seek higher education.

It would be Rud, then, who would pursue a college degree. Problem was, though, that Rud had decided he had had enough school. He wanted to go into business with his Uncle Sardis, who was managing to do very well without the benefit of a college education. On a trip back to New England to meet relatives, Rud spent time with his nineteen-year-old cousin Horatio Noyes, a student at Yale College, and had been dazzled by Noyes' stories of college life in New Haven. Sardis, who would be paying Rud's tuition, was also enthusiastic about a Yale education for the boy, but doubted that his nephew was ready for Yale. And besides, Rud was still steadfast in his opposition to further studies. Sophia would have none of that. "When boys are interrupted in their studies at his age they are apt to lose their ambition," she wrote to Sardis.

Sardis found a school for Rud in Norwalk, Ohio, which wasn't far from Sardis' home in Lower Sandusky. Rud enrolled in Norwalk Seminary, which was headed by the Reverend Jonathan E. Chaplin, a Methodist minister. It was the school where the son of Sardis' friend and neighbor Judge Ebeneezer Lane attended. In the years to come, Rud and Will Lane would become good friends.

Rud entered Norwalk Seminary in 1836. Chaplin's curriculum emphasized oration and writing. Soon after commencing classes, Rud composed and delivered a speech on the British statesman William Pitt. It was his first experience speaking before an audience. "I was not scared as much as most of the boys are the first time they speak," he wrote to his mother.

Rud spent a year at Norwalk, then returned home when the term concluded in the spring of 1837. Once again, Rud talked of dropping out of school and following his Uncle Sardis into business. Again, Sophia fumed. Rud even found his good-natured sister opposing his decision to drop his studies. At the time, Fanny was just finishing up her education at Putnam. In a letter to Rud, Fanny huffed, "Many is the time this winter I have wished myself in your place so I could go to college."

Sophia proposed to send Rud to Kenyon College in Gambier, Ohio, just some forty miles east of the Hayes home in Delaware. Sardis didn't think the boy was ready. At Norwalk, his nephew had been a bright student, but Rud often exhibited a propensity for laziness. Sardis thought Rud could use a year at a prep school. Sardis again consulted with his friend Judge Lane, who told him he planned to send his son Will to Isaac Webb's preparatory school in Middletown, Connecticut. Sardis decided to send Rud there as well. "I will not say I won't go, but I don't wish to go," Rud complained, upon hearing of his uncle's plans. The shock was tempered, though, when Rud learned he'd be rejoining Will Lane in Middletown.

Webb's school turned out to be just the right experience for a boy of slothful tendencies. A former Yale College tutor, Webb accepted only twenty boys per year. The tuition cost Sardis the considerable sum of $250 a year. For his money, Sardis was promised that his nephew would be exposed to "thorough study, faithful instruction and steady discipline."

Rud arrived in October 1837, and soon found that there were few opportunities to be lazy at Isaac Webb's school. In December, he wrote to his uncle: "We get up at half past 6 o'clock, breakfast at 7, prayers, and school begins at 9; dinner at 12; [study] at 1 till 4, then 6 till 9. I like this school very much indeed. I never heard of a school that I should like near so well. All the scholars like the school very much and that is more than can be said of most schools. We all like 'Mr. W' very much. I think he is the best calculated to take care of the parcel of boys of any man I most ever saw, for they soon find out that he is not to be trifled with, and at the same time that he is very pleasant when they suit him."

Despite the frantic pace of the work, Rud tried hard to maintain his sense of humor. He wrote that his French teacher "is a passionate old fellow. He looks more like a plump feather bed than anything else I know of!"

Rud was a popular boy with many friends who were drawn to him because of his good nature. His nickname was "Charley Bates"—the happy-go-lucky character in Charles Dickens' *Oliver Twist*.

Hayes entered Kenyon College in Gambier, Ohio, in 1838. Kenyon, a liberal arts college, had been founded fourteen years earlier by Philander Chase, the first Episcopal Bishop of Ohio, for the education of young men living west of the Alleghenies. The Kenyon library was outstanding at a time when the total number of books available in a college library was the most important factor in ranking it.

This is a page from Hayes' 1838 notebook. A common college assignment was for the student to copy passages from a textbook—and then to memorize them.

"What's in a name? that which we call a rose,
By any other name would smell as sweet;"
Romeo and Juliet
"These violent delights have violent ends,
And in their triumph die; like fire and powder
Which as they kiss, consume; the sweetest honey
Is loathsome in his own deliciousness,
And in the taste confounds the appetite;
Therefore love moderately; long love doth so;
Too swift arrives as tardy as too slow."
Shaks. R. & J.
"But, good my brother,
Do not, as some ungracious pastors do,
Show me the steep and thorny way to heaven;
Whilst like a puffed and reckless libertine,
Himself the primrose path of dalliance treads,
And recks not his own read." Hamlet

"And these few precepts in thy memory
Look thou character. Give thy thoughts no tongue

At Middletown, Rud developed an interest in politics. Sardis was an ardent Whig and now so was Rud. In 1836, the Whigs lost the presidential race to Martin Van Buren, a Democrat. Rud was one of the many Whig sympathizers who awaited with great anticipation the election of 1840, knowing that the presidency would be within the party's grasp. In 1837, he followed the successful mayoral campaign of Whig Aaron Clark in nearby New York City with great interest, writing, "The celebration of the New York victory in this city was splendid. There was nearly a constant roar of cannon throughout the day and in the evening three hundred dollars worth of fireworks was set off." Rud's admiration of the Whigs was probably helped along by Isaac Webb, a Whig who held a minor political office in Middletown.

Rud finished his year's studies in Middletown in the spring of 1838. By now, the fifteen-year-old had warmed up to the idea of going to college and told Sardis and his mother he wished to enroll at Yale. Isaac Webb didn't think the boy was ready for Yale and urged Sardis to enroll Rud for another year in Middletown. Sophia wanted him closer to home, though, insisting that he enroll at Kenyon. "If Rutherford lives he is to be a Western man," she declared in a letter to Sardis. Sophia had her way, and on November 1, 1838, Rud Hayes stepped onto the Kenyon campus.

Webb had prepared him well for college. Before being admitted to the freshman class, Hayes was tested on his knowledge of Latin, Greek, mathematics and grammar and sailed through all the examinations. He found his classes less than challenging; indeed, they were much easier than the strict routine that he had experienced under Webb. Also, the lighthearted Rud Hayes bristled under

Kenyon's many rules. A student could be
disciplined for such a minor infraction as eating
custard in his room. When Fanny wrote to Hayes,
urging him to learn to like his teachers, he replied,
"Well, I do like them—a great ways off." He also
complained about the food.

Fanny's letters cheered him, though, and he
managed to finish his freshman year in good spirits.
By the time he started his sophomore year, Hayes
had grown to like Kenyon and devoted himself to
his studies. He joined the Philomathesian Society,
the college literary and debating club, and soon
became one of the group's best debaters. By the
spring of 1840, he found himself wrapped up in the
long-awaited presidential campaign, which was
shaping up as a contest between President Martin
Van Buren and William Henry Harrison, the old
military hero whom the Whigs had drafted as their
candidate. Still just eighteen years old, Hayes wrote an

Rutherford B. Hayes, circa 1839, at age 17.

extensive "History of the Presidential Campaign of 1840," in which he left no doubt
as to who he believed was the better man.

"The long agony is over," Hayes wrote on November 5. "The 'whirlwind' has
swept over the land and General Harrison is undoubtedly elected President. I never
was more elated by anything in my life. His majority in this state about…twenty-
three thousand. Kentucky and everywhere else is going fine. Glorious!"

By the end of his junior year at Kenyon, Hayes blossomed into a dedicated
scholar. He was elected president of the Philomathesian Society and steered the
organization into staging politically charged debates. Among the topics tackled by
the Philomathesians during his tenure were the admission of Texas to the Union
and the veto power of the president. Hayes also helped bolster Kenyon's other
literary society, Nu Pi Kappa, which was faltering because it had been traditionally
composed of boys from southern states and by the 1840s many southern parents had
stopped sending their sons up north for college. To prop up Nu Pi Kappa, Hayes
worked out an agreement between the two societies in which geography would no
longer be a consideration in the selection of members.

Hayes started telling his friends that he intended to pursue a career in law,
which he hoped would lead to elective office. Just before finishing his junior year at
Kenyon, Hayes wrote in his diary what he hoped to accomplish as a senior: "I wish
to become a master of logic and rhetoric and to obtain a good knowledge of history.
To accomplish these objectives I am willing to study hard, in which case I believe I
can make, at least, a tolerable debater. It is another intention of mine, that after I
have commenced in life, whatever may be my ability or station, to preserve a

reputation for honesty and benevolence; and if ever I am a public man I will never do anything inconsistent with the character of a true friend and good citizen."

By his senior year Hayes had resolved to become a lawyer. He was now the top scholar on campus, studying philosophy, mathematics and chemistry. He wasn't so serious, though, that he had to give up his reputation as the class cut-up. He helped organize a fraternity, the Phi Zetas. Each member obtained a silver-headed walking stick and reveled in strolling about campus, flaunting their fancy sticks in front of their classmates. In letters home to his mother, he bragged about his drinking binges, although Sophia, a dedicated supporter of the temperance movement, knew full well that Rud was pulling her leg. Around campus, he was known as "Uncle Ruddy."

There was, however, trouble at home. Fanny had married during Hayes's freshman year and soon delivered a baby, Sarah. Sadly, the baby died two years later. Sarah's death drove Fanny into a deep depression, and by Hayes's senior year his sister's mental illness had grown so severe that she had to be institutionalized. As Rud prepared for graduation, it became clear to him that she was too ill to attend commencement exercises and watch her brother deliver the valedictory speech.

Graduation from Kenyon occurred on August 5, 1842. Sophia and Sardis traveled to Gambier to watch Rud take highest honors. By now, he had grown into a tall, handsome red-haired young man eager to start the next step in life. Hayes decided

On August 5, 1842, Hayes delivered the valedictory address at his graduation from Kenyon. The ceremonies lasted from morning until dusk. Hayes's oration on "College Life" came after speeches from his eight classmates, two poems, and eight musical pieces. He urged the younger students "to master what is profound and difficult" and "substantial" through disciplined study. That evening, he recorded his thoughts to his diary: "I felt myself all over, and to my astonishment I found I was 'the same old Rud,' not a single cubit added to my stature, nor a hairs breadth to my girth, on the contrary if anything I felt more lank & gaunt than common, much as if a load were off my stomach."

After graduation from Kenyon, Hayes spent several months reading William Blackstone's *Commentaries on the Laws of England* in the office of Sparrow and Matthews in Columbus. Mastering law, he thought, "would unlock the passport which is to conduct me to all that I am destined to receive in life." He resolved to study "with more attention," to read no newspapers, rise at seven, read Blackstone for six hours, and then "study reasoning and logic for two hours, German for two hours, and retire at ten." In 1843, after several "vexatious and tedious months," Hayes entered Harvard Law School, graduating in 1845. At Harvard he studied under Joseph Story and Simon Greenleaf, two of the nation's most distinguished jurists. Hayes noted in his diary his excitement at glimpses of John Quincy Adams and Daniel Webster. In addition, he found time to attend the theater, dabble in Latin and French, and read philosophy. At Harvard, he discovered that his "chief defect" was his "boyish conduct" and that he needed "greater mildness and affability."

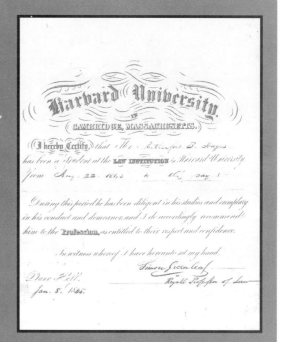

to attend Harvard Law School but before enrolling spent several months reading law under the guidance of Thomas Sparrow, an established Columbus, Ohio, attorney.

Hayes spent ten dismal months in Sparrow's office, running errands, sweeping up, and reading law books for six hours a day. The one bright spot in his experience with Sparrow was his opportunity to study politics up close. Columbus, the state capital, was a hotbed of Ohio politics.

Finally, Rud arrived at Harvard's venerable campus in Cambridge, Massachusetts, enrolling in August 1843. His teachers included Simon Greenleaf, a famed legal scholar, and Joseph Story, an associate justice of the U.S. Supreme Court. Unlike his teachers at Kenyon, whom he liked "a great ways off," Hayes had little but praise for Greenleaf and Story. In his diary, he wrote:

> Professors Story and Greenleaf illustrate and explain as they proceed. Mr. Greenleaf is very searching and logical in examination…he keeps the subject constantly in view, never stepping out of his way for the purpose of introducing his own experience. Judge Story, on the other hand, is very general in his questions so that a person well skilled in words affirmative and negative shakings of the head need never more than glance at the text to be able to answer his interrogatories. He is 'very fond of digressions to introduce amusing anecdotes, high-wrought eulogies of the sages of the law, and fragments of his own experience. He is generally very interesting, often quite eloquent…In short, as a lecturer he is a very different man from what you would expect of an old and eminent judge; not but that he is great, but he is so interesting and fond of good stories. His amount of knowledge is prodigious.

Hayes studied more than just law at Harvard. He read philosophy, gaining an appreciation for human rights and morality from James Beattie and John Locke. He learned about the power of eloquent argument by studying Cicero, and about ethics from Aristotle. Henry Wadsworth Longfellow was on the Harvard faculty at the time, and Hayes attended some of his lectures. He also studied French and German. And, of course, he followed politics. In the fall of 1844, he cast his first vote in a presidential election, awarding it to the Whig candidate, Henry Clay. For Hayes, it was a busy two years.

He graduated in the spring of 1845. With just a few days left of classes, Hayes wrote of his future in his diary:

> My labors have been to cultivate and store my mind. This year the character, the whole man, must receive attention. I will strive to become in manners, morals, and feelings a true gentleman. The rudeness of a student must be laid off, and the quiet, manly deportment of a gentleman put on—not merely to be worn as a garment, but to become by use a part of myself. I believe I know what true gentility, genuine good breeding, is. Let me but live out what is within, and I am vain enough to think that little of what is important would be found wanting.

His future would take him to a law practice and political career in Cincinnati. When the Civil War erupted, Hayes joined the Union Army, saw action against Stonewall Jackson and Jubal Early, and, by the end of the war, attained the rank of major general. Now a Republican, his war record helped him win a seat in Congress. Later, he won three terms as governor of Ohio and, in 1876, Hayes accepted the Republican nomination for president.

The presidency of Rutherford B. Hayes commenced on March 3, 1877, after a long campaign against Samuel Tilden that was not decided until well after election day. Following the election the previous November, the race hinged on disputed Electoral College votes in South Carolina, Florida, Louisiana, and Oregon. The dispute dragged on for months, and was settled when Hayes promised the southern states to withdraw the federal troops that had been keeping the peace since the end of the Civil War. The gesture won South Carolina, Florida, and Louisiana over to his side, and Hayes was declared the winner of the presidency with an electoral college vote of 185 to Tilden's 184.

Withdrawing those troops would have an impact on the lives of millions of Americans long after Hayes stepped down from the presidency after a single term in office. While the troops had been in the South, the lives and rights of the newly freed slaves were safeguarded. Without the troops to protect them, southern blacks were exposed to hatred and prejudice that would rob them of their civil rights—and very often their lives—for nearly a century. It was a sad ramification that the light-hearted Rud Hayes could never have envisioned.

—Hal Marcovitz

James A. Garfield
Chapter Twenty

It is fair to say James A. Garfield was a born student and teacher. A poor boy growing up without a father in rural, post-frontier Ohio, he had only limited opportunities and almost no money for practically the first half of his life. Nonetheless, at a very early age he discovered the enormous personal value of reading, which would help catapult him all the way to the White House.

Garfield was born November 19, 1831, in Orange, Ohio, a township emerging steadily from primitive frontier status to farming prosperity. He was the youngest of five children, and the last president to be born in a log cabin. His father, Abram, had traveled to Ohio from New York State, and his mother, the former Eliza Ballou, had lived in New Hampshire. When Abram and Eliza first settled in Ohio, in the years just before James' birth, the family lived on the bank of the Cuyahoga River near Lake Erie. Their region, known as the Western Reserve, was backward. They lived in a crude log home with a dirt floor (which in wet weather quickly became muddy) and a fireplace with chimney. Winters were brutal, but wet warmer weather brought malaria and other fevers.

Abram Garfield was a big, powerful man who knew little of books. His labor supported the large family in the Ohio backcountry. He helped build canals and was renowned as an unbeatable wrestler. In 1829, he bought land near the Chagrin River in Orange Township, and he built the cabin where James was born. He and Eliza became fervent churchgoers, joining the Disciples of Christ.

When James was not yet two, his father died from the ill effects of fighting a forest fire. Eliza and the children struggled to survive on their thirty-acre farm. James' older brother and sisters worked the fields and performed an endless, daily regimen of chores. Little James was too young to offer much help. Besides, as his mother later recalled, he was "rather lazy."

Jame's mother served as his first teacher. She read, told stories, and sang to all her children in the evenings. James was eager to learn. Unlike his older brother, Thomas, who had to forego education so he could help work the farm, James began attending the local school when he was three. Within a short time, he could read

James A. Garfield had the second-shortest tenure of all U.S. presidents—only two hundred days, eighty of which were spent as a helpless invalid. When he was shot and incapacitated in 1881, national debates were held about presidential disability and succession.

Garfield was the last chief executive to be born in a log cabin. He was preceded by at least six generations of Garfields born in America, an immigrant ancestor having come to Massachusetts Bay Colony as a follower of John Winthrop in 1630.

Abram Garfield, the father of James, and his wife Eliza Ballou, moved with their three children from central New York State to Ohio in 1827. Abram had obtained a construction work contract on the Ohio Canal. However, he abandoned this and became a pioneer farmer in Cuyahoga County, Ohio. James Abram, born in 1831, was his last child. Abram Garfield died two years later.

James A. Garfield knew a childhood of hard work. As a teenager, in the spring, he worked on the Ohio Canal usually cording and stacking lumber en route to the Lake Erie port of Cleveland. As a teenager, he also experienced a religious conversion and, like his parents, became a member of the Disciples of Christ, a group of Protestant churches that originated in the American frontier revival movement of the early nineteenth century. Garfield attended rural local schools, the Disciples' new school in Ohio's northeast "western reserve" area, the Eclectic Institute (later Hiram College), and he worked his way through a two-year program at Williams College, graduating with the class of 1856. He returned to the Eclectic Institute, first as a teacher then for many years as its principal. It was here that he experienced the full development of both his religious and his educational interests unhampered by sectarian restrictions.

Garfield's pre-political years revolved around Western Reserve Eclectic Institute. This photograph of the building and its students was taken in 1858, when Garfield was the principal. Founded in 1850 by the Disciples of Christ, the school, although avowedly nonsectarian, was heavily slanted toward Disciple religious tenets. The main aim of the school was to prepare a new generation of preachers to replace aged Disciple leaders. The chief educational emphasis was placed on a literal interpretation of the New Testament and on moral excellence, especially in abstinence from alcohol and from sexual misconduct. Garfield was a student at the school from 1851 to 1854.

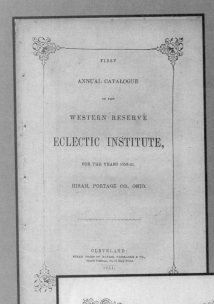

The rural isolation of co-educational Western Reserve Eclectic Institute—the nearest stagecoach route was five miles away—was considered to be most positive by Disciple elders. They feared travel would expose their students to urban temptations, especially to alcohol and sex. "Let us expose our children to the virus of pestilence," Eclectic Institute's first catalogue exclaimed, "let them fall by the touch of the Asiatic scourge, rather than expose them to the moral effluvia that poison the great pathways of public travel."

Eclectic had no endowment. It depended on fees paid by the approximately two hundred and fifty students to cover its operating expenses. When debts were pressing or fees in arrears, the school balanced its books by firing teachers. The course of study was similar to that of other rural Ohio schools: arithmetic, history, geography, science, the classics, and religious studies.

After leaving Eclectic Institute to study at Williams College, Garfield returned to the Hiram area as an experienced Disciple preacher with the prestige of having graduated from an Eastern college. Within a few years, Garfield was considered one of the foremost Disciple preachers in northeastern Ohio. Although Disciples avoided political issues, Garfield had utter disdain for slavery. Therefore, he enthusiastically backed the recently formed Republican Party during the 1856 presidential election because its main plank opposed the extension of slavery into new territories and states. He was elected to the Ohio State Senate in 1859 and subsequently to Congress as a Republican—and when the Civil War began in 1861, he helped assemble the 42nd Ohio Volunteer Infantry, which contained many of his Hiram students.

Bible passages to the family by the light of the hearth. He loved books and decided early that he wanted to attend college. He realized, however, that a college education was quite beyond the financial means of his family.

Books were hard to come by on the frontier. Consequently, James developed a personal affection for his books, and he borrowed others from neighbors. History was his favorite subject. He reread Samuel Goodrich's *History of the United States for the Use of Schools and Families* many times and memorized entire passages. He also enjoyed novels, a passion at least partly inspired by the folk ballads his mother sang. Books carried him to distant regions and lands. Most intriguing were stories about the sea. Harriet Boynton, a cousin who lived nearby, shared James's enthusiasm for novels, and they often read together.

As a teenager, James often dressed in a slovenly fashion. He was also absent-minded, clumsy, and accident-prone. "In many ways he was a blundering, careless boy," his wife wrote of him many years later. "Once he came near killing his cousin Silas Boynton by heedless use of an axe, and within a hair's breadth of ending his own life by plunging headlong down through a mill." He was a dreamy, moody youth who yearned to be far away from the hard, drab life of the settlements. For this reason, James half-heartedly worked on the farm and labored at odd jobs for neighbors, earning extra money to help his mother support the family.

In the words of one historian, James "had the reputation of being difficult—not mean and not dishonest, but sensitive, short-tempered, and, alas, not terribly hard-working." He did not take well to the jeers of other boys—feeling scorned because he was fatherless, poor, and plainly dressed. As a result, James was quick to fight if he interpreted a remark as an insult.

In one situation, he demonstrated an early zeal for equality and independence. He had taken a job as a resident farmhand in a neighboring township. His employer gave him a room and meals and paid him nine dollars a month to boil wood ashes into black salts, a frontier product useful for cleaning. As a fringe benefit, the host family let him read their books in the sitting room at night. But one evening, the mother of the family shooed him from the little chamber so her teenage daughter could privately entertain a suitor. James could not fault the justice of the rearrangement, but he was incensed by the woman's flippant remark that "servants" must withdraw and go to bed. James allowed that he was a lowly worker, but he didn't consider himself a servant. The next morning, he quit and walked home.

By this time, the Garfield family was living in a small frame house. James knew it was not the life for him. Whenever he could, Garfield visited the nearby Cleveland waterfront, where he listened to the tales of canal boat crews and admired the Lake Erie sailboats. Imagining what it must be like to voyage over the horizon, and drawing from the romanticized view of the world he found in novels, James had no accurate idea of the world outside the Western Reserve. "His conceptions of the outside world were often romanticized or distorted," wrote biographer Hendrik Booraem V. "All he knew was that he was missing something—he had no real idea what."

The schoolhouses of the Western Reserve were much like those of other rural regions, ranging from small, poorly built log structures to thin-sided frame shelters to temporary quarters within places of business or worship. When James was in his mid-teens, a new schoolhouse was built within sight of the family farm. Younger students sat on benches in the center of the single room, while older ones sat in desks placed around the walls. The teacher's desk was at the front, beside a wood stove.

A woman teacher usually instructed smaller children during the summer, while older children remained home to work. In winter, the older students joined the youngsters for classes that lasted two to three months, Monday through Saturday. Students—ranging in age from four to their early twenties—attended winter classes. Many of the older students were uninterested and disorderly during class, so school officials sought a male teacher for the winter term. In many schools, teachers were not much more educated than some of the students. The teacher might be attending a nearby college or academy (college preparatory school) and needed to earn money, or might be a young man or woman who lived in the village.

Year after year, the students studied Joseph Ray's *Rudiments of Arithmetic* and Jedidiah Morse's *Geography*, read from the *McGuffey Readers*, and struggled to master Noah Webster's *Speller*. While many boys would much rather work than pursue an education, James wanted to learn. This made tolerating an unqualified teacher a difficult task. During midterm in January 1848, he and a handful of other students dropped out and began trekking to a different school in the region after convincing their parents that the local instructor was "unfit to teach."

Several times each winter, villages would hold evening spelling contests, or spelling schools, at the schoolhouse. At times, the local students were pitted against students from nearby school districts, while at other times, anyone was welcomed to challenge the town scholars—and James, an excellent speller, proved to be the pride of Orange Township on these occasions. He also enjoyed singing schools, held on certain nights during winter. Traveling singing masters taught rhythm, notation, and harmony from a classic hymnal entitled the *Musica Sacra*.

When he was seventeen, Garfield's restlessness overcame him. He left home intent on becoming a sailor on the Great Lakes. When he tried to board a cargo vessel, though, the captain turned him away with a barrage of insults. Humiliated, the young man began navigating a towboat that carried animals along the Ohio Canal. More than a dozen times, he later recalled, he almost drowned after falling into the canal because he could not swim. His towboat days were cut short by a severe illness that landed him home in bed, shaking and feverish, for three months. When he finally began to recover, his mother asked him to give up his canal boat life to further his education.

Garfield agreed with his mother and traveled to Chester, Ohio, in March 1849 to enroll at Geauga Academy—a college preparatory school similar to a modern

Williams College, Mass.
Wednesday Eve. Oct 10th/55

G. M. Guernsey Dear Sir.
Will not our common
cause allow me to lay aside the formal-
ities of modern etiquette, and address
a letter to you without any long pre-
liminaries. I have just returned from a
class meeting we had, which was called
to consider the letter your Committee
has just sent us in reference to choosing
men to respond to the toasts to us—
There was any amount [...]
pulling — and knavery. but [...]
succeed, and two candidates [...]
were very kindly relieved of [...]
responding to any toasts on [...]
sion —
We hope that all our A[...]
nity Brethren of the Senior [...]
meet us there at the propo[...]
on Monday next and that we [...]
more intimately acquainted —

Williams College
Friday Oct. 12th 185[.]

G. M. Guernsey
Dr Sir,
The secret society
men are very mad to think
that they have been foiled
in their machinations, and
this morning one of their
men has gone away to be
gone two days. and it is
supposed he has gone to
Amherst. Please be on
the look out for breakers —
He is a Six footer. K.A.
They used very base means to
elect one of their men (a perfect
rascal) he speaker in respon
to a toast — but were de-
feated fairly and honorably

Please consider this
Strictly "inter nos" and
oblige Yours truly
J. A. Garfield

Garfield had clear handwriting and he was a prolific
letter and diary writer. Many of his eloquent college
letters have survived, including these examples
preserved in the Williams College archive. Most of
Garfield's letters dealt with college activities—the
subject of a debate, the new literary club, and his
opposition to secret fraternal societies.

CATALOGUE

OF THE

OFFICERS AND STUDENTS

AND

REGISTER OF SOCIETIES,

IN

WILLIAMS COLLEGE,

FOR THE ACADEMICAL YEAR

1855-56.

WILLIAMSTOWN, MASS.
1855.

FACULTY.

REV. MARK HOPKINS, D. D., PRESIDENT,
PROFESSOR OF MORAL AND INTELLECTUAL PHILOSOPHY.

EBENEZER EMMONS, A. M., M. D.,
PROFESSOR OF NATURAL HISTORY AND GEOLOGY.

ALBERT HOPKINS, A. M.,
PROFESSOR OF NATURAL PHILOSOPHY AND ASTRONOMY.

REV. NATHANIEL H. GRIFFIN, A. M.,
LAWRENCE PROFESSOR OF THE GREEK LANGUAGE AND LITERATURE.

REV. JOHN TATLOCK, A. M.,
PROFESSOR OF MATHEMATICS AND LIBRARIAN.

REV. ISAAC N. LINCOLN, A. M.,
PROFESSOR OF LATIN AND FRENCH.

PAUL A. CHADBOURNE, A. M.,
PROFESSOR OF CHEMISTRY AND BOTANY.

JOHN BASCOM, A. M.,
PROFESSOR OF RHETORIC.

ARTHUR L. PERRY, A. M.,
PROFESSOR OF HISTORY, POLITICAL ECONOMY, AND THE GERMAN LANGUAGE.

SENIOR CLASS.

SEMPER UBIQUE.

NAMES.	RESIDENCES.	ROOMS.
W. R. Baxter,	Cornwall, Vt.	9 E. C.
Stephen W. Bowles,	Boston.	1 E. C.
Henry Coon,	Cleveland, Ohio.	2 S. C.
Elijah Cutler,	Dorchester.	18 E. C.
Hamilton N. Eldridge,	Williamstown.	8 New St.
D. Maurice Evans,	New York Mills, N. Y.	16 E. C.
J. Edwards Fay,	Westboro'.	20 E. C.
James A. Garfield,	Hiram, Ohio.	23 E. C.
James Gilfillan,	Rockville, Ct.	4 S. C.
Charles S. Halsey,	East Wilson, N. Y.	18 E. C.
Abner Hazeltine, Jr.,*	Jamestown, N. Y.	14 E. C.
James King Hazen,	Canterbury, Ct.	15 S. C.
Clement Hugh Hill,	London, Eng.	4 S. C.
Silas P. Hubbell,	Champlain, N. Y.	Mr. Morey's.
Ferris Jacobs, Jr.,	Delhi, N. Y.	7 E. C.
H. M. Jones,	Victory, N. Y.	16 S. C.
Henry E. Knox,	Rock Island, Ill.	5 E. C.
John E. D. Lamberton,	Ware.	8 S. C.
Charles W. MacCarthy,	Potsdam, N. Y.	4 Chapel.
E. Newell Manley,	Richville, N. Y.	21 E. C.
James McLean,	Glasgow, Scotland.	17 E. C.
Robert Jay Mitchell,	Great Barrington.	19 E. C.
George B. Newcomb,	Brooklyn, N. Y.	19 E. C.
Henry M. Newcomb,*	Detroit, Mich.	Mr. Hoisington's.

* University student.

high school. Garfield, along with two companions, paid for lodging at a local house. On Saturdays, he chopped firewood and worked for a carpenter to earn money. "No greener boy ever started out to school," he recorded in his diary.

Garfield was inspired by his coursework at Geauga. Courses such as grammar challenged him, while algebra and natural sciences fascinated and intrigued him. He also took an interest in public speaking. Still, he interrupted his studies during his first long winter vacation at Geauga because he did not have enough money for another school term. After a desperate search for a job, he was hired as a country schoolteacher. In one of his classes, a bullying older boy was so domineering that the previous schoolmaster had quit. Garfield handled the matter by beating the antagonist in a brawl.

With $48 from his four-month teaching job, Garfield returned to Geauga Seminary. He excelled in his courses, which now included botany and Latin. And both students and faculty respected Garfield for his oratory. Still, the young man was horrified when selected by his teachers to deliver a speech at a formal academy program in July 1850. As it turned out, his delivery was masterful and eloquent, drawing hearty applause. Later, he boasted in his diary, "I am no longer a cringing scapegoat but am resolved to make a mark in the world."

But Garfield grew increasingly disturbed with the way the school was run. Meanwhile, he grew increasingly ashamed of his poor upbringing. The money he had made the previous winter did not go far. He wore patched, faded clothes and subsisted on a near-starvation diet. He sensed that the other students mocked his impoverished state. After the autumn term, he left Geauga and spent a year working as a country schoolteacher and carpenter.

At nineteen, he was ready for higher education. He enrolled at the Western Reserve Eclectic Institute in Hiram, Ohio. The Eclectic Institute—which one person described as "a cornfield with a solid, plain brick building in the centre"— was a brand new college founded by the Disciples of Christ, the Garfield family's church denomination. During this time Garfield, who had often skipped church as a youngster, was baptized in the frigid Chagrin River. And he took his newfound faith very seriously. He held in contempt those who indulged in swearing, partying, and drinking—and his early journals are filled with allusions to his religious faith.

Soon, he began preaching as a layman (non-ordained minister) at nearby churches. The polished sermons Garfield delivered as a preacher may have been most influenced by his three-year education at the Eclectic Institute. His understanding of Greek and Latin gave him an exceptional command of English, which he would parlay into highly effective oratory skills. He studied more hours than he slept, regularly covering much more homework than he was assigned. When he had mastered all the Greek and Latin materials the institute could offer, he and another student, Almeda Booth, supplemented their learning by reading other classical works together.

It was during this time at school that Garfield overcame his feeling of inferiority and rose to great popularity among the student body. Although he was still a poor young man, the Disciples' devout creed accepted a person's humble state. At the same time, he was a good athlete, almost six feet tall. He became a dynamic orator, and few could rival his academic record. The other students looked to him as a leader. Garfield was particularly proud of his talent as a speaker during debates. "I love agitation and investigation and glory in defending unpopular truth against popular error," he stated. In his first year at the Eclectic Institute, James defeated the unofficial champion of the lyceum, or debate society. And, to his credit, James later became friendly with his opponent.

With an impoverished family unable to support him, Garfield worked as a janitor and as a private tutor to other students so he could pay for his tuition. Money was not the only reason Garfield decided to tutor students, though. He had come to regard education as something that must be passed to the next generation. One of his clients, Lucretia "Crete" Rudolph, would eventually become Mrs. James A. Garfield.

In 1854, Garfield borrowed money from a friend so he could transfer to Williams College in Massachusetts. Again, he helped support himself by teaching, accepting the master's post for the winter term at a school in Vermont. Meanwhile, he thrived as a collegian, earning the respect of Williams's noted president, Mark Hopkins. His new studies included German, natural sciences, mechanics, logic, and political economy. In a letter to Lucretia, Garfield summarized his first-year routine at Williams: "Rise and attend prayers in the chapel at 5 and then recite one hour of Qunitillian. Then go a quarter of a mile to breakfast. At 9 o'clock, three times a week attend lectures on Philosophy and at 11 recite in Mechanics. At 4 p.m. Greek for an hour, then prayers. In addition to these there are occasional exercises in themes, debates and orations."

Garfield was additionally influenced by Ralph Waldo Emerson. Garfield wrote to a friend, "I must say he is the most startlingly original thinker I have ever heard...I could not sleep that night after hearing his thunderstorm of eloquent thoughts."

Hopkins, who insisted that students think for themselves, personally taught a course in moral philosophy to seniors. Garfield was one of his favorite students, and they spent hours discussing topics of mutual interest. It has been suggested that Garfield's decision to become a teacher was inspired by Hopkins. The college president later recalled of Garfield, "He was prompt, frank, manly, social in his tendencies, combining active exercise with habits of study, and thus did for himself what it is the object of a college to make every young man to do—he made himself a man."

Among other benefits, Garfield credited his experience at Williams with improving his debating skills. A classmate later remembered Garfield as "undoubtedly one of the greatest debaters ever seen at Williams College."

Garfield prepared diligently for debates and proved himself a brilliant leader of his debating team. He also was a mainstay of the Philologian Society, a Williams' literary group. He was elected an editor of the college literary journal and president of a theological society.

At the time, Garfield was the oldest student at Williams. Both his knowledge and physical prowess deeply impressed his classmates and made him very popular. He acquired a good sense of humor and mixed well socially. When Garfield graduated with honors from Williams, he was ranked second in his class of forty-five students. At commencement, he gave the "metaphysical oration," speaking on the tension between human nature and things spiritual.

Garfield immediately accepted a professor's post at the Eclectic Institute, teaching Greek and Latin. One year later, Garfield became the school's president at the age of twenty-six. He also preached on Sundays as a lay speaker for the Disciples of Christ. Now ready for marriage, he proposed to Lucretia. She came from an education-minded farm family. Her father had helped found the Eclectic

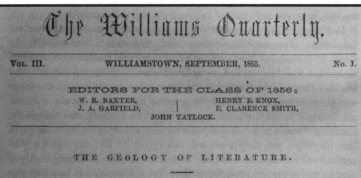

In the spring of 1855, Garfield became an editor of the *Williams Quarterly*, then in its third year of publication.

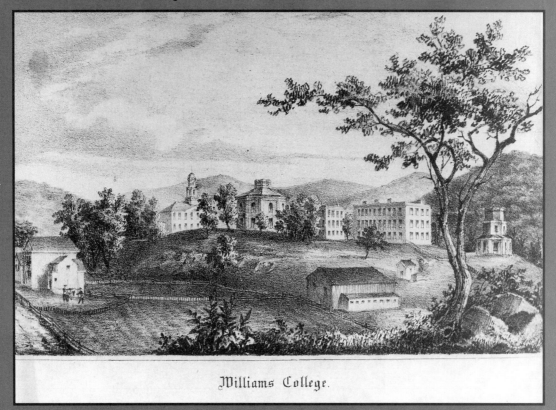

An illustration of Williams College, circa 1854

Williams College.

In 1854, James Garfield decided to enter Williams College in Massachusetts, a Congregational school known for its classical curriculum and moral atmosphere. Like Eclectic, Williams was located in an isolated area many miles from the nearest major stage road. There were about two hundred and fifty male students at the school, mainly from New England; most intended to enter the ministry. Though non-sectarian, religion permeated the school and its curriculum. Both morning and evening chapel and two church services on Sunday were mandatory. The method of instruction was conventional and rigid. The college library was inadequate for the student body. Mark Hopkins, a strict Calvinist minister known for his Socratic teaching style, was the college president and philosophy instructor. Years later, an unintentional remark made by President Garfield at a Williams alumni dinner, to the effect that his idea of a college would be fully met by a log in the woods with a student at one end and Mark Hopkins at the other, has become an aphorism that has passed into the lore of American education.

Garfield was dissatisfied with his religious education at Williams College. Being used to the extemporaneous sermons preached by the frontier Disciples who were called "brothers" and not "ministers," he expressed contempt for the dull religious lectures that were imposed upon the Williams student body. According to his letters and diary, Garfield often verbally clashed with his fellow students on various points of Disciple doctrine. At no point, he often repeated, had the biblical creation story been contradicted by science. His religious zeal led him to Disciple churches within a reasonable distance from Williamstown. Often, he preached at their services. "There were several immersions," he wrote during his first year at Williams, "and I think much good done. Nothing else could have kept me away from college, but I am glad I stayed." However, his visiting and staying at neighborhood Disciple churches continued through his senior year.

Garfield was twenty-five when he graduated from Williams College in 1856.

Institute, and while James attended Williams College, she taught school in Ohio. They were married in 1858 and eventually had seven children.

As president of the Eclectic Institute, Garfield remained committed to furthering his education. In 1860, he was admitted to the Ohio State bar and won a seat in the Ohio State Senate. As a state senator, Garfield expressed his ardent opposition to slavery by working hard for the presidential election of Abraham Lincoln. When the Civil War erupted in 1861, Garfield received an army commission at the rank of lieutenant colonel. By the mid-point of the conflict, he had become a major general.

In 1863, Garfield resigned from the army to take a seat in the U.S. House of Representatives, to which he had been elected the year before. He spent seventeen years in Congress, rising to become the Republican leader. At first, Garfield was a Radical Republican, calling for Confederate leaders to be executed or banished from the land and their property confiscated. Garfield felt such fiery animosity toward the rebels that he only half-heartedly endorsed Lincoln's re-election in 1864; he believed the president, in his eagerness to reunite the nation, would be too lenient on the South when the fighting ended. During the decade after the war, though, Garfield softened his stance and became a mediator among party factions.

In 1880, Garfield was elected to the United States Senate. That year at the Republican National Convention, he led the supporters of Ohio Senator John Sherman, nominating Sherman for president with a stirring speech that did more in the minds of delegates to enlarge Garfield's own image than to promote his friend. When the delegates split among the leading candidates through more than thirty ballots, frustrated delegates looked to Garfield as a compromise candidate. Garfield received sixteen votes on the convention's thirty-fourth ballot, fifty votes on the next, then a landslide three hundred and ninety-nine to win the Republican nomination. He went on to narrowly defeat Democratic Winfield S. Hancock to become America's twentieth president.

In an era of clamor for government and industry reform, progressives considered Garfield as weak and subject to corporate influences. On the other hand, he ordered a full investigation of the Star Route Scandal, a controversy over improper mail contract awards, even though he knew it probably would hurt members of his own political party. It was an affirmation of his lifelong principles. "A brave man," he once said, "is a man who dares to look the Devil in the face and tell him he is a Devil."

On July 2, 1881, only four months into his administration, an assassin shot Garfield in Washington, D.C. The wound was not immediately fatal. Garfield was taken to an ocean retreat in Elberon, New Jersey, where he died on September 19, 1881.

—Daniel E. Harmon

Chester A. Arthur
Chapter Twenty-one

hester Alan Arthur was sworn into office as America's twenty-first president on September 20, 1881, in what was anything but a festive inaugural gala. The official ceremony was staged not during an all-day, all-night Washington inaugural celebration, but in the dead of an exhausting, stressful night at his New York City residence. President James Garfield, shot by an assassin two months earlier, had hovered near death while the nation prayed. Vice President Arthur had hoped against hope that Garfield would survive. Amid the deep gloom of national tragedy, the vice president knew he might never be a popular president. Journalists and critics questioned the vice president's credentials. Would he be able to rise to the task of leading his country? Were his political friends behind the assassination? In fact, some detractors scoffed at the thought that the vice president was qualified for *any* position in public service. Still, when Garfield died, Arthur stepped into the daunting role of America's chief of state.

Chester Arthur was born October 5, 1829, in North Fairfield, Vermont. He had four older sisters; two more sisters and a brother would arrive later. Although he is remembered in history as a man of wealth, high fashion, and refinement, Arthur was not born into wealth, and his ancestors had known their share of hardships. Uriah Stone, a maternal great-grandfather, fought in frontier wars and lost his humble cabin in a flood. Others in his mother's lineage were hardworking farmers. Some were preachers and church elders.

His father, William Arthur, was partly crippled by a childhood foot injury. He was a college-educated Irishman who immigrated to Canada where he taught school. Eventually, he traveled to the United States to study law. William completely changed his life's course after attending a New England church revival. He was ordained as a Baptist minister in 1828, and he accepted his first call to a Fairfield church. He only earned $250 a year, so he remained a schoolteacher while also occasionally preaching for congregations in other towns.

During Chester's boyhood, the family moved often because his father preached in many different locales around Vermont and New York State. One

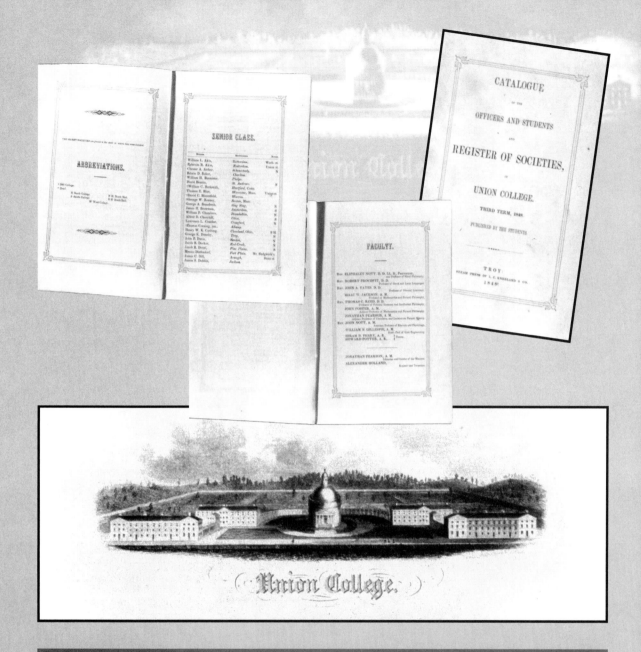

Union College.

Chester Arthur entered Union College in September 1848 as a sophomore. Union, in the old Dutch town of Schenectady, New York, traced its traditions to 1795. It was the first college chartered by the Board of Regents of New York State. When Arthur arrived at Union, Eliphalet Nott, a Presbyterian minister, was in his fifth decade as the school's president. Besides being an innovative educator, Nott was also a well-known inventor who had patented thirty different kinds of stoves, including an ingenious steamship boiler. School records do not reveal exactly what Arthur studied but it is known that he pursued the traditional classical curriculum. A friend recalled him as a tall, good-looking, slender youth with fashionably long hair and clear brown eyes. "In disposition," the friend wrote, "he was genial and very sociable and he had a good relative standing in his class though not a very diligent student." Arthur managed to be elected to Phi Beta Kappa in his senior year.

> *A brief Universal history from the Deluge to the present time.*
>
> Moses being the only man that survived the distruction of earth's inhabitants by water, after living some length of time in the open air, set his son Nebudchadnezzar to build Solomon's temple. In the course of which happened the confusion of languages, and this was the cause why the temple was left unfinished. About this period Alexander the Great after a siege of some months, took the tower of Babel by storm, and put all the inhabitants to the sword. But soon after he was attacted with vertigo, and fell into the bullrushes, where he was found by Pharaoh's daughter, and taken care of.
> While these things were going on in this quarter of the globe, Noah founded Egypt near the banks of the Amazon river, where the ruins are still to be seen. This place becoming powerful and renouned, principally by the great influx of Arabs, which literally crowed that fertile region, Napoleon Bonaparte fearing the consequences that might ensue from having so mighty a neighbor, hired

At Union, Arthur was a bit of a prankster. He jumped on and off of slow-moving trains at the nearby railroad station. He once threw the college bell into the Erie Canal. And he carved his name twice on the somber college buildings.

Three of Arthur's writings from his Union student days have survived. One is a humorous essay modestly titled "A brief Universal history from the Deluge to the present time." Page one is illustrated above.

The second of Arthur's student writings that has survived is a serious, reflective paper that reveals Arthur's fervent dislike of slavery.

reason they uprooted so frequently stemmed from Reverend Arthur's feisty, strongly stated opinions, which often clashed with those of many members and leaders of his congregations. Over the years, the reverend's annual income rose to as much as $550 a year, but this was a meager sum with which to support a large family.

Reverend Arthur probably introduced young Chester to the basics of education and reading while the boy spent time at home. Wherever they settled, Chester was enrolled at the local school. When he was nine, Chester's family moved to Union Village (Greenwich), near Saratoga, New York. Chester began attending an academy run by Principal James I. Lowrie, who later would recall Chester as a friendly, honest youth.

Even as a child, Chester showed natural leadership ability. When the Union Village children played together—perhaps building a dirt dam across a creek— young Chester would observe their progress carefully, and then he would suggest improvements. One Union Village boy recalled Chester's actions: "Pretty soon he would be ordering this one to bring stones, another sticks, and others sods and mud to finish the dam; and they would all do his bidding without question." Chester, meanwhile, never touched the muddy work himself. He enjoyed the outdoors, though. Fishing and hunting became lifelong pastimes.

In 1844 the Arthur family moved to Schenectady, New York, where Reverend Arthur accepted a call to another Baptist church. There, the minister befriended the president and faculty of Union College and found time to pursue his own quest for higher learning. Reverend Arthur was trained in the biblical and classical languages: Hebrew, Greek, and Latin. He became editor of a monthly magazine entitled *The Antiquarian and General Review*, which touched on topics including history, science, religion, and morals. At times, the *Review* exaggerated, or simply made up, stories to arouse emotional reactions from readers—a style of journalism typical of the era.

At 15, Chester followed in his father's editorial footsteps. While attending the Lyceum preparatory school, Chester edited the school newspaper, *The Lyceum Review*. Influenced by the reverend in a different way, Chester also took an early interest in politics. Reverend Arthur was outspoken in opposing slavery; he spent time with important abolitionists and served as cofounder of the New York Anti-Slavery Society. Meanwhile, Chester joined other Lyceum students in promoting Henry Clay, the Whig candidate for president in 1844. And while Chester expressed interests in politics, he still focused on his education. In 1845, Union College recognized Chester's advanced level of knowledge and admitted him as a sophomore.

Union, located in Schenectady, New York, was somewhat prominent among American colleges in the 1840s. It had a student body of approximately two hundred and fifty, and was overseen by a renowned president, Dr. Eliphalet Nott. Students followed one of three general courses of study: classical subjects, natural sciences, or civil engineering. Chester selected the classical, or traditional, curriculum. Subjects included advanced mathematics (algebra, trigonometry, geometry), science (geology, botany, chemistry, astronomy, anatomy, mineralogy, physiology), philosophy, rhetoric, economy, and French. Greek was a central part of the course work. Chester became familiar with the works of Horace, Livy, Homer, Thucydides, Herodotus, Homer, Xenophon, and other classical writers, and studied ancient history.

Under Nott's leadership, Union was a progressive college unlike most other institutions of the times. Nott's policy of accepting students who had been dismissed from other colleges for misconduct led detractors to nickname the school "Botany Bay"—the name of a British penal colony in Australia. Nott believed that teenagers and young adults must learn to discipline themselves rather than rely on older authorities for guidance at every turn.

Chester, like most adolescents, required discipline. His college pranks included heaving the college bell into the nearby Erie Canal, carving his name on campus buildings, and playing hooky from chapel. For the most part, though, he was forced to concentrate on his studies. Each morning began with breakfast and prayers at 6:30. Classes and recitations (students responding aloud during class) were held throughout the day, ending with a 7 P.M. study period.

A student's familiarity with recitations may explain the wide popularity of college debating societies in the mid-nineteenth century. Many U.S. statesmen gained some of their early oratorical experience as college debaters. Chester was elected president of one of Union's two debating clubs. He also joined Psi Upsilon, one of several fraternities at Union. When college classes were suspended during the winter months, Chester helped pay for his fees and board by teaching at nearby schools. Although he earned just fifteen dollars a month, the earnings meant much to his father, whose minister's salary alone could hardly support a child through college.

Overall, Chester was a good college student. In 1848, eighteen-year-old Chester Arthur graduated Phi Beta Kappa, ranked in the top one-third of his class. Arthur continued to teach through the remainder of that year, but he had decided to become a lawyer.

After briefly attending law school at Ballston Spa, New York, he pursued legal studies on his own at home. He still taught school and worked a stint as principal of a small academy for young students in North Pownall, Vermont. The academy conducted classes in the basement of a church. His students would remember the future president as a demanding master—but with a kind streak. Later, Arthur accepted a position as principal of an academy for older students in Cohoes, New York. Disruptive teenagers had given the Cohoes school a formidable reputation. Arthur wanted to instill order at the school without having to expel any students, so he identified the ringleaders and temporarily extracted them, one at a time, from the main class. He then told these students to return to Cohoes so they could apply themselves to learning, in harmony with others. His position was clear, and the boys understood. Here was a principal who seemed sincerely interested in seeing them better themselves, but who would take measures to keep order. "In two weeks time," one wayward student later wrote, "there was not a scholar in the room who would not do anything the teacher asked."

In 1853, Arthur began his practical legal education as an understudy of Erastus Culver, a noted New York City lawyer. At this period of history, even in major cities like New York, law schools were rare. Most aspiring lawyers learned the profession by reading law books under the guidance of an experienced practitioner. By the following year, Arthur had been admitted to the New York Bar and hired by Culver's law firm.

As a lawyer, Arthur became, like his father, a passionate abolitionist. He eagerly represented downtrodden African Americans. Early in his career, in a case that earned him enduring prestige, he sued a horse-car company in Brooklyn on behalf of an African-American woman, Lizzie Jennings. She had been ejected from a streetcar because of her race. He won a $500 judgment for Jennings—and the award was only a material token of an important precedent. The ultimate result was desegregation of New York City's transportation system. Only in his mid-twenties, the young lawyer had claimed a landmark legal victory.

In another famous case, the Culver firm helped win freedom for eight slaves being transported through New York State. The incident had occurred in 1852, but litigation and appeals lasted until 1860.

In 1856, Arthur partnered with Henry D. Gardiner to form their own law firm. Arthur had a talent for the courtroom. He was a personable character and a witty storyteller. But he had his sights on larger causes. That same year, he joined the Young Men's Frémont Vigilance Committee, formed to support John Charles Frémont as the fledgling Republican Party's first presidential candidate. Four years later, Arthur actively supported the candidacy of Abraham Lincoln.

However, Arthur did not only place his interest toward a career. In 1859, Arthur married Ellen Lewis Herndon, daughter of a naval officer. She was a Virginian, a cousin of one of his friends in Manhattan. They had three children. Ellen, a frail woman, would die at forty-two, shortly before Arthur became president.

Arthur had already been serving in the military when the Civil War started in 1861. He had joined the New York State Militia three years before and was serving as an engineering officer. By mid-1862, he had been promoted to quartermaster general. He did not see action on the battlefield—his role was to ensure that New York troops were properly supplied.

As it did with countless American families in the North and South, the war presented internal tensions for the Arthur family. Arthur's wife had many friends and relatives fighting for the

The third of Arthur's surviving college papers, pictured at left, is a portion of an acceptance speech delivered on May 8, 1847, after he was elected president of the Delphian Institute, the Union College debating society.

Confederacy. His sister, Malvina, was married to South Carolinian Henry Haynesworth, a Confederate civil servant. Arthur, who sided politically with the moderate Republicans (as contrasted with radicals who pressed for severe punishment of the rebels), yearned for the war's end and a return to family harmony.

Arthur returned to politics when he became a leader of the Republican organization of New York City in 1867. Soon after, he was made chair of the statewide Republican executive committee. In 1869, he was given a $10,000-a-year job as legal council to the tax commission of New York City. And in 1871, President Ulysses S. Grant appointed Arthur collector of customs for the Port of New York. He held the post for seven years, which made him very wealthy. New York was one of the world's busiest port cities, and the customs role—collecting duties (fees of commerce) from ships that docked there—was recognized as the most valuable political appointment in America. Arthur's pay and side benefits (which may have been collected through coercion and kickbacks) totaled as much as $50,000 a year—an enormous income at that time.

Arthur participated in a government system in which bribery and other forms of corruption were part of doing business. Even if unqualified, key political party officials were given lucrative appointments to administrative jobs such as the one Arthur held. Employees were expected to contribute substantial campaign funds to the party in control.

This amount of corruption couldn't be masked. Due to reform measures in 1878, Arthur lost his post as collector of customs. As a result, Arthur briefly returned to law practice, but power politics remained his destiny. In 1880, Arthur was among the delegates appointed by Senator Roscoe Conkling to the Republican National Convention in Chicago. Conkling supported the candidacy of former president Grant. Through a long series of inconclusive ballots, Grant repeatedly led his rivals but always fell short of a majority. The delegates ultimately nominated James A. Garfield as a compromise candidate. To soothe the anger of the Conkling faction, the convention chose Arthur as the Republican vice presidential nominee.

The selection of Arthur as Garfield's running mate drew fire from critics who deplored the conniving New York political machine, of which Arthur was a key figure. For the most part, however, voters took little notice of vice presidential candidates because they didn't expect a vice president to ever do anything of significance. The vice president in those years, unlike today, played only a minor role in the executive administration. "Because no politician of stature and prospects wanted to waste four years in semiparalysis," reflected historian Bernard A. Weisberger, "the nomination generally went to second-string party regulars with a regional following—men who largely lacked the leadership skills necessary should they suddenly be thrust into command."

The power brokers should have heeded history. Three times before (the most recent just fifteen years earlier), a vice president had been cast into the leading role when a president had died in office. When Garfield was assassinated in 1881, Arthur was publicly scorned and widely suspected of involvement in the crime. The assailant, Charles Guiteau, claimed he had acted on behalf of the Conkling political faction, although Republican leaders had refused to associate with Guiteau when he had tried to involve himself in their 1880 campaign. Still, the night after the shooting, Arthur twice visited Conkling's hotel room, which led to lingering suspicions. It soon became obvious, however, that Guiteau was suffering from a mental disorder.

But the rumors had done their damage. As a result, Arthur entered the White House amid a hailstorm of controversy. And so it is hardly surprising that Arthur did not appreciate the press and avoided reporters. Consequently, newspapers and satirical magazines of the day treated him with disrespect. So did Congress, which routinely overrode his presidential vetoes.

Historians have belittled his qualities to serve as president, and few give him very high marks for his performance in office. Historian Justus D. Doenecke observed, "there was little in his background to prepare him for executive leadership." In Weisberger's view, "Arthur was fortunate that he inherited the White House at a time when not much was expected or desired of its occupant." Other commentators were more kind. One of the most famous members of his generation, Mark Twain, estimated that "it would be hard to better President Arthur's administration."

Arthur surprised his detractors with a show of independence from his old political boss, Senator Conkling. He took measures to combat graft and favoritism. For example, he signed and supported the 1883 Pendleton Act, a reform bill that established the civil service system. Meanwhile, he made progress in foreign policy and refurbished the American naval fleet. "Overall," Weisberger surmised, "Arthur conducted a responsible, if undistinguished (and unimportant) presidency."

If not remembered for great achievements, Arthur clearly made a visible impression. A tall man with thick sideburns and mustache, he was a stylish dresser whose taste in fine clothes, banquets, and wine gave him a reputation as the "Gentleman Boss" and "Elegant Arthur." On most days, he changed clothes at least once so he wouldn't appear in the same attire. He had the White House redecorated and commissioned Louis Comfort Tiffany to design a lavishly expensive stained-glass petition in the main entrance. To some, he seemed to regard the presidency as much a social as administrative occupation. Arthur worked only from ten to four, and he spent considerable time entertaining—on some days, more than he spent dealing with the nation's business affairs. At times, dinner parties at the White House lingered past midnight— occasionally climaxed by late-hour social walks with friends through the capital city.

Perhaps these extended evenings spent with guests helped him stave off loneliness. His wife's untimely death shortly before he assumed the presidency was a horrible blow, made unbearable by the fact that he could not be at her bedside during her final hours. A portrait of her hung in the White House; the president ordered that fresh flowers be displayed with it each day.

Throughout his life, Arthur displayed qualities of leadership, style, and energy. His was a life of controversy and accomplishment. Chester A. Arthur died in New York City on November 18, 1886, following a battle with kidney disease.

—Daniel E. Harmon

Grover Cleveland
Chapter Twenty-two

Grover Cleveland was a man of physical and historical stature: a two-hundred-and-fifty-pound man with a bullish appearance. And his actions as a political figure ultimately added several presidential firsts to his legacy. He was the first president to get married while in office. He was the first Democrat to win the White House after the Civil War, following twenty years of Republican control of the office. And he was the first (and only) president ever to have personally administered capital punishment—while serving as sheriff in Buffalo, New York, approximately fifteen years before becoming the nation's chief executive, Cleveland had hanged two convicted prisoners.

Perhaps Cleveland's insistence on discipline had been cultivated by his family. Born as Stephen Grover Cleveland on March 18, 1837, in Caldwell, New Jersey, the future president's earliest influences were gleaned from his father Richard, a Presbyterian minister. The Clevelands had originally immigrated to America from England, and were a family with a long lineage of preachers and church leaders. Moreover, Grover's great-great-grandfather, Aaron Cleveland, had been a close friend of Benjamin Franklin in Philadelphia. Noted biographer Allan Nevins commented that the Cleveland clan was remarkable for its "piety and strength."

Some of the family's strength came from its numbers. Grover was the fifth of nine children. And the size of his family also influenced him greatly throughout his life. In his early years, Grover's casual education was enhanced by his older brothers and sisters, as well as by the practical teachings of his parents.

In 1841, Grover's parents decided to move the family to the village of Fayetteville in central New York. Fayetteville was about eight miles from Syracuse and only a mile from the Erie Canal.

Grover (who also was called Steve and later—even into adulthood—"Big Steve" by some of his friends) grew to be a hefty boy, full of energy and mischief. Along with his friends and older brother, Will, he played repeated pranks—carrying off yard gates and slipping into the school late at night to arouse villagers by clanging the bell. He also enjoyed sports with village boys and games with his family at home. Grover loved fishing

THE

CHRISTIAN OBSERVER.

N°. 3.] MARCH, 1802. N° 3. Vol. I

MISCELLANEOUS DEPARTMENT.

THE LIFE OF SIMON PETER, THE APOSTLE.

SIMON, the son of Jonah, a native of Bethsaida in Galilee, where he became acquainted with our Saviour, was settled at Capernaum, a city on the lake of Gennesareth, at which place he exercised the occupation of a fisherman, and was probably at that time a married man.

These scanty memoirs of the origin and early life of Simon, are little calculated to amuse curiosity. We have here a specimen of the biographical style of the sacred penmen; who all conspire in one design, and whether they write of Abraham, of Paul, or of Peter, mean to lead us to the knowledge of Christ, from whom those great men derived every valuable distinction. Whatsoever is irrelevant to this end, however curious or interesting, seems to be consigned to oblivion. Keeping this remark in view, as we delineate the character and record the life of Simon, it shall be our endeavour to illustrate the grace and power of the Redeemer, as they were displayed in that Apostle.

There is room to conjecture, that, previously to Simon's acquaintance with Jesus, he had been a disciple of John the Baptist, and, under his instructions had become acquainted with that repentance towards God, which is the best preparative to faith in Christ. This conjecture we found on the circumstance of his brother Andrew being one of the two disciples of John, to whom he pointed out Jesus Christ as the Lamb of God; as well as upon the readiness Simon shewed to wait on Jesus, and the distinguished reception he met with from him. No sooner had Andrew ascertained that Jesus was the Messiah, than he announced the discovery to Simon, as to one who also eagerly looked forward to his advent,

March, 1802.] *Life of Simon Peter, the Apostle.* 145

in learning the self-denying doctrines of the cross, than the scholars of Gamaliel were in unlearning the prejudices they had imbibed from their master. We therefore conclude, not only that the truth of Christianity was more strongly asserted, and the power of God more illustriously displayed, by their appointment; but that they were, in fact, the fittest instruments which the Jewish nation, at that time, furnished, and probably, for various reasons, the fittest instruments which human nature, in its present state, in any age or in any country, could furnish.

Here, however, there is a danger of pushing our conclusions to unwarrantable lengths. The partial advocates of an unlearned ministry should remember, that the gift of tongues superseded the painful discipline of schools and colleges; and that the luminous and energetic inspirations of the Spirit, would be degraded by a comparison with the slow deductions of reason, or the cold productions of mechanical rhetoric. We, who claim no such aids, must be content to burn our lamp, and to ply our studies; never however losing sight of this solemn truth, that it is the exclusive prerogative of religion, to make us truly wise, and good, and useful, and happy.

As a previous step to his exaltation to the Apostleship, Simon was called to a personal attendance on our Saviour. Under this great teacher, he was to be emptied of himself, and freed from those inveterate Jewish prejudices, which were likely to take strong hold of a mind constituted like his. His rude manners were also to be humanized by the benign converse of his Lord. From him he was to learn a doctrine without error. In him he was to behold an example without spot. And thus was he fitted, in common with the other Apostles, to receive the mantle of their ascending Lord. Would to God, that our young candidates for Holy Orders, considered well the solemn responsibility of the office to which they aspire! Then would they feel the force of the words of Moses: *Send by whom thou wilt send, but*

THE

CHRISTIAN OBSERVER,

CONDUCTED

BY MEMBERS OF THE ESTABLISHED CHURCH.

VOLUME I.

FROM THE FIRST OF JANUARY, TO THE THIRTY-FIRST OF DECEMBER, 1802.

FROM THE LONDON EDITION.

BOSTON:

PUBLISHED BY WILLIAM WELLS AND T. B. WAIT AND CO. BOSTON,

AND WHITING AND WATSON, NEW YORK.

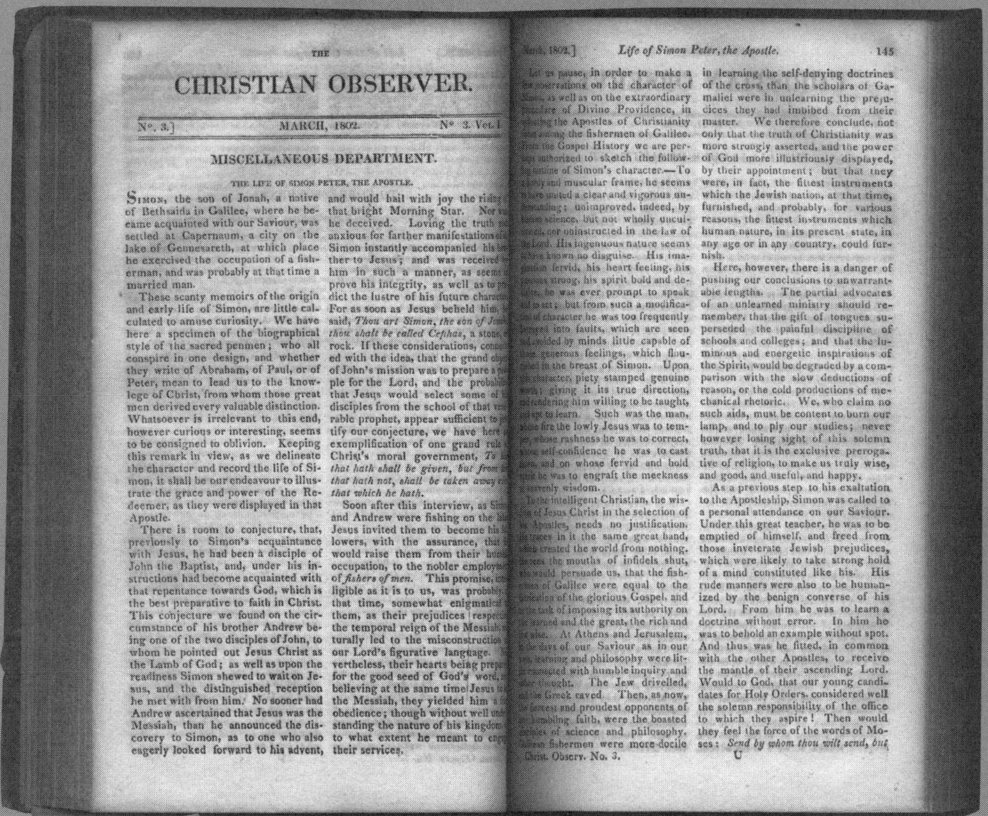

Allan Nevins, author of Grover *Cleveland: A Study in Courage* (1932), was the first historian to have access to Cleveland's personal papers. Nevins also conducted interviews and corresponded with family members, including Cleveland's widow. Nevins wrote that young Cleveland and his siblings were required to memorize the Westminster Catechism and the Bible. The Catechism, a statement of Calvinistic doctrine, has been the basis of American Presbyterianism since 1729.

Grover Cleveland, born in 1837, was the fifth of nine children. His father, an itinerant Presbyterian minister, had a profound intellectual influence on Cleveland. This devout man regularly read selections from the *Christian Observer* to his family. The weekly *Observer* was intended to provide all contemporary knowledge worth knowing. Nevins, in his biography of Cleveland, emphasizes the significance of the *Observer* in the education of the future president.

The *Christian Observer* began publication in London around 1800 and continued for at least fifty years. It contained, as the first issue stated, "information upon general subjects, with religious instruction, as to furnish such an interesting view of Religion, Literature, and Politics, free from the contamination of false principles, as a Clergyman may without scruple recommend to his Parishioners, and a Christian safely introduce into his Family." The pages shown above are from the first American edition (1802).

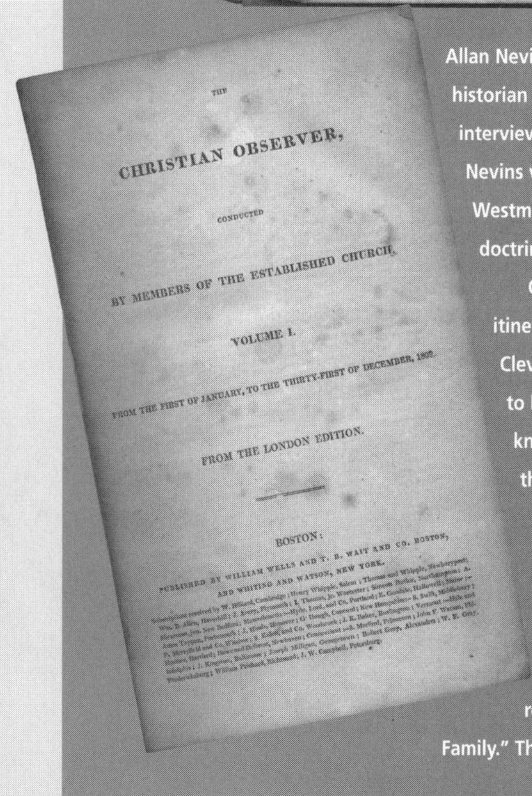

In his 1932 Cleveland biography, Allan Nevins lists the many books in young Cleveland's modest home and how the father encouraged his children to read. "Grover was taught many forcible ethical lessons," wrote Nevins. "He heard much of duty and self-improvement, and his parents spared no effort to lay a solid foundation for his character. One of the first productions of his pen that has been preserved is a brief essay, composed…at the age of nine, upon the value of time and the necessity of making the most of it in order 'to become great and good men'—an essay in which there are only two misspellings."

The Cleveland home library included Greek and Latin classics, books on theology and history, and the works of John Milton and William Shakespeare—but the most "entertaining volume in the collection was Bunyan's *Pilgrim's Progress*, which they all knew by heart," wrote Nevins.

The English writer John Bunyan's masterpiece *The Pilgrim's Progress from This World to That Which Is to Come* was published in two parts between 1678 and 1684. It is an allegory recounting a man named Christian's journey from the City of Destruction to the Celestial City. The second part describes how Christian's wife Christina makes the same pilgrimage. The popularity of *Pilgrim's Progress* rests on the spiritual fervor that permeates the story, a story that unites the eloquence of the Bible with the realism of common speech. It is considered one of the world's great works of literature.

The pages above are from an 1836 edition of *Pilgrim's Progress*.

and swimming in the local ponds and streams. In fact, as an adult, he frequently visited lakes of the Adirondack Mountains—Saranac Lake was his preferred fishing hole.

At the same time, Grover's lifelong dedication to a healthy work ethic had also been cultivated during his childhood. Grover helped tend the family garden, cut firewood, and performed other household chores. On one occasion, Grover lost the tip of a finger while operating a corn cutter. The church furnished Grover's father with a home, but the pay was meager. As the Cleveland children grew, they worked odd jobs to help financially support the family. When Grover was ten, his two teenage brothers were off working, one in a store in a neighboring town, the other on a farm fifteen miles away from home. At times, Grover would crawl out of bed hours before daylight and trudge to the Erie Canal to wave down passing cargo boats for local merchants, earning ten cents for his predawn errand.

Although Reverend Cleveland never earned the reputation of a brilliant theologian, he loved books and was, in the private sense, a lifelong student. In a letter to a friend, he relished the fact that after moving from Caldwell to Fayetteville he found "more opportunity to study than in my former location." Specifically, he reported that he was resuming his study of the German language. The minister had a notable library: volumes of classical literature, history, and theology. Consequently, the Cleveland children developed a love for reading. Grover's favorite book was John Bunyan's *The Pilgrim's Progress*. He and his siblings reread the work many times, memorizing whole chapters. And each week, they were also expected to read a periodical called the *Christian Observer*.

The devoutly religious Cleveland family practically spent every hour on Sunday reading Scripture or strolling in the home garden. The children were not allowed to work or play on that day.

Grover and his siblings were taught the values of honest work, diligence, self-improvement, and upright living. Their parents impressed upon them the importance of using their time wisely. For heroes, Grover marveled at the adventures and achievements of George Washington and Andrew Jackson.

Grover saw that achievement could be achieved through higher education. Grover's oldest brother, Will, enrolled at Hamilton College and became a minister, while another older brother became an engineer. "Indeed, the whole family circle constituted an excellent school for a growing boy," wrote Nevins. Grover's brief formal schooling began at Fayetteville's elementary school and continued at its academy for older students. His sister, Margaret, later remembered Grover as a diligent but not remarkable pupil. Although not a standout student, he was intelligent. His earliest preserved letter is lengthy and sophisticated. The letter, which thirteen-year-old Grover wrote to a sister while he was visiting relatives in Buffalo, contains a cheery description of his boat trip across the state as well as a detailed account of family life in western New York.

In 1850, the Cleveland family moved to Clinton, New York, because Reverend Cleveland had accepted a church administrative post that provided a substantial raise in salary—much needed to support his large family. Grover was sent to the local academy, the Clinton Liberal Institute, where his studies included math and Latin. Clinton was an intellectual center, the home of Hamilton College, which inspired Grover to one day pursue a collegiate education. But with the family continually struggling for money, any type of higher education would be difficult to achieve.

As a result, fourteen-year-old Grover accepted a job as a grocery clerk back in Fayetteville. He earned $1 a week, with free lodging; he and another young clerk shared a tiny room above the store, with no fireplace or comforts except a bed with a mattress of cornhusks. They were allowed to eat meals with the merchant's family.

Still, Grover continued his studies. Along with other teenagers inspired by intellectual yearnings, he formed a debating club in Fayetteville. They discussed a variety of topical questions, including, "Should a lawyer defend a criminal client if the client is known to be guilty?" and "Are Roman Catholic institutions 'a menace to the interests of the Union?'" (Grover argued "no" on both issues.)

In early 1853, Grover returned to Clinton to attend his sister Anna's wedding. He stayed on to study under a private tutor, planning to enroll for the autumn term at Hamilton College. But his plans for education were put on hold again when tragedy struck. In failing health, possibly because of the frequent travel required by his church position, Reverend Cleveland had decided he had to return to the pulpit. The salary would be only a fraction of what he had been earning in Clinton, but he had hoped the stability of parsonage life would enable him to recover his strength. He accepted a call to the church in Holland Patent, New York, where the family relocated in September. But he was not up to his duties. After preaching only one sermon in Holland Patent, he became bedridden and died a few weeks later.

By this time, Grover's older brothers and sisters were on their own, married or working. Grover and his younger siblings were obligated to care for their impoverished mother, so Grover postponed college and instead searched for a job. Of this decision, Nevins wrote, "He had been a boy; now he quickly became a man…. There was no question that he now had to stand upon his own feet. The family was too proud to accept help from its neighbors."

Within weeks, Grover joined his older brother, William, in New York City. There, William had obtained a post as head of the literary department at the New York Institution for the Blind. He managed to get Grover a job teaching the younger student residents the basics of reading, writing, math, and geometry. Grover also worked as a clerk for the institution's superintendent, and he and William were resident supervisors of the boys' dormitory. Grover's employment with the institution provided him with a regular paycheck, but little else. The institution's faculty and administration were dismal. The building was cold, the food unappetizing, and the discipline severe. By one account, "the children were treated more as inmates than pupils."

One ray of light for Cleveland originated from a friendship he had developed with Frances "Fanny" Crosby, a blind teacher and former student at the institution. At William's request, she took Grover under her wing and became like a mother lvi PREFACE TO THE ÆNEID.

of chief Use in compiling them, was to make *Virgil* his own Interpreter, and illustrate one Passage by comparing it with others that are parallel. This often proved the only Resource in Difficulties which were either entirely overlooked by Commentators, or where they disagreed among themselves.

As to the *Latin* Text, no pains have been spared to present it to the Reader in its genuine Purity and Correctness: For I all along compared the most celebrated Editions, namely, those of *H. Stephen, Heinsius, Emmenessius, Masvicius, Servius*, and *La Cerda*. And, for the Satisfaction of the Curious, I have also taken Notice of the most material of the various Readings from *Pierius, Servius, Stephen*, and others.

And that nothing might be wanting to render this Work complete, the Pointing, which in most Editions is exceeding erroneous, I have altered throughout, and endeavoured to set it to rights: considerable Instances of this the Reader will find in *Geor.* iv. 241. *Æn.* vii. 390. and *Æn.* ix. 140.

P. VIRGILII MARONIS

BUCOLICA.

ECLOGA I.

MELIBŒUS, TITYRUS.

MEL. TITYRE, tu, patulæ recubans sub tegmine fagi,
Silvestrem tenui musam meditaris avenâ:
Nos patriæ fines, et dulcia linquimus arva;
Nos patriam fugimus: tu, Tityre, lentus in umbrâ,
Formosam resonare doces Amaryllida silvas.

TRANSLATION.

MEL. YOU, Tityrus, lying all along under the Covert of *that* full-spread Beech, practise your woodland Lays on a slender oaten Pipe: We *are forced* to leave the Bounds of our Country, and our pleasant Fields; we fly our Country, *while* you, Tityrus, in the Shade, at Ease, teach the Woods to re-echo fair Amaryllis.

NOTES.

VOL. I. H

THE

WORKS OF VIRGIL,

TRANSLATED INTO

ENGLISH PROSE,

AS NEAR THE ORIGINAL AS THE DIFFERENT IDIOMS OF THE LATIN AND ENGLISH LANGUAGES WILL ALLOW:

WITH

THE LATIN TEXT AND ORDER OF CONSTRUCTION ON THE SAME PAGE;

AND

CRITICAL, HISTORICAL, GEOGRAPHICAL, AND CLASSICAL NOTES IN ENGLISH,

FROM THE BEST COMMENTATORS; BOTH ANCIENT AND MODERN.

BESIDE A VERY GREAT NUMBER OF NOTES ENTIRELY NEW.

For the Use of Schools, as well as of Private Gentlemen.

IN TWO VOLUMES.

FIRST AMERICAN EDITION,

CAREFULLY REVISED AND CORRECTED BY MALCOLM CAMPBELL, A. M. TEACHER OF LANGUAGES.

VOL. I.

NEW-YORK: PRINTED FOR

E. DUYCKINCK, No. 110 Pearl-street; T. & J. SWORDS, No. 160 Pearl-street; P. A. MESIER, No. 107 Pearl-street; and G. F. HOPKINS, No. 118 Pearl-street.

1803.

2 P. VIRG. MAR. BUCOLICA. Ecl. I.

TIT. O Melibœe, Deus nobis hæc otia fecit;
Namque erit ille mihi semper Deus: illius aram
Sæpe tener nostris ab ovilibus imbuet agnus.
Ille meas errare boves, ut cernis, et ipsum
Ludere, quæ vellem, calamo permisit agresti.
MEL. Non equidem invideo; miror magis; undique totis
Usque adeò turbatur agris. En ipse capellas
Protenus æger ago: hanc etiam vix, Tityre, duco:
Hic inter densas corylos modò namque gemellos,
Spem gregis, ah! silice in nudâ connixa reliquit.
Sæpe malum hoc nobis, si mens non læva fuisset,
De cœlo tactas memini prædicere quercus.
Sæpe sinistra cavâ prædixit ab ilice cornix.
Sed tamen, iste Deus qui sit, da, Tityre, nobis?
TIT. Urbem, quam dicunt Romam, Melibœe, putavi
Stultus ego huic nostræ similem, quò sæpe solemus
Pastores ovium teneros depellere fœtus.
Sic canibus catulos similes, sic matribus hœdos
Nôram; sic parvis componere magna solebam.
Verùm hæc tantum alias inter caput extulit urbes,
Quantum lenta solent inter viburna cupressi.

TRANSLATION.

TIT. A God, O Melibœus, hath vouchsafed us this Tranquillity; for to me he shall always be a God: a tender Lambkin from our Folds shall often stain his Altar *with its Blood*. 'Tis he hath licensed my Heifers to feed at large, as you see, and myself to play what *Tunes* I pleased on my rural Reed.

MEL. Truly, I envy you not; *but* rather am amaz'd *at your good Fortune*; now that all around there are such Confusions in the Country. Lo myself, sick *as I am*, drive far hence my tender Goats: This too, O Tityrus, I drag along with much ado: For here just now among the thick Hazles having yeaned Twins, the Hope of my Flock, she left them, alas! on the naked flinty Rock. This Calamity, I remember, my Oaks, struck *with Lightning* from Heaven, often presaged to me, had not my Mind been under Infatuation: Often the ill-boding Crow from an *old* hollow Oak presaged *it*. But tell me, Tityrus, who is this God of yours?

TIT. The City, Melibœus, which they call Rome, I foolishly imagined to be like this our *Mantua*, whither we Shepherds oft-times are wont to drive the tender Offspring of our Ewes. So I had known Welps like Dogs, so Kids like their Dams; thus was I wont to compare great Things with small. But that City hath raised its Head as far above others as the Cypresses use *to do* above the limber Shrubs.

NOTES.

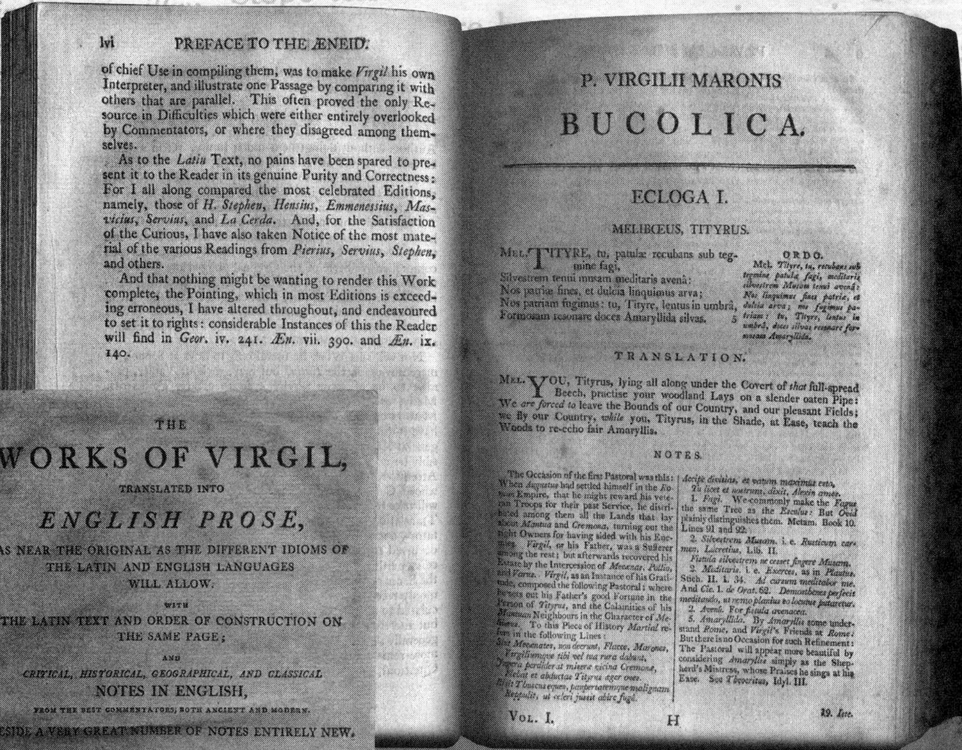

In the winter of 1850–51, thirteen-year-old Cleveland attended the town school in Clinton, New York. His sister Margaret wrote, "He was then, as I remember, a lad of rather unusual good sense, who did not yield to impulses—he considered well, and was resourceful—but as a student Grover did not shine. The wonderful powers of application and concentration which afterwards distinguished his mental efforts were not conspicuous in his boyhood." The school had two teachers. In his class of three, young Cleveland struggled through four books of the *Aeneid*, using his father's worn copy. He envied his wealthier classmates who could afford newer editions, with large print and explanatory notes to help them over the difficult passages.

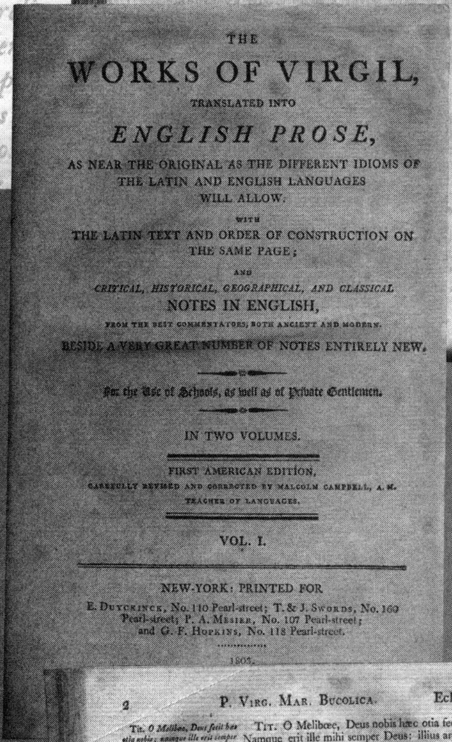

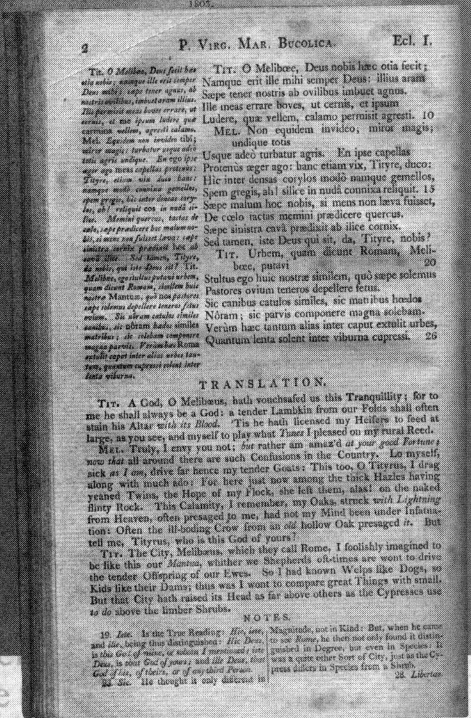

The deeds of Aeneas are the subject of the Roman poet Virgil's great epic, the *Aeneid*. After the fall of Troy, Aeneas escaped to Carthage, bearing his aged father on his back. Eventually, Aeneas went to Italy where his descendants founded Rome. Almost every Latin student of the nineteenth century read this work.

Several pages from an 1803 edition of Virgil's works are shown above. This edition is comparable to the ones used by young Cleveland's richer classmates as it contains an English translation as well as explanatory notes.

figure in the strange, busy city. Crosby, a gifted poet, eventually became one of America's most prolific hymn writers, composing more than 9,000 during her life. In Cleveland's free time, he read to Crosby and served as her scribe while she dictated her compositions.

Another eloquent figure, Reverend Henry Ward Beecher, notably influenced Cleveland during his time in New York. Beecher, a famous preacher in the years leading up to the Civil War and the brother of writer Harriet Beecher Stowe (*Uncle Tom's Cabin*), preached at nearby Plymouth Church. Cleveland was enthralled by Beecher's sermons, later describing the "fervid eloquence" that "captivated my youthful understanding."

Cleveland was never captivated, however, by his dreary employment at the New York Institution for the Blind. After only a year, he left the institute with a painful sympathy for its students and other downcast members of society. William Cleveland also left at that time to attend seminary and train for a career in ministry.

When Cleveland returned to Holland Patent, he worked odd jobs while improving his understanding of Latin by reading with a traveling tutor. He still hoped to attend college, but was beginning to despair. "How is a man going to spend four years in getting an education," he wrote to a sister, "with nothing to start on and no prospect of anything to pay his way with…. Until I see how I am going to get through, you don't catch me inside of College walls."

Cleveland did get an unexpected opportunity to attend college when Ingham Townsend, a local church elder and prominent citizen, offered to pay for Cleveland's college education if he agreed to enter the ministry. However, Cleveland declined the proposition. Instead, with a $25 loan from Townsend, the eighteen-year-old set out for the West hoping to earn a better living.

He went no farther than Buffalo, New York. While staying with relatives along the Niagara River, an uncle offered him a reasonably good job working on the family farm and keeping a livestock journal for his cattle-breeding business. Eventually, his uncle persuaded the Buffalo law firm of Rodgers, Bowen, and Rodgers to hire his bright, industrious nephew as a clerk. While performing work for the firm, Cleveland read law books and learned the legal profession.

Expecting little of the young clerk, the senior lawyer in the firm gave him a copy of Sir William Blackstone's commentaries on law and justice. Cleveland was left to his own supervision, practically ignored by the lawyers and staff at the firm. Basically, he had to make himself a lawyer. Biographer Nevins explained, "A law student then had to read hard, keep his eyes and ears open, and in a more or less unsatisfactory fashion school himself. It was a crude and uncertain way of learning law. But until the case system was introduced at Harvard by Langdell in the [1860s], even the colleges furnished no better method."

While working as a clerk, Grover was influenced by Dennis Bowen, one of the firm's three partners. Bowen was known not only for his thorough research in preparing cases, but also for his concern for justice above and beyond legal

> "I have to work pretty hard at present, as the senior clerk is absent. But it is better for me, as the more I do, the more I learn."

technicalities. Bowen was an effective arbitrator who was able to settle many matters before they reached the courtroom.

Besides law, Grover's time at the Rodgers firm taught him, if nothing else, to be a self-starter. At one point, the firm's clerk supervisor was away, as were his relatives at home. Grover wrote to his sister Mary, "I have to work pretty hard at present, as the senior clerk is absent. But it is better for me, as the more I do, the more I learn." Unlike his fellow clerks, he stayed at the office after hours, helping research cases for the firm's lawyers. Soon, he was so engrossed in his legal studies that he left the friendly home of his relatives to rent quarters near the law office in town, making it easier for him to work long hours.

After four years, Grover Cleveland was admitted to the bar in May 1859. Soon, he was made chief clerk at the Buffalo law firm, earning the handsome salary of $1,000 a year.

During the Civil War (1861–65), Cleveland opted not to fight. Having become a staunch supporter of the Democratic Party, he opposed the conflict. He paid another young man to substitute for him in the military draft—an accepted practice during the war. Meanwhile, Cleveland rose to prominence in local politics. He became a key campaign worker for Governor Horatio Seymour, and by the end of the war he had worked as assistant district attorney.

Five years later, he was elected sheriff of Erie County. On two separate occasions, he personally hanged convicted murderers. For Cleveland, it was a matter of principal: hanging was the punishment mandated by law, and he wouldn't order his deputies to perform an ugly responsibility unless he was willing to do the same.

As assistant district attorney and sheriff, Cleveland became known for his insistence on justice and his refusal to succumb to political corruption. He diligently fought illegal practices in the Buffalo area. The reputation he acquired would follow him into national politics—and his rise to national prominence was meteoric.

Cleveland was elected mayor of Buffalo in 1882. Within months, this forty-four-year-old bachelor lawyer of moderate means and slight name recognition was being touted as a candidate for New York governor. Running as a Democrat, Cleveland handily defeated his Republican opponent. Even as he took office in the state capital in 1883, national party movers and shakers were grooming him as their 1884 presidential candidate. Consequently, it came as no surprise when Cleveland was nominated at the 1884 Democratic convention in Chicago. In seconding the nomination to the convention, delegate Edward S. Bragg of Wisconsin pointed out that the public loved Cleveland "for himself, for his character, for his integrity and judgment and iron will." But above all, Bragg

46   INDEX TO STATUTES.

No.
Of trustee of separate neighborhood,.................. 147
Of trustees of colored schools,.................... 184
Of county clerks,....................... 169
Forms of, to be transmitted to trustees, &c., by superintendent,......................... 12, 185
Proceedings and penalties in case of neglect of town superintendents to make,.................... 45, 47, 48
Penalty for trustees making false report,........... 148
Public money not to be apportioned to districts from which no sufficient annual report shall have been received,......... 38

Apparatus.

For schools may be purchased,.................. 87

Appeals.

To superintendent,.................. 157, 165

Appendages to School House.

Taxes for,.................. 87
To be provided by trustees,.................. 107

Apportionment of School Moneys.

When to be made by superintendent,.................. 6
Ratio of,.................. 7
Increase of school moneys when and how to be apportioned,.................. 8
Proceedings when census is defective,.................. 9
Proceedings on erection or division of towns,.................. 10
To be certified to comptroller and county clerks,.................. 11
Library fund to be annually apportioned, amount of, and how to be appropriated,.................. 161
When and how to be apportioned by town superintendents among the several districts,.................. 33
Conditions of apportionment and when to be withheld, 35, 36, 38
To be equitably adjusted by town superintendents in case of alteration or formation of districts after date of annual report,.................. 40, 41
Disposition of moneys uncalled for in the hands of town superintendents for one and two years,.................. 42, 43
To be directed by superintendent in certain cases of accidental omission or non-compliance with law,.................. 39

Arms and Accoutrements.

When and to what extent exempt from warrants of collectors,.................. 398 (note.)

INDEX TO STATUTES.   47

No.
Assessments.

Of school moneys by board of supervisors on their several towns,.................. 20

Assessment of Taxes.

See Taxes and Tax List—Trustees.

Assessment Roll of Town.

Valuation of taxable property to be taken from,.................. 121

Authentications.

Of papers, acts and decisions of superintendent,.................. 5

B.

Black Boards.

Districts authorized to impose taxes for purchase of,.................. 87

Blank Books.

To be provided by trustees for use of districts, and what to contain,.................. 129

Board of Supervisors.

To assess an amount upon each town equal to that apportioned by superintendent,.................. 20
To require collector to pay such amount when collected, to commissioner,.................. 21
To hold special meeting in case of deficiency in amount raised the preceding year, for the purpose of supplying such deficiency,.................. 23
Duty of, on receiving from county treasurer, accounts of unpaid taxes of non-residents, furnished by trustees,.................. 118, 120

Book Case.

Districts may raise tax for purchase of, for district library.................. 158

Bonds.

To be given by collector of district when required by trustees, and amount and condition of,.................. 128

STATUTES

OF THE

STATE OF NEW-YORK

RELATING TO

COMMON SCHOOLS,

INCLUDING

TITLE II. OF CHAPTER XV. PART I. OF THE REVISED STATUTES,
AS AMENDED BY THE ACT CHAPTER 480, LAWS OF 1847.

WITH

FORMS AND REGULATIONS

RESPECTING PROCEEDINGS UNDER THOSE STATUTES.

Prepared pursuant to the directions of the Legislature,

BY THE SUPERINTENDENT OF COMMON SCHOOLS.

ALBANY:
C. VAN BENTHUYSEN, PUBLIC PRINTER.
1847.

INDEX

TO THE

STATUTES RELATING TO COMMON SCHOOLS.

The figures relate to the several sections as numbered.

A.

Alteration of School Districts.

No.
Without consent of trustees when to take effect,.................. 70

Annual Meeting of School Districts.

Provision for holding,.................. 90
When omitted, special meeting may be called and how,.................. 91
When superintendent may order meeting,.................. 92
When trustees may fix day for,.................. 93
Powers of inhabitants when lawfully assembled, 87, 96, 98, 99, 109, 158
Proceedings of, not invalidated by defective notice unless wilful and fraudulent,.................. 94
Notice of, how to be given and what to contain,...79, 89, 106, 107
Appeals from proceedings of, to superintendent,.................. 157
District librarian to be chosen at,.................. 87
Qualifications of voters at,.................. 84 to 86

Annual Reports.

Of superintendent, what to contain,.................. 1
Of town superintendent of common schools, to be made between 1st July and 1st August,.................. 44
What to contain,.................. 44
Of trustees of school districts,.................. 140, 141
Of trustees of joint districts,.................. 116

In 1855, eighteen-year-old Cleveland began to clerk in the offices of a Buffalo law firm. On the first morning, the elder partner placed a copy of William Blackstone's *Commentaries on the Laws of England* on Cleveland's desk, announcing, "That's where they all begin." Cleveland was left to learn law on his own.

In accordance with custom at the time, Cleveland was paid nothing during his first month or two. Then the law firm allowed him four dollars a week, a sum fixed as the precise amount necessary to pay his food, laundry, and lodging with the family of a fellow clerk.

In addition to being a factotum, Cleveland was required to read and understand the law books in the firm's small library. New York State recently had codified statutes dealing with public schools, and *Statutes of the State of New York Relating to Common Schools* (1847), a two-hundred-and-fifteen-page volume, was in the firm's library.

said, Cleveland was respected "for the [political] enemies he has made." Cleveland won the party's nomination by a landslide on the second ballot and went on to defeat Republican James G. Blaine in the national election.

Four years later, the Democratic Party unanimously nominated Cleveland for reelection. Opposition by political bosses in New York, however, swayed his crucial home state for Republican opponent Benjamin Harrison, costing Cleveland the presidency. In 1892, Cleveland was poised for a rematch. This time, a focused Cleveland carried New York and defeated Harrison by a narrow margin.

Perhaps Cleveland's dedication to politics played a major role in delaying his pursuit of marriage. On June 2, 1886, in the second year of his first term, a fifty-year-old Cleveland became America's first president to wed in the White House when he married Frances Folsom—a woman less than half his age. And even on this momentous day, he worked as usual at the White House—almost until the very hour of the evening ceremony. Amid all his political responsibilities, Cleveland fathered five children.

While Cleveland showed great discipline when fulfilling his presidential duties, honesty may have been his most memorable trait. In the opinion of one biographer, Cleveland compared favorably to George Washington: "Both were heavy, somewhat narrow, a little dull, inclined to be conservative; but both were of a sort to inspire confidence.... Neither was a gifted speaker or writer, but neither was afraid to say bluntly what was called for."

In an era of high corruption and wasteful government spending, the blunt-spoken Cleveland primarily used the presidency to veto congressional measures he felt might further such corruption and waste. He made political enemies because of it—and won public admiration. Apart from his watchdog measures, though, his record seems diminished compared to those of other chief executives. "A largely negative president," wrote historian Vincent P. De Santis, "he firmly believed it was his duty to prevent hurtful things from happening, rather than to make beneficial things take place.... Cleveland is therefore remembered less for his accomplishments (or his personal brilliance) than for his character—specifically, for his courage, firmness, uprightness, and sense of duty."

At times, his specific zeal for economy drew disbelief and scorn. In 1887, he vetoed a bill to aid drought-stricken farmers in Texas, proclaiming the measure unconstitutional. In another instance, he used military force to end a boycott by train workers who had suffered a dramatic pay cut, arguing that "though the people should support the government, the government should not support the people." In his later years, Cleveland lectured at Princeton University and was named president of the university board of trustees. In 1906, he took a lucrative leadership job with the insurance industry. He died on June 24, 1908, in Princeton, New Jersey.

—Daniel E. Harmon

Benjamin Harrison
Chapter Twenty-three

By the mid-nineteenth century, the Harrison family had a long and distinguished history in America—the family had settled in Virginia in 1632, less than twenty-five years after the colony had been founded. The Harrisons became plantation owners and mixed and married into Virginia plantation society. The fifth generation of Harrisons provided the Revolutionary-era leader Benjamin Harrison, who signed the Declaration of Independence. Benjamin's second-youngest son, William Henry Harrison, became a military hero for his battles against Native Americans and the British during the early years of the nineteenth century. He was elected president of the United States in 1840.

Before running for president, William Henry Harrison had retired from the military and politics and was living on a farm along the Ohio River near Cincinnati. While Harrison had been in politics—he had served as territorial governor of Indiana, as well as a stint in Congress—his son John Scott Harrison had managed the property. John Scott had been educated as a lawyer, but at his father's request had given up law to run the family farm. When William Henry Harrison retired, he gave his son a gift of additional land between the Ohio and Miami rivers.

John Scott Harrison was not a successful farmer. He frequently had to borrow from relatives to make ends meet. The farm grew most of the food the family ate, and some cash crops as well. It needed to provide a lot of food, because the Harrison family was growing quickly. John Scott and his wife, Elizabeth Ramsey Irwin Harrison, had twelve children, although only eight lived to maturity. Their second child, Benjamin, was born August 20, 1833, in North Bend, Ohio.

Ben Harrison was a typical farm child. He helped with daily chores, planting, and harvesting. Like other boys who lived in rural Ohio, Ben always was eager to find time for hunting and fishing.

Sundays were very special. Because churches were far away, the family developed their own Sunday services, which included hymn singing, often for hours at a time.

A one-room school had been built on the Harrison farm. It served the children of John Scott and their cousins who lived nearby. The children's

Just after his seventeenth birthday, Harrison entered Miami University at Oxford, Ohio. Miami, a school with high academic standards, was known as the "Yale of the West" because its curriculum was patterned very much after that of Yale. In 1850, Miami had about 250 students and six instructors.

Harrison was invited to become a member of the Miami Union Literary Society. He took advantage of the society's splendid program of group study, public speaking, and debating. At meetings, members debated religious and political questions of the day and were encouraged to have independent opinions and to speak them freely. In his last year at Miami, Harrison was elected president of the society. This was both an acknowledgment of his skill in public speaking and as a personal tribute of respect from his fellow students.

The above two illustrations are from the 1851 minutes of the Miami Union Literary Society, which list Harrison as a participant. The page on the left indicates that he was fined for disorderly conduct at a meeting.

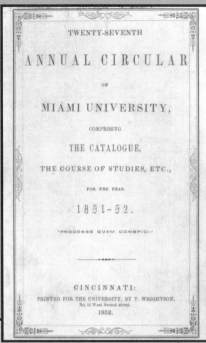

The above illustrations are from the 1852 Miami University Catalog—the cover and class lists (Harrison is included in the senior class).

Miami was the thirteenth university to be established in the United States, and the seventh state university. It compared most favorably in the matter of faculty and enrollment with the more renowned institutions of the day.

governess, Harriet Root, was the first teacher hired by John Scott. She noted in later years that Ben, her brightest student, was a very determined child.

The classroom had only rudimentary furniture—benches that were little more than log slabs with no backs pushed up to long tables. A fireplace provided heat, and there were a few windows. The students used whatever schoolbooks were available. Ben loved to read; fortunately, his grandfather William Henry Harrison had a large library, so the youngster had access to many books.

As the children grew older, a more experienced teacher was needed. John Scott hired Joseph Porter, a college graduate. While living with the family, Porter noted Ben's intelligence and encouraged John Scott to send him to a college in the East to complete his education. Heeding Porter's suggestion, John Scott Harrison decided his two older boys should have a college education. To prepare for this, he enrolled them in Cary's Academy (later Farmers College), a school located on a farm near Cincinnati. Cary's Academy was similar to an independent prep school. At the time, Ben was fourteen years old.

The school was fortunate to have an outstanding educator. Dr. Robert Hamilton Bishop had been teaching at colleges and universities for forty years. Before he came to Cary's Academy, he had been president of Miami University in Oxford, Ohio. Bishop instilled in his students the need for self-control and the need to develop all the facts in order to make decisions. He was a most important mentor for Ben. Later, Benjamin Harrison's biographers would comment on how much Bishop's philosophy typified Ben's adult conduct.

Ben attended Cary's Academy for three years. While there, he was able to remain very close to his family. At times, Ben was needed at home to help with farm work. When he left the school, Ben thanked his teachers for the care they had shown for his welfare and for his advancement in religious and scientific knowledge.

John Scott Harrison wanted to send his son to Harvard or Yale. But in 1850, he was experiencing another financial setback and such an expense was out of the question. It was decided that Ben would go to Miami University in Oxford, the "Yale of the West."

Miami University had suffered through a difficult 1848. Students had rebelled against harsh discipline. Many of the buildings had been damaged or destroyed. One observer noted the campus "looked like a horse barracks—broken doors and windows, weeds, brick and cinders in the yard, brush and locust shoots springing up beside the paths." A new president, Reverend W. C. Anderson, rebuilt the school both physically and academically. He expanded the faculty and updated the curriculum. Anderson returned the school to the prestigious level it had been prior to 1848.

It was in this troubled scene that Ben began his studies as a junior in the fall of 1850. But the school had all he needed to complete his transformation into an educated adult. During Ben's time there, the school's reputation grew, as did its student enrollment, from sixty-eight students to almost two hundred. The tuition was $30 per year.

This photograph, taken around 1858, is the earliest known photo of Miami University

Miami University, established in 1809, is located in Oxford, Ohio, thirty-five miles north of Cincinnati. The school is named for the Miami Indian Tribe that inhabited the area now known as the Miami Valley. In its early years, Miami was the principal training school for Presbyterian ministers in Ohio.

Living so far away from his family was hard on Ben. His father continually worried that Ben would fall into bad habits without proper guidance. Ben studied basic subjects, with Greek, Latin, science, and mathematics as the core. Later, classes in modern languages, history, political economics, geometry, astronomy, and art were added. From its start, Miami University had a religious orientation. Its board members were Presbyterian ministers. Chapel attendance was mandatory each morning and twice on Sunday. Many students went on to the ministry—a possibility Ben considered.

There was great emphasis on writing and debating. Ben joined the Union Literary Society. The society had its own extensive library to supplement that of the school, which was oriented toward ministerial studies. With the use of both libraries, Ben had access to books on history, law, and politics. The latter would be useful in his postgraduate career.

Ben was a student leader at Miami. He helped many of his classmates in courses they found difficult. He also developed a romantic friendship with Caroline Scott, daughter of Dr. John W. Scott, whom Ben had met while attending Cary's Academy. Caroline now attended the nearby Oxford Female Academy founded by her father. Their relationship deepened, and prior to his graduation they secretly became engaged.

Ben graduated from Miami University in June 1852. He participated in the graduation ceremonies by reading a speech titled "Poor of England." It was a commentary about the impact of the Industrial Revolution on the lower classes in England. The young man proposed that rampant poverty resulted from replacing private charity with "the compulsory provision of a legalized, soulless benevolence." He was very much in favor of personal responsibility during economic bad times. Later, this belief in Social Darwinism would cause him problems as president.

Many of Ben Harrison's teachers thought he would follow a career in the church. But after much reflection, Ben decided he would prefer to be a lawyer. His father had been advised to send him to Harvard, which at that time was the finest law school in the United States. But Ben's father was financially strapped, and both he and Ben knew they could not afford Harvard. Traditionally, there was another way to become a lawyer. This was to take a job as a clerk in an established firm and read law with a lawyer who served as a mentor. Two years of study usually was required before one could take a bar exam. Ben decided to follow this route. He read law with Storer and Gwynne, a prominent Cincinnati firm.

This apprenticeship was complicated by the fact that young Ben was in love and wished to marry Caroline. To add to his problems, the sister with which Harrison was living in Cincinnati was moving away. Ben did not have the funds necessary to live in a boarding house, so he had to return home. Harrison decided he would return to the family farm married to Caroline. The ceremony took place on October 20, 1853. (The

The earliest known photograph of Oxford Female Institute, taken around 1864

In 1849, John W. Scott opened the Oxford Female Institute in the west end of the town. His daughter Caroline, the future Mrs. Benjamin Harrison, was in the first graduating class. The school merged with Miami University in the 1910s.

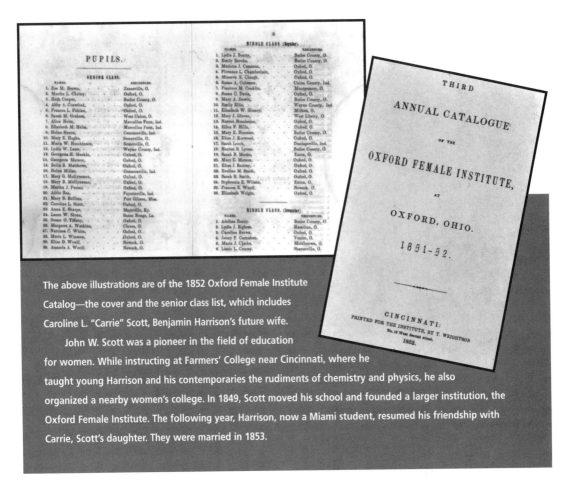

The above illustrations are of the 1852 Oxford Female Institute Catalog—the cover and the senior class list, which includes Caroline L. "Carrie" Scott, Benjamin Harrison's future wife.

John W. Scott was a pioneer in the field of education for women. While instructing at Farmers' College near Cincinnati, where he taught young Harrison and his contemporaries the rudiments of chemistry and physics, he also organized a nearby women's college. In 1849, Scott moved his school and founded a larger institution, the Oxford Female Institute. The following year, Harrison, now a Miami student, resumed his friendship with Carrie, Scott's daughter. They were married in 1853.

Harrisons would have three children, but only two would reach adulthood.) By this time, Ben's father had been elected to Congress and he left the farm to the newlyweds. Although Harrison worked as a farmer, he continued his legal studies, borrowing such books as he could until he was able to pass the bar exam in 1854.

The next question was where to establish his law practice. Harrison decided to move to Indianapolis, the capital of Indiana. It was a new city, and he felt he had a better chance to get started there. Having few connections, Harrison had to take whatever work he could find. To supplement his meager income as a beginning lawyer, he obtained a job as a court clerk for $8 a week.

One day he was asked by the county prosecutor to assist in a criminal trial. When it came time for closing arguments, the prosecutor was not there, so Ben had to plead the case. His opponent was former Ohio governor David Wallace. Harrison's performance impressed Wallace, and soon Wallace's son asked Ben to join their law firm. The younger Wallace was beginning a political career and needed a lawyer to assist his clients while he campaigned. Harrison soon became a very successful and respected lawyer. After his presidency, he would return to his law career.

The Harrison family had belonged to the Whig Party, but in the turbulent 1850s new political forces were emerging. After a crushing defeat in the 1852 election, the Whig Party disintegrated. A new political party, the Republican Party, emerged. It opposed the spread of slavery into the western territories. Republican leaders said that they would not interfere with slavery where it already existed, but they would oppose the further expansion of slavery in new states to be admitted to the Union. John Harrison thought the Republican Party would push the country into a civil war. However, Ben Harrison decided to join the Republicans. He gave the new party his unswerving allegiance. For Harrison, slavery was a moral evil which had to end.

In 1857, Ben Harrison was elected city attorney for Indianapolis. In 1860, he ran for Indiana Supreme Court reporter. Winning the position was a steppingstone into the state Republican power circle. During a subsequent campaign, Harrison spoke on a forum with his Democratic opponent. The other man spoke for four hours, and then turned the podium over to Harrison. With precision, he rebutted the Democrat point by point, but never included personal attacks. His success in this debate helped Benjamin Harrison win reelection as court reporter.

During the Civil War, Harrison helped raise the 70th Indiana Infantry and was appointed its colonel. By the end of the war, he was a brevetted brigadier general. Harrison was very popular with his troops—a popularity that he was unable to carry over into politics.

The Miami University commencement program, June 24, 1852. Harrison (whose name is incorrectly spelled as "Harris") is listed as giving an address on "The Poor of England." The original rough draft of this speech is in the Harrison papers at the Library of Congress. Lewis Ross, a fellow classmate, later wrote that Harrison "was a protectionist [on the tariff issue] at the age of 19...he is a protectionist still...his whole career has been illustrative of his desire to save his countrymen from the poverty which oppressed the 'Poor of England.'"

The post–Civil War presidency of Ulysses S. Grant was marred by corruption and scandal, causing the Republican Party to lose ground in Indiana. A movement was started to have Harrison run for governor of Indiana in 1876. Reluctantly he did, but it was not a successful campaign. Four years later, the Republicans regained control of the state government. Harrison decided to seek a Senate seat. At that time each state appointed its U.S. senators, and in 1880 Harrison was chosen as a senator from Indiana, serving from 1881 to 1887.

After Grover Cleveland was elected president in 1884, becoming the first Democratic president since before the Civil War, Harrison turned his attention to the 1888 election. The campaign against Cleveland would be fought over the tariff issue. Democrats saw the tariff as a device to keep prices high; Republicans argued that it protected business and the wages of the American laborer.

In 1888 Harrison was Indiana's "favorite son." He won the Republican nomination, defeating eight other candidates, and defeated the incumbent Cleveland, becoming the twenty-third president. Because he was inaugurated in 1889, one hundred years after George Washington had taken the oath of office, Benjamin Harrison was called the "Centennial President."

Harrison served one term, losing to Cleveland, his old opponent, four years later. There were many forces at work against Harrison's reelection. Democrats said he was cold and aloof. He was a prisoner of detail. He had 1,700 political positions to fill as president, and he insisted on doing this himself. His selections disappointed many party leaders. But he was determined to appoint only qualified people. Business and labor supporters turned against him for various reasons, especially for his uncompromising defense of a high protective tarrif.

Biographers have noted that Harrison lacked the charisma of Cleveland, and he had little sense for political compromise. Once he made up his mind, he was unmovable.

His 1892 reelection campaign fell under a pall with the death of his wife. Due to her illness and death Harrison did not actively campaign. After Cleveland was reelected, Harrison returned to Indianapolis. He found life lonely and decided to remarry. His second wife, Mary Lord Dimmick, was Caroline's niece and had nursed her during her final illness.

Harrison returned to the practice of law. He again had a very successful career, even arguing before the U.S. Supreme Court. His life centered around his family, his religion, the Republican Party, and his law practice.

Benjamin Harrison, the only grandson of a president who became a president, died on March 13, 1901.

—Harry Mortimer

VIEWS

OF

AN EX-PRESIDENT

BY

BENJAMIN HARRISON

BEING HIS ADDRESSES AND WRITINGS ON SUBJECTS
OF PUBLIC INTEREST SINCE THE CLOSE OF
HIS ADMINISTRATION AS PRESIDENT
OF THE UNITED STATES

COMPILED BY
MARY LORD HARRISON

INDIANAPOLIS
THE BOWEN-MERRILL COMPANY
PUBLISHERS

On March 4, 1889, Benjamin Harrison, the grandson of President William Henry "Old Tippecanoe" Harrison, became the twenty-third president of the United States. Harrison's education was one of privilege—he had unlimited access to a superb family library and he also had the encouragement of his grandfather and parents who were determined that he receive an outstanding education.

In 1896, Harrison, at age sixty-three, reflected on the value of his early schooling. He was thoroughly convinced that the "seeds of knowledge" ought to first be planted at the tender age of eighteen months, and that the wise parent should not neglect the child's education until the average school-going age of six or seven years. In an unprecedented essay written by a former president, Harrison pleaded with teachers to emulate his own education by introducing children to "a vast workshop, where the most subtle forces and the most intricate mechanisms are humming and whirling; into a vast picture gallery where thousands of canvases, great and small, are hung; into a great auditorium where on many stages clowns and tragedians are acting and reciting."

Harrison wrote this essay at the urging of his second wife. After his death in 1901, she had it published as a tribute. Illustrated above are pages from Mary Lord Harrison, *Views of an Ex-President* (1901).

William McKinley
Chapter Twenty-four

William McKinley joined a regiment of Ohio volunteers just a few weeks after Confederate troops bombarded Fort Sumter with cannon fire, touching off the Civil War. At the time, McKinley had been working as a teacher in Poland, Ohio, hoping to save enough money so that he could return to college. McKinley had spent a semester at tiny Allegheny College in western Pennsylvania, dropping out because of poor health and a lack of money.

It had been his intention to re-enroll at Allegheny. But when the Civil War began, McKinley found himself caught up in the patriotism of the hour. When the call went out for volunteers, McKinley enlisted as a foot soldier and served the entire four years of the war, participating in some of the conflict's bloodiest battles. Because of his intelligence, talent, and heroism, he rose quickly and steadily through the ranks. By the time he was mustered out in July 1865, William McKinley had achieved the rank of major.

When the war ended, McKinley was unsure of what he might do for the rest of his life. He was now twenty-two and too old (or so he thought) to return to Allegheny College. He could not see himself returning to his old profession as a schoolteacher, either. He thought only briefly about remaining in the army as a career officer, for he had been horrified by the cost of human life in war and knew he could never make fighting his profession.

Finally, he considered a career in law. Finding this acceptable to his conscience, McKinley wrote to his old regiment commander, a prominent Ohio attorney named Rutherford B. Hayes, to ask for advice. Hayes took a dim view of McKinley's intention to become a lawyer. Instead, he suggested McKinley look for a job with a railroad or perhaps seek a business opportunity. Hayes believed there would be plenty of opportunity for men who worked for the railroads, which were pushing westward steadily.

"With your business capacity and experience, I would have preferred Rail Roading or some commercial business," Hayes wrote. "A man in any of our Western towns with half your wit ought to be independent at forty in business. As a lawyer,

AGE 15   AGE 18   AGE 23

WILLIAM McKINLEY

William McKinley was not a prolific letter writer. He did not keep a diary. As a rule, his letters were either businesslike communications or straight to the point. Rarely did he comment on his personal life. The McKinley Papers in the Library of Congress are extensive, including more than eighty-five bound volumes, eighty-four letter books, and over one hundred manuscript boxes. The striking feature of the collection is its impersonal character, a formality and discretion that was typical of McKinley.

Charles S. Olcott wrote the authorized biography of the president, *The Life of William McKinley*, which was published in two volumes in 1916. McKinley's friends and associates cooperated with Olcott, and the writer integrated previously conducted interviews of many people who had known McKinley in childhood, youth, and during his studies both at Allegheny College and Albany Law School. Since the publication of *The Life of William McKinley*, later McKinley biographers have relied on Olcott's material for these years of his life.

The three photographs above were loaned to Charles S. Olcott by the McKinley family.

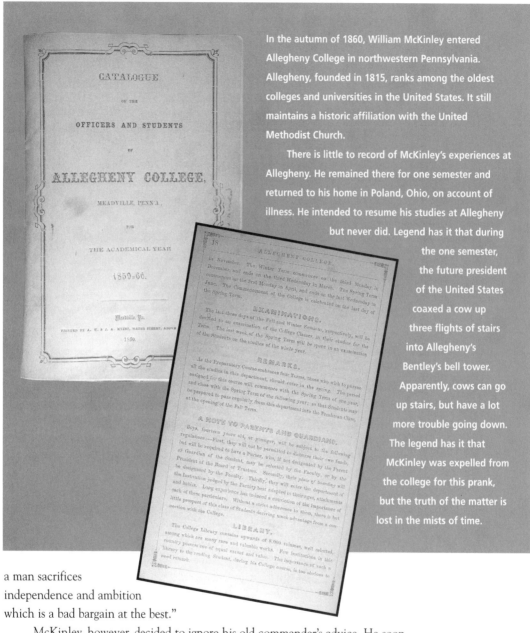

In the autumn of 1860, William McKinley entered Allegheny College in northwestern Pennsylvania. Allegheny, founded in 1815, ranks among the oldest colleges and universities in the United States. It still maintains a historic affiliation with the United Methodist Church.

There is little to record of McKinley's experiences at Allegheny. He remained there for one semester and returned to his home in Poland, Ohio, on account of illness. He intended to resume his studies at Allegheny but never did. Legend has it that during the one semester, the future president of the United States coaxed a cow up three flights of stairs into Allegheny's Bentley's bell tower. Apparently, cows can go up stairs, but have a lot more trouble going down. The legend has it that McKinley was expelled from the college for this prank, but the truth of the matter is lost in the mists of time.

a man sacrifices independence and ambition which is a bad bargain at the best."

McKinley, however, decided to ignore his old commander's advice. He soon enrolled in law school and established a legal practice in Canton, Ohio, then turned to politics. On their individual and different ways to success in law and politics, neither man would find it necessary to sacrifice ambition. In 1876 Rutherford B. Hayes would become president of the United States. Twenty years later, so would William McKinley.

William McKinley Jr. was born on January 29, 1843, in Niles, Ohio, a town just north of the city of Youngstown near the Pennsylvania border. He was the seventh of nine children in the family of William and Nancy Allison

McKinley. Grandfathers on both sides of the family fought in the War of Independence. William's father operated a small foundry—a place where metals were melted and poured into molds to make kitchenware, tools, bells, and other household implements.

Niles had a one-room schoolhouse where William learned his first lessons. Girls sat on one side, boys on the other. Benches and desks spanned the width of the room from wall to wall. The teacher, Alva Sanford, kept a rod on his desk and was known to use it. Children who didn't know their lessons were made to stand in the center of the room so they would serve as an example to their classmates.

William never had to stand in the center of the classroom. He was among the brightest students in class. An avid reader, he soon devoured the few books on the school shelves as well as the limited library his parents kept at home. Among the books he read as a boy in Niles were several novels by Charles Dickens as well as David Hume's *History of England* and Edward Gibbon's *Decline and Fall of the Roman Empire*, two books that would provide important lessons to a future world leader on the pitfalls powerful nations would do well to avoid. At home, the McKinleys subscribed to Horace Greeley's *Weekly Tribune*; its strong abolitionist theme would make a deep impact on William's views on slavery.

Education was important to Nancy McKinley and she made sure her children studied hard. Years later, she said, "My ideas of an education were wholly practical, not theoretical. I put my children in school just as early as they could go alone to the teacher, and kept them at it. I did not allow them to stay away."

William's mother believed so strongly in education, in fact, that she convinced her husband to move the family to another town because she was not satisfied with the opportunities available in Niles' tiny schoolhouse. William's older sister Anna taught in the Poland Academy, a private high school in the town of Poland, about six miles west of Youngstown. In 1852, the family moved there to ensure that William and his brothers and sisters had the opportunity for an education better than what was available in Niles. Poland Academy offered a curriculum far superior to what William had studied in Niles. The new school provided classes in arithmetic, English, grammar, literature, rhetoric, Latin, Greek, American history, and government.

The Methodist McKinleys were dedicated churchgoers. Nancy McKinley hoped her son would pursue a career in the ministry. She was encouraged in that belief by his prowess as an orator; at Poland Academy, he joined the school's literary club, as well as the Edward Everett Society, in which members gave speeches and participated in debates. He soon became president of the Society.

During William's matriculation at Poland, several of his fellow students were dismissed from the Edward Everett Society because they refused to donate $1 to help finance the Society's project to obtain a portrait of Everett, the American statesman and orator after whom the Society had named itself. As for McKinley, he paid his dollar.

The Edward Everett Society members also saved their money so they could buy a carpet for the group's meeting room. After pooling their funds, the Society members were able to procure a handsome green carpet decorated with hand-sewn wreaths. Once the carpet was laid in their meeting room, the members unanimously voted that no boots would be permitted there. The female members volunteered to knit slippers to wear instead, but the slippers were not ready by the next meeting. Thus for the first meeting of the Edward Everett Society to be conducted atop the club's glorious green carpet, William McKinley was forced to preside over the session in his stocking feet.

After a year at Poland Academy, William was visited by a friend, Robert B. Murray of Youngstown, who had just finished his freshman year at Allegheny College, about sixty miles northeast of Poland. Murray urged William to join him there as a student. Though the McKinleys were certainly not poor people, they were far from wealthy. When William's sister Anna volunteered to help pay his tuition, the McKinleys agreed that he should go to college. He and his cousin, William Osborne, arrived at Allegheny in the spring of 1860. They would share a room in Dr. Goe's boarding house just north of the campus.

William had always been a bright student, but his parents' decision to move to Poland so that he could receive a better education had also been of great value. His entrance exam scores were so high that he entered as a member of the junior class. His amazing memory astounded teachers as well as classmates; he learned almost immediately the faces, names, hometowns, and ambitions of all his fellow students—obviously, a talent that would serve him well later as a politician.

He joined the college oratorical society at Allegheny and soon became a leader. With the country edging toward Civil War, the Allegheny students often found themselves in debates over slavery. By now, William was a devoted abolitionist and frequently led the anti-slavery arguments during campus debates.

Elsewhere in the country, the debate over slavery was often more than just a war of words—indeed, just a few months before William's enrollment at Allegheny, the abolitionist John Brown had been captured and hanged for his raid on an arsenal at Harper's Ferry, Virginia. Sometimes, the debates at Allegheny threatened to turn violent as well. At one point, when a pro-slavery student proposed Jefferson Davis for the presidency of the United States, William proposed instead to settle the matter with his fists.

Such outbursts by William were rare, though. He was regarded as a polite student, friendly and well-dressed. He was known for his punctuality and devotion to services in the chapel. Years later, he recalled his time at Allegheny as "among the pleasantest memories of my life."

There may have been a bit of the prankster in him. A legend still circulates on the Allegheny campus that McKinley was responsible for leading a cow up to the belfry of Bentley Hall, the college administration building. (An alternate version

CIRCULAR AND CATALOGUE

OF THE

LAW SCHOOL

OF THE

UNIVERSITY OF ALBANY,

FOR THE

YEAR 1865-6.

ALBANY, N. Y.:
J. MUNSELL, 78 STATE STREE
1866.

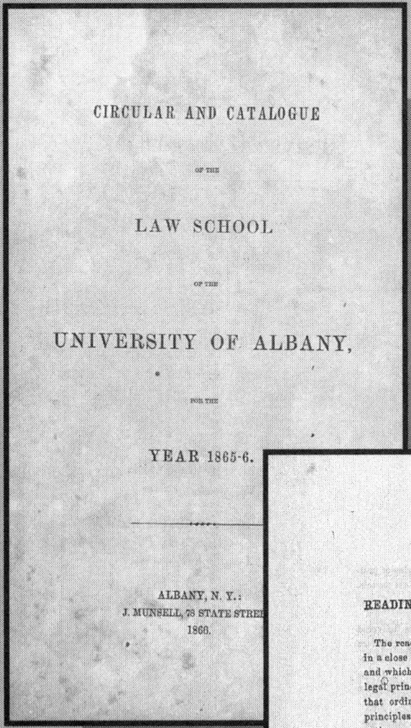

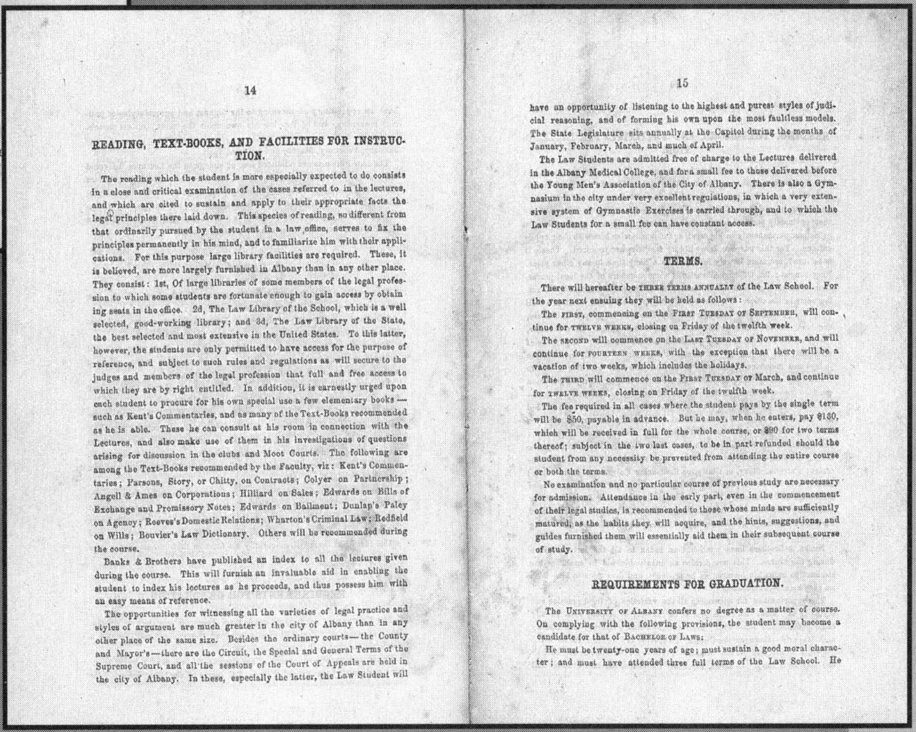

14

READING, TEXT-BOOKS, AND FACILITIES FOR INSTRUCTION.

The reading which the student is more especially expected to do consists in a close and critical examination of the cases referred to in the lectures, and which are cited to sustain and apply to their appropriate facts the legal principles there laid down. This species of reading, so different from that ordinarily pursued by the student in a law office, serves to fix the principles permanently in his mind, and to familiarize him with their applications. For this purpose large library facilities are required. These, it is believed, are more largely furnished in Albany than in any other place. They consist: 1st, Of large libraries of some members of the legal profession to which some students are fortunate enough to gain access by obtaining seats in the office. 2d, The Law Library of the School, which is a well selected, good-working library; and 3d, The Law Library of the State, the best selected and most extensive in the United States. To this latter, however, the students are only permitted to have access for the purpose of reference, and subject to such rules and regulations as will secure to the judges and members of the legal profession that full and free access to which they are by right entitled. In addition, it is earnestly urged upon each student to procure for his own special use a few elementary books — such as Kent's Commentaries, and as many of the Text-Books recommended as he is able. These he can consult at his room in connection with the Lectures, and also make use of them in his investigations of questions arising for discussion in the clubs and Moot Courts. The following are among the Text-Books recommended by the Faculty, viz: Kent's Commentaries; Parsons, Story, or Chitty, on Contracts; Colyer on Partnership; Angell & Ames on Corporations; Hilliard on Sales; Edwards on Bills of Exchange and Promissory Notes; Edwards on Bailment; Dunlap's Paley on Agency; Reeves's Domestic Relations; Wharton's Criminal Law; Redfield on Wills; Bouvier's Law Dictionary. Others will be recommended during the course.

Banks & Brothers have published an index to all the lectures given during the course. This will furnish an invaluable aid in enabling the student to index his lectures as he proceeds, and thus possess him with an easy means of reference.

The opportunities for witnessing all the varieties of legal practice and styles of argument are much greater in the city of Albany than in any other place of the same size. Besides the ordinary courts—the County and Mayor's—there are the Circuit, the Special and General Terms of the Supreme Court, and all the sessions of the Court of Appeals are held in the city of Albany. In these, especially the latter, the Law Student will

15

have an opportunity of listening to the highest and purest styles of judicial reasoning, and of forming his own upon the most faultless models. The State Legislature sits annually at the Capitol during the months of January, February, March, and much of April.

The Law Students are admitted free of charge to the Lectures delivered in the Albany Medical College, and for a small fee to those delivered before the Young Men's Association of the City of Albany. There is also a Gymnasium in the city under very excellent regulations, in which a very extensive system of Gymnastic Exercises is carried through, and to which the Law Students for a small fee can have constant access.

TERMS.

There will hereafter be THREE TERMS ANNUALLY of the Law School. For the year next ensuing they will be held as follows:

The FIRST, commencing on the FIRST TUESDAY OF SEPTEMBER, will continue for TWELVE WEEKS, closing on Friday of the twelfth week.

The SECOND will commence on the LAST TUESDAY OF NOVEMBER, and will continue for FOURTEEN WEEKS, with the exception that there will be a vacation of two weeks, which includes the holidays.

The THIRD will commence on the FIRST TUESDAY OF March, and continue for TWELVE WEEKS, closing on Friday of the twelfth week.

The fee required in all cases where the student pays by the single term will be $50, payable in advance. But he may, when he enters, pay $130, which will be received in full for the whole course, or $90 for two terms thereof; subject in the two last cases, to be in part refunded should the student from any necessity be prevented from attending the entire course or both the terms.

No examination and no particular course of previous study are necessary for admission. Attendance in the early part, even in the commencement of their legal studies, is recommended to those whose minds are sufficiently matured, as the habits they will acquire, and the hints, suggestions, and guides furnished them will essentially aid them in their subsequent course of study.

REQUIREMENTS FOR GRADUATION.

The UNIVERSITY OF ALBANY confers no degree as a matter of course. On complying with the following provisions, the student may become a candidate for that of BACHELOR OF LAWS:

He must be twenty-one years of age; must sustain a good moral character; and must have attended three full terms of the Law School. He

In 1866, McKinley entered Albany Law School in New York. He did not finish the course of study, which then consisted of only a single year, but left in the spring of 1867. He passed the Ohio bar examination and opened a law office in Canton. He was twenty-four.

The Albany Law School had a president and four professors. The faculty ranked as one of the most distinguished in the nation. Reuben H. Walworth, an outstanding jurist, had served as chancellor of New York for twenty years. Ira Harris taught "practice, pleadings, and evidence" while serving as a United States senator from New York, and Amasa Parker, who handled real estate, wills, and criminal law, had compiled and edited the major criminal decisions of the New York State Supreme Court. Albany Law was among the first schools to make use of the case method. The course of instruction consisted of three parts and a student could "enter any term while in progress, and complete his course by remaining until he has reached the point at which he commenced."

reports that it was a goat, a candidate perhaps more likely to have permitted itself to be led up—or carried—to a belfry.) The legend goes on to suggest that William may have been punished for the perpetration of this prank, and that the punishment included expulsion after just a single semester at Allegheny.

William did drop out of Allegheny College after one semester, but it is likely that he was forced to do so because of illness, and probably a lack of money—his father's fortunes seem to have taken a bad turn when the elder McKinley was forced to assume the debt of a brother. In any event, he was no longer able to help pay his son's costs at Allegheny. Left with only what his sister Anna provided, William returned home to Poland where he rested and regained his health. He also took a job in the Poland post office and later as a school teacher, hoping to save enough money to return to Allegheny.

"My wages were, I think, $25 a month, and I boarded around," McKinley recalled. "My parents, however, lived only three miles from the schoolhouse, and the most of the time I stayed with them and walked to school and back every day. Six miles would be a big walk for me now, I suppose, but it did not seem much then."

He would, however, never return to Allegheny as a student. Instead, he and his former roommate at Allegheny, cousin William Osborne, joined the Twenty-third Ohio Volunteer Infantry Regiment. McKinley took his oath as a soldier from General John C. Frémont, the famous American explorer who himself had run for president in 1856. "He pounded my chest and looked square into my eyes, and finally pronounced me fit for a soldier," McKinley recalled.

McKinley would fight with the Twenty-third Ohio Volunteers in some of the war's major battles. At the Battle of Antietam Creek in Maryland, he was promoted to second lieutenant for making his way through the midst of the fighting to bring food to hungry Union soldiers. More than 20,000 Union and Confederate troops were killed or wounded in a day's fighting at Antietam.

McKinley had initially intended to serve for three years, but found himself unwilling to return to civilian life until the fighting was over. By the time the war ended, McKinley was a major. He returned to Poland and, ignoring the advice of Rutherford B. Hayes, found work as a clerk in the office of Judge Charles E. Glidden, who presided over the courts of Mahoning County, Ohio. He worked a year for Glidden, and spent his free time reading the massive legal volumes that made up the judge's library. Glidden was impressed with McKinley's intelligence and hunger for knowledge, and concluded that his clerk would become a much better attorney if he attended a law school.

Currently, law school is generally required for anyone who wishes to practice in a courtroom in America, but in the 1800s few attorneys had the benefit of a formal legal education. Most attorneys learned their craft by clerking for established lawyers who would provide their training and eventually sponsor them in their applications to practice law. At the time, most law schools in America were of recent vintage. One such school was Albany Law School in New York State, which had been in operation for only fifteen years when William McKinley stepped onto its campus in 1866.

Perhaps because law schools were relatively new, the Albany school, with an enrollment of some one hundred and sixty students, was the fifth-largest law school in the country. Its faculty included Amos Dean, an attorney, and judges Amasa J. Parker and Ira Harris. At the time, the school offered a bachelor of laws degree, but few of its students matriculated long enough to win degrees. Instead, students would enroll for a semester or two, taking courses in the types of law they intended to practice. McKinley was to stay two terms.

Tuition was $50 per term. Once more, McKinley's sister Anna offered to help her brother with his tuition. And again McKinley saved money by sharing a room, this time with a friend, George F. Arrel, who would go on to become a prominent Youngstown attorney. Arrel would later recall McKinley as a "delightful companion. He was a sociable fellow, liked the theater, and was fond of good company. He worked very hard, often reading until one or two o'clock in the morning." A devout Methodist, McKinley never missed going to church and refrained from drinking and smoking.

McKinley's choice of classes illustrate his varied interests in the law. He attended lectures on how to write contracts and form partnerships as well as the rules surrounding the sale of real estate. He studied the U.S. Constitution and the constitution of the state of New York. He learned how to draft lawsuits for clients who believed they had been the victims of shady business transactions. He studied divorce law and learned how to defend clients charged in criminal cases.

Students at Albany had to participate in "moot courts," in which they role-played as attorneys. McKinley found that these mock trials were similar to the debates in which he had participated at Poland Academy and Allegheny College. Having always been a good debater, he excelled in the law school's moot courts.

Shortly after arriving at Albany, McKinley attended a reception for new students at the home of the prominent Judge Parker. During the reception, the judge's daughter, Grace, handed McKinley a bowl of ice cream—a desert he had never tasted. McKinley thought that she had given him a bowl of ruined custard, and promised her that he wouldn't tell anybody she had botched the recipe. Grace laughed and told McKinley that he was mistaken, the ice cream was just fine. Years later, in the White House, he met Grace Parker's niece and related the story to her. "You know, I was a simple country boy," he explained.

He left Albany Law School in 1867, returned to Ohio, and was admitted to practice before the Ohio courts. He soon established a thriving law practice in the city of Canton and married Ida Saxton, the daughter of an influential man who would assist McKinley later in his political career. That career was launched in 1878 when he won a seat in the U.S. House of Representatives. A Republican, he spent the next twenty-two years in and out of Congress, occasionally falling victim to gerrymandering—the unscrupulous redrawing of congressional districts by one party to gain advantage over its rivals.

In 1891 he won a term as governor of Ohio and served in that office until winning the presidential election in 1896. Foreign affairs dominated his presidency. It was a time in which many political leaders demand that United States flex its muscles and stand up to foreign powers.

In 1895, the people of Cuba had staged a rebellion against the Spanish, rulers of the island since the days of the conquistadors. Spain responded with a brutal repression of the Cubans, which prompted warmongering politicians in the United States to demand American intervention. McKinley resisted, but when the American battleship *Maine* exploded in Havana harbor, influential newspapers published by William Randolph Hearst and Joseph Pulitzer demanded an invasion of the island, even though there was no proof that the *Maine* had been sabotaged.

McKinley finally committed U.S. troops to what Secretary of State John Hay called "a splendid little war." The war in Cuba was brief and resulted in a clear victory for the United States; nevertheless, the Spanish-American War established the precedent of the United States exerting its influence over the politics of Latin American countries. In later years, that policy would have disastrous consequences for the United States in places such as Nicaragua, Chile, and Cuba.

McKinley ran for reelection in 1900. As his running mate, the incumbent selected a firebrand New York City politician named Theodore Roosevelt. McKinley easily won re-election, but his second term would be brief. On September 6, 1901, an anarchist named Leon Czolgosz emerged from the crowd at the Buffalo Pan-American Exposition and shot the president. William McKinley died eight days later.

—Hal Marcovitz

Catalogue of the Alumni of the
Albany Law School, 1851 to 1908

Name	Last known residence	Graduate of
Humphreys, David T.		
Huse, Hiram A.	Whitestown	
Ingersoll, Daniel W.	Hustisford, Wis.	
Jeroloman, John, Jr.	St. Paul, Minn.	Dartmouth
Johnson, James G.	Princeton, N. J.	Yale
Joyce, John T.	Salamanca	Princeton
Judson, Selden C.	Albany	
Kellogg, Rowland C.	St. Joseph, Mo.	
County Judge, Essex Co., N. Y.	Thousand Island Park	Hamilton
Kinne, Ephraim	Elizabethtown	
Kingston, George A.	Ovid	
Kip, William B.	Brasher	
Latta, B. Frank	Rhinebeck	
Losey, Henry E.	Allens Grove, Wis.	
Loucks, William	Poughkeepsie	
Love, John G.	Albany	Knox
Luce, Moses A.	Central Line, Pa.	Union
Marks, Constant R.	San Diego, Cal.	
Marston, Howard S.	Pittsfield, Mass.	Hillsdale
Martin, Wesley	Greenland, N. H.	Yale
McDonald, Theodore F.	Jamestown	
McKinley, William, Jr.*	Chenango Forks	
President United States	Canton, Ohio	
Mechling, John		
Moore, Watson W.	Brookville, Pa.	
Monroe, Daniel	13 William St., N. Y. City	
Monroe, Charles W.	Detroit, Mich.	Alleghany
Nelson, Seymour B.	Providence, R. I.	Michigan Uni.
O'Connor, Lewis H.	Cold Spring	Trinity
Olin, Stephen H.	Peoria, Ill.	
Oliver, William M.	32 Nassau St., N. Y. City	Chicago Uni.
Olmstead, Martin L.	East Springfield	Wesleyan Uni.
Osgood, Alpheus C.	Rochester	
Paige, E. Winslow	Manchester, N. H.	Genesee
Palmer, Francis	44 Cedar St., N. Y. City	Dartmouth
Parrish, George W.	Hume	Union
Peckham, George W.	Salem, Oregon	Madison Uni.
Perrin, William B.	Milwaukee, Wis.	Williamette Uni.
Phelps, Julian D.	Nashoa, Iowa	
Phelps, William B.	Atlantic, Iowa	
Porter, Jerome B.	Hinsdale	Dartmouth
Price, Robert W.	Warner, N. H.	Uni. of Vermont
Ransom, Washington H.	Centreville, Md.	
Reynolds, S. Edgar	Lockport	
Ridlon, Emery S.	Troy	Wash. and Jeff.
Roat, John H.	Kezar Falls, Me.	
Roase, Henry H.	Irving	Union
Saunders, Charles R.	Smithboro	
Sayles, Joseph I.	Westkill	
Schenck, Ferdinand S.	Rome	
Schermerhorn, George J.	Whitehall, Ill.	
Scott, John A.	5 Nassau St., N. Y. City	Princeton
Scripture, William E.	Andes	Union
Justice Supreme Court, N. Y.	Rome	
Shafer, M. Luther	280 Broadway, N. Y. City	Hamilton
Shepard, Theodore T.	Scio	
Showerman, Charles D.	Alexander	
Sill, Edward E.	Livonia	
*Deceased		Williams

34

UNION UNIVERSITY

DEPARTMENT OF LAW

CATALOGUE OF THE ALUMNI

OF THE

ALBANY LAW SCHOOL

1851 to 1908

1851 to 1908

Theodore Roosevelt
Chapter Twenty-five

Theodore Roosevelt learned to box when he was fourteen years old. He took up the sport to develop endurance—the boy suffered terribly from asthma—and to help him fend off the attacks of bullies. His father, a wealthy importer of European goods, visited several roughneck gymnasiums in New York City before finally deciding to entrust the physical education of his son to the able hands of John Long, trainer of some of the city's best prizefighters.

Young Roosevelt was an enthusiastic student. The boy loved sports and competition. After several months of studying with Long, Roosevelt was invited by his teacher to participate in a tournament he planned to stage among his students. First prize in each weight class was a pewter mug. Roosevelt and the other boys his age were entered as lightweights.

"It happened that I was pitted in succession against a couple of reedy striplings who were even worse than I was," Roosevelt later recalled. "Equally to their surprise and to my own, and to John Long's, I won, and the pewter mug became one of my most prized possessions. I kept it…and fear I bragged about it, for a number of years."

Roosevelt went on to become a zealous fan of prizefighting. Years later, as police commissioner of New York, Roosevelt could be found at ringside during some of the city's top boxing cards. After he became president of the United States, Roosevelt often invited top American boxers to visit the White House—as long as they agreed to spar a few rounds with him.

As a competitor himself, though, Roosevelt was destined never to enjoy again the success he found on that afternoon in John Long's gym. Seven years after capturing Long's pewter mug, Roosevelt fought for the lightweight title of Harvard University. His opponent was a senior named C. S. Hanks, who won the fight by bloodying Roosevelt's nose, apparently after the bell ending a round had already chimed. Roosevelt's friend and fellow student, the writer Owen Wister, attended the tournament. Here is how he described the incident:

> Time was called on a round, Roosevelt dropped his guard, and Hanks landed
> a heavy blow on his nose, which spurted blood. Loud hoots and hisses from

HARVARD COLLEGE.

⁘

CERTIFICATE OF ADMISSION.

Cambridge, *July 3,* 1876.

T. Roosevelt is admitted to the FRESHMAN Class in Harvard College, but can become a candidate for a degree only on condition of passing a satisfactory examination in the studies named below.

Chas F. Dunbar
Dean of the Faculty.

The examination required above will be in

Greek Poetry (no book),
Plane Trigonometry,
Botany.

A student who has received an admission condition may obtain its removal, within the year after his entrance, by excellence of College work in the special subject in which he was conditioned. Conditions not so removed can be made up only at the beginning of some subsequent academic year, at the regular examination for admission, or at such special examinations as may be authorized by the Faculty.

Theodore Roosevelt was admitted to Harvard College on condition of passing examinations in Greek poetry (without a book), plane trigonometry, and botany. He passed all three within one week of arriving at Harvard. This certificate was signed by Charles F. Dunbar, who in addition to being dean of the faculty, was Harvard's (and the nation's) first professor of political economy. Roosevelt received an 89 in Dunbar's course (known as Philosophy 7) in his junior year. In his *Autobiography,* Roosevelt praised Dunbar's lectures as "even more interesting" than his science courses.

Theodore Roosevelt, age eighteen (1876)

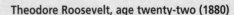
Theodore Roosevelt, age twenty-two (1880)

Theodore Roosevelt was born into a New York City family of wealth, culture, and privilege. Young Theodore's life was a challenging one because of health problems. Frail and troubled by poor vision and asthma, he undertook a rigid and vigorous exercise program that restored his health. His love of competitive sports and of the outdoor life is evident through his childhood interests in boxing, hunting, and horseback riding. He was also an avid science student. Roosevelt was educated by family members and private tutors. In 1876, he entered Harvard College. He had never sat in a classroom in his life. Nevertheless, when Roosevelt graduated in 1880, he was ranked twenty-first in a class of a hundred and seventy-one. Years later, Roosevelt credited Harvard mainly with providing him "an especially good time," but, according to his recollection, the college had not prepared him well for "the big world."

the gallery and floor were set up, whereat Roosevelt's arm instantly flung out to command silence, while his alert and slender figure stood quiet.

'It's all right,' he assured us eagerly, his arm still in the air to hold the silence; then, pointing to the time-keeper, 'he didn't hear him,' he explained, in the same conversational but arresting tone. With bleeding nose he walked up to Hanks and shook hands with him.

It was the gesture of sportsmanship. However, Roosevelt's true purpose in displaying such gallantry may have been to impress young Alice Lee, who sat in the spectators' gallery that afternoon and was soon to become his wife. It should be reported, though, that Roosevelt was at best just a fair boxer, and he wasn't much of an athlete in other sports either. His poor eyesight made it difficult for him to hit a baseball. His thin, wiry frame made him an unlikely blocker on the gridiron. Nevertheless, in the years to come, as Theodore Roosevelt rose higher in the ranks of influence and it became clear to all who knew him that he was destined for a role of importance, Roosevelt's former classmates were bemused to read in the official biographies of the future president that their fellow graduate of Harvard University, class of 1880, claimed victory for the lightweight title over C. S. Hanks.

That sort of embellishment of the truth was not unusual for Roosevelt, whose propensity to brag about himself could be found in his diary or his letters home, or in later years, in the way he manipulated news reporters so they would do his bragging for him. Theodore, his cousin Maud Elliot said about him, "always thought he could do things better than anyone else."

Theodore Roosevelt Jr. was born October 27, 1858, in a fashionable brownstone at 28 East Twentieth Street in New York City. The first Roosevelts had arrived in America in 1649 and soon established themselves as farmers, merchants, bankers, manufacturers, and engineers. By the time Theodore came along, the Roosevelts were among New York's wealthiest families. Theodore Roosevelt Sr. enhanced the family wealth when he married Martha "Mittie" Bulloch, the daughter of a Georgia plantation owner.

Theodore Jr. had an older sister, Anna, and two younger siblings, Elliott and Corinne. All four Roosevelt children received their early education at home. Annie Bulloch, the children's aunt and a boarder in the Roosevelt home, handled the teaching responsibilities.

The Roosevelts could have afforded the best private schools for their children, but Theodore Jr., who was called Teedie, suffered from severe asthma attacks and his parents feared that his life could be in danger if he boarded at a school far from home. Corinne was asthmatic as well, although her attacks occurred far less often and were much less severe. Except for a brief period when Teedie and Elliott attended classes down the street in the home of a private tutor named Professor McMullen, the Roosevelt children learned their lessons under the guidance of Aunt Annie Bulloch.

She was energetic and animated—a good storyteller who filled their heads with tales of American heroes who battled against overwhelming odds. The fact that most of her favorite heroes were southerners, such as Davy Crockett of Tennessee and Daniel Boone of Kentucky, may have been Annie's way of winning the children over to the noble cause of the South at a time when the Civil War was raging. Young Teedie was more interested in the adventures Annie related to him than in the politics behind them.

With no school chums to dominate his playtime, and under orders to stay indoors lest he find himself in the throes of an asthma attack, the boy eventually found his way into his father's well-stocked library. Teedie was most fascinated by the books he found on the shelves that included pictures of wildlife. In fact, the first book he paged through, which he was hardly able to read, was the explorer David Livingstone's *Missionary Travels and Researches in Southern Africa*. The boy spent hours flipping through the pages, studying the drawings of hippopotamuses, zebras, elephants, tsetse flies, and other exotic critters.

Soon, under Aunt Annie's guidance, Teedie became a voracious reader. Teedie attacked the books in the library, spending hours curled up in a softly upholstered red velvet chair. He was most interested in his father's books on the natural sciences, but soon developed a taste for adventure stories as well. He pored over stories of pioneers, trappers, cowboys, and frontiersmen authored by writer Mayne Reid. Another favorite author was Captain Frederick Marryat, the British author whose books enthralled Teedie with tales of adventure at sea. On a higher level were the stories of the American frontier written by James Fenimore Cooper and the patriotic poetry of Henry Wadsworth Longfellow. That type of reading undoubtedly had an influence on a future president who would preserve some 230 million acres of land by creating a system of national parks and forests.

It wasn't long before Teedie started putting his own thoughts down on paper. His fascination with wildlife led him, at the age of ten, to write a manuscript titled "The Broadway Seal." The book contained his observations on the body of a dead seal he had seen dockside at New York harbor while on an errand to buy strawberries. He followed next with "The Foregoing Ant," which purported to explain why ants always seem to walk forward. His third treatise was a far more comprehensive work titled "Natural History of Insects," in which he detailed his observations on beetles, dragonflies, ants, spiders, ladybugs, and lightning bugs, although he permitted himself to stray from his topic from time to time by discussing various birds and aquatic animals.

His parents indulged him. He turned his room into the "Roosevelt Museum of Natural History," filling it with all manner of plant and animal life—both living and dead. Occasionally, the museum exhibits found their way into the rest of the house. In the Roosevelt home, it was not unusual to hear a shriek emanating from the kitchen because the cook had been surprised by a toad launching itself out of a water pitcher.

Theodore Roosevelt's Harvard study room, 1876–80

Roosevelt lived off campus for all his four years at Harvard. His quarters were selected and furnished by Anna (Bamie), his adoring elder sister. Roosevelt's living space consisted of a study room and a small bedroom. ("I had Harry Chapin [TR's classmate and good friend] in here the other day to look at the new bookcase [pictured at left in this photograph]," he wrote Bamie in his sophomore year, "and after he had examined it he exclaimed, "Jove! Your family do act squarely by you!")

Harvard in the 1870s was a school for economically privileged young men. A survey of Roosevelt's class of 1880 shows that nearly two-thirds came from within a hundred-mile radius of the Harvard campus. More than half had graduated from Andover, Exeter, St. Paul's School, and other such prestigious New England preparatory academies. There were no female, black, foreign, or Jewish students in Roosevelt's class, although there were three Catholics.

Left card (page one, in Roosevelt's handwriting):

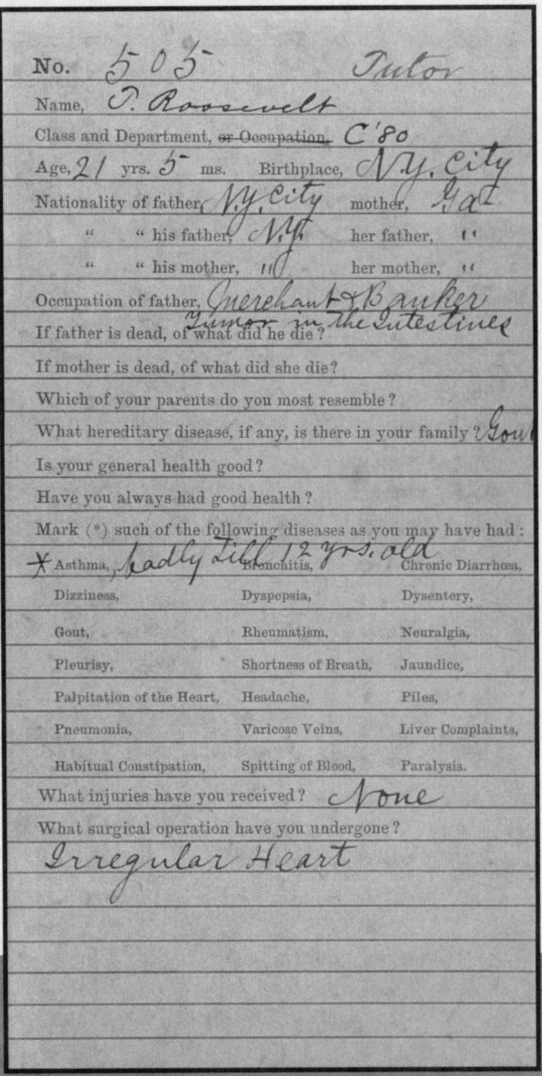

No. *5 05*   *Tutor*

Name, *T. Roosevelt*

Class and Department, ~~or Occupation~~ *C '80*

Age, *21* yrs. *5* ms.   Birthplace, *N.Y. City*

Nationality of father *N.Y. city* mother, *Ga*

" " his father *N.Y.* her father, "

" " his mother, " her mother, "

Occupation of father, *Merchant & Banker*

If father is dead, of what did he die? *Tumor in the Intestines*

If mother is dead, of what did she die?

Which of your parents do you most resemble?

What hereditary disease, if any, is there in your family? *Gout*

Is your general health good?

Have you always had good health?

Mark (*) such of the following diseases as you may have had:

✗ Asthma, *badly till 12 yrs. old*   Bronchitis,   Chronic Diarrhœa,

Dizziness,   Dyspepsia,   Dysentery,

Gout,   Rheumatism,   Neuralgia,

Pleurisy,   Shortness of Breath,   Jaundice,

Palpitation of the Heart,   Headache,   Piles,

Pneumonia,   Varicose Veins,   Liver Complaints,

Habitual Constipation,   Spitting of Blood,   Paralysis.

What injuries have you received? *None*

What surgical operation have you undergone?

Irregular Heart

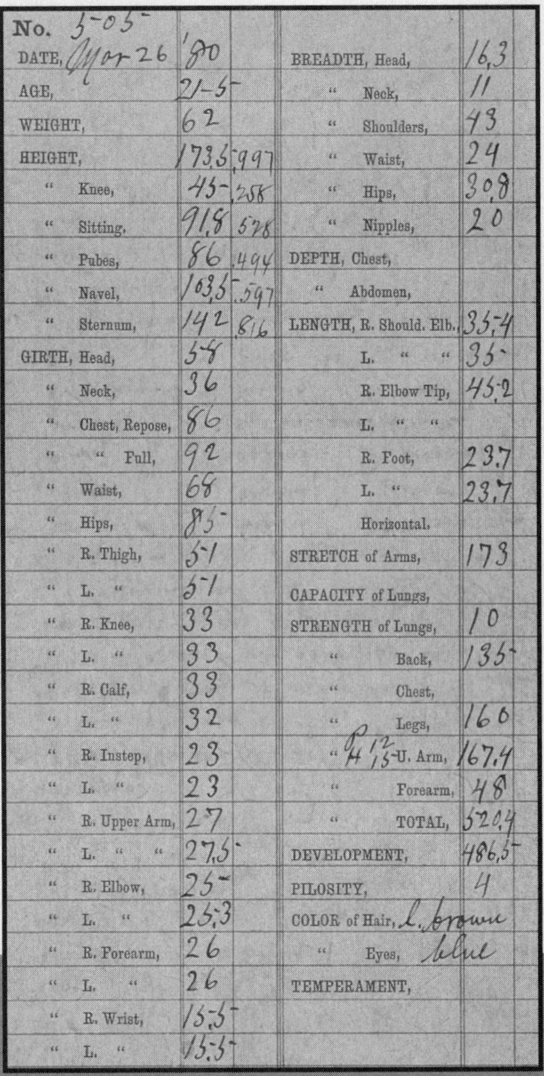

Right card (page two, measurements):

No. *5-05*			
DATE *Mar 26 '80*		BREADTH, Head,	16.3
AGE,	21-5	" Neck,	11
WEIGHT,	62	" Shoulders,	43
HEIGHT,	173.5	.997	" Waist,	24
" Knee,	45-	.258	" Hips,	30.8
" Sitting,	91.8	.528	" Nipples,	20
" Pubes,	86	.494	DEPTH, Chest,	
" Navel,	103.5	.597	" Abdomen,	
" Sternum,	142	.816	LENGTH, R. Should. Elb.	35.4
GIRTH, Head,	58		L. " "	35-
" Neck,	36		R. Elbow Tip,	45.2
" Chest, Repose,	86		L. " "	
" " Full,	92		R. Foot,	23.7
" Waist,	68		L. "	23.7
" Hips,	85-		Horizontal,	
" R. Thigh,	51		STRETCH of Arms,	173
" L. "	51		CAPACITY of Lungs,	
" R. Knee,	33		STRENGTH of Lungs,	10
" L. "	33		" Back,	135-
" R. Calf,	33		" Chest,	
" L. "	32		" Legs,	160
" R. Instep,	23		4 12/5-U. Arm,	167.4
" L. "	23		" Forearm,	48
" R. Upper Arm,	27		" TOTAL,	520.4
" L. " "	27.5-		DEVELOPMENT,	486.5-
" R. Elbow,	25-		PILOSITY,	4
" L. "	25.3		COLOR of Hair, *L. brown*	
" R. Forearm,	26		" Eyes, *blue*	
" L. "	26		TEMPERAMENT,	
" R. Wrist,	15.5-			
" L. "	15.5-			

Page one of Roosevelt's 1880 gymnasium card (left) is in his handwriting. From this card, we learn a great deal about Roosevelt, then twenty-one years, his family, and its history. Note the asterisk he placed to the left of "Asthma," adding "badly till 12 yrs. old." Under "surgical operation," he writes, "irregular heart." He also notes that gout is a "hereditary disease" running in his family. (While gout was a recurring illness in Roosevelt's family, it is not a hereditary illness. A cause is the consumption of rich foods usually associated with an affluent lifestyle such as that on both the maternal and paternal sides of his family.)

Roosevelt noted an "irregular heart" only a few days after he had completed a physical examination by Dr. Dudley A. Sargent, the college physician. Dr. Sargent listened to his breathing and to his heart. He then followed up with some advice. Sargent told Roosevelt that his heart had an irregular beat. The doctor warned Roosevelt that he must live a quiet life and to choose a sedentary occupation. He was to avoid physical exertion and undue excitement—he was never to run up stairs, for example. Roosevelt responded defiantly, telling the doctor that he would do exactly the opposite!

Page two provides an excellent description of Roosevelt's physical measurements, the most extensive such record for any American president at that age of life. Most measurements seem to be in inches, with Roosevelt's weight in kilos.

Aunt Annie Bulloch wasn't the only family member to contribute to the education of the Roosevelt children. Hilborne West, an uncle from Philadelphia, spent summers in New York and read Shakespeare to the children. In 1869 and 1872, Theodore Sr. and Mittie took their children on lengthy visits to Europe and the Middle East. Those trips—with their heavy emphasis on museums, historic sites, and culture—were regarded as educational experiences for the children.

For Teedie, the second trip was by far the most fascinating of the two. Now fourteen years old and well into his training as a boxer, his asthma was far less troublesome than it had been on the first trip abroad. The second trip included a slow, meandering voyage down the Nile River. The Roosevelts spent eight weeks traveling aboard a *dahabeah*, an Egyptian houseboat that never strayed far from the Nile's boggy shores. For Teedie, it was an opportunity to wade alongside the boat and sift through the reeds in search of unusual wildlife. From the deck of the *dahabeah*, Teedie shot birds and retrieved them for scientific analysis, spending hours dissecting the creatures and making careful notes about what he found beneath their feathers. "The bird collecting gave what was really the chief zest of my Nile journey," Teedie wrote. "I was old enough and had read enough to enjoy the temples and the desert scenery and the general feeling of romance; but this in time would have palled if I had not also had the serious work of collecting and preparing my specimens."

During that fall and winter, the Roosevelts were not the only westerners touring the Nile. The Roosevelts' boat spent several weeks traveling alongside a *dahabeah* carrying four students from Harvard University—Nathaniel Thayer, Augustus Jay, Francis Merriam, and Harry Godey. The Roosevelts and the four Harvard men became close friends. On December 31, Thayer, Jay, Merriam, and Godey joined other Nile travelers aboard the Roosevelt *dahabeah* for a party to welcome in the new year. Teedie, now just four years away from selecting a college, was undoubtedly influenced by the swagger and adventurous nature of the four lads from Harvard.

After touring the Nile, the Roosevelts spent several months in Europe, finally leaving Teedie and Elliott in the care of a German family in Dresden. It was in the Minkwitz home that Teedie became fluent in German. Later, he would also master French and Italian.

As a New Yorker, Roosevelt might have been expected to attend Columbia college or perhaps Princeton. But Harvard was regarded as the far superior institution when it came to scientific pursuits, and Roosevelt still intended to study for a career in the natural sciences. To help his son prepare for the rigorous Harvard entrance examination, Theodore Sr. hired a recent graduate named Arthur Cutler to tutor the boy.

Cutler provided rigorous college preparatory training for Teedie. He concentrated on mathematics, which was Cutler's specialty and Teedie's weakness. The Roosevelt children had been exposed to little in the way of mathematics training. Roosevelt worked hard under Cutler, devoting six to eight hours a day to his studies. "The young man never seemed to know what idleness was," wrote Cutler. "Every leisure moment would find the last novel, some English classic, or some abstruse book on natural history in his hand."

In the fall of 1876, after having squeezed three years of college preparation into two, Theodore Roosevelt Jr. entered Harvard. He had never sat in a classroom in his life; until setting foot in Cambridge, Roosevelt's entire education had been provided by family members or private tutors. Except for a brief period in the Minkwitz home, the boy had never spent time away from his parents. A student of lesser confidence may have been overwhelmed by the circumstances he faced at Harvard. Theodore Roosevelt, on the other hand, was not a student who lacked confidence.

Harvard is the oldest college in America; by the time Roosevelt arrived, it was well established as the preeminent college in America as well. That status was due largely to the efforts of Charles W. Eliot, who had been named president of the university seven years before Roosevelt enrolled as a freshman. Eliot enlarged the faculty, reorganized the law and medical schools, placed a new emphasis on the sciences, and, buoyed by an unprecedented fundraising campaign, built several new campus buildings. Ralph Waldo Emerson, Richard Henry Dana, Henry Wadsworth Longfellow, and Henry Cabot Lodge were members of the faculty. Clearly, Eliot hoped to attract the best students in America to Cambridge. In truth, though, Eliot had succeeded mainly in attracting the best students in Massachusetts. By the 1870s Harvard still drew most of its undergraduates from the wealthy and prominent Brahmin families of Boston. Even Theodore Roosevelt, the wealthy son of a prominent New York society family, was regarded as an outsider.

Roosevelt worked hard to overcome that stigma. He joined the appropriate clubs and societies, such as the Hasty Pudding Club and the socially important Porcellian Club. He joined the campus rifle team and even the glee club, although a student's ability to carry a tune was apparently not a prerequisite for membership. Roosevelt got himself elected vice-president of the Natural History Society, helped start the school's finance club, took dancing lessons, and joined the editorial board of the *Advocate*, the undergraduate literary magazine.

And he did get along with the Brahmin boys at Harvard. His father's money enabled him to live off-campus in a comfortably furnished suite of rooms that was the envy of many of his classmates. Roosevelt was also good-hearted and eager to please his friends; during semester breaks, he often had the Boston boys down to New York, where he entertained his classmates and impressed them with his family's wealth. He spent money on himself as well. During his last two years at Harvard, Roosevelt spent some $1,300 just on his wardrobe—a sum that today would total in the tens of thousands of dollars. Certainly, the Brahmin boys found themselves hard-pressed to find fault with his choice of clothes.

Academically, he met the challenge as well. He excelled in his classes, particularly the science courses which were, after all, the reason he had chosen

Harvard in the first place. His average was high enough for him to gain admission to the Phi Beta Kappa Society. Eventually, he would graduate twenty-first in a class of one hundred and seventy-one, although with typical Roosevelt bombast he would later claim to have graduated in the top ten percent. He often exasperated his professors with his enthusiasm. Nathaniel Southgate Shaler, his geology professor, is said to have once blurted out: "See here, Roosevelt, let me talk. I'm running this course."

It was at Harvard, though, that Roosevelt made up his mind that he would not pursue science as a career, perhaps coming to the realization that most of a scientist's work was carried out in the laboratory rather than the field. "I had no more desire to be a microscopist and section-cutter than to be a mathematician," he wrote. In his senior year, Roosevelt began work on a book titled *Naval History of the War of 1812*. The book, which found a publisher two years after Roosevelt left Harvard, marked the beginning of what would be a brief yet fulfilling literary career. What's more, the book remains the definitive source on its subject more than a century after its publication.

At Harvard, his favorite class was a unique course on political economy taught by Professor Charles Dunbar. As his time at Harvard drew to a close, Roosevelt confided to friends that following graduation, he had an interest in pursuing a career in New York City government.

His time at Harvard was not always carefree, however. Theodore Roosevelt Sr. died during his son's second year in Cambridge. The boy was devastated by the loss of his father, whom he had worshipped. After his father's funeral, Theodore spent many anguished nights alone in his room in Cambridge. "I have lost the only human being to whom I tell everything," he wrote in his diary, "never failing to get loving advice and sweet sympathy in return. …With the help of God I will try to lead such a life as he would have wished."

Eventually, he was able to overcome his grief with the help of Alice Lee, a Chestnut Hill girl he met through an introduction by his classmate and

Roosevelt in Rowing Attire, c.1877

At Harvard, Roosevelt was involved in numerous physical activities, including rowing, boxing, and wrestling. He rowed on the Charles River in a one-man shell (and posed for this photograph wearing a rower's skullcap and knee breeches, barefoot and bare-chested, arms folded and his whiskered face set in a defiant scowl.) Roosevelt was a person of incessant activity. He took dancing lessons and then went off on long hikes. He joined the Rifle Club, the Art Club, the Glee Club, and the Natural History Society, and he helped start a Finance Club. He joined the Hasty Pudding Club, the D.K.E. ("the secret society," novelist George Santayana wrote, "to which everybody of consequence belonged"), the aristocratic Porcellian, and several other social groups as well. His close friend Richard Saltonstall said, "He was always ready to join anything." Another classmate recalled that Roosevelt was "forever at it."

1876-77.

HARVARD COLLEGE.

By the regulations of the Faculty I am directed to print, at the end of each Academic Year, the names of all students who have attained seventy-five per cent of the maximum mark in any prescribed study, or seventy-five per cent of it in any elective study, and to send a copy of this publication to the father or other guardian of each student. A list of the members of the *Freshman* Class of 1876-77 who attained seventy per cent in any prescribed study, or seventy-five per cent in any elective study, will be found on the following pages.

The studies pursued by T. Roosevelt in which he did not attain these percentages, will be found among those below with the percentage attained by him in each.

C. J. WHITE,
Registrar of the Faculty.

1877-78.

HARVARD COLLEGE.

By the regulations of the Faculty I am directed to print, at the end of each Academic Year, the names of all students who have attained seventy-five per cent of the maximum mark in any elective study, or seventy per cent in any prescribed study, and to send a copy of this publication to the father or other guardian of each student. A list of the members of the *Sophomore* Class of 1877-78 who attained those percentages in any study will be found on the following pages.

The studies pursued by T. Roosevelt in which he did not attain these percentages, will be found among those below with the percentage attained by him in each.

His per cent on the work of the Sophomore year is *above* seventy. 82 1/8.

C. J. WHITE,
Registrar of the Faculty.

1878-79.

HARVARD COLLEGE.

By the regulations of the Faculty I am directed to print, at the end of each Academic Year, the names of all students who have attained seventy-five per cent of the maximum mark in any elective study, or seventy per cent in any prescribed study, and to send a copy of this publication to the father or other guardian of each student. A list of the members of the *Junior* Class of 1878-79 who attained these percentages in any study will be found on the following pages.

The studies pursued by T. Roosevelt in which he did not attain these percentages, will be found among those below with the percentage attained by him in each.

His per cent on the work of the Junior year is *above* seventy. Average 87+

C. J. WHITE,
Registrar of the Faculty.

1879-80.

HARVARD COLLEGE.

In accordance with the regulations of the Faculty, I herewith give the names of those students who have attained seventy per cent of the maximum mark in any study in the academic year 1879-80.

The studies pursued by T. Roosevelt in which he did not attain seventy per cent, will be found among those below with the percentage attained by him in each.

C. J. WHITE,
Registrar of the Faculty.

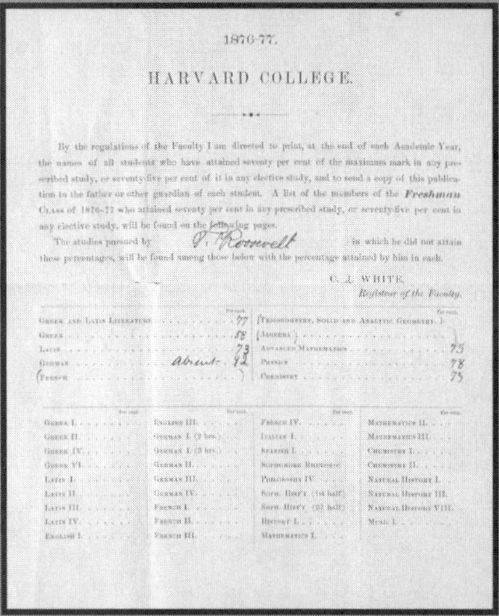

Charles William Eliot (1834–1926), one of the most influential American educators of the nineteenth century, was president of Harvard during Roosevelt's years at the college. When Eliot began his term of office in 1869, Harvard University consisted of the college, together with the schools of divinity, law, medicine, and dentistry. The total enrollment was less than 1,000 students, with a faculty of about sixty teachers. Forty years later, the university had added graduate schools of arts and sciences, applied science, and business administration. The enrollment stood at about 4,000 students and the faculty at nearly six hundred teachers.

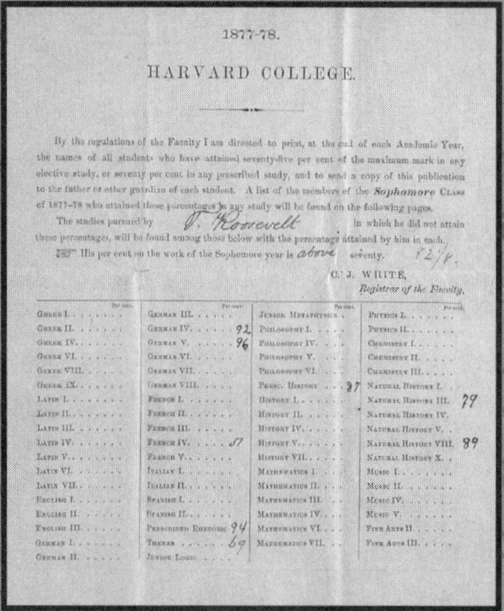

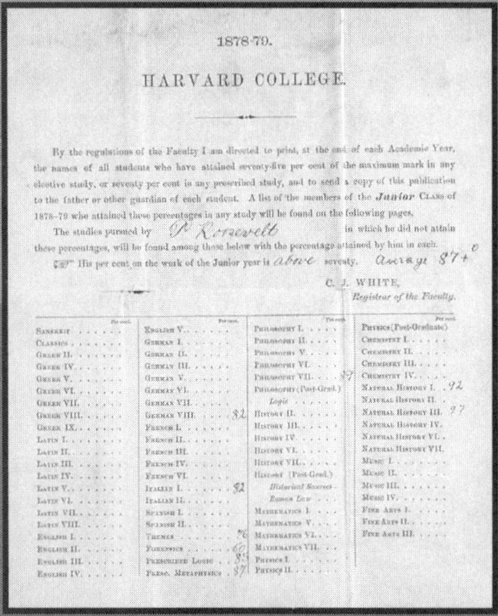

In Harvard College, the undergraduate part of the university, the most radical change introduced by Eliot was the elective system. He believed that the individual student should have a wide choice of courses so that he might rise to the highest stage of attainment in his chosen field. The Eliot course of study gave modern subjects such as English, French, German, history, economics, and above all, the natural sciences, equal rank with Latin, Greek, and mathematics so that a "liberal education" might be more closely related to contemporary life.

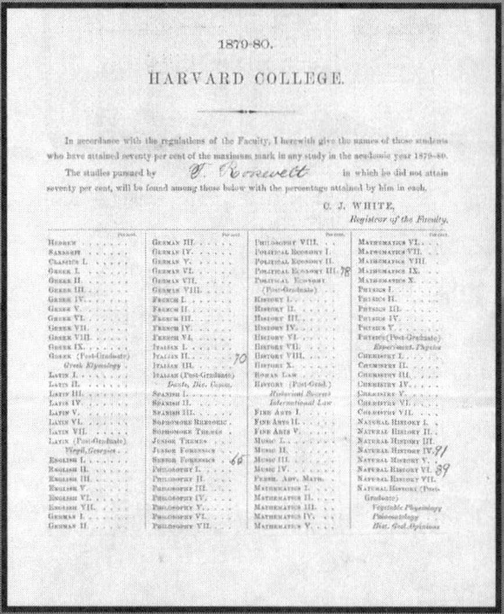

Roosevelt was probably oblivious to Eliot's changes. He never found any real intellectual excitement at the school, for all his good grades. He was never inspired to push himself academically. It does not seem that an instructor stimulated his intellectual curiosity. Nevertheless, Roosevelt was proud of his Harvard affiliation and he enjoyed being known as a Harvard man. Pictured above are Roosevelt's academic transcripts for his four years at Harvard College, 1876–80.

best friend, Richard Saltonstall. She was seventeen when they met, and he was nineteen. In his diary, he would describe her as "radiant," "bright," "cheerful," "sunny," "high-spirited," "enchanting," and "full of life." Theodore spared no expense to impress her. He had a horse shipped to Cambridge from New York, and paid the $900 a year expense of stabling the animal off-campus. He had a buggy shipped to Cambridge as well so he could take Alice riding in the afternoons. She was as smitten with her suitor as he was with her. Alice and Theodore married just a few months after his graduation. She died in 1884, shortly after the birth of their daughter Alice Lee, and only a few hours after the death of Roosevelt's own mother. Two years later, in 1886, Roosevelt married Edith Kermit Carow.

Harvard provided Roosevelt with an education, but he left Cambridge unsure of what to do with himself. He studied law for a short time, but found himself bored with the mundane details of the legal profession. Soon, though, a fulfilling career would find him. New York City Republican leaders, in need of a reform candidate for a state assembly seat, drafted Roosevelt for a slot on the 1882 ticket. Thus began an incandescent political career that would take him to the governorship of New York. Along the way, he was sidetracked by the Spanish-American War, during which his service with a volunteer cavalry regiment (the Rough Riders) in Cuba made Roosevelt a national celebrity. Roosevelt was a natural choice for the 1900 national ticket as the vice presidential candidate under incumbent William McKinley. When McKinley was killed by an assassin just eight months into his second term, Roosevelt took the oath as the nation's twenty-sixth president.

As president, Roosevelt negotiated the treaty that would lead to construction of the Panama Canal, mediated the end of the Russo-Japanese War, and oversaw the enlargement of the U.S. Navy that would make America a world military power—the source of his oft-quoted admonition to "Speak softly and carry a big stick." At home, he used the power of the federal government to break up the huge corporate trusts that he believed were restraining trade, oversaw the reconstruction of the White House, and invited the African-American educator Booker T. Washington to dine with him there. Roosevelt was perhaps the most important conservationist to serve as president, creating a system of national parks and forests that remains unparalleled in the world.

Of course, all that was very much in the future as he completed his education at Harvard. Just after leaving the university, Theodore Roosevelt summed it all up in his diary: "I have had just as much money as I could spend; belonged to the Porcellian Club; have had some capital hunting trips; my life has been varied; I have kept a good horse and cart; I have had a dozen good and true friends in college, and several very pleasant families outside; a lovely home; I have had but little work, only enough to give me an occupation, and to crown all infinitely above everything else put together, I have won the sweetest of girls for my wife. No man ever had so pleasant a college course."

—Hal Marcovitz

William Howard Taft
Chapter Twenty-six

William Howard Taft, the twenty-seventh president of the United States, did not want the job. Although he had previously served as Secretary of War to President Theodore Roosevelt, few who knew Taft considered him a politican. It would be during his tenure as chief justice of the United States Supreme Court, rather than during his term as president, that Taft would implement the ideas and beliefs instilled in him by a first-rate education.

William Howard Taft was born on September 15, 1857, in Cincinnati, Ohio, to Alphonso Taft and his second wife, Louise Torrey Taft. Alphonso had moved to Cincinnati after completing his legal studies at Yale in 1839. He rapidly made a name for himself as an outstanding lawyer and a civic leader in an increasingly prosperous city.

Alphonso's first wife, Fanny, died in 1852, leaving him with two young sons. Almost immediately, he began searching for another wife and a mother for his sons—and the following year, Alphonso married Louise Torrey, a woman from an old and distinguished New England family. According to Henry Pringle, Taft's first major biographer, Alphonso told Louise "she must read good books, cultivate her mind, and pay less attention to the vanities of life." Throughout her life, Louise obliged, partnering with her husband in maintaining a home in which intellectual pursuits held paramount importance.

This emphasis on stimulating the mind played a prominent part in the upbringing of the Taft children, who in time would number five boys and a girl. Will and his siblings were all raised in a household that not only preached intellectualism but lived it as well. Alphonso Taft was an avid reader and a member of Cincinnati's Literary Club, which counted among its members Rutherford B. Hayes, a future president of the United States, and Ainsworth R. Spofford, later to

"Great things have happened and luck came my way…and I want to say that whatever credit is due of a personal character in the honor that came to me, I believe is due to Yale."

The senior class photograph at Woodward High School, Cincinnati, 1874. William Howard Taft sits in the center, first row. The top hat Taft is wearing indicates that he was the class president.

Woodward High was among the first public schools in the nation to offer an adequate college preparatory program. The school maintained a traditional classical education that included a study of Latin, Greek, history, literature, mathematics, and elocution.

Taft served as president of the Woodward Alumni Association, 1883–84. When, as president-elect of the United States, he laid the cornerstone for a new Woodward building in November 1908, Taft praised "the thoroughness of the education I received at her hands."

YALE UNIVERSITY. "Old South Middle" Built in 1750.

Yale University was founded in 1701 as the "Collegiate School within his Majesties Colony of Connecticot [sic]." In that year, according to Yale tradition, ten Congregational ministers met, each with a gift of books, and the first class was held at the Reverend Samuel Russel's parsonage in Killingworth (now Clinton), Connecticut.

In 1716 the college moved to New Haven, because its citizens had outbid other communities in pledging money toward a new school building. Elihu Yale, a retired East India corporation merchant who had been born in New England and was then living in London, sent nine bales of East India goods that were sold at a public auction to raise money for the school. The institution, in gratitude, took his name. The first brick building, known as Old South Middle (pictured above, circa 1909) was finished in 1752 (it is now called Connecticut Hall); the first professorship and endowed chair in divinity were established in 1755. The *Yale Literary Magazine* is the oldest literary periodical in the United States; the *Yale Daily News* is the oldest daily college newspaper.

Yale University honored William Howard Taft, class of 1878, two weeks after he was inaugurated as president of the United States. "Great things have happened and luck came my way," the president told a gathering of undergraduates on March 18, 1909, "and I want to say that whatever credit is due of a personal character in the honor that came to me, I believe is due to Yale." In fact, Yale had been a part of Taft's life as far back as he could remember. His father, the president recalled, had walked from Townshend, Vermont, to Amherst Academy in Massachusetts to prepare for college. "There he heard that there was a larger college in New Haven, Connecticut, so he walked on from Amherst to New Haven," Taft told the students. "He walked back in the summer to help his father farm in Vermont, and he walked back again in the fall. He did not have a dress suit until the senior commencement (1833) when he hired a Baptist minister…to make it for him.…I tell you these stories to show you the influences that prevailed in our home, and they were Yale all through."

be Librarian of Congress. Alphonso and Louise regularly attended plays, the opera, and lectures by prominent men of the day, including one by Ralph Waldo Emerson, who often spoke at the Unitarian church they attended regularly.

Young Will began his education in the Sixteenth District School, a public school in Cincinnati's Mount Auburn section. In 1870, he entered a college preparatory program at Woodward High School, founded by William Woodward, an educator of national reputation. During these years, Will enjoyed an idyllic life filled with family, friends, sports, and other activities (he particularly loved baseball), and of course, his studies. He did very well at Woodward, seemingly with little effort. Will's school day ran from 8:30 A.M. to 1:30 P.M., and included courses in Latin, Greek, math, history, literature, and elocution. The future president graduated second in his class, earning an average of 91.5 for four years. This program of study more than adequately prepared him for matriculation at Yale, his father's alma mater.

If Woodward High School provided the necessary classical foundation for success at Yale, the intellectual atmosphere at home prompted Will to consider more contemporary social and political issues. The post–Civil War Reconstruction era was beginning to wind down, but new social issues remained at the forefront of the national consciousness, especially in a home as progressive as the one in which Will Taft came of age. Young Will had grown up in what would have been considered a very "forward-thinking" home. His father had publicly and vigorously supported the emancipation of slaves before and during the Civil War, and both his father and mother were extremely active in Cincinnati's intellectual and cultural life. Louise was involved in a variety of activities from charity work to the organization of the Cincinnati Art Museum, as well as an advocate of the then avant-garde kindergarten movement.

In 1874, the year William Howard Taft graduated from high school and left home for Yale, the United States was struggling with a variety of social concerns. The position of African Americans after the Civil War remained sharply disjunctive: the sixth black congressman was elected to the House of Representatives in that year, but sixteen blacks were lynched during August in Tennessee. Some American workers formed the anti-capitalist Social Democratic Workmen's Party. Across Taft's own home state of Ohio, the Women's Christian Temperance Union (WCTU) flourished, reaffirming both the continuing need for social reform in a rapidly changing America as well as women's central role in such movements. Circumstances and events such as these were discussed at length in the Taft household, and Will must have been listening closely, judging from the speech he gave at his high-school graduation. Influenced not only by the views he heard expressed at home, but also by the unique sight of both father and mother functioning as intellectual equals, he spoke on women's suffrage:

> However different man and woman may be intellectually, coeducation…
> shows clearly that there is no mental inferiority on the part of the girls.…
> Give the woman the ballot, and you will make her more important in the

William Howard Taft, from his 1878 Yale senior class album. Taft delivered the 1878 class oration and was second in a class of one hundred and twenty-one students.

William Howard Taft is the only person to serve both as president of the United States and as chief justice of the U.S. Supreme Court. He was the third generation in his family to enter the legal profession.

eyes of the world. This will strengthen her character.…Every woman would then be given an opportunity to earn a livelihood. She would suffer no decrease in compensation for her labor, on account of her sex.…In the natural course of events, universal suffrage must prevail throughout the world.

"Bill" Taft, as he was now called, arrived at Yale in the fall of 1874, with, according to historian David Burton, a "mastery of fact and a commitment to disciplined study, rather than a sense of an intellectual adventure on which he was about to embark." The future president had indeed been exposed to a variety of innovative ideas in his parents' home, but Yale was in the process of trying to turn those new ideas into a systematic program of study, so that the school's graduates would be well equipped to lead the country into what was clearly going to be a radically different era. Largely driven by the alumni, the university instituted curricular changes designed to expose its students to more science, political philosophy, and economics—areas of knowledge that seemed vital in an increasingly industrialized and urbanized America. In 1872, two men arrived at Yale who were emblematic of the school's ambition to meet the needs of a changing world and to influence that world as well. One was Yale's new president, Noah Porter, brought in to solidify the post–Civil War re-visioning of the school that had come to be known as "Young Yale." The other was William Graham Sumner, a sociologist and economist who profoundly shaped Taft's views on the functions of government—views that he would later act on both as president and as chief justice of the United States Supreme Court.

Bill Taft would not take a course with Sumner until his junior year. In his freshman and sophomore years, he was still obliged to take the courses that comprised Yale's traditional curriculum, based on the same classical education that had formed his high school experience. In his freshman year, he studied Greek and Latin; algebra, geometry, and trigonometry; botany; and the various arts of rhetoric, including composition and oratory. Oratory—the art of making effective speeches—would serve the future president, professor, and jurist well; in fact, his speeches were

This is a photograph of William Howard Taft's Yale "eating club." Taft is in the center of the last row, indicating that he was the club's president. Taft noted on this photograph, "Taken in 1878," and signed his name.

Observe the dress of the all-male club. Women were first admitted to the Yale graduate schools in 1892 but the university did not become fully coeducational and racially integrated until the late 1960s. Note the woman sitting in the first row looking away from the camera—and note the nonwhite male standing, right of illustration.

William Howard Taft also became a member of Yale's Skull and Bones secret society. Taft's father had been a founder of the organization in 1833. This secret undergraduate society extended membership to those whom the group thought had an outstanding personality and was a great force in undergraduate life. Throughout Taft's life, the memory of his election to Skull and Bones was precious to him. It represented the very best among all of the excellent phases of Yale life that he experienced. Skull and Bones was not a sleeping or eating club but a social organization with secret ceremonies. The organization competed with other groups for the outstanding leaders and honored men in each class. Taft returned to many of its meetings.

It is difficult to describe Yale of the 1880s, a time more than one hundred and twenty years ago. Yale itself was a shabby row of battered buildings. It had been founded because of religion. But the power of the place was unmistakable. Yale inspired loyalties in its graduates that were impressive. The customs of the college were delightful rather than negative. It seemed that old traditions and new experiences continually mingled and strengthened the Yale spirit. At least it did for Bill Taft. His link with Yale was never broken.

so well regarded that many collections of them have been published, including *Four Aspects of Civic Duty* (1907), *Popular Government* (1913), *The United States and Peace* (1914), and *The President and His Powers* (1924).

In Taft's junior year, some of Yale's new progressivism found its way into his course work. Bill began to study philosophy and the social sciences. His required readings now shifted from the classics to major contemporary seminal works that were challenging as well as profound. Required books included: Henry Fawcett, *Manual of Political Economy*; Francis Lieber, *On Civil Liberty and Self-Government*; Albert Schwegler, *History of Philosophy*; Theodore Woolsey, *Introduction to the Study of International Law*; Alexis Tocqueville, *Democracy in America*—and of course, the writings of William Graham Sumner, Yale's brightest intellectual.

Sumner taught at Yale from 1872 to 1909. In his many essays, he expounded his firm belief in laissez-faire economics, individual liberty, and the innate inequalities among people. He viewed competition for both property ownership and social status as resulting in a beneficial elimination of the ill adapted. For him, the middle class Protestant ethic of hard work, thrift, and sobriety was conducive to wholesome family life and sound public morality. He opposed the drift toward a welfare state that would impose taxes on the middle class, because poverty, he wrote, was the natural result of an inherent inferiority. In essence, Sumner adapted Charles Darwin's theory of natural selection—the concept of "survival of the fittest"—to the contemporary economic scene—no government social programs were necessary, as this would interfere with the natural order. This theory became known as "social Darwinism."

Sumner's influence was powerful, and young Bill Taft was swayed by most of his ideas. As Taft himself wrote half a century later, "I have felt that he had more to do with stimulating my mental activities than anyone under whom I studied during my entire course." He accepted Sumner's views about the rights of capital and private property in a free-market economy—ideas that were to be sorely tested in the compromises President Taft tried to achieve in controversies over tariff reform in 1909. He understood the need to protect American industries from overseas competition, but also saw the benefits in Sumner's advocacy of unrestrained free trade. Taft's ideological dilemma between these positions ended in the 1909 Payne-Aldrich Tariff, a solution that pleased no one, including the president.

Bill Taft decisively rejected Sumner's more extreme ideas, which included not just his version of Social Darwinism but also the acceptable use of force to protect and encourage free trade. No doubt Bill's parents played a crucial role in his partial acceptance of Sumner's ideas; his mother's activities in particular would have reinforced a sense that there were other, less economically driven things to be valued in society. But Bill also seems to have found support for these values at Yale as well, particularly in the classes of Henry A. Beers, with whom he studied English literature from Chaucer to Tennyson. As Burton wrote, Beers "appealed to the humane and kindly in Taft, of which there was a generous share, much as Sumner spoke to his prosaic side."

This May 14, 1877, letter from Yale to Taft's father informed Alphonso Taft that his son had accumulated sixteen demerits. To have accumulated only sixteen demerits by his junior year indicates that Taft was a well-behaved and punctual student.

In the letter, Yale's policy on demerits and expulsion of students is explained: "To secure regularity in attendance and propriety of conduct on the part of the students, marks are given for their delinquencies in both these respects. When the marks of a student amount to *sixteen*, notice of the fact is given to his parent or guardian. When they amount to *thirty-two*, a second notice is given. When they amount to *forty-eight*, he is suspended from the College."

Bill ended his undergraduate years at Yale with courses in the sciences, mental philosophy (a concept with its premise found in Noah Porter's *Human Intellect: with an Introduction Upon Psychology and the Soul*), and constitutional law. Overall, his years at Yale were very successful; he ranked third in his class as a freshman, won two composition prizes as a sophomore, and captured both a math award and an essay prize as a junior, the latter for an essay titled "Availability as a Ruling Consideration in the Choice of Presidential Candidates." His undergraduate achievements earned him the rank of second, or salutatorian, in his class of 1878. As salutatorian, he spoke at the graduation ceremony, on the topic of "The Professional and Political Prospects of the College Graduates."

Bill Taft's own prospects were, of course, quite good. Though he was to go on to law school in Cincinnati immediately after graduating from Yale, the foundation of his political, judicial, and intellectual persona were already in place, lodged firmly within him by both an excellent education and an upbringing that ensured a life-long predilection for careful consideration of new ideas, circumstances, and political realities. Taft's preference for the balanced viewpoint did not, however, suit the needs of the presidency in a time of political, economic, and social ambiguity. A more decisive—even partisan—approach to the problem of tariff reform, for example, would have served him, if not the country, better.

Taft's one term as president, from 1909 to 1913, was marked by increasing conflict between the progressive policies staunchly advocated by Theodore Roosevelt and the more conservative beliefs held by Taft. He continued Roosevelt's program of "trust-busting," or breaking up the coalitions of companies that exercised control over certain industries. His failure, however, to reduce the tariffs that protected American business from overseas competition earned him much criticism. The Ballinger-Pinchot controversy—a scandal concerning the transfer of public lands to private corporations—devastated Taft's political viability. He was not returned to office in 1912, and the historical verdict on his presidency has generally not been favorable.

Taft's post-presidential career was more successful—and far more to his liking. Immediately after his presidency he returned to his alma mater, Yale, and served as a professor of law from 1913 to 1921. In 1921, Taft realized a long-cherished dream when President Warren G. Harding appointed him chief justice of the United States Supreme Court. This was a position Taft had coveted since his early years of service to President Roosevelt, and it was as chief justice that Taft made his lasting mark. Though he wrote no memorable opinions, he is credited with significant administrative reform of the Court's operations and with upholding principles of private property, the rights of the individual (including those of minorities), and the limitation of governmental authority.

Taft's habits of thinking, which had proven too ponderous for the presidency, were perfectly suited to the Supreme Court, a body whose mandate is cautious deliberation. Today, some of his opinions would be considered controversial at best, more often than not upholding the rights of business at the expense of a labor force now understood to have been cruelly exploited at the time. Through much of his judicial career, Taft seems to have embraced many of the ideas of his old mentor at Yale, William Graham Sumner. At the time, however, Taft was respected for his adherence to a strict interpretation of the Constitution and for the intellectual rigor that he brought to his position as the nation's top jurist. Taft would serve as chief justice until February 3, 1930, when ill health forced him to retire. He died the following month. He was the first president to be buried in Arlington National Cemetery.

William Howard Taft came of age in a time when the United States had left behind the innocence of its national infancy. Continued expansion, the Civil War, urbanization, and industrialization all weighed heavily on a country still a bit too impressed, perhaps, by its own raw energy and optimism. As Taft progressed through his education, education itself progressed toward a more relevant curriculum meant to embrace "modernity". Ultimately, both Taft and his education had one foot in the past and one in the future, leading to a political ambivalence that often paralyzed Taft's presidency. In his later career as chief justice, however, ambivalence redefined itself as wisdom and perspective. It is in this phase of his life that both Taft and the education he received acquitted themselves admirably in the service of their country. To Taft, his appointment as chief justice was his greatest honor; toward the end of his life he would comment, "I don't remember that I ever was president."

—Pamela Fitzgibbon

Woodrow Wilson

Chapter Twenty-seven

"The president," Woodrow Wilson once wrote, "must above all things else, be a man of unbiased judgment, energy, determination, intelligence, moral courage, conscience." It is hard to argue with Wilson's vision for the presidency, but it should be pointed out that the man who would become the nation's twenty-eighth chief executive did not pen those words as he faced William Howard Taft and Theodore Roosevelt on the eve of the 1912 election. Rather, Wilson authored that statement in September 1878 as he was campaigning for the office of president of the Princeton College Baseball Association.

Wilson had the advantage in the race. He was already editor of the student newspaper, the *Princetonian*, and apparently more than willing to use the power of a press he controlled to further his own political ambitions. By the fall of his senior year, Wilson was an important member of the student body. In addition to serving as editor of the *Princetonian*, Wilson was elected speaker of the Whig Society, a campus literary group; founded the Liberal Debating Club, a semi-secret society for Princeton intellectuals; got himself elected secretary of the Princeton Football Club; and held a membership in the Alligators, a group of well-to-do students whose main purpose seems to have been to enjoy expensive dinners together while sketching plays for the football team on linen napkins.

Why Wilson believed he needed to add the presidency of the campus baseball association to round out his career as an undergraduate at Princeton remains a mystery. The job required the officeholder to see to the financial responsibilities of supporting the team and carried no guarantee of a place in the lineup. Nevertheless, on September 26, 1878, on the heels of a stirring editorial in the *Princetonian* suggesting that with a "good captain and an efficient president success is no longer a matter of doubt," members of the Princeton Baseball Club met to elect their officers for the coming year. Wilson's opponent was his classmate, Cornelius Cuyler, who appeared to be carrying a majority heading into the meeting. However, Wilson enlisted an ally, Charles Talcott, to call for a postponement of the vote. Talcott was able to sway a majority of the voters toward delaying the election—a ploy that

In 1873, Woodrow Wilson enrolled at Davidson, a small Presbyterian college in Piedmont, North Carolina. He was seventeen years old. He did not stay at Davidson long; Wilson's health seriously deteriorated and he returned home during his second semester. Until this point in his life, Wilson's education had been more or less informal. Family group reading sessions had been a custom. Wilson's father, a minister, assumed responsibility for educating his son. The father routinely read aloud from the novels of Charles Dickens and Walter Scott—and, of course, he read from the Bible. According to Ray Stannard Baker, Wilson's biographer, the first book the future president completed was Mason Weems's *The Life of George Washington*.

Wilson entered the College of New Jersey in September 1875. Presbyterian ministers had founded the school in 1746, making it the fourth-oldest institution of higher education in the United States (it would eventually be renamed Princeton University). Harvard, William and Mary, and Yale—the three American colleges that predated Princeton—were strongly supported by the colonies they served (Massachusetts, Virginia, and Connecticut, respectively) and each drew its students predominantly from that colony. The College of New Jersey was different. From the start, students came to Princeton from all of the colonies, making it a national institution before there was a nation. This tradition of a national academic Presbyterian-dominated school with a diverse student body attracted Wilson to the college.

The *Nassau Herald,* a yearbook, annually reported senior class polls. More than two-thirds of Wilson's class of 1879 stated that they intended to enter a profession. A majority replied that the "democratic spirit" had attracted them to the college. All but two class members declared they were members of a church.

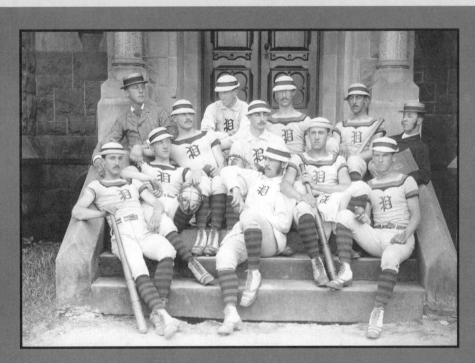

Undergraduate life at Princeton was undergoing significant changes in the late 1870s. What Woodrow Wilson later called the "sideshows"—extracurricular activities—were just beginning. Intercollegiate athletics were also getting underway. Princeton began a formal schedule of football games in 1876. By 1879, the baseball team was playing a fourteen game schedule. The 1879 team is pictured above. Wilson, the team manger, is in the upper left of the photograph, wearing a straw hat.

Wilson enjoyed baseball. As a student at Princeton, he and his fellow boarding house members formed a team called the "Bowery Boys." Wilson wrote in his diary that he often played baseball twice a day and once played every day for six days straight. In 1878, Wilson was elected president of the Princeton Baseball Association by the student managers. He resigned shortly afterwards at the urging of his mother, who advised him "to pursue studies connected with his future interests."

The Eumenean Society had as its objective "the acquirement of literary knowledge, the promotion of virtue, and the cultivation of social harmony and friendship."

12

Naval.

Phonography By Thomas W Wilson from Graham's Hand Book of Standard or American Phonography.

Comprising 25 lessons in the Corresponding Style of Phonography taking up 112 pages. Also full exemplification of the Reporting Style, together with full lists of word signs and contractions and a partial list of words in the Reporting Style. Also very copious exercises, both reading and writing, taking up about 58 pages. The best book on Phonography ever printed. I regard this book as a perfect gem and would not part with it, or the knoledge I have gained from it for anything.

Thomas W. Wilson

During his one year at Davidson College (1873–74), Wilson became an active member of the Eumenean Society. The Eumenean Society was one of Davidson's two undergraduate debating and literary clubs. It had as its objective "the acquirement of literary knowledge, the promotion of virtue, and the cultivation of social harmony and friendship." However, the lists of topics debated also indicate a keen interest in contemporary political and social issues.

Wilson had a clear and legible handwriting. He often was asked to take notes of student meetings.

While at Davidson, he also perfected his shorthand skills. Wilson's 1874 testimonial to phonography, a system of phonetic shorthand, illustrates both his excellent penmanship and his increased interest in shorthand. He concluded that Andrew Graham's book is the best "ever printed. I regard this book as a perfect gem and would not part with it."

worked in Wilson's favor. Four weeks later, the *Princetonian* reported that the postponed election for baseball club president had finally been held, and the winner was Thomas Woodrow Wilson, class of 1879.

The future president was born on December 29, 1856, in Staunton, Virginia, where his father, Dr. Joseph Ruggles Wilson, was minister of the First Presbyterian Church. Tom Wilson, as he was known in his childhood, had two older sisters and a younger brother. His mother, Jessie Woodrow Wilson, was the daughter of a Presbyterian minister. Soon, the family would move to Augusta, Georgia, where Reverend Wilson had been named leader of another church. Tom Wilson spent his earliest years growing up in Georgia while the ravages of the Civil War unfolded around him. "My earliest recollection is of standing at my father's gateway in Augusta, Georgia, when I was four years old, and hearing someone pass and say that Mr. Lincoln was elected and there was to be war," Wilson recalled years later. "Catching the intense tones of his excited voice, I remember running in to ask my father what it meant."

Reverend Wilson was an ardent supporter of the southern cause and made his church available as a hospital for wounded soldiers. Nevertheless, the Wilsons were largely unaffected by the war. Although they did not keep slaves, the Wilsons had the wherewithal to employ a butler and other servants. They even escaped the poverty and hunger that plagued the South during the post-war years. Reverend Wilson was paid well by his congregations, and Jessie Wilson had a modest inheritance that helped see the family through the difficult years of Reconstruction.

Woodrow Wilson would attend four colleges. He earned a law degree as well as a doctorate in political science, thus ranking him among the most educated of men to occupy the White House. Ironically, Wilson did not start formal schooling until he was twelve years old. Until then, Joseph and Jessie Wilson handled the chores of educating their children. They taught Tom and his siblings to read by reading to them. The Wilsons preferred British authors, because Joseph and Jessie were proud of their British ancestry. Stories authored by Charles Dickens and Sir Walter Scott were among the favorite selections read in the Wilson home. The first book that Tom Wilson read on his own is believed to be Mason Weems's *Life of Washington*.

In 1868, Tom entered his first classroom. His teacher was Joseph T. Derry, a former Confederate Army officer. Tom would spend just two years in Derry's private school, but would make long-lasting friendships with other Augusta boys, some of whom would go on to important political careers. His friends included Joseph R. Lamar, who would be appointed to the U.S. Supreme Court by President Taft, and Pleasant A. Stovall, whom Wilson would appoint minister to Switzerland.

In 1870, Reverend Wilson accepted a position at the Columbia Theological Seminary in South Carolina. Tom continued his education in Columbia, spending three years at a private school taught by Charles N. Barnwell. In 1873, at the age of sixteen, Tom Wilson left home to enroll in tiny Davidson College in North Carolina.

He spent a lonely, unhappy year at Davidson. Tom found the work difficult and struggled with his courses. Under Barnwell and Derry, Wilson had never been a particularly hard-working pupil. As a college student, Wilson continued a practice that would plague him until very late in his education as a graduate student—a tendency to loaf in his studies due to boredom.

At Davidson, though, he discovered a gift for oratory and debate and would, from then on, always be a leader among the debating societies at the schools he attended. It was also at Davidson that Wilson developed a fascination for American politics and made up his mind to study government and eventually enter government service.

Wilson fell ill at Davidson, beginning a lifelong struggle with dyspeptic ailments—stomach problems that would evidently account for his rail-thin physique. He dropped out of Davidson due to his illness and moved back with his parents, who were by then living in Wilmington, North Carolina. Tom spent a year recovering his health, then enrolled in Princeton College in New Jersey.

When Wilson arrived in 1875, Princeton did not have the reputation it enjoys today. While Harvard and Yale were modernizing their curriculums and raising money to attract top faculty members and erect grand lecture halls and dormitories, Princeton seemed mired in its old ways. A particular problem that incensed the students were the open cesspools and sewers that served the college—on a windy day, their odors would be swept across campus. Hazing, rowdiness, and cheating ran rampant. Freshmen were required to walk with canes on campus because of a tradition in which a sophomore could assault a freshman at any time in an effort to wrestle away his cane. Other freshmen had their heads shaved or were dragged by ropes in the nearby Raritan Canal. When a freshman defended himself by shooting a sophomore in the leg with a revolver, the police stepped in. That led to a faculty crackdown during Wilson's freshman year, which probably accounts for the fact that Wilson seems to have escaped the indignities of hazing during his matriculation at Princeton.

Over the next four years, Tom Wilson would study Latin, Greek, mathematics, religion, philosophy, history, French, psychology, and the physical sciences. His grades were respectable but hardly exemplary. He blamed himself, writing in his diary, "I have come to the conclusion that my friends have no doubt come to long ago and that is that my mind is a very ordinary one indeed. I am nothing as far as intellect goes. But I can plod and work."

It is more likely that Wilson was simply bored by the Princeton curriculum and did not find it challenging. When Wilson enrolled at Princeton, administrators were just beginning the process of improving the quality of the faculty and modernizing the courses of study. During Wilson's matriculation at Princeton, the student literary magazine commented, "Our weekly glimpses of certain fields of thought are as unsatisfactory as a five-minute stare through a telescope."

If he did show enthusiasm for any course of study, it was political science. As a descendant of British ancestors, Wilson found himself fascinated by Britain's form of government, and many of the essays and orations he wrote as an undergraduate suggested that Great Britain's parliamentary form of democratic government was far

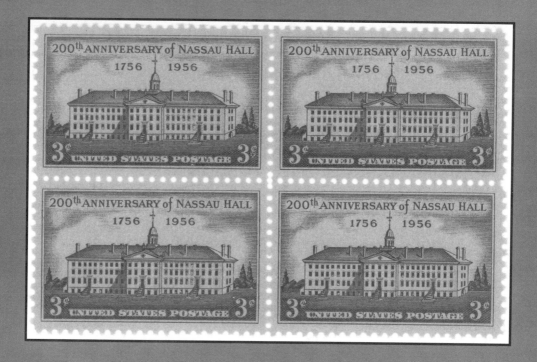

First class postage stamps issued in 1956 to commemorate the two-hundredth anniversary of Nassau Hall.

When construction of the College of New Jersey's Nassau Hall was completed in 1756, it was the largest stone building in the thirteen colonies. It has served as the model for numerous college campus buildings, including Hollis Hall at Harvard, University Hall at Brown, and Dartmouth Hall at Dartmouth.

Nassau Hall suffered an enormous amount of destruction during the American Revolution. Both British and American troops plundered the library and used the school's furniture for fuel. During the Battle of Princeton (1777), Nassau Hall changed hands three times. A cannonball fired by General George Washington's artillery passed through a prayer room window, destroying a portrait of King George II. A few years later, it was at Nassau Hall that Congress formally congratulated Washington on the successful termination of the war. At the request of the Princeton trustees, the general agreed to sit for a portrait by Charles Willson Peale. It was placed in the prayer room and in the frame once occupied by the King George II portrait.

Woodrow Wilson ranks among Princeton's greatest alumni. Wilson, who was president of the United States from 1913 to 1921, graduated from Princeton in 1879. In 1890, the Princeton Board of Trustees appointed Wilson, not yet thirty-four, professor of jurisprudence and political economy. And in 1902, Wilson was unanimously elected president of Princeton University, a position he held from 1902 to 1910.

Wilson developed a lifelong interest in phonetic shorthand after reading a series in *Frank Leslie's Boys' and Girls' Weekly*. In November 1872, a stenographic news reporter began writing more than fifty appealing articles popularizing the virtues of shorthand. Wilson's interest was immediate and sustained—he pasted forty-six articles into a scrapbook. He was sixteen years old.

Wilson made good use of his shorthand as an undergraduate student at Princeton. He seems to have compiled a verbatim record of the words of his professors—especially in his senior year, when he had become more proficient in note taking. However, more significant for Wilson's later political positions are the classroom notes of his graduate courses in history, law, and political science.

Several hundred of Wilson's shorthand notebooks have survived. They have been deposited with the Library of Congress and Princeton University. In 1963, the editors of the Woodrow Wilson Papers arranged the transcription of a shorthand diary that Wilson had kept during his freshman year at Princeton. It contains fifty-five closely written pages. It begins: "June 3rd: I now commence my diary which I have for some time contemplated. I am now 19 years old and am by the blessings of God in the enjoyment of excellent health. I have not employed the day to very much advantage having spent most of my time in loafing. My only reading today has been the life of Samuel Pepys prefixed to his diary in the

edition of '69. I like Pepys am writing my diary in shorthand but here the resemblance between his diary and mine cease."

There is no extant shorthand draft of Wilson's seminal essays that together form *Congressional Government*, his first book, but it is possible that he attempted one. Scholars do know that Wilson's father advised him to use shorthand as a drafting tool: "When you are first studying a given subject, place it upon paper in shorthand: —then make no direct use of that, but quitting it altogether, commence a fresh in long-hand as if you had not previously written at all. The one operation would give you the advantage of rapid and connected study—the other that of slow and connected expression."

Wilson intensively practiced his shorthand during the months prior to entering Princeton as a freshman student. He copied articles from *Frank Leslie's Weekly*. Among the articles that he copied was an entire series on geology. Above is a page from these articles in Wilson's shorthand. At the end of this lengthy exercise he wrote, partly in shorthand: "Finished 4/10/75." He was nineteen years old.

more effective than the bicameral model created by the U.S. Constitution. His reading material during this period included Thomas Macauley's *History of England*, several works by Samuel Pepys, the papers of Joseph Addison, and a significant amount of Shakespeare. Somehow, through all that study of Great Britain and its government, Wilson resolved to enter U.S. politics. As an undergraduate, he had calling cards made up for himself that read: "Thomas Woodrow Wilson, Senator from Virginia." Certainly, it did not escape Wilson's attention that the U.S. Senate was a forum for debate and oration—skills in which Wilson believed he excelled.

Wilson showed his leadership in the campus clubs and associations. He joined the Whig Society, a campus literary organization in which members wrote essays, delivered orations, and debated timely topics. Such societies, which were common on college campuses during the nineteenth century, were regarded as excellent training grounds for future lawyers, editors, teachers, and political leaders.

Wilson rose quickly in the ranks of the Whig Society. As a sophomore, he won second prize in a Whig competition for an oration titled "The Ideal Statesman." Eventually, he would serve a term as Whig Society speaker, the top position in the group. "He gave splendid addresses in extempore debate," recalled his classmate, Robert McCarter. "He was a careful speaker; he spoke without yelling. He prided himself on his ability to talk correctly and trained himself to think on his feet."

In his sophomore year, Wilson invited nine members of the Whig Society to join a group he called the Liberal Debating Club. The group took Whig Society debates a step further. Wilson drafted a constitution for the club, basing its bylaws on the debating rules that governed the British House of Commons. Members of the Liberal Debating Club studied political issues and met on Saturday nights to argue the merits of each side of the chosen topic for the week. Technically, the society was in violation of college rules. Members took a vow of secrecy, promising not to reveal to outsiders the nature of their debates. At the time, Princeton had outlawed fraternities, specifically because the groups demanded vows of secrecy from their members. Concluding that the Liberal Debating Club was harmless, Princeton administrators permitted Wilson's group to meet, and Wilson and the others continued to do so until they graduated two years later.

Wilson also took great delight in his membership in the Alligator Club, which was little more than a group of students with the means to rent a house off campus for the primary purpose of having fancy dinners. Wilson, who was receiving a generous allowance from his parents, was a dedicated Alligator. It was not unusual for the talk during Alligator Club dinners to focus on the fortunes of the Princeton baseball and football teams.

Wilson was, in fact, a fanatical sports fan. At the time, Princeton had just started playing intercollegiate sports. Wilson and his friends attended the games and became involved in the associations that supported the teams financially. Wilson used guile to win the presidency of the baseball association, although just a few weeks after wresting control of the group away from Cornelius Cuyler he resigned.

He was more enthusiastic about the football team and held office in the football association as well.

It was as editor of the *Princetonian*, though, that Wilson left his greatest mark as an undergraduate. Student newspapers were then, as they are now, feisty organs of the undergraduate community. Wilson, who took over the *Princetonian* in the spring of his junior year, was an enthusiastic proponent of that tradition. The *Princetonian*, Wilson wrote in his first commentary as editor, "will be an impartial record of college incident and a medium for a bold, frank, and manly expression of college opinion."

Under Wilson, the *Princetonian* complained about the college policy requiring students to pay their room and board in advance. The newspaper also campaigned for something to be done about the primitive campus sewage system. The *Princetonian* supported the plight of the poor Irish women who cleaned the dormitories—Wilson believed the ladies to be overworked. The newspaper attacked faculty members whom Wilson accused of giving too many tests, arguing that it led to cramming by students.

Faculty members and administrators weren't the only members of the Princeton community to feel the wrath of the newspaper's editor. *Princetonian* editorials criticized students for their sloppy dress, called on class members to donate to the football and baseball associations as well as other student organizations, and scorched members of the football team for refusing to play at their best. "The only thing worthy of serious reprehension in the playing of the team is the stubborn manner in which some of the men shut their eyes to the command of the captain," a *Princetonian* editorial huffed in the fall of 1878. "Until they learn to obey they will never learn to play with effect."

Wilson graduated from Princeton in June of 1879. His mediocre academic record ensured that he would be passed over for the main commencement honors. Wilson's only role during the three-day graduation celebration was the delivery of a short speech during a minor ceremony.

Still, Wilson would forever treasure his four years as an undergraduate at Princeton. He remained close to many classmates, continuing a correspondence with them that would last until the end of his life. A few weeks after leaving Princeton, Wilson wrote Charles Talcott, "Since Princeton I have not been in the brightest of moods. The parting after commencement went harder than I had feared even. It most emphatically and literally struck in."

Wilson was by no means finished with his education. He harbored ambitions to enter public life, and had concluded that his goal of a career as a lawmaker would best be reached by studying the law. Later, he wrote, "The profession I chose was politics; the profession I entered was the law. I entered the one because I thought it would lead to the other."

He entered the law school of the University of Virginia in the fall of 1879. At Virginia, Wilson proved himself every bit the type of student that he had been at Princeton, which means he compiled another mediocre academic record. Again, he

Woodrow Wilson's Princeton senior class photograph, 1879

found much more fulfillment in the extracurricular activities on campus. He joined the Jefferson Literary Society, a debating and speaking club similar to the Whig Society on the Princeton campus. He was admitted to Phi Kappa Psi, one of the most popular fraternities at Virginia, and was eventually elected chapter president. He even joined the university glee club, which traipsed around campus delivering sugary love songs beneath the bedroom windows of faculty members' daughters.

Unfortunately, all these extracurricular activities combined with his studies began to take its toll. In frail health, he was forced to leave the University of Virginia and abandon his studies halfway through his second year. He returned to his parents' home and spent the next year and a half recuperating and studying. It was around this time that he began going by his middle name, Woodrow.

After passing the Virginia bar examination in October of 1882, Wilson headed to Atlanta to establish a law practice with a Virginia classmate, Edward I. Renick. It was a disastrous undertaking. The firm of Renick & Wilson found few clients during that time, forcing Wilson to continue to accept—at the age of twenty-five— financial assistance from his father. Wilson also found himself bored with the

REGISTER OF STUDENTS.

56 SESSION. 1879-80.

The register of students at the University of Virginia, 1879–80. "Thos. Woodrow Wilson," as Wilson signed himself in the register (third from bottom), enrolled for classes in Junior Law, Senior Law, and International Law.

During his Princeton undergraduate years, Wilson often daydreamed. He repeatedly thought of himself as a United States Senator. He even had calling cards inscribed THOMAS WOODROW WILSON, SENATOR FROM VIRGINIA. Therefore, it seemed only natural when he decided to attend the University of Virginia for training in law.

John B. Minor was one of the two law professors at the school. Minor was known throughout the South as an outstanding legal scholar. Wilson considered him, next to his father, his greatest teacher. "The profession I chose was politics," Wilson later wrote, "the profession I entered was the law. I entered the one because I thought it would lead to the other."

minutiae of legal work, and was distressed to find that, at least in Atlanta, a career in law was not regarded as a stepping-stone into politics. In a letter to his fiancée, Ellen Axson, he grumbled, "Whoever thinks, as I thought, that he can practice law successfully and study history and politics at the same time is woefully mistaken."

He continued to suffer physical ills as well. His sensitive stomach acted up again, causing him to finally give up his law practice and return to his parents' home in North Carolina to recuperate.

By 1883 he was back in school—this time on a fellowship as a graduate student in history and politics at Johns Hopkins University in Baltimore, Maryland. At Hopkins, Wilson finally blossomed into a scholar. During his three years in Baltimore, he would author the book *Congressional Government*, an analysis of the bicameral form of legislative government in the United States, in which Wilson suggested the legislative and executive branches be combined as they are in England. The book also warned against the growing power of congressional committees, an issue that is still very much debated today. The book found a publisher in 1885. Although he left Johns Hopkins before completing his degree, he would later submit his published book as his thesis, and after taking the required examinations was awarded his Ph.D. in 1886.

Following Hopkins, Wilson accepted a teaching position at Bryn Mawr College in Pennsylvania. He found his way back to Princeton in 1890 as a professor of law and political science. Twelve years later, he was elected president of Princeton University.

In 1910, Wilson finally commenced a political career when he was elected governor of New Jersey. He entered the State House in Trenton as a reformer, and quickly came to the attention of national leaders of the Democratic Party. Two years later, he emerged from a divisive and bitter Democratic National Convention as his party's nominee for president.

To Wilson's advantage, the Republicans in 1912 were even more divided than the Democrats. The incumbent president, William Howard Taft, was running as the GOP candidate, while former Republican president Theodore Roosevelt campaigned as a third-party candidate. They split the Republican vote that fall, permitting Wilson to become just the second Democrat since the Civil War to win the presidency.

Wilson's eight years as president were dominated by events that unfolded in Europe. His decision to commit troops to the Allied cause in World War I broke the stalemate that had dominated the conflict since hostilities commenced in 1914. The success of the American Expeditionary Force under General John J. Pershing established the United States military as a formidable fighting force. Wilson also set out his "Fourteen Points" for a fair peace settlement; however, British and French negotiators weakened several of these in the Treaty of Versailles that was negotiated after an armistice was signed to end the war. In addition, the isolationist U.S. Senate refused to accept the establishment of the League of Nations, an organization supported by Wilson. Without U.S. might behind the League, the coalition of nations was largely ineffective.

JOHNS HOPKINS UNIVERSITY.

Candidates for admission are requested to answer, in their own hand-writing, the following questions. Candidates at a distance will be advised by mail, (after their replies to these questions have been received) whether they should present themselves for examination.

I. Date of application.

Sept. 18th 1883

II. State your name in full, year and place of birth, and present post-office address.

Woodrow Wilson, born in Staunton, Va., Dec. 28th 1856. Present address, Wilmington, N.C.

III. Name in full of your parent or guardian, and his post-office address.

Rev. Joseph R. Wilson, D.D., Wilmington, N.C.

IV. Enclose your credentials (a diploma, certificate or letter of recommendation), and give a list of them here.

I have a diploma from Princeton College, which I can present if necessary, and letters of recommendation which I presented last May, with an application for a fellowship and which are

V. Name the schools or colleges in which you have been taught, and the time of your residence in each.

One year ('73-'74) at Davidson College; four years at Princeton College ('75-'79) and one year and three months at University of Virginia law courses ('79-'80)

VI. State, somewhat freely, in your own way, the purpose which you have in view in coming to this University, and the studies you wish to pursue.

My purpose in coming to the University is to qualify myself for teaching the studies I wish to pursue, namely, History and Political Science, as well as to fit myself for those special studies of Constitutional history upon which I have already bestowed some attention

VII. State in what subjects you are prepared to be examined and indicate, by text-books or otherwise, how far your studies have gone.

I am prepared to be examined upon the Constitutional machinery of the English government (Bagehot's Eng. Constitution) upon the general course of colonial history, i.e. the history of the Eng. colonies in America (Lodge's Short History, Doyle's Virginia, Md., & the Carolinas, Scott's Constitutional Docts.) upon the phases of the Free Trade Controversy and upon other general topics of Political Economy which I have studied in Prof. Fawcett's writings and in the lectures of Prof. Atwater of Princeton. My preparation is one of general reading rather than of special training

Grad. Hist.
Name

Woodrow Wilson
Residence.

Wilmington, N.C.
Date.

Sept. 18, 1883.

In the autumn of 1883, Wilson gave up his almost clientless law practice in Atlanta and entered the graduate school of Johns Hopkins University to study history and political science. His handwritten admissions application, dated September 18, 1883, is pictured at left.

Wilson entered Johns Hopkins as a twenty-seven-year-old student still dependent on financial support from his family. Scarcely two years later, his book *Congressional Government* earned him an immediate reputation as a professional political scientist with great promise. A major reviewer hailed it as "one of the most important books, dealing with political subjects, which have ever issued from the American press." It ran through three editions in a year and it gave Wilson his first taste of fame. In 1886, Johns Hopkins awarded Wilson the Ph.D. degree by special dispensation, omitting the regular doctoral exams, with *Congressional Government* being accepted as his thesis.

There is no question that the education Thomas Woodrow Wilson received from Davidson to Johns Hopkins laid the groundwork for President Wilson to endure the challenges of a wartime presidency. True, he mostly coasted through his studies until he was challenged by the demands of graduate school, but Wilson long contended that there is more to education than what is taught in the classroom.

"There is always found to be a set of men in each class which pursues the 'classical' curriculum who stand below the honor list and are yet among the brightest men of their class," he once maintained in a *Princetonian* editorial. "These men are not infrequently hard and conscientious workers. They are often men who are sure to do their life work well and bring honor upon their college. They are preparing themselves, amidst the varied requirements of a general classical course, for the special work that awaits them after graduation."

—Hal Marcovitz

Alligator Club, circa 1879. Woodrow Wilson, first row and hatless, was the president of this Princeton eating club during his senior year at the college.

Warren G. Harding
Chapter Twenty-eight

When Warren G. Harding was a boy, his father owned a tiny, near-bankrupt newspaper in Caledonia, Ohio, named the *Argus*. George Tryon Harding knew little of journalism; Warren's father was a homeopathic physician who often invested his family's limited finances in questionable enterprises. The *Argus* was one such endeavor. So Dr. Harding left the editing and printing duties in the hands of the *Argus*'s longtime editor, Will Warner, who found he had a most able and willing assistant in Dr. Harding's ten-year-old son, Warren. After school each day, Warren would hurry to the *Argus* office, where he worked as a printer's devil: sweeping the floor, running errands, and feeding ink into the *Argus*'s creaky presses. After the paper rolled off the presses, Warren's job was to return the block letters of type used in the *Argus* headlines to their cribs. Soon, Warner taught the boy how to set type. Warren was thrilled to be a part of the inky business of publishing the *Argus*; indeed, it was much more preferable than cleaning out the barn, milking cows, or doing other chores around the Harding family farm just outside of town.

One night, after Warren Harding worked long hours helping to typeset a lengthy legal brief, Warner showed his appreciation for the boy by giving him a metal make-up stick—the ruler that old-time editors used to measure type. The ruler became one of Warren's most prized possessions; he would keep the stick as a good luck charm for the rest of his life.

Dr. Harding wouldn't own the *Argus* for long; he soon traded the newspaper for another business opportunity. But Warren's brief tenure at the *Argus* gave him a taste for journalism, and he intended to make the news profession his life's work. Seven years later, as a student at Ohio Central College, Harding and a classmate, Frank H. Harris, established *The Spectator*, the college's first student newspaper. Harding and Harris served as editors; they also sold advertising, oversaw circulation, and ran the presses at a nearby print shop. *The Spectator*, which was published six times during Harding's last year at Ohio Central, ran college news and gossip, humorous pieces, and hard-hitting editorials. "*The*

Warren Harding died in office on August 2, 1923, in the third year of his presidency. Harding's wife, Florence, destroyed most of the non-governmental records pertaining to his life. We do know that in the early 1870s he attended classes in several one-room schoolhouses, first in Blooming Grove and then in Caledonia, a small town (population about 600) in central Ohio. We also know that he was not interested in his formal studies. A childhood friend of Harding wrote, "Nobody ever saw him at hard study, but he shone at recitations. No other pupil had one-third as much time to give to things that were not in the curriculum. While others fought to win the prize, he sailed through on flowery beds of ease."

Harding's father recalled that he became curious "what Warren was doing to bring in such decent reports when he didn't seem to work. 'Oh, he's just naturally smart, I guess,' his teacher said. 'I never saw him working yet.'"

Warren Harding and his classmates, Blooming Grove, Ohio, 1872. Harding, last row center, was then seven years old. Note that the boy on the right is wearing a head covering which is probably a Mennonite cap.

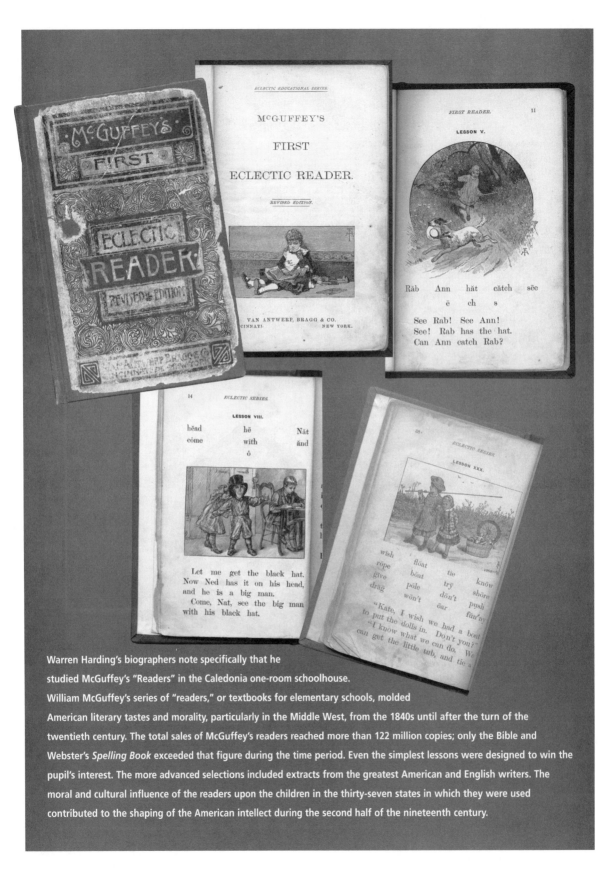

Warren Harding's biographers note specifically that he studied McGuffey's "Readers" in the Caledonia one-room schoolhouse.

William McGuffey's series of "readers," or textbooks for elementary schools, molded American literary tastes and morality, particularly in the Middle West, from the 1840s until after the turn of the twentieth century. The total sales of McGuffey's readers reached more than 122 million copies; only the Bible and Webster's *Spelling Book* exceeded that figure during the time period. Even the simplest lessons were designed to win the pupil's interest. The more advanced selections included extracts from the greatest American and English writers. The moral and cultural influence of the readers upon the children in the thirty-seven states in which they were used contributed to the shaping of the American intellect during the second half of the nineteenth century.

Spectator is taken by every family in our city excepting a few stingy old grumblers who take no more interest in home enterprise than a mule takes in a hive of bees," Harding wrote in one of the newspaper's editions.

It was typical Harding prose: homespun, light, humorous, and reflective of its author's small-town values. For Americans who would eventually find themselves emerging from a global war, confused by their role in the new world order, a certain amount of comfort could be found in what Warren G. Harding had to say.

Warren Gamaliel Harding was born November 2, 1865, in the village of Blooming Grove, Ohio, about thirty miles north of Columbus. His father had just returned from a brief service in the Civil War. Tryon—a name he preferred over George—had joined the Union Army late in the conflict, and his service had been confined to sentry duty in the nation's capital. Before leaving for duty, though, Tryon had married his school sweetheart, Phoebe Elizabeth Dickerson, whose family farm adjoined the Harding property. Warren would be the oldest of seven children born to the Hardings. (Another brother and sister died of childhood illnesses.) Phoebe wanted to name her first-born Winfield, but Tryon instead wanted the boy named after an uncle, Warren Gamaliel Bancroft. Tryon prevailed, but for years Phoebe insisted on calling the boy "Winnie."

She was his first teacher. Phoebe taught Winnie the alphabet by using flash cards. Under her guidance, Winnie memorized poems and short speeches, which he recited at church meetings and similar gatherings. In nineteenth-century America, this very popular practice was known as "declamation." Soon, it was known around town that Phoebe Harding's toddler was the best little declaimer in Blooming Grove.

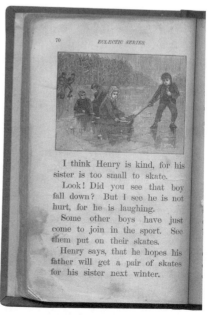

Reward of Merit cards were given by a teacher to a pupil for good behavior, scholarship, or attendance. This was one method used to maintain discipline in a rural one-room schoolhouse. These cards, popular in the late 19th century, usually were pasted into scrapbooks to show a child's accomplishments at school.

The Reward of Merit card pictured at the bottom was given to Warren Harding by his teacher in 1874. It can only be reproduced in black and white. However, these Reward of Merit cards were in bright colors, using the mid-nineteenth century technology of chromolithography, the first commercial reproduction of illustrations in color. Above are Reward of Merit cards from the same era.

When he was old enough, Warren began school in Blooming Grove's one-room schoolhouse, which had been built by his grandfather, Charles Harding. It was a rectangular brick building featuring two front doors—one for boys, one for girls—as well as a belfry on the roof, which housed the school bell. Inside were rows of wooden desks. Boys sat on one side, girls on the other. A potbellied stove heated the room.

Children who failed to learn their lessons wore the dunce cap, though it is unlikely that Warren ever suffered such an indignity. His schoolmaster, James Boggs, recognized the boy as bright, albeit not brilliant. Certainly, Boggs could tell Warren possessed a gift for declamation—he was best in class at reading the stories the students found in their *McGuffey's Eclectic Readers*.

The *Readers* were among the first mass-produced textbooks employed in American schools. They were conceived by William Holmes McGuffey, a University of Virginia professor who was among the first American educators to tackle the question of how to teach children to read. The first *Reader* was published in 1838, and as late as 1978 some schools in America were still using them. In between, some 120 million of the *Readers* were published. They remain in publication.

McGuffey initially published six *Readers*, although a spelling book and high school *Reader* were added later. They were arranged according to age and reading ability—beginning readers were started off with the *First Reader*, which included simple sentences broken down into their phonic elements. A typical McGuffey story, illustrated with drawings, would have found young Warren and his classmates following the exploits of a boy named George and his horse, Jack: "George is kind to Jack and Jack loves him, because he is kind."

When Warren was eight years old, his father decided to leave Blooming Grove for Caledonia, a town eight miles distant. Caledonia was a bit larger than Blooming Grove, although no metropolis. Since returning from the Civil War, Tryon had tried his hand at farming and then school teaching, finding neither to his liking. Finally, after acquiring some used medical books in a swap, he took up the practice of homeopathic medicine. In fairness to Tryon, it should be pointed out that he did more to learn the healing arts than simply page through dog-eared books that were no longer in print. Blooming Grove's doctor, Joseph McFarland, permitted Tryon to make the rounds with him and watch how he set broken bones and treated illnesses. Also, Tryon spent a year at the Western College of Homeopathy in Cleveland. By 1873, he was ready to open his own practice. There were not enough patients in Blooming Grove to support two doctors, so Tryon resolved to try his luck in Caledonia.

There may have been another reason for Tryon's decision to depart Blooming Grove. After the American Revolution, the Hardings were among the first settlers of Central Ohio. Warren's ancestors helped to found the little town, and Hardings would, over the years, build its schools and churches. Indeed, many long-time residents of Blooming Grove called it "Harding's Corners." Nevertheless, rumors persisted that one of Tryon's parents had been black—and central Ohio in the 1870s was a Ku Klux Klan center. This rumor, which one of Warren Harding's biographers called "the shadow of Blooming Grove," undoubtedly contributed to Tryon's decision to move his family to Caledonia.

In Caledonia, the Hardings first moved into a home near the center of town, although Tryon would soon buy a farm just outside of town. Warren and his sister, Charity, enrolled in the local school. Here again, Warren found his teachers relying mostly on *McGuffey's Readers*. By now, Warren was ready for *McGuffey's Second Reader*, in which he read Mason Weems's account of George Washington and the cherry tree. In the *Third Reader*, Warren read of the adventures of Napoleon Bonaparte and from that point on, he became a lifelong admirer of the French dictator. On Friday afternoons, the students would assemble for declamation contests. Warren was always an enthusiastic participant and winner of most of the events. Among the speeches he gave before his class were Patrick Henry's "Give Me Liberty or Give Me Death," as well as such other McGuffey standards as Felicia Hemans' poem of tragic youthful bravery, "The Boy Stood on the Burning Deck," and lyrics to the inspirational hymns of Scottish cleric Horatius Bonar. Other *McGuffey's Readers* included selections written by William Shakespeare, Sir Walter Scott, Henry Wadsworth Longfellow, Benjamin Disraeli, and Edgar Allan Poe.

As in Blooming Grove, Warren was regarded as one of the smartest pupils in school. "He studied his lessons, I don't know when," Tryon recalled later. "I never caught him at it and it used to worry me, so I asked his teacher what Warren was doing to bring in such decent reports when he didn't seem to work. 'Oh, he's just naturally smart, I guess,' his teacher said. 'I never saw him working yet." Warren's childhood friend, Jack Warwick, added, "Nobody ever saw him at hard study, but he shone at recitations."

In Caledonia, Warren also learned to play a cornet his father had obtained in a swap. Lessons were provided by the town harness maker and later a house painter, both of whom were members of the Caledonia Aeolian Band. Warren picked up the instrument quickly and in a short time was invited to join the band as well.

For a young boy growing up in Caledonia, life was idyllic. There were many games to play and many friends with whom to play them. There were trees for climbing, grassy fields for baseball, lakes for swimming, and haylofts for snoozing on lazy summer days. For a young boy willing to show some industry, there was work to do and money to be made. In addition to his job as a printer's devil at the *Argus*, Warren hired on at neighboring farms, found work helping crews building the Ohio Central Railroad, and became an expert grainer—the craft of staining and finishing wood. "I could do a bully job of graining," Harding recalled during the 1920 presidential campaign.

It was during those days in Caledonia that Harding learned to appreciate life in a small town. The men he admired in town were the blacksmith, wagon maker, sawmill operator, and, of course, the printer-editor. To Harding, people

Warren Harding at Ohio Central College, circa 1882

The photo at left is of Harding, circa 1882, in the Ohio Central College production of Jules Massenet's 1872 comic opera *Don Cesar de Bazan*.

In 1880, at age fifteen Warren Harding was sent to Ohio Central College. The school was more of a secondary or high school. Harding graduated first in his 1882 class. There were only two others in the class!

Ohio Central at Iberia was located about six miles east of Caledonia. In the 1850s, it had acquired a bit of fame as a militant abolitionist center. But, it never recovered from the sharp enrollment drop of the Civil War years. In 1882, the faculty consisted of three persons. There were three "courses" of study—the "Academic Course," priced at seven dollars a term; the "English Course," for six dollars a term; and the "Collegiate Course," for eight dollars a term. Shortly after Harding's 1882 graduation, the college was converted into a school for the blind. A few years later, it burned to the ground.

THE SPECTATOR.

SEMPER PARATUS ET EXCELSIOR.

VOLUME 1. IBERIA, OHIO, APRIL 22, 1882. NUMBER 2.

Warren Harding was co-editor of *The Spectator*, a short-lived Ohio Central student newspaper. A copy of the April 22, 1882 issue (vol. 1, no. 2) is in the Ohio Historical Society. The front page is reproduced above.

Harding never praised his alma mater. Indeed, he was highly critical of it. In an October 1894 edition of the *Marion Star*, he wrote, "In the 1860s it was quite a notable institution of learning, the course of study comparing favorably with any western institution. Later on, though the classical course was still taught, the institution became more like an academy and normal school."

who worked with their hands were people to be respected. "The shops and smithies were real wood and metal work establishments and not mere places for assembling parts already fabricated," Harding later recalled. "A buggy cost $250, and it was all made there—painting and all."

In 1880, Warren entered Ohio Central College in Iberia, just six miles east of Caledonia. It was his father's alma mater, although when Tryon had matriculated there some twenty years before, the school had operated under the name Iberia College. Warren was not quite fifteen years old. Tryon's land speculations, business swapping, and homeopathic medical practice had all ended in failures; the family was supported by Phoebe, who earned money as a midwife. Although cash was short in the Harding household, Warren's parents managed to scrape up the seven dollars they needed for Warren's tuition each semester. Warren also helped raise money for his education by holding a number of part-time jobs throughout his three years at Ohio Central.

The college was tiny, consisting of little more than a single classroom building in downtown Iberia. Its faculty included just three teachers—the Reverend John P. Robb, the president of the college and instructor in philosophy; Albert C. Jones, dean and professor of ancient languages; and the Reverend A.C. Crist, who taught mathematics and natural sciences. Later, Harding was critical of the college, claiming that the curriculum was not much more advanced than what a student could find in a public school. He wrote, "In the 1860s, it was quite a notable institution of learning, the course of study comparing favorably with any western institution. Later on though the classical course was still taught, the institution became more like an academy and normal school."

Harding studied science, history, philosophy, and literature. He surprised his professors as well as himself with his mathematical ability. Classmate Frank Harris recalled how the future president would appear to be stumped by a knotty problem of geometry, then suddenly produce an answer. Harris said Harding "would sit down with his face to the wall, head in hands and soak it up. Then when he was through, he would jump up with a yell and shout, 'Now, darn it, I've got you,' and slam the book against the wall."

Harding excelled in oration and debate. In his last year at Ohio Central he won his first election when he polled enough votes to win the presidency of the Philomathic Literary Society, the college debating club.

Harding also maintained a social life away from school. As an accomplished grainer, his skills were very much in demand in Iberia, and he never lacked for work to help him make ends meet. He did so well, in fact, that he was able to keep a horse stabled in Iberia—a luxury for most members of the student body and one that enabled him to impress the many girls of Iberia whose acquaintances he managed to make. Harris said he and Harding knew every girl within a five-mile radius of Iberia, and they "frolicked together as innocently as young pups."

Harding graduated in 1882, with a bachelor of science degree. He was evidently the valedictorian because he delivered the commencement address, a speech he titled

"It Can Never Be Rubbed Out." It should not go unreported, though, that the Ohio Central College Class of 1882 consisted of three students. Harding's class was the last to graduate from Ohio Central. Unable to attract students, the college was converted to a school for the blind, although that institution was soon out of business as well when the classroom building burned down.

Following graduation, Harding returned to the family home, which was now in the town of Marion, where his father had hoped to revive his medical practice. At his father's insistence, Harding briefly studied law by working in the law office of S.A. Court, a Marion attorney. Harding found it dismal, boring work. He was forced to read Court's law books for four or five hours a day—the type of labor he had never respected. "It was slow work and money ran out," Harding recalled. "Compelled to ask my father for some cash to keep the law mill grinding was humiliating for I realized that I was not earning a living."

Harding soon left Court's office and found a job as a teacher, then tried selling insurance. He finally found his true calling when he landed a job as a reporter at the *Marion Mirror*, the town's weekly newspaper.

Harding had loved newspaper work since his days as a printer's devil at the Caledonia *Argus*. What he didn't love about the work, though, was the *Mirror*'s 1884 support for Grover Cleveland and the Democratic Party. Marion was a Democratic town. But during his years at Ohio Central College, Harding had studied with interest the career of Alexander Hamilton, who by no stretch of the imagination could be regarded as a Democrat. Instead, Harding embraced Republican politics—and would find himself blanching as he read the *Mirror*'s editorials.

The *Mirror*'s competition in town was the *Marion Star*, a daily that seemed to stay in business one step ahead of a sheriff sale. Harding and two friends bought the four-page *Star* for $300. Harding installed himself as editor. He was nineteen years old.

Marion grew into a bustling little industrial city, and the *Marion Star* prospered. Harding remained a committed booster of his adopted city, and the businesses of Marion awarded him with advertising and, soon, a political career. A major influence in his career was his wife, Florence, the daughter of a Marion banker who believed her handsome husband was destined for high public office. Her parents opposed the match because of the continued rumors about Harding's black grandparent. But, she persisted—promising her parents that the marriage would be childless.

Harding eventually found his way into the Ohio State Senate and then served a term as lieutenant governor of Ohio. Soon his outstanding public speaking ability came to the attention of national Republican leaders. In 1912 he placed the name of William Howard Taft in nomination for the presidency at the Republican National Convention. In 1914 Harding won a term in the U.S. Senate in a landslide. That victory convinced the GOP that Harding was presidential timber.

Harding spent the next six years as little more than a backbencher in the Senate; nevertheless, in 1920 the GOP turned to him because after years under the wartime presidency of Woodrow Wilson, Republicans believed the American people would support a candidate with down-home values, interested more in their lives than in forging alliances with European leaders. His slogan during the 1920 campaign would be "Back to Normalcy." That fall, he defeated James M. Cox, the Democratic governor of Ohio, with an unprecedented majority.

The Harding presidency would be short and besieged by scandal. Federal investigators soon turned up evidence that Harding appointees in the Justice Department, known as the "Ohio Gang," were accepting bribes from bootleggers. Harding was said to have kept mistresses and fathered a child out of wedlock. In May 1921, after just two months in office, he had let himself be convinced by Interior Secretary Albert B. Fall to transfer oil reserves on public lands in the West from ownership by the Navy to the Department of the Interior. Shortly after the transfer was made, Fall signed oil leases with private oil speculators. Fall and other aides in the Harding administration would be convicted of corruption and sent to prison.

It is unlikely that Harding had a direct hand in the wrongdoing committed by his subordinates. However, there is no question that the twenty-ninth president of the United States should have realized that not everybody shared his small-town values, and he would have done well to have kept an eye on his associates.

"I grew up in a village of 600 and I know something of the democracy, the simplicity, of the confidence in—aye, better yet, of the reverence for government, and the fidelity to law enforcement, as it exists in the small community," Harding once said. "I do not believe that anywhere in the world there is so perfect a democracy as in the village. You know in the village we know everybody's business. I grew up in such a community, and I have often referred to it as a fine illustration of the opportunities of American life."

With scandal closing in, President Harding launched a nationwide speaking tour. After appearing in Alaska, Vancouver, and Seattle, Harding arrived in San Francisco. Already, he was exhausted and reported to be suffering from ptomaine poisoning. After spending five days resting in the Palace Hotel, Harding seemed to be improving, but suddenly, at 7:30 P.M. on August 2, 1923, the president died. The nation mourned this very popular president; the breadth of the scandals would not become known to the public for several months.

—Hal Marcovitz

Calvin Coolidge
Chapter Twenty-nine

It was an unusual foot race called the "plug-hat race." More than thirty juniors from Amherst College, dressed in outlandish outfits, were lined up on one end of the school's athletic field. They were required to carry canes in their hands and wear Derby hats on their heads. They all knew that the last seven men to reach the other end of the field would have to provide a dinner for everyone in the race and the very last would have to give a speech. When it was over, the loser was Calvin Coolidge.

The next month, on November 23, 1895, the runners gathered in Hitchcock Hall to eat their meal paid for by the seven losers. Coolidge was given the topic "Why I got stuck." Few men in the junior class knew him because he was quiet and shy, so they expected little from him. However, with clear, short sentences full of humor and wit, Coolidge amazed them all. One of his classmates recalled later, "The class had the surprise of its life. He spoke cogently, fluently, and with a good sense of humor….It was as if a new and gifted man had joined the class."

Many of the students at Amherst were sophisticated men from major cities such as New York and Chicago. Coolidge, however, was a farm boy from a tiny village in Vermont called Plymouth. Locals referred to it as the Notch, because of its location at the top of a valley in a bowl of hills. Eventually, the village would become known as Plymouth Notch. The village was remote, nestled among hills and farms in central Vermont. When Calvin was born on July 4, 1872, the ninety-sixth anniversary of the Declaration of Independence, Vermont had a population of only 333,000. Small towns like Plymouth were losing people every year. They left farms and moved to larger cities to seek jobs in industry. However, the Coolidge family loved their rural home and stayed in the Notch. Calvin's father, John, owned the town's one store. It was attached to the house and the post office. There was also a school, a church, and seven farmhouses with their barns. Beyond Plymouth Notch were other farms and open, unpopulated areas. Tourists today would find Plymouth Notch much the same as it was one hundred years ago.

The baby boy was given the name John Calvin Coolidge. He was usually called Calvin, sometimes Cal, or even Red Cal because of his flaming red hair. Calvin's first

BLACK RIVER ACADEMY, 1885.

Calvin Coolidge attended Black River Academy in Ludlow, Vermont, from 1886 to 1890. This small Baptist-supported coeducational high school was founded in 1835. For a modest tuition, middle-class children of rural southern Vermont studied history, English grammar, and American literature. Those who planned to go to college also studied Latin, Greek, and classical literature. There were three terms a year. Students could attend any one of the terms as the young men were needed on the farms and the young women worked as elementary school teachers. Coolidge excelled in Latin and in history. Four other boys and four girls were in Coolidge's 1890 graduating class.

In his autobiography, Coolidge acknowledged two of his teachers—George Sherman, who was also the principal of the school, and Belle Challis—both of whom lived to see him enter the White House. "Under their guidance," wrote Coolidge, "I beheld the marvels of old Babylon, I marched with the Ten Thousand of Xenophon, I witnessed the conflict around beleaguered Troy which doomed that proud city to pillage and flames. I heard the tramp of the invincible legions of Rome, I saw the victorious galleys of the Eternal City carrying destruction to the Carthaginian shore, and I listened to the lofty eloquence of Cicero and the matchless imagery of Homer."

Black River Academy closed its doors in 1938. The main building, pictured above, opened when Coolidge was a student. It now houses a museum of Academy ephemera and exhibits dealing with the Black River area.

Amherst College Dormitories and Chapel, Amherst, Mass.

Calvin Coolidge entered Amherst College in 1891. The Congregational college was chartered in 1825 originally to train indigent men for the ministry. By 1890, when the photograph above was taken, the school had about three hundred students and a reputation beyond the New England area as a sound, conservative educational institution. The school was neither too expensive for Coolidge nor too far from his home. Most of Coolidge's 1895 graduating class aspired to be lawyers or businessmen.

Anson D. Morse was the school's most prominent faculty member. He taught history and political science at Amherst from 1876 to 1907. Morse, apparently an excellent teacher, stressed his belief that political parties are the most effective way for expressing popular will. The United States, he wrote, through its freedom from deeply rooted antagonistic customs and institutions, was the most favorable area to study the movement toward a democracy. However, Coolidge did not like Morse's course. For Coolidge, history was always an array of facts unconnected with the present.

home in the Notch was a small five-room cottage, but when he was four the family moved across the road into a much larger home with a picket fence and apple trees.

Calvin's mother, Victoria Josephine Moor, was a beautiful woman known for her love of poetry and nature. After Victoria had their second child, Abigail, she became an invalid, probably from tuberculosis. Yet, she poured her love into Calvin and Abbie and began to encourage their learning while they were very young. Calvin's first educational tool was a set of blocks with Roman numerals and the letters of the alphabet carved on them. His mother taught Calvin to read and eventually introduced him to novels and the poems of Tennyson, which she loved to read. By the time he was three years old, Calvin knew his letters and numerals. By age five, he was ready to begin school.

John Coolidge, Calvin's father, not only ran the store but also managed his farm. He was active in politics and held many local offices, including justice of the peace, superintendent of schools, and tax collector. John Coolidge spent three terms in the state house, and later became a senator. When Calvin was two months old, John was elected to the state legislature. (Interestingly, when Calvin's son was two months old, Calvin was elected to the same office in Massachusetts.) John Coolidge was a quiet man who insisted on hard work and thrift. Yet, he was also a kind and soft-spoken father who encouraged his only son in his studies.

Calvin was close to his grandparents. His grandfather, Calvin Galusha Coolidge, called "Galoosh," lived in the Notch and, like his son John, held many political offices. He kept an assortment of animals, even a peacock, which fascinated his grandson. He spent much time with Calvin, teaching him to ride a horse and to work on the farm. He wanted Calvin to become a farmer and settle down in Plymouth. Calvin's maternal grandfather, Hiram Moor, lived right across the road and impressed Calvin by his love of reading and his broad general knowledge.

Grandmother Sarah Coolidge read books to Calvin and helped to build in him a strong sense of patriotism. Calvin heard the stirring stories of Daniel Thompson's *The Rangers, or the Tory's Daughter* and *The Green Mountain Boys*, books about Vermont during the Revolutionary War. As he grew older, Grandmother Coolidge gave her grandson a two volume set of Joel Tyler Headley's *Washington and His Generals*, as well as other popular biographies. Calvin developed a love of reading from his family and nourished it all his life.

Calvin was shy as a boy and remained that way all his life. Years later, he told a friend, "When I was a little fellow, as long ago as I can remember, I would go into panic if I heard strange voices in the house. I felt I just couldn't meet people and shake hands with them. Most of the visitors would sit with Mother and Father in the kitchen and the hardest thing in the world was to have to go through the kitchen door and give them a greeting." Sometimes Calvin would even run away when visitors came.

The stone schoolhouse where Calvin went until he was thirteen years old was just a few steps from the Coolidge home. It was a one-room ungraded school attended by children from the age of five through eighteen. Students sat on wooden benches around the room, two at a desk. Their bathrooms were two outhouses behind the school. They had a pail and dipper in the classroom for water. The school had a bare floor with a smoky stove in the center, used even on chilly summer days. Calvin remembered his school days in the Notch as "always being cold."

Teachers only had to pass a test given by the town superintendent to be considered as qualified to teach at the school. (Calvin passed the test when he was thirteen; Abbie passed it when she was twelve years old and taught a term at a school in a nearby town the same year.) There was a succession of teachers because the pay was low. Most taught for only one year. The twenty-five children who went there with Calvin were taught spelling, reading, writing, arithmetic, geography, government, some science, and both American and Vermont history. The younger children sat close to the teacher and recited the alphabet, while older children memorized poems and speeches. When the little children were finished, the older ones stood in front of the teacher to recite their pieces.

Victoria Coolidge became seriously ill when Calvin was twelve years old. One day in 1885, she called her children to her bedside and gave them her final blessing just before she died. As an adult, Coolidge recalled the sadness of that day: "We laid her away in the blustering snows of March. The greatest grief that can come to a boy came to me. Life was never to seem the same again." Sadly, his sister would die five years later.

When Calvin was thirteen, he finished his required studies. He was given an oral examination, which he passed. "In a school of about thirty, he was among the first half dozen," one teacher later recalled. "He was methodical, faithful, honest, and punctual." John Coolidge decided that his son should continue his education at the Black River Academy in Ludlow, Vermont, twelve miles south of the Notch. The academy, which Calvin's father, mother, and grandmother had all attended, was similar to a high school.

On a bitter cold day in February 1886, Calvin and his father got up before the sun and packed for the sleigh ride to Ludlow. Calvin was ready to begin a new school and was excited that he was leaving for his first big adventure. "As we rounded the brow of the hill, the first rays of the morning sun steamed over our backs and lighted up the glistening snow ahead," he later wrote. "I was perfectly certain that I was traveling out of the darkness into the light."

Ludlow, Vermont, was located on an important rail line and was filled with mills, churches, and stores. Although the town had no sewerage system or indoor plumbing, it was modern compared to the Notch. Black River Academy consisted of one building on a hill overlooking Ludlow. It had no dormitories, so students rented rooms in town. Most of Calvin's fellow boarders were older than he was and were young clerks and professionals working in Ludlow.

The academy offered three separate courses for students. One was the English Course, designed for students who wanted to sharpen their English skills and receive a business education. Another was the Latin-Scientific Course, which gave students an English education and also offered some background in Latin and science. The third course was the Classical, which helped young people prepare for college. Unsure of

Anti-Secret Society.

DELTA UPSILON.

AMHERST CHAPTER.

SENIORS.

John A. Bennett,   Lucius P. Merriam,
Edward W. Chase,   Charles Negley,
Henry Gibbons,   Granville W. Nims,
Henry A. King,   Floyd E. Sherman,
Caleb R. Layton,   Lewis Sperry,
Frank H. Loud,   David H. Woods.

JUNIORS.

Winfred B. Bancroft,   William C. Merrill,
Benjamin F. Brown,   Nathan Morse,
Salem D. Charles,   Howard B. Scott,
William E. Judd,   Charles G. Stearns,
George H. Mellen,   Foster R. Wait,
George Y. Washburn.

SOPHOMORES.

Charles Arnd,   Rudolph Kauffmann,
Frank I. Babcock,   Charles P. Littlefield,
David W. Goodale,   Millard F. Logan,
Frank A. Hosmer,   Warren Thompson,
Maurice P. White.

FRESHMEN.

Gerritt H. Chaffee,   John Howland,
Osman D. Clarke,   Knox Johnston,
George W. Cloak,   Samuel R. Johnston,
George N. Cross,   William A. McClure,
Robert Ely,   Charles H. Ricketts,
Franklin Ripley.

Amherst in the 1890s was a strong fraternity school. Although Coolidge moved into a rooming house, he intended to remain there until he was pledged by one of the nine fraternities. With that many fraternities represented on campus, it was difficult not to be rushed; however, Coolidge was repeatedly passed over. "I don't seem to get acquainted fast," the disappointed freshman wrote to his father. The young man was shy, withdrawn, and awkward. He could neither dance nor make small talk. He took no apparent interest in girls. He avoided sports and was almost always a spectator. Coolidge's rejection by the Amherst fraternities labeled him as being inferior, a "Barbarian." "A drabber, more colorless boy I never knew than Calvin Coolidge when he came to Amherst," wrote one of his fellow students.

Delta Upsilon was the leading fraternity on the Amherst campus. It was founded in the 1830s as part of the Anti-Masonic movement that opposed secret societies, including those on campuses. Delta Epsilon is the nation's oldest non-secretive college fraternity.

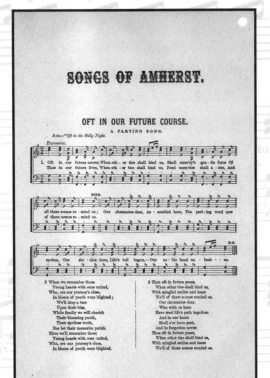

Amherst fraternities distributed song sheets to their members. The above illustrations are from an 1876 Amherst song booklet. Some of the other titles in the songbook include "First Time I Saw a Tutor" and "Amherst, Our Queen."

himself, he signed up for the English Course. The academy had three terms, fall, winter, and spring, each lasting about twelve weeks. There were three full-time faculty members when Calvin was there, the principal and two assistants. The principal, Henry Kendall, taught Latin and Greek, and his two assistants taught math, English, and history.

At first, Calvin had a difficult time at Black River Academy. He became very homesick and missed the farm. The structure was more formal and the grading was stricter than at the school in Plymouth, and the academy was also much larger, with approximately one hundred and twenty-five students. Coolidge rarely went to social events and did not feel comfortable around girls. In his first term he studied algebra, English grammar, and civil government. Algebra proved to be his most difficult subject and the study of the Constitution, in his government course, his favorite one.

In the fall of 1886, Coolidge changed to the Latin-Scientific Course and began to take Latin from Kendall. Later, he included Greek in his studies. He believed it was important for him to know these languages: "I found that the English language was generously compounded with Greek and Latin, which it was necessary to know if I was to understand my native tongue." He took a course in botany and continued his study of algebra. He wrote his father, "algebra is so hard that I do not half get my lessons. I did not do a single example today."

In time, Coolidge began to make friends among the townspeople and his fellow students. He began to feel at home at the academy, and his homesickness disappeared. Still, he enjoyed being by himself, taking long walks along the Black River and reading in the school library.

When George Sherman became principal of the academy in 1887, he encouraged more students to enroll in the Classical Course and go on to college. When Coolidge saw his grades improve during his second year, he was one of the students to enroll in the Classical Course.

In his junior year at Black River Academy, Coolidge developed a renewed interest in Latin. He enjoyed reading the speeches of Cicero. He also took rhetoric, the art of speaking, and wrote his own speeches. Principal Sherman revived the debating society at the academy, which Coolidge joined. He found that, in spite of his shyness, he could express himself through public speaking and debating.

In his senor year, Coolidge added history and French to his studies. French was hard for him, but he loved history. He discovered that his own country's ideas about democracy had come from Greece and Rome. For the rest of his life, he was grateful for the teachers at Black River Academy. "I owe much to the inspiration and scholarly direction they gave to my undergraduate days," Coolidge wrote. "They gave me a vision of the world when it was young and showed me how it grew."

Coolidge was seventeen years old when he graduated on March 21, 1890, in a class of nine. He gave one of the speeches during commencement, "Oratory in History." In it, Coolidge talked about how the spoken word had affected the actions of people throughout history. He mentioned many of the great orators whom he had studied at the academy, including Demosthenes, William Lloyd

Garrison, and Cicero. Sherman told Coolidge that he thought it was the best commencement speech he had ever heard.

After graduation, Coolidge expected to study further in a preparatory school before trying to gain admission to a university. However, Sherman encouraged John Coolidge to send Calvin to Amherst, Sherman's alma mater. As a result, young Coolidge was sent by train to Amherst, Massachusetts, in September to take his entrance exams. He became seriously ill on the way, was unable to complete his exams, and had to return home. Over the next several months, Coolidge made a slow recovery.

With George Sherman's help, Calvin enrolled at St. Johnsbury Academy in Vermont, in order to prepare for college. In April 1891, he began classes in algebra, Latin, and Greek. Once in school, Coolidge was uncertain about his progress, and wrote his father in May, "I do not know whether they will consider me up to the standard or not." However, just a week later, he wrote another letter to his father. "[The principal] told me he never had any one come into the class so late that did as well as I." Coolidge received the necessary approval from St. Johnsbury principal Dr. Putney, whom he described as "a fine drill-master, a very exact scholar, and an excellent disciplinarian," in just two months of review and was ready for Amherst.

Nineteen-year-old Coolidge, still shy by nature and uncertain of himself, entered Amherst College in early September of 1891. The all-male college had undergone major changes since George Sherman had graduated over a decade before. The school had been founded by Congregationalists, and when Sherman had been there most students had been studying to be ministers or teachers. By 1891, most Amherst graduates were going into business. Social life had also changed since Sherman had been a student. In 1880, only about 50 percent of students were members of a fraternity. When Coolidge arrived, more than 80 percent belonged to the nine fraternities on campus and the college's social life revolved around those organizations.

Since the few dormitories at Amherst were in poor shape, most of the students boarded and ate in private homes. Coolidge took a room in a home with one other college student and ate his meals down the street at another house. He quickly settled into a routine. Coolidge got up early every morning to study, went to the mandatory chapel at 8:30 A.M., and started classes at 9:00. He walked to the newly built Pratt Gymnasium four afternoons a week and exercised with his class. He attended the four required chapel services each afternoon and often studied until midnight to keep up with his study load.

As a freshman, Coolidge found that Latin and Greek were his most difficult courses because he found the professors boring. He thought they were good scholars but poor teachers. Algebra, the subject that had given him so much trouble at Black River Academy, actually helped keep up his grades. Coolidge wrote to his father in later September, "I do not suppose I know anything of college life but can say it more than meets my expectation in the large amount of work required. I recite 16 hours a week besides chapel, lectures and gymnasium."

Calvin Coolidge was an unhappy student at Amherst College. He was also extremely homesick and lonely. Donald McCoy, Coolidge's biographer, explains that Coolidge was, in the best New England backwoods tradition, "getting by." And getting by was important to Coolidge—he had to work twice as hard as the average student to get by academically.

In this November 17, 1892, letter to his grandmother Sarah A. Coolidge, the future president wrote, "The Library here has 60,000 volumes in it and I wish I could read many of them but I can only glance often at a few selected works, and I am often tempted to neglect my other duties to get more time to read." Coolidge, now a sophomore, also comments on the 1892 presidential election. He was surprised at the defeat of Benjamin Harrison, the Republican incumbent, by Grover Cleveland, the Democrat who had previously served a term as president.

Because social life at Amherst centered on fraternities, Coolidge hoped to be pledged to one. However, out of seventy-nine freshmen he was one of the thirteen who was not asked to join any fraternity. Those men who did not belong to fraternities were called *oudens*, a Greek word for "inferior."

Though Coolidge was isolated from fraternity life, he began to make friends with some of the men who ate at the same house he did. His personality was considered strange by some; other classmates liked the differences they found in this quiet boy from the hills of Vermont.

When Coolidge received his cumulative grade for the first term, he had a mark of two in a grading system in which five was perfect and one was failure. He seemed ready to give up when he wrote his father on January 6, 1892, "I hate to think I must stay here 12 weeks before I can go home again. I think I must be very homesick since my hand trembles so I can't write.… Each time I get home I hate to go away worse than before and I don't feel so well here now as the first day I cam here last fall." By the very next day, though, his attitude was already changing. "I am feeling better than I was last night; begin to feel at home some now."

By his final freshmen term at Amherst, Coolidge was not as homesick, but he was still not happy in college. After an enjoyable summer on the family farm, he returned to Amherst for his sophomore year. In the fall of 1892 he added rhetoric, geometry, and German to his schedule. His many hours of study were now beginning to pay off, and by the spring of 1893 he wrote home, "I drew a three; I feel pleased with the results of my work; perhaps ten men in the class, though probably less than that, got a four."

Coolidge began his junior year in the fall of 1893. His required subjects of Latin, Greek, and math were completed, and he was now able to take courses that were of real interest to him: Italian, English literature, and rhetoric. He also began studies in logic and public speaking under Professor Frink. As part of that course he was involved in weekly public debates and spoke during chapel. One of his most meaningful courses was history; it was taught by Professor Anson D. Morse, who stressed the impact of the frontier on the development of American democracy. Coolidge said that Morse's students "came to a clear comprehension not only of their rights and liberties but of their duties and responsibilities."

The professor who most permanently affected Coolidge, however, was Charles E. Garman, who taught philosophy. With dark, piercing eyes and a magnetic personality, students flocked to his course. Garman was a devout Christian who believed that students should develop through reason a faith that would guide their actions. Garman wrote textbooks and provided them to his students. He wrote pamphlets and gave them to his students before they were published. He demanded critical thinking of his students, saying, "Gentlemen, define your terms" and "Weigh the evidence." Coolidge was so impressed by Garman that he once wrote, "We looked upon Garman as a man who walked with God."

In November 1893, Coolidge spoke at the dinner that followed the plug hat race. During that speech, many of his classmates realized for the first time that Coolidge was an interesting person with a unique personality. He charmed his classmates when he joked about his own background on the farm: "You wouldn't expect a plow horse to make time on the race track or a follower of the plow to be Mercury." Then he concluded, "Remember, boys, the Good Book says that the first shall be last and the last first."

That dinner seemed to be a turning point in Coolidge's college career. He began to develop a circle of friends and to be appreciated by his class for his insights. As one classmate said, "Coolidge never said anything until the end, when some shrewd, keen, generally whimsical comment would seem to hit the thing on the head like a triphammer, or as though he had suddenly turned on the lights." During that same winter term, Coolidge received nearly a four in his marks, his highest at Amherst. In his senior year, he was asked to join a fraternity, Phi Gamma Delta, and became active in its business affairs.

Although his studies had been difficult for Coolidge when he began at Amherst in 1891, he graduated cum laude (with distinction) in 1895. For Coolidge, the years spent at Amherst were when he came to life. "In the development of every boy who is going to amount to anything there comes a time when he emerges from his immature ways and by the greater precision of his thought and action realizes that he has begun to find himself. Such a transition finally came to me." He believed that his success was a matter of his persistent effort: "It was not accidental but the result of hard work."

Commencement for the class of 1895 was held on June 26. Three students were selected by popular vote to give speeches at the commencement ceremonies. Coolidge had been elected to deliver the Grove Oration, a humorous speech about college life. He gave a witty message, with personal comments about the faculty of the school and members of his class. His oration was sprinkled with quotations from Shakespeare, Milton, and other famous writers.

Coolidge had often pondered what he would do after gradation. He had thought of returning to the Notch to run his father's store and later considered a career in law. Coolidge sought his father's advice about applying to a law school. John thought that his son should, instead, study law by working as an apprentice in a law firm. One of Calvin's classmates told him that there was an apprenticeship available at Hammond and Field in Northampton, only eight miles from Amherst. Coolidge wrote to them and was accepted by the firm. In September 1895, he moved to Massachusetts to begin the study of law.

Coolidge worked at Hammond and Field from eight in the morning until six each evening. During the day, he spent some of his time preparing writs, deeds, wills, and other documents and read some commentaries. In the evenings, he read speeches by renowned lawyers, studied Greek, translated some of the speeches of Cicero, and read a variety of things. "I read much in Milton and Shakespeare and found delight in the shorter poems of Kipling, Field and Rile," he later wrote.

Coolidge's classmates isolated him during his freshman and sophomore years. Then, during his junior year, he began to bud—ironically because he was a loser. In a traditional event, a "Plug Hat Race," the un-athletic Coolidge came in last. At an oyster stew and beer banquet for their classmates paid for by the seven losers, Coolidge, because he had finished last, was assigned to speak on the topic "Why I Got Stuck." Apparently, his dry humor and bland presentation won him the reputation of being a good sport and something of an undergraduate wit. Unknowingly, Coolidge concluded his talk with this almost-prophetic statement: "Remember, boys, the Good Book says that the first shall be last and the last shall be first."

Coolidge is wearing his "Plug Hat Race" outfit in this photograph. Each class member had to wear a Derby and carry a cane. The rest of the outfit was the creative part of the contest (Coolidge's classmates considered his outfit unimaginative). Then, each junior had to race the length of the college's athletic field wearing their "Plug Hat Race" outfit.

His main interest, however, was getting practical experience. Northhampton had a superior court with three civil and two criminal terms each year. Coolidge spent as much time as he could in the court each time it met: "I soon came to see that the counsel who knew the law were the ones who held the attention of the Judge, took the jury with them, and won their cases." He assisted his firm in preparing their cases and went to court with them to watch how they handled each case.

Finding the books in the office too daunting, Coolidge bought student textbooks and law cases on the major subjects needed for him to prepare for the bar exam. This allowed him to cut through the unnecessary details and to concentrate on the most important information. In June of 1897 he was examined by a committee and passed its examination. On July 4, 1897, his twenty-fifth birthday, and after twenty months of preparation, Calvin Coolidge was admitted to the bar in the state of Massachusetts. He wrote years later, "My formal period of education was passed, though my studies are still pursued." After a few more months with Hammond and Field, he opened his own law office in Northampton. He would practice law in that office until he became governor of Massachusetts in 1919.

Shortly after Coolidge settled into his own office, he became active in the Republican Party. Within two years he was elected to the Northampton City Council and then became chairman of the local Republican Party organization. He rose rapidly in politics, being elected to the state legislature in 1907. Coolidge was elected mayor of Northhampton in 1910. He was elected to the state senate in 1912 and served as its president from 1914–1915. In 1916, he was elected lieutenant governor, becoming governor in 1919. He would serve as governor of Massachusetts until 1921.

Politics was not the only significant thing for Coolidge in Northampton. He met Grace Anna Goodhue, who became his wife. Anna was on the faculty of the Clarke Institute for the Deaf. One day in 1903, she was watering flowers in front of the school when she saw Coolidge through an open window next door. He was shaving in front of a mirror, dressed only in a felt hat and long underwear. Her laughter drew his attention, and the two became friends. (Calvin would later explain that he wore the hat over his dampened hair to help control an "unruly lock of hair.") They were married on October 4, 1905, and eventually had two sons, John and Calvin Jr.

In 1921, Coolidge became vice-president of the United States under President Warren G. Harding. On August 2, 1923, while he was vacationing in the Notch at his father's home, Calvin Coolidge was awakened to be told that President Harding had died in San Francisco during a cross-country trip. Calvin Coolidge and Grace, along with John Coolidge, knelt in prayer. Then Coolidge took the oath of office from his father, a notary public and became the thirtieth president of the United States.

In 1924, Calvin Coolidge ran for president and was elected with 54 percent of the popular vote. He refused to run for a second term. Some said he lost interest in politics after the death of his son Calvin Jr. from blood poisoning. Others believed that he anticipated the economic downturn that would rock the United States and the world in October 1929. A man of few words, he stated simply, "I do not choose to run for President in 1928." Calvin Coolidge left office on March 4, 1929, and the Coolidges returned to Northhampton. On January 5, 1933, he died suddenly of a coronary thrombosis.

Calvin Coolidge was a man who believed deeply in individual responsibility and in working hard to accomplish goals. "Silent Cal" believed in actions over words. He once said what could well sum up his own character: "Nothing in the world can take the place of persistence. Talent will not; nothing is more common than unsuccessful men of talent. The world is full of educated derelicts. Persistence and determination alone are omnipotent."

—Bill Thompson

Herbert Hoover
Chapter Thirty

T he small boy walked into his father's empty blacksmith shop in West
Branch, Iowa. He watched tar bubbling in a huge kettle, then picked up a
burning stick. He was curious to know what would happen when he tossed
the stick into the kettle. The town newspaper reported the incident that resulted:
"Saturday afternoon a cauldron of tar which J. C. Hoover was heating for a coating
for fence wire took fire and immediately great clouds of fire and smoke were sent up,
causing much excitement among our people."

Men and women from all over town grabbed buckets and ran to help Jesse
Hoover put out the blaze. Jesse's youngest son, five-year-old Herbert, was nowhere
to be seen. He had run away in terror. However, in spite of the problems he caused
that day, Herbert never outgrew that curiosity and determination. These qualities
compelled him to learn and eventually helped him to become the thirty-first
president of the United States. Hoover's life is a powerful example of how much the
early years of a person's life define what that person becomes.

Herbert Hoover was born right across the road from his father's blacksmith
shop on August 1, 1874. His parents, Jesse and Huldah Hoover, called him Bertie
and later Bert. The Hoovers already had one son, Theodore ("Tad") who was three
at the time of Bertie's birth. In 1876, the family welcomed a third child, Mary, who
always went by the name of May. The three children grew up in a loving home,
surrounded by supportive relatives who lived in and around West Branch.

Jesse had opened his blacksmith shop after he was married and had moved his
wife into a tiny three-room cottage where Tad and Bertie were born. Jesse Hoover
eventually sold his blacksmith business and opened a farm implement store, which
offered everything from reapers and sewing machines to lightning rods and wagons.
Soon, the growing Hoover family moved into a larger home just down the street.

West Branch was a close-knit community that had been founded by Quakers.
The Quaker religious sect (more properly called "The Society of Friends") had been
established in England when certain Christians protested the religious formalism of
the Anglican Church. Facing persecution, many Quakers had emigrated to the

MAIN ENTRANCE AND MEMORIAL ARCH, LELAND STANFORD JR. UNIVERSITY.

Leland Stanford was a railroad builder, governor of California, and a United States senator. With his wife Jane, he founded Stanford University, endowing the school in memory of their son, Leland Jr., who had died in 1884, two months before his sixteenth birthday. Stanford, who had been at his son's bedside continuously from the time he had taken ill, fell into a troubled sleep after the boy's death. When he awoke, he turned to his grieving wife and said, "The students of California shall be our children." These words mark the real beginning of Stanford University.

Herbert Hoover was the youngest member of Stanford's first class—four hundred and sixty-five students, admitted in 1891. Hoover later wrote, "I happened to be the first boy to sleep in the Men's Dormitory [Encino Hall] before the university was formally opened—and so may be said to be its first student."

This rare postcard shows the ruined Stanford University Library. The April 1906 San Francisco earthquake caused serious damage to the university. However, the buildings, including the library, were rapidly repaired.

American colonies in the seventeenth and eighteenth centuries. Quakers emphasized the ideals of self-reliance, individualism, and thrift. They were also deeply committed to education and established many schools and colleges.

As a young child, Bertie was taken to Sunday meetings where the Quaker congregation sat in long periods of silence waiting for someone to speak. They believed that each person had an inner light and anyone could hear directly from God. From that early religious training he was taught to organize his life around Quaker ideals.

As good Quakers, Bertie's parents were committed to education. Both had attended a private school in West Branch run by Joel and Hannah Bean, two Quaker missionaries. Huldah had also studied at the University of Iowa and taught school for a short time before starting her family. She was Bertie's first teacher, and helped him learn to read and write. By the time he was ten he had read through the entire Bible.

Bertie's formal schooling began in the primary department at the West Branch School when he was five. "Who does not remember with a glow," he wrote as an adult, "some gentle woman who with infinite patience and kindness drilled into us those foundations of all we know today." Mollie Brown, one of Bertie's earliest teachers, described him as "industrious and determined.…He put his whole heart into it, whether it was coasting down Cook's hill on his home-made sled, or diving into the old swimming hole down by the railroad track, or getting a hard lesson in school. He worked with all his might."

A dentist in West Branch who knew Bertie as a boy also saw his strong-willed desire to learn. "Gradually there was born in the boy the determination to win an education," the dentist later related. "For so often I would say 'I don't know' in answer to his question. That would never satisfy him." Another teacher, however, remembered him as a more playful boy: "[He] learned rapidly and never made any trouble, but seemed more interested in getting out-of-doors to play than in books and studies."

In December 1880, a year after Bertie began school, his father died of typhoid fever. Although Jesse had left his wife with insurance, a new home, and some money, Huldah took in sewing and rented a room to a boarder to help provide for the children. She was determined to save the inheritance for their education. Huldah had been active in the West Branch Quaker meeting, teaching Sunday school and acting as its clerk. After Jesse's death, she became a Quaker evangelist and traveled around the countryside preaching.

Different Hoover relatives helped Huldah to raise her three children. For eight or nine months Bertie went to live with his aunt and uncle, Agnes and Laban Miles. Miles was an agent for the Osage Indian Nation and lived in Indian Territory [Oklahoma] with his family. Bertie loved to be outdoors and played with his cousins and young Osage braves from the tribe. They taught him to hunt and cook wild game over campfires he built by himself.

In February 1884, Huldah developed pneumonia. She died suddenly, only three years and two months after Jesse. Bert, who was nine, seemed unable to express much emotion. Twelve-year-old Tad, however, long remembered his sadness. "A lad of that age feels under these circumstances a helplessness and despair and a sort of dumb animal terror....The lady of the golden sunshine of the little brown house had gone away, and there were left only three small children, adrift on the wreck of their little world."

The three orphaned children were sent to live with various relatives. Bert went to stay with an aunt and uncle, David and Mary Hoover, who lived on a farm outside of West Branch with their son, Walter. There Bert planted corn, hoed the gardens, milked cows, and sawed wood. He didn't mind hard work. To earn extra money for firecrackers on the fourth of July, Bert picked potato bugs. His pay was one cent for a hundred bugs. He and his cousin went to a district school where Bertie continued his primary education.

When Bert was eleven, his life changed again. John Minthorn, Huldah's brother, wrote to the Hoovers in Iowa and asked that Bert be sent to live with him in Oregon. Minthorn had moved from Iowa to Newberg, Oregon, with his wife, Laura, and their three children. Once there, he became the superintendent of a new Quaker school, Friends Pacific Academy. (Minthorn was also a doctor; he had graduated from Jefferson Memorial Hospital in Philadelphia.) His seven-year-old son had died the year before, and he now asked that Bert be sent to live with him so he would receive a better education.

Bert was placed aboard a train on November 12, 1885, and sent to the Minthorn home in Oregon. Among the things Bert packed to go with him were two placards that had belonged to his mother. These read, "Leave me not, neither forsake me, O God of my salvation" and "I will never leave thee nor forsake thee." When Bert arrived in Newberg, he hung them over his bed. He was now separated from everyone he had ever known—including his brother and sister. He felt, as he wrote in his memoir, "lonely."

Once in Oregon, Bert was immediately enrolled in Friends Pacific Academy. The school had two divisions, the grammar school for young children and the academy, comparable to a high school today. The faculty consisted of John Minthorn, his wife, Laura, and a third teacher, W. R. Starbuck. The school day began at 9 A.M. with prayer and a twenty-minute talk on subjects Minthorn believed would build the character of the students. Classes continued until four in the afternoon. Bert entered the grammar school to begin his studies. That first year, Bert took six subjects: reading, arithmetic, geography and map drawing, writing and drawing, language lessons, and spelling.

Because it was a Quaker school, the catalogue was clear to point out what was expected from students: "Since immoral and sinful practices are incompatible with the highest mental or physical development, no one is desired as a student who is not willing to abstain therefrom." In spite of that strictness, Bert was allowed more educational freedom under John Minthorn than he had known in Iowa. Using his uncle's library, he read books that previously had been forbidden.

Bert had regular chores in the Minthorn household, which included feeding and watering his uncle's team of horses, driving cows to pasture and milking them, and splitting wood. There were many times that Bert traveled with his uncle when he called on patients. During those buggy trips, Dr. Minthorn would talk with his young nephew about physiology and health. "The long tedious drives over rough and often muddy forest roads," Hoover wrote in his memoirs, "became part of my education."

However, there were many fun times and opportunities to work for spending money. Bert explored the forests and streams of Oregon with other village boys and learned the art of fishing, a hobby he enjoyed all his life. He built dams in the nearby streams, played games with his cousins, and learned to swim. He also used some of his summer vacation time to earn extra money. Bert worked on a farm weeding onions, earning his board and fifty cents for an eleven-hour day. Later that same summer, he labored in a brickyard in Newberg.

In his second year at grammar school, Bert took arithmetic, American history, physiology, grammar, and physical geography. He was a good student and graduated from the grammar school in May 1887. At the commencement exercises he gave one of the speeches.

That September, his brother Tad came to join him from Iowa, and the two entered the academy together. Bert took algebra, bookkeeping, and rhetoric. He did well and was considered one of the best students in his class. For a while the two brothers lived together in a dormitory on the academy campus.

In 1888, when Bert was fourteen, Dr. Minthorn left the academy to start the Oregon Land Company with several partners. This was a real estate business operating out of Salem, thirty miles away from Newberg. When the Minthorn family moved to Salem, Bert chose to go with them rather than stay in school. He went to work as an office boy in the Oregon Land Company.

Arthur Diggles   R.E. McDonnell
Herbert Hoover   James White
SURVEYING SQUAD - STANFORD UNIVERSITY IN 1893

Herbert Hoover (seated, left) and other members of the Stanford University surveying squad, 1893.

Hoover majored in geology. A classmate later recalled that Hoover "practically lived in the geology laboratory." Various campus jobs and summer employment with the United States Geological Survey helped Hoover earn his way through four years of college. John Branner, the head of the Department of Geology and Mining, became his mentor and lifelong friend.

Herbert Hoover received his Bachelor of Arts in Geology degree from Stanford University in May 1895. Stanford used the pass/fail grading system, so it is not possible to rank the graduates. But according to his contemporaries, Hoover was considered an outstanding student in Stanford's first graduating class. He was not yet twenty-one years old.

Stanford University did a great deal for Hoover both professionally and personally. In turn, Hoover would do a great deal for Stanford. His most impressive contribution was to donate a specialized collection of documents on the causes and consequences of World War I (1914–18). The collection grew rapidly and soon became one of the largest archives and perhaps the most complete library in the world devoted to political, social, and economic change in the twentieth century. This collection led to the recruitment of scholars to use the documents in their work. Today, the Hoover Institution is one of the most distinguished academic centers in the United States dedicated to public policy research.

Bert threw himself wholeheartedly into his new occupation. He did some filing and mailing as well as managing the company's advertising. He developed new ideas about contacting prospective customers for the company. Bert learned accounting from the company bookkeeper and was taught typing by the office secretary, Laura Heulat. She admired Hoover a great deal. "H. H. was the quietest, the most efficient and the most industrious boy I ever knew in an office," said Heulat. "He knew everything about the office and the rest of us never tried to keep track of things. It was easier and quicker just to ask Bert about it."

Hoover did not neglect his education. A year after he arrived in Salem, he enrolled in the Capital Business College for evening classes. His teacher helped improve his algebra and geometry. In addition, she worked with him on Latin, but without a great deal of success. During that time, May came to Salem with her grandmother to live, uniting Bert with his sister for the first time in three years.

In Salem, Hoover's intellectual growth was aided by Jennie Gray, who took a personal interest in him. She befriended Hoover and spent much time helping him broaden his knowledge. She took him to the Salem library where she introduced the eager office boy to *Ivanhoe*, *David Copperfield*, and other works of literature previously unknown to him. Gray gave him a love of books, and Hoover felt she had opened his imagination to a new world.

After nearly three years working as office boy, Hoover began to consider his future education. He was influenced by Tad, who had finished at the academy and returned to Iowa to attend college. Bert also knew there was money left from his father's small estate that had been saved by the Hoover family exclusively for the children's education. At the same time, a mining engineer from the East visited the land company office and talked to Hoover. He told him about the outdoor life of an engineer, the excitement of the newly opened West, and the intellectual challenges the field of engineering offered. Hoover became very interested and this conversation had a profound effect on his life.

Bert investigated several colleges and decided to become an engineer himself. After a visit to a mine in the Cascade Mountains, he became fascinated by geology. His increased zeal for learning was noticed by those in the Oregon Land Company office. One of the partners, Ben Cook, spoke glowingly of the young office boy, "He was on the jump whenever there was anything to do but the moment he was through, out would come his geometry or algebra or history, and he'd sit, shoulders hunched over the little table in the corner, preparing for college."

A notice appeared in the Salem newspaper about the same time that caught Hoover's attention. Entrance exams were being conducted in Portland for a new college that was to open in California. It was called Stanford and was being built on the 80,000-acre ranch of wealthy Senator Leland Stanford, thirty miles south of San Francisco. In spite of Uncle John's misgivings about his nephew considering such a "godless" school, Hoover went to Portland and spoke with Professor Joseph Swain, who allowed him to take the exams.

Swain wrote about Hoover, "I observed that he put his teeth together with great decision and his whole face and posture showed his determination to pass the examination at any cost. He was evidently summoning every pound of energy he possessed to answer correctly the questions before him." Although Hoover did not do well on the exam, Swain was impressed by his determination and his zeal for engineering. Since Stanford needed such students, Swain asked Hoover to come to California early, study under tutors, and take the exams over again at Stanford.

At the end of August 1891, just after his seventeenth birthday, Hoover boarded the train in Salem for his trip to California. Swain, a Quaker himself, had talked with John Minthorn and won his approval to allow Hoover to enter Stanford. When he arrived, Hoover found that Stanford College was still incomplete. Only a few buildings were finished, and the roads were dusty and rutted. Yet there was an excitement in the air and great enthusiasm about the new school being established.

In 1885, Leland and Jane Stanford announced that they were donating several thousand acres of their Palo Alto estate and an initial endowment of $5 million for the construction of a major university, one that from the outset would be non-traditional. Stanford would be coeducational in a time when most universities were all-male; non-denominational when most were associated with a religious group; and avowedly practical, graduating "cultural and useful citizens," when most institutions of higher learning focused only on the former. Frederick Law Olmsted, the eminent landscape architect who had designed New York's Central Park, developed the general plan for long, low, mission-style buildings connected by arcades to form a double campus quadrangle.

Land values in the Palo Alto area soared. This is an 1889 promotional advertisement for real estate in the university area—the university opened two years later.

As soon as he arrived, Hoover contacted the tutors Swain had appointed to work with him. They were Lucy Fletcher and Eleanor Pearson, whose horses he groomed as payment for their help. Because of their assistance, Hoover qualified in arithmetic, geography, geometry, and U.S. history. However, he needed expertise in one more subject in order to be admitted. He remembered the many talks he had with his Uncle John about anatomy and health. That night he studied two books on physiology and qualified in that subject the next day. He entered as a "conditional" student, because his skills in English composition were so poor. He would need to write an acceptable essay before his graduation.

Bert settled in the new men's dorm, Encino Hall, as the youngest member of his class. On October 1, 1891, he went to the opening exercises of the new Leland Stanford Junior University. He was deeply impressed by the speeches of Senator Stanford and the new president, Dr. David Starr Jordan. "Remember," Stanford urged, "that life is, above all, practical; that you are here to fit yourselves for a useful career....learning should not only make you wise in the arts and sciences, but should fully develop your moral and religious natures."

Hoover declared mechanical engineering as his major and began his first semester. His freshman courses were solid geometry, algebra, trigonometry, two classes in drawing, and mechanical engineering. In January of the next year, a new professor, Dr. John Branner, began teaching geology. "I came under the spell of a great scientist and a great teacher," said Hoover, who quit his courses in drawing and signed up for Branner's geology course. The two developed a friendship that lasted over Branner's lifetime.

There was no tuition at Stanford, and Hoover had some money from his father's small estate. However, he still needed income to pay for his room, board, and supplies. He found a job in the university office and later accepted an offer from Dr. Branner to work for him, typing in the geology department. Hoover also began a laundry business for the students and a campus newspaper route. As these businesses grew in popularity, he subcontracted both of them to other students and received a small income from them.

Though Hoover was an enterprising young businessman and a good student, he was not socially outgoing. He was known by the faculty as quiet, shy, and reserved. He did not enjoy casual conversation and was a person of few words. "When he did offer an opinion," wrote biographer Eugene Lyons, "it was succinct and impressively to the point, so that his presence among [the students] registered—not dramatically, as in the case of extroverts, but slowly, like an unfoldment."

When Stanford began, it had a pass/fail grade system. All that is known about Hoover's freshman grades is that he passed all of his courses. He also became active in several student organizations. He joined the Geology Club and gave a paper at one of its meetings. He was a shortstop on the baseball team and then became the team's financial and scheduling manager. Hoover was more interested in activities where he could contribute instead of socialize.

In the summer of 1892, Branner helped Hoover land a position as a member of a geological team doing a survey in Arkansas. Through his work, Hoover began to learn more about people. He discovered that even though people in Arkansas were suspicious about what the team was doing, they always showed him hospitality. Hoover was always able to get a room at night in their homes, and people refused to take money from him even though they were poor and in need themselves.

When Hoover returned to Stanford to begin his sophomore year, he changed his major to geology. He took courses in mineralogy, paleontology, inorganic chemistry, and geology. He continued to work with Professor Branner, becoming more involved in geological matters. In the spring of his sophomore year, he helped build a huge topographical relief map of Arkansas, which was displayed at the 1893 Chicago World's Fair. As a result of his work, Hoover received fifteen hours of credit.

During the first semester of his junior year, Hoover took courses in paleontology, mineralogy, surveying, chemistry, and philosophy. In his second semester he added chemistry, calculus, and assaying to his schedule. In addition, he attended lectures in other subjects, such as evolution, biology, and the reconciliation of science and religion.

While in college Hoover was a typical student who enjoyed life with his classmates. A friend, Will Irwin, remembered the time Hoover and their classmates argued over who was the fastest runner. They all ran around a cinder track that night and Hoover won. Then he confessed that he had cut across the center of the field in the dark. His competitors hauled him to the bathroom and dunked him in the tub.

One of Hoover's most valuable experiences occurred outside the classroom during his junior year. During Stanford's first year, many organizations, including fraternities, had been formed on campus. Over the next two years, fraternity men had gained the control of most student offices. Those not in the fraternities—the barbarians, or "Barbs," including Hoover—decided to declare war against the "Frats" and win as many offices as they could. In the elections of April 1894, the Barbs won all of the important positions on campus.

Hoover helped write a new constitution, which made all student activities subject to the approval of the student body. It was approved and went into effect that year. Most of the campus organizations had previously acted independently. One, football, was beginning to reap large amounts of cash in game receipts with no accountability. Hoover was elected the first student financial manager and handled the finances of the many campus groups. He set up a system of accounts for all student enterprises and published the results regularly in the college newspaper.

In the summer of 1894, Hoover was hired by the United States Geological Survey as part of a team mapping the High Sierras around Lake Tahoe. He worked for Dr. Waldemar Lindgren, a leading geologist who eventually became chief geologist of the U.S. Geological Survey, and later was a professor of geology at the Massachusetts Institute of Technology. Hoover saw Lindgren not only as a great engineer but also as a great teacher. With Lindgren and other members of the survey team, Hoover felt "their illuminating conversations around the fire embraced a vast amount of objective observations…. A great amount of engineering lore and practice seeped into my mind." Lindgren considered the young Stanford student the best assistant he ever had, because Hoover was eager to learn and precise in his work. When the survey maps were printed, Lindgren placed Hoover's name next to his. It was the Iowa boy's first public recognition and it always had a special place in his heart.

Hoover got back to campus late for his senior year, but was awarded eight hours of credit for his work with Dr. Lindgren. He took German that semester but flunked it, the only course he failed at Stanford. He was so involved in campus activities and geological work off campus that he earned no college credit that semester. In the spring of his senior year, Hoover had to take a heavy load, which included nineteenth-century European history, ethics, and several advanced courses in geology. With the help of a compassionate professor, he finished the English essay he needed in order to graduate.

While working in the geology department that senior year, he met Lou Henry, a freshman from Monterey, California. She also had been born in Iowa and loved to ride horses, camp outdoors, and fish. Years later, Hoover wrote, "I felt it my duty to aid the young lady in her studies…. And this call to duty was stimulated by her whimsical mind, her blue eyes, and a broad grinnish smile that came from an Irish ancestor." He took her to every social event that year, and after he graduated, corresponded with her for three years until she completed college. They were married on February 10, 1899.

Herbert Hoover graduated from Stanford University on May 29, 1895, with a degree in geology. He was a good student, although not a top scholar. However, he was an independent thinker with great determination to succeed. "According to Branner and [Hoover's] other instructors," wrote Will Irwin, "the remarkable thing about his university work was its originality. He attacked all problems, even of pure mathematics, in his own way, and went forward to brilliantly original results." Throughout his life he gave financial support to Stanford and thought of the school as his family.

Because of an economic recession that year, Hoover's first job was shoveling dirt and rock at the bottom of Reward Mine in Grass Valley, California, at $2 for each ten-hour shift. A year later, the Stanford graduate went to San Francisco and was able to find office work with Louis Janin, a prominent mining engineer. Janin sent Hoover to survey several mines. His reports were so complete that Janin recommended him for a job with the London firm Bewick, Moring, and Company. Hoover was hired and sent to inspect and develop the firm's gold mines in western Australia. In 1897, the twenty-three-year-old sailed for Australia to begin a successful career as a mining engineer.

In 1899, Hoover was transferred to China. Within three years, he was a millionaire because of the mining commissions that he earned. He and his wife Lou survived the 1900 Boxer Rebellion. In China the Hoovers learned Mandarin. While living in Asia, the Hoovers became the parents of two sons, Herbert Jr. and Allan. Hoover formed his own mining engineering firm in 1908, and his wealth and reputation increased. Yet, he still found time for reading. He devoured works on history, sociology, economics, and philosophy. In addition, he and his wife translated a sixteenth-century mining book from Latin into English.

In 1914, President Woodrow Wilson asked Hoover to head the American Relief Committee, formed to help Americans stranded in Europe at the outbreak of World War I. He served in several governmental agencies during the war years and was an economic advisor to Wilson at the Versailles Peace Conference. From 1921 until 1928, he was Secretary of Commerce under Presidents Harding and Coolidge.

In 1928, Hoover ran for president as the Republican Party candidate. He defeated Democrat Alfred E. Smith. President of the United States was Hoover's first and only elected office. The Great Depression began during his term, leading to his defeat for reelection in 1932.

Hoover served as chairman of relief organizations in Europe during World War II. After the war, he was appointed by President Truman to supervise European food relief. Later, Truman asked him to head what became known as the Hoover Commission. Its purpose was to help streamline the executive branch of government. Eventually, a majority of the commission's recommendations were accepted. Because of his broad commitment to public service, by the end of his life Herbert Hoover had received eighty-four honorary degrees and seventy-eight medals and awards.

Hoover died on October 17, 1964, at the age of ninety. Although he was widely criticized for his performance as president, biographer Eugene Lyons remarked, "What has impressed me profoundly as I studied the data of his life is Hoover's wholeness and genuineness. There is nothing phony, nothing petty… in his story."

Herbert Hoover was a man who never departed from those things he had learned. Both his Quaker background and his years at Stanford had taught him to be useful to his country and of service to others. As an orphan himself, he showed special compassion for children caught up in two world wars as he worked for their relief. Another of Hoover's biographers, George Nash, wrote, "When Herbert Hoover died he had spent a half century of his life in public service. It was a record that in sheer scope and duration may be without parallel in American history."

—Bill Thompson

Franklin D. Roosevelt

Chapter Thirty-one

F ranklin D. Roosevelt ranks as one of the most controversial presidents in
American history. His administration (1933–1945) confronted two of the
most important events of the twentieth century—the Great Depression and
World War II. In handling these momentous problems, Roosevelt became a larger-
than-life hero to millions—a president who could just do no wrong. Likewise, due
to the fundamental changes in the nation's economy caused by his policies, millions
of others came to hate "that man in the White House" because, they claimed, he
undermined states' rights and individual liberty. Nevertheless, even his detractors
agree that Franklin D. Roosevelt left an indelible mark on the United States.

Roosevelt died in office on April 12, 1945, less than three months after his
inauguration for an unprecedented fourth term. He wrote no memoir, no
autobiography, no account of his personal inner feelings and motivations. There
is excellent documentation of the facts of Roosevelt's life, but despite collections
of his personal letters, the reminiscences of family, friends, and others who were
associated with Roosevelt in every conceivable way, and the many thoughtful
studies that have been written about his life and presidency, the essence of
Roosevelt the man remains elusive. Although because of illness he lost the use of
his legs at age thirty-nine, Roosevelt never allowed himself to indulge in self-
pity. He chose instead to face all the obstacles that confronted the people who
had placed their trust in him. While others lacked the courage to depart from
the old accepted rules of American politics, Roosevelt repeatedly took
unprecedented risks. His dynamic leadership never ceased to convey a sense of
trust, of assurance, and of bravery.

Franklin Delano Roosevelt was born at his family home, Springwood, in Hyde
Park, New York, on January 30, 1882. Hyde Park is a small village overlooking the
Hudson River about eighty miles north of New York City and five miles from the
town of Poughkeepsie. By the time of Franklin's birth, several generations of
Roosevelts had made their homes in the beautiful Hudson River valley. It is
thought that the first Roosevelt in America came from Holland in the 1640s.

Franklin Roosevelt was born to a wealthy family—a family that had enjoyed immense privilege for many generations, a family that was far removed from the great world of the underprivileged. From the porch of their stately manor at Hyde Park, New York, was a magnificent view of the Hudson River valley and the Catskill Mountains beyond. Herds of cattle grazed the land, and rolling hills, fields of grain, greenhouses, grape arbors, flowering gardens, goats, dogs, and stables for riding horses and racing trotters filled the panorama.

Outwardly, Roosevelt's youth was a happy, privileged existence. It was a sequestered life in which his playmates were almost always countless cousins and the children from neighboring estates. Before he was fifteen, Franklin had accompanied his parents on eight European trips, each of several months duration. In Europe his parents socialized with the wealthy aristocracy. He was taken to the English manors of friends and relatives, to the French Riviera, and frequently to German spas. The summer when he was nine, his parents enrolled him for six weeks in a school in southern Germany in the hope of improving his German. The Europe he knew was that of the elite. With the exception of servants, rarely did young Franklin have contact with people who worked for their living.

Hyde Park had a fine family library. Before he had reached fourteen, Franklin had read Alfred Thayer Mahan's epoch-study *The Influence of Sea Power Upon History, 1660–1783* (1890) as well as books written by Mark Twain, Rudyard Kipling, and Francis Parkman. (At the Roosevelt Museum, one can read margin notes and comments made by young Franklin in many of these books.) One afternoon, his mother found him engrossed in reading *Webster's Unabridged Dictionary*. She asked "what on earth" he was doing. He replied that he was reading the dictionary because "there are lots of words I don't understand" and that he was "almost half way through."

In the autumn of 1896, Roosevelt's parents entered him at the Groton School in Massachusetts. Their aim was to prepare Franklin for college. This was the first time that Franklin would be attending a formal school, and the first time that he would be separated from his loving and doting parents. Mrs. Roosevelt recorded Franklin's departure in her diary: "We dusted his birds and he had a swim in the river….I looked on. And with heavy heart. It is had to leave our darling boy. James and I both feel this parting very much."

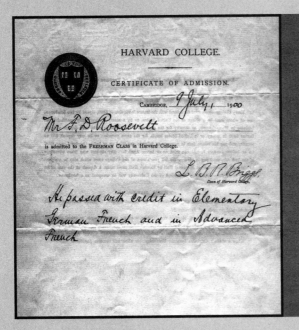

is admitted to the FRESHMAN CLASS in Harvard College.

Harvard College in 1900 was, as it had been for some two hundred and fifty years, a school for the sons of America's most distinguished and wealthy families. Almost immediately, Franklin Roosevelt, now eighteen, plunged into a wide range of social, athletic, and extracurricular activities. He seemed released from the confines of Hyde Park and Groton. He tried out for nearly every athletic team but made only one intramural football team. Although he was now more than six feet tall, he weighed only one hundred and forty-five pounds, which was much too light for the varsity team. He was too slow for the track team and not strong enough to succeed at rowing. Though he joined the freshman glee club, in his sophomore year he lost out to better voices.

Franklin's wealthy father, James Roosevelt, had purchased Springwood and over the years had increased his land holdings to more than a thousand acres.

James Roosevelt's first wife died in 1876. Four years later, when James was fifty-two, he married Sara Delano, a sixth cousin who was half his age. Like her husband, Sara Delano came from an extremely prosperous merchant family. Sara had traveled to China as a girl, attended school abroad, and moved in the prominent social circles of London and Paris.

James Roosevelt had inherited a comfortable fortune and his greatest concern, especially after his second marriage, was his country squire's life among the Hudson River gentry. His financial investments yielded sufficient money to enable this type of luxury. Their marriage was serene until broken by James's death in 1900 at age seventy-two (Franklin was then eighteen).

Franklin had a secure and idyllic childhood. His half-brother was an adult when Franklin was born, so Franklin faced no rivals for the love and devotion of his parents. He grew up as an only child with the loving and doting attention of both parents and every privilege of an aristocratic boyhood. There were always servants at Springwood—a butler, cooks, maids, gardeners, and horse grooms. After Franklin's birth, James and Sara were able to continue their extensive travels and their life of affluence.

In later years, Sara Delano Roosevelt claimed that neither she nor her husband ever tried to influence young Franklin against his own tastes and inclinations. However, it is hard to imagine a mother more closely attached to a son or more preoccupied with monitoring his life and activities. His strong-willed mother expected that Franklin would, in due time, continue in the Delano and Roosevelt traditions of overseeing the family fortune. "I know that traditionally every mother believes her son will one day be president," Sara remarked in 1932, "but as much as I love tradition and believe in perpetuating good ones, that is one to which I never happened to subscribe."

Young Franklin rarely had contact with people who worked for their living. When he accompanied his parents on business trips in the United States, they traveled in a private railway car. Franklin's boyhood was the happy one of a young patrician—frequent trips abroad, summers swimming and sailing at the family vacation home on Campobello Island off the coast of Maine, and part of almost every year spent in New York City. However, Hyde Park remained Franklin Roosevelt's true home. Throughout his life—even when he was president—Roosevelt returned to this magnificent estate. Perhaps no president had a happier or more secure childhood than did Franklin Roosevelt.

James Roosevelt took an active interest in the Hyde Park public school but it probably never occurred to Sara to send Franklin there. She kept her son in an insulated world as long as she could. Young Franklin was educated by private tutors and governesses. His governesses were all European, and learning foreign languages made up a large part of Franklin's early education. He became fluent in French and could write German fairly well. (During World War II Roosevelt was able to converse with the French leader Charles de Gaulle, who refused to speak anything but French.) One governess assigned Franklin the task of writing essays in French

Groton was spartan compared to the comforts of Hyde Park. Franklin's six-by-ten-foot room was sparsely furnished. A curtain substituted for a door. The boys were awakened at 7 A.M.; breakfast was at 7:30; morning chapel at 8:15; and then off to classes. Dinner was served at noon followed by more classes and compulsory athletics. At supper, the boys wore blue suits, starched white collars and black patent-leather shoes. Evening chapel followed supper and then study hour. Endicott Peabody, headmaster of the Groton School, wrote, "He was a quiet, satisfactory boy, of more than ordinary intelligence, taking a good position in his Form, but not brilliant. Athletically, he was rather too slight for success. We all liked him."

A postcard shows the chapel at Groton as it appeared when Roosevelt attended the school.

Franklin D. Roosevelt, center, is photographed with the Groton School baseball team, October 1899. The curriculum at Groton stressed the classics. For example, in his first year, Franklin studied Latin, Greek, algebra, English literature and composition, ancient history, general science, and Bible studies. Franklin ranked in the top quarter of students throughout his four years at Groton. Never a great student, never overly popular with his fellow classmates, he did enjoy the distinction one year of being Groton's champion "high kicker" in football. He was not much of an athlete, and his principal contribution to the Groton School's sports program was to manage the school's baseball team.

on the social inequalities of the time. These essays, which have survived, may have been Franklin's first exposure to problems beyond the comfortable world of his loving family and their affluent friends. His teachers traveled with the family so that he could have his lessons anywhere in the world. Sara remained in total charge of her son's education and a governess either deferred to her wishes or left.

Franklin got along easily with the adults in his life. But when he was playing with children his own age, Sara noticed that he was inclined to be bossy and controlling. His earliest playmates were Edmund and Archibald Rogers, who lived on an estate near Springwood. At age six, Franklin began spending two hours each day at the Rogers' home learning reading, writing, and German from their governess. He soon was able to write short notes in German to his mother, which she lovingly preserved. Sara, determined for Franklin to improve his German, enrolled him in a public school in Germany for six weeks during one of the family's European trips. This was Franklin's only exposure to a public school, and his only exposure to the schedule of a schoolboy until he entered Groton five years later.

At age nine, encouraged by his mother, Franklin started a postage-stamp collection to which he continuously added, even when president. The extended Roosevelt/Delano families were involved in shipping and trading, especially with the Far East, so Franklin was always asking his relatives to send him mail and to bring him stamps. No country was omitted from his collection. When he went to Groton, and later Harvard, he took his stamp collection with him. During World War II, when as president he traveled to the Casablanca and Yalta conferences, his stamp collection accompanied him in a large wooden crate. Spending time with his collection provided a way for Roosevelt to relax. His formidable knowledge of world geography and of the most obscure potential battle sites—gained from philately—impressed his military aides. His collection became one of the world's largest, numbering scores of albums for practically every country.

Aside from formal subjects, Franklin was tutored in carpentry—making model boats, birdhouses, and toys. Like his distant cousin Theodore Roosevelt, Franklin developed a keen interest in ornithology (the branch of zoology concerned with the study of birds). He collected birds' eggs and nests, carefully recording his observations in a notebook. When he was eleven, he wrote a composition on "Birds of the Hudson River Valley" that so impressed his maternal grandfather that he gave Franklin a life membership in New York's American Museum of Natural History. Franklin even learned taxidermy, but soon left the messy job of stuffing his birds to the servants. Photography also fascinated young Franklin. Using an expensive tripod-mounted Kodak camera, he took dozens of family photographs, as well as self-portraits made using a timer. Many of these photos are on display at the Roosevelt Museum at Hyde Park.

Above all, Roosevelt's parents influenced his education by welcoming him into their adult world. They introduced him to their well-educated friends. With them, he attended cultural events, such as museums, the theater, and the opera in both Europe and the United States.

Throughout his life, Franklin Roosevelt loved reading. Springwood had an extensive library and Franklin was allowed to explore all of its offerings to his heart's content. He was a fast reader with a powerful memory, devouring books quickly and retaining startling amounts of information. As a teenager, Franklin especially liked books about the sea and naval history. (Sailing on his father's boat, the *Half Moon*, was a favorite hobby.) Before he had reached the age of fourteen, Franklin had completed

Franklin D. Roosevelt (right) playing the part of senile Uncle Bopaddy in W. S. Gilbert's *The Wedding March*, the Groton School senior class play, February 22, 1900.

Franklin Roosevelt majored in history and government, with English and public speaking as minors. He was not a great student, and did not take his studies seriously. As a result, his grades were usually a "gentleman's C." Extracurricular activities and social life were much more important to him. Charming, handsome, and extremely wealthy, Roosevelt took a cruise in the Caribbean with his mother and missed the first six weeks of Frederick Jackson Turner's famous course on the role of the frontier in American history. The few samples of his undergraduate writing that have survived are mediocre and uncritical.

1900–01.

HARVARD UNIVERSITY.

FACULTY OF ARTS AND SCIENCES.

The grade attained by *F. D. Roosevelt* ...in each of his studies for the year 1900–01 is given below.

GEORGE W. CRAM, *Recorder.*

Subject	Course	Half Course	Subject	Course	Half Course	Subject	Course	Half Course	Subject	Course	Half Course
SEMITIC			GERMAN			ECONOMICS			ENGINEERING		
SEMITIC			GERMAN			ECONOMICS			MILITARY & NAVAL SCI.		
SANSKRIT			GERMAN			ECONOMICS			PHYSICS		
GREEK			FRENCH			ECONOMICS			PHYSICS		
GREEK			FRENCH 2a		C+	PHILOSOPHY			PHYSICS		
GREEK			FRENCH			PHILOSOPHY			CHEMISTRY		
GREEK			FRENCH			PHILOSOPHY			CHEMISTRY		
GREEK			FRENCH			PHILOSOPHY			CHEMISTRY		
LATIN B		C+	ITALIAN			FINE ARTS			CHEMISTRY		
LATIN			ITALIAN			FINE ARTS			CHEMISTRY		
LATIN			SPANISH			ARCHITECTURE			BOTANY		
LATIN			SPANISH			MUSIC			BOTANY		
CLASSICAL PHIL.		C	ROMANCE PHIL.			MUSIC			ZOÖLOGY		
ENGLISH 28			COMP. LITERATURE			MATHEMATICS			ZOÖLOGY		
ENGLISH			CELTIC			MATHEMATICS			GEOLOGY 4		C
ENGLISH			SLAVIC			MATHEMATICS			GEOLOGY 5		C
ENGLISH			HISTORY 1		C	MATHEMATICS			GEOLOGY		
ENGLISH			HISTORY			ENGINEERING			MINERALOGY		
GERMAN			HISTORY			ENGINEERING			MINING		
GERMAN			GOVERNMENT 1		C	ENGINEERING			ANTHROPOLOGY		
			GOVERNMENT			ENGINEERING			HYGIENE		

The standing of every student in each of his courses is expressed, on the completion of the course, by one of five grades, designated respectively by the letters A, B, C, D, E. Grade E in any course denotes failure to fulfil the requirements of the course. "*Abs.*" indicates failure to obtain credit for the course, owing to absence from the final examination.

The standing of every student in each of his courses is expressed, on the completion of the course, A, B, C, D, E. Grade E in any course denotes failure to fulfil the requirements of the course. "Abs."

Alfred T. Mahan's *The Influence of Sea Power on History*. Years later, he fondly recalled the boyhood hours spent reading old naval logs and reports found in his maternal grandfather's attic. Undoubtedly, his mother's stirring stories of her seafaring ancestors and her own travels to Asia as a young woman greatly contributed to his interest.

Roosevelt's tutors generally informed Sara that he was a good student. However, Franklin was never subjected to competition or comparison with other students. He did not receive formal grades and report cards. While he had a vast memory, he displayed no tendency to think critically about the multitude of facts trapped in his mind. They seemed to be just another of his collections, neatly organized and easily retrieved at a moment's notice. His early school exercises show no attempt to connect these facts or to find any deeper meaning in them.

Sara and James Roosevelt began making plans for their son's teenage education early. When he was one year old, they placed his name on the future entrance list of the Groton School in Massachusetts. At that time, Groton was still the dream of Endicott Peabody, an autocratic yet inspiring Episcopal minister from a wealthy New England family. Peabody had been educated in England, and he dreamed of founding a school for American boys modeled after Eton and Harrow, the famous English boarding schools. Peabody planned to keep his school small and to maintain a family atmosphere with a strong emphasis on Christian ethics, athletics, and the virtues of public service. Friends of Sara and James Roosevelt had donated the land for Groton. Peabody and his educational ideas impressed the Roosevelts. Sara Roosevelt especially liked the idea that the school would be small. By the time Franklin entered Groton, however, it had become a prep school for rich boys and its graduates formed the top echelon of the social and business elite in the United States.

Franklin Roosevelt entered Groton in 1896. His Hyde Park friend Edmund Rogers entered the school with him, and his nephew "Taddy" Roosevelt (the grandson of James and his first wife), was a class ahead. Although the school offered a six-year program for boys between the ages of twelve and eighteen, Sara and James could not part with young Franklin, around whom their life centered, until he was fourteen. His enrollment at Groton marked the first time Roosevelt would attend a formal school in the United States, and the first time he would be separated from his loving parents. At Hyde Park, Franklin had been the center of attention; at Groton, he was one of one hundred and ten students, most of whom had already been at the school for two years.

The four years Franklin spent at Groton (1896–1900) made a lasting impact on him. He adapted himself readily to sharply different circumstances. Compared to the comforts of Springwood, Groton was spartan. His small room was sparsely furnished, and a curtain substituted for a door. Franklin had to conform to a rigid daily structure. Breakfast was at 7:30 A.M., morning chapel at 8:15, and then off to classes. Dinner was served at noon, followed by more classes and compulsory athletics. At supper, the boys wore blue suits, starched white collars, and black patent-leather shoes. Then followed evening chapel and study-hour, along with a nightly handshake from Reverend and Mrs. Peabody.

Much of what is known of Franklin's time at Groton comes from the chatty letters he sent to his parents. "I am getting along finely both mentally and physically," he wrote in his first letter home. The tone of his letters is persistently cheerful and optimistic, and at times a bit overdramatic.

There were nineteen students in Franklin's class, all boys from similar upper-class backgrounds. Compared to his classmates, Franklin was quiet and reserved. Nevertheless, he sang in the choir, played intramural football, criticized the food, and fully conformed to Groton's mores. The boys in his class had already formed friendships; Roosevelt was an outsider who had to work his way into the group. Some of his classmates, finding him priggish and superficial, called him the "feather duster." To make matters worse, he had a slight accent as a result of his European travels and his extensive study of foreign languages. He worked to lose his accent, which the other students considered an affectation. Although he was never overly popular with his classmates, one year Franklin did enjoy the distinction of being Groton's champion high-kicker, setting a school record.

The Groton years left Roosevelt with a belief that children of the upper classes had a duty to society—especially to the underprivileged. Undoubtedly this belief came from Endicott Peabody, who constantly worried about the poor and needy. Peabody's biographer describes him as something of a Christian Socialist concerned about the morals of the masses but almost oblivious to the economic and social problems caused by the industrial revolution. This remarkable man apparently stamped his values on almost every Grotonian. Roosevelt formed a lifelong friendship with Peabody. When Franklin married, Peabody performed the ceremony, and when Franklin took his first oath of office as president in 1933, Peabody recited the prayer.

"Very good," wrote Headmaster Peabody on the first monthly report to Franklin's parents. "He strikes me as an intelligent and faithful scholar and a good boy." The curriculum at Groton stressed the classics—in his first year, Franklin studied Latin, Greek, algebra, English literature and composition, ancient history, science, and the Bible. During his time at the school Franklin's grades averaged slightly less than B, and he ranked in the top quarter of students. In his final report, Peabody wrote, "He has been a thoroughly faithful scholar and a most satisfactory member of this school. I part with Franklin with reluctance." In an interview conducted during Roosevelt's 1932 presidential campaign, Peabody rephrased his observations: "[Franklin] was a quiet, satisfactory boy, of more than ordinary intelligence, taking a good position in his Form, but not brilliant. Athletically he was rather too slight for success. We all liked him."

Franklin D. Roosevelt entered Harvard University in 1900, when he was eighteen years old. Harvard was then, as it had been throughout its history, a school for the sons of America's most distinguished and wealthy families. Many of Roosevelt's Groton classmates entered Harvard with him. They lived in the same luxurious private suites of rooms, ate at the same Groton table rather than in one of the large common dining halls, and joined the same social clubs. Their world expanded only slightly to include graduates of other exclusive New England prep schools.

Franklin Roosevelt's main interest at Harvard became the undergraduate daily newspaper, the *Harvard Crimson*. In 1902, during his junior year, he was elected editor-in-chief. He wrote all the editorials, and for some years liked to describe himself as a former newspaperman, who through his editorials had fought for reform at Harvard. In reality, he had sought no reform more drastic than the laying of boards on the muddy paths between the Harvard buildings.

At Harvard, Roosevelt seemed released from the confines of Springwood and Groton, and he plunged into a wide range of extracurricular activities. He tried out for nearly every athletic team, but made only one intramural football team— although he had grown to six-foot-one, he weighed just one hundred and forty-five pounds, much too light for the varsity football squad. He was too slow for the track team, and not strong enough to succeed at rowing. Though Roosevelt joined the freshman glee club, in his sophomore year he lost out to students with better voices.

Thanks to Roosevelt's excellent preparation at Groton, he completed most of the course work for the B.A. degree in three years. Roosevelt's main interest during his senior year became Harvard's undergraduate daily newspaper, the *Harvard Crimson*. While a junior he was elected editor-in-chief of this four-to-eight page tabloid, and work on the newspaper occupied much of his senior year.

Roosevelt, who majored in American history and government with minors in English and public speaking, was not a great student. He did not take his studies very seriously, and as a result his grades were often a "gentleman's C." Harvard offered students a great deal of academic freedom and a top-quality faculty, but Roosevelt was unimpressed with his Harvard education. He later complained that it had offered him complicated theories but little in the way of practical and useful information. "I took economics courses in college for four years," he later remarked, "and everything I was taught was wrong."

When Roosevelt was a freshman, his father died. James Roosevelt bequeathed to his son an annual income of about $6,000. (In 1900 a male school teacher earned about $500 a year, so $6,000 was indeed a small fortune.) Franklin Roosevelt was charming and handsome, as well as wealthy; in addition, his distant cousin Theodore Roosevelt became president of the United States in 1901. Because of his name and family connections, Roosevelt attended a seemingly endless series of parties on the Boston-Cambridge circuit. That social activities, rather than scholarship, occupied most of his time at Harvard can be seen from a line written to his mother: "Am doing a little studying, a little riding and a few party calls."

Sara Roosevelt inherited Springwood and the rest of James's estate. (She had already inherited more than a million dollars when her father died two years earlier.) In his will, James Roosevelt had stipulated that he wanted Franklin "under the supervision of his mother." Sara immediately assumed this role, renting an apartment in Boston to be near her son—"near enough to the University," she noted in her diary, "to be on hand should he want me and far enough removed not to interfere in his college life."

The presence of Franklin's mother so close to Harvard gained him a reputation as a "mama's boy." And, while many a young lady drawn to this handsome young Harvard man was put off by his domineering mother's influence, Franklin learned how to tactfully handle her. Sometimes he gave parties in his mother's lavishly furnished apartment, but at other times he attempted to remain independent of her presence. However, he spent the summers following his freshman and junior years with her touring Europe, with time left for sailing at Campobello.

The most important event of Franklin's years at Harvard was his engagement to a fifth cousin, Anna Eleanor Roosevelt. Franklin had known Eleanor since she was a child, but their relationship did not blossom into romance until his senior year, 1903–04. Their engagement was announced in November 1904.

At first, Franklin had avoided telling his mother about his growing interest in Eleanor. When he finally announced his intention to marry his cousin, Sara Roosevelt was shocked. She was not pleased at the thought of another woman in her son's life, and tried to cool the relationship by urging the couple to wait before formally committing themselves. In an attempt to have Franklin forget Eleanor, she took him on a Caribbean cruise. And on hearing about a minor diplomatic post available in London, Sara attempted to use her connections to secure the position for Franklin so that he would have to leave the country. In the end, her efforts failed: their wedding took place in New York City on March 17, 1905. Franklin was twenty-three and Eleanor twenty-one. President Theodore Roosevelt, Eleanor's uncle, gave the bride away in a ceremony and reception that was the high point of the New York social scene that year. "Well, Franklin," the president said in his high-pitched voice, "There's nothing like keeping the name in the family."

Franklin and Eleanor delayed their honeymoon so that he could finish his first year at Columbia University Law School. He had failed two courses and had to

Franklin Roosevelt, age twenty-two, in formal portrait for Harvard University, April 1904. The most important event of Roosevelt's years at Harvard was his engagement to his fifth cousin, Anna Eleanor Roosevelt. Franklin had known Eleanor from the time they were children, but their relationship did not blossom into romance until his senior year in 1903. Their engagement was announced in November 1904 and their marriage took place in New York City on March 17, 1905. President Theodore Roosevelt, Eleanor's uncle, gave the bride away. The president was the main attraction at the wedding while the bride and groom were virtually ignored.

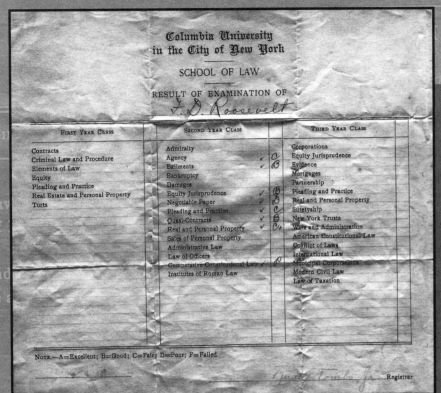

Columbia University
in the City of New York

SCHOOL OF LAW

RESULT OF EXAMINATION OF

F. D. Roosevelt

FIRST YEAR CLASS	SECOND YEAR CLASS		THIRD YEAR CLASS
Contracts	Admiralty		Corporations
Criminal Law and Procedure	Agency	✓ C	Equity Jurisprudence
Elements of Law	Bailments	✓ B	Evidence
Equity	Bankruptcy		Mortgages
Pleading and Practice	Damages		Partnership
Real Estate and Personal Property	Equity Jurisprudence	✓ B	Pleading and Practice
Torts	Negotiable Paper	✓ B	Real and Personal Property
	Pleading and Practice	✓ C	Suretyship
	Quasi-Contracts	✓ B	New York Trusts
	Real and Personal Property	✓ C+	Wills and Administration
	Sales of Personal Property		American Constitutional Law
	Administrative Law		Conflict of Laws
	Law of Officers		International Law
	Comparative Constitutional Law	✓ D	Municipal Corporations
	Institutes of Roman Law		Modern Civil Law
			Law of Taxation

NOTE.—A=Excellent; B=Good; C=Fair; D=Poor; F=Failed

Registrar

Franklin Roosevelt entered Columbia University Law School in the fall of 1904, squeezing class work into a full social calendar with less than happy results. Although the Columbia law faculty was one of the most distinguished in the nation, the professors elicited little response from Roosevelt. In the spring of his third year, he passed the New York State Bar examinations. He did not bother to finish his law school courses. Now twenty-five, he seemed perfectly suited to lead the life of a country squire just as his father had. Franklin and Eleanor had an annual income from trust funds of more than $12,000. (An average factory worker at that time earned about $300 per year.)

Twenty-two years later, in the autumn of 1929, Governor Franklin Roosevelt of New York was invited to address the Columbia Law School alumni dinner. Columbia's President Nicholas Murray Butler sat next to him. At some point during the evening, Butler was heard joking with the governor: "You will never be able to call yourself an intellectual until you come back to Columbia and pass your law exam." Roosevelt laughed and threw back his head. "That just shows how unimportant the law really is," he said.

pass make-up exams for these classes. Then, in June 1905, they took a grand European trip on which their family connection to President Roosevelt led to lavish treatment wherever they went. On their return to New York City, the young couple lived in a small house that had been rented and furnished by Franklin's mother.

Eleanor, however, was often unhappy. For most of her married life she had to live near Franklin's mother, who refused to fade into the background of the couple's life. "For the first year of my married life, my mother-in-law did everything for me," Eleanor later recalled. Franklin and Sara Roosevelt continued to have a warm relationship, and Sara remained a central figure in Franklin's life until her death in 1941. A depressed Eleanor repeatedly confided to her tear-stained diary her fear that Franklin had been attracted to her Uncle Theodore, not to her.

In the spring of 1907, Franklin Roosevelt passed the New York State bar examination and decided not to finish his degree at Columbia. Law school, he concluded, had no relationship to the actual practice of the law. Now twenty-five, he seemed perfectly suited to lead the life of a country squire, just as his father had done. The Roosevelts had an annual income from their trust funds of more than $12,000. (By contrast, a factory worker at that time earned about $300 per year.) Franklin and Eleanor Roosevelt's first child, Anna Eleanor, was born in 1906, followed by James in 1907, Franklin Jr. (who died shortly after his birth in 1909), Elliott in 1910, a second child named Franklin Jr. in 1914, and John in 1916. As Eleanor noted, for the first ten years of her marriage she was "just getting over having a baby or about to have one."

Roosevelt possessed an average legal mind. His looks, winning personality, and family connections soon brought him a law partnership, but the legal profession bored him. Politics, however, lit a fire in Roosevelt. His outgoing personality made him an obvious choice for public office. He served in the New York state legislature and as assistant secretary of the navy in Woodrow Wilson's administration before running for vice president on the Democratic ticket in 1920. After this losing race, his public career seemed to have come to an end when he was stricken with poliomyelitis and lost the use of his legs. But Roosevelt, with the assistance of his wife Eleanor, worked hard to return to politics. In 1928, he was elected governor of New York. Four years later, he was elected president of the United States, even though at the time his views on most national issues were unknown.

Franklin D. Roosevelt was given the best educational opportunities available to any American of his day. But academic subjects never really interested him. As a child he encountered no competition for the love, acceptance, and admiration of everyone that mattered to him. At Groton, and again at Harvard, he had to learn to compete and to succeed. Within his insulated experiences, he learned the skills that enabled him to face the broader world beyond. When he died in 1945, Roosevelt had made enemies who despised him and everything for which he stood, but he had also gained the love and respect of millions of people throughout the world.

—Fred L. Israel

Harry S. Truman
Chapter Thirty-two

Although today he is admired for his honesty, simplicity, and straightforward style, Harry Truman was not the most popular of presidents. He was thrust into the position in 1945 after the death of one of the most beloved presidents of all time, Franklin D. Roosevelt. After four terms in office, Roosevelt was the only president most young Americans had ever known. He proved a tough act to follow. Truman took over near the end of World War II, and was soon faced with the most critical decisions in the nation's history.

Truman was entirely different in background, education, and style from his predecessor. While Roosevelt had been born into wealth and privilege, Truman's life and upbringing were far more typical for Americans of the time. In the early years of the twentieth century, the United States was still a nation of farmers, though farmers and immigrants were moving into large cities in unprecedented numbers. Young Harry grew up on his grandparents' farm in Missouri and, as a young man, worked the farm alongside his father and brother. Truman lived most of his life in Independence, Missouri. It was small-town America, but closely connected to both urban and rural life. Kansas City, ten miles from Independence, was booming and growing into the largest city between St. Louis to the east and San Francisco to the west.

Of all the twentieth-century presidents, Harry Truman had the least amount of formal education. He was the only president elected in the century who did not attend college. Although this lack of education made Truman unusual for a modern day president, it made him quite typical at a time when the majority of Americans his age had not even finished high school. A late bloomer, he did not settle on a career in politics until he was thirty-eight years old. The years between completing his formal schooling and choosing his ultimate career served as a rather long apprenticeship. Numerous work, educational, and social experiences went into preparing him for his presidency.

Harry Truman was born in the small town of Lamar, Missouri, on May 8, 1884. He was the oldest of John and Martha "Mattie" Truman's three children.

Reading history was Truman's passion.

As a boy Harry read avidly. He claimed—doubtless with some exaggeration—to have completed every book in the Independence Public Library—even the encyclopedias—by the time he graduated from high school.

Reading history was Truman's passion. On his twelfth birthday, his mother gave him an impressive four-volume set of books, bound in leather and trimmed in gold, entitled *Great Men and Famous Women: A Series of Pen and Pencil Sketches of the Lives of More than 200 of the Most Prominent Personages in History*. These books were anthologies of essays from Harper's and other leading American and English magazines. The authors included Edward Everett Hale, Thomas Macaulay, and young Theodore Roosevelt; the subjects ranged from Moses to President Grover Cleveland. By the time he was sixteen, Truman had read Jacob Abbott's twenty-two volumes of biographical studies of famous people of the ancient and medieval worlds. "Reading history, to me, was far more than a romantic adventure," wrote Truman. "It was solid instruction and wise teaching which I somehow felt that I wanted and needed."

A postcard shows Independence High School as it appeared at the turn of the century. Harry Truman graduated from Independence High School in 1901, when he was seventeen years old. He enjoyed all of his high-school subjects but did best in history.

When Harry was three years old, the family moved to the farm of Mattie's parents located not far from Kansas City. Truman's earliest memories were of farm work. It was here that his mother taught him how to read. When he had trouble making out the letters in the family Bible, Mattie took him to an eye doctor who fitted him with the thick glasses he wore for the rest of his life. The doctor and his parents warned Truman not to break them, so his opportunities to play rough games and sports were limited. Instead, young Truman spent a great deal of time reading.

The Trumans took an interest in their children's educations. In 1890, the family moved to the nearby town of Independence specifically because its schools were superior to those in the country. In Independence, John Truman operated a livestock business in addition to working a small farm. He was an ambitious man who failed in several business ventures in his efforts to get ahead. A hard-working perfectionist, he expected his children to do the best job possible, whether they were weeding the garden or studying for school. All the Truman children performed regular daily chores. Harry and his brother, Vivian, split the firewood, fed and watered animals, weeded the garden, mowed the lawn, and raked leaves in fall.

Truman's parents enrolled him in Sunday school at the Presbyterian Church. The Trumans were Baptists, but Mattie found the Presbyterian minister to be a most educated man. At church Truman first set eyes on Elizabeth "Bess" Wallace, who would one day become his wife. Class distinctions among white people were determined by religion in Independence, where much of the town's social life revolved around church functions. Presbyterians were the social elite; the Baptists ranked considerably lower. Through Sunday school and his own reading, Truman became familiar with the Bible and was able to quote numerous verses by heart— particularly the Sermon on the Mount: "Ye are the salt of the earth...Let your light so shine before men, that they may see your good works." He claimed he had read the Bible "three times through" by the time he was thirteen years old.

At age eight, Harry began first grade at the Noland School in Independence. He contracted diphtheria during second grade and missed most of the school year when complications developed. He was tutored during the summer to catch up to his classmates and did so well that he skipped third grade. At the Noland School, Harry received excellent grades in spelling, reading, deportment (conduct), arithmetic, language, and handwriting. (Although Harry was originally left-handed, his teachers made him learn to write with his right hand, a common practice at that time.) Years later, his first-grade teacher remembered him fondly, as would most of his teachers. He remembered them fondly as well. Truman took pride in having been a bit of a teacher's pet. He learned early in life that he could succeed by establishing a good rapport with people.

When the Trumans acquired a piano, Harry began to take lessons. At first, his mother, who had studied art and music at a women's college, taught him. He quickly moved on to lessons from his next-door neighbor, and when his ability to learn quickly outstripped her ability to teach, he began taking piano lessons twice a week in Kansas City. Harry showed talent. He loved music, especially the great classical works. He was apparently a favorite with his piano teacher as well. Mrs. Grace White opened a new world for him. Harry practiced at least two hours every day, often beginning at five o'clock in the morning. Mrs. White, a gifted teacher, took him to concerts in Kansas City when outstanding pianists performed. She took him to hear the Polish composer Ignacy Jan Paderewski play the piano at a Kansas City recital. Mrs. White introduced young Harry to him after the concert. At the time, Truman was trying to learn a work composed by Paderewski, his "Minuet in G." To his surprise, the composer sat down at the piano and demonstrated a stanza that was giving Truman trouble. (Years later, Truman entertained Winston Churchill and Josef Stalin with the same piece when they met at Potsdam near the end of World War II.)

Harry Truman took piano lessons in Kansas City for five years, even after he graduated from high school. He gave them up when he could no longer afford them. He recalled many times in later years that he had considered a career as a professional pianist. Although he moved on to other interests, Truman continued to enjoy classical music for the rest of his life.

When Truman was growing up, a high school education was not essential. Jobs were available to boys who finished sixth grade, and many went directly to work after finishing elementary school. Most boys who went on to high school were preparing for college and a professional career. Harry's parents were probably behind Truman's drive to continue his education through high school. Young Harry took on his first paying job during his freshman year. He worked before and after school at Clinton's drug store. After three months, his grades suffered. His father ordered him to quit and concentrate on his school work, making it clear that he thought school was more important.

High school lasted three years and included English, Latin, public speaking (known as rhetoric), logic, mathematics, science, and history. History was always Truman's favorite subject. An enthusiastic reader, he claimed to have read every book in the Independence Public Library by the time he was seventeen. His favorites were always history books, particularly biographies. For his twelfth birthday, his mother presented him with a four-volume set of books called *Great Men and Famous Women*. He was especially interested in military history and military leaders. His favorite book of the set was a volume called *Soldiers and Sailors*. The generals he most admired were Hannibal, Andrew Jackson, and Robert E. Lee. In Latin class, the students read Julius Caesar's account of his military campaigns. Truman and two friends were so inspired by a description of a bridge that Caesar's army built across the Rhine River that they spent days building a wooden model to match it. His favorite writers were Mark Twain and the poet Alfred Lord Tennyson. He continued to carry a copy of Tennyson's *Locksley Hall* in his wallet throughout his presidency. The one subject that always gave Truman trouble was spelling. His spelling difficulties would continue to plague him in his letters as an adult.

Truman also enjoyed Latin and algebra study sessions with his cousins, Nellie and Ethel Noland, and with Bess Wallace, who lived across the street from the Nolands. Cousin Ethel would remember, "I don't know whether they got much Latin read or not because there were a lot of fun going on." In Truman's senior year, he was on the staff of the school's first yearbook, which students voted to name *The Gleam* after Tennyson's romantic poem *Merlin and the Gleam*, which every tenth grader memorized. Truman graduated in 1901 at the age of seventeen. There were twenty-four girls (including Bess Wallace) and eight boys (including Charlie Ross, who later served in the White House as Truman's press secretary) in his graduating class. We do not know his high school grades because the school records were destroyed in a fire. He claimed to have been a good student, and we know that he and his teachers maintained contact for many years. In his memoirs, Truman repeatedly expressed admiration and gratitude to them, most of whom were unmarried women who devoted their lives to teaching. Truman felt he had learned human values from these women, values that surmounted book knowledge. From his teachers and parents, Truman

Harry Truman is in the back row, fourth from left, in this photograph of the Independence High School graduating class of 1901. Bess Wallace, his future wife, is on the far right of the second row. The class valedictorian, Charlie Ross, is seated at the far left of the front row; Ross and Truman would maintain a lifelong friendship.

learned the need for hard work and honesty. He learned to respect honesty, straightforwardness and simplicity, characteristics for which he is admired.

Around the time of Truman's high-school graduation, John Truman's business failed, leaving him with huge debts that affected the family for years to come. If college had been on Harry's horizon, it was no longer a possibility. He became interested in the U.S. Military Academy at West Point, partly because he was fascinated by military history, but mostly because it offered a free college education. His dreams of becoming a great general and attending the alma mater of his hero, Robert E. Lee, were not to be—but this was not for lack of trying. He and a friend, who was interested in an appointment to the Naval Academy at Annapolis, prepared together for the entrance examinations. They studied history and geography with their high school history teacher, Margaret Phelps. The panorama of history, as taught by Miss Phelps, began with Adam and Eve. Truman's efforts came to naught when he failed the eye exam and was told he was ineligible for the academy.

Rather than marching at West Point, Truman enrolled in a course at Spalding's Business College, a business school in Kansas City. He studied bookkeeping, stenography, and typing. Over the next few years, he worked at several entry-level jobs. Kansas City offered abundant choices for culture and leisure, and Truman enjoyed them, particularly concerts and the theater. He was working as a bank clerk when his family moved back to his grandparents' farm. Truman followed and spent the next eleven years as a farmer.

All the while, Truman was ambitious, but his ambitions were ill defined. He wanted to succeed and make something of himself, especially after he began courting Bess Wallace. He did not intend to spend his life as a farmer and tried several business ventures, all of which eventually failed. In his letters to Bess, he joked about a career in politics.

Politics fascinated John Truman, and he openly shared this interest with his oldest son. In 1900, Harry had worked as a page during the Democratic National Convention, which met in Kansas City. There he heard William Jennings Bryan, the populist Democratic presidential nominee who had broad support in farm areas. Bryan became his political hero. Despite his Democratic leaning, Truman also left work to hear Republican President Theodore Roosevelt speak in 1903.

While Harry was working on the farm, John Truman received a politically appointed job as road overseer in their portion of the county. The upkeep and repair of country roads was performed by local men with their horses. For the work, the men received a rebate on their school tax. Almost no one wanted the overseers job. When his father died in 1914, Harry took over this patronage position. Although it involved a great deal of work for little pay, it served Truman well later in his political career when he undertook the improvement of all the county's roads.

Truman led an active social life. He joined numerous organizations, including the Missouri National Guard. When the United States entered World War I in 1917, Harry volunteered for the army. He could have opted out of the war. At thirty-three, he was too old to be drafted. As a farmer, he was exempted from serving because farmers were considered essential at home. Also, his poor eyesight would have exempted him. However, he passed the eye exam and joined, helping first with recruiting efforts before he was sent to training camp. Both in the national guard and in the army, Truman served in the artillery, in which crews positioned and fired mounted cannons.

Military training and service served to further Truman's education. It helped him to see new possibilities within himself. He once said, "a leader is a man who has the ability to get other people to do what they don't want to do, and like it." During World War I, Truman discovered that he had this ability. Army companies elected their own junior officers, and to his surprise Truman found himself elected a first lieutenant. He had expected to serve as an enlisted man, not an officer. After some training in the United States, Truman was shipped off to France ahead of his company to attend artillery school. Most of the other officers at the school were college graduates and found the coursework considerably easier than did Truman. Once his company arrived, he was responsible for its training. He became the soldiers' instructor in surveying, engineering, trigonometry, and logarithms; mathematical calculations were necessary to make certain the large guns were aimed accurately. After the company's training ended, Truman was given command of a notoriously unruly group of men. He quickly established discipline and earned their loyalty and respect.

Between taking command in July 1918 and the Armistice in November 1918, Truman saw a considerable amount of action. He discovered that he could keep his cool while under fire and that other men would follow him. He was soon promoted to captain. The men he led and the loyalty he inspired in them served Truman well later when he had to campaign for votes. He had an extraordinary ability to remember people and until his death he exchanged letters with members of his World War I battery. Eventually his World War I friends became political supporters. Truman remained in the army reserves for many years and took part in training exercises every summer.

By the time the war ended, Truman was 35 years old and had still not really settled on what he wanted to do in life. He married Bess Wallace in 1919 (the Trumans would have one daughter, Mary Margaret). That same year Truman and an army buddy opened a men's clothing store. Because of a business recession, the business failed. Truman refused to declare bankruptcy, however, and spent the next fifteen years paying off his share of the debts.

Truman finally discovered his true calling when he ran for county judge in 1922. After taking office, he realized that he was an effective administrator and that he enjoyed the work. He made one more attempt at a formal education when he

Views of the main square of Independence, Missouri, circa 1909. When he was about thirteen years old, Truman began working at J. H. Clinton's drugstore in the center of town. He worked before and after school; it was his first paying job. "There must have been a thousand bottles to dust and yards and yards of patent-medicine cases and shelves to clean," Truman wrote years later to his daughter, Margaret. Truman recalled:

> I can remember the first $3.00 I received for working a week—seven days from seven o'clock until school time and from four o'clock until ten at night, all day Saturday and Sunday. I had to wipe off bottles, mop the floor every morning, make ice cream for sodas, and wait on customers. . . . That three silver dollars looked like three million and meant a lot more. I bought a present for Mamma and tried to give the rest of it to my dad and he wouldn't take it. It was as I say a great day all around when I got the $3.00.

enrolled in the Kansas City School of Law. It was the only law school in Kansas City, and it offered only night classes taught by local attorneys. In all, Truman took fourteen courses and received good grades. However, he did not continue after his second year, probably due to outside obligations and the pressure of supporting a family. The Kansas City School of Law awarded him an honorary degree in 1945.

Although Truman lacked the intellectual sophistication of an Ivy League education, his life experiences left him with common sense and an ability to work well with people. These qualities served him well when he led the U.S. at a challenging time in its history. During the first months of his presidency he made the decision to drop atomic bombs on Japan, which hastened the end of World War II. Truman also understood the challenges presented by the Cold War with the Soviet Union. He sent American troops to aid South Korea when it was attacked by North Korea in 1950. His 1948 decision to desegregate the armed forces preceded the civil rights movement of the 1950s and 1960s. Truman's middle-class, middle-American background helped him to understand the people he felt it was his duty to serve as president.

—Anne Marie Sullivan

Dwight Eisenhower
Chapter Thirty-three

W hen Dwight Eisenhower was fourteen years old he suffered what he believed was a minor scrape to his knee. That was hardly unusual. Dwight was a skinny but scrappy boy, quick with his fists but just as quick running away from tacklers on the football field or snaring grounders on the baseball diamond. Scraped knees and elbows, swollen lips, bloody noses, black eyes, and similar injuries were all common occurrences in the Eisenhower household. This time, however, the scraped knee proved to be a major problem when it became infected. The year was 1904, and penicillin would not be discovered for another twenty-four years.

The infection caused Dwight to fall into a delirium. A doctor was summoned to the Eisenhower home in Abilene, Kansas. For two weeks, the boy slipped in and out of a coma as the infection spread. Finally, with the infection creeping toward his abdomen, Dwight's physician feared that the boy's life was in danger. To save his life, the doctor decided that the infected leg had to be amputated.

During one of his rare periods of consciousness, Dwight heard his parents discussing the operation. Horrified, Dwight summoned his older brother Edgar to his bedside and made him promise not to let anybody cut off his leg. "Under no circumstances would they amputate my leg," Dwight recalled years later. "I'd rather be dead than crippled, and not be able to play ball." Edgar Eisenhower, who was two years older than Dwight, kept his promise. He slept on the floor of his brother's room, ready to scuffle with any surgeon who approached his brother intending to amputate.

After two more weeks, the infection subsided. Soon, Dwight's health returned, as did his quickness and competitiveness. On two good legs he would become a star athlete at Abilene High School and would later dazzle spectators as a halfback on the football team of the U.S. Military Academy in West Point, New York.

After his playing career was over, Dwight Eisenhower would call on the same determination that helped him endure a life-threatening infection to rise through the ranks of the U.S. Army and, as supreme commander of Allied forces in Europe, lead his troops to victory over Nazi Germany in World War II—an accomplishment that would pave the way to his election as the nation's thirty-fourth president.

Third Street looking East, Abilene, Kansas.

Dwight Eisenhower grew up with a liking for his hometown Abilene that he never lost. Third Street (pictured above in a photo taken about 1909) was Abilene's main street. On one side lived affluent families in stately Victorian homes, while on the other side were the simple wooden houses of working-class families such as the Eisenhowers.

Dwight Eisenhower was an average boy growing up in a small town in Kansas. He had ambition, but it was vague and unfocused.

Dwight is in the front row, second from left, in this 1901 photograph of his fifth-grade class at Lincoln Elementary School. Lincoln, one of two elementary schools in Abilene, lacked electricity and indoor plumbing. Younger students used slates for writing, paper being reserved for the fifth and sixth graders. About two-thirds of Eisenhower's class entered the town's high school.

David Dwight Eisenhower was born October 14, 1890, in Denison, Texas, a town just south of the Oklahoma border, where his parents had moved after his father's business failed. David and Ida Eisenhower had been married in 1885. As a wedding gift, David's father gave the couple one hundred and sixty acres of Kansas wheatland near Abilene, but David had no interest in farming and sold the acreage to buy a general store in the nearby town of Hope. Within two years, the business had collapsed.

By then, the Eisenhowers were the parents of a son, Arthur, and were soon to be parents of a second boy, Edgar. David Eisenhower found work cleaning locomotive engines in Denison. Soon, he summoned his family to join him. They lived in a small rented home—really not much more than a shack—in Denison, not far from the railroad roundhouse. Ida Eisenhower hated Denison and she hated Texas, but she toughed it out and refused to complain. It is likely that Dwight and his brothers inherited their silent determination and toughness of spirit from their mother.

David Dwight was the Eisenhower's third son. Ida Eisenhower named him David, after his father, but she never called him David, insisting that she did not want the boy to be confused with his father. She also abhorred nicknames, believing them undignified, and did not want her son called by the shortened name "Dave." Dwight, she was certain, could never be shortened into a nickname. Soon after his birth, Ida noted her son's name in the family Bible as "Dwight David."

(Much to her chagrin, her son Edgar would become known as "Big Ike" while Dwight was first "Little Ike" and eventually just "Ike," as people learned they could boil all those sounds in the Eisenhower name down to a single, friendly syllable.)

In Denison, the Eisenhowers lived just above the poverty line but Ida Eisenhower was a clever and resourceful woman who was able to feed and clothe her family despite her husband's paltry salary of $10 a week. Finally, David Eisenhower's brother-in-law, the foreman of a creamery in Abilene, offered David a job as a mechanic at the salary of $50 a month. David accepted, and the Eisenhowers returned to Abilene. The pay was not that much better than it was in Denison, but in Abilene the Eisenhowers would be back with family.

When the family returned to Abilene, eight-year-old Dwight was enrolled in Lincoln Elementary School, which was across the street from the family home at 201 South East Fourth Street. Dwight later described himself as a "lackluster" student; this is too modest an assessment, however, as he earned excellent grades throughout his school years. At Lincoln Elementary he enjoyed spelling bees and mathematics contests, regarding them as an outlet for his competitiveness. Later, in high school, Dwight would prove to be so gifted in geometry that he quickly solved every problem in his textbook, forcing his teacher to search elsewhere for problems that would challenge him.

"The introduction of plane geometry was an intellectual adventure, one that entranced me," Dwight Eisenhower later wrote. "After a few months, my teachers conducted an unusual experiment. The principal and my mathematics teacher called me to the office and told me that they were going to take away my textbook. Thereafter, I was to work out the geometric problems without the benefit of the book. In other words, the propositions, as well as the auxiliary problems, would be, for me, originals. This was a fascinating challenge and particularly delightful because it meant that no advance study was required. They said that for the remaining months, unless the experiment was terminated by them, I would automatically receive an A-plus grade."

His real love, though, was reading history. Mostly, he enjoyed books about great battles, particularly those that described the tactics and strategies of the ancient Greek and Roman generals. Later, he would extend his interest in military history to the American Revolution. This interest in military history should not be regarded as the initial sign that Eisenhower was destined for a future as a military leader. Dwight Eisenhower did not entertain the notion of soldiering as a career until he was twenty years old, and only then because a friend told him that the military academies did not charge tuition.

In addition, while he was fascinated by stories of warfare and quickly learned the dates and places of major battles, he was far less interested in the political reasons that prompted great armies to clash. "The battles of Marathon, Zama, Salamis, and Cannae became as familiar to me as the games (and battles) I enjoyed with my brothers and friends in the school yard," Eisenhower wrote years later. "I could never seem to get it into my head that all these things had happened two thousand years earlier—or that possibly I would be better advised to pay at least a little attention to current, rather than ancient affairs. Among all the figures of antiquity, Hannibal was my favorite."

David and Ida Eisenhower did all they could to discourage their son's interest in military science. The Eisenhowers were members of the River Brethren, a fundamentalist Protestant Christian church formed by former Mennonites from Pennsylvania; later, the Eisenhowers joined a congregation of Jehovah's Witnesses. As part of their religious beliefs, the Eisenhowers were pacifists. To cure her son of his interest in the art of war Ida Eisenhower locked his history books in a closet. She hid the key, but Dwight soon discovered its location and, whenever his mother was out of the house, he would unlock the closet and pore though his volumes of military history. "Whenever mother went to town to shop or was out working in her flower garden I would sneak out the books," he admitted in his memoirs.

Both David and Ida Eisenhower were dedicated readers; they filled their home with books, which were relatively rare among families living on the Great Plains. Each evening after dinner, David Eisenhower would gather his large family together and read the Bible. The boys were required to read passages from the Scriptures as well. The boys looked on the after-dinner Bible readings as a chore that had to be endured, and in their later lives none of the Eisenhower brothers would become devoted churchgoers.

The Eisenhowers had a large family. In addition to his older brothers Arthur and Edgar, Dwight had three younger brothers, Roy, Earl, and Milton. (A seventh son, Paul, was born into the Eisenhower family but died before his first birthday.) David Eisenhower was a stern, humorless man who demanded total obedience from his sons. He punished misdeeds severely, usually by a beating with his belt or a hickory switch. But David also believed in education—he had gone to college for a year himself before dropping out to marry and open the general store. One of his most severe beatings was administered to Edgar when David Eisenhower found out the boy was playing hooky from school to work at a part-time job. In later years, none of the boys—all of whom were beaten by their father at one time or another—would suggest that the thrashings were undeserved. "Had it not been for the application of leather, prolonged and unforgettable, my brother might have become an unhappy handyman in Kansas," Dwight explained. As it turned out, Edgar became a successful lawyer and a millionaire.

Dwight attended the seventh and eighth grades at Garfield School in Abilene, then in September 1904 enrolled as a freshman in what passed for Abilene High School—a few rooms on the first floor of city hall. The building also served as a jail and firehouse. (When a fire bell disrupted classes, male students were often drafted to help pull the fire engine through town.) At Abilene High, Dwight and his classmates learned English, history, mathematics, geography, and foreign languages. For the most part, Dwight was an A student.

It was during his freshman year at Abilene High that Dwight suffered the knee infection. The resulting illness forced him to drop out of school for the remainder of the year. When he returned to school in the fall of 1905 to repeat his

Abilene High School's baseball team, 1909. Dwight Eisenhower is in the front row, fourth from left.

Eisenhower had the good fortune to attend high school in a brand-new building with a newly hired faculty. "None of us could complain in our final high-school years about the competence or enthusiasm of our teachers," he recalled.

ABILENE CITY SCHOOLS
HIGH SCHOOL CREDIT SHEET

PUPIL'S NAME: _Dwight Eisenhower_   FILING INITIAL: _E._

STUDY	GRADE 1ST T	GRADE 2ND T	YEAR	TEXT	TEACHER	REMARKS
English 1	88	88	05-06			
Algebra 1	93⁷	93⁷	05-06			
Latin 1	93⁶	93⁶	05-06			
Physical Geog. 1						
Latin Comp	95⁴	95⁴	05-06			
Rhetoricals	86	86	05-06			
English 2	82+	82+	06-07	Johnson Lit	Daisy Martin	Lake Classics
Algebra 2	90-	90-	06	Wentworth	C. H. Brooks	2 yr Last half
Latin 2	85+	85+	06-07	Caesar	Lavonia Donica	Harper & Tolman
Ancient History 2	88+	88+	06-07	Myers	Pauline Sleth	
Geometry 2	97+	97+	07	Phillips Fisher	C. H. Brooks	First half
German 1	93⁷	93⁷	05-06	Cont in Otis		
English 3	I	II	07-08	Quackenbos	E. Dickinson	Classics
Geometry 3	I+	I	07-08	Phillips Fisher	M. Everette	
Latin 3	II	II	07-08	Cicero	L. Donica	
German 2						
Botany 1						
Eng Hist		I+	07-08	Higginson Channing	P. Williams	
Civics		II	07-08			
English 4	II+	II+	'08-'09	Quackenbos	Lucy Dickinson	Johnson Simonds Classics
Latin 4						
German 3						
Physics 1	I	I+	08-09	C and C	C. H. Kesler	
American History 1	II+	II+	08-09			
Chemistry 1						
Econ	II+	I	08-09		J. H. R. Field	

I hereby certify that the above is a true copy of the records in Abilene High School.

Date _____   Principal _____

In 1904, Abilene High School consisted of five teachers and the principal, who also taught. The school was on the second floor of the city hall; the city jail and the town fire department were on the first floor. One room of the school served as a chapel, and teachers took turns conducting the daily devotional. In 1905, during Eisenhower's sophomore year, the school moved into a new building.

Several of the textbooks Eisenhower used as a student have survived. Interestingly, he scrawled in the margins his evaluation of his teachers: "good," "cross," one was scorned with "nothing." History, both ancient and modern, was Eisenhower's favorite subject. He idolized George Washington and he was fascinated by accounts of the Revolutionary battles of Trenton and Princeton, and by the encampment at Valley Forge.

Pictured above is Dwight Eisenhower's Abilene High School transcript.

freshman year, he started classes in a new red-brick building the community had erected to house the high school.

During the late 1860s, the dozen log huts that made up Abilene briefly became a boomtown at the junction of the Chisholm Trail and the Kansas-Pacific Railroad. Herds of Texas steers were driven to the stockyards there for transit to Chicago and the East. Education was not of primary interest to most residents. Some of the citizens of Abilene wondered why the town needed a high school in the first place. High school was still regarded as a luxury in the rural farm community; most boys dropped out of school following their elementary-school years to work in the fields or learn a trade. Jobs at the creamery were also plentiful. But all of the Eisenhower boys went to high school, even though if they had gotten jobs their wages would have helped out at home. When Dwight arrived for classes in the fall of 1905 there were thirty-four students enrolled at Abilene High School, twenty-five of them girls.

Somehow, the school managed to field baseball and football teams. Sports had long been Dwight's passion. The money he earned at odd jobs or by selling home-grown vegetables door-to-door was spent on sports equipment. As a high-school sophomore Dwight weighed one hundred and fifty pounds—small by football standards. He was a fierce competitor, though, and a leader on the team. In 1906, Dwight's first year on the football team, Abilene High School won all seven games it played by lopsided scores.

Dwight insisted on fair play and a strict adherence to the rules: no piling on after a tackle, no cheap shots at the other players. When Dwight caught one of his teammates violating the rules, his face would flush with anger and he would loudly and publicly dress down the other player. One time, when Abilene faced a team with an African-American player in the line, none of his teammates would play center—the position responsible for blocking the black student. Dwight, who never played center, volunteered for the assignment and spent the entire afternoon overmatched by the larger lineman. Nevertheless, at the end of the game Dwight shook hands with the fellow. "Rest of the team was a bit ashamed," he wrote later.

The Abilene team played much better than it looked. The team had just two footballs—one for practice, the other for games—and the school had no money for uniforms or equipment. The players provided their own uniforms: old sweaters as jerseys, saddle pads that were cut down and converted into shoulder pads, and stocking caps for helmets.

Dwight organized and became first president of the Abilene High School Athletic Association, which took on the responsibility of raising money for uniforms and sports equipment. The association also arranged travel to away games—usually, Dwight talked a friendly trainman into letting the team members ride in a freight car. The association was also responsible for finding opponents, which became something of a challenge due to Abilene's fierce reputation on the field. In Dwight's junior year, he could find only four opponents willing to face Abilene.

Dwight graduated from Abilene High School in May 1909. His brother Edgar was also a member of that graduating class, having dropped out of school for a time to work. The school yearbook, *The Helianthus*, identified Dwight as "Best Historian and Mathematician." Edgar was the real star of the class, though. The other students voted him most likely to be elected president of the United States.

The commencement speaker was Henry J. Allen, editor of the *Witchita Beacon* and a future Kansas governor and U.S. senator. Allen told the graduates, "I would sooner begin life over again with one arm cut off than attempt to struggle without a college education." His speech made a deep impression on Dwight.

Edgar and Dwight both wanted to go to college, but there was no money to pay the tuition. Edgar wanted to attend the University of Michigan, where he intended to study law. Michigan would have been fine with Dwight as well; in fact, any college with a football team would have suited him. Finally, the two boys came up with a plan. Dwight would work for a year, and his wages would help pay for Edgar's first year of school. In the second year, Edgar would drop out and take a job, which would help pay Dwight's college tuition for the first year. That fall, Edgar left for Michigan while Dwight found a job in the ice house at the creamery.

Dwight Eisenhower's year of labor stretched into two when his brother talked him into staying home for another year. During that time he earned a promotion to second engineer in the ice house, a position that required him to work from 6 P.M. to 6 A.M. He often had little work to do, which provided an opportunity to invite in friends from time to time for a few hands of poker—a game he loved and played meticulously, using his talent as a mathematician to constantly figure the odds. (Well into his White House years, the president steadfastly refused to draw to an inside straight.)

One of the friends who often came by the ice house was Everett Hazlett, son of an Abilene physician. Hazlett had received a congressional appointment to the U.S. Naval Academy in Annapolis, Maryland, but had flunked the entrance examination. While Eisenhower was working, Hazlett was spending a year studying to retake the test. It was Hazlett who first told Eisenhower that he could go to a military academy for free, an idea that intrigued Eisenhower. Hazlett urged him to write to Kansas's senators and ask for an appointment to Annapolis.

Eisenhower received a reply from Senator Joseph Bristow, who said that he awarded appointments to the academies to the boys who placed highest on a test. Eisenhower was one of eight candidates who showed up in Topeka on October 4, 1910, to take the test. He finished with the second-best score, hurt by surprisingly low marks on the history questions. Senator Bristow's examination had focused more on the reasons great battles were fought than on who had led the armies.

In any event, the senator could make two appointments. The young man with the highest score was given first choice; he selected Annapolis. Eisenhower was offered a place at the U.S. Military Academy at West Point. He was disappointed, as he had hoped to accompany his friend Hazlett to the Naval Academy.

June 9th 1911

En route to West Point, twenty-year-old Dwight Eisenhower stopped in Chicago to visit his high school friend Ruby Norman. She took this snapshot June 9, 1911, on South Michigan Avenue.

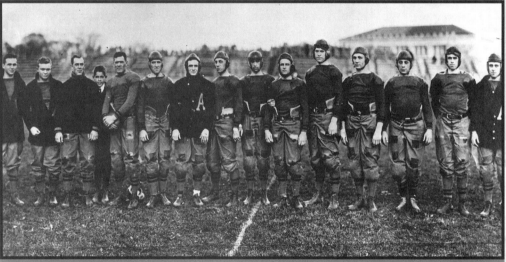

These two photographs show the West Point football team in 1912. In the top photo, Eisenhower is in the middle row, third from left. Omar Bradley, who also gained fame as a general during World War II, is in the back row, fourth from left. In the bottom picture, Eisenhower is second from left and Bradley is second from right.

Eisenhower considered appealing to Bristow, but in the end he accepted West Point. It was hard to pass up free tuition.

First, though, he had to pass West Point's entrance examination. Eisenhower had not been to school in two years, so he re-enrolled in Abilene High School to refresh his memory in chemistry, physics, and mathematics. He breezed through the Abilene courses, easily passed the West Point examination, and in June 1911 boarded a train for a long ride east.

Before leaving he did, of course, have to tell his pacifist parents that he was off to join the U.S. Army. "The only person truly disappointed was mother," he wrote. "She believed in the philosophy of turn the other cheek. She was the most honest and sincere pacifist I ever knew, yet at the same time she was courageous, sturdy, and self-reliant. It was difficult for her to consider approving the decision of one of her boys to embark upon military life."

Eisenhower arrived in West Point a twenty-year-old plebe, two or three years older than most of his classmates. On campus, he encountered a life most unlike that which he had known on the Kansas plains. Eisenhower had learned discipline and to obey his elders, but even the threat of a thrashing from his father did not compare to the intimidation he faced at the academy. Drill instructors, upperclassmen, and teachers were constantly barking orders at Eisenhower and the other plebes. Hazing was a way of life at West Point. Plebes were forced to stand in uncomfortable and exaggerated postures of attention, eat their meals with their feet raised off the floor, do countless push-ups, and perform ridiculous tasks, like collecting ants from an anthill. Eisenhower endured all with a steely resolve to succeed, but others were far less successful. His first roommate dropped out after a short time. (When Eisenhower became an upperclassman, he refused to haze the younger students.)

Eisenhower had been one of the best students at Abilene High School, but making good grades at West Point was much more difficult. During his four years at West Point his classroom performance was good but not great. He graduated sixty-first out of a class of one hundred and sixty-four.

West Point did have a football team, and Eisenhower made the squad on the first day of practice. By now, his skinny frame had filled out with muscle. Before the first game that fall, Army's star halfback, Geoffrey Keyes, sustained an injury. The coach played Eisenhower at halfback, and he responded by leading the team to two straight victories. His accomplishments on the gridiron were even written up in the *New York Times*.

Eisenhower's career in intercollegiate athletics would last only two seasons. In November 1912, shortly before the all-important game against Navy, he injured his knee during cavalry practice, tearing the cartilage and tendons. Eisenhower's football career was over, and the injury nearly ended his army career as well. Although the knee healed, army doctors refused to allow him to join the cavalry, which in those days was the most glamorous branch of the service. Instead, the doctors recommended Eisenhower for a career as an artillery officer, which would have required him to do little more than oversee large guns positioned at strategic defensive points on the coasts. Rather than accept that duty, Eisenhower decided to resign. He changed his mind when he was approved for infantry service.

He graduated from West Point in June 1915 and was commissioned as a second lieutenant. Eisenhower's rise through the ranks was steady and he would find himself serving under some of the army's greatest generals—John J. Pershing, Douglas MacArthur, and George C. Marshall among others. Eisenhower was promoted to brigadier general shortly before the Japanese attack on Pearl Harbor in December 1941, and was soon placed in command of Allied forces in the European theater of the war. He was in charge of the 1942 North Africa campaign, and as supreme Allied commander oversaw the D-Day invasion of France in June 1944. This invasion contributed greatly to the liberation of Europe and ultimate defeat of Nazi Germany. By the end of the Second World War, Eisenhower was perhaps the most popular U.S. hero.

Dwight Eisenhower, formal West Point cadet portrait, 1915.

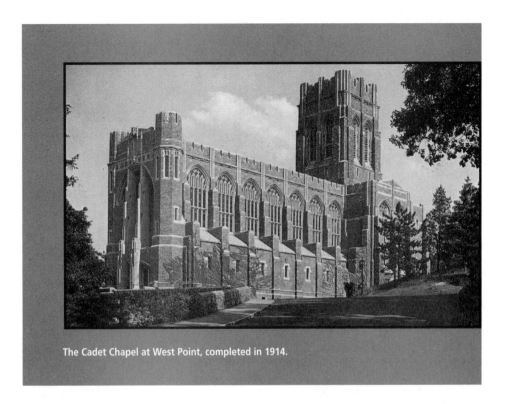

The Cadet Chapel at West Point, completed in 1914.

After the war, Eisenhower accepted the presidency of Columbia University in New York, then returned to the military to serve as commander of the multinational forces under the newly formed North Atlantic Treaty Organization. In 1952, the Republican Party convinced him to run for president. Eisenhower easily won election, and was reelected four years later. During his two terms as president, he forced the communist Chinese to accept terms ending the Korean War by threatening the use of nuclear weapons. At home, he launched the U.S. space program and sent troops to Little Rock, Arkansas, to enforce a federal court ruling that ordered the desegregation of schools. When his term ended in January 1961, Dwight Eisenhower and his wife Mamie retired to their farm in Gettysburg, Pennsylvania.

In March 1968, Eisenhower suffered his fourth heart attack in thirteen years. He would spend the last year of his life in Walter Reed Army Hospital in Washington, D.C. A few weeks before he died, Eisenhower was visited by General Vernon Walters, a long-time friend. Eisenhower told Walters that he did not expect to leave the hospital alive, but that he was satisfied with the way his life had turned out. "How can I complain when all the daydreams of my youth have been fulfilled?" he said. Dwight D. Eisenhower died on March 28, 1969.

—Hal Marcovitz

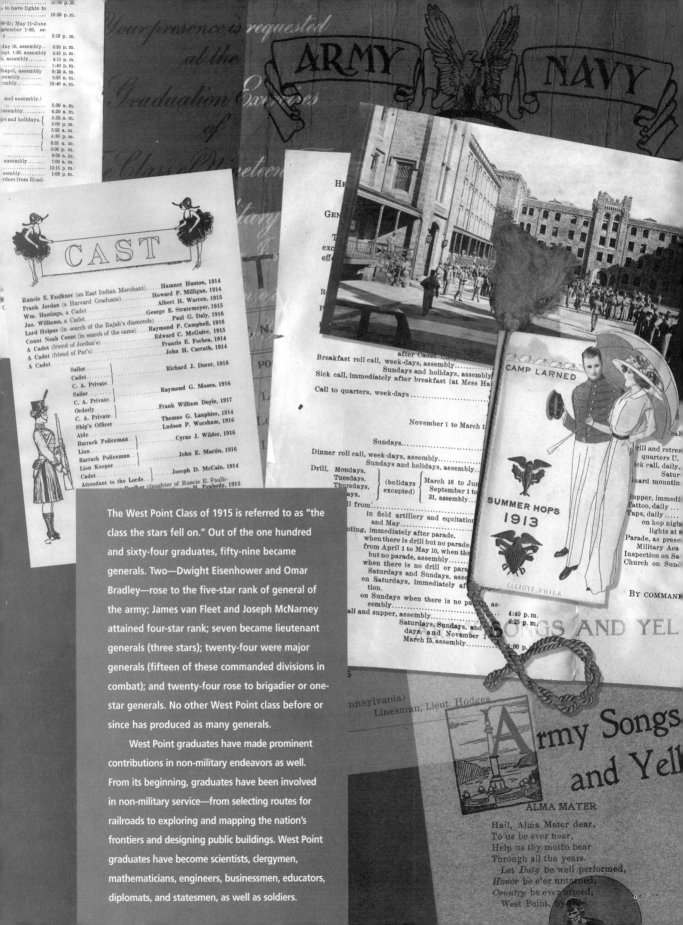

The West Point Class of 1915 is referred to as "the class the stars fell on." Out of the one hundred and sixty-four graduates, fifty-nine became generals. Two—Dwight Eisenhower and Omar Bradley—rose to the five-star rank of general of the army; James van Fleet and Joseph McNarney attained four-star rank; seven became lieutenant generals (three stars); twenty-four were major generals (fifteen of these commanded divisions in combat); and twenty-four rose to brigadier or one-star generals. No other West Point class before or since has produced as many generals.

West Point graduates have made prominent contributions in non-military endeavors as well. From its beginning, graduates have been involved in non-military service—from selecting routes for railroads to exploring and mapping the nation's frontiers and designing public buildings. West Point graduates have become scientists, clergymen, mathematicians, engineers, businessmen, educators, diplomats, and statesmen, as well as soldiers.

John F. Kennedy
C h a p t e r   T h i r t y - f o u r

Like so many public figures in his lifetime—Joseph P. Kennedy, Harry Truman, Lyndon B. Johnson, to mention just a few—John F. Kennedy had a profound regard for the importance of education in an individual's life and, collectively, in the life of the nation.

Kennedy saw trained intelligence, particularly an understanding of history and the analytical skepticism it encouraged, as essential ingredients of a democracy. He greatly admired Thomas Jefferson, whom he saw as possibly the country's smartest and most cerebral president. Kennedy once told a group of Nobel laureates they were the greatest collection of brains ever assembled at the White House—with the exception of when Thomas Jefferson dined there alone. Kennedy also liked to quote Jefferson's observation that, "if a nation expects to be ignorant and free, in a state of civilization, it expects what never was and never will be." In a 7,500-word message to Congress in 1963, Kennedy described education as "the keystone in the arch of freedom and progress." He believed that federal monies could improve the "quality of instruction" and reduce "alarming" drop-out rates. Federal dollars were also needed to help colleges meet a projected 100 percent increase in enrollments by 1970 and a 50 percent rise in students attending secondary schools.

Kennedy saw ideas as a powerful influence on history and as essential to successful leadership. "The men who create power make an indispensable contribution to the nation's greatness," he said in a speech honoring the poet Robert Frost at Amherst in October 1963, "but the men who question power make a contribution just as indispensable, especially when that questioning is disinterested, for they determine whether we use power or power uses us."

Kennedy himself was a published author. His first book, *Why England Slept*, a revised version of his 1940 Harvard honors thesis, probed questions about how England had allowed itself to become vulnerable to Nazi Germany by neglecting its national defense. His second book, *Profiles in Courage*, published in 1956, celebrated American politicians who risked their careers by opposing majority sentiment. The

Kennedy John

RIVERDALE COUNTRY SCHOOL

Upper School Scholarship Report

Form_____

Physiology

Physics

RIVERDALE COUNTRY SCHOOL

Kennedy John

Upper School Scholarship Report

Form _IA_ for period ending _Feb 25_, 19_30_

SUBJECTS:

Chemistry		
Civics		
Drawing		
English		C 3
French		D 3
General Science		
Geography		A 1
German		
Greek		
History		
Latin		
Manual Training		
Mathematics		B+2
Music		
Penmanship	B 2	
Physiology		
Physics		

Average ____ C+

Absence ___2___ Demerits _____

Creditable, Jack 75th

Head Master.

Now for Honors

(over)

SYSTEM OF MARKING

Letters stand for achievement, and **may** be interpreted as follows:

A	high honors
B+	honors
B	good
C+	fair
C	minimum passing
D	failure
F	bad failure

Numbers represent the master's estimate of the boy's effort, and may be interpreted as follows:

1	exceptional effort
2	commendable effort
3	fair effort
4	indifferent effort
5	exceptionally poor effort

Reports are issued three times per term.

John Kennedy attended the Riverdale Country School in Riverdale, New York, from 1928 to 1930. On this report card, dated February 25, 1930, the encouraging headmaster noted, "Creditable, Jack. Now for Honors." According to the system of marking, Kennedy, nearing his thirteenth birthday, was a fair student who showed only moderate effort in his schoolwork.

book won a Pulitzer Prize and gave Kennedy standing as an uncommonly thoughtful senator worthy of consideration for the presidency.

Kennedy's regard for ideas grew out of at least three influences—his family setting, his childhood and adult struggles with health problems, and his exposure to teachers and fellow students at some of America's most distinguished educational institutions.

His mother and father were warm advocates of reading and exchange of ideas that introduced the young John Kennedy to the pleasure of books and the stimulation of debating ideas. Rose Kennedy encouraged a respect for book learning that registered forcefully on her nine children. Joe Kennedy's influence was even more decisive in encouraging his offspring to think for themselves. Family meals were occasions for discussions that kept his children abreast of current events and challenged them to argue against accepted truths. Sending his two eldest sons, Joseph Jr. and John, to study in England with Harold Laski is a case in point. When Joe Jr. graduated from Choate in 1933, his father decided that some exposure to Laski, a prominent socialist academic at the London School of Economics, would be a valuable experience. Rose considered this "a little wild and even dangerous," but Joe, convinced it would encourage greater independence and sharpen his son's ability to argue the case for a more conservative outlook, ignored his wife's concern. And when Joe Jr. returned after a summer trip to Russia with Laski and described the advantages of socialism over capitalism, Joe told Rose, "If I were [Joe and Jack's] age[s] I would probably believe what they believe, but I am of a different background and must voice my beliefs." Joe Sr. made it clear that he cared much less about their different outlooks than that they had reached independent judgments.

Jack's medical ills also made him more thoughtful and respectful of ideas. Considerable amounts of time in bed recovering from childhood maladies and subsequent chronic intestinal and back problems helped him develop lifelong reading habits that served him during his political career. More important, a variety of possibly life-threatening and painful ailments—spastic colitis, Addison's disease, the malfunctioning of his adrenal glands, unrelenting back difficulties, and chronic prostate infections (prostatitis)—moved Kennedy to be more reflective than he might otherwise have been about human nature and the human condition. It made him fatalistic but also intensified his determination to live life to the fullest. As a result of this, he refused to be intimidated by accepted wisdom and was open to unconventional ideas.

Kennedy's formal education reinforced and intensified his attraction to the proposition that a trained mind ensured a richer, more productive life. This was not evident at the start of his schooling. After attending the local Edward Devotion public school in Brookline, Massachusetts, for two years, when Jack was seven he and nine-year-old Joe Jr. were sent to a local private school, Dexter. There, unlike at Devotion, which had shorter hours, they could be supervised from 8:15 A.M. until

4:45 P.M. This schedule freed Rose Kennedy to give more attention to her daughter Rosemary, who was mentally retarded and required home tutoring. Rose also saw Dexter as a guard against the mischief—the "state of quixotic disgrace," she called it—for which Joe Jr. and Jack had an affinity. To their father, Dexter, an elite institution, would bring his sons together with their Beacon Hill counterparts, the offspring of social register families like the Storrows, Saltonstalls, and Bundys.

In September 1927, after the Kennedy family moved to Riverdale, New York, Jack began attending the private Riverdale Country Day School, where he excelled in his studies in the fourth and fifth grades. In the sixth grade, however, when Joe Jr. went to the Choate boarding school in Wallingford, Connecticut, Jack's work suffered, falling to a "creditable" 75, a report of February 1930 stated. Despite his undistinguished school record—or possibly because of it—Joe and Rose decided to send Jack to private boarding school as well. But instead of Choate, Rose enrolled Jack in the Canterbury School in New Milford, Connecticut. This was an exclusive Catholic academy run by a priest and staffed by fourteen teachers for ninety-two students. Of the twenty-one students in the school's 1930 graduating class who continued on to college, seven went to Yale, seven went to Princeton, and one went to Harvard.

Although attending a boarding school marked Jack Kennedy as a privileged child, he did not appreciate being sent so far away from home. He was homesick and struggled to make a creditable record. English, math, and history were fine, but he felt a little overwhelmed by science and Latin; poor grades in these subjects drove his average down to 77. "In fact, his average should be well in the 80s," the headmaster recorded. In a letter to his mother, Jack admitted he was "doing a little worrying about my studies, because what [the headmaster] said about me starting of[f] great and then going down sunk in."

In the fall of 1930, when he was thirteen, Jack was more interested in current events and sports than any of his studies. Football, basketball, hockey, squash, skating, and sledding were his first priorities, but feeling closed off in the cloistered world of a Catholic academy made him increasingly eager to keep up with the state of the world. He wrote to his father from Canterbury, "Please send me the Litary [sic] Digest, because I did not know about the Market Slump until a long time after, or a paper. Please send me some golf balls." A missionary's talk one morning at mass about India impressed Jack as "one of the most interesting talks that I ever heard." It was all an early manifestation of what his later associate Theodore C. Sorensen described as "a desire to enjoy the world and a desire to improve it; and these two desires, particularly in the years preceding 1953, had sometimes been in conflict." In 1930, however, pleasure seeking clearly stood first.

After a year at Canterbury School, Jack was not keen to return, but wished instead to follow Joe Jr. to Choate. Joe Sr. acquiesced to his son's request, and in September 1931 Jack joined his older brother at the storied New England academy. Choate was not quite on a par with the older, more elite, prep schools of Andover,

CANTERBURY SCHOOL

NEW MILFORD, CONNECTICUT

Record of John Kennedy, Form II

From November 1 to December 6, 1930.

Any average from 90% to 100% is accounted "Very Good"; from 80% to 90% "Good"; from 70% to 80% "Fair"; from 60% to 70% "Poor"; and below 60% "Unsatisfactory".

SUBJECT	DAILY WORK	EFFORT AND APPLICATION	FORM AVERAGE
English II	86	Good	71.69
Latin II	55	Poor	64.35
History II	77	Good	67.00
Mathematics II	95	Good	61.69
Science II	72	Good	66.62
Religion II	75	Fair	78.46
AVERAGE: 77.00			

This report is not quite so good as the last one. The damage was done chiefly by "Poor" effort in Latin, in which Jack got a mark of 55. He can do better than this. In fact, his average should be well in the 80's.

N.H.

Rose and Joseph Kennedy decided to send their son Jack to a boarding school. He was enrolled in the Canterbury School in New Milford, Connecticut, an exclusive Catholic academy run by a Catholic priest and staffed by fourteen Catholic teachers for ninety-two students. Of the twenty-one students in the school's 1930 graduating class going to college, seven went to Yale, seven to Princeton, and one to Harvard.

His fair academic work at Canterbury corresponded with an undiagnosed illness that restricted Kennedy's activities. Between October and December 1930, he lost nearly six pounds. In May 1931, Kennedy left school with appendicitis and did not return. He completed his year's work with the help of a tutor at home.

Exeter, St. Mark's, or St. Paul's, but it was distinctive enough—part of a wave of boys' boarding schools that had been founded in the 1880s and 1890s.

Within sharp bounds, Jack rebelled against school and, indirectly, parental authority at Choate. His schoolwork continued to be uneven—strong in English and history, subjects in which he had substantial interest, and mediocre at best in languages, which required the sort of routine discipline that he found difficult to maintain. His low grades in Latin and French compelled him to attend summer session in 1932, at the end of his freshman year. Rose later remarked on how concerned they were about Jack's health during his Choate years. But "what concerned us as much or more, was his lack of diligence in his studies; or, let us say,

Kennedy's classmates and teachers remembered him as a charming, irreverent young man with a sense of humor and a passion for sports and the good life.

School _____ Choate _____

Quarter of Class and School Rank ___ 65/110 ___

Plan of Admission ___ N ___
(O–Old Plan, N–New Plan, H–Honor Plan)

Weighted Admission Record ___ 68 ___

Scholastic Aptitude Test ___ B C ___

FRESHMAN ADVISER'S REPORT.

Name of Freshman: John F. Kennedy

Student's choice of a field of concentration:

First Choice ___ Government ___
Second Choice ___ History & Literature ___

Are there any reasons for his first choice which seem to you to establish for him a special claim?

He is planning to do work in Government. He has already spent time abroad studying it. His father is in that work.

So far as you can judge, do his course grades at mid-years give a fair picture of his intellectual powers?

He will probably do better on the whole.

Information about his interests or personal traits which you think might be helpful to those responsible for assignment to a field of concentration, to a House, or to a Tutor. Have you any suggestions as to type of Tutor?

He would like to live with his brother in Winthrop. Well oriented, normal.

Any additional comments may be written on the reverse side of this sheet.

Date 3/19 ___ Signature of Adviser ___ E.P. Little ___

Please return by March 13th to Chairman of the Board of Advisers, 9 University Hall.

John Kennedy attended Harvard College from 1936 to 1940. During his first two years, his academic record was unimpressive. Pictured above is his freshman "adviser's report," dated March 19, 1937.

Kennedy's classmates and teachers remembered him as a charming, irreverent young man with a sense of humor and a passion for sports and the good life. While the university policy stressed the importance of merit, social snobbery still dominated undergraduate life.

John Kennedy's Harvard "tutorial record" from 1937–38. Kennedy's tutor noted that he was ill during a good deal of the year. Nevertheless, the tutor predicted, while Kennedy would "never be very original, he has ability, I think, and gives promise of development."

TUTORIAL RECORD—19_37_–_38_

Class 40   Name John F. Kennedy   House Winthrop   Concentration Govt   Plan

Special Field

Correlation Field

READING AND ESSAYS

Ford – Dictatorship in the Modern World
Hoover – Germany Enters Third Reich
Mussolini – Autobiography
Seldes – Sawdust Caesar
Finer – Mussolini's Italy
Marx – Communist Manifesto
Lenin – State and Revolution
Armstrong – We or They
Beard – Economic Basis of Politics
Lindsay – Essentials of Democracy
   Essay on These three books
Arnold – Folklore of Capitalism

COMMENTS

Kennedy was ill during part of the year, and did no very large quota of tutorial work. Though his mind is still undisciplined, and will probably never be very original, he has ability, I think, and gives promise of development.
Plan A recommended

Date   Tutor   1

lack of 'fight' in trying to do well in those subjects that didn't happen to interest him.…Choate had a highly 'structured' set of rules, traditions, and expectations into which a boy was supposed to fit; and if he didn't, there was little or no 'permissiveness.' Joe Jr. had no trouble at all operating within this system; it suited his temperament. But Jack couldn't or wouldn't conform. He did pretty much what he wanted, rather than what the school wanted of him."

During his years at Choate, Jack remained more interested in contemporary affairs than his classes. But although he "conspicuously failed to open his schoolbooks," Choate's headmaster recalled, he "was the best informed boy of his year." One classmate remembers that Jack was able to answer between 50 and 60 percent of the questions on the popular radio quiz show *Information Please*, while the classmate could only get about 10 percent of them right. Jack's academic work was good enough in his junior and senior years to allow him to graduate in the middle of his class and gain admission to Princeton, which he attended briefly before transferring to Harvard in the fall of 1936.

During his first two years at Harvard, Jack largely continued the pattern he had established at Choate. His academic record was unimpressive: a B-minus in Government the first year and a B in English the second were offset by grades of C and C-plus in French, History, and a second Government course, his major interest.

Jack's Harvard classmates and teachers remember a charming, irreverent young man with a fine sense of humor and a passion for sports and the good life. He certainly showed no overt interest in the campus activism provoked by the Depression, FDR's New Deal, and the challenges to democracy and capitalism from fascism, Nazism, and communism. There is no indication that he read any of the

This is a handwritten page from John Kennedy's December 14, 1939, class notes for Government 18, "New Factors in International Relations: Europe." Kennedy was then in his junior year at Harvard. The course instructor would become Kennedy's senior thesis advisor.

popular progressive journals of the day—the *Nation*, *New Republic*, or *New Masses*—or gave much, if any, heed to the parades and protest demonstrations organized by students eager to have a say in public affairs. He had little use for doctrinaire advocates who "espoused their causes with a certitude which he could never quite understand."

His focus remained on the extracurricular and social activities he found more enjoyable, and stamped him out as one of the many students at Harvard more interested in earning the social standing attendance and graduation provided than the book learning needed to advance a career. Although James Bryant Conant, who became Harvard's president in 1933, stressed the importance of "meritocracy"—a university focused more on the intellect and character of its students than their social origins—social snobbery continued to dominate the undergraduate life of the university. Jack's first two years on campus were a reflection of these mores. Football, swimming, golf, and service on the Smoker and Annual Show committees occupied his freshman year, while junior varsity football and swimming, the Spee and Yacht clubs, and service on the business board of the *Harvard Crimson* filled his second year.

During these two years, however, Jack gave indications that he had more than a passing interest in public issues. His academic work began to demonstrate a substantial engagement with political leadership and how influential men changed the world. He read several books on recent international and political history, and more revealing, he wrote papers on King Francis I of France and Enlightenment philosopher Jean-Jacques Rousseau. His essays focused on the uses of political and intellectual power to alter human relations.

Nothing may have contributed to Jack's affinity for politics more than his repeated trips to Europe between 1937 and 1939, especially after his father became ambassador to Britain in 1938. The excursions became as much an opportunity for Jack to school himself about European power politics as about the traditional historical sites tourists visited in Western and Eastern Europe. The trips sparked Jack's interest in writing about the origins of Britain's appeasement policy and the coming of World War II. Jack's compelling central argument was one originally made by Alexis de Tocqueville over a hundred years before: popular rule does not readily lend itself to the making of effective foreign policy. Democracies, Jack asserted, have a more difficult time than dictatorships in mobilizing resources for their defense. Only when a pervasive fear of losing national survival took hold could a democracy like Britain or the United States persuade its citizens to "give up their personal interests, for the greater purpose."

Jack's thesis and later book marked the beginning of his entrance into politics. Some biographers have seen Jack's decision to run for Congress in 1946 as the result of his older brother's death in World War II and Joe Sr.'s pressure on Jack to replace his brother, who intended to run for high office. But Jack's interest in politics was more the product of his Harvard education and travels than of his

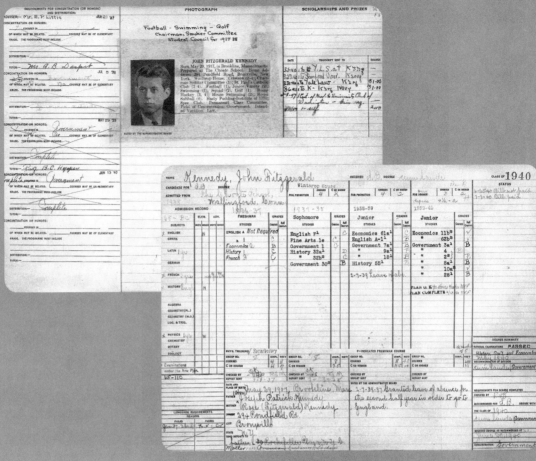

John Kennedy graduated from Harvard College in June 1940, *cum laude*, with a major in history and government. These pages are his Harvard transcript.

JOHN FITZGERALD KENNEDY	S.B. cum Laude June 20, 1940	Field of Concentration Government
Name of course	Description	Instructor

1936-37:

English 1	History and Development of English Literature in Outline	Professor Munn
Economics A	Principles of Economics	Professor Burbank
History 1	European History from the Fall of the Roman Empire to the Present Time	Professor Merriman
French F	Introduction to France	Professor Morize

1937-38:

English F^1	Public Speaking	Asst. Professor Packard
Fine Arts 1e	Interpretation of Selected Works of Art: an Introduction to Art History	Professor Koehler
Government 1	Modern Government	Professors Holcombe and Elliott
History 32a^1	Continental Europe; 1815-1871	Professor Langer
History 32b^2	Continental Europe; 1871-1914	Professor Langer
Government 30^a	New Factors in International Relations: Asia	Asst. Professor Hopper

1938-39 Fall Term:

Economics 61a^1	The Corporation and its Regulation	Professor Mason
English A-1^1	English Composition	Messrs. Davis, Gordan, Bailey and McCreary
Government 7a^1	The National Government of the United States: Politics	Professor Holcombe
Government 9a^1	State Government in the United States	Professor Hanford
Government 18^1	New Factors in International Relations: Europe	Associate Professor Hopper
History 55^1	History of Russia	Asst. Professor Karpovich

1939-40:

Economics 11b^a	Economics of Socialism	Dr. P. M. Sweezy
Economics 62b^a	Industrial Organization and Control	Professor Mason
Government 3a^1	Principles of Politics	Professor Elliott
Government 4	Elements of International Law	Associate Professor P. S. Wild
Government 2^1	Theses for Honors	Members of the Department
Government 8a^1	Comparative Politics: Bureaucracy, Constitutional Government and Dictatorship	Professor Friedrich
Government 10a^a	Government of the British Commonwealth of Nations	Professor Elliott
Government 26^1	Modern Imperialism	Associate Professor Emerson

^{1} Indicates 1st half year course; ^{a} Indicates 2nd half year course.

John Kennedy spent the summer of 1939 traveling in Europe, ostensibly researching his senior thesis. His father, Joseph P. Kennedy, was Franklin D. Roosevelt's ambassador to Great Britain, so young Kennedy had access to an array of prominent people. Kennedy thought that the outbreak of war on September 1, 1939, would delay his Harvard senior year. In this September 13, 1939, letter to the college registrar, Kennedy, now twenty-two, explained that his father had sent him to Glasgow to assist the more than two hundred American citizens rescued by a British destroyer after a British liner carrying 1,400 passengers from Liverpool to New York had been sunk by a German submarine. The embassy staff had been so rushed because of the war that no regular member could be spared. This was Kennedy's first experience in hands-on diplomacy.

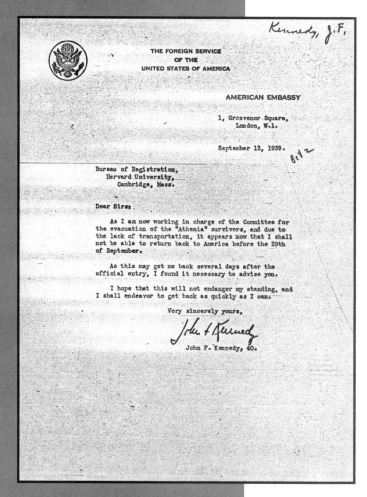

brother's demise and his father's insistence on a public career. Part of the message Jack took away from Choate and Harvard was that much was expected of those to whom much had been given. Jack saw his entrance into politics as a case of public service privileged Americans educated at private boarding schools and Harvard were trained to give.

Jack's regard for quality education registered forcefully on his presidency. During his thousand days in the White House, he repeatedly argued the case for expanded federal aid to education. He believed it essential if the United States were going to compete effectively in the Cold War. He saw a better educated population as not only raising the country's standard of living but also as a way to make America more attractive to Third World countries being wooed by communists promising a better life.

Although tensions over segregation, complaints that federal aid would undermine traditional ideas about separation of church and state, and budget constraints defeated Kennedy's legislative requests, he would surely have passed education bills in a second term when, like Lyndon Johnson, he would have had large congressional majorities. No comprehensive assessment of John F. Kennedy's life and political career can neglect his schooling and subsequent views on education.

—Robert Dallek

A photograph of the 1936 Harvard freshman swimming team. John Kennedy is in the back row, third from left.

Lyndon B. Johnson

Chapter Thirty-five

Rebekah and Sam Johnson spent months trying to talk their boy into going to college, but young Lyndon always refused. He hated studying, and disliked the restrictions on his time and behavior that had been placed on him in high school. Still, Rebekah and Sam persisted. Rebekah Baines Johnson was a woman of culture and refinement. She was a college graduate herself—rare for a woman in Texas's backwater Hill Country. She directed the plays at the local high school and gave elocution lessons in the parlor of the Johnson home. When Lyndon graduated from high school, she urged him to attend the nearby Southwest Texas State Teachers College.

Sam Johnson's efforts to get his son into college were more halfhearted. Sam was a farmer and high school dropout who lacked the refinement and education of his wife. He certainly knew the value of a college degree, however—he had served in the Texas legislature, working side-by-side with men who had gone to college. When it came to giving fatherly advice about what direction to take in life, Sam Johnson would often relay some ill-advised homespun wisdom to his boy, which Lyndon often found difficult to accept. "My daddy always told me that if I brushed up against the grindstone of life, I'd come away with far more polish than I could ever get at Harvard or Yale," Lyndon Johnson said years later. "I wanted to believe him, but somehow I never could."

By early 1927, Lyndon was eighteen years old and working on a road construction crew in rural south-central Texas. The back-breaking labor paid just two or three dollars a day, but at night Lyndon was free to go to dances and saloons and run with his friends, who were constantly on the lookout for ways to have fun and get into mischief.

One night in February 1927, Lyndon Johnson went to a dance in the town of Fredericksburg, not far from the Johnson home. Things had not been going well for him on the road crew. Lyndon had gotten into an argument with his boss and was probably going to lose his job. That night in Fredericksburg he wore a white silk shirt and swaggered around the dance hall, looking for trouble. It didn't take long

Johnson's biographer Robert Dallek noted that, "At school, Lyndon was constantly in trouble. His early academic work was good. However, he began to have behavior problems in the higher elementary grades. He wouldn't do his homework, and even rebelled against going to school. One observer in the Johnson home remembers that Rebekah [LBJ's mother] 'had a hard time getting him up in the morning and getting him to school.' A record of his school attendance from 1920 [when Johnson was in the eighth grade] shows that out of 180 school days he was absent 50 times and was tardy on 30 of the 130 days he was present." Pictured below is Johnson's third-grade report card.

"Never trouble another for what you can do for yourself"

PUPILS

PROMOTION--Satisfactory averages on all subjects; or a general average standing of 70 with no yearly average on any one study below 50 will be required for promotion. To be promoted this card must be presented upon your entrance in school next year.

"There is nothing so kingly as kindness and nothing so royal as truth."

Certificate of Promotion.

THIS CERTIFIES THAT Lyndon Johnson has attained the required standard in conduct and in the branches of study for promotion and is hereby promoted from Third Grade or year of course to Fourth Grade or year of course

Given this .... day of ....

Carrie Ytt Teacher

.... Superintendent

"The best part of knowledge is that which teaches us where knowledge leaves off and ignorance begins."

Published By C. A. Bryant Co., Dallas, Texas.

"He that ruleth his own spirit is greater than he that taketh a city"

TEXAS
TEACHERS' MONTHLY REPORT
TO PARENTS

Johnson City Public Schools

PUPIL Lyndon Johnson

Age 7 grade or year of course 3

School .... District No. 4

Year 1915 1916

Carrie Ytt, Teacher.

TO PARENTS

The school can do but little without the hearty co-operation of the home. We therefore send you a report each month to keep you informed as to the conduct, standing and progress, that you may better assist us in accomplishing satisfactory results. To this end we request you to examine this report carefully each month to give due credit and praise for all good marks, and remove, if necessary, the principal cause of all poor ones--irregularity in attendance and improper conduct.

Should there be any delay in the presentation of this report or any neglect in its preparation, or anything of any unsatisfactory character, you will confer a favor by calling attention to it immediately. Frequent visits by parents encourage teachers and pupils.

L C Fawcett Superintendent.

"Never put off till tomorrow what you can do today"

Published By C. A Bryant Co., Dallas, Texas

Scale of grading: A+ = 95-100 C+ = 75-80 D+ = 65-70

Report for year beginning .... day of .... 191.... and Ending .... day of .... 191....

Sept. Oct. Nov. Dec. Jan. Feb. Mch. Apr. May June Yearly Avg. Pace Reached

Reading, Spelling, Writing, Drawing, Arithmetic, Grammar, Geography, Physiology, Agriculture, Texas History, U. S. History, Civics, Composition, Physical Geography, Literature, General History, Algebra, Geometry, Physics, ..., Application, Department, Days Absent, Times Tardy

TO THE TEACHER

This report contains full information regarding the attendance, deportment and progress of the pupil. Fill the blanks regularly and carefully at the close of each month and send them to parents promptly. See that they are returned with proper signatures. Make all entries with pen and ink. Exercise such care that it will not be necessary to erase. The manner in which your reports are made will be a good index to the general character of your school. If rightly used, this report will prove to be a valuable medium of communication between you and the parents. Have frequent written tests on work passed over by all pupils. Require thorough work. Let your test be fair and sufficient. Honest patrons will sustain the honest teacher. Frequently bring or send work of your pupils to this office for inspection by other schools.

SCALE OF GRADING

E-excellent; 90-100. V-very good; 80-90. G-good; 70-80. F-fair; 60-70. P-poor; 50-60. Marks below F on studies and below 90 on conduct are considered unsatisfactory.

The parent or guardian will please sign below and return promptly to teacher.

Sept. ....
Oct. Rebekah B. Johnson
Nov. Rebekah B. Johnson
Dec. Rebekah B. Johnson
Jan. ....
Feb. ....
March ....
April ....
May ....

"The best thought of the community must be in close sympathy with the schools."

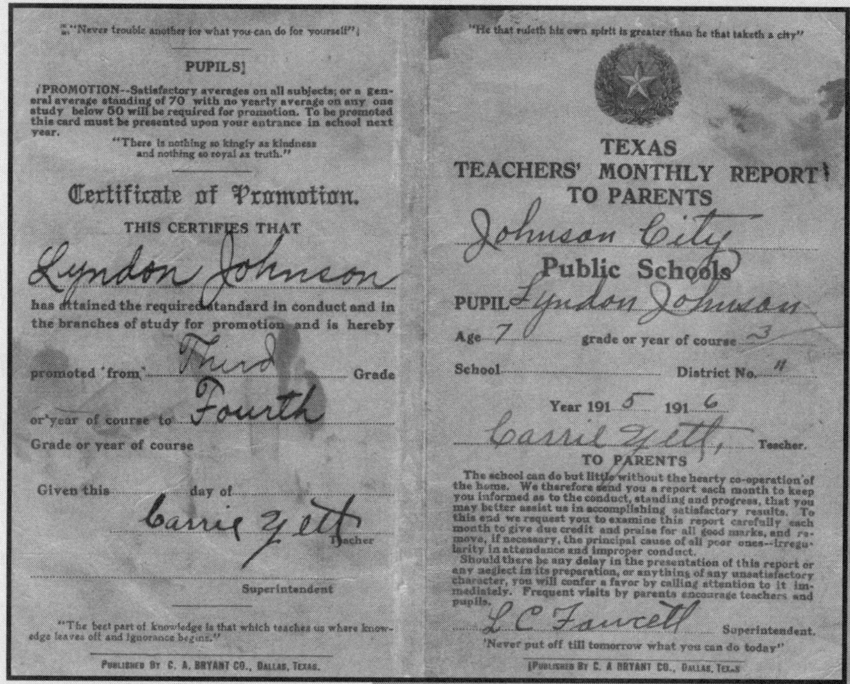

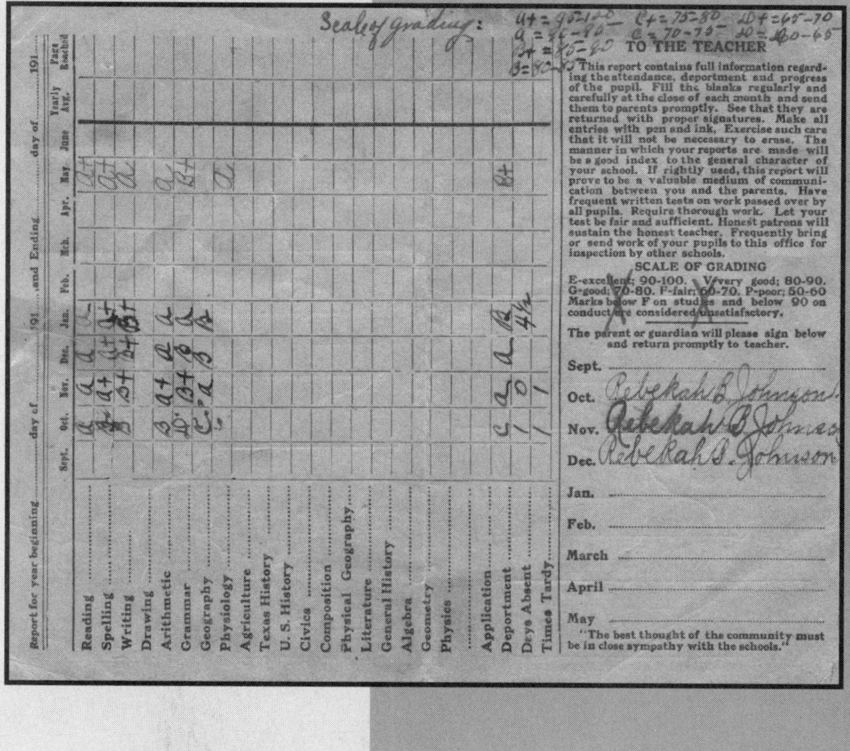

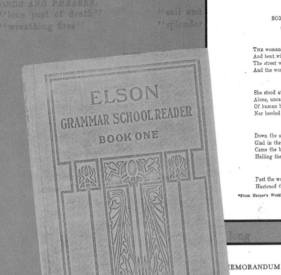

54   Elson Grammar School Reader Book One

VOCABULARY:
task—work; business; toil; labor.
gal'-lant—brave; noble; high-spirited.
faith'-ful—trustworthy; honest; sincere.

WORDS AND PHRASES:
"lone post of death"   "sail and shroud"
"wreathing fires"   "splendor wild"

SOMEBODY'S MOTHER*
(AUTHOR UNKNOWN)

1

The woman was old, and ragged, and gray,
And bent with the chill of the winter's day.
The street was wet with the recent snow,
And the woman's feet were aged and slow.

2

She stood at the crossing and waited long
Alone, uncared for, amid the throng
Of human beings who passed her by,
Nor heeded the glance of her anxious eye.

3

Down the street with laughter and shout,
Glad in the freedom of "school let out,"
Came the boys like a flock of sheep,
Hailing the snow piled white and deep.

4

Past the woman so old and gray,
Hastened the children on their way,

*From Harper's Weekly. Copyright, 1878, by Harper & Brothers.

Somebody's Mother   **55**

Nor offered a helping hand to her,
So meek, so timid, afraid to stir,
Lest the carriage wheels or the horses' feet
Should crowd her down in the slippery street.

5

At last came one of the merry troop,
The gayest laddie of all the group;
He paused beside her and whispered low,
"I'll help you across if you wish to go."

6

Her aged hand on his strong young arm
She placed, and so, without hurt or harm,
He guided her trembling feet along,
Proud that his own were firm and strong.

7

Then back again to his friends he went,
His young heart happy and well content.
"She's somebody's mother, boys, you know,
For all she's aged and poor and slow;

8

"And I hope some fellow will lend a hand
To help my mother, you understand,
If ever she's poor, and old, and gray,
When her own dear boy is far away."

9

And "somebody's mother" bowed low her head,
In her home that night, and the prayer she said,
Was, "God be kind to the noble boy,
Who is somebody's son and pride and joy."

MEMORANDUM   10✓

THE WHITE HOUSE
WASHINGTON

June 7, 1968

MR. PRESIDENT:

Last week on a ride around the Ranch, you told us about a
poem which influenced you as a boy -- the story of a boy
who shows compassion for an old woman. You mentioned
that it may have appeared in the 5th grade edition of
Elson's Readers.

Your memory was 100% accurate. The Library of Congress
couldn't find the book, but the Office of Education did.

Here is the poem.

Ervin Duggan

Attachment

In the last months of his presidency, Lyndon Johnson became increasingly reflective about what had shaped his thinking process that led to the social programs called the "Great Society." Ervin Duggan described one such incident.

Ervin Duggan, assistant to the president, to President Lyndon B. Johnson, June 7, 1968. Elson, *Grammar School Reader* (1911), book one, fifth grade, pp. 54–55.

for him to find it. Lyndon provoked a fight with a hulking farm boy, who responded by unleashing a torrent of fists that the tall and lanky Lyndon Johnson could not fend off. With his fancy white shirt covered in blood, Lyndon limped home, his nose and spirit broken. "It made him realize he wasn't 'cock of the walk,'" recalled his cousin, Ava Johnson Cox.

The next morning, while Rebekah Johnson nursed her boy's wounds, Lyndon told her he was ready to go to college. He said, "All right, I'm sick of working just with my hands and I'm ready to try and make it with my brain."

Johnson City is located in Blanco County, Texas, about twenty-five miles west of the state capital of Austin. It was founded in 1879 by James Polk Johnson, a nephew of Lyndon's grandfather, Sam Johnson Sr. The Johnsons were a prominent family in Hill Country by the time Lyndon Baines Johnson was born on August 27, 1908, but they were by no means wealthy citizens. Few people in Hill Country were well off in those days. People in Blanco County were poor and mostly illiterate. Their land produced few crops. Indoor plumbing was a rarity in Blanco County homes. Electricity was nonexistent.

The thirty-sixth president of the United States was born on his father's farm near the town of Stonewall, on the north bank of the Pedernales River, the oldest of five children. Rebekah Johnson sent her boy to the local one-room Junction School when he was four years old, a year before most children were expected to begin school. Clearly, he was not ready for the experience. He was bright enough—by that age Lyndon was already reading—but he was shy and unwilling to participate in class. When the teacher, Kate Deadrich, told Rebekah that Lyndon refused to read aloud in class, she told her to let Lyndon read while sitting on her lap. It worked. Still, Lyndon didn't last too long in Miss Kate's class. After three months, he contracted whooping cough and had to stay at home for the rest of the school year.

Rebekah Johnson had never enjoyed the pioneer life on the farm near Stonewall. In September 1913, she convinced Sam to buy a home in Johnson City, about ten miles from the farm. Sam bought one of the finest homes in Johnson City, but it was hardly luxurious. Johnson City, with a population of about three hundred, had no paved roads, no gas lines to provide heat and light, and just a few telephones and automobiles. The downtown consisted of a saloon, diner, barbershop, drugstore, three churches, and a courthouse. There was also an elementary school, where Lyndon was enrolled shortly after his family moved to Johnson City.

Now a bit older and out of his shell, Lyndon Johnson was a rambunctious and ill-behaved boy who craved attention and exasperated his parents. Every night when Sam would get home from the farm, he would ask, "Well, what has Lyndon done today?" When Rebekah or his younger sisters would tell on him, Lyndon could often count on receiving a thorough spanking from his father. At school, he would underachieve well into his high school years. He refused to do his homework or study for tests and was often truant from school. In 1920, Johnson City school records showed that of one hundred and eighty days of school, Lyndon Johnson was absent fifty times and tardy thirty times.

Luzia Casparis, one of his elementary school teachers, described him as a "little hellion." Once, when Lyndon had gone several days without turning in his homework, Casparis told him he would have to remain inside for recess to make up the work. When the bell rang for recess, Lyndon defiantly walked out of the school, spitting at his teacher as he walked by. To punish the boy, Casparis locked him in a storage room. Lyndon pounded on the door and screamed so loudly that when she finally relented and let him out, he burst through the doorway so hard that he fell and bloodied his nose.

At the end of the 1922 school year, Lyndon was so far behind in his school work that he was told he would have to go to summer school or be held back. To make up the work, Sam and Rebekah sent their son to a private school in San Marcos, about thirty miles from Johnson City. Within a week of his arrival, Lyndon had bought so much ice cream and candy for his friends that he had spent all the pocket money Sam had given him for the entire eight-week course. When he hitchhiked home to ask for more money, Sam took him right back to San Marcos without giving him another penny.

Eventually, Lyndon Johnson began to emerge as a leader among students— certainly not in academics or in extracurricular activities, but by the force of his personality. "If there was an argument, he had to win," recalled Emmette Redford, who grew up with Johnson. "If he'd differ with you, he'd hover right up against you, breathing right in your face, arguing your point with all the earnestness…I got disgusted with him. Sometimes I'd try just to walk away, but…he wouldn't stop until you gave in."

His talent for arguing led Lyndon to join the debating club at Johnson City High School. It was one of the few extracurricular activities in which Lyndon would participate. In 1921, at the age of thirteen, he won his first debating contest, when he placed first in a meet in Fredericksburg for a speech titled "Texas: Undivided and Indivisible," a response to a persistent proposal by local politicians to split up the vast state into several smaller states. As a high school student, his skills earned him a trip to the finals of a debating competition in San Marcos. When he lost the competition, he was so distraught by the judges' decision that he threw up in the men's room.

Back at Johnson City High School, he was no more interested in academics than he had been in elementary school. The exception was civics class. By the time Lyndon took high school civics he already knew far more about how government worked than most boys his age. For years, Lyndon had sat on the front porch of the Johnson City home listening to Sam Johnson and his political cronies gossip about affairs in Austin. His high school civics class was taught by Scott Klett, who had attended law school at the University of Texas and was, therefore, far more educated than most everyone else

His talent for arguing led Lyndon to join the debating club at Johnson City High School.

The High School Department
OF THE
Johnson City Public School
ASSISTED BY MRS. S. E. JOHNSON
PRESENTS THE PLAY
"An Old Fashioned Mother"
THURSDAY NIGHT, MAY 3RD, 1923.

CAST OF CHARACTERS.

Deborah Underhill .... A Mother in Israel
        Annie Rae Ottmers.
Widder Bill Pindle .... Leader of the Choir
        Georgia Cammack.
Miss Lowizy Loviny Custard ..... Plain Sewing and Gossip
        Louise Casparis.
Isabel Simpscott .... The Village Belle
        Kittie Clyde Ross.
Gloriana Perkins .... As Good as Gold
        Margaret Johnson.
Sukey Pindle .... The Widder's Mite
        Josefa Johnson.
John Underhill .... The Prodigal Son
        Lyndon Johnson.
Charley Underhill .... The Elder Brother
        Garland Galloway.
Brother Jonah Quackenbush ...... A Whited Sepulchre
        John Dollahite.
Jeremiah Gosling, "Jerry" .... A Merry Heart
        Truman Fawcett.
Enoch Rone .... An Outcast and a Wanderer
        Cecil Redford.
Quintus Todd .... The County Sheriff
        Charley Hunnicutt
    The Village Choir.

Time: Twenty years ago. Place: The village of Canton in Northern New York.

SYNOPSIS.

ACT I—Settin' Room at the Underhill Farmhouse. An afternoon in late March. The Good Samaritan.

ACT II—Same scene, three years later. A winter afternoon. A Mother's Love.

ACT III—Same scene, two years later. A morning in autumn. The Prodigal Son.

ADMISSION, 15C AND 25C

Program, Johnson City High School Senior Play, *An Old Fashioned Mother*, 1923. Lyndon Johnson played "John Underhill, the Prodigal Son."

in town. Lyndon was fascinated by the lessons on government that he learned in Klett's class. Johnson City was also the seat of government of Blanco County, which meant the courthouse was located in the center of town. Recalled Emmette Redford: "There wasn't anything in town except three churches and a courthouse, and although Lyndon and I gave some attention to what was going on in the churches…we were more interested in what happened at the courthouse."

In 1920, the Johnson family fell on hard times when cotton prices suddenly dropped. The year before, Sam Johnson had gone heavily into debt to buy his parents' four-hundred-and-thirty-three-acre farm from his brothers and sisters. In 1919, cotton prices had risen to forty cents a pound. A year later, Sam Johnson's crop suffered from flooding in the winter and a hot spell in the summer. When a national recession and an international cotton surplus forced cotton prices to tumble to eight cents a pound, Sam was ruined. Even though he gave up his seat in the legislature and sold the farm, Sam still found himself drowning in bills that totaled $40,000—a debt that, after Sam's death in 1937, Lyndon and his brother and sisters would have to repay.

Johnson City High School only went up to the eleventh grade. What's more, the school was unaccredited, meaning that colleges did not regard its graduates as prepared to take their courses. In May 1924, Lyndon Johnson graduated from Johnson City High. His parents wanted him to attend Southwest Texas State Teachers College, but to enroll there that fall he would have to attend classes on the San Marcos campus over the summer, essentially taking twelfth-grade courses. Reluctantly, Lyndon enrolled, but lasted just a few weeks. He bristled under the workload and didn't believe he was up to the challenge. "Going to school as just another poor boy—well, that wasn't something Lyndon wanted to do," said his cousin, Elizabeth Roper Clemens.

Meanwhile, he continued his hell-raising ways. Not yet sixteen years old, Lyndon had started drinking. Despite Prohibition—the federal law that made alcoholic beverages illegal—Lyndon and his friends found ways to buy liquor, which they drank until they were drunk. They drove recklessly around Blanco County, daring the local sheriffs to chase them. Once, they burned down a barn. Said his grandmother, Ruth Baines: "That boy is going to end up in the penitentiary—just mark my words."

Instead of going to prison, Lyndon went to California. That July, Lyndon and four friends climbed into a beat-up Model T Ford and headed west. Lyndon's friends decided to look for jobs in California. Lyndon wasn't sure what he would do when he got there and planned on staying for just a few weeks. Instead, he spent two years in California, finding a job as a clerk in a San Bernardino law practice headed by a cousin, Tom Martin.

Martin promised to teach Lyndon the law, but it soon became clear that cousin Tom was managing to stay just a step ahead of the law himself. Martin was a drunk who rarely showed up in the office. Whenever Lyndon managed to contact

In May 1924, Lyndon Johnson completed the eleventh and final grade at Johnson City High School. This photograph shows members of the school's junior and senior classes. Not yet sixteen, Johnson was the youngest member of the class; he is in the back row, fifth from left.

his cousin with a question on how to handle a matter for a client, Martin told the young clerk to take care of the problem himself. Lyndon did the best he could, but was concerned that he could be in trouble with authorities for practicing law without a license. When Martin stopped paying Lyndon, he was forced to take a job as an elevator operator. Finally, in the fall of 1926, Lyndon returned home to Johnson City. His parents pressed him to go to college, but again he refused. Sam pulled some strings and found his son a job on a Texas Highway Department road crew. That was the job Lyndon held until the following February, when he argued with his boss and then said the wrong thing at the wrong time to a Fredericksburg farm boy with, as his cousin Ava recalled, "fists like a pile-driver."

After committing himself to attend college, Lyndon Johnson was one of 700 students matriculating at Southwest Texas State Teachers College when he arrived on campus in March 1927 to begin his college education. Although he would eventually become an honor student, at first Lyndon had no more interest in his studies than he had displayed in high school. Still, Lyndon aimed to make the best of his college experience.

Most of his fellow students came from backgrounds similar to Lyndon's— they were from small Texas towns in Hill Country, and most of them were from

Lyndon Johnson attended Southwest Texas State Teachers College at San Marcos from March 1927 to August 1930. Known as San Marcos, this small provincial school had little standing in the world of higher education. It opened in 1903 as a state "normal school" to train public school teachers. It became an accredited four-year college in 1925.

In this December 13, 1929, letter to his mother Rebekah Baines, Johnson describes the courses he registered for at San Marcos. "My schedule of classes is as follows: English 119—(a course in journalism) History 225 (American Diplomacy), Education 222 (a course in statistics), Education 252 (Practice Teaching), Religion (a study of the life of Jesus)," he wrote. "My courses this term have been unusually hard. They have required a great deal of application but the reward that application brings far overshadows the time spent. This has been my best college year."

poor families. As so-called "scholarship students," they held jobs on campus to help pay their way. Lyndon's first job was collecting trash—a chore he shared with several other students, most of whom complained about the work. Not Lyndon. Unlike the other students, Lyndon saw that there were better jobs on campus and understood the way to land one of the more desirable jobs was to impress the people who gave out the work. Lyndon went about picking up the trash with such unabashed zeal that he soon won a promotion to janitor's assistant. He spent just a short time in that job, landing a much-desired appointment as messenger in the office of Cecil Evans, the college president.

Lyndon had no intention of stopping there, either. Instead of simply carrying messages from building to building, Lyndon took on other duties in Evans' office: answering phones, announcing the arrival of visitors, and, after a brief time, acting as an appointment secretary for the president. Evans was grateful for the help and soon found himself relying on Lyndon, even taking him to Austin whenever he had business in the state capital. As the son of a former legislator, Lyndon knew many of the Texas lawmakers as well as the legislature's staff members, and he often used those contacts to steer Evans to people who could help the college.

In class, Lyndon excelled in debating, as he had done in high school. He grew close to Harry Greene, a political science professor and coach of the debating team, and would often spend hours at the end of each day with Greene, engaging his mentor in long-winded dialogues.

Although he had made himself into an influential member of the president's staff and had made a good friend on the faculty, Lyndon was still far from the center of student power on campus. A great deal of power was held by the leaders of the Black Stars, a campus fraternity that controlled the membership on the Student Council and, therefore, the flow of some $12,000 of the college's money into student activities. The problem was, though, that since the Black Stars were made up of athletes, most of the money went to the athletic teams. The school newspaper, literary magazine, music club, debating society, and other groups received few dollars from the Black Stars–led Student Council. Lyndon attempted to join the Black Stars but was rejected because he wasn't an athlete. So, Lyndon resolved to form a rival group, which he called the White Stars, and aimed to use his group to wrest control of the purse strings from the Black Stars.

It took three years. Lyndon's strategy was to slowly build up membership in the White Stars and run opposition slates for Student Council seats. In the first year, the White Stars won five seats on the council and took control of the student newspaper and literary magazine. Lyndon himself assumed the editorship of the paper, the *College Star*. During the second year, he used his influence to help assign jobs to the scholarship students. Relying on the old political patronage technique of awarding jobs to supporters, Lyndon gave the jobs in the library, bookstore, and administrative offices to White Stars supporters. Backers of the Black Stars were assigned to pick up the trash.

The final step toward taking control of the campus occurred in Lyndon's third and final year in San Marcos. Lyndon realized that to control the Student Council completely, the White Stars would have to elect the council president. Lyndon decided not to run himself; he believed his three-year effort to squash the Black Stars had made him too many enemies on campus. Instead, he convinced his best friend, Bill Deason, to run for president. The Black Stars slated their own candidate: Dick Speer, one of the most popular boys on campus.

Lyndon launched a relentless campaign for Deason. He organized teams of campaign workers to fan out across campus to round up support for the White Stars candidate. The White Stars worked for weeks, but the night before the vote a head count showed Deason still twenty votes behind Speer. The White Stars caucused to look over the poll numbers and most of them, including Deason, concluded that the election was out of reach. Lyndon wouldn't hear of defeat, however. He told the other White Stars: "The rest of you may go to bed, but I'm not." Lyndon headed out into the cold and drizzly Texas night. He went from boarding house to boarding house on campus, getting in people's faces, twisting arms, and making promises. Lyndon Johnson drew from all his talents as a debater to persuade ironclad Black Stars supporters to change their minds. "His greatest forte," Deason would later comment, "is to look a man in the eye and do a convincing job of selling him his viewpoint." When the votes were counted the next day, Deason was declared the winner by eight votes.

The Deason campaign was the beginning of a political career for Lyndon Johnson that would soon take him to Washington as a member of the U.S. House of Representatives (first elected in 1937) and then the Senate (first elected in 1949). In 1951, Johnson was elected the majority whip. In 1953, Johnson used all his political skills to convince his fellow Democratic senators to elect him minority leader. In 1954, when Democrats won control of the Senate, Johnson found himself majority leader—one of the most powerful jobs in the U.S. government.

In the midst of building a political career, Johnson found time to have a family. In 1934, he married Claudia Alta Taylor. Johnson called her "Lady Bird," a nickname she had been given as a small child by a nursemaid. The Johnsons would raise two daughters.

After losing the Democratic presidential nomination in 1960, Lyndon Johnson joined John F. Kennedy on the national ticket, winning election as vice president in November 1960. When Kennedy was assassinated in 1963, Johnson took the oath of office as president. A year later, "LBJ" was elected president to his own four-year term in a landslide victory.

As president, Johnson aimed to wipe out poverty in the United States. He signed legislation creating educational, medical, and housing programs for poor people, pledging to "build a great society, a place where the meaning of a man's life matches the marvels of man's labor." He also signed legislation ensuring civil rights to minorities, ending the decades-old practice of prohibiting African Americans

Transcript of Lyndon Johnson's grades at Southwest Texas State Teachers College. In August 1930, Lyndon Johnson received his B.S. degree in Education and History from Southwest Texas State Teachers College. "I never worked so hard in all my life," Johnson said later.

and other minorities from using restaurants, restrooms, train stations, and other public facilities that had been reserved for "whites only." And Johnson was a vigorous supporter of space exploration; during his presidency, he fully backed manned space travel, clearing the way for the first lunar landing in 1969. Despite these social advancements, Johnson's presidency will always be shadowed by the Vietnam War and his decision to escalate U.S. involvement in the conflict.

In the spring of 1968, Johnson shocked the nation when he announced on national television that he would not seek reelection. Johnson soon retired to his ranch near Johnson City. He died on January 22, 1973.

—Hal Marcovitz

Richard M. Nixon
Chapter Thirty-six

As he would often remind people during his years in public service, Richard Milhous Nixon was born into a poor, hardworking family. Yet the Nixon family valued education. Though he graduated from high school in the depths of the Great Depression, a combination of hard work, determination, and the support of his family gave Richard the opportunity for both a college education and a post-graduate degree.

The families of both of Richard Nixon's parents were deeply rooted in America. On his father's side, he was descended from James Nixon, who had arrived in Delaware from Ireland during the 1700s. On his mother's side, Franklin Milhous had immigrated to Pennsylvania from Germany—by way of England and Ireland—in 1729. Members of the Nixon family had served in both the American Revolution and the Civil War.

Richard Nixon was born on January 9, 1913, in a house that had been built by his father. He joined a family that included his father, Francis "Frank" Nixon; his mother, Hannah Milhous Nixon; and older brother Harold, born in 1909. A year later, Frank and Hannah Nixon had a third son, Francis Donald Nixon. Their early years were filled with hardship. Frank owned an orchard, but this business was not nearly as fruitful as he had hoped. Times were tough and it proved difficult to make ends meet. The business venture failed in 1922, two years after a fourth child, Arthur, was born. Frank Nixon sold the house in Yorba Linda, California, and moved his family to Whittier. Here, Frank opened a gas station to which a grocery store was soon attached. Though it was a demanding enterprise, this business eventually achieved modest success.

The young Nixons had started school in Yorba Linda, but Harold and Richard transferred to East Whittier Elementary in 1922 when Richard was in the fourth grade. Much of their education, however, came from their parents and from the social and religious life within the large Quaker community in Whittier. The family attended Quaker services at least twice a week, and young Richard served as the church organist when he was still in grade school.

Richard Nixon is seated in the front row, extreme right, in this 1919 photograph of his first grade class, Yorba Linda, California.

"I started first grade in Yorba Linda's schoolhouse when I was six," Nixon wrote in his *Memoirs* (1978). "My mother had already taught me to read at home, and this head start enabled me to skip the second grade. After homework and chores, I often sat by the fireplace or at the kitchen table immersed in a book or magazine. We took the *Los Angeles Times*, the *Saturday Evening Post*, and the *Ladies' Home Journal*. Aunt Olive, my mother's youngest sister, and her husband, Oscar Marshburn, lived in nearby Whittier and subscribed to the *National Geographic*. Nearly every time I visited them I borrowed a copy. It was my favorite magazine."

Nixon was not a boy who enjoyed pranks. "He was very mature even when he was five or six years old," his mother Hannah Nixon recalled in a 1960 interview. "He was interested in things way beyond the usual grasp of a boy his age. He was thoughtful and serious. 'He always carried such a weight.' That's an expression we Quakers use for a person who doesn't take his responsibilities lightly."

Much of Nixon's education came from his parents and from the social and religious life within the large Quaker community in Whittier.

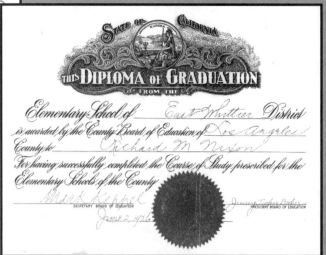

East Whittier Graduating Exercises

WEDNESDAY, JUNE 2, 1926
7:30 P.M.

Opening Song--"Banner of Liberty" - *H. W. Loomis*
    THE CLASS

Invocation--
    REV. T. W. RINGLAND

Songs--"Homeward" - - - *Stanley Avery*
    "The Birds' Singing School" - *Earl Towner*
    THE CLASS

Scripture Reading--
    REV. T. W. RINGLAND

Violin Solo--"Humoreske" - - - *Devorak*
    BARBARA MAY COGBURN
    MARGARET MITCHELL, Accompanist

Address--
    DR. WALTER F. DEXTER

History of the Class--
    RICHARD M. NIXON, Class President

Piano Solo--"Rustle of Spring" - - *Sinding*
    MARGARET MITCHELL

Talk by the Class Valedictorian
    RUTH LILLY MCGEE

Class Poem--
    BARBARA MAY COGBURN

Class Song--
    THE CLASS

Presentation of the Class--
    MISS EVELYN G. FLOWERS

Presentation of Diplomas--
    MR. D. R. MAHLING, President of School Board

Song--"America"
    CLASS AND AUDIENCE

Benediction--
    REV. T. W. RINGLAND

CLASS ROLL

Hazel Irene Bell	Ruth Lilly McGee
Tillie Calleros	Mabel Mitchell
Barbara May Cogburn	Margaret Ruth Mitchell
Estelyn Davis	Richard M. Nixon
Edward Flutot	Claire Ruth O'Neill
Eliza J. Gaskill	Harriett Louise Palmer
Cecilia B. Harris	Elizabeth Rees
Irene Hewitt	Emma Louise Renken
Doris M. Hinshaw	Margaret Alice Samson
Elden Hostetler	Linniel Edward Taylor
Opal Mae Johnson	Julia Mae Tompkins
Russell E. Johnson	Viola Ruth Ware
George Loomis	Joe Watkins
Salvador R. Lopez	Mildred Wright
Joe Lord	

A program for the East Whittier Elementary School graduating exercises, held on June 2, 1926, and Nixon's elementary school diploma.

Richard Nixon was a conscientious student. A classmate recalled, "Dick very seldom came out and played. He was usually studying, and there were remarks and cracks made about it." Another classmate remembered, "He was a little different from the rest of us. He was a kid you respected. He knew everyone, but he was very good in class, and when you talked to him you always had his full attention. He was friendly, but not a guy you'd put on a backpack and go fishing with."

There were twenty-nine students in Nixon's eighth grade class. He was the class president and delivered a brief talk on the "History of the Class."

    The Nixon boys would also learn early the value of hard work. They were pressed into service to help out at Frank Nixon's store, and they spent their school vacations doing farm work to add cash to the Nixon family coffers.

    At home, Richard Nixon's parents were a study in contrasts. Hannah Nixon was a kind, gentle, and thoughtful woman whom Richard would later often refer to as "a saint." Frank Nixon, on the other hand, was an outspoken and often angry man. His anger came from the fact that he was a barely educated laborer battling to succeed while competing with more established businessmen. While Hannah was a serene influence on the home, Frank often went off on frightening tirades.

Frank Nixon was not, however, irrational in his ranting and raving. His opinions were generally well reasoned and supported by facts. From his father, Richard learned to debate, but he also learned the value of knowing facts that would sustain his points of view. To gain these facts, Richard became an avid newspaper reader when he was still in grade school. Thanks to his father's inspiration, and to his own study and hard work, Richard emerged as an accomplished debater in an era when public debates were seen as a form of entertainment. His first debate before an audience—on the merits of renting versus owning real estate—set the stage for his future behind a podium as a political figure.

Just as he inherited his father's skill as a debater, Richard inherited much of his father's bitterness. The years of poverty and struggle, both before and after the orchard business failed, had made a deep impression on him. He would develop an appreciation for diligence and hard work, but on the dark side, he also resented people of privilege who seemed to have wealth handed to them. Like Frank Nixon, Richard developed an inferiority complex that would affect his outlook for the rest of his life. In high school, when he drove a delivery truck for his father, Richard was so ashamed to be doing this kind of work that he went out of his way to not be seen in the truck by his classmates.

Richard entered high school in the fall of 1926 in nearby Fullerton, but transferred to Whittier High School for his junior and senior years. Despite having to work in all of his spare time, he was an above-average student. He joined the debate team and soon became one of its stars. Though he was bashful and withdrawn around small groups of fellow students, he had no fear of speaking to crowds. As a result, he became a prizewinning orator and honed important skills as a public speaker that would be vital in his later career.

His time in high school was bracketed by two of the most tragic events that a young person could experience—the death of two siblings. His seven-year-old brother Arthur became sick in August 1925, just as Richard was entering the eighth grade. Doctors were unable to find a cause for his illness and he died a few weeks later. Then, about the time he graduated from Whittier High School in 1930, Richard found out that his older brother Harold had been diagnosed with tuberculosis, a widely feared and often deadly respiratory disease. Treatment at a sanitarium in the dry air of northern Arizona was recommended, and Harold was hospitalized at an institution in Prescott. Hannah Nixon moved to Arizona to be with her son, and wound up working on the janitorial staff to help pay his bills. Two years later, in March 1933, Harold passed away.

The early 1930s were trying times for the Nixon family. Harold was ill, Hannah was away from the rest of the family, and family finances were stretched thin. This already-difficult situation was complicated by the fact that Frank and Hannah had a late-in-life fifth son in 1930. Little Edward Nixon arrived in the world just as the Nixons' next-youngest son, Francis Donald, was turning sixteen and as Richard was graduating from high school.

In the meantime, Richard had been accepted to Whittier College, a Quaker institution in his hometown that his mother had attended. This was all the Nixons could afford. Though he had also applied for scholarships to prestigious Ivy League schools back east, including Harvard and Yale, the family situation clearly made it impossible for him to leave home. He started classes in the fall of 1930 and lived at home to help out with household chores while his father cared for the new baby.

Young Richard Nixon's character had been forged in adversity and shaped by tragedy. In college, he developed a reputation as a serious student. He appeared so somber to many fellow students that he would eventually earn the nickname "Gloomy Gus."

Despite this, his talent for public speaking made him a well-known campus figure at Whittier. It might be said that while everyone came to know him, few people knew him well. He was elected president of his freshman class and he became co-founder, with his friend Dean Triggs, of a new fraternity that was known as the Orthogonian Society.

One can clearly see Nixon's influence in the founding principles of the Orthogonians. The society was created as a reaction to the Franklin Society, a group of men who wore tuxedos and fancied themselves as being "upper crust." It was here that Nixon's resentment of the wealthy upper class came out. He imagined himself as a "common man." Orthogonians wore open-necked shirts and were deliberately informal. Most of the members, like Nixon, were working their way through school. Orthogonians were self-described as "square shooters"—men who said what they meant and did not hide behind pretense. For much of his career, Nixon would characterize himself as such a person.

Though just a freshman, Richard Milhous Nixon was elected as the first president of the Orthogonians. He even penned the lyrics to the fraternity's song, which closes with the phrase, "Brothers together we'll travel on and on, worthy of the name of Orthogonian." The Orthogonian Society remains at Whittier College to this day.

When he was a sophomore, Nixon joined the debate team. Just as he had in high school, he emerged as a renowned debater, and he won numerous intercollegiate contests for Whittier College. He also went out for football. He made the team, but was not nearly so skilled on the field as behind the podium. As a result, he spent most of his brief pigskin career on the bench. Nevertheless, he was to be greatly influenced by Coach Wallace Newman, who Nixon recalled as having been an inspiration to the young men, teaching them important life skills, such as honesty and fair play, as he was teaching them plays.

On the academic side, Nixon was an excellent student. Math and science were a challenge for him, but he breezed through history, studying under the esteemed history professor Paul Smith.

Perhaps his most influential teacher at Whittier College was Albert Upton, professor of English and literature. An expert in Aristotelian logic, Upton was

Nixon said that he had two unfulfilled ambitions—to direct a symphony orchestra and to play an organ in a cathedral.

Richard Nixon loved music. He began to play the piano before he was five years of age. Nixon said that he had two unfulfilled ambitions—to direct a symphony orchestra and to play an organ in a cathedral. During a concert that was part of his 1969 presidential inauguration ceremony, as pianist Andre Watts was playing, Nixon's aunt leaned over and whispered to the President, "Now Richard. If thee had practiced more on the piano, thee could have been down there instead of up here!"

Nixon is in the back row standing, second from the right in this 1929 photograph of the Fullerton High School orchestra.

Richard Nixon (back row, third from left) with the other members of the Whittier High School debating team, circa 1930. At Whittier High, Nixon joined a myriad of clubs—the Latin Club, the school newspaper, the school orchestra, the football team, and the debating team. Mrs. Clifford Vincent (front row, center), the teacher/coach of the debating team, recalled, "He was so good it kind of disturbed me. He had the ability to kind of slide round an argument instead of meeting it head on, and he could take any side of a debate."

Program

⚜

Presiding: JOHN F. D. AUE, Managing Editor, Whittier News.

Selection—Prince of Pilsen . . . . *Luders*

The Stars and Stripes Forever . . . . *John Philip Sousa*
Whittier Union High School Orchestra

Address of Welcome:
MR. O. C. ALBERTSON, District Superintendent
Whittier Union High School District

ORATIONS:

1. The Constitution and the Duty of the Citizens . . . . . *Helen Cox*
2. Our Privileges Under the Constitution . . . . . . *Richard Nixon*
3. The Constitution, its Contribution to World Peace *Leland Klingerman*
4. The Individual, His Rights and Duties Under
   the Constitution . . . . *Karl Von der Ahe*
5. Our Constitution—Practical and Ideal . . . . . *Hilla Willard*
6. The Constitution in the Upbuilding of the United States *Henry Meyers*
7. The Vitality of the Constitution . . . . . . *Robert McArthur*

Come to the Fair . . . . *Easthope-Martin*

Nightfall in Granada . . . . *L. Bueno*
Whittier Union High School

A loving cup donated by Whittier Union High School will be presented
to the winner.

JUDGES:

HON. LEON R. YANKWICH, Judge of the Superior Court, Los Angeles.

MR. W. C. HAY, President, Blue Diamond Company, Los Angeles.

MR. WM. CAREY MARBLE, President, The John C. Marble Company, Los Angeles.

GEORGIA P. BULLOCK, Judge of the Municipal Court, Los Angeles.

HON. WALTER S. GATES, Judge of the Superior Court, Los Angeles.

PACIFIC COAST GRAND FINALS

On Friday evening, May 10th, at the Shrine Civic Auditorium, Los Angeles, the winning orators representing Arizona, California, Idaho, Nevada, Oregon, Utah, Washington and the Territory of Hawaii will compete for the right to represent this section in the National Finals to be held at Washington, D. C., on May 25th. The Chief Justices of the Supreme Courts of the states concerned will be present to act as judges for the event. A presiding officer of national prominence has been secured. A combined band from the High Schools of the City of Los Angeles will furnish music for the occasion. There will be no charge for admission. Reservations for seats for the Pacific Coast Finals may be had by writing Alan Nichols, Contest Director, Oratorical Contest Department, Los Angeles Times.

In the spring of 1929, sixteen-year-old Richard Nixon entered an area-wide oratorical contest sponsored by the *Los Angeles Times*. The subject was the Constitution of the United States. Nixon called his speech "Our Privileges Under the Constitution." He won the contest. These pages are from Nixon's program for the contest.

Nixon attended Fullerton High School in his freshman and sophomore years and Whittier High School for his junior and senior years. After graduating from high school in 1930, young Nixon, whom his class had voted "best all-around student," was awarded a scholarship to Harvard University. But he could not take advantage of this educational opportunity, because his family could not afford to pay his traveling and living expenses.

highly regarded for his theories involving fundamental thinking processes based on semantics, cognitive psychology, and problem solving. He greatly influenced the future president by defining the conceptualization, qualification, and classification of language. From Upton, Nixon would learn a great deal about analyzing and solving problems.

As a senior, Nixon was elected student-body president, a crowning achievement to his campus career. In 1934, he graduated summa cum laude and second in his class with a bachelor's degree in history.

His academic success at Whittier earned Nixon a scholarship to the Duke University Law School in Durham, North Carolina. At Duke, Nixon avoided campus politics until his senior year, concentrating on his studies and on part-time jobs that he took to help out with expenses. These included work in the campus library and at the National Youth Administration. Academically, he received praise for a 1936 term paper in legal ethics that was entitled, "Automobile Accident Litigation: The lawyer versus the public." Again, his interests were colored by his image of himself as a common man and as a champion of underdogs.

As a senior, he was elected president of the Duke Bar Association, and he joined the honorary legal fraternity known as the Order of the Coif. In June 1937, Richard Nixon graduated third in his class of twenty-five with a Bachelor of Laws degree.

While at Duke, Nixon had decided that he would like to pursue a career with the Federal Bureau of Investigation. His application was turned down, so he returned to Southern California to practice law. He was admitted to the California bar in the autumn of 1937, and he joined the Whittier law firm of Wingert & Bewley. The firm had as one of its clients the city government of La Habra, California, a small city about halfway between Whittier and Yorba Linda.

Nixon set up a branch office in La Habra for Wingert & Bewley, and he soon became a full partner in the firm (renamed Bewley, Knoop, & Nixon). In La Habra, Nixon found himself performing a variety of tasks. He might be doing tax work one day and in court on a criminal case the next. It was a diverse career for the young attorney.

In 1940, Nixon was named to the board of trustees of his alma mater, Whittier College, a post that he would retain until 1968, the year he was elected president of the United States. In his spare time between l937 and 1940, Nixon joined an amateur theater troupe, and it was here that he met a young schoolteacher named Thelma Catherine Patricia "Pat" Ryan. Pat Ryan and Richard Nixon were married on June 21, 1940.

Nixon had planned to apply for a job at a larger law firm, possibly in Los Angeles. However, in 1941, shortly before the United States entered World War II, the Nixons moved to Washington, D.C., where Richard Nixon took a government job as an attorney with the Office of Price Administration. After the

Japanese attack on Pearl Harbor and the subsequent U.S. declaration of war in December 1941, Nixon applied to join the armed forces. He earned a commission as a lieutenant, junior grade, in the U.S. Naval Reserve on June 15, 1942. He went on active duty two months later, and was sent for aviation training at the Naval Training School at Quonset Point, Rhode Island.

Beginning in May 1943 Nixon served in the South Pacific with the Combat Air Transport Command at Guadalcanal. In December 1944, Nixon, now a full lieutenant, was assigned to the Navy Bureau of Aeronautics office in Washington, D.C. He served for four months at the Navy Department offices in the nation's capital, and was then transferred to the Bureau of Aeronautics as an officer in the contract termination office. Though he was based in New York City, his work took him to various cities on the East Coast.

Richard Nixon left active duty with the navy in March 1946, and he and Pat returned to California. They had been lured back, in part, by a group of Republican businessmen who had asked Nixon whether he'd like to go into politics. If so, they said they would be willing to finance his run for the Twelfth District seat in the U.S. House of Representatives that had been held for five terms by a Democrat named Horace Jeremiah "Jerry" Voorhis. Nixon agreed to take up the challenge of running for office.

During the campaign, it was suggested that Voorhis, who had socialist leanings, was a communist sympathizer. In 1946, in Southern California, there was little sympathy for communist sympathizers. Nixon handily won the election, in part because of the communism issue and in part because of his skills in debate and public speaking.

In Washington, Nixon was assigned to the House Un-American Activities Committee. It was here that he would make a name for himself during the committee's investigation of a former State Department aide named Alger Hiss, who was accused of being a communist subversive. Nixon would soon rise to national prominence, nurturing the image of himself as a tireless crusader against communism.

Though he was easily reelected to Congress in 1948, Nixon had larger ambitions. In 1950, California had an open seat in the U.S. Senate, and Nixon decided to run for that office. His Democratic opponent was Helen Gahagan Douglas, a former actress and the wife of Hollywood leading man Melvyn Douglas, who had already served three terms in the House of Representatives. Touring the state in a station wagon equipped with a public address system, Nixon stated his case to voters. He built on his reputation as an anti-communist by accusing his opponent of communist leanings. Also during the 1950 campaign, Nixon turned his long-held disdain for the rich and privileged into a useful campaign tool. Because the Douglases were seen as wealthy, Nixon was able to paint his opponent as being "out of touch" with the "common man." Douglas, who considered Nixon's campaign tactics to be unfair and underhanded, coined the nickname "Tricky Dick" for her opponent, an epithet that would be continually resurrected for the rest of his

Friends College, Whittier, Cal.

633

Richard Nixon attended Whittier College from 1930 to 1934. Whittier had about four hundred students. More than half had graduated from the town high school and most, like Nixon, lived at home. "I was not disappointed," Nixon recalled, "because the idea of college was so exciting that nothing could have dimmed it for me."

The postcard above shows the school as it appeared around 1930, when Nixon arrived on campus. The school had been started as Friends Academy in 1887. By 1930, it was nonsectarian but, as its catalogue stated, was "devoted to higher education with a constant overtone of Quaker responsibility in the social order." Of the eighty-five graduates in Nixon's class of 1934, only twelve settled out of state and more than twenty lived their lives within walking distance of the college.

political career. Despite being characterized as a trickster, Nixon saw his victory in the hard-fought 1950 election as that of an underdog triumphing over adversity.

After two years in the Senate, Nixon went on to serve two terms as vice president under President Dwight D. Eisenhower, from 1953 to 1961. In 1960, he ran unsuccessfully for president against John F. Kennedy, losing one of the closest elections in history. Two years later, hoping to recapture the magic of his successful congressional campaigns, he ran against incumbent California governor Edmund G. "Pat" Brown. When Nixon lost the 1962 gubernatorial race, he was bitter. He told a television audience that he was quitting politics forever—"You won't have Dick Nixon to kick around anymore."

Despite this promise, Nixon returned to the national stage six years later with a successful 1968 campaign for president, in which he defeated Democrat

"Ever since I first played in high school, football has been my favorite sport," Nixon recalled in his *Memoirs*. "As a 150-pound seventeen-year-old freshman I hardly cut a formidable figure on the field, but I loved the game—the spirit, the teamwork, the friendship. There were only eleven eligible men on the freshman team, so despite my size and weight I got to play in every game and to wear a number on my sweater. But for the rest of my college years, the only times I got to play were in the last few minutes of a game that was already safely won or hopelessly lost."

Nixon is in the back row, center, in this 1931 photograph of part of the Whittier College football team.

Richard Nixon (top row, fifth from left) and his Duke University Law School Class, 1937.

"One day during my last year at Whittier," wrote Nixon, "I saw a notice on the bulletin board announcing twenty-five $250 scholarships to the new Duke University Law School in Durham, North Carolina. I applied."

Hannah Nixon said that the proudest day of her life was when the letter arrived stating her son had won a scholarship—"yes, even prouder than the day Richard became Vice President."

"I was able to maintain the grades I needed to keep my scholarship and I became a member of Duke's law review," wrote Nixon. "My three years at Duke provided an excellent legal background."

Hubert Humphrey. Nixon was reelected in 1972 by a wide margin, but almost immediately found himself embroiled in the Watergate scandal. As reports of presidential misconduct grew, Nixon ultimately decided to resign the presidency on August 9, 1974.

It is unfortunate that today the reputation of President Richard Milhous Nixon is shaded by the dark cloud of Watergate. In his early life, Nixon's character seems to have been quite the opposite of the chief executive who sanctioned a criminal cover-up. If any lesson can be drawn from the sad climax of Nixon's career, it is how a serious misdeed can undo the positive results of a life of hard work and dedication.

—Bill Yenne

Gerald Ford

Chapter Thirty-seven

T he University of Michigan can usually be counted on to field one of the
nation's best college football teams. That has not always been the case. In
the fall of 1934, the team was crippled by the loss of many of its most
talented players through the previous spring's graduation. The players who
remained on the team were young and inexperienced, and it soon became clear that
Michigan's varsity was outclassed by most of its opponents. The Wolverines lost
their first two games that season, falling in each contest by lopsided scores.

As the team prepared for its third game, against Georgia Tech, the Wolverines
found themselves faced with another problem. One of the team's best players was
Willis F. Ward, an African-American track star who played pass receiver. In the
1930s, black athletes were just beginning to be accepted onto college campuses in
the northern states. That was not true in the still-segregated South. As the game
with Georgia Tech approached, administrators from the southern school made it
clear their team would refuse to take the field if Ward played.

Michigan coach Harry Kipke soon capitulated and ordered Ward to stay home
for the Georgia Tech game. That decision sent a wave of anger through the
Wolverine squad. One of the players most upset by Kipke's decision was Jerry Ford,
the team's center. Ford had grown close to Ward because the two players roomed
together during Michigan's road games. If Ward could not take the field, Ford told
his friend, he would sit out the game as well. It was Ward who talked Jerry into
playing. "Look," Ward told Jerry, "the team's having a bad year. We've lost two
games already and we probably won't win any more. You've got to play Saturday.
You owe it to the team."

Jerry changed his mind, deciding that the best way to react to Georgia Tech's
racist attitude was on the field. That Saturday, Michigan played its best game of the
season. Early in the game, one of the Georgia Tech players taunted the Michigan
team for including a "nigger" on its squad. When play resumed a few minutes later,
Ford laid such a savage block on that player that he had to be carried off the field
on a stretcher. Michigan went on to win that day by a score of 9 to 2. It would be

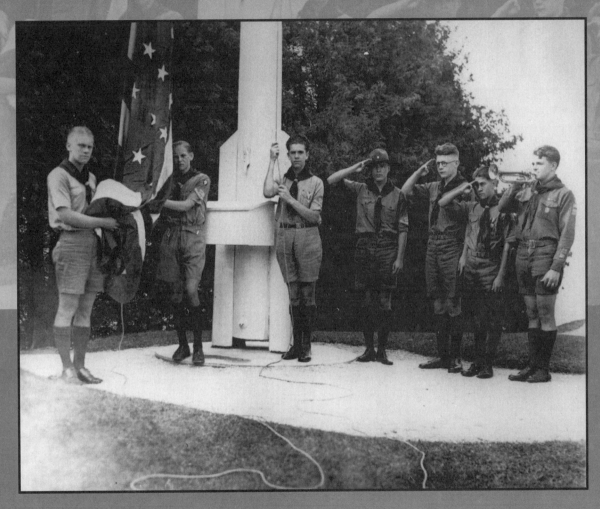

Gerald R. Ford, the only president to become an Eagle Scout, holds the flag as he and his fellow members of the Eagle Scout Guard of Honor prepare to raise the colors over Fort Michilimackinac at Mackinac Island State Park, Michigan. This photograph was taken in August 1929. The troop served as guides for tourists during the summer months.

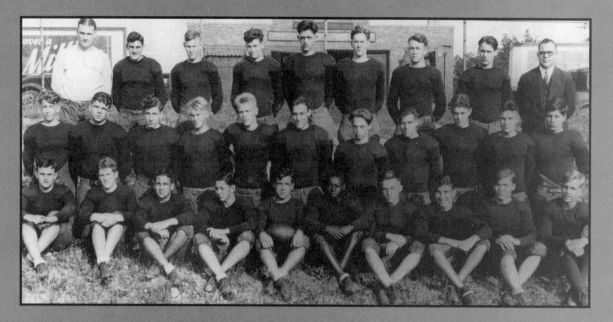

South High School football team, Grand Rapids, Michigan, 1930. Gerald Ford is in the second row, fifth from left. Clifford Gettings, upper left, was the coach. Many considered Gettings the most important faculty member at South High.

In his autobiography, Gerald Ford devotes more than fifty pages to his childhood and education. He mentions no book or teacher that had any influence on him, except Gettings. Ford did recall that "as a child I had a hot temper, which Mother taught me to control—most of the time. A strict disciplinarian, she would ridicule me and show me how foolish I looked when I got angry and said stupid things.... One time she gave me the poem 'If,' by Rudyard Kipling. 'Read this and profit from it,' she said. 'It'll help you control that temper of yours.'" Ford does not write whether he read this inspirational poem or if her advice had an effect upon his temper. Ford's recollection of his school years deals with the fierce competition and exultation of the football field.

Ford spent many hours speaking with his close friend Jerald F. terHorst about his early life and education. TerHorst, in his biography of the former president, mentions no book that Ford had read. Again, the emphasis is Ford's participation in sports.

Football was much more important in Grand Rapids when Ford was growing up during the 1920s than it is today. There were fewer competing attractions. There was no television. Very few students had an automobile available to them. Student social life focused on what one did after the Saturday afternoon football game. School district boundaries were fixed on a city region basis. School bussing did not exist. Football rivalry between high schools also involved neighborhood pride. And, the football coach, rather than the teaching staff, helped to determine the reputation of a school.

Football was the biggest influence on Ford's education. It brought him national attention as a teenager. His skill on the field enabled him to obtain a university education and a law degree. It enhanced his courtship of Betty Bloomer, who studied under the famous dancer Martha Graham, and who believed, as Ford did, in physical grace and fitness. In Ford's sophomore year at Grand Rapids South High School, he played center on the city championship football team. He was named to the All-city and All-state teams.

Ford's popularity extended beyond South High. In 1930, the Majestic Theater, the largest in downtown Grand Rapids, joined a midwestern promotional contest to identify the most popular high school senior in fifty participating cities. Theater patrons wrote their candidates' name on ballots and dropped them in lobby boxes. As the Grand Rapids winner, Ford traveled to Chicago where he met the boys and girls of the other cities. Then, it was a train trip to Washington, D.C., for five days of sight-seeing. Apparently, the future president drew no inspiration from the trip. "Ending up in Washington was just about the farthest thing from my mind," he wrote. "Back then I had absolutely no interest in politics or a career in government." Ford wanted to become a famous baseball player!

the only game that Michigan won that year, but for Jerry Ford and his teammates, it was perhaps the sweetest victory of their college careers.

Gerald R. Ford Jr., who would go on to become the nation's thirty-eighth president, was born in Omaha, Nebraska, on July 14, 1913. His name at birth was Leslie Lynch King Jr. His mother, Dorothy, divorced his father when the boy was two, taking him to her parents' home in Grand Rapids, Michigan. In Grand Rapids, she met and married Gerald R. Ford Sr., who adopted her son, gave him his name, and raised Jerry as his own. Over the years Jerry would have only brief contact with his biological father.

Dorothy and Gerald Ford Sr. would become the parents of three more sons— James, Richard, and Thomas Ford. The Fords were a close-knit family who met the challenges of life in Depression-era America through diligence, hard work, and a commitment to small-town values. Gerald Ford Sr. started his own paint company, which mostly sold its products to the many furniture factories located in Grand Rapids. During the Depression, Jerry's stepfather struggled to make a profit and the Fords often found themselves scrimping to make ends meet.

Jerry started kindergarten at Madison Elementary School in Grand Rapids in 1918. Even at that age, Jerry was athletic and loved sports. He recalled playing football and softball on the gravel playground behind the school building, and coming home with torn clothes and skinned knees. He spent just two years at Madison, and then enrolled in East Grand Rapids Elementary School when his family moved to a new home across town.

Jerry struggled with a stuttering problem as an elementary school student, but outgrew it by the age of ten. "Some words gave me fits and it was a struggle for me to get them out," Ford would later recall. "I don't know what caused the problem."

Although he cured his own stutter, Jerry soon confounded his teachers with a different sort of peculiarity—he was ambidextrous, meaning he could write and do other tasks with equal ability with either hand. "My parents and early teachers... became quite concerned and tried to make me use my right hand all the time. After a while, they gave up and I continued switching hands as I'd done before," he said.

By the time Jerry entered South High School in Grand Rapids, sports were an important part of his academic life. He competed on the baseball, basketball, and track teams, but his main sport was football. As a sophomore, he played center and linebacker on the South High School team that won the city championship. Even as a sophomore, his teammates looked to him as a leader.

Although he was a star athlete, Jerry was hardly anybody's idea of a "Big Man on Campus." He was quiet, did not date much, and was regarded by many of his fellow students as something of a square. Jerry was the only student at South High School who made it a point of wearing a suit and tie every day.

Jerry's performance in the classroom did not measure up to his achievements on the football field. Other than sports, Ford participated in few extracurricular activities at South High. He was a good student, earning solid B's in most subjects, but there were exceptions. He struggled with mathematics, usually able to attain only grades of C, but he excelled in history and political science, often earning A's. "Jerry and I were the best pupils in the class," Virginia Berry, Jerry's classmate in American history, later recalled. "Our teacher gave weekly exams and the way it went was one week I would get a 96 and Jerry a 93, next week he'd get a 97 and I'd get a 94. I sat in the back of the room and Jerry up front, and every time exams were returned he would come back to see what my grade was. He didn't resent if I got a better grade, he was just checking. We both got As in that subject, the only two in the class."

Well after his political career started, Jerry regretted not being a better student of English or speech in high school. "Nothing in life is more important than the ability to communicate effectively," he said.

In the fall of 1929 the American stock market crashed, sending the country into a deep economic depression. The family paint business suffered, and Jerry's stepfather was barely able to keep the business running. His employees agreed to work for pennies while he struggled to keep the plant in operation. The Fords felt the sting as much as anyone in town. Gerald Ford Sr. was no longer able to make the mortgage payments on the East Grand Rapids home. The bank took over the property, and the Fords were forced to move into a smaller home in another part of town.

By then, Jerry was a junior in high school. He was a star on the football team and participated in other

Gerald Ford's high school graduation picture, 1931.

"Athletics, my parents kept saying, built a boy's character," Ford recalled. "They were important, but not nearly as important as attaining good grades. My parents made sure that I did my homework and pressed me to excel. In chemistry and other science courses, I received average grades. In Latin, which I disliked, it was a struggle to earn C's. Math was not too difficult. In the courses I really enjoyed, history and government, I did very well."

These pages are from Gerald Ford's Grand Rapids South High School transcript.

Ford was elected to the National Honor Society at the end of his junior year (1930). The society, which had been established the previous year by the Association of Secondary School Principals, honored those students in their junior year who distinguished themselves in scholarship and in athletics.

Ford ranked in the top five percent of his two-hundred-and-twenty-member graduating class, with an overall grade average of 89.58 percent. Latin was his poorest subject, and history and physical training were his best subjects.

sports as well. The Fords' new home was several miles away from South High School. Instead of transferring to a closer high school, Jerry chose to finish his education at South High. This meant he had to rise early every morning to ride a bus into town, where he transferred to another bus that took him to South High. The ride each way took nearly an hour. Jerry didn't mind the ride to school, as it gave him an opportunity to study before class. But on the way home, Jerry was often weary from football practice and had to struggle to stay awake so he wouldn't fall asleep and miss his stop. Eventually, Jerry scraped together $75 that he had earned from part-time jobs and bought an old Model T Ford that he drove to school.

"The car ran beautifully during the football season, but then cold weather set in," Ford remembered. "One December day, the temperature fell below zero and there was snow on the ground. Because I didn't know much about cars, I hadn't bothered to pour antifreeze into the radiator. I parked the car at school, attended varsity basketball practice and drove home for dinner that night. As I pulled into the driveway, I noticed clouds of steam rising up from the engine. I lifted the hood, saw that the motor was a fiery red and decided, incredibly, that what I needed was something to keep the car warm all night. Some old blankets were lying in the garage. I laid them on top of the engine and went inside to eat. Just as we finished the family meal, we heard fire engine sirens loud and close. We looked out the window and my poor car was in flames." The hot engine had ignited the blankets

Jerry had placed on the hood to keep the car warm. The car was a total loss. Jerry hadn't bothered to buy insurance for the vehicle, so his entire investment of $75 went up in smoke. The next morning, he was back on the bus.

By the end of his senior year at South High, Jerry very much wanted to attend college but there was no way his parents could afford the tuition. Arthur Krause, the principal of South High School, arranged for Jerry to receive an athletic scholarship from the University of Michigan. The scholarship covered Jerry's tuition of $100 a year. By today's standards this would be a paltry sum for a college education, but for the Depression-era families in the 1930s it was well beyond most people's means.

The scholarship took care of the tuition, but there were other costs, such as books and room and board. Harry Kipke, the Michigan football coach, found Jerry a job waiting on tables in a university hospital dining room. An aunt and uncle promised to send him two dollars a week for pocket money. He arrived on campus in Ann Arbor in the fall of 1931. "So the hotshot center from Grand Rapids came to live at Michigan in a third-floor 10-by-10 room way in the back of the cheapest rooming house I could find," Ford said. "I shared the rent—$4 a week—with a basketball player. We each had a desk and a bed, which pretty much exhausted the floor space, and there was one small window between us."

Things did improve. Soon after enrolling at Michigan, Jerry joined the Delta Kappa Delta fraternity, and was able to move into a nicer room in the Deltas' fraternity house, although he had to work as a dishwasher to pay his rent. He majored in economics and political science. Again, his grades reflected the work of one who was certainly committed to his studies, although he hardly stood out academically. He finished with a B average, scoring A's in just four courses over his four-year college career: American government, economics, European history, and labor studies.

After the disappointing football season of 1934, Jerry finished his classes at Michigan in the spring of 1935 with little notion of what to do following graduation. He thought he would like to take up the study of law, but was aware that he could not afford tuition to a law school. His performance on the Wolverines' varsity football team prompted two football teams to make him offers to play professionally. The Detroit Lions and Green Bay Packers each offered him contracts to play for them in the fall of 1935, but in that era professional football was not the sport that it is today. It was considered a minor-league sport at the time, played in small stadiums before few fans. Each team offered him contracts that amounted to about $2,800 a year. Ford turned them down.

When Coach Kipke learned that the Yale University football team, coached by his friend Raymond "Ducky" Pond, was looking for an assistant coach, he contacted Pond and recommended Ford as a candidate. Pond invited Ford to visit the Yale campus in New Haven, Connecticut, to talk about the job. "Everywhere I went [at Yale], I discerned an atmosphere of scholarship, dignity, and tradition,"

✶ ALL-STAR EAST TEAM ✶
ROSTER

This photograph shows Gerald Ford on the field of Michigan Stadium at the University of Michigan, Ann Arbor, 1933. Ford was a second-stringer until his senior year.

Ford graduated from South High School in 1931. His football achievements won him a scholarship to the University of Michigan. At Michigan, Ford was as popular as he had been in high school.

In 1934, Ford's final year on the football team, Michigan lost seven of its nine games. But, Ford's outstanding abilities as a center and linebacker won him an invitation to play in the East-West Shrine Game in San Francisco on January 1, 1935. (Pictured are the cover and pages from the game program.) Ford's fifty-eight minutes on the field were good enough to win him offers from the Green Bay Packers and the Detroit Lions to play professional football.

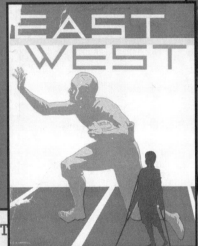

BENEFIT SHRINERS HOSPITAL FOR CRIPPLED CHILDREN

✶ ALL-STAR EAST T
ROSTER

No.	Name	College	Position	Age	Weight	Home Town
5	Borden, Lester	Fordham	R. End	22	179	
10	Hartwig, Charles	U. of Pitt	L. Guard	22	190	
11	Veller, Donald	Indiana	Quarter	23	158	Roodhouse, Ill.
14	Steen, James	Syracuse	L. Tackle	21	200	New Rochelle, N.Y.
16	Munjas, Miller	U. of Pitt	Quarter	23	185	Bellaire, O.
17	Weinstock, Isadore	U. of Pitt	Fullback	21	196	Wilkes-Barre, Pa.
18	Brominski, Edward	Columbia	R. Half	22	171	Sweyerville, Pa.
21	Shepherd, William	Western Maryland	J. Half	25	185	Clearfield, Pa.
22	Leeper, Harry	Northwestern U.	L. End	21	186	Fort Wayne, Ind.
23	Ford, Gerald	U. of Michigan	Center	21	197	Grand Rapids, Mich.
33	Whalen, Edward	Northwestern U.	R. Guard	22	182	Chicago, Ill.
34	Nott, Douglas	U. of Detroit	L. Half	23	188	Ann Arbor, Mich.
37	Akerstrom, George	Colgate	Center	22	187	Whitestone, L.I.
41	Monahan, J. Regis	Ohio State	L. Guard	21	210	Pittsburgh, Pa.
43	Lund, Francis	U. of Minnesota	L. Half	21	189	Rice Lake, Wis.
48	Brocke, Lewis	Colgate	R. Tackle	21	200	Bayside, L.I.
49	Larson, Frank	U. of Minnesota	R. End	22	188	Duluth, Minn.
70	Bengtson, Philip	U. of Minnesota	R. Tackle	21	208	St. Paul, Minn.
74	Pacetti, Mario	U. of Wisconsin	Guard	21	210	Kenosha, Wis.
83	Boganski, Joseph	Colgate	R. End	22	180	New Britain, Conn.
88	Purvis, Duane	Purdue	R. Half	22	194	Mattoon, Ill.
99	Barclay, George	U. of N.C.	R. Guard	23	184	Natrona, Pa.

✶ ALL-STAR WEST TEAM ✶
ROSTER

No.	Name	College	Position	Age	Weight	Height	Home Town
00	Berry, Roy	Tulsa U.	Half	22	157	5.7	Shawnee, Oklahoma
4	Salaino, Joe	Santa Clara	Quarter	22	167	6.0	Tacoma, Wash.
7	Fuqua, Raymond	Southern Methodist	End	22	185	6.0	Shreveport, La.
10	Sobrero, Frank	Santa Clara	Half	21	197	6.1	Oakland, Calif.
13	Warburton, Irvine	U.S.C.	Quarter	21	148	5.6	Los Angeles, Calif.
18	Clemens, Cal	U.S.C.	Half	21	197	5.11	Los Angeles, Calif.
21	Meier, Franklin	Nebraska U.	Center	21	175	6.1	Lincoln, Neb.
28	Siemering, Lawrence	U.S.F.	Center	24	210	6.2	Lodi, Calif.
30	Mucha, Rudolph	Washington U.	Guard	21	190	5.10	Chicago, Ill.
31	Barber, Jas.	U.S.F.	Tackle	22	215	6.3	Manteca, Calif.
33	Hilliard, Bohn	Texas U.	Half	25	168	5.10½	Orange, Texas
35	Stancy, Jas.	Oklahoma U.	Guard	22	200	6.2½	Altus, Oklahoma
41	Stojack, Frank	Washington State	Guard	22	205	5.11½	Tacoma, Wash.
45	Hubbard, Wesley	Olympic Club	End	23	190	6.0	San Jose, Calif.
48	Theodoratus, Geo.	Washington U.	Guard	22	240	6.2	Sacramento, Calif.
50	Carter, Clyde	Southern Methodist	Tackle	25	205	6.1½	Denton, Texas
51	Mahbin, Geo.	Kansas State	Tackle	25	217	6.3	Greenville, Texas
54	Nachtman, Allen	St. Mary's	Full	25	215	6.6	St. Helena, Calif.
69	Pennisi, Felix	St. Mary's	End	21	190	6.0	Los Angeles, Calif.
70	Ullin, Woodrow	Washington U.	Tackle	21	193	6.1	Centralia, Wash.
75	Morse, Ray	Oregon U.	End	23	195	6.1½	Portland, Ore.
76	Sulkosky, Paul	Washington U.	Full	21	195	5.10½	Puyallup, Wash.

OFFICIAL SOUVENIR PROGRAM

All Star East
vs.
All Star West
Tenth Annual Game American Football

KEZAR STADIUM

Tuesday, January 1, 1935.
Military Pageant 1 p.m.
Kickoff 2 p.m.

Auspices of Islam, Asbraz and Ben Ali Temples, A.A.O.N.M.S.,
for the Benefit of the San Francisco Unit
Shriners' Hospital for Crippled Children

PRICE TWENTY-FIVE CENTS

(right-hand column, partially visible home-town listing)

No.	Home Town
00 Ber	
4 Sala	
7 Fuq	
10 Sob	Oakland, Calif.
13 Wa	Angeles, Calif.
18 Clen	Angeles, Calif.
21 Mei	Lincoln, Neb.
28 Sien	Lodi, Calif.
30 Muc	Chicago, Ill.
31 Bar	Manteca, Calif.
33 Hill	Orange, Texas
35 Stac	us, Oklahoma
41 Sto	acoma, Wash.
45 Hub	an Jose, Calif.
48 The	amento, Calif.
50 Car	Denton, Texas
51 Mac	enville, Texas
54 Nich	Helena, Calif.
69 Pen	Angeles, Calif.
70 Ulli	entralia, Wash.
75 Mor	Porland, Ore.
76 Sulk	yallup, Wash.

J. REGIS MONAHAN
Ohio State
Left Guard

GEORGE AKERSTROM
Colgate
Center

GERALD FORD
U. of Michigan
Center

FRANK LARSON
U. of Minnesota
Right End

HARRY LEEPER
Northwestern U.
Left End

DOUGLAS NOTT
U. of Detroit
Left Half

EDWARD BROMINSKI
Columbia
Right Half

GEORGE BARCLAY
U. of C.
Right Guard

Ford said. "At the end of my second day, Pond offered me $2,400 a year if I would join him as an assistant and also coach the freshman boxing team. I knew nothing about boxing, but I promised to take instruction at the Grand Rapids YMCA before returning that fall."

Ford had another reason to jump at Pond's offer—he wanted to enroll in Yale Law School. He asked Pond whether he could take law classes while working as a coach. Pond thought his duties with the team would take up too much of his time, but he promised to relay the request to Yale's law school deans. Looking over his grades from Michigan, the deans doubted that Ford could handle his classes in addition to his coaching responsibilities. They turned down his request, but Ford decided to take Pond's offer anyway, hoping eventually to change their minds.

Ford started work at Yale in August 1935, and soon realized Pond had been correct—coaching football was a full-time job and he had been foolish to think he could have squeezed in law school during his spare time. Yale's varsity team had a good year, winning six games and losing three. Ford spent the next summer working as a ranger at Yellowstone National Park. The next fall he returned to Yale, where he helped coach a team that won the Ivy League championship. Two of the players on that team were Robert Taft Jr. and William Proxmire, both of whom would go on to serve in the U.S. Senate.

After the season, Ford again found time on his hands. This time, instead of working at a national park, Ford returned to Ann Arbor, where he took law classes at the University of Michigan. He scored B's in two classes, then returned to Yale in the fall of 1937. Again, he asked permission to take classes while coaching football. Pond reluctantly agreed, but Ford still had to convince the law school deans. This time, they agreed to let him take two classes in the spring semester, after football season. They cautioned Ford that he would have to score well in those classes to be accepted as a full-time student.

"They were reluctant—98 of the 125 members of the freshman class had made Phi Beta Kappa as undergraduates, they pointed out—but they finally agreed to let me take two courses that spring," Ford recalled. "I earned two more B's. Satisfied that I could do the work, they withdrew their rejections and accepted me full time."

Ford worked hard and graduated as a member of the Yale Law School Class of 1941. He graduated in the top 25 percent of the class, demonstrating that he certainly was up to the challenge of Yale. Among his classmates at Yale were Cyrus Vance, a future secretary of state; Potter Stewart, a future member of the U.S. Supreme Court; and Sargent Shriver, who would marry the sister of President John F. Kennedy, head the Peace Corps, and run for vice president on the Democratic ticket in 1972.

Following graduation, Ford returned to Grand Rapids, where he started a law practice with Philip Buchen, an old friend from his days living in the Delta

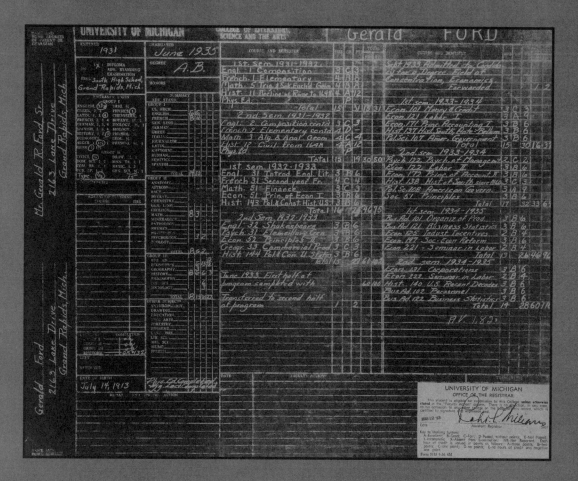

Gerald Ford's transcript from the University of Michigan, which he attended from 1931 to 1935. Ford graduated from the University of Michigan with a 1.82 grade-point average and a liberal arts degree. He received A's in four courses during his four years at the university—European History from the Decline of Rome to 1648, Western Civilization Since 1648, Labor I, and American Government.

Kappa Delta fraternity on the Michigan campus. There was little time to devote to the practice of law, though. Just a few months after Ford returned to Grand Rapids, the Japanese launched an attack on the U.S. naval base at Pearl Harbor. Ford enlisted in the U.S. Navy and saw action in the South Pacific during World War II aboard an aircraft carrier.

He returned to Grand Rapids following the war and resumed the practice of law. In 1948, he won his first election, a seat in the U.S. House of Representatives. He took a brief time off during that campaign to marry Elizabeth Bloomer, whom everyone called Betty. Jerry and Betty Ford would raise four children, Michael, John, Steven, and Susan.

A Republican, Ford remained in the House throughout the 1950s, turning down offers from GOP leaders in Michigan to run for governor and the U.S. Senate. Instead, Ford gained stature and influence in the House, and in 1963 was elected chairman of the House Republican Conference—the third most important leadership post in the GOP caucus.

Coach Gerald Ford (rear row, third from left) and the Yale University Boxing Team, 1936. When the Yale University football coach needed an assistant, he offered Ford $2,400 per year—then a fairly good salary—to work as assistant line coach, junior varsity coach, and as coach of Yale's boxing team. "Of boxing," said Ford, "I knew next to nothing. No, that's not right. I knew absolutely nothing."

Ford accepted the job, hoping to realize two dreams at once—to stay in football and to pursue a long-nurtured aspiration to attend law school. However, the admissions officer was convinced that he could not handle both law school and a full-time job. Finally, in 1938, Ford obtained permission to take two courses on a trial basis. He did sufficiently well to be allowed to increase to a full-time program the following semester. "I was warned that of the 125 law students entering that year," said Ford, "ninety-eight were Phi Beta Kappa, and that was clearly another league from the one I had been in. Somehow, I got by."

After the assassination of President Kennedy in November 1963, Ford was appointed to the Warren Commission, which investigated the assassination and concluded that there had been no conspiracy to kill the president, and that gunman Lee Harvey Oswald had acted alone. Over the years, skeptics have criticized the conclusion and the evidence on which the commission relied, but no one has ever been able to offer convincing proof of a conspiracy to kill the president.

In 1965, with Democrats in control of Congress, Ford was elected House Minority Leader, the top GOP leadership post in the House.

In 1972, while President Richard M. Nixon was on his way to scoring a landslide victory in his reelection campaign, reports surfaced that a group of burglars employed by the president's campaign committee had been arrested with electronic eavesdropping equipment during a break-in at the Democratic National Committee office in the Watergate office complex in Washington.

The scandal that grew out of the break-in became known as Watergate. In late 1973, a separate scandal engulfed Vice President Spiro T. Agnew, forcing him to resign amid charges that he evaded income taxes. When Agnew resigned, Nixon selected Ford to serve as the new vice president.

In August of 1974, the Watergate scandal finally caught up with Nixon. He became the first president to resign from office, and Ford was sworn in to take his place. As such, Ford became the only president in history to have been appointed to the job under the terms of presidential succession spelled out in the U.S. Constitution.

For Ford, it would be a brief stay in the White House. Soon after taking office, he decided to issue a presidential pardon for Nixon, preventing prosecutors from seeking indictments against the former president. That decision haunted him as the 1976 election approached. During the race that fall against Democrat Jimmy Carter, Ford committed a major blunder when he declared during a televised debate that "there is no Soviet domination of Eastern Europe, and there never will be under a Ford administration."

The former Soviet Union had, of course, dominated many of the Eastern European countries since the closing days of World War II, sponsoring puppet regimes in Poland, Romania, East Germany, and other countries, and marching troops into Czechoslovakia to stifle rebellions. Ford tried to clarify his remarks following the debate, but Americans found themselves doubting his competency as president and Carter won the election of 1976.

After taking the oath of office and being sworn in as the nation's thirty-ninth president, Jimmy Carter's first words were, "For myself and for our nation, I want to thank my predecessor for all he has done to heal our land."

—Hal Marcovitz

Jimmy Carter
Chapter Thirty-eight

From the time he was a boy, Jimmy Carter wanted to become a naval officer. Growing up in a rural Georgia town named Plains, Jimmy had never seen the ocean, much less the huge U.S. Navy battleships and destroyers he hoped one day to command. His interest was piqued by his Uncle Tom Gordy, who had joined the Navy as an enlisted man and was, as the recruiting posters promised, seeing the world. Every few weeks, young Jimmy would receive a picture postcard from Uncle Tom announcing his latest port of call. Soon, Jimmy had a collection of postcards from Marseille, Gibraltar, Amsterdam, Athens, the Panama Canal, Pearl Harbor, Manila, Hong Kong, Pago Pago, and Sydney, among other places. Occasionally, Uncle Tom would send a gift—a model sampan, for example, or a tiny enameled box with oriental dragons painted on it. Jimmy treasured these gifts, for they had planted the hope that he would be a Navy man, too.

On June 30, 1943, with the Second World War raging in Europe and the South Pacific, eighteen-year-old Jimmy Carter took a major step toward fulfilling his dream when he stepped onto the campus of the U.S. Naval Academy in Annapolis, Maryland. He was sworn in as a "plebe"—a freshman student soon to face three years of vigorous training, testing, and physical endurance. Jimmy had studied hard and prepared himself for years for this opportunity, and he resolved that no task at Annapolis would cause him to fail in his goal of graduating as an officer of the U.S. Navy.

However, Jimmy had not counted on the rituals of hazing at the academy. For decades, hazing was a common practice on many college campuses, but no place was it practiced with such relish and cruelty as on the campuses of America's military academies—Annapolis and West Point, where future officers of the U.S. Army are trained. Plebes at both schools found themselves at the beck and call of upperclassmen, who could force them to perform ridiculous and demeaning chores simply to provide amusement for other students. Sometimes, the plebes at Annapolis were woken up early and forced to run through the campus obstacle course chased by sadistic upperclassmen. Plebes were told to row heavy boats

Plains, Georgia

A view of Main Street in Plains, Georgia, taken around 1976. Few presidents have had such close ties with the town where they were born and raised. The rural southern culture of Plains, which revolves around farming, church, and school, had an enormous influence on molding the character and shaping the political policies of the thirty-ninth president of the United States.

The Plains High School basketball team, 1940. Jimmy Carter is in the back row, second from left (number ten).

In his *Memoirs* and in many interviews and speeches, Carter has stated that the principal influences on his education were his hometown of Plains, Georgia; the Plains High School; the Plains Baptist Church; and his studies at the United States Naval Academy at Annapolis, Maryland.

against the current across the Severn River, which flowed through the campus. Other times, plebes were told to snap to attention and recite inane poems or sing songs. Jimmy endured the hardships of hazing, knowing it was part of the Annapolis experience. He forced himself to do whatever the upperclassmen commanded, until the day a senior told him to stand at attention and sing the Civil War song "Marching Through Georgia." Jimmy flatly refused.

The song, written by Henry Clay Work in 1865, celebrates the victory of the Union Army under General William Tecumseh Sherman, whose "March to the Sea" helped destroy the Confederacy. Sherman led his men on a cruel rampage through Georgia and other states, burning farms and looting homes as they swept aside rebel resistance. Before their march was over Sherman's men destroyed Georgia's capital, Atlanta.

Jimmy Carter did not have much interest in the history of the Civil War, but because he grew up in the South, he had come to respect the rebel cause and the sacrifices his ancestors had made for a fight they believed was just. To Southern whites, "Marching Through Georgia" was regarded as an insult. The song contains these lyrics:

Sherman's dashing Yankee boys will never make the coast!
So the saucy rebels said 'twas a handsome boast
Had they not forgot, alas! To reckon with the Host
While we were marching through Georgia.

Plebes who refused an upperclassman's orders found themselves subjected to severe punishments. They were told to bend over and grab their toes so their rumps could be paddled with wooden soup spoons or planks of wood. In the dining hall, they were forced to eat their meals while sitting under their tables. Or, they may have been ordered to assume a sitting posture at the table, but instructed not to let their posteriors touch their chairs. After a few minutes, the pain of stooping while eating could become unbearable. Jimmy endured the punishments, but for the remainder of his year as a plebe he steadfastly refused to sing "Marching Through Georgia."

Years later, as Carter was campaigning for the presidency of the United States, he visited Phoenix, Arizona. To welcome him, a high school marching band played "Marching Through Georgia." Jimmy Carter, whose warm and wide smile had captivated voters, suddenly grew sullen. "Doesn't anybody realize that's not a southern song?" he asked.

James Earl Carter Jr. was born October 1, 1924, in Plains Hospital. He was the first U.S. president born in a hospital. His father was James Earl Carter Sr., a prosperous but by no means wealthy farmer and storekeeper whom everyone called Earl. His mother, Lillian Gordy Carter, had been educated as a nurse. In keeping with southern custom, she was called Miss Lillian. Jimmy was the oldest of the Carters' four children.

For Jimmy, childhood was a Huck Finn existence. He rarely wore shoes or a shirt in the spring and summer. He fished for eels and catfish in the Kinchafoonee Creek. He climbed trees and went hunting for possums and raccoons with his father. His playmates were mostly the African-American children of the poor farm workers who lived in shacks on his father's land. Jimmy would have few white friends until he enrolled in the Plains school. Like every Southern town during the 1920s, Plains was segregated. That meant white children went to one school while black children went to another.

Jimmy entered Plains School in September 1930, one month before his sixth birthday. The school was relatively new. It had been erected just nine years before. First through eleventh grades were taught in the same building. The elementary school was housed in the east wing while high school students took classes in the north and west wings.

Jimmy was one of the brightest children in the elementary school wing, a fact attributed mostly to the influence of Miss Lillian. She was a voracious reader who passed her love for books on to her children, particularly Jimmy. When he was five years old, Jimmy's godmother sent him the complete works of the French writer Guy de Maupassant. Jimmy was too young to read the stories then, but he would eventually read them all. In the third grade, Jimmy received a prize for reading the most books. The reward for the contest was lunch at the teacher's house.

Many of the students at the school in Plains went on to college, which was a remarkable achievement for children of the rural South during the Great Depression. Carter—and nearly everyone else who went to school in Plains from the 1920s to the 1950s—attributed the school's success to one woman, Julia Coleman. "I have never known of a teacher who had such a profound impact on students as she did," Carter said years later.

Miss Julia, as she was known around school, inspired her students to see beyond the tiny world of Plains and the rural South. She urged them to read, of course, but not just schoolbooks. Miss Julia's students read poetry and developed an interest in art and music. She engaged them in conversations about national and international events and forced them to become debaters. She had a particular talent for recognizing intelligence in her students and challenging them to make the most of their abilities.

Jimmy spent his eighth-grade year in Miss Julia's classroom. At the conclusion of the year, Miss Julia recommended that Jimmy read *War and Peace* over the summer. The 1,400-page novel about Napoleon's invasion of Russia is not an easy read for most adults; for a thirteen-year-old boy it might have proven to be an overwhelming task. But Jimmy resolved to read the book, thinking at first it was a Western adventure featuring gun-toting cowboys and Indians on the warpath. Of course, *War and Peace* has nothing to do with cowboys and Indians. Written between 1863 and 1869 by Russian author Leo Tolstoy, the novel is complicated, featuring more than five hundred characters whose lives are affected by the war between Russia and France early in the nineteenth century. The overwhelming theme of the book is that war is evil, and while princes and army generals may find fame and valor in the fighting, it is ordinary people who suffer the most. Jimmy finished the book that summer and, in fact, would read Tolstoy's masterpiece again two more times by the time he was an adult. No book would have more of an effect on his outlook during his four years as president, or in the years that followed, during which he served his country as an internationally known diplomat. The message of *War and Peace*, Carter said later, was "to show that the course of human events—even great historical events—is determined ultimately not by the leaders, but by the common ordinary people. Their hopes and dreams, their doubts and fears, their courage and tenacity, their quiet commitment to determine the destiny of the world."

Despite his love for reading, Jimmy was hardly what anyone would call "bookish." He was athletic and competed on the basketball and track teams. He joined the Future Farmers of America. He took up woodworking, an avocation that would become a lifelong passion. He dated girls, worked in his father's store, and went hunting and fishing.

"The course of human events…is determined ultimately not by the leaders, but by the common ordinary people. Their hopes and dreams, their doubts and fears, their courage and tenacity, their quiet commitment to determine the destiny of the world."

Carter is in the front row, right side (squatting down) in this photograph of the Plains High School class of 1941.

The First Baptist Church in Plains, Georgia, where President Carter still teaches a Sunday school class. (This photo was taken around 1976.) The church website states, "This unique situation gives us an opportunity to share with many people who have never before had any close exposure to the Gospel message. This opportunity also represents a responsibility which we take very seriously."

He also maintained his fascination with the Navy. While still in elementary school, Jimmy wrote to Annapolis asking for the school's catalog without, of course, revealing his age. The catalog became a much-cherished possession and Jimmy read and re-read it many times, memorizing the criteria he would have to meet in order to be accepted as a midshipman. "It was the driving force in my life," he said later.

Some parts of the catalog puzzled him, though. For example, he fretted for years that his toothy smile would cause him to be turned down. The catalog warned that candidates who suffered an overbite—referred to in the catalog as a "malocclusion of the teeth"—would not be considered.

The malocclusion turned out to be a trivial issue that would have no effect on his application to Annapolis. His grades would not stand in his way, either. As he approached graduation, Jimmy's grades were among the best at Plains High School; he would have been valedictorian had it not been for an ill-advised prank. Jimmy and some friends played hooky just a few weeks before graduation. They were caught and punished. In Jimmy's case, the punishment included denial of valedictory honors. Still, when Jimmy graduated from Plains High School on June 2, 1941, he was one of three commencement speakers.

Nevertheless, the one handicap that Jimmy could not overcome was the lack of political influence required to obtain an appointment to Annapolis. Backing by the local member of Congress was necessary to obtain admission to the service academies. In Sumter County, the congressman was Democrat Stephen Pace. Earl Carter knew his son's ambitions, and he knew it would take Pace's help to win Jimmy an appointment to Annapolis. By 1938, Earl Carter was an influential farmer and businessman in Sumter County. He contributed money to Pace's congressional campaign that year as well as in 1940 and helped campaign for him in Plains. However, when Jimmy graduated from Plains High School Pace decided to secure an appointment to Annapolis for another boy.

Pace promised to reconsider Jimmy in 1942. In the meantime, he recommended to Earl and Lillian that they send their boy to Georgia Southwestern College, a tiny two-year school located in the nearby town of Americus. The school was small, consisting of just some two hundred students. It included just one classroom building, two dormitories, and a gymnasium. Tuition was $204 a year, which Earl paid.

Georgia Southwestern was not Annapolis, but Jimmy made the most of his time at the school. He knew he needed to keep his grades up, so he studied hard. He also joined the basketball team and got involved in student activities. He joined a fraternity and was elected vice president of the freshman class. During his first semester at Georgia Southwestern he lived at home and took a bus to Americus for classes. He moved into a dormitory for his second semester. His baby brother Billy had been born that year and Jimmy felt crowded at home, sharing the modest Carter family house in Plains with his parents, two sisters, and a baby.

Congressman Pace made good on his promise to Earl and won an appointment for Jimmy to Annapolis in 1942. By then, the Japanese had attacked Pearl Harbor, drawing the United States into World War II. It is likely that if Jimmy hadn't been appointed to the academy, he would have been drafted and sent off to combat as an enlisted man. Still, he would have to wait yet another year before enrolling at Annapolis. Jimmy lacked a background in the science and engineering courses he would need as a midshipman. The Navy recommended that he spend a year at Georgia Institute of Technology in Atlanta, where he could study science and also take courses in navigation and seamanship as a member of the Reserve Officers' Training Corps. Jimmy agreed, and enrolled that fall at Georgia Tech.

Jimmy hated city life. He joined few college organizations and rarely spent a weekend on the Atlanta campus, preferring instead to take the bus home to Plains. He studied hard, though, and at the end of his year at Georgia Tech placed in the top 10 percent of his class and made honor roll.

Finally, in the summer of 1943, he started classes at Annapolis. Ordinarily, the service academies require four years to obtain a degree, but during World War II the Army and Navy were both in need of young officers so the courses were accelerated so that they could be completed in three years.

Carter and the other midshipmen rose at 6:15 A.M. every morning and spent their entire day in class or field training of some sort. They had little time to themselves, and even their weekends were dominated by their studies. Jimmy endured it all—the study, physical tests, discipline, and even the hazing. "He would never let it out," said Arthur Middletown, one of his classmates at Annapolis, "never kick a chair or throw a book like the rest of us."

Slowly, Carter inched his way toward graduation. Each summer, the midshipmen were assigned to duty aboard warships. In the summer of 1944, Carter saw duty aboard the U.S.S. *New York*, an old battleship that patrolled the North Atlantic. Mostly, the *New York* seemed to spend the war dodging torpedoes launched from German U-boats. During Carter's summer aboard the *New York*, a U-boat torpedo clipped the ship's propeller. The *New York* made for port for repairs, but the damaged propeller caused the ship to lurch violently all the way home. It was an exciting summer. Carter held a variety of jobs aboard the *New York*. His favorite job was manning a forty-millimeter antiaircraft gun during alerts. His least favorite job was cleaning toilets that had a habit of overflowing on the old ship.

During Carter's second summer as a midshipman, he was called on deck along with the rest of the crew to hear a radio transmission broadcast by President Harry Truman. While standing at attention on deck, Carter heard the president announce that an atomic bomb had just been dropped on the Japanese city of Hiroshima. World War II was over. Jimmy Carter would not, at least in the foreseeable future, be serving as an officer aboard a navy ship during a time of war.

Jimmy Carter graduated from Annapolis in June 1946 and was commissioned an ensign in the U.S. Navy. A few days later he married Eleanor

DRESS PARADE, U. S. NAVAL ACADEMY, ANNAPOLIS, MD.

PICKERING PHOTO   1A3129

Looking Across Smoke Park, showing Seaward Terrace of Bancroft Hall.   22

U. S. Naval Academy, Annapolis, Md.   60666

Colored postcards show scenes at Annapolis, circa 1941–45.

The United States Naval Academy at Annapolis, Maryland, was established in 1845 as an undergraduate college to prepare young people to be effective naval and marine officers. The four-year course of study is similar to that of leading technical colleges except that in addition to scientific and cultural studies, there are specialized courses relating to the sea and to the profession of the naval officer.

Jimmy Carter graduated from the Naval Academy in 1946 with the accelerated class of 1947.

Midshipmen Preparing for Sailboat Drill, U. S. Naval Academy, Annapolis, Md.

OFFICIAL U. S. NAVY PHOTOGRAPH   1B-H2267

Rosalynn Smith in a small ceremony in Plains. Rosalynn was a friend of Jimmy's sister Ruth; she had started dating Jimmy a year earlier. The Carters would raise a family of three sons and a daughter.

Carter's Navy career would eventually lead him into service under Admiral Hyman Rickover, who spearheaded the Navy's efforts to develop nuclear submarines. During the program, though, Carter was forced to resign his commission when his father died and Miss Lillian asked him to return to Plains to take over the family farm and business. He reluctantly agreed, and on October 9, 1953, Jimmy Carter left the U.S. Navy and the career he had dreamed about since first receiving his Uncle Tom's postcards as a boy.

Carter entered politics in 1962, winning a disputed election to a seat in the Georgia State Senate. Initially, it appeared that Carter had lost the election, but he was able to prove that his opponent's victory was based on widespread voting fraud. He appealed, and a judge threw out votes cast by people either dead or in prison. The subsequent recount showed Carter the winner. In 1966, he lost the Democratic primary for governor of Georgia, but ran for the position again in 1970 and won. He became one of the first southern politicians to support racial integration. *Time* magazine featured him on its cover in 1971, and both the *Washington Post* and *Life* magazine declared Carter a representative of the "New South."

In 1972, Carter sought to win his party's vice presidential nomination at the Democratic National Convention. His campaign fell short and Carter was left off the ticket. He resolved to make another run for a national ticket in 1976, this time as his party's presidential nominee. When the 1976 campaign began, Carter was a little-known former governor of a southern state, and political experts gave him little chance of winning the Democratic nomination in a field that featured such heavyweight contenders as Congressman Morris Udall and Senators Henry Jackson and Birch Bayh. But the public seemed to connect with his down-home ways and Southern charm, and Carter scored impressive victories in the early primaries and was soon viewed as the front-runner. That fall, he defeated the incumbent president, Gerald R. Ford, who found himself weighed down by his pardon of President Richard M. Nixon following Nixon's resignation from the White House in the aftermath of the Watergate scandal.

As president, Carter became a defender of international human rights. In September 1978 he hosted a historic summit to encourage peace talks between Egypt and Israel. At home, though, his efforts resulted in far fewer successes. He was unable to rescue the economy from a deep recession. Meanwhile, America's stature as a world power suffered during Carter's presidency. In 1979, militant Islamic students in Iran seized the U.S. embassy and held members of the diplomatic staff hostage for fourteen months. When a military rescue attempt failed in the Iranian desert, Carter took the blame. Ultimately, he was unable to negotiate the release of the hostages before the election of 1980, and he lost to Republican Ronald Reagan.

Carter has spent his post-presidential years as an active member of the world community. He has traveled from country to country, crisis to crisis, using his talents as a negotiator to help broker cease-fires, bring relief to famine-stricken areas, and ensure free elections. He also became an active volunteer for Habitat for Humanity, helping to build homes for the needy in the United States and abroad. In 2002, he was awarded the Nobel Peace Prize.

During his acceptance speech in Oslo, Norway, Jimmy Carter talked about the influences on his life. He mentioned Julia Coleman, saying, "When I was a young boy, this teacher introduced me to Leo Tolstoy's novel *War and Peace*. She interpreted that powerful narrative as a reminder that the simple human attributes of goodness and truth can overcome great power. She also taught us that an individual is not swept along a tide of inevitability but can influence even the greatest human events."

—Hal Marcovitz

Ronald Reagan
Chapter Thirty-nine

When Ronald Reagan arrived at tiny Eureka College in Illinois in the fall of 1928, he found what he thought was a sleepy campus composed of aging ivy-covered classroom buildings and dormitories, streets lined with shady elm trees, and a creaky old football stadium that came alive on Saturday afternoons. At Eureka, the young man who would become the fortieth president of the United States found a way to escape the hard times his family knew in nearby Dixon.

Eureka College, however, was on the verge of rebellion in the fall of 1928. Students and faculty members were quite vocal about demanding changes in the way college president Bert Wilson and the board of trustees had run the school for decades. Eureka's administrators complied with strict rules set down by the school's sponsor, the Disciples of Christ Church. Daily chapel attendance was mandatory, and dancing at campus events was prohibited. Even students caught attending dances at such harmless off-campus affairs as American Legion–sponsored mixers were severely punished. Women had to adhere to a strict dress code that required skirts to be worn down to their calves.

The students wanted the rules to be eased. For the most part, faculty members were sympathetic to the students' complaints. The faculty had its own complaints about President Wilson. They believed the curriculum was outdated. They felt the college, a shoestring operation to begin with, was nevertheless suffering because of Wilson's parsimonious attitude and his willingness to cut budgets. When Wilson proposed combining several departments, laying off six professors and cutting the salaries of others, what had long been a quiet contrariness by teachers about Wilson's administration suddenly became a very public show of rancor.

The students wanted Wilson to resign. Student leaders proposed a strike—they wanted all students to stay out of classes until Wilson stepped down. Late in the fall, the students met in the school chapel to debate the issue. Although the upperclassmen were leading the revolt, they felt a freshman should propose the strike. The upperclassmen were too close to graduation and feared that if the ploy failed, they would be dismissed from school and denied their diplomas.

...we wore knee pants and black stockings and when our shoes wore out we put cardboard in the bottoms...

Ronald Reagan, age eight, is in the second row at far left with his hand on chin in this 1919 photograph of his third-grade class at Tampico Grade School, Illinois. Nellie Darby, his teacher, is at upper right. Reagan's best grade school chum Denison (whom Dutch called Newt) later told an interviewer that they "attended all the silent Westerns, gaining free admission by carrying coal to the Opera House where they were shown." Denison recalled:

[On Sundays] we wore knee pants and black stockings and when our shoes wore out we put cardboard in the bottoms and when we got holes in our stockings we painted in shoe polish to cover 'em up. We stole a few grapes and some apples. . . .We had this janitor at the school. In the fall we'd all come down and help him rake up the leaves and we'd stay for a big marshmallow roast. We didn't play ball on Sunday. . . . We had to go to church and then have the family dinner and not much rough play.

In 1920, the Reagan family settled in Dixon, Illinois, a small town of nearly 8,200 residents about a hundred miles west of Chicago. The Reagans lived in a modest rented three-bedroom house—their fifth new town and seventh house in the previous nine years. Dutch, now nine years old, remembered his childhood in Dixon as the happiest period of his life. "We didn't know we were poor because the people around us were of the same circumstance," wrote the future president. Dixon was Ronald Reagan's first permanent home. "All of us have a place to go back to. Dixon is that place for me," he later wrote. "There was the life that shaped my mind and my body for all the years to come after."

Reagan was enrolled in the fifth grade at South Central Grammar School, a five-minute walk from his home. He then attended South Dixon High School, transferring to North Dixon in his sophomore year.

During his junior year at North Dixon High School, 1926–27, Reagan played guard for the varsity football team. The caption for this photograph in the 1927 school yearbook, *The Dixonian*, read, "'Dutch,' the lightest but fastest guard on the team, won his letter through sheer grit. With 'Dutch' returning to the squad, things look good for Dixon in 1927." Reagan excelled in athletics and he also had strong interests in dramatics, creative writing, drawing, and school politics.

The freshman selected to stand before the student body and propose the strike was Ronald Reagan. He was a popular member of the freshman class, a leader among his fellow students and, as a member of the drama club, somebody who appeared at ease in front of an audience. Although hardly a student radical, Reagan accepted the challenge.

"I'd been told that I should sell the idea so there'd be no doubt of the outcome," Reagan recalled. "I discovered that night that an audience had a feel to it and in the parlance of the theater, that audience and I were together. When I came to actually presenting the motion there was no need for parliamentary procedure; they came to their feet with a roar—even the faculty members present voted by acclamation. It was heady wine."

For Reagan, this would be one of his first opportunities to use his natural powers as a communicator to persuade an audience of his position—it was even reported that one of the female students in attendance that evening fainted under the spell of his rhetoric.

The student strike commenced the day after Thanksgiving break. For the next week, only eight of the school's two hundred and twenty students attended classes (two of the students were President Wilson's daughters). Reporters swarmed to the tiny Eureka campus to report the news about the student uprising. On December 7, 1928, President Wilson submitted his resignation to the board of trustees and the students returned to classes.

Years later, when Reagan was governor of California, he encountered a similar student uprising at the University of California at Berkeley over a series of cuts in the university's budget proposed by the state government. As governor, Reagan was far less sympathetic to the plight of the Berkeley students and faculty members who supported them than he had been as a leader of the Eureka campus uprising. "It is disturbing to see supposedly mature members of the academic community inciting students to intemperate acts with inflammatory charges," he huffed at the time.

Of course, by then, Ronald Reagan had received a thorough schooling in the conservative ideology that would come to dominate his political career and eventually his presidency.

Ronald Wilson Reagan was born February 6, 1911, in Tampico, Illinois, a small town about ninety miles west of Chicago. He was the second son of Jack and Nelle Reagan. His mother was a devoted churchgoer, his father a shoe salesman and hopeless alcoholic.

Although the Reagans were of Scotch-Irish ancestry, the little boy was called "Dutch" almost from the moment of his birth. Upon seeing his second son in the hospital, Jack called him a "fat little Dutchman."

There is no question the Reagans were a close family, but life was a struggle for them. Jack Reagan's jobs in the shoe business were invariably low-paying; his drinking put a further strain on the family. By the time Dutch entered the first grade at Filas Willard School in February 1916 in Galesburg, a town near the Iowa border, the Reagans had already been forced to move three times.

Still, Nelle Reagan brought warmth to the home. Dutch and his older brother Neil loved snuggling close to their mother while she read to them. They particularly loved adventure stories, such as the exploits of the Three Musketeers or King Arthur and the Knights of the Round Table.

Dutch could read before he entered the first grade. Nelle Reagan taught her son to read in the parlor of their Galesburg home by having him follow her fingers as she pointed to words on the page. "One evening," Reagan later recalled, "all the funny black marks on the paper clicked into place."

The fact that little Dutch could read at age five was a source of pride among the Reagans. Nelle would often invite neighbors in to listen to her boy read articles from the Galesburg newspaper.

During Dutch's second year at Filas Willard, Jack Reagan's drinking cost him his job and the family was forced to move again, this time to nearby Monmouth, Illinois. Jack found a job selling shoes in the E.B. Colwell Department Store, and Dutch and Neil enrolled in Monmouth Central School.

Dutch did not adjust easily to school in Monmouth. He was nearsighted and had trouble reading the blackboard, but his parents were unaware of his problem and no effort was made to correct his vision. He also made few friends in Monmouth; evidently, his classmates were jealous of him. "He was startling to look at, not only good-looking but he had this air about him," recalled a Monmouth classmate, Gertrude Crockett. "I used to turn around in class just to stare back at him. His jaw was always set—as though somebody was going to take a poke at him and he was ready for the punches… I looked at his thrust-out chin every day and wondered, 'Why?'"

Other classmates were much more cruel. Dutch would often be chased home from school by bullies; later, when he returned to Monmouth to campaign for the presidency, he told local citizens that his mad dashes home were the only times in his life when he had been truly terrified.

In the summer of 1919 the Reagans moved again, this time back to Tampico, where Jack had the opportunity to manage a shoe store. Dutch entered the third grade that fall at Tampico Grade School. He wasn't much for studying, but he was generally an "A" student because he discovered he had a photographic memory. Dutch's favorite subject was American history; he could easily recall the dates of battles and scored well on tests.

It was at this time that Dutch developed a love for football—a sport he much preferred over baseball because his poor eyesight made it hard for him to hit the ball. Each day, he would hurry home from school for the sandlot games his friends played in his Tampico neighborhood. "We chose up sides, backed up to the limits of the field, and one of us kicked off," he recalled. "Then, screaming and waving our arms we descended on the unlucky kid who caught it. Everyone piled on top of him."

In December 1920 the Reagans moved once again. Jack had become part owner of the Fashion Boot Shop, a shoe store in Dixon, a small town about seventy-five miles west of Chicago. Jack Reagan's finances would improve little in Dixon, however. Although he managed the store, he was in debt to his partner and brought home little money over the next few years. Nevertheless, this was the last time the Reagan family had to move. Dixon became Dutch's permanent home until he left for college.

Located along the Rock River, Dixon was then a town of some ten thousand people. All the streets were lined with trees. On the main street, Galena Avenue, a visitor might stay at the town's largest hotel, the Nachusa House, where Abraham Lincoln spent a night in 1856 when he arrived in town to debate Stephen A. Douglas. Dixon's South Central Grammar School, where Dutch enrolled, was a red brick building erected during the Civil War. The Reagans rented a house on South Hennepin Avenue. The rent was $23 a month, which Jack Reagan was hard-pressed to meet. The family did find the money for eyeglasses for Dutch, though; by then, his eye problems had been diagnosed.

During their summers in Dixon, Nelle started taking Dutch to the Chautauqua shows held on campgrounds outside of town. Often staged beneath large tents, the Chautauqua shows included Bible readings and other religious lectures, but there were also theatrical productions. This was probably Dutch's first exposure to any sort of live theater. Neil, the more rebellious of the two Reagan

In April 1927, the North Dixon High School junior class presented Philip Barry's play *You and I*. (In 1923, *You and I*, a comedy about life and manners among the socially privileged, had been performed one hundred and seventy times on the Broadway stage.) Reagan and Margaret "Mugs" Cleaver, his high school girlfriend, received top billing playing sweethearts. They are shown sitting on the sofa in the top picture. Dutch is kneeling and playing the banjo in the bottom photograph (detail to the right).

children, did all he could to stay away from the Chautauqua shows, but Dutch was an enthusiastic member of the audiences.

In the summer of 1925, now a tall, muscular lad of fourteen, Dutch found work on a construction crew building the foundation for a Catholic church in Dixon. Dutch's job was to swing a pick. He spent all summer working for the crew and earned the princely sum of $200. Certainly, the impoverished Reagans could have used that money, but Nelle insisted that Dutch put the cash away for college. She was determined to see her children go to college even though most boys in Dixon dropped out of school in the eighth grade to take jobs in the local factories.

After a year at South Dixon High School, Dutch transferred to North Dixon High. There he was a member of the football team, though he sat on the bench most of his sophomore season. He was an excellent swimmer, though, and in the summer of 1926 found a job as a lifeguard in Dixon's Lowell Park. He earned $18 a week for a job he worked at seven days a week, usually twelve hours a day. He gave swimming lessons to young children, delivered the raw hamburger to the lunch stand in the mornings, showed off by performing swan dives off the diving platform, and of course made sure nobody drowned. In seven summers at Lowell Park, he was credited with saving seventy-seven lives.

At North Dixon High, Dutch befriended a young English teacher named B. J. Fraser who convinced him to join the drama club, which Fraser coached. The fact that Margaret Cleaver was also a member probably had a lot to do with Dutch's decision to join. The daughter of a local minister and the prettiest girl in Dixon,

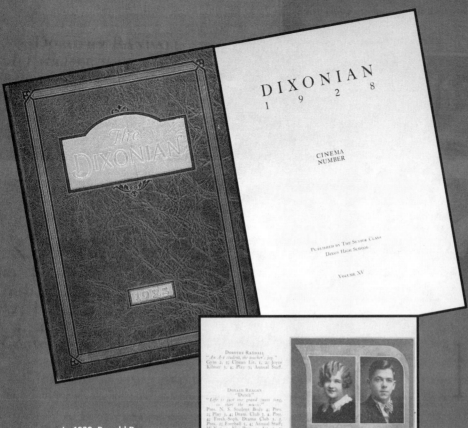

DIXONIAN
1 9 2 8

CINEMA
NUMBER

Published by The Senior Class
Dixon High School

Volume XV

In 1928, Ronald Reagan was the art director of the senior class yearbook, *The Dixonian*. His design and drawings are remarkably predictive of his future life. Described as the "Cinema Number," the book was designed with sections illustrated so that the campus was the "Studio." The teachers were "Directors," the students the "Cast," their activities the "Stage," and athletics "Filming." Reagan wrote a poem for the yearbook. The first stanza described a credo he would live by his entire life:

"I wonder what it's all about and why
we suffer so, when little things go wrong?
We make our life a struggle,
When life should be a song."

Reagan was president of the senior class; vice-president of the Boys Hi-Y, a club with the aim of promoting "clean speech, clean sports, clean living, and clean scholarship"; and a member of both the varsity basketball team and the varsity football team. "He was the perfect specimen of an athlete, tall, willowy, muscular, brown, good-looking," remembered his friend Bill Thompson. During his senior year, Reagan also narrated a football game in which he did not play on the local Dixon radio station. A typo in the senior class yearbook listed him as "Donald" Reagan. Under his name appeared this assessment from his classmates: "Life is just one grand sweet song, so start the music."

Margaret was Dutch's steady girlfriend for most of his high school years. In his senior year, Dutch was president of the drama club. Until then, the club performed plays only for audiences composed of North Dixon students; Dutch convinced Fraser to open the plays to the public.

"He possessed a sense of presence on the stage, a sense of reality," Fraser recalled of his best student. "He fit into almost any kind of role you put him into. Wisecracking, hat-over-the-ear, cigarette-in-the-mouth reporter—he could do that as well as any sentimental scenes."

Dutch was more than just a performing artist. He submitted sketches, short stories, and poetry to the school yearbook, and several examples of his work were published.

In the classroom Dutch was a good student but hardly a scholar. He scored good grades, but relied more on his photographic memory to pass tests than on any devotion to study. On the football field, he had become a tough, gritty player unafraid of physical contact. His coach played him on the line because he wasn't fast enough to carry the ball.

As his graduation from North Dixon High approached, Dutch had his sights firmly set on attending Eureka College. Garland Waggoner, a former North Dixon football star, had gone to Eureka on a football scholarship and Dutch was anxious to follow in Waggoner's footsteps. Margaret Cleaver was also heading for Eureka. For a time, however, the school seemed out of reach. Even though he had saved about $400 from his summer jobs, Dutch lacked the resources to pay the tuition at Eureka.

In September 1928, he accompanied Margaret to Eureka and met with Dean Samuel Harrod. He asked Harrod for a football scholarship. Harrod sent him to see the football coach, Ralph "Mac" McKinzie. The coach thought Reagan was too scrawny for the team but liked his enthusiasm and told school administrators to grant Dutch an athletic scholarship that would pay for half his education. Even with the financial aid, a year of school at Eureka cost Reagan $365.

To help make ends meet, Reagan washed dishes in the Tau Kappa Epsilon fraternity house, where he lived, and also found a job busing tables in the dining room of the girls' dormitory. He majored in economics, but the classroom was not his favorite place on campus. He carried a "C" average throughout his college years. He much preferred drama club rehearsals—where he often had the lead male role— or working for the student newspaper, or football practice, even though he was far from a star on the Golden Tornadoes.

"He was nearsighted you know; couldn't see worth a damn," Coach McKinzie recalled. "Ended up at the bottom of the heap every time and missed the play because he couldn't see the man or the ball moving on him....He was very skinny at the time, and not quite as fast as the other fellows....He was a plugger, but Eureka wasn't in a position to gamble because we were not a top team even in the local area. I kept him off the field so that the other young men who were a little more aggressive playing football could carry the ball."

And yet, for years after his matriculation at Eureka Reagan would recall with fondness his experiences on the team and the guidance in life he received from McKinzie. In 1982, he returned to Eureka as president to give a speech on the fiftieth anniversary of his graduation from the school. He told this story to the students:

> I know what it's like most of the time to play up-field. One day, a bunch of us on campus decided that we ought to have a better field. The townspeople joined in and better equipment was provided, and the field was better graded. The up-hill part was in those days there were 250 of us here; in those days we were playing against schools that were 10 times your size. One day, we asked Mac…we said we were a little tired sometimes of 50 percent seasons. We said, 'Why don't we have a schedule where we could look forward to [winning]. And he said 'Sure, I could give you a schedule like that.' And he named a few of the schools we could play. But he said, 'What would you rather remember, that you played on the same field as a team that played Iowa the week before in the Big 10, and maybe you lost by a touchdown,' which we did, 'Would you rather do that, or would you rather play against a bunch of set-ups just because you could have a score at the end of the game that would put you out front.' We got the idea. I mention sometimes about playing football for Eureka…and I say I played against George Russo who was eight years all-pro tackle with the Chicago Bears. This little school with the elms on the campus used to be known and admired by everyone we met as having the greatest spirit of anyone that they played.

Reagan graduated from Eureka in the spring of 1932. He had his diploma, but no idea what he wanted to do with it. He soon found the answer at a small radio station in Davenport, Iowa, where he worked as a sports announcer. One of his jobs was to broadcast Chicago Cubs games by reading Western Union dispatches over the air. The telegrams gave him only the briefest of descriptions of the game; Reagan would compensate by making up dramatic details of the action while a station engineer played recorded sounds of crowd noises and cheering to accompany Reagan's descriptions.

Reagan's radio career led to a Hollywood screen test, which led to a steady if unspectacular career in the movies. He was tall with boyish good looks and a homespun, small-town charm. In 1940, Reagan married actress Jane Wyman. The couple raised two children but would divorce in 1948. Wyman said the marriage fell apart because her husband started ignoring their family for what was a growing interest in political activism. She also found him boring. "If you ask Ron Reagan what time it is, he will tell you how to make a watch," she said.

Reagan had always been a liberal Democrat, but in 1947 he was elected president of the Screen Actors Guild and used his position to help expel communists from the union—although he was certainly a fierce defender of guild members he believed were unjustly accused by the zealous communist hunters of the era. Still, it was clear that

Reagan was growing more conservative as he guided the union into the 1950s. In 1952 and 1956, he headed the Democrats for Eisenhower organization, which was established to help elect the Republican candidate, Dwight D. Eisenhower, president.

In 1952, Reagan married Nancy Davis, a little-known actress who was the daughter of a wealthy Chicago physician. Nancy gave up her acting career to raise two children the Reagans had together. She became a member of a Southern California circle of wealthy conservative Republican women that included Betsy Bloomingdale, whose husband founded the credit card company Diners Club, and Mary Jane Wick, wife of an important California financier. Certainly, Nancy was an influence in her husband's turn to the right. So was the movie star Dick Powell, a good friend of the Reagans and a staunch Republican.

Meanwhile, Reagan's best years in film were behind him, so he turned to the then-infant medium of television, where he signed on to host General Electric Theater, a widely popular series of dramas. The job required him to tour the country acting as a celebrity spokesman for GE. It also required him to visit GE appliance factories where he met many of the company's executives—virtually all of them political

A 1927 photograph of sixteen-year-old Ronald Reagan in his uniform as a lifeguard at Lowell Park Beach, Illinois. When he was fifteen, Reagan began working summers at Lowell Park Beach, a popular swimming spot on the Rock River two miles upstream from Dixon. Its sandy shore gave way to a few yards of mud before sloping precipitously to depths where the undertow could be extremely strong. During his seven years as a lifeguard, Reagan was credited with seventy-seven rescues, several of which made the front page of the *Dixon Telegraph*. "Pulled from the Jaws of Death" was the headline on August 3, 1928. Reagan took great pride in saving lives. On a nearby log, he carved a notch for each rescue with his jackknife. "How many you got now?" Reagan would be asked. "You count 'em," he would reply. One of the "jokes" in the 1928 *Dixonian* was:

DROWNING YOUTH: "Don't rescue me. I want to die."
DUTCH REAGAN: "Well, you'll have to postpone that; I want a medal."

Reagan was paid eighteen dollars a week. He saved most of this money for anticipated college tuition. (Reagan was one of only 8 percent of his North Dixon High School graduating class of 1928 who went on to college.) "You know why I had such fun [at being a lifeguard]?" Reagan asked in his memoirs. "Because I was the only one up there on the grand stand. It was like a stage. Everyone had to look at me."

In September 1928, Reagan enrolled at Eureka College in Illinois, a small school run by the Disciples of Christ, a church whose credo his mother had embraced. A football hero of Dutch's had attended the school and his girlfriend, Margaret Cleaver, also was studying there. "I fell head over heels in love with Eureka," Reagan later wrote. "It seemed to me then, as I walked up the path, to be another home. I wanted to get into that school so badly that it hurt when I thought about it." Reagan was able to afford the tuition because he had saved several hundred dollars from his summer lifeguard job, received a partial athletic scholarship, and worked for his board by washing dishes at a local fraternity house.

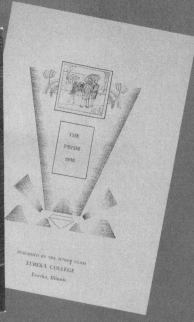

Eureka College competed fiercely for football talent because a star player and a winning team attracted students. Eureka's elders disdained athletics, because the school's main commitment was to teaching a Christian doctrine. But without a competitive football team, the school lost many prospective students.

When Reagan attended the school, Eureka had an enrollment of two hundred and twenty students but it bore few resemblances to other college campuses. It was a small rural school with strict standards of student behavior. For example, dancing was not allowed.

All of the character traits that Reagan had exhibited at North Dixon High School were reinforced at Eureka College. He never was a great student. Reagan recalled that his enthusiasm was in "drama, sports, and politics and not always in that order." Reagan played first-string guard on the football team, worked on the school newspaper and yearbooks, became president of the Booster Club, was captain of the basketball cheerleaders, and appeared in most college plays, usually having the lead role.

Reagan was a feature writer for the *Prism*, Eureka's yearbook.

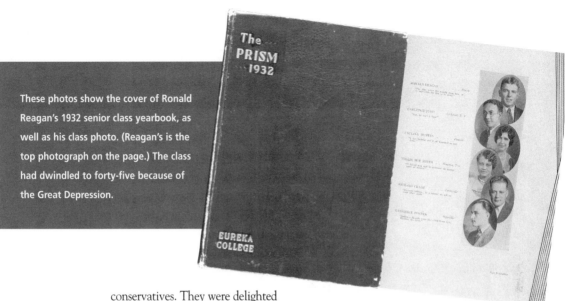

conservatives. They were delighted to share their political views with Reagan, telling him about the evils of big government and their belief that government should keep its hands off business. By the early 1960s, Reagan was committed to the cause of conservatism.

In 1966, he answered an invitation by California Republicans to run for governor. He overwhelmed the state's Democratic governor that fall, beginning a political career that culminated in his election as president in 1980. That year, he ran against President Jimmy Carter, who was unable to solve the nation's severe economic problems. Carter also fell out of favor with the American people because he had been unable to negotiate the release of U.S. hostages captured in an embassy takeover by fundamentalist Muslim students in Tehran, Iran.

Preaching a distrust of big government as well as a promise to turn America into a strong military force, Reagan was elected in a landslide over Carter, and then easily won reelection four years later. He made good on his promise to make the United States into a military power of unprecedented might. The Reagan arms build-up was so successful that it is regarded as a main factor leading to the collapse of the Soviet Union.

Reagan remained immensely popular with the American people throughout his presidency. He never forgot the values he learned growing up in a small town or attending college on a tiny campus. Returning to Eureka to make a speech, Reagan said, "Those big assembly-line diploma mills may teach…but you will have memories, you will have friendships that are impossible on those great campuses, and just are peculiar to this place.…Yes, this place is deep in my heart. Everything that has been good in my life began here."

—Hal Marcovitz

George H. W. Bush
Chapter Forty

Henry L. Stimson graduated from Phillips Academy in Andover, Massachusetts, in 1883, and from there went on to a busy career in public service. By 1942, when he was invited back to Andover to be the commencement speaker for that year's graduating class, Stimson was serving as secretary of war under President Franklin D. Roosevelt.

By then, the world was at war. The previous December, Japanese planes launched from a naval task force had attacked the U.S. Navy base at Pearl Harbor in Hawaii, sinking eighteen U.S. ships, destroying two hundred airplanes, and killing or wounding more than three thousand servicemen. The surprise attack led to the United States's involvement in World War II. When Stimson addressed Andover's Class of 1942, America was preparing for a long conflict and desperately needed young, able-bodied men to take up arms.

During his address to the Andover graduates, Stimson told the boys that a soldier should be "brave without being brutal, self-confident without boasting, part of an irresistible might, but without losing faith in individual liberty." Nevertheless, Stimson counseled the Andover graduates to stay in school and begin their college educations before joining the armed forces.

One of the graduates in the audience that day was George H. W. Bush. The previous December, he had been stunned by the surprise attack on Pearl Harbor and resolved then to enlist in the Navy at the earliest opportunity. Although George had been accepted at Yale University, he aimed to be a Navy pilot and decided college could wait. His parents, teachers, and now even Secretary Stimson urged him to change his mind, but George was steadfast in his plan to enlist.

Shortly after commencement exercises concluded George's parents, Prescott and Dorothy Bush, encountered their son in the hallway of Andover's Cochran Chapel. Prescott asked George whether Stimson's words had changed his mind. "No sir," George responded. "I'm going in."

Prescott shook hands with his son, and then began to cry.

A few days later, George Bush celebrated his eighteenth birthday by going to

The 1947

YALE BANNER

FOUNDED 1841

▲

VOLUME CVI

▲

Published For
YALE UNIVERSITY
NEW HAVEN   CONNECTICUT

The

YALE BANNER

1947

In the late 1940s, Yale University was suddenly crowded by new students. Some were returning students who had left for the armed services during World War II; others were veterans who sought a college education under the G.I. Bill. Enrollment increased about 60 percent to a record of nearly eight thousand undergraduates.

Some students were jammed into dormitories of the residential colleges. Others lived with faculty and alumni around New Haven. Some three hundred students were temporarily housed in the gymnasium. Complicating the problem was the influx of married students, often with their young children. To house them, one hundred Quonset huts were rapidly erected near the Yale Bowl. Each of the forty-eight-by-twenty-foot metal structures was divided into two three-room apartments.

CAPT. G.H.W. BUSH '48

Although
George had been
accepted at
Yale University,
he aimed to be
a Navy pilot and
decided college
could wait.

George H. W.
Bush, wearing
his baseball
uniform, sits on the Yale Fence. For
generations, Yale students sat on
the fence at the corner of Chapel
and College Streets. Each class,
except freshmen, had a specific
place where they perched
themselves, smoked, laughed,
chatted, and sang together. Being
photographed "sitting on the fence"
is a Yale tradition.

the U.S. Navy recruitment office in Boston and enlisting as a seaman second class. By that summer he was enrolled in aviator cadet school in North Carolina.

George Bush was far from the most academically talented student at Andover. He was athletic, to be sure, but there were better athletes at Andover. But no boy at Andover beat him to the recruitment office, and no member of the Andover Class of 1942 would accomplish as much in combat as George Bush.

George Herbert Walker Bush was born on June 12, 1924, in Milton, Massachusetts, where his family was living temporarily while Prescott Bush worked as an executive for a rubber products company. There was wealth on both sides of young George's family. The Bushes were distant relatives of King Henry III of Great Britain, making George a thirteenth cousin of Queen Elizabeth II. Prescott was the son of Samuel Bush, who had made a fortune as a manufacturer of parts and equipment for railroad cars. Samuel sent his children to private schools and the best colleges. Prescott graduated from Yale and, after making his mark as an executive with a talent for rescuing troubled companies, turned to investment banking and later politics. In 1952, he was elected to the U.S. Senate representing Connecticut, where the family had moved soon after George's birth.

George's mother was also born into wealth. She was the daughter of George Herbert Walker, whose ancestors had emigrated to America in the early seventeenth century. By the time Dorothy Walker married Prescott Bush, the Walkers were the owners of one of the nation's largest dry goods companies and

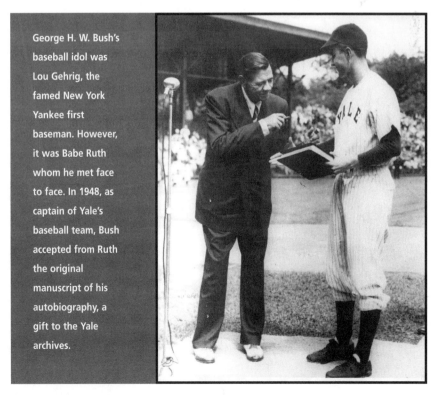

George H. W. Bush's baseball idol was Lou Gehrig, the famed New York Yankee first baseman. However, it was Babe Ruth whom he met face to face. In 1948, as captain of Yale's baseball team, Bush accepted from Ruth the original manuscript of his autobiography, a gift to the Yale archives.

George Herbert Walker was president of a prosperous New York investment banking firm. Dorothy Walker and her family spent their summers in a seaside home in Kennebunkport, Maine, and their winter vacations in a shooting lodge in South Carolina known as Duncannon.

George Bush was the second of five children born to Prescott and Dorothy. George's older brother, Prescott Jr., was called "Pressy" by everyone in the family. George had a nickname, too. He was called "Poppy," an unusual nickname for a little boy. He came by the nickname because the children called Grandfather George "Pop." George was, then, "Little Pop," and soon simply "Poppy."

George Bush grew up in Greenwich, a wealthy Connecticut suburb of New York City. The Bush children spent their childhoods amid mansions, estates, and servants. In 1929, the American stock market crashed, plunging the country into an economic catastrophe known as the Great Depression. Hundreds of thousands of people were thrown out of work, and many found themselves standing in lines for bread. In the Midwest, thousands of citizens of Oklahoma and other Plains states were forced to give up their homes when their crops failed. To George Bush and the other privileged children who grew up in Greenwich in the 1920s and 1930s, however, that world was far-removed and virtually unknown.

There were twenty public schools in Greenwich when George was growing up. He would never set foot in any of them, at least not as a student. George Bush began his education at the age of five when his parents enrolled him in the private Greenwich Country Day School. The school was located on the estate of the Warner family of Greenwich and sprawled over some eighteen acres. His parents wanted to wait until he was six before sending him off to school, but Pressy, who was twenty-one months older than George, was already going to school and George complained that he was lonely at home without his brother.

Each morning, the Bush family chauffeur dropped Prescott Sr. off at the Greenwich train station for his commute into New York, then stopped by Greenwich Country Day School to let Pressy and Poppy out for classes. Later, the chauffeur made another stop—at Rosemary Junior School, the private girls' school in Greenwich where sister Nancy attended. At the time, Greenwich Country was an all-boys school.

The school day was long. It commenced at 8:30 A.M. and lasted until 6 P.M. Ordinarily, children are dismissed from school in the mid-afternoon and can be expected to spend the remainder of their afternoons playing together in their neighborhoods, doing their chores, or working in after-school jobs. There were no "neighborhoods" in Greenwich where children could meet after school for games of stickball or marbles, however, and children from wealthy families did not need jobs to earn extra money. Also, parents were rarely home in the afternoons to supervise their children's play. Greenwich Country Day School was charged with looking after its students long after most public school children had been dismissed from classes.

TORCH

GEORGE HERBERT W. BUSH
JOHN CLARK CALHOUN, JR.
CHARLES HALSEY CLARK
WILLIAM JUDKINS CLARK
ENDICOTT PEABODY DAVISON
EUGENE DINES, JR.
WINTHROP PALMER ELDREDGE
WILLIAM RICHARD EMERSON
GORDON NESBITT FARQUHAR
RICHARD ELWOOD JENKINS
                    HOWARD SAYRE WEA...

TORCH

University Honor Society
FOUNDED 1916

GEORGE HERBERT W. BUSH
JOHN CLARK CALHOUN, JR.
CHARLES HALSEY CLARK
WILLIAM JUDKINS CLARK
ENDICOTT PEABODY DAVISON
EUGENE DINES, JR.
WINTHROP PALMER ELDREDGE
WILLIAM RICHARD EMERSON
GORDON NESBITT FARQUHAR
RICHARD ELWOOD JENKINS

VANDERVEER KIRK
ROBERT PERKINS KNIGHT
ARTHUR KEEFE MOHER
THOMAS WILDER MOSELEY
FRANK O'BRIEN, JR.
JOHN JOSEPH O'NEILL
GEORGE HAROLD PFAU, JR.
JOHN GRANDIN ROHRBACH
DAVID OWEN WAGSTER
SAMUEL SLOANE WALKER, JR.

HOWARD SAYRE WEAVER

Back Row: Emerson, Farquhar, Clark, C. H., Bush, Clark, W. S., Wagster, Walker.
Second Row: Pfau, Knight, Weaver, Dines, Moseley, Rohrbach, Moher.
Front Row: O'Brien, Calhoun, Kirk, Davison, Eldredge.

63

This page from the 1947 Yale yearbook shows the members of the Yale Honors Society. George Bush is in the center of the back row.

Bush was also selected as a member of a more exclusive organization. Yale's Skull and Bones, founded in 1833, was (and remains) a secret intellectual and fraternal society. The Bonesmen met in padlocked windowless rooms that were filled with the same sorts of knickknacks and worn leather chairs found in the old clubs of an English university. Bonesmen were required to leave a room if they ever heard the words "Skull and Bones" uttered by non-members. Likewise, Bonesmen were forbidden even to say the name in conversation with those who were not members. Each year, fifteen graduating members of this exclusive group were replaced by an equal number of inductees.

For George H. W. Bush, being tapped for Skull and Bones was a thrill that he had long dreamt about. His father had been a Bonesman, as had other relatives and family friends. Bush's Skull and Bones contemporaries became his lifelong friends. They formed a core of a network that assisted his future career both in business and in politics.

George and the one hundred and forty other Greenwich students wore uniforms—knickers as well as black sweaters with orange stripes on the sleeves. Poppy Bush and his classmates studied history, geography, mathematics, English, Latin, music, nature studies, and art. Athletics were stressed— students played baseball, soccer and, when the pond froze over in the winter, ice hockey.

Discipline was strict, particularly under George Meadows, an Englishman who became headmaster in 1936. He was very tough on miscreants who talked during assembly, making them stand on their chairs until dismissed, and gum-chewers, who were sentenced to eat a whole pack of gum while standing at attention in front of the student body.

George remained at Greenwich until the spring of 1937, and then enrolled at Phillips Academy in the fall of that year. By setting foot onto the Andover campus he entered one of the nation's most prestigious private boarding schools. Children who attend the school, known familiarly as Andover, are expected to go on to careers in law, literature, the arts, or business. Among the graduates of Andover are actors Jack Lemmon and Humphrey Bogart, artist Frank Stella, photographer Walker Evans, author Edgar Rice Burroughs, and inventor Samuel F. B. Morse. Noted journalists, as well as members of Congress, governors, and justices of the U.S. Supreme Court, have attended Andover as well.

The school, which is located twenty-one miles north of Boston, was founded in 1778 by Samuel Phillips Jr. Paul Revere designed the school seal while John Hancock, then serving as governor of Massachusetts, signed Andover's incorporation papers. The school's charter admonishes its students to understand that "goodness without knowledge is weak…yet knowledge without goodness is dangerous."

When George Bush commenced his education at Andover, the Great Depression still hovered over the lives of ordinary Americans. At Andover, though, Bush was just as shielded from the horrors of poverty as he had been back home in Greenwich. In fact, students were instructed not to leave campus for visits to the town of Andover, just past the school's border.

President Franklin Roosevelt was held very much in disdain by the faculty, administrators, and even the students of Andover. Roosevelt, the son of a wealthy New York family, had grown up in circumstances similar to the average Andover

> Bush excelled more on the athletic field than he did in the classrooms at Andover. He was one of the tallest boys in school, and played basketball, soccer, and baseball.

student, yet around the Andover campus his liberal New Deal programs were despised. Roosevelt's New Deal used government funding—and, therefore, the taxes paid by the wealthy—in an attempt to pull the United States out of the Depression. At Andover the student newspaper, the *Phillipian*, referred to Roosevelt as a "betrayer of his class."

George Bush may have agreed with the editorial policy of the *Phillipian*, but at the time he was not in the habit of sharing his views publicly. During the five years he spent at Andover, George joined many extracurricular clubs, both social and academic, but throughout that time he displayed a nonchalant attitude toward politics and social activism. Bush became a very popular boy on campus mostly because he had a talent for staying out of scrapes. He was friendly with everybody, earning their respect because of his pleasant nature and sense of humor. His teachers liked him because he was well behaved.

He never impressed his teachers with his academic prowess. Although he did not lack intelligence—in college, he would make Phi Beta Kappa—his teachers at Andover recalled that George was for the most part a mediocre student. "His grades in my course were not very good," said Andover teacher Hart Day Leavitt. "He was in my eleventh-grade English class, but my remaining impression is he just sat in the class and handed in his papers."

Bush excelled more, though, on the athletic field. He was one of the tallest boys in school—by his senior year he was already standing six feet tall. He played basketball, soccer, and baseball. He was elected captain of the soccer and baseball teams because he was the most enthusiastic member of the teams, and his teammates found themselves infected with his enthusiasm.

"He was a very well-liked kid," recalled Frank DiClemente, the Andover physical education teacher and baseball coach. "You never heard that guy say anything bad about anybody. If he had anything to say about a person, it would be in a positive sense."

Even the outbreak of World War II didn't seem to dampen George's enthusiasm. On campus, Headmaster Claude Moore Fuess convened a special assembly to report the news of the Japanese attack to the student body. Bush was a member of the senior class, and he was planning to enroll at Yale after graduating the following spring. During that assembly, though, he resolved to enlist in the Navy.

During Christmas vacation that winter, George returned home to Greenwich and attended a dance at the Round Hill Country Club. At the dance he met a sixteen-year-old girl named Barbara Pierce, who was soon to become his fiancée. She was a student at an exclusive girls' prep school in Charleston, South Carolina, and was home for the holidays as well. Barbara Pierce's mother, Pauline Robinson Pierce, was the daughter of an Ohio Supreme Court justice. Her father, Marvin Pierce, was a magazine publisher and descendant of former U.S. president Franklin Pierce.

George H. W. Bush and Barbara Pierce married in January 1945. He was not yet twenty-one and she was a year younger. In September, Bush entered all-male Yale University. Veterans comprised more than half of his class—and one-quarter of them were married with wives living in New Haven. On July 6, 1946, Barbara gave birth to their first child, whom they named George Walker Bush.

At Yale, as well as at every major college, veterans assisted by government benefits under the G.I. Bill changed the traditional campus scene. The Bushes were fortunate to live in an apartment with a shared kitchen within a sprawling house on New Haven's Hillhouse Avenue. The house had been subdivided into thirteen separate apartments.

In these cramped quarters, Bush studied and helped raise his infant son. He majored in business and economics. In his senior year, Bush won the Gordon Brown Prize for "all around student leadership" and he was elected to Phi Beta Kappa, the national undergraduate honor society.

These photographs show George Bush holding his infant son in their New Haven home (top) and George W. on his father's shoulders (left). Both were taken in April 1947.

Following the holidays, George returned to Andover while Barbara went back to Charleston. They kept in touch by writing letters. That spring, George graduated from Andover and kept his promise to himself to enlist in the navy. On August 6, 1942, he reported for duty in Chapel Hill, North Carolina, where he began training as an aviation cadet.

At the start of the war, the navy declared that a would-be pilot needed at least two years of college to be considered for aviator training. The Battle of Midway changed the navy's thinking. Fought in early June of 1942—just as Bush was accepting his diploma at Andover—Midway became the first significant naval aviation battle of the war. The battle was fought in the skies over the Midway Islands by planes launched from Japanese and American aircraft carriers. (The two enemy fleets never came into contact with one another.) American air power prevailed, delivering a blow to Japan's attempts to seize the islands and stage a future invasion of Hawaii. Nevertheless, the battle convinced the U.S. Navy that it needed pilots, and there would be too few available if two years of college was a prerequisite. The college rule was waived, opening the doors to aviation cadet school to high school graduates.

Bush would undergo pilot training for some eighteen months. His training took him to seven navy bases and included stopovers in North Carolina, Minnesota, Texas, Florida, Massachusetts, Rhode Island, and Virginia. During that time, he learned to fly a torpedo bomber called the Avenger—a single-engine plane designed to take off from an aircraft carrier and deliver a torpedo or depth charges aimed at an enemy target. The training was grueling and hazardous. Bush had to learn how to perform takeoffs and landings from the deck of a carrier, which pitched and heaved in choppy ocean waters. What's more, many of those carrier maneuvers had to be performed at night when visibility was low.

"One can practice carrier landings on land forever without knowing the thrill of actually landing on a moving ship at sea," Bush said years later. "There's something about the isolation, the ocean, the tiny carrier below that gets the adrenaline flowing."

On June 6, 1943, George Bush was commissioned an ensign in the U.S. Navy. He was issued a set of gold wings that were pinned to his uniform designating him a naval aviator. Bush, who had not yet turned nineteen, was at the time the youngest pilot in the U.S. Navy. After more training he was assigned in February 1944 to a squadron of torpedo bombers aboard the U.S.S. *San Jacinto*, a newly commissioned aircraft carrier dispatched to duty in the South Pacific.

By the time the war was over George Bush had flown fifty-eight missions, logging 1,228 hours as a military pilot. He made one hundred and twenty-six carrier landings. He was shot down twice, but managed to escape injury and capture, and was awarded the Distinguished Flying Cross—the military's highest award for valor by a pilot. In August 1945 the war ended after the United States unleashed atomic bombs on the Japanese cities of Hiroshima and Nagasaki. Less than a month later, George Bush received an honorable discharge from the U.S. Navy.

George Bush had married Barbara the previous winter. Now, he was anxious to get on with his education. He enrolled in Yale for the fall 1945 semester. The couple found an apartment in New Haven, Connecticut. Bush took up the study of business and economics. He was in the largest freshman class in the history of the college, a fact attributed to the massive discharge of men from the armed services and the government's commitment to help pay for their college educations through the G.I. Bill of Rights.

Bush made Phi Beta Kappa at Yale and completed the requirements for what is ordinarily a four-year degree in three years. The easygoing, friendly attitude that made him popular at Andover also made him many friends at Yale. In Yale's case, his friends turned out to be very influential because Bush was invited to join Skull and Bones.

Fraternities and sororities are very common on college campuses. Many of them have their roots in the literary societies of colonial days—clubs composed of students who met on their own, outside the influence of the faculty, to practice their writing and oratory skills. Over the years, many such groups have adopted customs and rituals they prefer to keep secret. Perhaps no group has maintained the custom of secrecy with such dedication as Yale's Skull and Bones. The members, known as Bonesmen, meet in a windowless clubhouse known as the Tomb, which is located on High Street in New Haven. The club was established in 1832. Its members have included Supreme Court justice Potter Stewart, President William Howard Taft, *Time* magazine publisher Henry Luce, journalist William F. Buckley Jr., and U.S. senator John F. Chafee.

Each year, fifteen Yale men are asked to join. Women are barred from membership. Whatever goes on behind the doors of the Tomb is, of course, a closely guarded secret. Nevertheless, for years following their experiences at New Haven, Bonesmen regard themselves as members of a select group, always ready to come to the aid of one another. Soon after Bush left Yale, a fellow Bonesmen named Neil Mallon would give him his start in the oil exploration business in Texas.

Other than Skull and Bones, Bush's other great passion on the Yale campus was the baseball team. Once again, his teammates elected him captain. He played first base and was regarded as a gifted fielder. When the Yale baseball team won two regional championships during his two years on the team, pro scouts stopped by to see if any members of the team were worthy of major league contracts. The team's sure-handed first baseman caught their eye until they saw his batting average—a paltry .239 his first year, a respectable but hardly impressive .269 in his second season.

George Bush graduated from Yale in the spring of 1948. He would pursue a career in the oil business in Texas, switching to politics in the 1960s. He served two terms in the U.S. House of Representatives and was appointed by Republican administrations to posts that included ambassador to the United Nations, special envoy to China, and director of the Central Intelligence Agency.

In 1980, he campaigned for president and ran a strong second in the Republican primaries to eventual nominee Ronald Reagan, who asked him to join the ticket as the party's vice presidential candidate. Bush spent eight years as Reagan's vice president, then was elected president in 1988. His single term in office was marked by his decision to wage war in the Persian Gulf to drive an invading Iraqi army out of neighboring Kuwait. Although victory in the 1991 Gulf War boosted Bush's popularity, his inability to revive the country's sagging economy led to his defeat at the hands of Democrat Bill Clinton in the 1992 election.

He left active politics following his loss to Clinton, but in January 2001 he stood by his son, George W. Bush, as the former governor of Texas—who had followed his father to Andover and Yale—took the oath of office as the nation's forty-third president. The two Bushes became the first father and son to serve as presidents since John Adams and John Quincy Adams two centuries ago.

—Hal Marcovitz

Bill Clinton

Chapter Forty-one

I n the summer of 1963, when Bill Clinton was sixteen years old, he
participated in Boys' Nation, a weeklong convention in Washington, D.C.,
meant to teach young people about the government of the United States. For
Clinton and the other Boys' Nation "senators," the trip would involve more than
just sight-seeing tours of landmarks and government buildings. The American
Legion, which sponsored the event, expected the boys to elect officers, participate
in debates, and take votes on resolutions that would address many of the same
issues faced by Congress.

To take part in Boys' Nation, Bill Clinton won the position of senator at his
home state's convention at an Arkansas summer camp. He spent the week
campaigning, going from cabin to cabin each night so he could introduce himself to
the hundreds of boys in attendance. Each morning, he rose early and stationed
himself at the entrance of the cafeteria where he shook hands with the boys as they
arrived for breakfast. He recruited many friends at the camp, and they fanned out
and urged their friends to vote for Bill Clinton for Boys' Nation senator.

Bill Clinton was a born campaigner. He won the election in a landslide.

William Jefferson Blythe III was born on August 19, 1946. His father, Bill
Blythe Jr., died in a car accident three months before his son's birth. When Bill was
two years old, his mother Virginia decided she needed an education in nursing in
order to support her son. She made the sacrifice of living away from him for the
next two years, attending nursing school in New Orleans and sending Bill to live
with her parents, Elbridge and Edith Cassidy, in their home in Hope, Arkansas, a
tiny town near the Texas border.

It was Edith Cassidy who first recognized the boy's intelligence. Under her
guidance, Bill learned to read before he was three years old. "From the beginning,
Bill was a special child—smart, sensitive, mature beyond his years," recalled
Virginia. "He remembers my sitting him down in that house on Thirteenth Street
and telling him about his real father. He must have been four or five at the time,
but talking with him at that age was like talking with a grown friend."

Bill learned to read before he was three years old. "From the beginning, Bill was a special child—smart, sensitive, mature beyond his years," his mother recalled.

Bill Clinton attended Hot Springs High School, 1960–64. During the summer between his junior and senior years, Clinton participated in Boys' Nation, an American Legion–sponsored program to help students learn about the U.S. government and its operation. For Clinton, the highlight of the program was a visit to the White House, where President John F. Kennedy greeted the group. Clinton was in the front, so when Kennedy finished his prepared remarks and stepped forward to greet the delegates, the first hand the president clasped was that of sixteen-year-old Bill Clinton. Later in his life, Clinton often said that this was the moment he decided on a political career.

This photograph ranks among the most popular requested from the White House during Clinton's years as president.

A REALISTIC APPROACH TO STUDENT GOVERNMENT

BILL CLINTON

CANDIDATE

PRESIDENT OF THE STUDENT COUNCIL

MAR. 8 1967

Georgetown, the nation's oldest Roman Catholic university, was founded in 1789. The school was the idea of John Carroll, the first Catholic bishop in the United States and the first archbishop of Baltimore. His goal was to establish a college so that young Catholic men would no longer be compelled to go abroad for a higher education. Their alternative was to matriculate at the non-sectarian University of Pennsylvania, which alone among America's colleges welcomed Catholics. The Georgetown curriculum was modeled on that of the typical classical academy. Georgetown has always been open to students of all religious faiths. George Washington's two nephews attended the school in the late 1790s.

In 1919, the university inaugurated the Georgetown School of Foreign Service to train students who intended to enter diplomatic service or become employees of corporations involved in international business. Bill Clinton, who graduated fourth in his high school class of three hundred and sixty-three students, chose to attend Georgetown because of the university's School of Foreign Service. His goal was to combine the practical experience of working for a member of Congress with the more regimented course work of the college. The nation's capital and Georgetown promised academic challenge, social excitement, and political possibility.

Bill Clinton entered Georgetown University in 1964. Clinton's easy-going manner, coupled with his intelligence, charm, and sincerity, overcame any reservations his more affluent classmates may have felt about the economically underprivileged boy from one of the poorest states in the nation. Recalling those days, Clinton said, "I'd never been out of Arkansas really very much, and there I was with people from all over the country and all over the world." Those people must have liked Clinton because they elected him president of his freshman and sophomore classes.

While at Georgetown, Clinton always held at least one part-time job to supplement his family's financial support. He was able to juggle many activities and still maintain a 3.57 grade-point average.

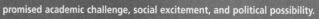

Meanwhile, Virginia met car salesman Roger Clinton. Roger loved to gamble and roam the bars in search of fun. Virginia thought she could tame his wild spirit, and they married in 1950. Roger and Virginia Clinton and Virginia's son Bill moved into a small house in Hope.

Virginia enrolled her boy in school as Bill Clinton, a name Bill would legally adopt at the age of fifteen to form a bond with his younger stepbrother, Roger Clinton Jr. From early on, Bill impressed his teachers will his eagerness to learn. Some of his teachers weren't quite sure what to make of the boy who always knew the answers. In the second grade, he raised his hand so much that his teacher regarded him as a pest and gave him a "D" in behavior. That would be Bill's last poor grade. For the rest of his school years he was an "A" student who seemed far ahead of his classmates.

Roger Sr. was originally from the Arkansas city of Hot Springs, and that's where the family moved in 1952. Bill's stepfather lost money in the car business in Hope and decided to give it up and try farming. The family found a farm on the edge of Hot Springs, but it became clear that Roger Clinton was not the type of man who could drag himself out of bed to milk the cows. Roger enjoyed the nightlife too much to keep farmers' hours. Virginia had no intentions of becoming a farm wife, either. By now she had become a nurse-anesthetist, and found her skills in demand by Hot Springs surgeons. After just a few months, the Clintons moved to a home on Park Avenue in Hot Springs, and Roger Clinton found a job as a salesman.

Bill's interest in politics and government may have started as early as the summer of 1956, just after he completed the fourth grade. That year, the political conventions were being televised and Bill found himself much more interested in the intrigues and dramas unfolding on the floors of the convention halls than in such typical childhood television fare as *Howdy Doody* and the *Mickey Mouse Club*. "I was hooked on politics then and there," Clinton said later. "It got to me in a way on television that no amount of reading in the newspapers about candidates running for office and politics in general could impact me."

Most people in Hot Springs were Republicans. Bill was an independent thinker, though, and as he grew older he became partial to the Democratic Party's liberal politics. In 1960, as a student at Central Junior High School in Hot Springs, Clinton closely followed the presidential election pitting Republican Vice President Richard M. Nixon against the young Democratic senator from Massachusetts, John F. Kennedy.

"My teacher in ninth-grade civics class was Mary Marty, and she had the class debating the merits of the two candidates for the White House," Clinton recalled. "Mrs. Marty and I were the only ones who were for the [Kennedy] ticket. Being that Hot Springs is the seat of government for Garland County and is heavily Republican, my teacher and I were like outcasts in an environment that had everyone else rooting for Nixon."

On November 8, 1960, fourteen-year-old Bill Clinton stayed up all night watching the election returns on TV. "What a rewarding moment it was for me when Nixon made his concession speech," Bill said.

Bill Clinton soon entered Hot Springs High School. He was clearly one of the brightest students in school. What's more, he was a natural leader. Bill joined many school clubs and held numerous leadership positions; he won his first election in 1961 when his classmates voted him president of the sophomore class.

At home, though, things were not going as well. Bill's stepfather was an alcoholic who abused Virginia. There were many angry confrontations between his parents; Bill would shut himself off in his room to escape the fighting. Bill had taken up the saxophone and would often rely on the instrument to help him escape the raucous fighting elsewhere in the house, practicing music to drown out the voices of Virginia and Roger.

When Bill arrived at Hot Springs High School his talent was recognized by Virgil Spurlin, the music teacher and band director. Spurlin appointed Bill the band major, a job that went to the school's most accomplished musician. Spurlin recognized Bill's intelligence and popularity and knew he would be a vast help in organizing the annual Arkansas statewide band competition, which Hot Springs High School hosted. The festival featured performances by one hundred and forty high school bands from throughout Arkansas.

Clinton worked hard to help Spurlin coordinate the festival while still finding time to practice and compete with the Hot Springs High School band himself. He also joined the Stardusters, the Hot Springs dance band. Clinton and some friends also formed a jazz combo that played in the high school cafeteria during lunch hour. They wore dark sunglasses, which prompted their classmates to call the group the Three Blind Mice. At home, the walls of his bedroom displayed the numerous medals and awards he received for winning saxophone competitions. By the time he entered his senior year in high school, he was being urged by his teachers to major in music at college.

Spurlin recalled, "One time down in Camden, Arkansas, I believe he was in a stage band, and he was a soloist, and he received the outstanding soloist for the state in this particular case. And it wasn't just the fact that he was an accomplished musician, but he had to read music of all kinds of moods and different kinds of music, from jazz to classical to everything in the book, and he just did a phenomenal job in that."

As tempting as the idea of a career in music seemed, in the summer of 1963 Bill was picked to attend Boys' Nation, where he made up his mind to pursue a career in politics and government. Bill Clinton left for Boys' Nation on July 19, 1963. For the next week, Bill and the other senators lived in dormitories at the University of Maryland. Their days were filled with trips to Cabinet departments, lunches with members of Congress and sessions to draft resolutions that would be placed before all one hundred Boys' Nation senators for a vote.

In the summer of 1963, the rights of African Americans were still very much in dispute. In 1962, President Kennedy had been forced to send United States marshals to Mississippi so that a black student, James Meredith, could be admitted to the all-white University of Mississippi. Eight months later, Kennedy sent U.S. marshals as well as federal troops to the University of Alabama to ensure that two black students would be permitted to enroll there.

The Boys' Nation senators drafted a resolution supporting civil rights for African Americans. Bill was one of the major voices for civil rights at the convention. He worked hard rounding up votes for the civil rights resolution, using the same political skills that had won him votes just a few weeks before at the state convention in Little Rock.

He found opposition on the convention floor. Two of the southern senators—Pete Johnson of Alabama and Tommy Lawhorne of Georgia—were committed to defeating the civil rights resolution. One morning, they confronted Bill in the University of Maryland cafeteria. They told Bill that the southern senators had to stick together to defeat the resolution. Soon, Bill and the other two boys were shouting at one another. Bill refused to budge, though, and Johnson and Lawhorne had to back off. Ultimately, the civil rights resolution won by a small margin.

The next morning, the senators boarded buses on the University of Maryland campus for what was to be the final activity—a tour of the White House and a meeting with President Kennedy.

When the other boys showed up to board the buses, they found Bill already standing in line. He had arrived first because he intended to sit in the front seat of the first bus so that he could be first off the bus. That way, Bill was sure he could be first to meet the president. When the buses arrived at the White House Bill leaped out of his seat and hurried to the front of the line. He found a place just to the right of where Kennedy was expected to stand on the White House lawn to greet the boys.

Just before ten o'clock in the morning, Kennedy stepped out of the White House to address the Boys' Nation senators. He told them that he had read a newspaper story that morning about their convention and was impressed with their resolution calling for civil rights. When he concluded his speech, the president stepped forward and extended his hand to greet the senators. The first hand he shook was Bill Clinton's.

Bill graduated from Hot Springs High School in May 1964. He was neither valedictorian nor salutatorian, but his grades placed him fourth in the class, and he was picked to deliver the benediction, typically a brief prayer to close the ceremony. Bill turned it into a rousing salute to the graduates, challenging them to do their best in life. "Lord, make us care so that we will never know the misery and muddle of a life without purpose, and so that when we die, others will still have the opportunity to live in a free land," he told his three hundred and sixty-two fellow graduates.

There was no question where Bill intended to go to college—the nation's capital. He picked Georgetown University and enrolled in the college's School of Foreign Service, drawn to a curriculum that would train him for a future in the service of his national government. From the moment Bill stepped on campus that fall, he was off and running in a college election. He launched a vigorous campaign for president of the freshman class. He developed a platform and staged a rally, complete with a makeshift band composed of college students, and was easily elected president. After the election, Georgetown's student magazine reported, "Bill Clinton, who looks and sounds like an amiable farm boy, is the latest to ascend to the position of status supremacy known as freshman class president."

Bill was a top student at Georgetown, taking courses in political science, philosophy, and comparative cultures. He also became active in the anti-war movement. With opposition to the Vietnam War growing, many college students took part in anti-war demonstrations and opposed the Selective Service, the draft that required young men to enter the military and fight in Vietnam. On October 21, 1967, Bill was one of 55,000 people who attended an anti-war march that ended at the Lincoln Memorial. The next spring, Bill campaigned for U.S. senator Robert F. Kennedy, whose presidential campaign called for American withdrawal from Southeast Asia.

While attending Georgetown, Bill won a part-time job on the staff of the Senate Foreign Relations Committee, which was headed by Senator J. William Fulbright, an Arkansas Democrat. The young college student and the scholarly senator from Arkansas would form a bond stemming from that experience, and in the future Fulbright would mentor Bill as his political career began to rise.

Bill worked as a clerk in the committee's documents room. His duties included sorting mail and filing reports, clipping stories about foreign relations from daily newspapers and running errands for committee members. For Clinton, by now an avowed political junkie, it was like working in Disneyland.

Just after starting work for Fulbright's committee, Bill wrote to his grandmother Edith Cassidy: "It is of course exciting to be here around all the senators and already this year I've seen the president....There's not much time to do anything but study and work, but I love being busy and hard work is good for people."

In April 1968, just before Bill graduated from Georgetown, civil rights leader Martin Luther King Jr. was assassinated in Memphis, Tennessee. The assassination touched off rioting in many American cities, including Washington. Bill volunteered to work for the American Red Cross, driving food into riot-torn Washington neighborhoods because commercial truckers refused to deliver supplies to grocery stores. The organization painted a large red cross onto Bill's white Buick, which he used to make the deliveries. Carolyn Staley, a friend from Hot Springs, helped Bill make some of the deliveries. "It was very dangerous," she recalled. "We raced through red lights and all. But Bill just had to be there. Before we left the shelter, we were advised to pull hats and scarves over our faces because we were

In 1968, Bill Clinton was awarded a Rhodes Scholarship to attend Oxford University in England, one of the world's oldest and most prestigious universities. A 1901 bequest of Cecil Rhodes established these scholarships for the purpose of promoting unity among English-speaking nations. Until 1976, candidates had to be unmarried males between the ages of nineteen and twenty-five. It was Rhodes' wish that, while at Oxford, the scholars would choose instruction at the various colleges comprising the university in accordance with their own interests.

The card pictured here shows the Arms of the Colleges at Oxford University.

After studying at Oxford, Clinton entered the Yale University Law School in 1971. Even though he received a full scholarship, Clinton held various part-time jobs. He taught at a local community college, researched civil suits for a New Haven law firm, and worked briefly for a local city councilman. Clinton had little difficulty with his course work. Friends recalled how he could miss lectures, but borrow their notes to prepare for his exams by studying the night before.

white. We got out and walked throughout the city and saw the burning, the looting, and were very much brought into face-to-face significance with what was going on."

During his final few months at Georgetown, Bill applied for admission to Oxford University in England on a Rhodes Scholarship. He had been urged to make the application by Senator Fulbright, himself a Rhodes scholar in 1924. The honor is awarded to thirty-two American men and women to study at Oxford for up to three years and is considered a prestigious honor.

It took more than good grades to earn the Rhodes Scholarship. Clinton was an "A" student and recommended highly by Fulbright, but he also had to win over committees of Rhodes interviewers in Little Rock and New Orleans. Clinton impressed the committees with his knowledge of world affairs. He breezed through his interviews in Little Rock, and then left for New Orleans. On his way, he stopped in the airport and bought a copy of *Time* magazine to read on the plane. The cover story of the magazine that week reported news of the world's first heart transplant, which in 1968 was regarded as radical surgery. When Bill Clinton arrived in New Orleans one of the things the Rhodes interviewers quizzed him about was heart transplants. Clinton was able to handle the questions easily, thanks to the knowledge he had gained just hours before simply by reading a magazine story.

When Clinton learned he had been selected as a Rhodes scholar, he immediately called his mother. Getting Virginia on the phone, he said, "Well, mother, how do you think I'll look in English tweeds?"

Clinton spent two years at Oxford. He studied international politics, philosophy, and economics, concentrating on study of the Soviet Union, then one of the world's superpowers. Away from the classroom, Clinton loved to dawdle after meals in the school cafeteria, engaging in dialogues with other students. Fellow Rhodes scholar Doug Eakely recalled that the younger English students "were in constant fascination with Bill and he with them. They were so verbally facile. It was expected that you would not just eat and run but eat and talk and debate the great issues of the day until you were thrown out of the dining hall. Bill was always in the thick of it."

In 1969, while still studying in England, Bill received his U.S. military draft notice. After much thought, he decided to make himself available for the draft. He was found to be qualified to serve and was placed in the draft lottery. On December 1, 1969, Clinton received his lottery number, which was high enough to assure that he would never be called into service.

Clinton returned to America in 1970 and enrolled in the law school of Yale University. In the United States, law school has often been an important stop on the path followed by many political leaders as they prepare to become lawmakers. Clinton may have gone to Yale to study for the bar examination, but what he mostly practiced at the school was politics. Immediately after stepping onto the campus in New Haven, Connecticut, Clinton signed up to work for a U.S. Senate candidate named Joe Duffey. Duffey and his aides recognized a born political organizer when they saw one, and Clinton was soon assigned the task of running the campaign in the city of New Haven as well as its suburbs. Clinton worked hard in the campaign, rising early in the morning to round up volunteers, distribute campaign literature in neighborhoods, produce mailings, and step in for Duffey at candidates' events whenever he had to. He slept little and ate on the run.

Duffey finished a distant second in the race, but to Clinton the campaign was hardly a waste of time. Although it turned out to be a losing effort, he gained valuable experience. Clinton was certain that after earning his law degree, he would return to Arkansas to run for public office himself.

After law school, Bill returned to Arkansas where he found a college teaching job while he planned his first political campaign. He failed in that campaign—a race for Congress—but in 1976 won the position of state attorney general. Two years later he won his first term as governor. He served two years but was defeated in the 1980 gubernatorial election. He was reelected governor in 1982 and served four more consecutive terms.

During the 1980s, his leadership and success in governing Arkansas came to the attention of national Democratic Party leaders. In 1992, Bill Clinton won his party's nomination for president, then defeated President George Bush in the fall campaign.

As president, Clinton led his country through a period of tremendous economic growth. Few people were out of work during his administration. Clinton also signed trade agreements with Mexico and Canada and new laws to crack down on crime and control handguns. His wife, Hillary Rodham Clinton, whom he had met at Yale and married in 1975, became a popular though controversial first lady. After the Clintons left the White House Hillary Clinton won election to the U.S. Senate representing New York, becoming the first former first lady in history to be elected to a major political office.

Bill Clinton's administration was also marked by scandal. He was only the second president in U.S. history to be impeached. Members of Congress believed he had lied when asked questions under oath about his romantic relationship with a young woman who worked in the White House. Clinton denied the relationship, but later admitted that it had occurred. Opinion polls reported that a majority of American people believed he was doing a good job as president. Ultimately, the Senate was unable to find the votes to remove him from office, and he finished his presidency and left the White House in January 2001.

"If you live long enough, you'll make mistakes," Bill Clinton once said. "But if you learn from them, you'll be a better person. It's how you handle adversity, not how it affects you. The main thing is never quit, never quit, never quit."

—Hal Marcovitz

George W. Bush
Chapter Forty-two

T
he Second Gulf War, launched by the United States in the face of strident opposition by some of America's oldest allies, again brought into sharp focus the acuity of George W. Bush. Throughout the 2000 election campaign puzzlement regarding Bush's capacity to serve as the single most powerful man in the world had persisted, continuing into his first year in the White House. His brash Texas folksiness, inexperience with (and seeming indifference to) world affairs, and a regular tendency to mangle the English language were all recurring themes in the early months of his presidency.

This shadow disappeared in the immediate aftermath of the national tragedy on September 11, 2001. The president rose to meet America's greatest crisis since Pearl Harbor, immediately commanding respect and support at home and abroad. For the next two years his Gallup approval rating remained high—even as the stock market lost 20 percent of its value and confidence in the economy went into sharp decline. While protestors around the world demonized the president for invading Iraq, within the United States he managed to preserve a strong political base by projecting a confident leadership style, one that seems to reflect unflinching ability to transform world affairs. Thus the paradox of a notable public figure often viewed as a casually educated and mostly inexperienced lightweight who has embarked on the most ambitious foreign policy crusade since Woodrow Wilson set out after World War I to remake the world in America's image.

In *Bush at War*, Bob Woodward relates a rare but telling piece of presidential introspection. Bush mused to the author about taking command of his national security team in the immediate aftermath of September 11. "If I have any genius or smarts," he told Woodward, "it's the ability to recognize talent, ask them to serve and work with them as a team." Missing from the quotation but implicit in it is the message that the "team" would follow a determined leader filled with a mission and devoid of self-doubt.

Whatever lethargy may have once possessed him, Bush immediately found resolve as wartime commander in chief. While only the unfolding of tumultuous events and the sharp judgment of historical perspective will determine the relative

George W. Bush is part of a distinguished American political family. His paternal grandfather, Prescott Bush, was a U.S. senator from Connecticut from 1952 to 1962, and his father, George H. W. Bush, served as the forty-first president of the United States from 1989 to 1993. George W. is the second president to be the son of a president— John and John Quincy Adams being the first father and son to have each achieved the nation's highest political office.

George W. Bush graduated from Phillips Academy, Andover, in 1964. He received his BA in History from Yale University in 1968 and his MBA from the Harvard Business School in 1975.

George W. Bush with his father George H. W. Bush and his mother Barbara Bush. Young George was nine years old when this photo was taken in the summer of 1955.

wisdom or folly of Bush's international venture, one principal aspect of it is already unmistakably clear. However much he is coached by significant others, the new American worldview is that of George W. Bush.

Once the conventional wisdom concerning Bush's major aides—Dick Cheney, Donald Rumsfeld, Colin Powell, and Condoleezza Rice, along with Paul Wolfowitz and Richard Perle—held that the inexperienced president needed heavyweights to tell him what to think, what to do, and how to do it. As events after September 11 now clearly indicate, however, they function less as advisors and more as managers of this president's ideas. Tactics and strategy are surely open for discussion. But general objectives and Bush's fixed determination to achieve them are not. Perhaps the strongest impression left by *Bush at War* is of the president's command style. Unlike John F. Kennedy in the Cuban Missile Crisis or Lyndon B. Johnson in the Vietnam War, Bush did not seek advice, options, or multiple scenarios. He issued orders. Perhaps this decisive clarity is instinctively transmitted to popular opinion. It certainly stands at variance with earlier perceptions of the man.

One legitimate question for debate is the source of his self-confidence. Primary is the influence of the Bush Dynasty, now in its fifth generation of permanent power but only dimly appreciated as an experience that provided all the training necessary to live life and play a dominant role in the affairs of the nation. The comparison between Bush's formal and informal education is revealing. It is often remarked that George W. Bush, afforded the best educational opportunities available in the United States, responded by insisting upon intellectual mediocrity. In fact, Bush's three academic experiences are almost insignificant in his "education." A study of President Bush's education must be rooted more in family training and experience than in prep school, college, or university. In the fullest sense, young Bush brought to his elite educational experience a value system fully forged in the wild oil frontier of West Texas and the upper-class haunts of the children of Houston's business aristocracy.

His formal education began prosaically enough at Sam Houston Elementary School in Midland, Texas. After the family moved to Houston in 1959, the young man was enrolled at the Kinkaid School, a private and exclusive redoubt for the children of Houston's petrobusiness elite. Two years later, deferring to his parents' wishes at the age of fifteen, he went off far away to Andover, Massachusetts, to Phillips Academy.

For most of American history Phillips Academy, or just "Andover" (the names are used interchangeably), twenty miles north of Boston, has been steeped in the traditions of the upper class. A daunting legacy hovered over the legendary campus, the nation's oldest boarding school. Its hundred-odd buildings have been inhabited by generations of graduates whose success touched every corner of American life. In 1960 it remained a refuge for the boys of the American elites, entrance based largely if not exclusively on family prominence, connections and, as with the Bushes, lineage. His father, graduated nineteen years earlier, had been named, in then-familiar parlance, "Best All Around Fellow" in his class.

> "He was one of the cool guys.... He rose to a certain prominence for no ostensible, visible reason.... Obviously, he inherited some extraordinary political skills."

The academic and social structure of Phillips Academy resonated with eternal verities, discipline, particularly punctuality, religiosity, and continuous academic and sports activity. The roughhousing atmosphere of the playing fields and residence halls reflected the kind of muscular Christianity favored by Theodore Roosevelt for the young men of the American elite. Young Bush, not blessed with the athletic skills of his father, more than compensated socially. He did try baseball, gave rock music a whirl, and became head cheerleader. Arguably the most popular boy due to his exuberant infectious personality, Bush drew into his circle peers who did excel at sports and scholarship. They became his admirers and friends, some on a lifelong basis. More importantly, young Bush began to exhibit at Andover characteristics that would mark his maturity as a politician.

In an interview with Bill Minutaglio for *First Son: George W. Bush and the Bush Family Dynasty* (1999), an Andover schoolmate tried to describe the essence of the teenaged George W. Bush. "George was always part of a small group of seven or eight guys who were really, well, you have to call them the big men on campus. He was one of the cool guys.... He rose to a certain prominence for no ostensible, visible reason.... Obviously, he inherited some extraordinary political skills."

Bush would need them. Northeastern winters lasted forever for the young Texan. Inside the classrooms, moreover, he perceived the academic sophistication of his peers as an obstacle course that he had no particular interest in testing. Instead he concentrated on being mischievous, the leading boy prankster whose peers admired his nerve in testing the limits of order and pomposity. "I'm sure he took some things seriously," another classmate recalled, "but he was more interested in social standing than what grades he had in order to get into Yale." Bush and his friends "would walk around with a certain confidence, bravado, a little swagger," Minutaglio wrote in *First Son*. As head cheerleader the swagger took center stage. As "High Commissioner" of an informal but elaborately organized stickball league, young Bush presided with mock solemnity as judge and jury in mediating the endless arguments that competitive boys have in their games. Mock solemnity, wigs, disguises, top hats, and pranks. As another classmate recalls for Bill Minutaglio, "It's very hard to get below the surface of George, he is so facile and so personable.... He was already who he was, but being at Andover gave him a chance to hone his skills."

In June 1964 George W. Bush graduated from Andover and returned to Texas to begin his real education, just at the moment when the Bush Dynasty's torch was passed to his father. In Connecticut, Senator Prescott Bush announced his retirement at about the same time that, in Houston, George H. W. Bush sought to replace him in the upper

George W. Bush's 1968 senior class photograph, and the title page from *The Old Campus*. The 1968 Yale class was the last for an all-male student body.

During George W.'s four years at Yale, his father was involved in political campaigns that attracted national publicity. In 1964, the senior Bush ran unsuccessfully for the United States Senate from Texas and two years later he was elected to the House of Representatives. George W. was involved in each campaign.

THE OLD CAMPUS
1968

A YALE BANNER PUBLICATION

chamber. Thus the recent Andover graduate, on his way to Yale, returned home to join his father's campaign for the United States Senate. At eighteen, his real education began.

Although Republican John Tower had won a special Senate election in 1961, serious Republican candidates were still strange characters across an endless Texas landscape filled with habitual Democrats. This was particularly so in 1964, when the almost manic campaign of President Lyndon Baines Johnson dominated both state and national political attention. In Texas, with the president claiming possession of nearly all of the political spectrum, George H. W. Bush ran toward the right-wing fringes, opposing civil rights, nuclear test ban negotiations with the Soviet Union, foreign aid, anti-poverty initiatives, and Martin Luther King Jr. Beyond political issues, however, Bush faced the even more daunting hurdle of his manner and lineage.

With his son alongside, Bush exerted great effort in a flawed attempt to disguise his gentlemanly manner and northeastern bearing. Traveling in a bus caravan dubbed "The Bandwagon for Bush," he gamely listened at stop after stop to the Black Mountain Boys working up a country and western performance, accompanied by a chorus of Republican women, the "Bush Bluebonnet Belles," offering such rustic verse as "Oh, the sun's gonna shine in the Senate someday! George Bush is going to chase them liberals away!"

Amidst the rhetorical hokum, George Bush seemed inauthentic. Never convincing in western garb, he remained in the mind's eye in blue blazer and rep tie, reflecting the country club gentility of his Greenwich, Andover, and Yale roots, the picture of a well-bred Yankee aristocrat created over generations of wealth and political influence. He embodied the great dynasty that Bushes and Walkers represent. (However strenuously the family continues to deny the "dynasty" appellation, there is no other term for the century-long melding of privilege and power routinely exercised by the Bush and Walker families.)

In the Gilded Age of the last three decades of the nineteenth century the modern American industrial and commercial aristocracy took its form as a permanent elite, insuring succeeding generations access to wealth and its rewards, including political power. Samuel Prescott Bush (1863–1948), great grandfather to President George W. Bush, was born in New York but became a steel and railroad baron in Columbus, Ohio. His impressive dossier includes serving as the first president of the National Association of Manufacturers, then as now the nation's most powerful industrial lobby. Also a founding member of the United States Chamber of Commerce and a Federal Reserve director, Samuel P. Bush became an adviser to President Herbert Hoover and a member of his administration. Noted for his prominent role in civic associations, Bush, a varsity athlete in football and baseball, also helped establish the sport of football at Ohio State University.

Samuel's son Prescott, father to a president and grandfather to another, added great luster to the family's standing. Born in 1895 to wealth and status, he was properly educated in prep school, on to Yale, varsity baseball and football, nationally known golfer, Skull & Bones, World War I combat as a field artillery captain in front-line service in France, before careers on Wall Street and in the United States Senate.

In 1921, Prescott Bush married Dorothy Walker, from another powerful family of merchants and bankers. Her grandfather, David Douglas Walker, made a fortune in dry goods and rose to prominence in civic affairs in St. Louis. Dorothy's father, George Herbert Walker, a founding partner of Wall Street's oldest and most powerful private investment house, Brown Brothers Harriman, became a confidante of Franklin Delano Roosevelt. The congenialities shared by the Bush-Walker family included golf, the favored sporting indulgence of the elite in those generations. Prescott Bush achieved international recognition as an amateur champion. His wife's father, the Wall Street banker, gave the family name to the Walker Cup competition between American and British teams.

The essence of the family's story over the past half-century is the move from the New England patrician class to the hard-knuckle cultural bramble of Texas. Remarkably resilient and successful in building an oil fortune in the havoc of the West Texas oil patch, George H. W. Bush moved the family base to Houston, capital city of the American petrochemical industry, solidified his class and caste base in the opulent suburbs, and watched his family grow under the discipline of the redoubtable Barbara Walker Bush. In 1964, in running for the Senate, Bush sought to emulate his ancestors and in-laws, observed every day by his eldest son.

The impact of family dynamics in the socialization of the forty-third president cannot be overestimated. For ten years after his sixth birthday, young George watched his two principal role models with great intensity. His grandfather, elected to the Senate in 1952, periodically arrived in Midland, a commanding Yankee patrician visiting the family's outpost on the oil derrick frontier. Also during these years, Poppy began his own strenuous efforts to build a political profile of his own. A relentless civic man, involved in his church, service clubs, and philanthropic campaigns, George H. W. Bush genuinely liked his peers, the rising class of accomplished men who wrenched fortunes out of the petroleum landscape. Moving among them with his loopy smile, mouth slightly agape, exchanging a joke or a confidence, shaking all hands, purring the small talk that is coin of the realm for politicians, George H. W. Bush became a natural aristocrat on this untamed society. There are few less likely sites for a Yale Club than Midland, Texas, but there it was, with dinner dances and strenuous tennis matches, filling up with rising men compatible with Bush values. Here became an incubus for the Republican Party in Texas, which would send Bush forward to vie for a Senate seat in 1964.

Because the summer vacation of 1964 ended before the election campaign, George W. headed for New Haven to follow family tradition at Yale. After settling in briefly, the young man returned to Houston for the final hours of the election. His father, crushed by over 300,000 votes by the incumbent Democrat, Senator Ralph Yarborough, reacted with typical aplomb. He empathized with the feelings of disappointed family and friends, and avoided bitterness toward political adversaries who had defeated him through a campaign marked by caricature and crude innuendo. Bush the war hero and successful oilman disappeared into the caricature of an outsider, an interloper sent by shadowy intriguers to somehow hoodwink Texans. Provincialism triumphed, and an observant son carefully noted it. There would never be a question of the son's authenticity as a Texan.

Back at Yale, Bush would confront a daunting legacy. His grandfather had at Yale been a scholar, varsity athlete in football and baseball, championship-caliber golfer, member of the famed "Whiffenpoof" singers, and served on the Yale board. His father had, if anything, done even more at Yale as student, baseball captain, and as a kind of peer-respected student statesman. George W., naturally assuming that his generation of Yalies would be similarly commissioned to service and status, found instead frustration bordering on bitterness. During his freshman year, in the direct aftermath of his father's political defeat, young Bush had an encounter that would permanently sour his feelings toward Yale.

This most galling event came about in a chance meeting on campus—when Bush introduced himself to Yale's famously controversial university chaplain, William Sloane Coffin, a nationally prominent antiwar activist. As a Yale senior in 1948, Coffin had been "tapped" for the secret Skull and Bones Society by its leader, George H. W. Bush. A generation later, in the wake of the elder Bush's crushing political defeat at the hands of Senator Yarborough, Coffin said to the younger Bush, "Oh, yes, I know your father. Frankly, he was beaten by a better man." This moment provided a kind of negative epiphany for the young man from Texas. Resolutely positioning himself outside of Yale's turbulent Sixties mainstream, Bush chose the safety of a fraternity culture increasingly marginalized and trivialized by most of his peers.

Much of the consternation he felt as an undergraduate grew out of the counterculture that invaded American campuses both great and modest. Elevated for the first time in American colleges and universities were the values inimical to established traditions of family, country, and noblesse oblige embraced by his forebears. Public figures like his father and grandfather were routinely excoriated as standard-bearers of a society whose primary institutions and policies were found by increasingly radicalized students as not only deficient but positively malevolent.

Teach-ins, sit-ins, street demonstrators, challenges to professors and college administrators, alliances with populist fringe groups, Marxist and Freudian analyses of self and society—all struck young Bush as shockingly wrongheaded. Traditionalists at Yale and elsewhere did attempt to counter the radicalization of campus life, including many Republican and conservative student groups, but Bush remained resolutely apolitical. He retreated into the safety of fraternity life, with its ubiquitous social activities featuring alcohol, parties, intramural sports, pursuit of young women, and assorted weekend adventures.

It was a comfortable routine of intramural sports and fraternity fun. His style became centered on the Delta Kappa Epsilon fraternity, the legendary DKE, the quintessential fun-and-games refuge for athletes and the descendants of Yale's elite. His father, perhaps naturally, had been chapter president, a position that George W. succeeded to for his senior year.

The recollections of his fraternity brothers are filled with nostalgic warmth for the chapter president who made it to the White House. Obviously, and despite the vastly different proportions, George W. Bush's young undergraduate peers recognized and followed certain personality traits that a dubious national political world would come to accept only haltingly a generation later. "He's the great sun around which a universe revolved," a DKE told Bill Minutaglio. "He radiated star quality, but never in an unapproachable way."

Over the following four years the young Texan made lifelong friends—and a few detractors as well. In the latter category, one would prove a continuing nemesis. Gary Trudeau, author of the syndicated and widely read cartoon series "Doonesbury," knew Bush casually at Yale when the Texan served as DKE rush chairman. Years later, Trudeau would sardonically tell Ted Koppel on *Nightline* that when it came to deciding how many kegs of beer for a party, "I have to say, George Bush showed great leadership qualities during those meetings." Trudeau routinely mocks President Bush as an invisible person beneath a ten-gallon hat spouting inanities. The continuing ridicule of Bush, certainly less pervasive as his accomplishments have produced great popular approval, is nonetheless rooted in the modest biography he brought to the White House. In large part, the arrogant anti-intellectualism of his career at Yale continued to resonate.

Even the prize of the DKE presidency, a trophy in his father's time, became devalued in the fevered political context of the Sixties. The once-mighty sway of the so-called Greek System of fraternity and secret society membership atrophied to become the fodder for condescension. Ensconced in this narrowing world of fun and foolishness, with academic responsibilities casually tolerated, George W. Bush and his like-minded associates spent the mid-Sixties pleasantly enough.

The focus of his senior year centered on the "tapping" of Bush for the ultra-secret elite society, Skull and Bones. Formed at Yale in 1832 out of a recondite hodgepodge of Germanic mysticism, it pledged generations of members to absolute secrecy. In its campus "tomb" on High Street, a two-story house with lounges, library, dining room, and an "inner temple," the selected handful of that year's seniors came into contact with Bonesmen of old, collectively the generations of the elite from Wall Street, corporate America, Washington, and world capitals. Alexandra Robbins's *Secrets of the Tomb* (2002) recounts the extraordinary list of famous and powerful Americans tapped for Skull and Bones—a litany of the aristocracy, including family dynasties named Bundy, Harriman, Lord, Rockefeller, Taft, and Whitney, as well as the Bushes. Revered by the members and derided by critics, Yale's secret societies enclosed young men in a self-congratulatory world in which the insiders found much of college's values, even as they misbehaved. George W. Bush's minor scrapes with the police, commonplace enough among fraternity carousers of that era, would later provide fodder for tall tales of youthful indiscretion. He did not much like Yale even as he grew more self-confident.

His alienation from Yale's purported snobbishness, its "heavy" intellectualism, its estrangement from loyalty, tradition, and the purported commonsensical mind of the American electorate, served to reinforce Bush's commitment to tradition. He

DELTA KAPPA EPSILON

DKE

Class of 1968
R. H. Allen, Robert E.L. Beebe, Daniel M. Bogel, D. Bergman, Roland W. Betts, George W. Bush, C.E. Thomas Cleveland, Edgar M. Cullman, Millard D. Davidson, David W. Davis, Robert J. Dieter, John R. Emmons, Donald B. Ensenat, James D. Fisher, Steven L. Freshman, G. Gregory Gallico, Matthew D. Gay, R. Hoseeler, Robert T. Hume, Clay Johnson, Collister Johnson, Paul B. Jones, Robert J. Keith, D. Knuth-Winterfeldt, Donald W. Koerbin, Kenneth R. Kurtz, Franklin H. Levy, James B. Lockhart, Peter F. Markle, Samuel Martin, Stephen W. Mayberg, Frederick V. Mc-Carthy, Allan McDowell, Livy Miller, David B. Patterson, Joseph E. Potter, Clark F. Bandt, Robert A. Reisner, Steven R. Rummel, John T. Sartore, Robert T. Savage, William H. Sawyer, Donald A. Schollander, Kenneth B. Schulman, Steven M. Shapiro, J. Courtney Shevelson, Chris C. Taylor, Robert J. Ternes, D. Townsend, Paul Tully, Joseph T. Ward, William B. Wemple, Kenneth E. White, Ronald F. Whitney, Geoffrey B.H. Woglom.

Class of 1969
Robert E. Arras, John B. Babcock, Charles W. Banta, Francis A. Boyer, Timothy P. Brisey, Richard D. Bruin, H. Douglass Connell, Walter J. Cummings, David M. Darst, Bardfute W. Davenport, Mark B. Dayton, Steven Dixon, Brian J. Dowling, William Evans, Jerry Du'v. Gary, J. P. Goldsmith, Timothy Harris, David Heckler, John M. Hemingway, Calvin Hill, Robert G. Hoban, J. William Howerton, John M. Keeling, Merritt B. Kleber, Phillip M. Laughlin, Robert E. Levin, Frederick Livingston, Richard E. Lunien, William McKenna, John E. Mackey, Walter A. Martini, Kimball B. Morsman, B. Owens, William A. Palmer, Charles S. Peck, Daniel Petric, James L. Pomeranz, Alexander Bechter, Charles P. Resor, B. Rothstein, Ralph S. Sando, Jonathan Stern, Duane A. Selander, Robert J. Sokolowski, Karl A. Spangenberg, Frank J. Sprole, Gregory N. Thomas, Daniel M. Tucker, John B. Waldman, A. Weller, Michael M. Wood, Scott A. Williams, James N. Worreston.

Class of 1970
Gerard D. Cameron, Gordon H. Clack, Glenn E. DeChabert, Wayne H. Ewing, Harvey F. Greber, William A. Harper, Charles B. Hogas, Gerard B. Hughes, Terrence J. Jackson, Stephen C. Jones, William H. Kotz, Bradford A. Lee, Joseph D. Messinger, Van Midgely, Samuel R. Miller, George Noble, Jeff D. Palmer, Robert Potts, Peter A. Radice, William B. Seyfluch, William H. Starbuck, James B. Stryker, Edgar L. Taplin, John C. Train, Chris Trower, Todd Wheeler, Richard C. Whittlesey, Edward M. Wright, Jeff Almquist, Woody Britton, Wayne Cutler, Larry Dautch, James Dempsey, Pete D'Chellis, Tony Gaslevich, Charles Stewart.

George W. Bush attended Yale from 1964 to 1968 (this photograph was taken in 1965). He was the fourth generation to do so.

Bush was elected president of the Delta Kappa Epsilon fraternity—his father's former fraternity. (His name appears in the second line under "Class of 1968"; the DKE house is pictured on the right.) Bush was also "tapped" for membership in Skull and Bones, his father and grandfather's club. Almost all who knew Bush as a fellow student have described his charismatic and exuberant personality.

left New Haven with no doubts that he, like his father and grandfather before him, represented that older, wiser American polity. He would eventually pursue these values not as a New England Yankee Ivy Leaguer, but as its stylistic opposite.

Embedded in this family socialization is religiosity, a force that has gathered momentum in recent years in defining and shaping President Bush's view of himself and his domestic and foreign policies.

His family insists that social class does not matter while all the time seeing the world through the natural assumptions of who should prevail, i.e., achievement through family lineage, association with similar others, respect for economic accomplishment, and use of government to promote and protect this ethic which allows success on the highest levels with a value system determined by the simple ethos of market capitalism.

Attracted by the practicalities of the bottom line, Bush has learned to dismiss those abstractions that challenge it. As president, he professes to see no hypocrisy between his own admission to elite schools based on moderate academic qualifications and his opposition to Michigan's preferential formula according weight to race. He asked the Supreme Court to rule the Michigan system unconstitutional, noting that "African-American students and some Hispanic students and Native American students receive 20 points out of a maximum of 150, not because of any academic achievement or life experience, but solely because they are African-American, Hispanic or Native American." Family legacy, yes. Skin color counterbalancing racism, no. It would be difficult to explore this contradiction, and so he ignores it, confident that his family's traditions are sufficient. His SAT scores (566 verbal, 640 math) were no obstacle to elite matriculation in the system that prevailed then and now, for the children of alumni, particularly rich and influential alumni.

Another "practical" tenet of family faith is revealed religion, although the style and content of religious practice has changed substantially over the Bush generations. In its March 10, 2003, cover story, *Newsweek* explored the role of religion in defining the most controversial aspects of the Bush presidency. The account traces the family's religious bent over the years down to the establishmentarian Episcopalian traditions when they lived in Yankee Connecticut. The move to Texas gradually led to an opening to the religious right, fundamentalist, evangelical, born-again Christianity that became such a potent force in the Republican Party's capture of power in the South in the 1980s. As George W. assumed a surrogate's power in his father's political rise, the firmest vase lay on the religious right, where the son found a spiritual home in mid-life. He has often cited biblical study and the personalized relationship with the Deity for his rescue from excessive drinking. As a friend put it, "Good-bye Jack Daniels, hello Jesus." As Bush observed to a clergymen's group, "There is only one reason that I am in the Oval Office and not in a bar. I found faith. I found God. I am here because of the power of prayer."

All American presidents are required, as a matter of political necessity, to pay some level of obeisance to religious observance, of course. For the forty-third president, however, religion is revealed and fundamental, not intellectual and abstract. The veteran Washington journalist Elizabeth Drew referred to his "messianic streak." The far side of George W.'s "aw shucks" regular guy persona is his sense of destiny: if something is big enough and important enough, he believes it is his destiny to right it. As his formal educational experiences taught him to suspect rationality and intellectualism, space opened for his personal religious experience.

By the time of his 1968 graduation, Bush's father had been elected to Congress from a Houston district, and in 1970 again lost an attempt at a Senate seat before winning nomination as U.S. ambassador to the United Nations. George W.'s resume proved much more modest. He returned home and entered into the much-debated process through which he avoided active duty in the Vietnam War by securing a much-coveted Texas Air National Guard commission. With the sons of other prominent Lone Star State families, he spent parts of the next years flying jet planes safely away from the murderous conflict in Southeast Asia. Settling into a relaxed bachelor lifestyle with similarly inclined young people, he tended to re-create his Yale lifestyle while slowly pondering the future. Unsatisfying jobs and low-level dabbling in Republican politics followed, and five years passed.

In 1973, Bush and eight hundred others began in the MBA program at Harvard Business School. The prestige of this degree rested largely on its alumni, whose careers in the United States and around the world constituted an interlocked system of power and influence. The pedagogy rested on case studies, specific examples of situations relying on facts to be analyzed and policy options to be taken. For the first time, the twenty-seven-year-old Bush took with great interest to a kind of formal education. Avoiding grand theorizing, social policy, and abstruse academic subjects, Bush fully and successfully took on the curriculum and interacted positively with his like-minded classmates. Nonetheless, the unstable world of the Nixon presidency dominated the climate within which the business school stood isolated in its commitment to entrepreneurial capitalism.

Bush again resolutely shunned campus turmoil, and concluded that Harvard, like Yale, had little to teach him about his own value system. After two years, he headed straight for the life his father had trail blazed a generation earlier: the wild oil fields. George W. Bush returned to his childhood home, Midland, Texas.

Formal education had ended. In sum, he more or less despised Phillips Academy, Yale and Harvard; each in its own way the antithesis of the values lived and learned by the family in Texas. Years later, during his father's 1992 reelection campaign, according to Minutaglio's *First Son*, George W. fulminated about "of what he hated about the cynics in the northeastern media, all those guilt-laden intellectuals who had everything in common with the arrogant, suffocating products of Yale and Harvard."

As a boy and young man during time spent in Andover, New Haven, and Cambridge, Bush insulated himself from the dominant campus ethos, successfully

In 1968, George W. Bush joined the Texas Air National Guard. He served as a F-102 fighter pilot. When the commanding officer of the unit asked him, "Why do you want to join?" Bush replied, "I want to be a fighter pilot because my father was." George H. W. Bush had been the youngest commissioned officer in the U.S. Navy during World War II.

"There is only one reason that I am in the Oval Office and not in a bar. I found faith. I found God. I am here because of the power of prayer."

shutting out "the Sixties" which howled about him preaching values and habits repugnant to his family tradition. The worldview that has come to mark his presidency is largely shaped by those years. Scion of a generations-old dynasty of wealth and power, George W. Bush's nature and nurture comprised the only education he would ever need.

The process of linking the biographical elements in the career of a public person is certainly an inexact art form. Aspects of George W. Bush's public persona seem to have discernible roots, however. Never comfortable with the easy pragmatism and relativism so common among political people, he has always implicitly trusted people who meet the definition of character worked out by the Bush Dynasty.

As president, he appointed as his principal officers men whose fervently held beliefs matched his own. Sure of themselves to the point of dogmatism, Cheney, Rumsfeld, Wolfowitz and their outriders were brought into positions of high power not to advise President George W. Bush so much as to carry out their vision by a president who believed in it as strongly as they did themselves. Rooted in a clear sense of righteousness, a businessman's notion of common sense, with the marketplace the judge of value and reward, fundamental religious verities and the clear superiority of American institutions, the Bush administration would pursue a breathtaking restructure of U.S. domestic and foreign policy.

At home, no president since the ill-fated Herbert Hoover had trusted his fortunes so much to the foibles of supply-side economics, where fiscal and monetary policy concentrating on tax cuts benefiting the privileged and powerful would pass down through society to increase the general welfare. Abroad, the export of U.S. democratic institutions to areas of the globe and cultural traditions with no experience with it (or apparent taste for it) constituted an idealism that harkened back eight decades to Woodrow Wilson's failed plans to "make the world safe for democracy."

From the vantage point of the spring of 2003, therefore, the pending question concerns not at all the willingness of Bush to attempt a historic shift in global balance of power. Rather it is the wisdom of that vision. Unlike all his predecessors stretching back to Roosevelt and Truman, Bush seems almost anxious to give up the multilateral framework within which the United States clearly played the role of leader of alliance systems. Upon the wisdom of unilateralism Bush has staked his reputation and most likely his presidency. He remains remarkably self-assured in knowing what he knows. Otherwise, he shows little curiosity. In sum, an irregular education.

—J. F. Watts

A Selective Guide to Presidential Biographies

This listing is a sampling of the biographies available dealing with the lives of the presidents of the United States. Many of these titles have been reprinted; the date listed is that of the original publication. The bibliographies and footnotes in each of the following books should be useful for further study. This bibliography is based upon Tom Trescott and Dan Weinberg, "The Essential Presidential Book Shelf: A Selective Readers' and Collectors' Guide," *The Rail Splitter*, vol. 7 no. 4 (Spring 2002).

George Washington (Federalist, 1789–1797)

James Thomas Flexner's *George Washington* (four vols., 1965–1972) is thoroughly researched and well written. Essential for studying the life of the first president.

Douglas Southall Freeman's *George Washington: A Biography* (seven vols., 1948–1957) is a distinguished work by an eminent historian. Volumes one and two deal with Washington's early life. This is the definitive portrait of Washington.

George Washington: The Man Behind the Myths (1999), by William Rasmussen and Robert Tilton, is an outstanding combination of narrative, analysis, and visual imagery. The authors give an original analysis of Washington's public and private lives.

John Adams (Federalist, 1797–1801)

Page Smith's *John Adams* (two vols., 1962) was the first major biography of Adams completed after the publication of the Adams Papers. First rate.

John Adams: A Life (1992), by John Ferling, is an excellent one-volume work.

David McCullough's *John Adams* (2001) is a popular and well-written biography by a Pulitzer Prize winner.

Thomas Jefferson (Democratic-Republican, 1801–1809)

Dumas Malone's *Jefferson and His Times* (six vols., 1948–1981) is one of the greatest contributions to American historical literature in the twentieth century. Volume one, *Jefferson the Virginian* (1948), deals with young Jefferson.

Thomas Jefferson and the New Nation: A Biography (1970), by Merrill Peterson, is perhaps the best one-volume life of the third president.

James Madison (Democratic-Republican, 1809–1817)

Irving Brant's *James Madison* (6 vols., 1941–1961) is the definitive work on Madison. Brant's *The Fourth President: A Life of James Madison* (1970) is a masterful condensation of the multi-volume original.

James Madison: A Biography (1971), by Robert Ketcham, is a well-written review of Madison's life.

James Monroe (Democratic-Republican, 1817–1825)

Harry Ammon's *James Monroe* (1971) is a good survey of Monroe's life.

William Cresson's *James Monroe* (1946) is a scholarly biography of Monroe.

John Quincy Adams (Democratic-Republican, 1825–1829)

John Quincy Adams (1972), by Marie Hecht, is a good survey of Adams' life.

Lynn Parsons's *John Quincy Adams* (1998) is a well-written recent biography.

Andrew Jackson (Democrat, 1829–1837)

The definitive biography of Jackson is Robert Remini's three-volume *Andrew Jackson* (1977–1984). Volume one, *Andrew Jackson and the Course of American Empire, 1767–1821* (1977), covers Jackson's early life.

Marquis James's *Andrew Jackson* (two vols., 1933–1937) was considered the standard life of Jackson until the Remini study.

Martin Van Buren (Democrat, 1837–1841)

Denis Lynch's *An Epoch and a Man: Martin Van Buren and His Times* (1929) is the best available biography of Van Buren.

John Niven's *Martin Van Buren and the Romantic Age of American Politics* (1983) is the first modern biography of Van Buren based extensively on his personal papers.

William Henry Harrison (Whig, 1841)

Old Tippecanoe: William Henry Harrison and His Times (1939), a sympathetic biography by Freeman Cleaves, is an excellent survey of Harrison's early life.

Dorothy Goebel's *William Henry Harrison* (1926) remains essential to the study of Harrison. Goebel also wrote the excellent article on Harrison for the *Dictionary of American Biography*, volume eight.

John Tyler (Whig, 1841–1845)

Oliver Chitwood's *John Tyler: Champion of the Old South* (1939) is a scholarly work on a complex personality, the first of the accidental presidents.

The essential book on Tyler is Robert Seager's *And Tyler Too: A Biography of John and Julia Tyler* (1963).

James K. Polk (Democrat, 1845–1849)

Eugene McCormac's *James K. Polk* (1922) is an excellent account of the first "dark horse" in a presidential race.

Charles Sellers's *James K. Polk* (two vols., 1957–1966) is a carefully researched study.

Zachary Taylor (Whig, 1849–1850)

K. Jack Bauer's *Zachary Taylor: Soldier, Planter, Statesman of the Old Southwest* (1985) is a balanced and thoroughly researched biography of a complex personality.

The definitive life of "Old Rough and Ready" is Holman Hamilton's two-volume Zachary Taylor (1941–1951).

Millard Fillmore (Whig, 1850–1853)

Millard Fillmore: Biography of a President (1959), by Robert Rayback, is a good biography of an underrated president.

Franklin Pierce (Democrat, 1853–1857)

Franklin Pierce: Young Hickory of the Granite Hills (1931; revised 1958), by Roy Nichols, is a discerning portrait of Pierce, and the only scholarly biography of the man. Nichols expanded his research on Pierce with a series of articles that appeared in numerous journals.

James Buchanan (Democrat, 1857–1861)

Philip Klein's *President James Buchanan: A Biography* (1962) is a scholarly biography of one of the most misunderstood chief executives.

Abraham Lincoln (Republican, 1861–1865)

David Donald's outstanding 1995 biography *Lincoln* won the Pulitzer Prize.

The Last Best Hope of Earth: Abraham Lincoln and the Promise of America (1993), by Mark Neely Jr., is an excellent one-volume analysis.

With Malice Toward None: The Life of Abraham Lincoln (1977) by Stephen Oates is another worthwhile study of the sixteenth president.

Carl Sandburg's *Abraham Lincoln* (six vols., 1926–1939) is essential for understanding Lincoln. Sandburg captured the essence of the Lincoln myth and its importance to Americans.

Benjamin Thomas's *Abraham Lincoln: A Biography* (1952) was the classic one-volume life of Lincoln until publication of the Donald study.

Andrew Johnson (Republican-Union, 1865–1869)

Hans Trefousse's *Andrew Johnson: A Biography* (1989) is a full-length biography written by the foremost authority on the Reconstruction period.

Ulysses S. Grant (Republican, 1869–1877)

William McFeely's *Grant: A Biography* (1981) won the Pulitzer Prize.

Ulysses S. Grant: The Triumph over Adversity, 1822–1865 (2000) is the first of two projected volumes by Brooks Simpson.

Jean Smith's *Grant* (2001) is a recent work that is exhaustively researched and wonderfully written.

Rutherford B. Hayes (Republican, 1877–1881)

Harry Barnard's *Rutherford B. Hayes and His America* (1954) is an excellent biography.

Ari Hoogenboom's *Rutherford B. Hayes: Warrior and President* (1996) is a comprehensive biography.

James A. Garfield (Republican, 1881)
The best account of Garfield and the "gilded age" is Allan Peskin's *James Abram Garfield* (1978).

John Taylor's *Garfield of Ohio* (1970) is a fine study of the president who served only six months before he was assassinated.

W. W. Wasson's *James A. Garfield: His Religion and Education* (1952) is a well-documented monograph.

Chester A. Arthur (Republican, 1881–1885)
The only full-length biography of Arthur is Thomas Reeves's *Gentleman Boss: The Life of Chester Alan Arthur* (1975). It is an excellent book.

Grover Cleveland (Democrat, 1885–1889; 1893–1897)
Allan Nevins's *Grover Cleveland* (1932) is the best biography of Cleveland, written by one of the great twentieth-century American historians. Nevins interviewed Cleveland family members and also had access to the president's personal papers.

While Nevins stresses Cleveland's courage, Alyn Brodsky emphasizes his integrity in *Grover Cleveland: A Study in Character* (2000).

Benjamin Harrison (Republican, 1889–1893)
Harry Sievers's *Benjamin Harrison* (three vols., 1952–1968) is the only comprehensive biography. Volume one, *Hoosier Warrior, 1833–1865* (1952) deals with Harrison's education.

William McKinley (Republican, 1897–1901)
Margaret Leech's *In the Days of McKinley* (1959) is an important analysis of McKinley.

H. Wayne Morgan's *William McKinley and His America* (1963) is a masterful study.

Theodore Roosevelt (Republican, 1901–1909)
Power and Responsibility: The Life and Times of Theodore Roosevelt (1961) is an excellent study by William Harbaugh.

David McCullough's superb biography of young TR, *Mornings on Horseback* (1982), won the National Book Award.

Nathan Miller's *Theodore Roosevelt: A Life* (1992) is an excellent one-volume study.

Two volumes by Edmund Morris, *The Rise of Theodore Roosevelt* (1979) and *Theodore Rex* (2001), promise to become the definitive biography.

William Howard Taft (Republican, 1909–1913)
Henry Pringle's *The Life and Times of William Howard Taft* (two vols., 1939) remains the best biography of the only president who also served as chief justice of the Supreme Court.

Woodrow Wilson (Democrat, 1913–1921)

August Heckscher's *Woodrow Wilson* (1991) is the best one-volume study.

Arthur Link's five-volume *Wilson* (1947–1955) is outstanding. Volume one, *The Road to the White House* (1947), deals with Wilson's early years.

Woodrow Wilson (1978), by Arthur Walworth, received the Pulitzer Prize for biography.

Warren G. Harding (Republican, 1921–1923)

Francis Russell's *The Shadow of Blooming Grove: Warren G. Harding and His Times* (1968) is still the best biography of Harding.

Calvin Coolidge (Republican, 1923–1929)

Donald McCoy's *Calvin Coolidge: The Quiet President* (1967) is an objective scholarly biography.

William Allen White's *Puritan in Babylon: The Story of Calvin Coolidge* (1938) is a well-written biography by a famous newspaper editor.

Herbert Hoover (Republican, 1929–1933)

David Burner's *Herbert Hoover* (1979) is a scholarly biography.

George Nash's *The Life of Herbert Hoover* (three vols., 1983–1996) will be the definitive study. It has been subsidized by the Hoover Presidential Library Association. Volume one, *The Engineer, 1874–1914* (1983), covers Hoover's education in great detail.

Franklin D. Roosevelt (Democrat, 1933–1945)

James MacGregor Burns's *Roosevelt* (two vols., 1956–1970) was the first complete biography of Franklin D. Roosevelt. It has maintained its reputation and is still a standard biography of FDR.

FDR: A History (five vols., 1972–2000) is a sweeping chronicle, incomplete due to the death of author Kenneth Davis.

Frank Freidel's *Franklin D. Roosevelt* (four vols., 1952–1973) focuses on Roosevelt's life through the first two years of the New Deal. Volume one is indispensable for understanding FDR's education.

Harry S. Truman (Democrat, 1945–1953)

Robert Ferrell's *Harry S. Truman: A Life* (1994) is a first-rate biography.

A Man of the People: A Life of Harry S. Truman (1995), by Alonzo Hamby, is a scholarly well-written biography.

David McCullough's *Truman* (1992) received the Pulitzer Prize.

Dwight D. Eisenhower (Republican, 1953–1961)

Stephen Ambrose's comprehensive biography *Eisenhower* (two vols., 1983–1984) remains the best study to date.

John F. Kennedy (Democrat, 1961–1963)

Robert Dallek's *An Unfinished Life: John F. Kennedy, 1917–1963* (2003) is an outstanding and engrossing biography.

Nigel Hamilton's *JFK: Reckless Youth* (1992) is the first of a projected multi-volume study that takes JFK through his first election to Congress.

Jack: The Struggles of John F. Kennedy (1980) and *JFK: The Presidency of John F. Kennedy* (1983), both by Herbert Parmet, were considered the best biographies of Kennedy until publication of the Dallek volume.

Lyndon B. Johnson (Democrat, 1963–1969)

The first three volumes of Robert Caro's yet-to-be-completed biography *The Years of Lyndon Johnson* (1982–2002) are the most detailed life of LBJ. Volume three takes LBJ through his Senate years.

Lone Star Rising: Lyndon Johnson and His Times, 1908–1960 and *Flawed Giant: Lyndon Johnson and His Times, 1961–1973* (1991–98), both by Robert Dallek, are excellent studies of LBJ. Dallek has made great use of the Johnson papers and of numerous oral histories deposited in the LBJ presidential library.

Richard M. Nixon (Republican, 1969-74)

Stephen Ambrose's *Nixon* (three vols., 1987–1991) is a balanced, thorough, and compelling study of Nixon. Volume one, *The Education of a Politician, 1913–62*, is a superb account of these years.

Roger Morris's *Richard Milhous Nixon: The Rise of an American Politician* (1990) is the first of a projected two-volume study.

Gerald R. Ford (Republican, 1974–1977)

There is no good biography available. The best is James Cannon's *Time and Chance: Gerald Ford's Appointment with History* (1993).

Jimmy Carter (Democrat, 1977–1981)

No good biography is available. The best available account of Carter's education is his own book *An Hour before Daylight: Memoirs of a Rural Boyhood* (2001).

Ronald Reagan (Republican, 1981–1989)

William Pemberton's *Exit with Honor: The Life and Presidency of Ronald Reagan* (1998) is the first biography to make extensive use of the material at the Ronald Reagan Presidential Library.

George H. W. Bush (Republican, 1989–1993)

Herbert Parmet's *George Bush: The Life of a Lone Star Yankee* (1997) is a well-written and well-researched study.

Bill Clinton (Democrat, 1993–2001)

No good biography is available, and Clinton's personal papers are still closed to researchers. The best account is the highly selective journalistic account by David Maraniss, *First in His Class: A Biography of Bill Clinton* (1994).

George W. Bush (Republican, 2001–)

The best available book is J. H. Hatfield's *Fortunate Son: George W. Bush and the Making of an American President* (2001).

Internet Resources

http://www.archives.gov/presidential_libraries/index.html
The National Archives and Records Administration holds papers, records, and other historical material related to each of the presidents, and oversees the operation of presidential libraries.

http://memory.loc.gov/
The American Memory collection of the Library of Congress contains a large amount of written, photographic, and audiovisual material useful to understanding American history and the development of education in the United States.

http://www.whitehouse.gov/history/presidents/index.html
This area of the official White House website contains biographies and portraits of each president.

http://www.pbs.org/wgbh/amex/presidents/index.html
This page contains links to brief overviews of each president's life and times, drawn from a public broadcasting series called *The Presidents*.

http://www.americanpresidents.org
This website is based on C-SPAN's *American Presidents: Life Portraits* series. It contains biographical facts and reference materials for each president.

http://www.ipl.org/div/potus/
This database covers the presidents' family lives, schools attended, cabinet members, election results, acts in office, and miscellaneous life events. It also contains many links.

http://showcase.netins.net/web/creative/lincoln/speeches/educate.htm
This web page contains Abraham Lincoln's quotes on the importance of education.

http://www.ux1.eiu.edu/%7Ecfrnb/index.html
The History of American Education Web Project includes short informational articles, biographies of influential educators, and illustrations of educational materials from various periods of American history.

http://www.pbs.org/kcet/publicschool/roots_in_history/index.html
The website "School: The Story of American Public Education" was developed to supplement a PBS series with the same title.

http://www.cedu.niu.edu/blackwell/
The Blackwell History of Education Museum and Research Collections hold many rare and interesting examples of textbooks used in U.S. education over the past two hundred years.

http://www.ed.gov/index.jhtml
The official website of the U.S. Department of Education.

Photo Credits

3: Courtesy of the Mount Vernon Ladies'
   Association

4: private collection

7: The University Archives and Record Center,
   University of Pennsylvania

8: Manuscript Division, Library of Congress

11: Manuscript Division, Library of Congress

12: Manuscript Division, Library of Congress

13: Manuscript Division, Library of Congress

16: Courtesy of the Harvard University Archives

19: Courtesy of the Harvard University Archives

20: Courtesy of the Harvard University Archives

22: Courtesy of the Harvard University Archives

28: Earl Gregg Swem Library,
    The College of William and Mary

31: Earl Gregg Swem Library,
    The College of William and Mary

32: Earl Gregg Swem Library,
    The College of William and Mary

35: Earl Gregg Swem Library,
    The College of William and Mary

37: Earl Gregg Swem Library,
    The College of William and Mary

43: Seeley G. Mudd Manuscript Library,
    Princeton University

46: Seeley G. Mudd Manuscript Library,
    Princeton University

47: Seeley G. Mudd Manuscript Library,
    Princeton University

50: Seeley G. Mudd Manuscript Library,
    Princeton University

51: Seeley G. Mudd Manuscript Library,
    Princeton University

54: Earl Gregg Swem Library, The College of
    William and Mary

56: Earl Gregg Swem Library, The College of
    William and Mary

59: Earl Gregg Swem Library, The College of
    William and Mary

63: Courtesy of the Harvard University Archives

64: Courtesy of the Harvard University Archives

68: Courtesy of the Harvard University Archives

71: Courtesy of the Harvard University Archives

72: Courtesy of the Harvard University Archives

75: Courtesy of the Harvard University Archives

77: private collection

78: private collection

82: private collection

84: private collection

88: private collection

95: Eggleston Library, Hampden-Sydney College

96: The University Archives and Record Center,
    University of Pennsylvania

99: The University Archives and Record Center,
    University of Pennsylvania

100: The University Archives and Record Center,
     University of Pennsylvania

103: The University Archives and Record Center,
     University of Pennsylvania

104: private collection

105: The University Archives and Record Center,
     University of Pennsylvania

107: Earl Gregg Swem Library,
     The College of William and Mary

108: Earl Gregg Swem Library,
     The College of William and Mary

111: private collection

117: Wilson Library,
   University of North Carolina, Chapel Hill
118: Wilson Library,
   University of North Carolina, Chapel Hill
121: Wilson Library,
   University of North Carolina, Chapel Hill
123: Wilson Library,
   University of North Carolina, Chapel Hill
127: Old Military and Civil records,
   National Archives and Records
   Administration
130: private collection
131: private collection
137: private collection
138: private collection
142: private collection
144: private collection
147: George J. Mitchell Department of Special
   Collections and Archives,
   Bowdoin College Library
148: George J. Mitchell Department of Special
   Collections and Archives,
   Bowdoin College Library
151: George J. Mitchell Department of Special
   Collections and Archives,
   Bowdoin College Library
152: George J. Mitchell Department of Special
   Collections and Archives,
   Bowdoin College Library
155: Bowdoin College Museum of Art
159: Waidner-Spahr Library, Dickinson College
161: Waidner-Spahr Library, Dickinson College
162: Waidner-Spahr Library, Dickinson College
165: Waidner-Spahr Library, Dickinson College
166: Waidner-Spahr Library, Dickinson College
169: private collection
171: private collection
172: private collection
174–75: private collection
176: private collection
179: private collection
180: private collection
183: private collection
184: Division of Historical Resources, North
   Carolina Department of Cultural Resources
189: private collection
193: West Point Museum Art Collection,
   United States Military Academy

194: West Point Museum Art Collection,
   United States Military Academy
197: Records of the U.S. Military Academy,
   Record Group 404,
   National Archives and Records
   Administration
198: private collection
201: West Point Museum Art Collection,
   United States Military Academy
203: Rutherford B. Hayes Presidential Center
204: Rutherford B. Hayes Presidential Center
207: Rutherford B. Hayes Presidential Center
208: Rutherford B. Hayes Presidential Center
209: Rutherford B. Hayes Presidential Center
210: Rutherford B. Hayes Presidential Center
213: Archives of Hiram College
214: Archives of Hiram College
217: Williams College Archives
218: Williams College Archives
221: Williams College Archives
222: Williams College Archives
225: Archives of Union College
226: New-York Historical Society
229: New-York Historical Society
233: private collection
234: private collection
237: private collection
240: private collection
243: Miami University of Ohio Archives
244: Miami University of Ohio Archives
246: Miami University of Ohio Archives
247: Miami University of Ohio Archives
248: Miami University of Ohio Archives
249: Miami University of Ohio Archives
251: private collection
253: private collection
254: Pelletier Library, Allegheny College
257: Archives of Albany Law School
261: Archives of Albany Law School
262: Theodore Roosevelt Collection,
   Harvard College Library
264: Theodore Roosevelt Collection,
   Harvard College Library
267: Theodore Roosevelt Collection,
   Harvard College Library
268: Theodore Roosevelt Collection,
   Harvard College Library
271: Theodore Roosevelt Collection,
   Harvard College Library

272: Theodore Roosevelt Collection, Harvard College Library
275: Manuscripts and Archives, Yale University Library
276: private collection
278: Manuscripts and Archives, Yale University Library
279: Manuscripts and Archives, Yale University Library
280: private collection
282: Manuscripts and Archives, Yale University Library
285: Seeley G. Mudd Manuscript Library, Princeton University
286: E. H. Little Library, Davidson College
289: private collection
290: Seeley G. Mudd Manuscript Library, Princeton University
293: Seeley G. Mudd Manuscript Library, Princeton University
294: The Albert and Shirley Small Special Collections Library, University of Virginia
296: The Ferdinand Hamburger Archives of The Johns Hopkins University
297: Seeley G. Mudd Manuscript Library, Princeton University
299: private collection
300: private collection
301: private collection
302: private collection
305: private collection
306: Archives and Library Division, Ohio Historical Society
311: private collection
312: private collection
315: private collection
316: private collection
319: Archives and Special Collections, Amherst College
322: Archives and Special Collections, Amherst College
325: private collection
326: private collection
329: Herbert Hoover Presidential Library
331: private collection
337: Franklin D. Roosevelt Library
339: (top) Franklin D. Roosevelt Library; (bottom) private collection
340: Franklin D. Roosevelt Library
341: Franklin D. Roosevelt Library
342: Franklin D. Roosevelt Library
345: Franklin D. Roosevelt Library
347: Franklin D. Roosevelt Library
348: Franklin D. Roosevelt Library
351: Harry S. Truman Presidential Library and Museum
352: private collection
355: Harry S. Truman Presidential Library and Museum
359: private collection
361: private collection
362: Dwight D. Eisenhower Library
365: Dwight D. Eisenhower Library
366: Dwight D. Eisenhower Library
369: Dwight D. Eisenhower Library
370: Dwight D. Eisenhower Library
372: Dwight D. Eisenhower Library
373: private collection
374–375: private collection
376: John F. Kennedy Library
380: John F. Kennedy Library
381: John F. Kennedy Library
382: John F. Kennedy Library
383: John F. Kennedy Library
385: John F. Kennedy Library
386: John F. Kennedy Library
387: John F. Kennedy Library
389: Lyndon B. Johnson Library and Museum
390: Lyndon B. Johnson Library and Museum
393: Lyndon B. Johnson Library and Museum
395: Lyndon B. Johnson Library and Museum
396: Lyndon B. Johnson Library and Museum
399: Lyndon B. Johnson Library and Museum
401: The Richard Nixon Library and Birthplace Foundation
402: The Richard Nixon Library and Birthplace Foundation
405: The Richard Nixon Library and Birthplace Foundation
406: The Richard Nixon Library and Birthplace Foundation
409: private collection
410: Wardman Library, Whittier College
411: The Richard Nixon Library and Birthplace Foundation
413: Gerald R. Ford Library and Museum
414: Gerald R. Ford Library and Museum
416: Gerald R. Ford Library and Museum

417: Gerald R. Ford Library and Museum
419: Gerald R. Ford Library and Museum
421: Gerald R. Ford Library and Museum
422: Gerald R. Ford Library and Museum
424: private collection
426: Corbis
429: Jimmy Carter Library and Museum
430: private collection
433: private collection
437: Ronald Reagan Presidential Library
438: Ronald Reagan Presidential Library
441: Ronald Reagan Presidential Library
442: Ronald Reagan Presidential Library
445: Ronald Reagan Presidential Library
446: Ronald Reagan Presidential Library
447: Ronald Reagan Presidential Library
449: Manuscripts and Archives,
    Yale University Library
450: Manuscripts and Archives,
    Yale University Library

451: Manuscripts and Archives,
    Yale University Library
453: Manuscripts and Archives,
    Yale University Library
456: George H. W. Bush Presidential Library
    and Museum
461: private collection
462: (top) private collection; (center, bottom)
    Georgetown University Archives
467: private collection
471: George H. W. Bush Presidential Library
    and Museum
474: Manuscripts and Archives,
    Yale University Library
479: (top right) George H. W. Bush Presidential
    Library and Museum; (left, lower right)
    Manuscripts and Archives,
    Yale University Library
482: George H. W. Bush Presidential Library
    and Museum

Contributors

Editor Fred L. Israel is professor emeritus of American history, City College of New York. He is the author of *Nevada's Key Pittman* and has edited *The War Diary of Breckinridge Long* and *Major Peace Treaties of Modern History, 1648–1975* (five vols.) He holds the Scribe's Award from the American Bar Association for his joint editorship of the *Justices of the United States Supreme Court* (four vols.). For more than twenty-five years Professor Israel has compiled and edited the Gallup Poll into annual reference volumes.

General Editor Arthur M. Schlesinger jr. holds the Albert Schweitzer Chair in the Humanities at the Graduate Center of the City University of New York. He is the author of more than a dozen books, including *The Age of Jackson*; *The Vital Center*; *The Age of Roosevelt* (three vols.); *A Thousand Days: John F. Kennedy in the White House*; *Robert Kennedy and His Times*; *The Cycles of American History*; and *The Imperial Presidency*. Professor Schlesinger served as Special Assistant to President Kennedy (1961–63). His numerous awards include the Pulitzer Prize for History; the Pulitzer Prize for Biography; two National Book Awards; the Bancroft Prize; and the American Academy of Arts and Letters Gold Medal for History.

Associate Editor Michael Kelly has his doctorate degree in history from the State University of New York, Stony Brook. Dr. Kelly is the author of a forthcoming biography of Senator Robert Wagner. He teaches at the Gilman School.

Associate Editor Hal Marcovitz is a staff writer for *The Morning Call*, Allentown, Pennsylvania. He has written several biographies of presidents for teenagers.

Robert Dallek has taught at Columbia, UCLA, and Oxford. He is professor of history at Boston University. He is the author of a two-volume biography of Lyndon Johnson and *An Unfinished Life*, a biography of John F. Kennedy. Professor Dallek has won the Bancroft Prize, among other awards for scholarship.

J. F. Watts is Dean of the Humanities, City College of New York. He has written extensively on American political and social history.

Bill Thompson majored in history at Boston University. He holds a Master of Divinity degree and is a Presbyterian minister. Mr. Thompson is the author of several books for teenagers.

Daniel E. Harmon is an author and editor. His short story collection *The Chalk Town Train & Other Tales* has received critical acclaim. Mr. Harmon is associate editor of *Sandlapper: The Magazine of South Carolina*.

Anne Marie Sullivan received her baccalaureate degree from Temple University. She is a writer and editor.

Bill Yenne is the author of numerous popular books, including *Astronauts: The First 25 Years of Manned Space Flight*.

Pam Fitzgibbon is a writer. She teaches at the Park School, Baltimore.

Harry Mortimer has two law degrees from Georgetown University. He served as General Counsel, First Fidelity Bank Corp.

Index

Abbot, Samuel, **68**
Abbott, Jacob, **351**
abolitionists, 96, 101, 145, 255, 256
    See also slavery
Abraham Lincoln and Men of His Time (Browne), **171**
Adams, Abigail (Nabby), 62, 70
Adams, Abigail Smith (Mrs. John Adams), 25, 62, 64–66, 67–69, 70, 73
Adams, Charles, 62, 68–69
Adams, Deacon John, 17, 21
Adams, Elihu, 17
Adams, Hannah, 17
Adams, John, 13, 26, 38, 39, **59,** 62, 66, 67–70, 73, 74, 86, 91, **204,** 459, 471
    birth of, 14
    career of
        law, 24–25, 64–65
        teaching, 22, 24
    early education of, 17–18, 21
    at Harvard University, 15, **16, 19,** 21–22, **23**
    presidency of, 25
    schooling at home, 17
    subjects studied by, 18, 21
Adams, John Quincy, 25, 34, 85, **204,** 459, 471
    birth of, 62
    career of
        law, 74
        politics, 74–75
    death of, 75
    early education of, 66, 69
    at Harvard University, 67, **71,** 73–74
    schooling at home, 62, 64–65, 68, 70
    subjects studied by, 65, 66, 67, 69, 70, 73

    at the University of Leyden, 69
Adams, Louisa Catherine Johnson (Mrs. John Quincy Adams), 74–75
Adams, Peter, 17
Adams, Susanna Boylston (Mrs. Deacon John Adams), 17
Adams, Tom, 62
Addison, Joseph, 10, 15, 110, 291
Aeneid (Virgil), 122, **147, 237**
Agnew, Spiro T., 423
Akenside, Mark, 60
Albany Law School, **257,** 259, **261**
Allegheny College, 252, **254,** 256, 258
Allen, Henry J., 368
Allen, John, 177
Allen, Moses, 48
American Bible Society, **171**
American Party, 145
American Revolution (1775-81), 12, 13, 15, 27, 36, 38, **50,** 52–53, 61, 64–65, 67, 70, 80–81, 109, 149, **176**
The American Spelling Book (Webster), 139–140, **169,** 170, 216
The American Universal Geography (Morse), **137,** 140
American Whig Society, 47–48, **49**
    See also literary societies
Amherst College, 310, **312, 315, 316,** 318–321
Ampudia, Pedro de, **131**
Ancient History (Rollin), 65, **104**
Anderson, W. C., 245
Andover. *See* Phillips Academy (Andover)
Annapolis. *See* U.S. Naval Academy (Annapolis)
Argus, 298, 304, 308

numbers in **bold italic** refer to captions

Arrel, George F., 259
Arthur, Chester A.
 birth of, 224
 career of
  law, 228–229
  military, 229–230
  politics, 230–231
  teaching, 228
 death of, 231
 early education of, 227
 subjects studied by, 227–228
 at Union College, *225, 226,* 227–228, *229*
Arthur, Ellen Lewis Herndon (Mrs. Chester A.
 Arthur), 229, 231
Arthur, William, 224, 227
Athenaean Society, 153
 See also literary societies
athletics, *340,* 404, *410, 426,* 428, 444–446
 George H. W. Bush, *450, 451,* 455, 458
 Dwight Eisenhower, 360, *365,* 367, *370,* 371
 Gerald Ford, 412, 414–416, 418–420, *422*
 John F. Kennedy, 379, 384, *387*
 Theodore Roosevelt, 262, *264,* 265, *271*
 Woodrow Wilson, 284, *285,* 291–292
Ayers, Elisha, 129–130, 132

Baines, Ruth, 394
Baker, Ray Stannard, 285
Barbour, Philip P., 109
Bard, Simeon Ingersoll, 150
Barnwell, Charles N., 287
Barry, W. T., 51
Bayh, Birch, 434
Bean, Joel and Hannah, 326
Beecher, Henry Ward, 238
Beers, Henry A., 281
Belcher, Jonathan, 41
Berkeley, Norborne (Baron de Botetourt), 36
 See also College of William and Mary
Berry, Virginia, 416
Bibb, George, 97
Bible, 2, 29, 65, *138,* 163, *169, 171,* 353, 364
 See also religion
Biddle, Nicholas, 85
Bingham, Caleb, *189*
Bingham, William, 164
Birchard, Sardis, 205, 206, 207, 209
Bishop, Robert Hamilton, 245
"blab" schools, 170

Black, Samuel, 122, 124
Blackstone, William, 37, 60, 62, 74, 141, *142,*
 156, *210,* 238, *240*
Blaine, Ephraim, 164
Blaine, James G., 164, 241
Blaine, Robert, 164
Blair, James, 97
Bliss, William W. S., 128, 134
Bloomingdale, Betsy, 445
Blount, William, 83
Blow, John, *108*
Blythe, Bill, Jr., 460
Blythe, William Jefferson, III. *See* Clinton, Bill
Bogart, Humphrey, 454
Boggs, James, 303
Bolívar, Simón, 98
Booraem, Hendrik, V., 216
Booth, Almeda, 219
Booth, John Wilkes, 181
Boston Massacre, 25, 64
 See also American Revolution (1775–81)
Botetourt Medals, 36, *37*
Bowdoin, James, *72, 155*
Bowdoin College, *72, 147, 148,* 150, *151,*
 153–154, *155,* 156
Bowen, Dennis, 238–239
Boynton, Harriet, 215
Boynton, Silas, 215
Boys' Nation, 460, *461,* 464–465
Brackenridge, Alexander, *166*
Brackenridge, Henry, 48–49
Brackenridge, John A., 173
Bradford, William, 47, 49
Bradley, Omar, *370, 375*
Bragg, Edward S., 239, 241
Branner, John, *329,* 332–333, 334
Breasted, James Henry, *104*
Breckinridge, John C., 190
Bristow, Joseph, 368, 371
Brown, Edmund G. "Pat," 410
Brown, John, 256
Brown, Mollie, 326
Browne, Robert H., *171*
Bryan, William Jennings, 356
Bryant, Lemuel, 22
Buchanan, Elizabeth Speer (Mrs. James Buchanan
 Sr.), 163, 164
Buchanan, James
 birth of, 160, 163

at Dickinson College, 158–160, **161,** 164–167
early education of, 163–164
as president, 167
schooling at home, 163
subjects studied by, **162,** 164, 165–166
Buchanan, James, Sr., 160, 163, 164
Buchanan, Mary, 163
Buchen, Philip, 420–421
Buckley, William F., Jr., 458
Bulloch, Annie, 265–266, 269
Bulwer-Lytton, Edward, 112, **198**
Burke, Edmund, **148**
Burr, Aaron, 38, 47, 86, 92–93, 133
Burroughs, Edgar Rice, 454
Burton, David, 278
Bush, Barbara Pierce (Mrs. George H. W. Bush), 455–457, 458, **471,** 476
Bush, Dorothy Walker (Mrs. Prescott Bush), 448, 451–452, 476
Bush, George H. W., 469, 471, 473–476, **482**
birth of, 451
career of
military, 448, 451, 457–458
politics, 458–459
early education of, 452, 454
at Phillips Academy, 448, 451, 454–455, 457
subjects studied by, 454, **456**
at Yale University, **449–450, 453, 456,** 458
Bush, George W., 98, 459
birth of, **456**
career of
politics, 470, 472, 475, 483
Texas Air National Guard, 481, **482**
early education of, 472
at Harvard Business School, 471, 482
at Phillips Academy, 471, 472–473
at Yale University, 471, **474,** 476–480
Bush, Nancy, 452
Bush, Prescott, 448, 451–452, 471, 473, 475–476
Bush, Prescott, Jr., 452
Bush, Samuel, 451, 475
Bush at War (Woodward), 470, 472
Butler, Nicholas Murray, **348**

Caldwell, Joseph, 124, 125
Caldwell, Zenas, 153
Camm, John, **54**
Campbell, Archibald, 53, 55
Capital Business College, 330
Carey, Matthew, **4, 138**

Carroll, John, **462**
Carter, Billy, 431
Carter, Eleanor Rosalynn Smith (Mrs. Jimmy Carter), 432, 434
Carter, James Earl, Sr., 427, 431, 434
Carter, Jimmy, 423, 447
birth of, 427
career of
military, 432, 434
politics, 434–435
early education of, 427–428
at Georgia Institute of Technology, 432
at Georgia Southwestern College, 431
at Plains High School, **426, 429,** 431
at the U.S. Naval Academy, 424, 426–427, 431–433
Carter, John, **35**
Carter, Lillian Gordy (Mrs. James Earl Carter Sr.), 427, 431, 434
Carter, Ruth, 434
Casparis, Luzie, 392
Cassidy, Elbridge and Edith, 460, 466
Castle, Amos, 139–140
Catlin, George, **193**
Chadwick, Joseph, **16**
Chafee, John F., 458
Challis, Belle, **311**
Chaplin, Jonathan E., 205–206
Chapman, Robert, 119, 122, 125
Chase, Philander, **207**
Cheney, Dick, 472, 483
Cheney, Zaccheus, 140, 143
cherry tree, 2, **3, 4**
See also Washington, George
civil rights, 211, 229, 398–399, 465, 466, 468
Civil War (1861–65), 115, 145, 168, 181, 190, 199, 200, 211, **214,** 223, 229–230, 239, 249, 252, 258, 266, 287, 426
See also secession
Clark, Aaron, 207
Clarke Institute for the Deaf, 323
Clary, Joseph, 143–144
Clay, Henry, 34, 85, 115, 134, 145, 211, 227
Cleaver, Margaret "Mugs," 441, 443, **446**
Cleland, Thomas, 129
Clemens, Elizabeth Roper, 394
Cleveland, Aaron, 232
Cleveland, Frances Folsom (Mrs. Grover Cleveland), 241

Cleveland, Grover, 250, 308, *318*
    birth of, 232
    career of
        law, 238–239, *240*
        politics, 239, 241
        teaching, 236, 238
    childhood of, 232, 235
    at the Clinton Liberal Institute, 235–236
    death of, 241
Cleveland, Margaret, 235, *237*
Cleveland, Mary, 239
Cleveland, Richard, 232, 235–236
Cleveland, Stephen Grover. *See* Cleveland, Grover
Cleveland, William, 232, 235, 236, 238
Cleverly, Joseph, 18, 21
Clinton, Bill, 459
    birth of, 460
    at Boys' Nation, 460, *461,* 464–465
    career of
        politics, 469
    at Central Junior High School, 463
    at Georgetown University, *462,* 466, 468
    at Hot Springs High School, *461,* 464, 465
    at Oxford University, *467,* 468
    subjects studied by, 466, 468
    at Yale University Law School, *467,* 468–469
Clinton, De Witt and George, 92, 93, *193*
Clinton, Hillary Rodham (Mrs. Bill Clinton), 469
Clinton, Roger, Jr., 463
Clinton, Roger, Sr., 463, 464
Clinton, Virginia (Mrs. Roger Clinton), 460, 463,
    464, 468
Cliosophic Society, 47–48, 49
    See also literary societies
Coffin, William Sloane, 477
Coke, Edward, 37, 60, 74
    See also Blackstone, William
Coleman, Julia, 428, 435
College and Academy of Philadelphia. *See*
    University of Pennsylvania
College of New Jersey. *See* Princeton University
College of Philadelphia. *See* University of
    Pennsylvania
College of William and Mary, 26, *28, 31, 35,* 41,
    44, 97, *107,* 129, 285
    and the Church of England, *54*
    Thomas Jefferson, 27, *32,* 33–34, 36
    James Monroe, 53, *54,* 57–58, 60
    and Phi Beta Kappa, *56, 59*

    John Tyler, *108,* 109–110, *111,* 112–113
Collinson, Peter, *103*
Columbia College, 89, 373
Columbia University Law School, 347–349
The Columbian Class Book (Lowe), *176*
The Columbian Orator, 187, *189*
Commentaries on the Laws of England (Blackstone),
    74, 141, *142,* 156, *210, 240*
Complete History of England (Smollett), 65
Conant, James Bryant, 384
Congressional Government (Wilson), 295, *296*
Conkling, Roscoe, 230–231
The Conquest of Canaan (Dwight), 73
Conrad, Robert T., *131*
Constitutional Convention (1787), 2, 41, *46,* 51
Continental Congress, 25, 38, *46,* 61, 65, 76, 96, 167
Cook, Ben, 330
Cook, James, *75*
Coolidge, Abigail, 313, 314
Coolidge, Calvin
    at Amherst College, 310, *312, 315,*
        318–321, *322*
    birth of, 310
    at Black River Academy, *311,* 314, 317–318
    career of
        law, 321–323
        as president, 323
    death of, 323
    early education of, 313–314, 318
    subjects studied by, *311,* 314, 317, 318, 320
Coolidge, Calvin, Jr., 323
Coolidge, Calvin Galusha, 313
Coolidge, Grace Anna Goodhue (Mrs. Calvin
    Coolidge), 323
Coolidge, John, 310, 313, 314, 318, 321, 323
Coolidge, John (son of Calvin), 323
Coolidge, Sarah (Mrs. Calvin Galusha Coolidge),
    313, *318*
Coolidge, Victoria Josephine Moor (Mrs. John
    Coolidge), 313, 314
Cooper, James Fenimore, *198,* 266
Copley, John Singleton, 70
copying (rote learning), 6, *8, 11, 159, 207*
Court, S. A., 308
Cowper, William, 163
Cox, Ava Johnson, 391, 395
Cox, James M., 309
Crawford, Andrew, 170
Crawford, Jane and James, 78

Crist, A. C., 307
Crittenden, John J., 132, 134
Crittenden, William, 109
Crockett, Gertrude, 440
Crosby, Frances "Fanny," 236, 238
Culver, Erastus, 228–229
Cutler, Arthur, 269–270
Cuyler, Cornelius, 284, 291
Cyropedia (Xenophon), 67
Czolgosz, Leon, 260

Dallek, Robert, 389
Dalton, Tristram, 22
"dame schools," 17, 18
Dana, Francis, 70
Dana, Richard Henry, 270
Darby, Nellie, *437*
Dartmouth College, 150
Davidson, Robert, 158, 159, 160, 165, 167
Davidson College, 285, *286,* 287–288
Davie, William Richardson, 81
Davis, Jefferson, 256
Dawkins, Henry, *42*
Day, Jeremiah, *179*
de Gaulle, Charles, 338
De Santis, Vincent P., 241
Deadrich, Kate, 391
Dean, Amos, 259
Dearborn, Henry, 126, 128, 133
Deason, Bill, 398
Decimal Arithmetic (Cocker), 21
Declaration of Independence, 15, 25, 27, 34, 38,
    39, 41, *45,* 47, 61, 76, 87, 101
The Decline and Fall of the Roman Empire (Gibbon),
    74, *121,* 255
Delta Epsilon, *315*
Delta Kappa Delta, 418, 420–421
Delta Kappa Epsilon, 477–478, *479*
    See also fraternities
Democracy in America (Tocqueville), 281
Democratic Party, 93, 114, 124, *152,* 156, 157,
    190, 239, 241, 295, 308
Democratic-Republican Party, 61, 85, 89, 91, 149
    See also Democratic Party
Derry, Joseph T., 287
The Dialectic, 197, 199
Dialectic Society, 116, 119, *121,* 124, 125
    See also literary societies
Dickens, Charles, 255

Dickinson, John, 164, 166–167
Dickinson College, 158–160, *161,* 164–167
DiClemente, Frank, 455
Dill, John and Lin, 173, 177
Doenecke, Justus D., 231
Dorsey, Azel, 170
Douglas, Helen Gahagan, 408
Douglas, Stephen A., 178, 181, 190
Douglas, William, 29–30
Drew, Elizabeth, 481
Dromgoole, George, 125
Drummer, Henry E., 178
Duffey, Joe, 469
Duggan, Ervin, *390*
Duke University Law School, 407, *412*
Dunbar, Charles F., *263,* 271
DuPonceau, Pierre S., 60
"Dutch." *See* Reagan, Ronald

Eakely, Doug, 468
Early, Jubal, 211
Eastman, Seth, *194*
Eaton, John, *84, 121*
Eclectic Institute (Hiram College), 213, *214,*
    219–220, 221, 223
economics (classical), 110, *111,* 115, 281
Edward Everett Society, 255–256
    See also literary societies
Eisenhower, Arthur, 362, 364
Eisenhower, David, 362–363, 364
Eisenhower, Dwight, 410, 445
    at Abilene High School, 360, 364–368, 371
    birth of, 362
    career of
        military, 372–373
        as president, 373
    death of, 373
    early education of, *362,* 363
    subjects studied by, 363–364, *366*
    at West Point Academy, 360, 368–372, *375*
Eisenhower, Earl, 364
Eisenhower, Edgar, 360, 362–363, 364, 368
Eisenhower, Ida, 362–363, 364, 371
Eisenhower, Mamie (Mrs. Dwight Eisenhower), 373
Eisenhower, Milton, 364
Eisenhower, Paul, 364
Eisenhower, Roy, 364
Elements of Moral Philosophy (Fordyce), 15
Eliot, Charles W., 270, *272*

Elliot, Maud, 265
Emerson, Ralph Waldo, 220, 270, 277
English Grammar (Kirkham), **172**
"English school," 29
Episcopalian Church, 26, 33, 44, 49–50
    See also religion
An Essay Concerning Human Understanding
    (Locke), 15
Eugene Aram (Bulwer-Lytton), 112
Eumenean Society, **286**
    See also literary societies
Eureka College, 436, 438–439, 443–444, **446,** 447
Evans, Cecil, 397
Evans, Walker, 454
Expository Notes (Burkett), 49

Fairfax, Thomas (Lord Fairfax), 10, 12
Fairfax, William, 10
Fall, Albert B., 309
Fauquier, Francis, 27, 34
Federalist Papers, 51
    See also Madison, James
Federalist Party, 89, 91, 92, 119, 124, 150
Fillmore, Abigail Powers (Mrs. Millard Fillmore),
    141, 143, 144
Fillmore, Millard
    birth of, 139
    career of
        law, 141, **142,** 143–144
        politics, 144–145
        teaching, 140–141, 143, 144
        wool-carding, 136, **137,** 139, 140–141
    early education of, 139–140
    subjects studied by, 140
Fillmore, Nathaniel, 136, 139, 141
Fillmore, Olive, 136
Fillmore, Phoebe (Mrs. Nathaniel Fillmore), 139,
    141
*First Son: George W. Bush and the Bush Family
    Dynasty* (Minutaglio), 473, 478, 482
Fithian, Philip Vickers, 41
Fitzpatrick, John C., **8,** 9
Fletcher, Lucy, 332
Flexner, James Thomas, 5
Ford, Betty Bloomer, **414,** 421
Ford, Dorothy (Mrs. Gerald R. Ford Sr.), 415
Ford, Gerald, 434
    birth of, 415
    career of

law, 420–421
    military, 421
    politics, 421, 423
    as Yale University football coach, 418,
        420, **422**
    as Eagle Scout, **413**
    early education of, 415
    at South High School, **414,** 415–418, **419**
    subjects studied by, 416, 418, **421**
    at University of Michigan, 412, 415, 418,
        419, 420, **421**
    at Yale University Law School, 420
Ford, Gerald R., Sr., 415, 416
Ford, James, 415
Ford, John, 421
Ford, Michael, 421
Ford, Richard, 415
Ford, Steven, 421
Ford, Susan, 421
Ford, Thomas, 415
Four Books of Architecture (Palladio), 38
Fox, Charles James, 187
Franklin, Benjamin, **4, 59,** 66, 67, 124, **138,** 232
Franklin's Almanac (Franklin), **138**
Fraser, B. J., 441, 443
fraternities, 209, 228, 293, **315, 316,** 318, 320, 321,
    333, 397–398, 404, 418, 421, **453,** 458, 477–480
Frémont, John Charles, 229, 258
French and Indian War (1754-63), 13
Freneau, Philip, 48–49
Frost, Robert, 376
Fry, J. Reese, **131**
Fry, Joshua, 26
Fuess, Claude Moore, 455
Fugitive Slave Act, 135, 145
    See also slavery
Fulbright, J. William, 466, 468
Fulton, Robert, 124

Gardiner, Henry D., 229
Gardinier, Aaron, 90–91
Garfield, Abram, 212, 213
Garfield, Eliza Ballou (Mrs. Abram Garfield), 212, 213
Garfield, James A., 230
    assassination of, 213, 223, 224, 230
    birth of, 212
    career of
        maritime, 216
        as president, 223

teaching, 213, *214,* 219, 220, 221, 223
early education of, 212, 215–216, 219
at the Eclectic Institute, 219–220
schooling at home, 212
subjects studied by, 219, 220
at Williams College, 213, *214,* 220–221, *222*
Garfield, Lucretia "Crete" Rudolph (Mrs. James A. Garfield), 220, 221, 223
Garfield, Thomas, 212
Garman, Charles E., 320
Gentleman's Calling (Allestree), 9
Gentleman's Magazine, 10, *11,* 15
Geography Made Easy (Morse), *137*
Georgetown University, *462,* 466, 468
Georgia Institute of Technology, 432
Georgia Southwestern College, 431
Gettings, Clifford, *414*
Giles, William Branch, 97
Glidden, Charles E., 258
Godey, Harry, 269
Gordon, George (Lord Byron), 53
Gordy, Tom, 424
Graham, Andrew, *286*
Graham, Mentor, 178
Granger, Daniel, 205
Grant, Hannah Simpson (Mrs. Jesse Grant), 192
Grant, Hiram Ulysses. *See* Grant, Ulysses S.
Grant, Jesse, 192, 193, 194–195, 196, *197*
Grant, Julia Dent (Mrs. Ulysses S. Grant), 200
Grant, Ulysses S., 181, 230, 250
    birth of, 192
    career of
        military, 200
        as president, 200–201
    death of, 201
    early education of, 194–195
    subjects studied by, 195, 197, 199
    at West Point Academy, 193, 195, 196–200, *201*
Gray, Jennie, 330
Great Awakening, 41
    See also religion
Great Britain, 47, 48–49, 52, 53, *54,* 57–58, 60, 67, 86, 384, *386*
    and the Boston Massacre, 25, 64
    and the War of 1812, 133, 149
Great Compromise, 134–135, 145
    See also slavery
Great Depression, 335, 336, 415, 416, 452, 454–455

Greene, Harry, 397
Greenleaf, Simon, 210
Gridley, Jeremy, 24–25
Griffith, R. McKinstry, 196
Groton School, 337, *339, 340, 341,* 343–344
Grover Cleveland: A Study in Courage (Nevins), *233, 234,* 236
Guiteau, Charles, 230–231
Gulf War (1991), 459

Hale, Edward Everett, *351*
Hale, John P., 150
Hamilton, Alexander, 51, 86, 92, 124, 308
Hamilton, William, *82*
Hamilton College, 235, 236
Hampden-Sydney College, 94, *95,* 97–98, 100–101
Hanaford, Phoebe Ann, *180*
Hancock, John, *23,* 67, 454
Hancock, Winfield S., 223
Hanks, C. S., 262, 265
Hanks, John, *180*
Harding, Charity, 304
Harding, Charles, 303
Harding, Florence Kling (Mrs. Warren G. Harding), 299, 308
Harding, George Tryon, 298, 301, 303–304, 307
Harding, Phoebe Elizabeth Dickerson (Mrs. George Tryon Harding), 301, 307
Harding, Warren G., 283, 323
    birth of, 301
    career of
        journalism, 298, 301, *306,* 308
        politics, 308–309
    death of, 299, 309
    early education of, 299, *300, 302,* 303–304
    at Ohio Central College, 298, *305–306,* 307–308
    schooling at home, 301
    subjects studied by, 307
Harris, Benjamin, 18
Harris, Frank, 307
Harris, Frank H., 298
Harris, Ira, 259
Harrison, Anna Symmes (Mrs. William Henry Harrison), 102
Harrison, Benjamin, 241, *318*
    birth of, 242
    career of

law, 247–249, 250
    as president, 250, *251*
at Cary's Academy, 245
early education of, 242, 245
at Miami University, *243, 245*–247, *249*
subjects studied by, 246
Harrison, Benjamin, V, *35,* 94, 96, 102, 114
Harrison, Caroline Scott (Mrs. Benjamin
    Harrison), 246, 247–248, 250
Harrison, Carter Bassett, 97
Harrison, Elizabeth Bassett (Mrs. Benjamin
    Harrison V), 96
Harrison, Elizabeth Ramsey Irwin (Mrs. John Scott
    Harrison), 242
Harrison, John Scott, 242, 245, 249
Harrison, Mary Lord Dimmick (Mrs. Benjamin
    Harrison), 250, *251*
Harrison, William Henry, 90, 114, 208, 242, 245, *251*
birth of, 94
career of
    medical, 101–102
    military, 102
    politics, 102, 105
death of, 105
early education of, 97
at Hampden-Sydney College, 94, *95,* 97–98,
    100–101
subjects studied by, 97–98, 100, *104*
at the University of Pennsylvania Medical
    School, *96,* 101
Harrod, Samuel, 443
Harrison, Nathaniel, 97
Harvard, John, 21
Harvard Business School, 471, 482
Harvard Crimson, 345, 346, 384
Harvard Law School, 210–211
Harvard University, 17, *20,* 41, 67, *72,* 285, *406*
    John Adams, 15, *16, 19,* 21–22, *23*
    John Quincy Adams, 67, *71,* 73–74
    buildings of, *16,* 270
    cost of, 68
    finances of, *63, 64*
    John F. Kennedy, *381, 382,* 383–386, *387*
    Franklin D. Roosevelt, *337,* 344–347
    Theodore Roosevelt, 262, *263, 264, 267,*
    270–273
Harvard University Archives, 15
Hawthorne, Nathaniel, 146, 149, 150, *151, 152,*
    153, 157

Hay, John, 260
Hayes, Fanny, 202, 205, 206, 208, 209
Hayes, John, 159, 165
Hayes, Lorenzo, 202
Hayes, Rutherford, Sr., 202, 205
Hayes, Rutherford B., 252, 254, 258, 274
    career of
        as president, 211
    diary of, *204,* 208–209, 210, 211
    at Harvard Law School, 210–211
    at Kenyon College, 202, 207–209
    schooling at home, 205
    subjects studied by, 206, 207, *210,* 211
    at Webb's Preparatory School, *203,* 206–207
Hayes, Sarah, 202
Hayes, Sophia (Mrs. Rutherford Hayes Sr.), 202,
    205, 206, 207, 209
Haynesworth, Henry, 230
Haynesworth, Malvina Arthur, 230
Hazel, Caleb, 170
hazing, 371, 424, 426–427, 432
Hazlett, Everett, 368
Hearst, William Randolph, 260
Henderson, Robert, 122, 124
Henley, William, 53
Henry, Patrick, 50, 96, 109, 304
Herndon, William H., 178, 181
Heulat, Laura, 330
Hill, A. P., 200
Hill, William, 187
Hiss, Alger, 408
The History of Charles V (Robertson), 70
History of England (Hume), 70, 74, 110, 255
The History of England (Macauley), 70, 291
A History of Kentucky Baptists (Spencer), *171*
History of Philosophy (Schwegler), 281
History of the Saracens (Ockley), *148*
*History of the United States for the Use of Schools and
    Families* (Goodrich), 215
Hollis, Thomas, *68*
Holyoke, Edward, 14, 15
    See also Harvard University
Hoover, Allan, 334
Hoover, David and Mary, 327
Hoover, Herbert, 475, 483
    birth of, 324
    at Capital Business College, 330
    career of
        engineering, 334

office clerk, 328, 330
politics, 335
surveying, 333–334
death of, 335
early education of, 326–328
at Stanford University, *325, 329,* 330–334
subjects studied by, 328, *329,* 330, 332, 333–334
Hoover, Herbert, Jr., 334
Hoover, Huldah (Mrs. Jesse Hoover), 324, 326, 327
Hoover, Jesse, 324, 327
Hoover, Lou Henry (Mrs. Herbert Hoover), 334
Hoover, Mary, 324, 330
Hoover, Theodore ("Tad"), 324, 327, 328, 330
Hoover Institution, *329*
Hope, Matthew B., *50*
Hopkins, Mark, 220, *222*
hornbook, 17–18
Houston, William Churchill, *46*
Howe, William, 67
Humane Society, 101
    See also abolitionists
Hume, David, 47, 49, 60, 70, 74, 110, *148*
Humphrey, Hubert, 412
Humphreys, David, 5
Humphries, William, 79
Hungerford, Benjamin, 136, 139, 140
Hunter, Cyrus L., 80
Hunter, Humphrey, 80
"Ike." *See* Eisenhower, Dwight
Iliad (Homer), 67, 97
The Influence of Sea Power Upon History (Mahan), 337, 341, 343
Innes, James, *54, 58*
The Instructor (Fisher), *11*
Introduction to the Study of International Law (Woolsey), 281
Irving, Washington, *198*
Irwin, Will, 333, 334

Jackson, Andrew, 93, 102, 109, 124, 188, 235
    birth of, 78
    career of
        law, 83
        military, 81, 85
        politics, 85
    childhood of, 76
    early education of, 79–80
    subjects studied by, 79

Jackson, Andrew, Sr., 78
Jackson, Elizabeth Hutchinson (Mrs. Andrew Jackson Sr.), 78–79, 80, 81, *84*
Jackson, Henry, 434
Jackson, Hugh, 78, 80–81
Jackson, Robert, 78, 81
Jackson, Thomas "Stonewall," 200, 211
Janin, Louis, 334
Jay, Augustus, 269
Jay, John, 51, 86
Jefferson, Jane Randolph (Mrs. Peter Jefferson), 26
Jefferson, Martha Wayles Skelton (Mrs. Thomas Jefferson), 38
Jefferson, Peter, 26, 29, 30
Jefferson, Thomas, 2, 13, 25, 50, 51, *59,* 60–61, 73, 76, 86, 91, 110, 113, 119, 149, 376
    birth of, 26
    career of
        law, 37
        politics, 38
    at the College of William and Mary, 27, *32,* 33–34, 36
    death of, 39
    early education of, 29–30, 33
    subjects studied by, 29, 30, 33–34
Jefferson Literary Society, 293
    See also literary societies
Jehovah's Witnesses, 364
    See also religion
Jennings, Lizzie, 229
Johns Hopkins University, 295, *296*
Johnson, Andrew
    apprenticeship education of, *184,* 186, 187
    birth of, 185
    career of
        politics, 182, 188, 190, 191
        as tailor, 186, 188
    childhood of, *183, 184,* 185
    death of, 191
Johnson, Claudia Alta Taylor "Lady Bird" (Mrs. Lyndon B. Johnson), 398
Johnson, Eliza McCardle (Mrs. Andrew Johnson), 188
Johnson, Jacob, 185
Johnson, James Polk, 391
Johnson, Lyndon B., 387, 472, 475
    birth of, 391
    career of
        as law clerk, 394–395
        as president, *390,* 398–399

death of, 399
early education of, 389, 391–392
at Johnson City High School, 392–394, **395**
at Southwest Texas State Teachers College,
388, 394, 395–398, **399**
subjects studied by, 392, **396**
Johnson, Mary McDonough (Mrs. Jacob Johnson),
185, 186
Johnson, Pete, 465
Johnson, Rebekah Baines (Mrs. Sam Johnson),
388, 389, 391–392, **397**
Johnson, Sam, 388, 391–392, 394, 395
Johnson, Sam, Sr., 391
Johnson, William, 185, 186
Jomini, Henri, 199
Jones, Albert C., 307
Jones, James A., 97
Jones, Joseph, 55, 57
Jordan, David Starr, 332

Kansas City School of Law, 359
Kellogg, Alvan, 140, 143
Kendall, Henry, 317
Kennedy, John F., 410, 420, **461,** 463, 465, 472
assassination of, 398, 423
books by, 376, 378
career of
as president, 386–387
early education of, **377,** 378–380, 382
at Harvard University, **381, 382,** 383–386, **387**
illnesses of, 378, 380, **382**
subjects studied by, 379, 380, 383, **385**
Kennedy, Joseph, Jr., 378, 379, 382, 384, 386
Kennedy, Joseph P., 378, 379, **380, 386**
Kennedy, Robert F., 466
Kennedy, Rose (Mrs. Joseph P. Kennedy), 378,
379, 380
Kennedy, Rosemary, 379
Kenyon College, 202, 207–209
Keyes, Geoffrey, 371
King, John, 164, 167
King, Leslie Lynch, Jr. *See* Ford, Gerald
King, Martin Luther, Jr., 466, 475
See also civil rights
Kipke, Harry, 412, 418
Klett, Scott, 392, 394
Knox, James, 120
Knox, John, 42
Knox, William, **175**

Kramer, John Matthias, **103**
Krause, Arthur, 418

Ladies Calling (Allestree), 9
Lamar, Joseph R., 287
Lane, Will, 206
Langdon, Samuel, 67
languages, 29, 30, 34, 43, 48, 69, 70, 87, **88,** 269,
317, 338, 340
Laski, Harold, 378
Lawhorne, Tommy, 465
Lawrence, Abbot, 145
Leavitt, Hart Day, 455
Lee, Richard Henry, 96, 101, 102
Lee, Robert E., 181, 200, 356
Leipner, Andrew, 100, 101
Lemmon, Jack, 454
Lessons in Elocution (Scott), 173, **175**
Lever, Charles James, **198**
Lewis, Lloyd, 199
Lewis and Clark, **148**
Library of Congress, 6, 38, **253, 290**
*The Life and Memorable Actions of George
Washington* (Weems), 2, **4,** 173, 285, 287
Life of Abraham Lincoln (Scripps), **171**
Life of Andrew Jackson (Parton), **77,** 85
The Life of Franklin Pierce (Hawthorne), **152**
Life of George Washington (Ramsay), 5
The Life of William McKinley (Olcott), **253**
Lincoln, Abraham, 134, 182, 190, 200, 223, 229
assassination of, 181, 190
birth of, 168
career of
as ferryman, 173, 177
law, 178
politics, 177–178, 181
early education of, 170
subjects studied by, 170, 173, **175, 176**
Lincoln, Mary Todd (Mrs. Abraham Lincoln), 178
Lincoln, Nancy (Mrs. Thomas Lincoln), 168,
170, **171**
Lincoln, Robert Todd, 178
Lincoln, Sarah, 170
Lincoln, Sarah Bush Johnston (Mrs. Thomas
Lincoln), 170
Lincoln, Thomas, 168, 170, 177
Lindgren, Waldemar, 333–334
Linnaeus, Carl, **103**
Litchford, James, 187

Literary Commonplace Book (Jefferson), 33
literary societies, 47–48, *49,* 73, 98, 113, 116, 119, *121,* 153, 167, 188, 197, 199, 208, 221, *243,* 255–256, 286, 291, 293
Livingston, Robert R. and Edward, 92
Locke, John, 60, 124, 153, 211
Locke, Samuel, 22
Lodge, Henry Cabot, 270
Long, John, 262
Longfellow, Henry Wadsworth, 150, *151,* 211, 266, 270
Longstreet, James, 200
Louisiana Purchase, 38
  See also Jefferson, Thomas
Lowrie, James I., 227
Luce, Henry, 458
Luzerne, Chevalier Anne Cesar de La, 62
The Lyceum Review, 227
Lyons, Eugene, 332, 335

Macaulay, Thomas, *351*
Madison, Ambrose, 40
Madison, Dorothea "Dolley" Payne Todd (Mrs. James Madison), 51
Madison, Frances (Mrs. Ambrose Madison), 40, 43
Madison, James, *127*
  birth of, 40
  career of
   politics, 49–51
  early education of, 41, 43–44
  illnesses of, 48
  at Princeton University, 41, *42,* 44, *46,* 47–49
  schooling at home, 40, 43
  subjects studied by, 43, 44, 47, 49
Madison, James, Sr., 40
Madison, James (Bishop), 112–113
Madison, Nellie Conway (Mrs. James Madison Sr.), 40
Mallon, Neil, 458
Malone, Dumas, *28*
Malthus, Thomas, *111*
Manual of Political Economy (Fawcett), 281
"Marching Through Georgia," 426–427
Marryat, Frederick, *198,* 266
Marsh, Joseph, 14, 21
Marshall, George C., 372
Marshall, John, 27, 34, 55, 57, 59, 113–114
Marshburn, Olive and Oscar, *401*
Martin, Alexander, 44

Martin, Thomas, 41, 44, 49
Martin, Tom, 394–395
Marty, Mary, 463
Mason, John Y., *117*
Maury, James, 30, 33
Mayhew, Joseph, 21
McArthur, Douglas, 372
McCarter, Robert, 291
McCay, Spruce, 83
McClellan, George B., 200
McCormick, James, 159, 165
McCoy, Donald, *318*
McCullough, David, 25
McDaniel, Blackston, 188
McDonald, Ephraim, 120
McFarland, Joseph, 303
McGuffey, William (*McGuffey's Readers*), *3, 300,* 303, 304
McKinley, Anna, 255, 256, 259
McKinley, Ida Saxton (Mrs. William McKinley), 259
McKinley, Nancy Allison (Mrs. William McKinley Sr.), 254–255
McKinley, William, *253*
  at Albany Law School, *257,* 259
  at Allegheny College, 252, *254,* 256, 258
  assassination of, 260, 273
  birth of, 254
  career of
   law, 252, 254, 258–259
   military, 258
   politics, 259–260
  early education of, 255
  at Poland Academy, 255–256
  subjects studied by, 255
McKinley, William, Sr., 254–255
McKinzie, Ralph "Mac," 443–444
McNairy, John, 83
McNarney, Joseph, *375*
Meadows, George, 454
Mercer, John, 57, 58
Meredith, James, 465
Merriam, Francis, 269
Mettauer, Joseph, *95,* 97, 100
Mexican-American War (1846-48), 109, 134, 156, 200, *201*
Miami Union Literary Society, *243,* 246
  See also literary societies

Miami University, *243, 244,* 245–247, *249*

Middletown, Arthur, 432
Miles, Agnes and Laban, 327
Milhous, Franklin, 400
Milton, George Fort, 188
Milton, John, 163, *175, 234*
Minor, John B., *294*
Minthorn, John, 327–328, 331
Minthorn, Laura, 327–328
Missionary Travels and Researches in Southern Africa (Livingstone), 266
Monroe, Andrew, 57
Monroe, Elizabeth, 57
Monroe, Elizabeth Jones (Mrs. Spence Monroe), 52, 55, 57
Monroe, Elizabeth Kortright (Mrs. James Monroe), 61
Monroe, James, 27, 34, 114
    birth of, 52
    at Campbelltown Academy, 53, 55, 57
    career of
        law, 60–61
        military, 58–60
        as president, 61
    at the College of William and Mary, 53, *54,* 57–58, 60
    death of, 61
    schooling at home, 55
    subjects studied by, 57, 58, 60
Monroe, Joseph, 57
Monroe, Spence, 52, 55, 57
Moody, Theodore L., *148*
Moor, Hiram, 313
Moore, John Trotwood, *84*
The Moral Philosopher (Morgan), 24
Morgan, John, *96*
Morison, Samuel Eliot, 15
Morris, Robert, 101, 102
Morse, Anson D., *312,* 320
Morse, Jedediah, *137,* 140, 216
Morse, Samuel, *137*
Morse, Samuel B., 454
Moseley, William D., *118,* 124
Murray, Joan Hills, 205
Murray, John (Earl of Dunmore), 57, 58
Murray, Robert B., 256

Nash, George, 335
National Honor Society, *417*
Naval History of the War of 1812 (Roosevelt, Theodore), 271

Nevins, Allan, 232, *233, 234,* 236, 238
The New American Practical Navigator (Bowditch), *159*
The New and Complete System of Arithmetic (Pike), 170, 173
New England Primer, 18
New Guide to the English Tongue (Dilworth), 170, *172*
New Salem Debating Society, 177–178
New York Institution for the Blind, 236, 238
Newman, Wallace, 404
Nichols, Roy Franklin, 150, 153
Nixon, Arthur, 400, 403
Nixon, Edward, 403
Nixon, Francis, 400, 402–403
Nixon, Francis Donald, 400, 403
Nixon, Hannah Milhous (Mrs. Francis Nixon), 400, *401,* 402, 403, *412*
Nixon, Harold, 400, 403
Nixon, James, 400
Nixon, John, 76
Nixon, Richard M., 423, 434, 463
    birth of, 400
    career of
        law, 407–408
        military, 408
        politics, 408, 410–411
    at Duke University Law School, 407, *412*
    early education of, 400, *402*
    at Fullerton High School, *406*
    and music, *405*
    subjects studied by, 404, *405*
    at Whittier College, 404, 407, *409, 410*
    at Whittier High School, 403, *406*
Nixon, Thelma Catherine Patricia "Pat" (Mrs. Richard M. Nixon), 407–408
Noel, Nicholas, 66
Noland, Nellie and Ethel, 354
Norman, Ruby, *369*
Nott, Eliphalet, *225,* 227–228
Noyes, Horatio, 205
Nu Pi Kappa, 208
    See also literary societies

O'Hara, Kean, 132, 133
O'Hara, Theodore, 132
Ohio Central College, 298, *305–306,* 307–308
"old-field" schools, 79–80
"Old Hickory." *See* Jackson, Andrew
"Old Man Eloquent." *See* Adams, John Quincy

"Old Rough and Ready." *See* Taylor, Zachary
"Old Tippecanoe." *See* Harrison, William Henry
Olmsted, Frederick Law, *331*
On Civil Liberty and Self-Government (Lieber), 281
Orations (Cicero), 98, *147*
Orthogonian Society, 404
    See also fraternities
Osborne, William, 256, 258
Oswald, Lee Harvey, 423
Oxford Female Academy, 246, *247, 248*
    See also Miami University
Oxford University, *467,* 468

Pace, Stephen, 431
Page, John, *28*
Paradise Lost (Milton), 65
Parker, Amasa J., *257,* 259
Parker, Grace, 259
Parsons, Theophilus, 74
Parton, James, *77,* 85
Pate, Samuel, 177
Peabody, Endicott, *339,* 343, 344
Peale, Charles Willson, *289*
Pearson, Eleanor, 332
Pearson, Eliphalet, *71*
Perle, Richard, 472
Perret, Geoffrey, 199
Pershing, John J., 295, 372
Phelps, Margaret, 356
Phi Beta Kappa, 27, *56, 59,* 67, 73, *225,* 228,
    271, 455, *456,* 458
Phi Gamma Delta, 321
Phi Kappa Psi, 293
Phi Zeta, 209
    See also fraternities
Philanthropic Society, *121,* 125
    See also literary societies
Phillips, Sam, Jr., 454
Phillips Academy (Andover), *71,* 448, 451,
    454–455, 457, 471, 472–473
Philologian Society, 221
    See also literary societies
Philomathean Literary Society, 188
    See also literary societies
Philomathesian Society, 208
    See also literary societies
Pickett, George E., 200
Pierce, Anna Kendrick (Mrs. Benjamin Pierce), 149
Pierce, Ben (brother of Franklin), 150

Pierce, Benjamin, 146, 149, 156
Pierce, Elizabeth Andrews (Mrs. Benjamin
    Pierce), 149
Pierce, Franklin, 455
    birth of, 149
    at Bowdoin College, *147, 148,* 150, *151,*
        153–154, *155,* 156
    career of
        law, 156
        politics, 156–157
    death of, 157
    early education of, 146, 149–150
    subjects studied by, *147,* 150, 154
Pierce, Jane (Mrs. Franklin Pierce), 156–157
Pierce, Marvin, 455
Pierce, Pauline Robinson, 455
The Pilgrim's Progress (Bunyan), *234,* 235
Pitcher, John, 173
Pitt, William, 187, 206
Pleasants, Robert, 101
Polemic Society (debating society), 188
Polk, Ezekiel, 120
Polk, James K., 115, 134
    birth of, 119
    career of
        politics, 125
        shop clerk, 120, 122
    early education of, 122
    illnesses of, 120
    subjects studied by, *118,* 122, 124
    at the University of North Carolina, 116,
        117, 118, 119, 122, 124–125
Polk, Jane Knox (Mrs. Sam Polk), 120
Polk, Sam, 119–120
Polk, Sarah Childress (Mrs. James K. Polk), 122
Polk, William, 120, 122
Pond, Raymond "Ducky," 418, 420
"Poppy." *See* Bush, George H. W.
Porter, Joseph, 245
Porter, Noah, 278, 282
Powell, Colin, 472
Powell, Dick, 445
Presbyterian Church, 41, 44, *233*
    See also religion
Princeton University, *45, 46,* 47–49, *50,* 119, 125,
    284–285, 287, 288, 291–292, *293,* 295, 383
buildings of, *42, 289*
founding of, 41, 44
James M. Madison Jr., 41, *42,* 44, *46,* 47–49

Woodrow Wilson, 284–285, 287, 288, **289,** 291–292, **293**
Princetonian, 284, 287, 292, 297
Pringle, Henry, 274
Profiles in Courage (Kennedy), 376, 378
Proxmire, William, 420
Psi Upsilon, 228
    See also fraternities
Pulitzer, Joseph, 260
Puritans, 17, 18, 21
Putnam, James, **24**

Quakers ("The Society of Friends"), 324, 326, 327, 328, 400, 404, **409**
    See also religion

Randolph, Edmund, 113
Reagan, Jack, 439, 440
Reagan, Nancy Davis (Mrs. Ronald Reagan), 445
Reagan, Neil, 439, 440–441
Reagan, Nelle (Mrs. Jack Reagan), 439, 440–441
Reagan, Ronald, 434, 459
    birth of, 439
    career of
        cinema, 444
        politics, 447
        radio and television, 444–445, 447
    early education of, **437, 438,** 439–440
    at Eureka College, 436, 438–439, 443–444, **446,** 447
    at North Dixon High School, **438,** 441–443
    at South Dixon High School, **438,** 441
    subjects studied by, 443
Reconstruction, 182, 277, 287
    See also Civil War (1861-1865)
Redford, Emmette, 392, 394
Reid, Mayne, 266
religion, 18, 24, 29, 49–50, 149, 212, 213, 219, **222, 233,** 235, **311,** 324, 326, 327,328, 353, 364, **430,** 480–481
    and universities, 17, 33, 41, **42,** 44, **54,** 101, 116, **117,** 119, **254,** 318, 436, **446, 462**
Remini, Robert V., **78, 82**
Renick, Edward I., 293
Republican Party, 145, 178, 181, 201, 223, 230, 249–250, 295, 308, 323, 335, 373, 480
Republican-Union Party, 190
Revere, Paul, **16,** 454
Revolutionary War. *See* American Revolution (1775–81)

Rhodes, Cecil, **467**
Ricardo, David, *111*
Rice, Asa, 143–144
Rice, Condoleezza, 472
Rice, Nathan, 65
Rickover, Hyman, 434
Riney, Zachariah, 170
Roane, Archibald, 85
Robb, John P., 307
Robertson, Donald, 41, 43–44
Rogers, Edmund and Archibald, 340, 343
Rogers, Elias, 143
Roman History (Goldsmith), **148**
Roosevelt, Alice Lee (Mrs. Theodore Roosevelt), 265, 271, 273
Roosevelt, Anna, 265, **267**
Roosevelt, Anna Eleanor, 349
Roosevelt, Anna Eleanor (Mrs. Franklin D. Roosevelt), 346–349
Roosevelt, Anna Lee (Mrs. Nicholas Longworth), 273
Roosevelt, Corinne, 265
Roosevelt, Edith Kermit Carow (Mrs. Theodore Roosevelt), 273
Roosevelt, Elliott, 265, 269
Roosevelt, Elliott (son of Franklin), 349
Roosevelt, Franklin, Jr., 349
Roosevelt, Franklin D., **386,** 448, 454–455, 476
    birth of, 336
    career of
        politics, 349
    at Columbia University Law School, 347–349
    death of, 336, 349, 350
    early education of, 338, 340, 343
    at Groton School, **337, 339, 340, 341,** 343–344
    at Harvard University, **337,** 344–347
    stamp collecting, 340–341
    subjects studied by, **340,** 341, **342,** 344, 346
Roosevelt, James, 338, 343, 346
Roosevelt, James (son of Franklin), 349
Roosevelt, John, 349
Roosevelt, Martha "Mittie" Bulloch (Mrs. Theodore Roosevelt Sr.), 265, 269, 273
Roosevelt, Sara Delano (Mrs. James Roosevelt), 338, 340, 343, 346–347, 349
Roosevelt, Theodore, 260, 274, 282–283, 295, 341, 343, 346, 347, 349, **351,** 357, 473
    birth of, 265

career of
  as president, 273
  early education of, 269–270
  at Harvard University, 262, *263, 264, 267,*
    270–273
  illnesses of, *264,* 265, *268*
  schooling at home, 265–266, 269
  subjects studied by, 271
Roosevelt, Theodore, Sr., 265, 269, 271
Root, Harriet, 245
Rosecrans, William S., 200
Ross, Charlie, 354, *355*
Ross, Lewis, *249*
Rousseau, Jean-Jacques, 60, 74, 384
Rowe, Nicholas, 60
"Rud." *See* Hayes, Rutherford B.
Rudiments of Arithmetic (Ray), 216
"Rules of Civility," 6, *8,* 9, 10
    See also Washington, George
Rumsfeld, Donald, 472, 483
Rush, Benjamin, 101–102, 159, 164–165
Russel, Samuel, *276*
Russell, Joshua, 160, 163
Russo, George, 444

Saltonstall, Richard, *271,* 273
Sanford, Alva, 255
Santa Anna, Antonio López de la, *131,* 134
Santayana, George, *271*
Sargent, Dudley A., *268*
Saunders, John Hyde, *28*
Savage, John, *183, 189*
Scott, John W., 246, *247, 248*
Scott, Walter, *198*
Scott, William, 136
Scott, Winfield, 109, 156
secession, 115, 167, 181, 182, 190
    See also Civil War (1861–65)
Secrets of the Tomb (Robbins), 478
    See also Skull and Bones
Selby, James J., *184,* 185–186, 187
Semple, James, 109
Severance, Frank H., *144*
Seymour, Horatio, 200, 239
Shakespeare, William, 65, 66, 79, 89, 173, *175,*
    205, *234,* 291
Shaler, Nathaniel Southgate, 271
Sharon, James R., 163, 164
Shaw, John, 73

Shelby, Isaac, 132
Shepard, William B., 125
Sherman, George, *311,* 317, 318
Sherman, John, 223
Sherman, William T., 200, 426
Shields, Patrick Henry, 97
Shippen, William, *100,* 101
Short, William, *59*
Shriver, Sargent, 420
"Silent Cal." *See* Coolidge, Calvin
Silvester, Cornelius, 90, 91
Silvester, Francis, 89–91
Skull and Bones, *279, 453,* 458, 475, 477, 478, *479*
slavery, 5, 12, 40, 87, 96, 109, 129, 134–135, 145,
    157, 178, 181, 182, 190, *214,* 223, *226,* 227,
    249, 256, 277
    See also abolitionists; Civil War (1861–65)
Small, William, 27, *28,* 33–34, 36
Smith, Adam, 47, 70, 110, *111*
Smith, Alfred E., 335
Smith, Paul, 404
Smith, Samuel Stanhope, 47
Smollett, Tobias George, 110
social activities
  Chester A. Arthur, 231
  George W. Bush, 473, 477–478
  Calvin Coolidge, 313, *315,* 317, 318,
    320–321, *322*
  Ulysses S. Grant, 199
  Warren G. Harding, 307
  Herbert Hoover, 332
  Thomas Jefferson, 34
  John F. Kennedy, 384
  Franklin D. Roosevelt, *342,* 346
  Theodore Roosevelt, 270, *271*
  Harry S. Truman, 357
  George Washington, 9–10, 12–13
  Woodrow Wilson, 291, *297*
    See also fraternities; literary societies
Social Democratic Workmen's Party, 277
Sorensen, Theodore C., 379
Southwest Texas State Teachers College, 388, 394,
    395–398, *399*
Soviet Union, 423, 447
Spalding's Business College, 356
Spanish-American War, 260, 273
Sparhawk, Thomas, *23*
Sparrow, Thomas, 210
Spectator, 10, 15, 40, 43, 44, 110

The Spectator (Warren G. Harding's), 298, 301, **306**
Speer, Dick, 398
spelling, 6, **77,** 79–80, **169,** 170, 188, 205, 216, 354
Spofford, Ainsworth R., 274
Spurlin, Virgil, 464
Staley, Carolyn, 466
Stanford, Jane, **331**
Stanford, Leland, **325,** 330, **331,** 332
Stanford University, **325, 326, 329,** 330–334
Starbuck, W. R., 328
Stark, John, 146, 149
Staunton, Virginia, 287
Steele, Richard, 10, 15, 110
Stella, Frank, 454
Stephens, Alexander, 134
Stephenson, James White, 80
Stewart, Potter, 420, 458
Stimson, Henry L., 448
Stith, William, **32**
Stockbridge, Joseph, **23**
Stockton, Richard, **45**
Stokes, John, 83
Stone, Uriah, 224
Story, Joseph, 210
Stovall, Pleasant A., 287
Stowe, Harriet Beecher, 238
Stuart, John Todd, 178
"subscription school," 195
Sumner, William Graham, 278, 281, 283
Supreme Court, 109, 114, 158, 274, **278,** 283
Swain, Joseph, 330–332
Swaney, James, 170

Taft, Alphonso, 274, 277, **282**
Taft, Fanny (Mrs. Alphonso Taft), 274
Taft, Louise Torrey (Mrs. Alphonso Taft), 274, 277
Taft, Robert, Jr., 420
Taft, William Howard, 295, 308, 458
    birth of, 274
    career of
        as president, 281, 282–283
        on Supreme Court, 283
    death of, 283
    subjects studied by, 277, 278, 281–282
    at Woodward High School, **275,** 277
    at Yale University, **276,** 278–282
Talcott, Charles, 284, 292
Taney, Roger B., 158
Tarleton, Banastre, 81

Tatler, 15, 110
Taylor, Hancock, 129
Taylor, James, 173
Taylor, Margaret Mackall Smith (Mrs. Zachary Taylor), 134
Taylor, Richard, 129, 133
Taylor, Sarah Strother (Mrs. Richard Taylor), 128, 129
Taylor, William, 133
Taylor, Zachary, 145, **201**
    birth of, 128
    career of
        military, 126, **127,** 128, **131,** 132, 133–134
        as president, 134–135
    early education of, 129–130, 132–133
    subjects studied by, 132–133
Tecumseh, 102
Tennant, William, **42**
Tennent, Gilbert, 41
terHorst, Jerald F., **414**
Thaxter, John, 65, 66, 69
Thayer, Nathaniel, 269
Thayer, Sylvanus, 193
Thompson, Bill, **442**
Tiffany, Louis Comfort, 231
Tilden, Samuel, 202, 211
Tocqueville, Alexis de, 384
Tom, John, 160, 163
Tower, John, 475
Townsend, Ingham, 238
Trefousse, Hans L., 188
"Tricky Dick." *See* Nixon, Richard M.
Triggs, Dean, 404
Trudeau, Gary, 478
Truman, Elizabeth "Bess" Wallace (Mrs. Harry S. Truman), 353, 354, **355,** 356, 357
Truman, Harry S., 432
    birth of, 350
    career of
        farming, 356–357
        military, 357
        politics, 357, 359
    early education of, 352–353
    at Independence High School, **352,** 354–356
    at Kansas City School of Law, 359
    and music, 353–354
    at Spalding's Business College, 356
    subjects studied by, 353–354

Truman, John, 350, 352, 356–357
Truman, Martha "Mattie" (Mrs. John Truman), 350, 352–353
Truman, Mary Margaret, 357, **358**
Truman, Vivian, 352–353
Trumbull, John, 73
tuition costs, 5, 165, 195, **203,** 206, 245, 259, **305,** 307, 332, 376, 431, 443, **445**
Turner, Frederick Jackson, **342**
Twain, Mark, 231, 337, 354
Tyler, Henry, 109
Tyler, John, 27, 96
    birth of, 106
    career of
        law, 113–114
        politics, 114–115
        as president, 114–115
    at the College of William and Mary, **108,** 109–110, **111,** 112–113
    subjects studied, 110, 112
Tyler, John, Sr., 106, 109, 112, 113, 114
Tyler, Letitia Christian (Mrs. John Tyler), 114
Tyler, Mary Armistead (Mrs. John Tyler Sr.), 106, 109
Tyler, Samuel, 113

Udall, Morris, 434
Unabridged Dictionary (Webster), 337
Union College, **225, 226,** 227–228, **229**
Union Philosophical Society, 167
    See also literary societies
Union Society, 98
    See also literary societies
United Methodist Church, **254,** 259
    See also religion
University of Alabama, 465
University of Buffalo, **144,** 145
University of California at Berkeley, 439
University of Leyden, 69
University of Michigan, 412, 415, 418, **419,** 420, **421**
University of Mississippi, 465
University of North Carolina, 116, **117, 118,** 119, **121,** 122, **123,** 124
University of Pennsylvania, **7, 96, 99, 100,** 101, **103, 105, 462**
University of Virginia, 38, 39, 51, 292–293, **294**
Upshur, Abel P., 113
Upton, Albert, 404, 407
U.S. Military Academy at West Point. *See* West Point Academy
U.S. Naval Academy (Annapolis), 424, 426–427, 431–433

Van Alen, James and John, 89, 93
Van Buren, Abraham, 86–87, 89
Van Buren, Marie (Mrs. Abraham Van Buren), 87, 89
Van Buren, Martin, **84,** 86, 94, 114, 145, 207, 208
    birth of, 87
    career of
        law, 89–92, 93
        politics, 91–93
    early education of, 87, 89
    subjects studied by, 89
van Fleet, James, **375**
Van Ness, John P., 91
Van Ness, William, 89–90, 91–93
Vance, Cyrus, 420
The Vicar of Wakefield (Goldsmith), **78,** 79
Vietnam War, 399, 466, 481
Vincent, Mrs. Clifford, **406**
Voorhis, Horace Jeremiah "Jerry," 408
Voyages and Adventures of Captain Robert Boyle (Chetwood), 140

Waddell, Moses, 97
Waggoner, Garland, 443
Walker, David Douglas, 476
Walker, George Herbert, 451–452, 476
Wallace, David, 248
Wallace, William, 79, **82**
Walters, Vernon, 373
Walworth, Reuben H., **257**
War and Peace (Tolstoy), 428, 435
War of 1812, 53, 102, 114, 134, 136, 149, 202
Ward, Willis F., 412
Warden, David B., 87, 89
Warner, Will, 298
Warwick, Jack, 304
Washington, Augustine, Jr., 9
Washington, Augustine "Gus," Sr., 2, 6, 9
Washington, Booker T., 273
Washington, George, 25, 27, 36, 38, 41, 52, 59, 74, 96, 163, **176,** 235, 241, **289, 366**
    birth of, 5
    career of
        as president, 2
        surveying, 12
    and the cherry tree, 2, **3, 4**
    honorary degree, **7,** 67

and the "Rules of Civility," 6, **8,** 9, 10
    schooling at home, 5–6
    subjects studied by, 6, 13
    and Virginia society, 9–10, 12–13
Washington, Lawrence, 6, 9–10
Washington, Mary, 5–6
Watergate, 411, 423, 434
Waterhouse, Benjamin, 69
Watson, James, 60
Watts, Andre, **405**
Wayne, "Mad" Anthony, 102
The Wealth of Nations (Smith), 70, 110, **111**
Webb, Isaac, **203,** 206, 207
Webster, Daniel, 98, 105, 146, 149, 150
Webster, Noah, 139–140, **169,** 170
Weed, Thurlow, 144–145
Weems, Mason, 2, **4,** 5, 173, 304
Weir, Robert Walter, 197
Weisberger, Bernard A., 230, 231
Wentworth, John, 22
West, Benjamin, 70, 124
West, Hilborne, 269
West Point Academy, 356, **374–375**
    Dwight Eisenhower, 360, 368–372, **375**
    Ulysses S. Grant, 193, 195, 196–200, **201**
Western Reserve Eclectic Institute. *See* Eclectic
    Institute (Hiram College)
Wetsel, Lewis, 129, 132
Whig Party, 94, 102, **104,** 105, 114–115, 134, 145,
    156, 178, 207, 249
Whig Society, 284, 291
    See also literary societies
White, Grace, 353
White, Joseph, 81
Whitefield, George, 41
Whittemore, Amos, 136
Whittier College, 404, 407, **409, 411**
Why England Slept (Kennedy), 376
Wick, Mary Jane, 445
Wiley, David, 98
Willard, Joseph, 67, 73, **75**
Willard, Nahum, 24
William and Mary College. *See* College of William
   and Mary
Williams College, 213, **214, 217, 218,** 220–221, **222**
Wilson, Bert, 436, 438–439
Wilson, James, 164
Wilson, Jessie Woodrow (Mrs. Joseph Ruggles
   Wilson), 287

Wilson, Joseph Ruggles, 287
Wilson, Woodrow, 308, 335, 349, 483
    birth of, 287
    career of
       law, 293, 295, **296**
       as president, 295, 297
       teaching, 295
    at Davidson College, 285, **286,** 287–288
    early education of, 287
    at Johns Hopkins University, 295, **296**
    at Princeton University, 284–285, 287, 288,
      289, 291–292, **293**
    schooling at home, 287
    subjects studied by, 288, **290**
    at University of Virginia, 292–293, **294**
Winthrop, John, 15, 213
Wirt, William, 114
Wister, Owen, 262, 265
Witherspoon, John, 41, **42, 45, 46,** 47, 48–49,
   124, 125
    See also Princeton University
Wolfowitz, Paul, 472, 483
women and education, 112–113, **279, 331**
Women's Christian Temperance Union
   (WCTU), 277
women's suffrage, 277–278
Wood, Molly and Rachel, 83
Wood, Walter, 141, **142,** 143
Woodward, William, 277
Work, Henry Clay, 426
World War I (1914-18), 295, **329,** 335, 357
World War II, 335, 336, 350, 359, **370,** 372, 384,
   407–408, 421, 424, 431–432, 448, 455,
   457–458
Wright, Silas, 45
The Writings of George Washington (Fitzpatrick), 9
Wyman, Jane (Mrs. Ronald Reagan), 444
Wythe, George, 27, 34, 37, 61

Yale, Elihu, **276**
Yale University, 41, **179,** 205, 285, 418, 420, **422**
    George H. W. Bush, **449–450, 453, 456,** 458
    George W. Bush, 471, **474,** 476–480
    founding of, **276**
    William Howard Taft, **276,** 278–282
Yale University Law School, 420, **467,** 468–469
Yarborough, Ralph, 476, 477
Yates, William, **28**

Brazeal